THE LIMITS OF EMPIRE

THE
LIMITS OF EMPIRE

The Roman Army in the East

REVISED EDITION

by

BENJAMIN ISAAC

CLARENDON PRESS · OXFORD

Oxford University Press, Walton Street, Oxford OX2 6DP

Oxford New York Toronto
Delhi Bombay Calcutta Madras Karachi
Kuala Lumpur Singapore Hong Kong Tokyo
Nairobi Dar es Salaam Cape Town
Melbourne Auckland Madrid
and associated companies in
Berlin Ibadan

Oxford is a trade mark of Oxford University Press

Published in the United States
by Oxford University Press Inc., New York

Revised edition 1992
First issued as a Clarendon Paperback 1993

British Library Cataloguing in Publication Data
Data available

Library of Congress Cataloging in Publication Data
Isaac, Benjamin H.
The limits of empire : the Roman army in the East
Includes bibliographical references.
1. Middle East—History—To 622.   2. Rome—History—Empire, 30
B.C.–476 A.D.   3. Rome—Army—History.   4. Imperialism.   I. Title.
DS62.I83   1990   937'.06—dc20   89–37163
ISBN 0–19–814952–2

1 3 5 7 9 10 8 6 4 2

Printed in Great Britain
on acid-free paper by
Biddles Ltd., Guildford and King's Lynn

For E. I.-E.

PREFACE

THIS work is the result of many years of rumination and of fieldwork carried out in Israel. Throughout that period I have been connected with the University of Tel Aviv, but the decisive stages in the development of the book have been two years leave: the first, 1980–81, I spent as a visiting member at the Institute for Advanced Study, Princeton, NJ, and the second, 1985–86, as a visiting fellow of All Souls College, Oxford. I am grateful to these two institutions for their remarkable hospitality and to my University for granting me leave of absence.

The entire typescript was read by various friends, colleagues, and relatives to whom I owe many suggestions and corrections: John Mann and Fergus Millar commented on the entire text in various stages. I also received detailed comments on the first half of the book from David Kennedy and on an early, brief version from Glen Bowersock. Carol Glucker carefully read part of an intermediate version. Zeev Rubin contributed helpful remarks on Chapter V. Ida Isaac saw all versions of the entire text and contributed sagacious advice. I am grateful to others for suggestions and information: Shimon Applebaum, Denis van Berchem, Moshe Fischer, Mordechai Gichon, Paul Hyams, Arthur Isaac, Marlia Mango, Israel Roll, Margaret Roxan, Alla Stein, Zvi Yavetz. I should like to mention in particular colleagues who work in countries inaccessible to me: Thomas Bauzou, David Graf, David Kennedy, Thomas Parker, Maurice Sartre. They all helped me to avoid errors of fact, but none are responsible for any opinions expressed in this book. The information they supplied was all the more important because I have been unable to visit in person large and important parts of the Middle East, a fact which must be stressed at the outset. Since the political reasons for this deficiency are unlikely to disappear in the very near future I publish this book acknowledging the flaws which may be the result.

The book may have gained in interest by the inclusion of material from Talmudic sources which are not accessible to most classical scholars. It is therefore a great pleasure to make separate mention of the generous assistance provided by Aharon Oppenheimer. During many years of collaboration he has contributed much information regarding Talmudic sources and Jewish history. He provided me with information and extensive comments on all the sources cited in this book and has patiently corrected all I wrote on related subjects.

Jonas Greenfield and Naphtali Lewis kindly showed me relevant documents from the Babatha archive (Yadin papyri) before publication.

The maps were prepared by Shabtai Isaac and drawn by Ora Paran of the Institute of Archaeology, Tel Aviv University. I am grateful for the generous assistance provided by the Institute. I am further indebted to Professor M. Gichon and Dr D. L. Kennedy for supplying various illustrations.

I should further like to thank the hard-working staffs of a number of libraries, first of all that of the University of Tel Aviv, but also those where I have been a visitor: the National Library and the library of the Institute of Archaeology in Jerusalem; the Firestone Library, the library of the Institute for Advanced Study and the Speer Library in Princeton; the Ashmolean Library, the Bodleian, and the Codrington Library of All Souls College in Oxford; the British Museum in London; the University Library and those of various institutes in Amsterdam.

I am indebted to the Oxford University Press for undertaking publication of this book, and in particular to Mr John Cordy, who prepared it for the printers and offered numerous suggestions for the improvement of clarity and style.

Finally I ought to thank my computer which never lost any information and assisted me in every manner I could think of.

Tel Aviv   B.I.
January 1989

REVISED EDITION

By the time this revised edition went to press various reviews of the book had been published. Some of these approve of my ideas while noting they go too far. Others express agreement but regret that I do not go far enough. A few accept my views *in toto* or reject them altogether. All, however, agree that the book contains much useful— and sometimes even interesting information. It is in this sphere that a revised edition can contribute something, for obviously it would be impossible to modify this work so as to satisfy all my critics. I have therefore left the text unchanged, apart from the correction of minor, typographical, and other errors. A postscript, printed at the end of the book after the index, contains various additions, mostly concerning recent literature which came to my notice after the text went to press in January 1989. I also include some references to ancient and modern literature which I had missed while writing this book. This is followed by an additional bibliography.

Unchanged are a few allusions to current affairs: valid when this book was written, they are now strangely out of date, such as 'the current Nato doctrine'. They are still instructive as a reminder of contemporary setting.

I am grateful to various colleagues who gave me additional factual information, or pointed out errors in the text. Finally I should note that this edition was prepared while I enjoyed the amenities of a Fellowship at Dumbarton Oaks, Washington, DC.

B.I.

Tel Aviv
February 1992

CONTENTS

List of Illustrations   x

Abbreviations   xi

Acknowledgements   xiv

Introduction   1

   I. Rome and Persia   19

  II. Consolidation and Internal Unrest   54

 III. The Army of the Principate: An Army of Occupation   101

 IV. The Army of the Fourth Century   161

  V. Enemies and Allies after Septimius Severus   219

 VI. Army and Civilians in the East   269

VII. The Military Function of Roman Veteran Colonies   311

VIII. Urbanization   333

 IX. Frontier Policy—Grand Strategy?   372

Epilogue   419

Appendix I. Roman Army Sites in Judaea   427

Appendix II. Antioch as Military Headquarters and
         Imperial Residence   436

Postscript   439

Bibliography

  Books and Monographs   451

  Articles   466

  Maps   490

Additional Bibliography   491

Index   497

LIST OF ILLUSTRATIONS

FIGURES

1. Bostra, with the site of the legionary fortress   124
2. Dura-Europos, with the military camp   148
3. Palmyra: plan   166
4. Palmyra: the military quarter   167
5. Ein Boqeq: oasis and castellum   190
6. Upper Zohar fort   192
7. Mezad Thamar and vicinity   194
8. Mezad Thamar: plan   195
9. Tsafit Tower and vicinity   196
10. Tsafit Tower: plan   197
11. Der el-ʿAtrash: plan   202
12. Qasr Beshir: plan   203
13. Dibsi Faraj: the defences   258

MAPS

(at end)

A. The Near East, showing areas covered by Maps I–IV
B.   I. The North-East
   II. Cappadocia
  III. Syria and Northern Mesopotamia
  IV. Judaea and Arabia

ABBREVIATIONS

AAAS	*Annales Archéologiques Arabes Syriennes*
AAES	*American Archaeological Expedition to Syria, Part III*
AASOR	*Annual of the American Schools of Oriental Research*
ADAJ	*Annual of the Department of Antiquities of Jordan*
AE	*Année épigraphique*
AFRBA	S. Mitchell (ed.), *Armies and Frontiers in Roman and Byzantine Anatolia*
AJA	*American Journal of Archaeology*
ANRW	*Aufstieg und Niedergang der römischen Welt*
b.	Babylonian Talmud
BAR	*British Archaeological Reports*
BASOR	*Bulletin of the American Schools of Oriental Research*
BCH	*Bulletin de Correspondence Hellénique*
BE	J. et L. Robert, *Bulletin épigraphique*
BEO	*Bulletin d'Études Orientales*
BIAL	*Bulletin of the Institute of Archaeology, London*
BIES	*Bulletin of the Israel Exploration Society*
BJb	*Bonner Jahrbücher*
BMB	*Bulletin Musée de Beyrouth*
BMC	*Catalogue of Coins in the British Museum*
BROB	*Berichten van de Rijksdienst voor het Oudheidkundig Bodemonderzoek*
CAH	*Cambridge Ancient History*
CCSL	*Corpus Christianorum Series Latinae*
CE	*Chronique d'Égypte*
CII	J. B. Frey, *Corpus Inscriptionum Iudaicarum*
CIL	*Corpus Inscriptionum Latinarum*
CIS	*Corpus Inscriptionum Semiticarum*
CJ	*Codex Justinianus*
CP	*Classical Philology*
CQ	*Classical Quarterly*
CR	*Classical Review*
CRAI	*Comptes-rendus de l'Académie des Inscriptions et Belles-lettres*
CSEL	*Corpus Scriptorum Ecclesiasticorum Latinorum*
DE	E. de Ruggiero, *Dizionario Epigrafico di antichità romane*
DOP	*Dumbarton Oaks Papers*
DRBE	P. Freeman and D. Kennedy (ed.), *The Defence of the Roman and Byzantine East*
EFRE	D. H. French and C. S. Lightfoot, C. S., *The Eastern Frontier of the Roman Empire*

FGH	F. Jacoby, *Die Fragmente der griechischen Historiker*
FHG	C. Müller, *Fragmenta Historicorum Graecorum*
GCS	*Die Griechischen Christlichen Schriftsteller der ersten drei Jahrhunderte*
GJ	*Geographical Journal*
HSCP	*Harvard Studies in Classical Philology*
HTR	*Harvard Theological Review*
IEJ	*Israel Exploration Journal*
IGBR	G. Mihailov, *Inscriptiones Graecae in Bulgaria Repertae*
IGLS	L. Jalabert and R. Mouterde, *Inscriptions grècques et latines de la Syrie*
IGR	R. Cagnat et al., *Inscriptiones Graecae ad Res Romanas Pertinentes*
ILS	H. Dessau, *Inscriptiones Latinae Selectae*
INJ	*Israel Numismatic Journal*
Jb RGZM	*Jahrbuch des Röm.-Germ. Zentralmuseums, Mainz*
JAOS	*Journal of the American Oriental Society*
JARCE	*Journal of the American Research Center in Egypt*
JEA	*Journal of Egyptian Archaeology*
JESHO	*Journal of the Economic and Social History of the Orient*
JHS	*Journal of Hellenic Studies*
JJS	*Journal of Jewish Studies*
JNES	*Journal of Near Eastern Studies*
JQR	*Jewish Quarterly Review*
JRAS	*Journal of the Royal Asiatic Society*
JRS	*Journal of Roman Studies*
LCM	*Liverpool Classical Monthly*
m.	Mishnah
MAMA	*Monumenta Asiae Minoris Antiqua*
MEFR	*Mélanges d'Archéologie et d'Histoire de l'École Française de Rome*
Mem. Ac. Inscr.	*Mémoires de l'Académie des Inscriptions*
MUSJ	*Mélanges de l'Université St. Joseph*
NC	*Numismatic Chronicle*
Not. Dig. Or.	*Notitia Dignitatum Orientis*
OGIS	W. Dittenberger, *Orientis Graeci Inscriptiones Selectae*
PAES	*Publications of the Princeton University Archaeological Expeditions to Syria*
PBA	*Proceedings of the British Academy*
PBSR	*Papers of the British School at Rome*
PEFQSt	*Palestine Exploration Fund Quarterly Statement*
PEQ	*Palestine Exploration Quarterly*
PG	J.-P. Migne, *Patrum Graecorum Cursus Completus: series Graeca*
PL	J.-P. Migne, *Patrum Latinorum Cursus Completus: series Latina*
QDAP	*Quarterly of the Department of Antiquities of Palestine*
RA	*Revue Archéologique*

RB	*Revue Biblique*
RE	Pauly-Wissowa-Kroll, *Real-Encyclopädie der classischen Altertumswissenschaft*
REA	*Revue des Études Anciennes*
REG	*Revue des Études Grecques*
REJ	*Revue des Études Juives*
REL	*Revue des Études Latines*
RMD	M. M. Roxan, *Roman Military Diplomas*
RN	*Revue Numismatique*
SCI	*Scripta Classica Israelica*
SDB	*Supplément au Dictionnaire de la Bible*
SEG	*Supplementum Epigraphicum Graecum*
SHA	*Scriptores Historiae Augustae*
SMR	*Studien zu den Militärgrenzen Roms*
TAPA	*Transactions of the American Philological Association*
TLL	*Thesaurus Linguae Latinae*
tos.	Tosefta
y.	Jerusalem Talmud
YCS	*Yale Classical Studies*
ZDMG	*Zeitschrift der Deutschen Morgenländischen Gesellschaft*
ZDPV	*Zeitschrift des Deutschen Palästina-Vereins*
ZPE	*Zeitschrift für Papyrologie und Epigraphik*

ACKNOWLEDGEMENTS

1. Bostra, with the site of the legionary fortress. From the plan in D. L. Kennedy and D. N. Riley, *Rome's Desert Frontier From the Air* (London, 1990), 125.

2. Dura-Europos, with the military camp. From *The Excavations at Dura Europos: Preliminary Report, the Ninth Season* (1944).

3. Palmyra: plan. From M. Gawlikowski, *Le Temple Palmyrénien* (1973), p. 11, fig. 1.

4. Palmyra: the military quarter. From J. Starcky and M. Gawlikowski, *Palmyre* (1985), Pl. viii.

5. Ein Boqeq: Oasis and castellum. From the plan supplied by Prof. M. Gichon.

6. Upper Zohar fort. From R. Harper, *Hadashot Arkheologiyot (Archaeological Newsletter)* 89 (1987), p. 54.

7. Mezad Thamar and vicinity. From M. Gichon, *Saalburg-Jahrbuch* 33 (1976), p. 81, fig. 2.

8. Mezad Thamar. From the plan drawn by D. Chen, supplied by Professor M. Gichon.

9. Tsafit Tower and vicinity. Supplied by Prof. M. Gichon.

10. Tsafit. From the plan by D. Chen, supplied by Prof. M. Gichon.

11. Der el-'Atrash: plan. From D. Meredith, 'The Roman Roads and Stations in the Eastern Desert of Egypt'. *Journal of Egyptian Archaeology* 11 (1925), Pl. xii.

12. Qasr Beshir. From *The Roman Frontier in Central Jordan*, ed. S. Thomas Parker (1987), Vol. ii, fig. 88 on p. 469.

13. Dibsi Faraj: the defences. From R. Harper, 'Excavations at Dibsi Faraj, Northern Syria, 1972–74', *Dumbarton Oaks Papers* 29 (1975), p. 323.

INTRODUCTION

THE traditional view of the Roman empire holds that the republic was a period of expansion, the principate one of successful defence against barbarian attack, the late empire one of less successful defence and retrenchment. Past generations could look upon the growth of the empire with admiration, free from moral qualms. European imperialists were convinced that it was a good thing for a civilization they considered superior (their own as well as Rome) to rule barbaric natives.[1] Both the republic and the principate were admirable, the republic as a period of dynamic expansion, the principate as one of stability and defence of what had been achieved. In our time of doubts, anguish, and egalitarianism it is no longer easy to admire an expanding empire. Self-determination is held to be a right. Infringement of that right is seen as immoral. Accordingly, views of the Roman republic are now ambiguous.[2] That leaves us with the Roman Peace of the principate as an object of admiration. From the moment when Augustus put a stop to expansion the empire became laudable in modern eyes, for it defended civilization against the barbarians and thus laid the basis for our own achievements. In fact this is not true for Augustus. It has been shown to what extent this period, in spirit as in fact, was one of aggressive expansion.[3] Even so, however, the old view of the principate after his time still persists. One of the achievements of the principate is held to be the development of a system of frontier defence that allowed the citizens of the empire to live in peace and quiet. Hence 'Roman Frontier Studies'. The frontier also is considered a suitable object for comparison with the frontiers of modern states organized to keep out the armies of neighbouring states.

We have, accordingly, two fields of association, or objects of comparison: the Roman empire with the European empires now defunct, and the frontiers of the Roman empire with those of modern nations. However, these comparisons are inappropriate. The European colonial empires were all far away from the motherland. The natives stayed in

---

[1] For discussion see C. M. Wells, *The German Policy of Augustus* (1972), preface.

[2] William V. Harris, *War and Imperialism in Republican Rome, 327–70 BC* (1979), has helped in shaping and clarifying opinions.

[3] P. A. Brunt, in his review of Chr. Meyer, *Die Aussenpolitik des Augustus*, *JRS* 53 (1963), 170–6; Wells, ch. 1; 249 f.

their own environment, and the colonies were never incorporated in any real sense. The difficulties which the former colonial powers now face in absorbing into their own society great numbers of their former subjects are a recent phenomenon which belongs to post-colonial history. The Roman empire grew by conquering and absorbing neighbouring peoples, one after the other. The subjects in the provinces lost their identity as peoples and became, if they were lucky, Roman citizens. All this was ignored by the older scholars who identified with empire builders and admired Rome. Modern Europeans, on the other hand, who disapprove of foreign conquest and the suppression of liberty, still find much to praise in the principate because it is assumed to be a period of the defence of the provinces against barbarian invaders, since modern states may legitimately defend their borders against attack.

I have the dubious advantage of living in a country that has to defend its borders and has also been an occupying power for twenty years. This is not to suggest that these are preconditions for—or a guarantee of—superior insight, but it may serve as a relevant frame of reference. It is often ignored by Roman historians that the forces of an empire never have the sole duty of defending the border. They are armies of conquest and occupation, as well as defence. The work of an army of occupation is basically different from that of a fighting army, but there is not usually a single, clear-cut process of reorganization which marks the transition. The work of an occupying army is rarely morally edifying in terms of military glory or plain human decency. It requires very special checks and balances for an occupation to be civilized in modern terms. These did not exist in the Roman empire. Roman historians should not overlook the fact that the Roman army was in many areas and periods an army of occupation or an internal police force and should try to realize the consequences for those who suffered occupation. A further essential function of the Roman army was the maintenance in power of the ruler. The many civil wars that were fought cannot simply be treated as so many irregularities. They were the result of a situation in which only the army kept an emperor in power and only a rival with an army could bring him down. There was no state security police,[4] no people's militia, of the kind that secure political control independently of the army for modern monarchies or dictatorial regimes. Part of these functions was performed by the army. The focus of these activities is to

---

[4] This is not to deny that there were troops which undertook part of the duties normally carried out by security forces, e.g. the *frumentarii*, P. K. Baillie Reynolds, *JRS* 13 (1923), 168–89; B. Rankov, *Britannia* 18 (1987), 243–9.

be sought in the capital and cannot therefore be the subject of this book, but the loyalty of the population in the frontier provinces was important as well and it was the responsibility of the army to secure it.

A view often encountered in histories of the Roman empire is that Rome, in the first and second centuries AD, created static lines of defence and thus passed to a rigid strategic defensive. As a result the 'barbarians' slowly gained the initiative. One of the central themes pursued in several chapters is the nature of 'the frontier'. An attempt is made to show that the concept of the boundary of the empire, both in Roman eyes and in historical perspective, was different from that found in the modern literature. The political boundary of the empire was irrelevant as a concept, and the military boundary was never organized as a 'line of defence'. The limits of the empire, if at all defined, were expressed in terms of power and military action. The only clearly demarcated boundaries were those of provinces, so it is argued, and the consequences of this different conception have in part determined the arrangement of the book.

A related subject is the offensive or defensive character of Roman diplomacy and warfare. It is very often hard to determine whether an army is engaged in defence or offence. Every move forward can plausibly be explained as having for its sole purpose the protection of what one has. Similarly it is not always easy to determine whether an attacker was indeed fighting a war of his own choice. Historians of the principate often assume that every move by the Romans was aimed at establishing a secure frontier. Even if it were true—and this study will argue that it is not—that is a view which oversimplifies. Two parties are needed to fight a war, and both have motives. While a war is being fought the aims of both sides will change in accordance with developments in the field, and whatever is achieved may be completely different from what what was anticipated. Nor is it necessarily true that a consensus exists on each side as regards aims and methods.

All this may seem commonplace. It is, however, often ignored by the historians of the principate. Discussions are usually confined to asking, for instance, whether Trajan intended to conquer Parthia for economic reasons, to establish a secure frontier, out of sheer megalomania, or for a combination of reasons. Otherwise it is often quietly assumed that the safety of the provinces was of primary concern to the Roman authorities.

This work considers such matters for one particular part of the empire. The eastern frontier is less well-known, archaeologically, than those of central and western Europe, but occasionally there are good

literary sources which help in clarifying matters. This is not a 'History
of the Roman Frontier in the East', nor an attempt to provide a
comprehensive work of reference. It is an attempt to clarify various
aspects of Roman aims in the East, from the Caucasus to Sinai. The
arrangement is not historical or geographical, but topical. It is hoped
that the book will convince historians and archaeologists that various
matters may legitimately be reconsidered. The subjects of discussion
will be the relationship first with Parthia, then with Persia, in the light
of Roman imperialism after the republic, and the Roman army as an
instrument for the occupation of Judaea and Arabia and—a related
topic—the slow penetration of the desert. An attempt is then made to
say something of the life of civilians living under occupation. This
includes a section on the role of army units based in cities (a
phenomenon characteristic of the eastern provinces), a discussion of
extraordinary levies in the light of evidence from Talmudic sources,
and reflections on imperial propaganda in the provinces. Two chapters
deal with Roman policy regarding urbanization in the region: first, the
function of veteran settlements in the implementation of imperial
policy in the provinces; second, the extent of Roman support for
urbanization. At issue here again is the activeness or passiveness of the
Roman imperial government,[5] which is relevant, in this book, in so far
as it touched on life in the eastern frontier provinces. The central issue
here is security, for the achievements of a sovereign state as an
organization depend above all on its success in providing for the
physical security of its subjects. Economic prosperity cannot exist
without security, but security can exist without prosperity.
Bureaucratic organization and the judicial system are not treated in
this book for various reasons: because they are the subject of F. Millar's
comprehensive treatment, but also because they cannot be isolated
regionally. The development of urbanization, however, can be discussed on a regional basis and is therefore treated in two chapters. The
final chapter is a general consideration of Roman politics and strategy,
the motives which led to the decision to go to war and the function of
'frontier systems'.

The common denominator of these subjects consists of three questions: first, what were the Roman aims in the eastern provinces through
various periods? Second, what did the Romans do to achieve results?
Third, what was the effect on the population?

---

[5] F. Millar, *The Emperor in the Roman World* (1977), 399–410, discusses the acquisition of city-
status but not the question whether the Roman authorities actively and financially promoted
urbanization in the provinces.

The most influential recent book on frontier studies is E. N. Lut-twak's *Grand Strategy of the Roman Empire*. It is a lucid study, but it is based on secondary literature. It reinterprets interpretations by historians and archaeologists and is a systematization, not of historical material, but of modern scholarship. Hence it is based on the same a priori assumptions. The present book, on the other hand, attempts to find in the sources information on more diverse functions of the army than are usually depicted. It will try to show that the Roman army functioned as an army of conquest or was organized for conquest even in long periods of peace, but also that in certain areas it served first and foremost as an army of occupation, which could evolve into an internal security force in some parts.

The image of the Roman empire that underlies Luttwak's *Grand Strategy* and the works of the historians and archaeologists whom he follows presumes that Roman sovereignty and control could exist in the way it did only thanks to positive qualities of organization and management. This concept entails a conviction that a large and lasting empire must in itself represent a victory of order and civilization over forces of disintegration which are inevitably at work in every society. Other views of Roman rule may legitimately be maintained, and this book attempts to describe Roman control over a significant part of the Near East as functioning despite numerous deficiencies. These are encountered in obvious shortcomings in the preservation of internal security, severe and yet sometimes ineffectual repression of internal unrest, a lack of organization, at least by modern standards, numerous negative aspects of military control in the provinces, and the cost of maintaining the army in particular and the empire as a whole. As part of these costs may be listed the many extraordinary taxes and compulsory services imposed on the civilian population for the benefit of the army and administration, partly sanctioned by law, partly exacted despite imperial efforts to curb them. The question to be asked then is how Roman control over the Near East was in fact maintained despite these shortcomings. It would be idle to pretend that clear-cut answers could be produced in the present book, but at least the problems and some answers are now better defined.

These questions touch upon a theme of general interest in the study of ancient society, namely the degree of rationalization reflected by the social organization as known to us. This is a topic that requires consideration in general, but in particular as regards the Roman imperial army with its strict discipline and order. One may legitimately wonder whether these seemingly modern characteristics do not induce modern students to attribute anachronistic standards of rationality, complexity, or sophistication. This is now commonly accepted in the case of the ancient economy, but may perhaps be considered in other spheres as well. Finally, it may be added that these are matters of debate in the study of history in general. The extent to which major events are determined, or merely influenced, by the designs and the will of individuals is a subject of interest for every period of history.

Interpretation of Archaeological Evidence

The fact that an attempt can be made to reconsider basic matters, after almost two centuries of 'Frontier Studies', is due to the nature of the evidence as well as the way it is handled. Traditional military history used to study specific battles: Cannae, Alesia, and so on. The tools were descriptions in literary sources and knowledge of the terrain. Modern 'frontier studies' combine information from literary sources with the results of archaeological exploration and the analysis of inscriptions. The use of archaeology is particularly difficult because so much induction is involved in the interpretation of physical remains.

The remains of military installations are of great interest, but it will be argued in this book that it is a fallacy to assume that one can easily understand why a particular site was chosen for a fort. Any attempt to reach such an understanding springs unavoidably from a series of assumptions regarding the Roman behaviour. These are not often explicitly stated in reliable sources. Usually almost nothing is known of the relationship with the subject population among which the army was stationed. Students tend to assume that there was constant pressure exerted on the frontier, but that need not be true. Conversely very little is known of internal problems in the provinces. A recent study which considers the relationship between the distribution of Roman troops and native settlements in Britain has shown entirely unexpected results.[6]

Even the interpretation of inscriptions requires much induction. Career inscriptions list titles, functions, and places, but they usually no more give an impression of how the men actually spent their time than excavated army camps tell us what entire units were doing.

There are therefore serious difficulties in forming a synthesis based on such material. These vary between different areas. In the eastern provinces archaeology has made far less progress than in the West.

---

[6] D. J. Breeze, *Proc. Soc. Antiq. Scotland* 115 (1985), 223–8. Troop concentrations are found in relatively unpopulated regions.

Much of the evidence consists of chronological sequences of occupied sites which have been established by surveys only. Surveys unaccompanied by excavation cannot provide a reliable chronology. Even if the pottery can be dated with confidence—often it cannot—excavation will frequently show that a site was occupied in periods not represented by pottery picked up on the surface. All this makes it hard to provide a synthesis based on archaeological material. This is not meant to disparage the hard work of many archaeologists in the field. After a long period of relative stagnation a major effort is now being made to explore the remains of the Roman and Byzantine periods in the eastern provinces, work often carried out under difficult circumstances. However, even in the best-explored western provinces it is still difficult to distil history from artefacts.

Talmudic Sources

Talmudic literature contains a substantial number of passages that are historically significant, and these are cited regularly as sources for the history of Judaea in the Roman period.[7] But there are considerable difficulties in their evaluation as a historical source, for the aim of this literature was not historiography: it was the formulation of *halakhah* and *midrash*, *aggadah* and moral discourse. *Halakhah* is exposition and interpretation of the traditional law, based on the Bible. *Aggadah* is homiletic explanation of the Bible text. The *midrashim* are commentaries on the Bible which contain both halakhic and midrashic material.

It is in the nature of such subjects that they reflect historical events as well as daily life. For a historian to extract historical reality from this material is difficult but possible, while at the same time he will find an advantage in the very fact that this is not historical literature: statements are accordingly made with a definite candour and without the bias inherent in literature which has historiographical aims itself.

Talmudic texts are divided by subject and contents into various categories: the halakhic literature is topically arranged, while the midrashic literature is compiled in correlation with the verses of the Bible books. A chronological division is further made into tannaitic and amoraic literature: the *tannaim* were active in the first and second centuries AD, the *amoraim* from the third to the fifth centuries. Finally there is a geographical distinction between Palestinian and Babylonian

[7] As already noted in the Preface, Aharon Oppenheimer has generously assisted me in the selection and interpretation of these sources.

literature. A rule usually accepted holds that the relative authenticity of the sources may be determined by proximity in space and time. This rule has indeed a certain validity, but it must not be followed as if it were an absolute law. A relatively late work may contain early material, while a work edited at an earlier date could contain material which is close in time to the date of its redaction. For instance, a Babylonian work may contain authentic material relating to Palestine, while the same material may appear in a Palestinian source in a version altered by editors whose very closeness to the location led them to introduce changes.

The sources of Talmudic literature have been developed in different manners: some are the fruit of dialectical reflection in the Study House, while others have a background in reality. Naturally it is only the latter group which may form a basis for historical conclusions. When the name of the author of a *halakhah*, interpretation, or saying is transmitted, this is often helpful in establishing the date. Sometimes, however, later sages report in their own name words which belong to earlier periods. For the verification of authenticity it will not suffice to rely on the mere period of the sage in whose name the source is transmitted. It is necessary to examine the contents of the source, its subject, as well as its historical context.

Periods of revolts, persecution, and crisis have left their imprint in the form of increased dynamism in the development of *halakhah* and in the formation of *aggadah*. Since these are precisely the periods when there would be changes in the imposition of taxes and the methods of levying them, this may explain the existence of many sources regarding Roman taxes. However, here too caution is required, for people always tend to complain of the burden of taxation, particularly when they live under foreign rule. Obviously one cannot accept at face value sources which describe in rhetorical language the heavy burden of Roman taxation.

It is especially important to verify the version of the sources discussed. Talmudic questions in general, and halakhic subjects in particular, were considered by sages of both earlier and later periods; and the later generations tended not to appraise and examine the historical context of the material. Despite the holiness of the subject matter in the eyes of the copyists, these nevertheless occasionally introduced distortions precisely in the sources which are of special interest to the historian. He must therefore verify as carefully as possible the version of the source with which he is concerned before drawing historical conclusions.

Excessive zeal in the application of these rules of criticism to each and every halakhic or aggadic source could result in the neutralization of Talmudic literature as historical source material. However, the evidence of a group of testimonies found in different works and interpreted in combination still justifies historical investigation. Many problems may be left unresolved, and we often have to be satisfied with more or less likely guesses which do not lead to definite conclusions. But critical analysis of groups of sources relating to specific subjects in well-defined periods—such as the activities of the Roman army of occupation and Jewish attitudes towards it, or taxation, the subject of Chapter VI—is valuable for our understanding of these matters.

Geographical Outline

This book is concerned with the broad area of Roman activity which stretches from the Caucasus in the north to the Red Sea in the south. It is a very diverse region, and there is only one feature which justifies treating it as if it were a unit of the empire that can be discussed in isolation, namely the fact that this was the eastern boundary of the empire and its hinterland for seven centuries, from Pompey's eastern campaign in 63 BC till the Islamic conquest. This book considers various themes that all centre around the Roman exercise of power, with the army as its main instrument; the Roman concept of a 'frontier' is central to these themes; and the 'frontier in the East' is usually conceived as a separate entity. Whether this is correct is another matter and will have to be considered. However that may be, a brief geographical and historical introduction must be given here in order to provide a concrete definition of our field of study.

South of the Caucasus, in the west was Colchis with two ports, Phasis 'where for ships is the farthermost run',[8] and Dioscurias, a market-place where seventy tribes came together.[9] All spoke different languages. Farther east lived the Iberians in what is now eastern Georgia, a fertile country 'shut in by rocks, forts, and rivers which flow through ravines'.[10] Between the Iberians and the Caspian lived the Albani, 'pastoralists more than the Iberians and closer to the nomadic way of life but not savage'.[11] Their land was fertile as well. These peoples lived in river valleys that ran parallel to and south of the Caucasus range, the main rivers being the Phasis (Rioni) and Cyrus (Kura). The region was never fully incorporated into the empire, but

---

[8] Strabo xi 2. 16 (497).   [9] Loc. cit.   [10] Strabo xi 3. 4 (500).   [11] Strabo xi 4. 1 (501).

stations on the south-eastern shore of the Black Sea were occupied by the Roman army, and the peoples of the entire region were considered to be dependent and under obligations of various kinds.

These valleys are separated from the Mesopotamian plain by the formidable Armenian plateau. This is a country now physically partitioned between the Soviet Union, Turkey, and Iran, and in antiquity the subject of an interminable tug-of-war between Rome and Parthia/ Persia. In the words of Tacitus: 'This people has been inconstant of old, because of the character of the men and their geographical position, bordering, as they do, far along our province and extending far to Media. They are situated between the two major empires and are often hostile to them, out of hatred towards the Romans and jealousy of Parthia.'[12] Its ancient boundaries were as follows: on the west it bordered on the Euphrates, Cappadocia, and Commagene, on the south on modern Kurdistan, on the east on Media Atropatene. The northern boundary has already been indicated. In the Roman period distinction was made between Armenia Major, east of the Euphrates, and Armenia Minor, a separate kingdom west of the river. Almost ninety per cent of Armenia lies above 1000 metres. The region consists in fact of a number of plateaux of varying heights, between 1000 and 2000 metres, separated by deep river valleys. These are the two branches of the Upper Euphrates, the Kara and the Murat; the Araxes, which joins the Kura before issuing into the Caspian; and the Acampsis (Çoruh) which reaches the Black Sea near Batumi. Finally there is the Tigris, several tributaries of which have their sources in Kurdistan. Conically shaped mountains can be distinguished from afar, notably Mount Ararat, 5165 metres high, near the modern border between Turkey and the Soviet Union. The country is further marked by a number of lakes, three of them of great size: Van, Sevan, and Urmia. Because of its volcanic origin the soil is fertile and can be cultivated in the valleys. There were two main cities, Artaxata (near modern Yerevan) in the north and Tigranocerta (Martyropolis, modern Silvan)[13] in the south.

Communication overland is virtually impossible except through the deep river valleys. Most of these run roughly east–west, and consequently Armenia is primarily accessible along two major routes from Cappadocia in the west and from Media Atropatene in the east. A

---

[12] *Ann.* ii 56: 'Ambigua gens ea antiquitus hominum ingeniis et situ terrarum, quoniam nostris provinciis late praetenta penitus ad Medos porrigitus; maximisque imperiis interiecti et saepius discordes sunt, adversus Romanos odio et in Parthum invidia.'

[13] For the identification, R. Syme, *AFRBA*, 61–70.

major north–south route runs inland from Trapezus (Trabzon) on the Pontic coast to the plain which extends south of Armenia. It negotiates, from north to south, first, the Zigana pass, and then the Antitaurus range and the Kurdish Taurus. Thence one reaches north-western Syria and northern Mesopotamia (Ergani Pass). Where the important east–west roads cross this route the Romans chose their main stations: at Satala, Melitene, and Samosata. From the east the whole region can best be penetrated along the valleys of the Kura in the north and the Araxes in the south. In antiquity these formed the easiest routes to Media.

To the south the Euphrates and Tigris descend to a plateau at 200–500 metres, with a range of lower mountains which do not exceed 2000 metres. Here, at the edge of the plain, lie a number of significant towns: Zeugma, Edessa, Constantina, Mardin, Dara, Nisibis. This is the age-old route linking Anatolia and Syria with Mesopotamia. Here we have reached the northern arc of the 'Fertile Crescent', a zone of land that allowed crop cultivation and the development of urban life. It comprised the lands along the shore of the Mediterranean, the parts of Northern Mesopotamia just mentioned, and descended into Babylonia.

Along the Mediterranean coast stretches a fertile strip of land which is nowhere broader than 200 kilometres. In the north Mount Amanus (summit 2224 m.) forces all travellers from Anatolia to Syria to pass through the so-called Cilician Gates, near Iskenderun (Alexandretta, Alexandria ad Issum), scene of great battles for the sovereignty of Syria. Then one reaches Syrian Antioch at the point where the Orontes cuts through the mountains. This is the first of a series of great cities spread along the coast down to the port of Gaza. Approximately half-way there is a double mountain ridge, the Lebanon and Anti-Lebanon which reach a height of 3000 metres and enclose the fertile Beqaʿ valley. Through this valley flow the Orontes northwards and the Litani to the south. Along the Orontes one finds another group of ancient towns, protected by mountains on both sides. The Jordan Valley, the natural continuation of the Beqaʿ, descends to a level of almost −400 metres where the Jordan discharges into the Dead Sea. South of the Dead Sea the Wadi ʿAravah constitutes an inland depression which terminates at the ancient Red Sea port of Aela (ʿAqaba, Elath).

The Jordan River depression is separated from the coastal plain by the hills of Galilee and the Mountains of Samaria and Judaea. West of the ʿAravah is the Negev Desert, which is linked with the land bridge of Sinai and thence with Egypt and the Sahara. The Negev is a desert, but was settled by the Nabataeans and, in the Byzantine period, by their successors. It has seen a remarkable development of urban life, made possible by highly developed techniques of irrigation. The Sinai consists of two parts, the land bridge in the north, which is a sandy waste, and the peninsula with its colourful granite mountains in the south. The summit of Mount Catherine reaches a height of 2637 metres. It bears the name of the monastery which was the principal focus of interest in the region in the Byzantine period. Egypt, 'the key of the land and the sea',[14] cannot be ignored in any discussion of the Roman East, but it is as much a part of Africa as of Asia. And a large subject in itself. Sinai, therefore, is a suitable boundary for the area discussed in this book.

Lines of communication are dictated by the peculiar topography of the region. Traffic is always possible along the coast road from Alexandria in Egypt to the Cilician Gates. Parallel north–south routes run along the Orontes, through the Beqaʿ Valley, and over the ridge of Samaria and Judaea past Jerusalem. Travel inland is possible through a number of gaps in the hill-system such as the Valley of Jezreel or the ancient road from Berytus to Damascus.

The area east of the Jordan is a plateau which varies in height from 800 to 1700 metres, thus exceeding by 700 metres the highest mountains west of the river. It is divided by deep wadis which run east to west and drain into the Jordan Valley. The western part of the plateau is suitable for settlement thanks to an adequate water supply and easy north–south communications, a line which connects the Red Sea and the Arabian peninsula with southern Syria (the King's Highway, *via Nova Traiana*). Along this line were situated the three most important cities of the region: Gerasa, Philadelphia, and Petra. Another road ran farther east, parallel to the King's Highway, through level but arid terrain. The southern part of Transjordan is a desert, like the Negev to the west of it. The main arteries of the Roman road system therefore roughly resemble the Greek letter *pi*: there are two main north–south routes, the coast road and the route through the valley of the Orontes, proceeding southwards to the Arabian peninsula. They both link up with the main west–east road which connected Byzantium (Constantinople) with Mesopotamia.

The Transjordanian plateau, like the hills and mountains west of the Jordan, is chiefly limestone. North of the Yarmuk, that is, east and north-east of the Sea of Galilee, one reaches basalt and volcanic rock. In

---

[14] Tacitus, *Ann.* ii 59: 'claustraque terrae ac maris', in the most widely cited description of that province.

this area the capital of Roman Arabia, Bostra, was situated west of the volcanic mountain of the Jebel Druz (1732 m.). Between this town and Damascus are the notorious lava fields of the Leja. To the south-east stretches a chain of water holes in a long, wide depression, the Wadi Sirhan, an old caravan route through the desert and a region of transhumant pastoralists. Throughout history it has served as the gateway from Syria into Arabia, and Jawf, at its south-eastern end has been described as 'a splendid oasis, a great caravan centre, a strong Nabataean outpost'.[15]

East and south of the old Roman provinces was the Syrian desert, enclosed by the semicircle of the 'Fertile Crescent'. The Romans here were confronted with nomadic Bedouin, a confrontation which could not be avoided because the desert formed the shortest connection between their settled lands and the cultivated parts of Mesopotamia. A key position on the routes from the Mediterranean to the Euphrates was occupied by Palmyra, a magnificent city in an oasis in the Syrian Desert.

The Euphrates is an alpine river as far as ancient Zeugma, where it enters the plain and becomes navigable (a town nearby is called Bireçik = opening). There are no further tributaries of importance. The Khabur and Balikh are dry in summer, but they are significant as lines of movement and settlement. Both banks of the Euphrates and the river itself formed an important highway leading to Babylon, Seleucia, and the Persian/Arabian Gulf. Along it there were many stations, some forming the terminals of desert highways. One of these was Dura Europos, one of the most remarkable excavated sites in the Near East. The Tigris, like the Euphrates, is alpine in Armenia and navigable only from Mosul, near ancient Nineveh. Unlike the Euphrates, the Tigris is fed by a number of significant tributaries further downstream, such as the Greater and Lesser Zab, and the Diyala which descends from the Iranian plateau.

The Mediterranean coast enjoys a moderate climate. Otherwise this is a region of extreme heat and drought, most of it being desert. Armenia, however, is hot and dry in summer and very cold in winter. Military campaigns were impossible there in the cold season.

All that has been said so far will show that there were many peculiarities and difficulties which the Romans faced when they conquered the area. The fertile strip of land along the coast had all the characteristics of other Mediterranean parts of the empire. It could be

---

[15] N. Glueck, *BASOR* 96 (1944), 7–17.

subdued and incorporated along familiar lines. The Jews, of course, caused difficulties, but that had nothing to do with geography, except for the fact that they inhabited a country through which the strategic link between Africa and Asia ran. Beyond it, however, was the desert, inhabited by transhumant pastoralists who had to be handled in different ways. One of the tasks of this book will be to see whether these problems were solved and, if they were, how it was done.

More important, in Roman eyes, was the confrontation with Parthia/Persia. As will be clear from the preceding pages, this encounter took place in several areas and different manners. Geography dictated that military campaigns were inconceivable along the shortest routes between, say, Ctesiphon, the Parthian capital, and Damascus, for the Roman army would not embark on a major campaign in the desert if it could be avoided. The natural routes to be followed by the Roman and Parthian/Persian armies followed either the Euphrates or the Tigris. The Euphrates could be reached by a number of roads in northern Syria—if Palmyra and the desert were avoided. The Tigris route usually entailed following the routes further north by way of Carrhae or Edessa. The cities of northern Syria therefore were usually the bases of operations for the Roman army and the targets for the Parthian and Persian armies. The Roman conquest of Northern Mesopotamia changed matters, as will be emphasized below.

A second region of confrontation was Armenia, a difficult country for large armies. As already noted, it was best accessible along east–west lines from Cappadocia and Media Atropatene. In the Byzantine period there was a third theatre of operations, the lands south of the Caucasus, the coastal area (Colchis) and modern Georgia.

Historical Outline

Direct Roman involvement east and south-east of Cappadocia began with Pompey's campaign in the region. The Roman conception of empire entailed that any region where Roman troops had set foot had become subject to the Roman will. Rome could decide whether to exercise the resulting prerogatives, what obligations to impose or not. For the constituent parts of Syria, Judaea, and the Nabataean kingdom this meant that direct Roman control was extended gradually. The process whereby this happened has often been discussed and will not be traced in detail here. As soon as Syria had become part of the empire, the confrontation with Parthia was a matter of course. However, before the second century AD the campaigns undertaken by Roman armies did not in fact extend Roman influence beyond the limits reached by Pompey. Significant change could be effected either in Armenia, or in Mesopotamia, or conceivably farther north, in the Caucasus. An attempt to conquer Armenia was made under Nero by the ambitious Corbulo. It ended in failure. Another full-scale war was prepared in the same direction, further northward, but given up because of trouble with Vindex in the west. Drastic action was taken half a century afterwards by Trajan, who annexed Arabia and conquered Armenia and Mesopotamia as far as the Gulf. As is well known, the only lasting result of these enterprises was the least significant element, his annexation of Arabia. Yet another half century later another ambitious general, Avidius Cassius, campaigned in Mesopotamia with uncertain results.

A definite change came in the second half of the second century when northern Mesopotamia was conquered by Septimius Severus and permanently occupied. This had far-reaching results, for the border between the two empires was now closer to the Parthian capital than to that of Syria. In times of war Roman reinforcements had to come from a greater distance, and the Parthian army could reach Roman territory with greater ease. Roman lines were greatly extended, while those of the Parthians much shorter than before: the difference was some 300–400 kilometres. No less significant is the change in the nature of the frontier, for previously the border was marked by the Euphrates. The river flowed through fertile territory only in the north, and here it coincided with the traditional boundary between Commagene and Osrhoene, two nominally independent vassal states. After the Roman conquest of northern Mesopotamia the border ran through territory which had been under Parthian hegemony, and it separated cities and their territories which were inhabited by peoples with a common language and culture. It was an artificial line imposed by the outcome of military campaigns, and neither party was satisfied with it.

Before the Severan conquest wars between Rome and Parthia occurred at intervals of fifty years or more. In the following century there was no generation of Syrian peasants or citizens of Antioch that did not see legions marching past on their way to the border. These wars no longer resulted in the conquest of large territories. There was never any decisive gain for either party, but occasionally the Romans suffered serious defeats. The Parthian dynasty of the Arsacids fell and was replaced by the Sassanians, perhaps not accidentally, less than twenty years after the Roman conquest of northern Mesopotamia: the revolt of Ardashir, formerly a vassal of the Parthians in Persis (Fars), coincided with Caracalla's invasion of Parthia. The change in regime led to changes in religion, government, and society in Persia. In the mid third century a large Roman army was destroyed and many cities in the Roman provinces were sacked, which proves—if proof is needed—that the conquest of northern Mesopotamia did not protect Syria against invasion. These disasters were followed by the remarkable attempt of Palmyra, briefly successful, to create a separate eastern empire. The attempt itself, even if it failed, is indicative of the social, economic, and political changes that the Roman empire had undergone in the course of the centuries.

More important, in Sassanian Persia the Zoroastrian religion played a central role, something it had never done among the Hellenized Parthians. Similarly, with the Christianization of the Roman empire, here too religion became a driving force in politics. Religious ideology and sectarian conflict generated or aggravated social conflict within the Byzantine empire and at the same time began to play a role in the complicated relationship between Byzantium and Sassanian Persia. It will have to be seen how important a factor religion became in warfare in the third and fourth centuries.

In the Byzantine period the conflict extended to the region south of the Caucasus. Reports of invasions, especially those of the Huns, show that the tribes north of the mountain range were more of a danger than before, and this led to the militarization of the region, which consequently converted it into another area of confrontation between Rome and Persia.

There was a period of relative quiet in the fifth century which saw merely two brief wars, in 421–2 and 441–2. The periods of peace may partly have been caused by exhaustion from the catastrophic invasions from the North at the end of the fourth century and the beginning of the fifth. At an uncertain date in the late fourth to early fifth century the status of Armenia changed. Instead of a contested separate state it was divided between the two empires. This may have been one of the factors that helped in preserving the peace for much of the fifth century, and it changed the nature of warfare in the sixth. In the sixth and seventh centuries major wars again were fought between the two empires with, at times, disastrous results for both parties. It is even possible that the fatigue caused by these wars made it easier for the Islamic armies to conquer the Near East. In 591 Byzantine troops entered the Persian capital to restore Khusro Parwez to the throne after the attempt at usurpation by Vahram. On the Roman side Antioch was captured and sacked in 540. In 606–7 and 610–28 parts of Syria, including Antioch, were again overrun and occupied by Persia, the first extended occupation by Persia of any part of this province since the conquest by Pompey. This, however, was exceptional. Usually the expeditions gave the impression of being raids undertaken only for the sake of inflicting damage and acquiring loot.

This was certainly true of the raids undertaken by the Saracen allies of both parties. The infliction of economic and moral damage clearly was their only function. In northern Mesopotamia matters were different. The fortified cities here were the focus of the wars. They served as strategic bases, as objects of siege warfare, and their acquisition was the ultimate aim of the campaigns. The role of the Bedouin allies and of the fortified cities from the fourth century onwards will be topics of discussion. At the heart of the conflict between Rome and Persia throughout the Byzantine period lay the regions east of the Euphrates, occupied by Septimius Severus at the end of the second century. However, despite occasional territorial changes made in the course of the centuries, it seems that the aim of the wars, from the second century onward, was primarily an adjustment of the balance of power, not the destruction of the other empire or the elimination of its presence east of the Cilician Gates in the case of the Romans, and below the Iranian Plateau in the case of the Persians. The aim was not the mastery of the Near East, let alone the destruction of the other power. The latter was achieved only by Islam.

To a distant observer there is nothing in the numerous clashes between these two powers which would make them qualify as 'just wars' on either side. Neither do they seem to have been unavoidable. It is worthwhile, however, to attempt to uncover the motives which led to hostilities, to see whether anything can be said of the war aims, whether the powers just 'muddled into war', as Lloyd George said when speaking of the First World War, or rationally calculated what they might gain or lose in terms of economy, power, and prestige, when they undertook major campaigns.

These matters can be discussed at some length because there are relatively many texts which consider the wars between Rome and Parthia/Persia. It is clear that the primary victims of the wars were the inhabitants of northern Mesopotamia on both sides of the border, and those of northern Syria. The campaigns and the raids of Persia's Saracen allies did not usually reach southern Syria, Arabia, and Palestine. The principal military challenge here is usually held to be the confrontation with nomadic tribes from the desert. While it is recognized that the Jews were rebellious till the suppression of the Bar

Kokhba revolt in 132–5, it is usually assumed that there were no serious internal difficulties for the Roman authorities within the Roman provinces. Both assumptions will be questioned in this book. For this region we have a single remarkable source of information in the books of Flavius Josephus. Later centuries have not provided any sources that allow the composition of a continuous narrative, and every discussion is necessarily an exercise in the interpretation of random items of evidence.

However, it is worth considering these matters, because the interpretation by modern scholars of the accumulated evidence regarding Roman frontier policy is based on—and has reinforced—a specific view of the nature of Roman rule and of life in the Roman frontier provinces. This view, exemplified by the theories of a 'Grand Strategy' already mentioned, stems from impressions—and they are no more than that—regarding the rational and moral values of Roman rule and society. It is a view that underlies current trends in the evaluation of the literary sources on wars fought by the empire and in the interpretation and evaluation of scattered and incomplete facts regarding the military occupation of frontier districts. Furthermore, as already suggested, it may be constructive to reconsider the degree of rationality of Roman military organization. The Roman imperial army has long been an object of admiration. The fact that it was extraordinarily effective in battle does not necessarily imply that it was a sophisticated instrument when used as an army of occupation or defence.

Every exercise in historical interpretation attempts to present a view of what is often called the quality of life in a society of the past. This book argues that there is scope for modification of our conception of some aspects of Roman rule in the provinces.

I

ROME AND PERSIA

—Vous n'aimez pas les Marsouins?
—Nous les haïssons.
—Pour quelle raison les haïssez-vous?
—Vous le demandez? Les Marsouins ne sont-ils pas les voisins des Pingouins?
—Sans doute.
—Eh bien, c'est pour cela que les Pingouins haïssent les Marsouins.
—Est-ce une raison?
—Certainement. Qui dit voisins dit ennemis.

(Anatole France, L'Île des Pingouins)

MUCH has been written about the motives for individual Roman campaigns against Parthia, later Persia, and there is no agreement.[1] This is not surprising, given the fact that even the origins of the Second World War have been a subject of debate. Roman policy in the East in general reminds one of a statement made in another context:

The interests of security on the frontier, and of commercial relations, compel the more civilized state to exercise a certain ascendancy over neighbours whose turbulence and nomadic instincts render them difficult to live with. . . . The state must abandon the incessant struggle and deliver its frontier over to disorder, which renders property, security and civilization impossible; or it must plunge into the depths of savage countries, where the difficulties and sacrifices to which it is exposed increase with each step in advance . . . The greatest difficulty is in knowing where to stop.

This is a pronouncement made by Prince Alexander Gorchakov, Russian foreign minister in 1864, cited in a recent book about Afghanistan and the Soviet Union.[2]

---

[1] See the observations by John Mann, 'The Frontiers of the Principate', *ANRW* ii. 1, 508–533, esp. 509 f., and Mommsen's discussion of the confrontation of Rome and Parthia, *Römische Geschichte*, v. 355–8, esp. 358, cited below, p. 28.

[2] Henry S. Bradsher, *Afghanistan and the Soviet Union* (Duke University Press, 1983), 3 ff., a discussion of 'the age-old tendency for any powerful nation to seek the territorial limits of its power, to seek to fix a secure and stable frontier'. For the full text of the document, W. K. Fraser-Tytler, *Afghanistan: A Study of Political Developments in Central and Southern Asia* (third ed., revised by M. C. Gillett, 1967), 333–7.

A similar attitude existed in Britain towards the gradually expanding colony in South Africa:

Once embarked on the fatal policy of establishing a frontier in South Africa
and defending that frontier by force, there seems to be neither rest nor peace
for us till we follow our flying enemies and plant the British standard on the
walls of Timbuctoo. To subdue one tribe is only to come in contact with
another equally fierce, impractical [*sic*] and barbarous . . .[3]

At another level there is the elementary truth that perceptions of
aggressive and defensive behaviour vary. History, ancient and modern,
is replete with wars initiated by major powers able to produce rational
arguments that they are defending their own basic security. Yet such
wars are frequently considered obvious cases of imperialist expansion
by other parties or uninvolved observers. There is, however, no
evidence that this pattern applied to Roman behaviour in the East. It is
not at all clear that ancient ideology demanded that a war was initiated
only in defence of one's interests.[4]

The Roman Assessment of the Relationship

It is not surprising that we have no authentic knowledge of the Persian
attitude toward the Roman empire, since the primary sources are
Greek and Roman and there is very little first-hand information from
the Persian side. It is, however, remarkable that there is so little to be
found in ancient literature on the Roman attitude toward the Parthians
and Persians. Modern students can rely on very few genuine statements
made in antiquity and have to depend mostly on their own interpretation of the events. This is often influenced by an anti-Oriental interpretation of history that is very common in western historiography and
usually starts from the introductory treatment of the wars between
Persia and the Greeks: 'The line separating the Orient and the West
was clearly demarcated by the Greeks; Aryan Persia was relegated by
them to the East.'[5] It is a view often marked by ethnic or cultural
prejudice, as in the following incorrect pronouncement: 'It is almost
enough to point out that it is impossible to translate the word
"freedom", *eleutheria* in Greek, *libertas* in Latin, or "free man", into any
Near Eastern language, including Hebrew, or into any Far Eastern

---

[3] *The Times*, cited below, n. 59.
[4] On attitudes in the republican period, W. V. Harris, *War and Imperialism in Republican Rome,*
327–70 BC (1979), chapter V. For more on this subject see below, chapter IX.
[5] E. Bayer, *Grundzüge der griechischen Geschichte* (1964), 60.

language either, for that matter.'[6] An otherwise impeccable essay describes the Persian reliefs at Naqsh-i-Rustam and Bishapur, which celebrate victories over the Romans, in peculiar terms: 'This is history seen through the other end of the telescope.'[7] That is a remarkable slip of the pen for a scholar who undoubtedly knew what one sees through an inverted telescope. It is to be noted that modern prejudice often echoes ancient pronouncements.[8]

The relationship between Rome and Persia is necessarily interpreted in the light of the available information on the actual course of events, since there is not much in ancient literature on the aims or motives of either party. A few statements, however, are relevant and may be discussed.

Strabo described the Parthians as powerful but virtually part of the empire.[9] Tacitus states that Artabanus III, in AD 35, demanded restoration of the old border between Persia and Macedonia.[10] It may be noted that the reign of Artabanus III was a period of great political instability.[11] Later Dio reports hearing that Ardashir laid claim 'not only to Mesopotamia but also to Syria, threatening that he would regain all that the Persians once possessed as far as the Hellenic Sea, because it was his inheritance from his forefathers.'[12]—a claim of which Herodian gives a similar, though more verbose, account.[13] In the fourth century Shapur II wrote to Constantius that he might claim all the lands of his forefathers as far as the Strymon, but he would be satisfied with the handover of Armenia and Mesopotamia.[14]

There are several points to be made. First, not all such reports are true, particularly if they derive from a hostile source. Second, in diplomacy and war one must distinguish between words and deeds.

---

[6] M. I. Finley, *The Ancient Economy* (1973), 28. Yet every Hebrew dictionary lists several words used from Old Testament times onward to denote freedom.

[7] J. B. Ward-Perkins, 'The Roman West and the Parthian East', *PBA* 51 (1965), 175–99, esp. 178.

[8] e.g. Dio lxxi 25. 1: references in Marcus' speech to his troops about eastern legions; Herodian ii 10. 6–7, a speech attributed by Herodian to Septimius Severus at the time of the latter's bid for power: 'Witty and sophisticated jests, that is what the Syrians are good at, especially those in Antioch.' See also an inscription cut in the rock in Sinai (Wadi Mukatteb): 'Cessent Syri ante Latinos Romanos' (*CIL* iii 86). Gibbon is full of similar pronouncements, for instance on Severus Alexander: 'His virtues, as well as the vices of Elagabalus, contracted a tincture of weakness and effeminacy from the soft climate of Syria, of which he was a native.' For a recent example see S. L. Dyson, *The Creation of the Roman Frontier* (1985), 274: 'Service in the border areas must have seemed a relief to many Romans after dealing with thieving Greeks, mendacious Syrians and decadent Egyptians'.

[9] vi 4. 2 (288).   [10] *Ann.* vi. 31.

[11] Richard N. Frye in F. Millar, *The Roman Empire and its Neighbours* (²1981), 250.

[12] lxxx 3.   [13] vi 2. 2.

[14] Ammianus xvii 5. 4 f; also xvii 14. 1.

Tacitus suggests that Artabanus was, in fact, interested in Armenia. Third, Tacitus considered Artabanus' claim mere boastfulness, and Dio adds that there would have been no cause for worry if only the Roman army had been in any shape to fight. There are reports of a mutiny among the troops in Mesopotamia that resulted in the assassination of the governor.[15] The *Historia Augusta* tells of disciplinary problems that arose among troops stationed in Antioch and Daphne. In 218 there had been unrest among the troops in Syria because they were kept in tents during the winter in spite of apparently peaceful conditions.[16]

It is possible, although there is no evidence of this, that Romans genuinely believed the Persian empire to constitute a danger. Regarding the Parthian attack in 51 BC Debevoise observed that both the Roman commanders and the historians failed to understand the tactics employed by the enemy. The Parthian campaign was a cavalry raid, carried out by a limited number of fast moving horsemen, whose aim was not conquest and occupation, but booty and the destruction of Roman property.[17] This may well have been true of other Parthian campaigns for which we have less documentation to provide an impression of the Roman reactions and interpretations.

Generally speaking in diplomacy and war the relationship between the perception of danger and preventive attack is often confusing. History is full of empires whose motive—or justification—for continued expansion was the need to protect the frontier. However, there is little evidence that this was so in the case of the Romans. The only apparent exception I can think of is Josephus' story about the annexation of Commagene:[18] *if* the client king had been disloyal (he was not) and *if* the Parthians had wanted to attack (they did not) it would have been dangerous for the Romans not to occupy Samosata (they did). Josephus nowhere else suggests that the Parthians constituted a danger in these years. Before the Jewish War he represents Agrippa II as saying that Parthia would do nothing to violate the treaty with the Romans,[19] and afterward Vologaeses I gave Titus a gold crown when they met at Zeugma to celebrate the suppression of the Jewish revolt.[20] Otherwise we know only of the claims made by Ardashir discussed above.[21] Finally, it is to be noted that all available sources deny that

---

[15] Dio lxxx 3. 1; 4. 1–21; Herodian vi 4. 7, with Whittaker's note, Loeb, vol. ii, p. 107; Eutropius viii 23; SHA, *Severus Alexander* 53; Georgius Syncellus, *Chron.* 674; Zosimus i 18.

[16] Dio lxxviii 28. 2 (iii 436).

[17] N. C. Debevoise, *A Political History of Parthia* (1938), 96.

[18] See below, p. 39.   [19] *BJ* ii 16. 4 (379; 389).   [20] *BJ* vii 5. 2 (105).

[21] Cf. Syme, *CAH* xi. 1422 ff.: 'Parthia no menace.' See also below, n. 136.

there was any practical need for Severus' Persian campaign, while that of Caracalla is said to have been undertaken because the emperor 'wanted to acquire the Parthian kingdom for himself'.[22]

It is often claimed that there was an important difference between the Parthian and Sassanian attitude.[23] For the present it may be observed that the few sources quoted do not support this view, as Artabanus, in AD 35, made the same claims as Ardashir in the third century.

Julian, in his panegyric in honour of Constantius, claims that the Persians, in the reigns of Constantine and Constantius, had planned to conquer all of Syria and to plant settlers there after capturing the cities.[24] The war was actually fought for control of Nisibis. Persia's real demands are explicitly formulated by Ammianus in his report on the negotiations that preceded the war in 357–8. Shapur II wrote to Constantius that he might have demanded all the ancestral territory as far as the Strymon and the boundary of Macedonia, but in fact he offered peace in exchange for Armenia and Mesopotamia.[25] Constantius in reply insisted on the preservation of the status quo in Armenia and Mesopotamia;[26] and it was on this condition that the Romans offered peace in 359.[27] Shapur refused and invaded Mesopotamia. For the raid carried out by Shapur I we have a brief statement in the only contemporary Persian source to the effect that 'Caesar lied again and acted unjustly in Armenia'.[28]

Elements of Roman ideology may be distinguished in the criticism of Hadrian's decision not to proceed with Trajan's policy of expansion. Fronto, writing in the time of Lucius Verus, says:

Lucius who had either to take new citizens by a levy for the Parthian war, or out of the serving legionaries (*ex subsignanis militibus*), demoralized by dull and lax service, chose the stoutest men. For after the Emperor Trajan's time the armies were almost destitute of military training, Hadrian being energetic enough in mobilizing his friends and eloquently addressing his armies and generally in the appliances of war. Moreover he preferred to give up, rather

---

[22] For Severus' campaign, Dio lxxv 5, 9–12 (Boissevain iii 366–50); Herodian iii 9. 1; SHA, *Severus* 15. 1. The latter two sources claim that desire for glory had been the only motive. For that of Caracalla, Dio lxxviii 1. 1; Herodian iv 10. 1.

[23] See e.g. R. N. Frye, *The History of Ancient Iran* (1984), 239 and 293. As regards the Roman–Parthian relations Frye concludes that the conflict mostly concerned a matter of honour, particularly concerning Armenia, but he takes seriously the western sources on Sassanian expansionism.

[24] *Or.* i 27 A–B.   [25] Ammianus xvii 5. 5–6.   [26] xvii 14. 1–2.   [27] xvii 14. 9.

[28] The *Res Gestae Divi Saporis*, Honigmann and Maricq, pp. 12 f., para. 10–19, cf. comments on pp. 131 ff.; E. Kettenhofen, *Die römisch-persischen Kriege des 3. Jahrhunderts n. Chr.* (1982), 38. On the wars between Rome and Persia in the fifth century, see below, ch. V.

than to hold with an army, the provinces which Trajan had taken in various wars, and which now required to be organized.[29]

Fronto had a particular dislike of Hadrian.[30] Criticism of Hadrian's abandonment of Trajan's new provinces in the East is repeated by later authors.[31] The tone of contemporary dispute in hostile circles is undoubtedly represented by Fronto's claim that under Hadrian army discipline deteriorated, to be restored by Lucius Verus.[32] It is probable that the matter of army discipline was already an issue during the reign of Hadrian, to judge from the unique inscription recording Hadrian's inspection and report in Africa.[33]

The attitudes of the Roman upper class towards the army are a highly interesting subject, but this is not the place to discuss them. It is probably true to say that the upper class always feared the army; hence the insistence of many authors that it be kept in order by discipline.[34] Yet it is clear that this was a particularly familiar topic among the proponents of an activist frontier policy—one of their motives being that it kept the army away from mischief at home. Fronto echoes Tacitus on the eastern army under Corbulo. The idleness of the troops, says Tacitus, was a greater problem than the perfidy of the enemy. The Syrian legions had become lazy as a result of the long years of peace.[35] Pliny praises Trajan for restoring military discipline after Domitian had allowed it to deteriorate.[36] Against this Dio, who approved of Hadrian's eastern policy and found the expeditions of his own time wasteful and superfluous, emphasizes that Hadrian revived military training and discipline and thus preserved the peace without going to war.[37] Herodian severely criticizes Severus for undermining miiltary discipline.[38] While Herodian favoured an activist policy such as was indeed pursued by Severus, he disliked this particular emperor; so it is perhaps more correct to say that the maintenance of military discipline

---

[29] *Princ. Hist.* 10, translation C. R. Haines, Loeb, p. 207.

[30] As noted by E. Champlin, *Fronto and Antonine Rome* (1980), 95. For Fronto on Hadrian and the Roman army, R. W. Davies, *Latomus* 27 (1968), 75–95.

[31] Aurelius Victor xiv 1; Eutropius, *brev.* viii 6. 2; Festus xiv 4; xx 3.

[32] On military discipline, J. B. Campbell, *The Emperor and the Roman Army* (1984), 190–8, 300–11, 409 f.

[33] *ILS* 2487; 9133–5.   [34] As argued by Professor J. C. Mann in a letter.

[35] *Ann.* xiii 35. The same attitude appears in Tacitus' judgement of governors, *Agricola* 16. 3; cf. *Hist.* i 60.

[36] *Pan.* 18, 1; cf. *Ep.* viii 14. 7; x 29. 1.

[37] lxix 9. 1–6 (229 f) and see the comments by Millar, *A Study of Cassius Dio* (1964), 66 f. Dio, who had mixed feelings about Trajan, acknowledges that he kept the soldiers well in hand after his victory and did not allow them to become conceited and arrogant, as happens usually (lxviii 7. 5).

[38] iii. 8. 4 f. Cf. ii 6. 14 on Didius Julianus.

was one of the standard subjects of debate in a discussion of any emperor's merits.[39] Julian claims that the troops in the East were disaffected or even mutinous when Constantius took over command.[40] In the preceding period of peace they had become lax, and Constantius had to drill them in person before they could fight the Persians.[41] After the disaster at Adrianople in 378 complaints of slack discipline were uttered repeatedly.[42]

Another point should be made regarding Corbulo and his 'lax and demoralized' army. Corbulo fought a difficult mountain war in the Armenian highlands with troops accustomed to service in Syria. Such a war is hard for any army, and it may be relevant to cite a history of more recent warfare in the same region: 'A notable lesson of the successive Russo-Turkish wars over the same terrain and under similar climatic conditions is the progressive capacity of man to endure and overcome hardships imposed by the natural conditions.'[43] In other words, Corbulo's troops went through a natural and unavoidable process of acclimatization described by Tacitus in a biased manner.

It is clear that there were divergent views on eastern policy in various periods. The SHA author is nowadays accepted as giving a fairer assessment of Hadrian's eastern policy: 'He therefore abandoned all the territories across the Euphrates and Tigris, following the example, as he said, of Cato who pronounced the Macedonians free because he could not protect them.'[44] The implications of this assessment are twofold. First, as is now generally recognized, it shows that Trajan's conquests had been effectively lost by the time of his death. Second, it follows that Hadrian gave up Mesopotamia because he could not afford to reconquer it. Aristides insists that Antoninus Pius kept the army in a

---

[39] Dio lxxviii 3. 5 quotes rumours circulating at the time of Caracalla's murder in Mesopotamia, that the army was demoralized and untrained. Dio considered Caracalla a vain and foolish emperor.

[40] *Or.* i 18 D; 20 D.

[41] Ibid. 21 C.

[42] Zosimus iv 23: Sebastianus, appointed general, observed that the officers and soldiers led a disorderly and scandalous life and were ready only to flee and pray. He requested permission to form an élite unit of two thousand men. However, Libanius (*Or.* xxiv 3–5), weighing accusations that lack of discipline and training was the cause of the disaster, denies that the soldiers and officers were in any way lesser men than previous generations. Somewhat later, however, he is critical of the officers in the Syrian army at Antioch, who exploited and robbed their men to the detriment of discipline and fighting spirit. This then is followed by a passage idealizing the army of the past (*Or.* ii 37–40; similarly *Or.* xlvii 32 f.).

[43] W. E. D. Allen and P. Muratoff, *Caucasian Battlefields* (1953), 7.

[44] SHA, *Hadrian* 5. 3: 'quare omnia trans Euphraten ac Tigrim reliquit exemplo, ut dicebat, Catonis, qui Macedones liberos pronuntiavit, quia tueri non poterant.' On the implications of this passage for the interpretation of republican policy see Harris, 144 f.

state of preparedness through exercise and discipline; that is to say, the army did not necessarily deteriorate in times of peace.[45]

Dio's criticism of the annexation of Mesopotamia is well-known.[46] Severus claimed that he had added a large territory to the empire and had made it a bulwark of Syria, but Dio himself insists it was all a waste of money and a cause of constant war. Rome had now annexed peoples who were neighbours of Parthia and was therefore constantly fighting other peoples' wars. Apart from being an interesting observation in itself, this shows that there existed internal criticism of the ideology that demanded periodical expansion of the empire.[47] It is not, however, moral criticism, nor an objection to expansion in principle. Neither Severus nor Dio claimed this was a war of defence. Dio stresses that Severus had selected the wrong area for expansion: the conquests were not profitable, and the new subject peoples caused trouble. Elsewhere he represents Maecenas as advising Augustus against further conquests.[48] It is important to note that Dio was not motivated by a biased attitude towards Severus in general in expressing his criticism. He is no less critical of Trajan's motivation in undertaking his Parthian war: 'He would say that he had gone further than Alexander and wrote accordingly to the Senate, while he could not even keep what he had conquered.'[49] Yet he had a high regard for Trajan[50] and approved of his Dacian war.[51]

This echoes Strabo's attitude, which was one of profound admiration for the empire: it encompassed all that was worth having and left aside infertile regions and those inhabited by nomads.[52] According to the Roman conception of empire no distinction was made between vassal kingdoms on the periphery and directly administered regions. They were all equally part of the empire. The vassal kingdoms included, in fact, that of the Parthians; Germany was being conquered (this was written before Varus); and in the north and east parts were all the time being added to the empire.

---

[45] *Roman Oration*, 87.

[46] lxxv. 3 (ed. Boissevain, 340): ἔλεγέ τε μεγάλην τέ τινα χώραν προσκεκτῆσθαι καὶ πρόβολον αὐτὴν τῆς Συρίας πεποιῆσθαι. ἐλέγχεται δὲ ἐξ αὐτοῦ τοῦ ἔργου καὶ πολέμων ἡμῖν συνεχῶν, ὡς καὶ δαπανημάτων πολλῶν, αἰτία οὖσα. δίδωσι μὲν γὰρ ἐλάχιστα, ἀναλίσκει δὲ παμπληθῆ, καὶ πρὸς ἐγγυτέρους καὶ τῶν Μήδων καὶ τῶν Πάρθων προσεληλυθότες ἀεὶ τρόπον τινὰ ὑπὲρ αὐτῶν μαχόμεθα.

[47] On this passage see F. Millar, *Brittannia* 13 (1982), 1. Note also the judgement in the *epitome de Caesaribus* 20. 5: 'fuit bellicosissimus omnium, qui ante eum ferunt'.

[48] lii 18. 5; 37. 1 (ed. Boissevain ii, 341; 407).

[49] lxviii 29. 1; cf. 33. 1: the whole war was fruitless.

[50] lxviii 6–7.

[51] lxviii 6. 1: undertaken because of 'past acts', yearly tribute paid to the Dacians, increased power and arrogance.

[52] vi 4. 2 (288); xvii 3. 24 (839).

Appian likewise held that the Romans had conquered all that was worthwhile and profitable to conquer.[53] He too stresses the need for selective expansionism: 'possessing the best parts of the earth and the sea they generally prefer to preserve their empire by good judgement rather than extend it indefinitely over poor and profitless barbarian peoples.' Pausanias notes with approval that the Romans refrain from superfluous conquests and praises the peace kept by Antoninus Pius.[54] Here too the emphasis is on caution versus unprofitable adventures. Aristides mentions wars as a thing of the past.[55]

These three all lived in the time of Antoninus Pius. Like Strabo and Dio they represent Greek culture, but this was not a factor of decisive importance. Herodian, writing toward the middle of the third century, resembles Strabo in admiring expansionist policy: according to wise advice given to Commodus, it would be wonderful for the new emperor 'to return in triumph, leading home barbarian kings and governors as prisoners in chains. This was what made your Roman predecessors great and famous.'[56] One is reminded of Corbulo's 'beatos quondam duces Romanos'.[57] Procopius, in the sixth century, still found that the noble king is rightly praised for striving to enlarge his realm.[58]

In literature, therefore, expansionist policy is both praised and criticized. It is, of course, not at all uncommon for empires to expand, internal criticism notwithstanding. An editorial in *The Times* of 1853 observes:

So long as the Governor of the Cape shall have a large military force at his disposal, supported at the expense of this country, we doubt not that he will always find enemies against whom to direct it, and so long as we encourage our colonists, relying on our military protection, to scatter themselves over a vast continent without the support of a concentrated population, we must expect every succeeding mail to bring us the same tale of losses and disasters.[59]

The ancient sources and the editorial just cited all speak exclusively in terms of utility, of cost and benefit, in addition to the desire for glory

[53] *Praef.* 7/25–8: ὅλως τε δι' εὐβουλίαν τὰ κράτιστα γῆς καὶ θαλάσσης ἔχοντες σώζειν ἐθέλουσι μᾶλλον ἢ τὴν ἀρχὴν ἐς ἄπειρον ἐκφέρειν ἐπὶ βάρβαρα ἔθνη πενιχρὰ καὶ ἀκερδῆ, ὧν ἐγώ τινας εἶδον ἐν Ῥώμῃ πρεσβευομένους τε καὶ διδόντας ἑαυτοὺς ὑπηκόους εἶναι, καὶ οὐ δεξάμενον βασιλέα.

[54] i 9. 5; viii 43.

[55] *Roman Oration* 70 f.

[56] I 6. 6: καλὸν δέ σοι χειρωσαμένῳ πάντας αὐτοὺς καὶ τὴν ὑπὸ τῇ ἄρκτῳ ἀρχὴν ὠκεανῷ ὁρίσαντι ἐπανελθεῖν οἴκαδε θριαμβεύοντί τε καὶ δεσμίους ἀπάγοντι καὶ αἰχμαλώτους βασιλεῖς τε καὶ σατράπας βαρβάρους. Τούτοις γὰρ οἱ πρὸ σοῦ Ῥωμαῖοι μεγάλοι τε καὶ ἔνδοξοι γεγόνασι. Cf. C. R. Whittaker's comments, Loeb vol. i, p. lxxiii. For these matters see also below, ch. IX, p. 374.

[57] Tacitus, *Ann.* xi 20. 1.

[58] *Bell*, ii 2. 14: *de aedificiis* i. 1. 6. Cf. Averil Cameron, *Procopius* (1985).

[59] Editorial, 28 February 1853, cited by John S. Galbraith, *Reluctant Empire: British Policy on the South African Frontier 1834–1854* (1963), 3.

on the part of the emperor. Nowhere is it argued that one should refrain from foreign conquest for moral reasons or from considerations of justice or humanity. The same can be noticed in the oration attributed by Josephus to Agrippa II, a last attempt to dissuade the Jews from their rebellion. Independence and foreign domination are equated with freedom and slavery. It is desirable to be free if you can. It is natural that the stronger power will subject the weaker. These are not matters of right or wrong but of logic, cost, and benefit. The authors who criticize uncontrolled expansion all wrote in the same period, and it is only natural to assume that opinions on such subjects varied from period to period. It is quite possible that, by the end of the reign of Augustus, there was a widespread feeling that the empire was large enough. That is no proof, however, that this remained so ever after.

Rome's Persian Wars

In modern literature it is very common to speak of Rome's need to defend herself against Parthia, 'whose power was the only "systemic threat" to Rome . . .'[60] Yet it may be noted that Mommsen assessed the relationship differently. In discussing the ongoing conflict between Rome and Parthia he observes that the coexistence of two equal major powers was incompatible with the Roman character, or perhaps even with ancient politics in general. 'The Roman empire accepted only the sea or undefended land as its frontier. The Romans grudged the weaker but militant Parthian state its position of power and took from the Parthians what they could not abandon. Hence the relationship between Rome and Iran was a continuous struggle for control of the left bank of the Euphrates.'[61] In fact, except in the 150s, Parthia never took the initiative in attacking Roman territory, nor is there any evidence that it ever laid claim in earnest to the Syrian region.

A brief survey of well-known facts should suffice. Before the first war between the two empires there were three treaties concluded by Sulla, Lucullus, and Pompey (in 66 BC). Each time the initiative came from Parthia, and Rome responded by bullying and insulting without actually entering into conflict with Parthia.[62] As soon as Syria and Pontus were brought into the empire in the first century BC Rome ceased to recognize the Euphrates as the boundary delimiting the

---

[60] The description by Edward N. Luttwak, *The Grand Strategy of the Roman Empire* (1976), 19, who in matters like this could only follow what appeared to be general agreement among ancient historians.

[61] T. Mommsen, *Römische Geschichte* v, ch. 9, esp. p. 358.

[62] Detailed analysis by A. Keaveney, *AJP* 102 (1981), 195–212; *AJP* 103 (1982), 412–428.

spheres of influence of the two states.[63] In 51 BC Parthian incursions into Syria were repelled. These, however, followed preparations for an invasion made by Gabinus in 65 BC and Crassus' actual invasion and defeat at Carrhae in 54,[64] and were followed in turn by Caesar's preparation for a grand Parthian campaign.[65] During the Civil Wars there was a clear tendency on the part of the losers to call in the aid of the Parthians against their Roman enemies. In 45 BC Q. Caecilius Bassus (a Pompeian), shut up at Apamea by Caesarian forces, appealed to the Parthians for aid. Pacorus forced the abandonment of the siege.[66] In 40 Labienus persuaded the Parthian king to invade Roman territory. This resulted in the only large-scale Parthian invasion of Roman territory (41–38) and was followed by Antony's unsuccessful campaign into Media Atropatene (Azerbaijan) and beyond in 36.[67] In the same years the Hasmonaean Antigonus offered money to the Parthian king in exchange for support against his rival Hyrcanus.[68] The Parthians were popular with the subject peoples, for the Roman governors had mistreated them, while the Parthian Pacorus was just and mild.[69] Later, in 35/4, Sextus Pompeius offered the Parthians his services.[70]

AD 52–63: Corbulo's eastern campaigns turned a diplomatic conflict regarding Armenia into a military one. 57–8: The invasion of Armenia transformed that state into a client with a garrison of Roman troops. 61–2: Tigranes of Armenia, supported by Corbulo, invaded Adiabene. Corbulo threatened Vologaeses with an invasion of Mesopotamia and made actual preparations. Bridgeheads were thrown across the Euphrates.[71] Caesennius Paetus invaded Armenia. Vologaeses demonstrated against the Syrian frontier. Paetus was defeated and surrendered in Armenia. The end result was the withdrawal of Roman troops to Syria and Cappadocia and an agreement on Armenia. The activist policy did not come to an end, however, as appears from the

---

[63] P. A. Brunt, 'Laus imperii', in P. D. A. Garnsey and C. R. Whittaker, *Imperialism in the Ancient World* (1978), 159–91, esp. 170 f. Keaveney, op. cit., traces an increased tendency towards confrontation on the part of the Roman leaders in the East.

[64] According to Plutarch, *Crassus* 16, the expedition was undertaken out of sheer megalomania: Crassus dreamt of 'Bactria, India, and the Outer Sea'. A. D. H. Bivar, *Cambridge History of Iran*, iii. 1. 49 f., however, sees it in the light of the dynastic struggle in Parthia: Crassus came to the support of Mithradates who was besieged in Seleucia.

[65] Appian, *BC* ii 110: scheduled to last three years; 16 legions; 90,000 infantry; 10,000 cavalry. Mommsen is quite clear about Rome's ambitions beyond the Euphrates: *Römische Geschichte* iii. 148 f.

[66] Cicero, ad Att. xiv 9; Dio xlvii 27; Appian, *BC* iv 59.

[67] For the geography, Bivar, 63 f.

[68] Debevoise, 105–18.   [69] Dio xlviii 24. 8; xlix 20. 4.

[70] Appian, *BC* v 133; Dio xlix 18; Livy, *ep.* cxxxi.   [71] Tacitus, *Ann.* xv 3; 5.

plans made for massive intervention in the North-East and for an Ethiopian campaign (discussed below).

112–14: In renewed conflict Trajan annexed Armenia. 115–16: A Parthian campaign was followed by annexation; Seleucia and Ctesiphon were taken and three new provinces organized. However, it all ended in failure and withdrawal.[72]

155: The Parthians invaded Armenia but subsequently withdrew. 161: Armenia was invaded for a second time. An Arsacid was placed on the Armenian throne. The Cappadocian and Syrian troops were defeated. The Parthians raided or threatened to raid Syrian cities. Parthian troops withdrew from Syria and remained in Armenia, which they failed to defend in 163. Avidius Cassius led a Parthian campaign deep into Mesopotamia. Seleucia and Ctesiphon were plundered.[73] This was followed by the plague in the Roman army and its withdrawal. However, Dura-Europos was permanently occupied by Roman troops, and it is quite possible that Roman garrisons were left in various parts of northern Mesopotamia. It should be kept in mind that this began as a war for control of Armenia.

194–8: Septimius Severus led to Parthian campaigns. Seleucia was captured and Ctesiphon plundered.[74] Northern Mesopotamia was annexed as a province.[75]

215–17: Caracalla marched against Adiabene. He died at Carrhae. According to Dio and Herodian the pretext for the campaign was that Artabanus had refused Caracalla the hand of his daughter, but in reality he wished to occupy the Parthian kingdom.[76] Macrinus met with a reverse near Nisibis. Then followed a negotiated peace.

[72] F. A. Lepper, *Trajan's Parthian War* (1948); M. G. Bertinelli, 'I Romani oltre l'Eufrate', *ANRW* ii. 9. 1 (1976), 3–22. For the capture of Ctesiphon, Honigmann, RE Suppl. 4, s.v. 'Ktesiphon'., col. 1111 f. A considerable number of Roman coins, the latest of 115/16, have been found at Seleucia, cf. R. H. McDowell, *Coins from Seleucia on the Tigris* (1935), 194, 232. For Seleucia and Ctesiphon, A. Oppenheimer, in collaboration with B. Isaac and M. Lecker, *Babylonia Judaica in the Talmudic Period* (1983), 179 ff. For Trajan's organization of the province, A. Maricq, *Syria* 36 (1959), 254 ff. = *Classica et Orientalia* (1965), 103–11. For evidence regarding the military occupation of Armenia in those years, J. Crow, *DRBE*, 80 f.

[73] The sources: Dio lxxi 2 (iii 246); Ammianus xxiii 6. 23–24; SHA, *Verus* 8. 3–4, *M. Antoninus* 8. 6; Orosius vii 15. 2; Fronto, *principia historiae*, ed. Haines, Loeb, ii. 209. See Bertinelli, 23–31; Debevoise, 246–53; for the chronology, A. Birley, *Marcus Aurelius* (1966), 161.

[74] Dio lxxvi 9. 3–4 (iii 77); SHA, *Severus*, 16. 1; Herodian iii 9. 9–12. For the expedition, Bertinelli, 32–45; Debevoise, 259–62. For the chronology of the campaign, Millar, 143; J. Hasebroek, *Untersuchungen zur Geschichte des Kaisers Septimius Severus* (1921), 119 f. Archaeological evidence from Seleucia consists of a cache of coins the latest of which dates to 198/9, cf. McDowell, 91 f, 130, 235.

[75] The first prefect of the new province is now known from an inscription discussed by D. L. Kennedy, *ZPE* 36 (1979), 255–62. The precise date of the formation of the new province, 195 or 198, is not quite certain.

[76] Dio lxxix 1 (Boissevain, p. 403); Herodian iv 10. 1.

While there is an overwhelming lack of ancient sources that explicitly discuss the reasons for the wars between Rome and Persia, the survey of known facts given above clearly shows a consistent pattern of Roman expansionism in Mesopotamia. There were periods of Roman inaction and periods of an activist policy. It cannot be shown that the safety of the Roman province of Syria was consistently threatened by Persian ambition. Raids into Syria were always part of the Parthian strategy, but it is not at all clear that the Parthians—or the Sassanians, for that matter—had any desire permanently to occupy these lands. When the Roman army operated in Armenia a successful Persian raid into Syrian territory was the most effective move to bring Roman troops back to this province (e.g. in 62). It is no coincidence that in 359 it was a Roman deserter, Antoninus, who persuaded the Persian king not to waste time in Mesopotamia, but to press on to the Euphrates crossings.[77] This is not to suggest that the impact of the Parthian invasion of 40 BC and its repercussions in Asia Minor were negligible:[78] the memories of that event may well have had a long-term effect on Roman attitudes toward Parthia. The same may be said of Shapur I's invasion three centuries later.[79] Yet Shapur's own report of his victories nowhere registers any permanent claim on territories west of the Euphrates.[80] The first campaign is represented as a war of defence in all sources. During the second campaign, according to the text, forts and cities 'of the Roman people' were conquered (but not permanently occupied). During the third campaign conquests, pillage, and devastation are recorded. There is no suggestion that any of the territories mentioned really belonged to the Persian kingdom, there was no attempt permanently to occupy any parts west of the Euphrates, and the treatment of prisoners of war followed the traditional Persian pattern: deportation and collective settlement in a foreign land. These wars were followed by yet another Roman expedition which devastated Babylonia as far as

[77] Ammianus xviii 10. 1; cf. xix 1. 3, 6 and xviii 8. 1.

[78] D. Magie, *Roman Rule in Asia Minor* (1950), 430 f., with n. 10 on pp. 1280 f. In 39 BC Aphrodisias was granted its freedom, apparently as a reward for its resistance to the Parthians, J. Reynolds, *Aphrodisias and Rome* (*JRS* Monographs 1, 1982), document 8.

[79] Gordian invaded Persia in 243. The date of the first Persian expedition is uncertain. It varies according to different sources: 252, 253, 255/6. The third campaign, which resulted in the capture of Valerian, began in 259 or 260. Zosimus i. 27, 2; Ammianus xxiii 5, 3; Zonaras xii 23, p. iii 141. 3–6 (Dindorf); Syncellus, *Chronographia* pp. i 715 f. (Dindorf); *Orac. Sib.* xiii; Syrian Chronicle of 724 (*CSCO* iii, p. 149. 20); E. Honigmann and A. Maricq, *Recherches sur les Res Gestae Divi Saporis* (1953), par. 10–19, pp. 12 f., with comments on pp. 131–42; A. Alföldi, *Studien zur Geschichte der Weltkrise des 3. Jahrhunderts* (1967), 138–53; Kettenhofen, 38 ff.; S. James, *Chiron* 15 (1985), 111–24.

[80] Edition of the Greek text with Middle Persian and Parthian in transcription by A. Maricq, *Syria* 35 (1958), 295–360.

Ctesiphon. Odenathus of Palmyra may have reached Ctesiphon twice, in 263 and 266/7.[81] According to the *Historia Augusta* Aurelian was murdered while on his way to Persia with a large army.[82] In 283 Carus took Koke (Be Ardeshir) and Ctesiphon.[83] T. Barnes has argued that Galerius too reached Ctesiphon during his campaign in 296–7.[84] In 363 Julian operated in the area, and in 591 Byzantine troops entered Ctesiphon to restore Khusro II to the throne.[85] Severus Alexander and Gordian III invaded the Persian part of Mesopotamia but did not reach the South.[86] Under Constantius Rome and Persia fought numerous battles, all in northern Mesopotamia.[87]

The striking element in this survey is the fact that no part of Syria or Cappadocia was ever occupied by Persia for any length of time. What Persia never accepted was a Roman takeover in Armenia or expansion east of the Euphrates. As part of their efforts to drive out the Romans from these areas or to block further advance the Persians would threaten Syria when they could. Luttwak expresses similar views on the Roman relationship with Parthia. However, he agrees with many others in considering Sassanian policy radically different from that of the Parthians: 'Sassanid expansionism transcended the scope of Arsacid ambitions, which had been limited to Armenia'. And he goes on to say: 'A bare chronology suffices to illustrate the continuity of the Sassanid threat'.[88] However, all the chronology illustrates is that the Persians did not accept the Roman presence east of the Euphrates. Before the seventh century the Persians reached Antioch only twice, the Romans southern Mesopotamia again and again.[89]

It has been pointed out that the partition of Mesopotamia divided a

[81] Cf. A. Alföldi, *Studien*, 188–95. For the sources, J. Eadie, *The Breviarium of Festus* (1967), 92 f. and 144 f.

[82] SHA, *Aurelian* xxxv 5. No other source mentions Aurelian's declaration of war against Persia. His death in or near Perinthos while marching eastward is well attested: Zosimus i 61. 3–62. 1; Aur. Vict. *Caes.* 35. 8, etc.

[83] Festus, *Breviarium*, 24 and parallel sources (cf. Eadie, 93–5; add: Euagrius, *HE* iii 41, *PG* lxxxvi 2, col. 2689a).

[84] *Phoenix* 30 (1976), 183. The evidence is explicit only for Armenia.

[85] Theophylactus Simocatta v 6. 7.

[86] For Alexander's campaign, SHA, *Severus Alexander* 50. 5; 54. 7; 55; Herodian vi 4–6 (with Whittaker's notes in the Loeb ed., ii. 102–21); cf. A. Jardé, *Études critiques sur la vie et la regne de Sévère Alexandre* (1925), 83–5; for relevant evidence from Hatra, A. Maricq, *Syria* 34 (1957), 288–305. For the war of Gordian, Eutropius ix 2; SHA, *Gordian*, 34; cf. P. W. Townsend, *YCS* 4 (1934), 126–32; Loriot, *ANRW* ii. 2 (1975), 657–787, esp. 757–75; E. Kettenhofen, *AFRBA*, 151–71.

[87] Evidence in Eadie, 149–51.

[88] 150–2.

[89] Dr Kennedy rightly observes that Ctesiphon was much more exposed to attack than was Antioch behind Mt. Silpius.

people which formed to a certain extent a homogeneous unit with a common language and shared historical traditions.[90] The conquest and annexation of part of this area brought about a state of permanent conflict between Rome and Persia. Neither party was satisfied with the status quo. However, the long-term effects of the Roman conquest of northern Mesopotamia will be discussed below, in Chapter V.

Roman and Byzantine rule in the East lasted seven centuries. The border remained more or less static for an extended period, during the two and a half centuries following the Byzantine loss of Nisibis in 363.[91] In this period there were no major changes because neither power succeeded in effecting them in the many wars that were actually fought.

The Distribution of Troops

The next subject to be discussed is the geographical distribution of Roman troops. As observed frequently in this book, without further information conclusions about strategy which are drawn from the disposition of an army are usually speculative, more so, at any rate, than many historians seem to think. Yet with due caution something can be said, and indeed something must be said, as so much has been concluded by other students on the basis of this sort of information. It is usually claimed that the army was organized for defence in the Flavian period, and the term 'Euphrates limes' is employed. That term is not applicable, as has been shown elsewhere.[92] It can equally well be argued from the organization and disposition of the Roman army in the East that it was geared for aggressive diplomacy or even offensive warfare rather than defence, at least until the Byzantine period. The Flavian reorganization of the East can in fact be seen in an aggressive light. Client states were eliminated and their populations brought under direct administration, roads were constructed, and legions moved forward to the Euphrates.

In this chapter the Roman army in Judaea is not discussed, nor is that in the province of Arabia after its annexation in 106, an omission which requires explanation. The arrangement of this book is topical, since it attempts to present ideas on what the army did and what it was there for in different periods and different locations. The army in

---

[90] J. B. Segal, 'Mesopotamian Communities from Julian to the Rise of Islam', *PBA* (1955), 109–41. For similar observations on Armenia, Mommsen, *Römische Geschichte* v. 356 f.

[91] Ammianus xxv 8. 13–9.2 for the surrender of Nisibis. Before 363 Nisibis frequently changed hands. It was, in the words of the Babylonian Talmud, Qidushin 72a, one of the cities which Rome 'sometimes swallows and sometimes spits out'. For the city, Oppenheimer, 319–34.

[92] Isaac, *JRS* 78 (1988), 125–147.

Judaea, Arabia, and western Syria had, so it will be argued, functions
different from those elements of the eastern army based in forward
locations on the Euphrates. The troops in Judaea and Arabia were
armies of occupation which, as long as they served there and were not
transferred elsewhere, performed tasks different from those carried out
by troops stationed in an area of confrontation with Persia. After the
summary of events given above there is no need of further argument to
prove that there was no connection at all between the military occupation of Judaea and Arabia and the confrontation between Rome and
Persia, as long as the road-system in these provinces was safe enough to
allow troops from Egypt and Africa undisturbed passage on their way
to the Euphrates in case of need. From the first century BC to the
seventh century AD no Parthian or Persian troops reached Southern
Syria, Arabia, or Palestine. When the Roman army collapsed under
Valerian, the Persian forces made for Asia Minor and left the southern
sector in peace.[93] The Roman army as a force of occupation, rather
than conquest or defence, is the subject of Chapter III, and that is
where the troops stationed in the hinterland will be discussed.

Syria and Cappadocia

Evidence for Flavian road-construction in Syria is so far rather limited,
but the little that does exist is significant for two reasons: first, the only
road marked by earlier milestones is the coast road from Antioch to
Ptolemais, constructed when the latter city became a Claudian Roman
veteran colony (see below, Chapter VII); and second, there is no
parallel evidence from Judaea, where inscribed milestones are very
numerous (see below in the section on Judaea). This is not to suggest
that there were no roads before the Romans started setting up
milestones.[94]

   There is, however, some evidence to show that in the Flavian period
increased attention was paid to the physical state of the road-system.
Best known from Syria, and most significant, is the milestone of AD 75
marking the road from Palmyra to Sura on the Euphrates.[95] It is

[93] See the list of cities pillaged by Shapur I, in his *Res Gestae*, 27–34 (A. Maricq, *Syria* 35 (1958), 312 f.).

[94] It is an interesting question to what extent the Romans were indeed pioneers in road construction in the provinces, just as it is difficult to determine whether the earliest milestones on a road actually reflect its construction or merely the beginnings of imperial propaganda. For the west J. C. Mann, *Britannia* 18 (1987), 285 f., argues that roads were an established feature of the pre-Roman, Celtic world. R. Chevallier, *Roman Roads* (1976), 1–15, says something of pre-Roman roads, but does not define the difference made by Roman activity.

[95] H. Seyrig, *Syria* 13 (1932), 276 f. (*AE* 1933. 205); cf. G. W. Bowersock, *JRS* 63 (1973), 133–40.

inscribed with the name of M. Ulpius Traianus, who, as legionary legate in 69, was responsible for the construction of the road from Caesarea to Scythopolis. The existence of a Roman road from Palmyra to the Euphrates seems to imply the simultaneous existence of roads from Damascus and from the coast to Palmyra. This, in other words, is evidence of the organization of a link between southern Syria and the Euphrates, which, before the publication of this milestone, was attributed to Diocletian. Once it is known that there was such a road to southern Syria the possibility may be considered that there were others. Milestones, like many other categories of inscriptions, provide minimum information. They indicate that the lack of certain information can no longer be used as an *argumentum e silentio*.[96]

Another milestone of 75–76 was found near the crossroads where the Apamea–Palmyra and Chalcis–Emesa roads meet.[97] A milestone of 72 was found on the Apamea–Raphanaea road.[98] Raphanaea was a legionary base and an important station in the system which linked northern Syria with the interior of southern Syria. That this milestone was set up in 72, before M. Ulpius Traianus became governor of Syria, may serve as a warning not to ascribe actions to the initiative of individual governors without decisive evidence.

A third milestone of 75 may have marked a canal in the neighbourhood of Antioch.[99] Its editor has argued that the canal was part of the logistic infrastructure constructed in the reign of Vespasian to prepare for a future Parthian campaign. Another element of this project would have been the construction of a port at Seleucia in Pieria which served the newly constituted *classis Syriaca*.[100] This remains to be proved. It has been shown, however, that the construction of the canal in the vicinity of Antioch would allow transportation by water over a substantial part of the journey from the coast to Zeugma on the Euphrates.[101]

A bridge over the Chabinas (Cendere) between Samosata and Melitene, repaired in AD 200, in the reign of Severus, may have been

---

[96] For the concept, F. Millar in M. Crawford, *Sources for Ancient History* (1983), 92–7.

[97] W. van Rengen in *Actes du colloque Apamée de Syrie 1969–71*, ed. Janine et Jean Ch. Balty (1972), 108–10 (*AE* 1974. 653); for a photograph, *ANRW* ii. 8. 120 f., pl. viii. 2.

[98] van Rengen, *Actes*, 108 f. (*AE* 1974. 652). For a photograph, *ANRW* ii. 8, pl. viii, 1.

[99] D. van Berchem, *Museum Helveticum* 40 (1983), 185–96; *BJb* 185 (1985), 47–87, revised reading of the inscription on pp. 85 f. For another canal dug by the city of Antioch in 73–4, L. Robert, *CRAI* 1951, 255, referring to texts now fully published by D. Feissel, *Syria* 62 (1985), 77–103.

[100] van Berchem, *BJb*, 61–4. A new harbour was constructed by army units at Seleucia Pieria and completed in AD 346; references in G. Downey, *A History of Antioch in Syria from Seleucus to the Arab Conquest* (1961), 361, with n. 198.

[101] van Berchem, *BJb*, 65–71.

constructed in the reign of Vespasian.[102] At Aini, a little distance north of Rumkale on the Euphrates, a hydraulic installation was constructed in 73 by a vexillation of the legion III Gallica, although the local community paid for the work.[103] In Asia Minor too roads were built in this period.[104]

Legions and Auxiliaries

The disposition of the legions in the eastern frontier zone now appears to be less clearly understood than was suggested by Ritterling, who thought that Syria in the Flavian period had three legions, III Gallica, IV Scythica, and VI Ferrata.[105] Josephus tells us that X Fretensis remained in Jerusalem after 70,[106] while XII Fulminata was transferred to Melitene in Cappadocia.[107] Ritterling assumed that, at the same time, the newly created legion XVI Flavia was established at Satala, thus forming the second legion of Cappadocia.[108] Cappadocia would then have been a consular province with two legions since 70. This hypothesis was not generally accepted.[109] There are now even better reasons to doubt its validity. The milestone of 75 from near Antioch records work carried out '[pe]r milites legionum (quattuor), [III Gal]l(icae), IV Scyt(hicae), VI Ferr(atae), XVI Fl(aviae), [ite]m cohortium (viginti), [item?] Antiochensium . . .' So soldiers of four legions were at work in Syria in 75, and these included XVI Flavia. Van Berchem therefore suggested that there may at first have been four legions in Syria and one in Cappadocia. This is possible. If it is true, Suetonius was not aware of it when he wrote that Vespasian sent legions to Cappadocia and appointed a consular governor (*Vesp.* 8. 4). However, if this was done in two stages, Suetonius need not have been aware of it.

It must be noted that the inscription from Antioch records work carried out by vexillations, not by entire legions, and a vexillation could

---

[102] *IGLS* 38; cf. V. W. York, *JHS* 18 (1898), 315, no. 20: 'the letters are all so doubtful that it is useless to hazard any conjecture as to the Emperor referred to'. For the Severan repair, *IGLS* 39–40. For the date see J. B. Leaning, *Latomus* 30 (1971), 386–9. Drawing and photographs of the bridge in J. Wagner, *Antike Welt*, 1985 (Sondernummer), figs. 50, 56, 58, 63 f., 66.

[103] *IGLS* 66. A vexillation of the legion IV Scythica is attested at Arulis, between Rumkale and Zeugma: *IGLS* 67–81.

[104] D. Magie, *Roman Rule in Asia Minor* (1950), ii. 429 f., nn. 12–14. For the road-system in Asia Minor, various publications by D. H. French: *ANRW* ii. 78. 698–729; *Roman Roads and Milestones in Asia Minor*, Fasc. 1, *The Pilgrim's Road* (1981); *AFRBA*, 71–102.

[105] *RE* xii (1924), s.v. legio, col 1271 f.   [106] *BJ* vii 1. 2 (17). See below, p. 427.

[107] Ibid. (18). For the site, T. B. Mitford, *ANRW* ii. 7. 1186; *DE* iv, s.v. limes, 1317 f.

[108] Op. cit., 1707. For the site of Satala, Mitford, *ANRW*, 1187; *DE*, 1314 f.

[109] References in van Berchem, *Museum Helveticum* 40 (1983), 190, n. 29. For the known auxiliary forts in Cappadocia, Mitford, *ANRW*, 1188–92; *DE*, 1314–19.

have been transferred for temporary duty from Cappadocia. That, however, seems neither necessary nor likely, particularly because we can be fairly certain that the total of twenty cohorts mentioned in the inscription from Antioch represents the total number present in the province. That possibility was mentioned by van Berchem.[110] It is confirmed by a point made by D. Kennedy in a discussion of the meaning of the numeral in the title of the cohors XX Palmyrenorum.[111] He tentatively suggested that the Palmyrenes were the twentieth cohort in Syria. It was raised perhaps in 194.[112] He further observed that the two complementary diplomas of the year 88 for Syria list eight *alae* and nineteen cohorts.[113] It may therefore be assumed that the number of cohorts in Syria varied, from the Flavian period onward, between nineteen and twenty.[114] The *Antiochenses* mentioned will have been a local militia.[115] As observed by van Berchem, it will have been easier to detach infantry for a building project than cavalry.[116] More important: generally speaking there seems to be no evidence that cavalry ever built anything.[117]

The auxiliary troops in Cappadocia appear to have been fairly constant.[118] A total of 4 *alae* and 15 or 16 cohorts are known from Arrian and inscriptions—4 *alae* and 10 cohorts being mentioned by Arrian. Three of the cohorts are *milliariae*. Added up that would make some 11,500 men, a number roughly equal that of the legionaries. In both Cappadocia and Syria Tacitus' statement holds true that the numbers of legionaries and auxiliaries were approximately the same.[119] Of the troops in Cappadocia 5 *alae* and 7 cohorts are listed in the *Notitia* as serving under the *dux Armeniae*. A number of forts have been identified with more or less certainty.[120] These are found along the main road

---

[110] *Mus. Helv.*, 191.

[111] *ZPE* 53 (1983), 214–16.

[112] As argued by J. C. Mann, in M. M. Roxan, *Roman Military Diplomas 1978–1984*, Appendix II, 218.

[113] Cf. R. Mellor, *The J. Paul Getty Museum Journal* 6–7 (1978–9), 173–84; Roxan, *RMD* no. 3; *CIL* XVI. 106.

[114] Note also the existence of a cohors XII Palaestinorum, below, ch. III, p. 106.

[115] According to the revised reading in *BJb* 185 (1985), 85 ff.

[116] *Mus. Helv.*, 192 .

[117] As pointed out to me by Professor J. C. Mann.

[118] Mitford, *ANRW*, 1189; M. Speidel, *AFRBA*, 16 f. Cf. the older list in G. L. Cheesman, *The Auxilia of the Roman Imperial Army* (1914), 159 f. There is no military diploma for the Cappadocian auxilia. The evidence derives from the list in Arrian, *Acies contra Alanos*, 1–14 and 18; *periplus* 3 and 9 f.; from scattered inscriptions; and from the *Not. Dig. Or.* 38.

[119] *Ann.* iv 5. 6: 'at apud idonea provinciarum sociae triremes alaeque et auxilia cohortium, neque multo secus in iis virium: sed persequi incertum fuit, cum ex usu temporis huc illuc mearent, gliscerent numero et aliquando minuerentur.'

[120] Mitford, *ANRW*, 1188–91. Note the auxiliary fort of Tell el Hajj (= Eragiza of the

from Trapezus to Commagene, about a day's march apart between the two legionary bases, as observed by Mitford, a feature which, once again, may serve to emphasize that such structures must be seen as part of a network of communications rather than a linear barrier.

Legionary Bases

The transfer of the legion XII Fulminata to Melitene in AD 70 is certain, as it is recorded by Josephus.[121] There is no evidence when Satala became a permanent base, but the road to Satala from the west is marked by milestones of 76.[122] The first military inscription from the site does not, apparently, antedate the second century.[123] At Trapezus (Trabzon) two separate vexillations are attested, one from each of the permanent Cappadocian legions.[124] This is yet another piece of evidence to show the widespread use of legionary vexillations in cities in the eastern provinces.

It is usually assumed that Cyrrhus, a site 70 kilometres north-west of Aleppo, was replaced as legionary base by Zeugma on the Euphrates in AD 18.[125] The evidence is as follows. In 18 Cyrrhus served as wintercamp.[126] We are not informed that it was abandoned. In 49 a *castra* was placed at Zeugma, which may suggest that it was not then a permanent base.[127] Josephus states that the Legion X Fretensis was based on the Euphrates before the Jewish war (Zeugma?).[128] On the other hand, Diploma *CIL* xvi 42 of AD 98 was awarded to a soldier born at Cyrrhus, presumably the son of a soldier. Cyrrhus therefore may still have been a base around the fifties. We need more evidence.

Peutinger Table?) on the right bank of the Euphrates between Hierapolis and Barbalissos which has been excavated partly. It was occupied first by the cohors I Milliaria Thracum, which is later attested in Judaea, and then by a cohors II Pia Fidelis. It is said to have been abandoned following the Roman conquest of northern Mesopotamia. For a brief summary with references to preliminary reports, P. Bridel and R. A. Stucky, *Le Moyen Euphrate: Actes du Colloque de Strasbourg 1977* (1980), ed. J. Cl. Margueron, 349–53.

[121] *BJ* vii 1. 3 (18). For Melitene see also p. 139 below.

[122] Cf. T. B. Mitford, *JRS* 64 (1974), 166; *SMR* ii (1977), 507–9; *ANRW*, 1186–92. Very little is known of the fortresses at Satala and Melitene, J. Crow, *DRBE*, 84–6. See also below, p. 139. For Commagene, H. Hellenkemper, *Studien*, 461–71.

[123] Mitford, *JRS*, 164, no. 3 (*AE* 1971. 465).

[124] Ibid. 163; *AE* 1975. 783; A. Bryer and D. Winfield, *The Byzantine Monuments and Topography of the Pontos*, i (1985), 181, and ii, pl. 109a. For Trapezus see also pp. 40, 48, 50.

[125] The site of the legionary base at or near ('apud') Zeugma has not been established with any certainty; the stamped tiles found near Belçik are not conclusive in themselves. J. Wagner, *SMR* ii (1977), 517–39, esp. 523 f.; J.-P. Rey-Coquais, *JRS* 68 (1978), 67; L. J. F. Keppie, *DRBE*, 415. For Cyrrhus and Zeugma as cities see also below, p. 139; for military inscriptions from Cyrrhus, *IGLS* 148–52; for Cyrrhus, E. Frézouls, *ANRW* ii. 8. 164–97. Note also the inscription that mentions Q. Marcius Turbo: E. Frézouls, *Syria* 30 (1953), 247 f.

[126] Tacitus, *Ann.* ii 57. 2.   [127] *Ann.* xii 12. 3: 'positisque castris apud Zeugma'.

[128] *BJ* vii 1. 3 (18).

Samosata, capital of Commagene, became part of the province of Syria in 72.[129] Ptolemy mentions it as a legionary base.[130] The earliest evidence from the site seems to be from the reign of Commodus.[131] Raphanaea definitely was a legionary base before the Jewish war and afterward.[132] It is possible that there was a (temporary?) military presence also at Beroea (Aleppo)[133] and at Apamea.[134]

The Annexation of Commagene

It is quite possible that the desire to station a legion at Samosata was one of the reasons for the annexation of Commagene. Caesennius Paetus, as governor of Syria c.72, reported to Vespasian that Antiochus of Commagene was conspiring with Parthia.[135] He accordingly received instructions to invade the kingdom and annex it. There was no resistance. According to Josephus the report of Paetus was untrue, but Vespasian had to act in the light of the information he received. 'For Samosata, the largest city of Commagene, lies on the Euphrates so that it would offer the Parthians, if they had such plans, an easy crossing and safe base.' Josephus does not go to any trouble to present it as anything

[129] Josephus, *BJ* vii 7. 1–2 (219–43); for the chronology, D. Kennedy, *Britannia* 14 (1983), 186–8 and cf. R. D. Sullivan, *ANRW* ii. 8 (1977), 797 f.; for the town, Oppenheimer, 436–42.

[130] v 14. 8.

[131] *CIL* vi 1408 f. Cf. Ritterling, *RE* xii, 1765 f. A dedication found in Cilicia, *AE* 1950. 190; *BE* 1949. 190 is not, in fact, informative regarding Samosata, as suggested by J.-F. Rey-Coquais, *JRS* 68 (1978), 67.

[132] Josephus, loc. cit. For the site, *IGLS* iv 1400 (*CIL* 14165.13), which mentions the wife of a tribune of the VI Ferrata and clearly dates from before the transfer of this legion to Arabia and Judaea in the second century. At an uncertain date it became the headquarters of the legion III Gallica. One inscription found on the spot mentions this legion (*IGLS* iv 1399). There is one manuscript of Ptolemy's Geography (codex Vaticanus 191, non vidi), which adds 'L III' after the name of the place, as noted by J.-P. Rey-Coquais, *Arados et sa perée* (1974), 167. Of course legionary vexillations may have been outposted at any time. See now Malavolta's long treatment of the eastern provinces in continuation of Forni's article in *DE* iv, fasc. 41–43/1–2, 4 (1982–5). For military inscriptions from the site, *IGLS* 1399, 1401.

[133] *IGLS* 178–81. The first two of these inscriptions refer to serving soldiers, but the evidence is meagre.

[134] Inscriptions cited by W. van Rengen, in *Apamée de Syrie; Bilan de recherches archéologiques 1965–68*, ed. Janine Balty (1969), 100, no. 4; id., *Bilan de recherches . . . 1969–1971* eds. Janine et Jean Ch. Balty (1972), 98, no. 1, and 100–2, no. 2. Two of these appear to be tombs of serving officers of the legion II Parthica who died when their unit was on its way to or from a war in Mesopotamia, in the reign of Caracalla or Severus Alexander. The third records a man who was a *protector* and that might suggest a later date, not before the middle of the third century. There are now reports of the discovery of numerous military tombstones at Apamea (I have not seen Balty, *CRAI* 1987).

[135] Josephus, *BJ* vii, 7. 1 (224): τὰ γὰρ Σαμόσατα, τῆς Κομμαγηνῆς μεγίστη πόλις, κεῖται παρὰ τὸν Εὐφράτην, ὥστ᾽ εἶναι τοῖς Πάρθοις, εἴ τι τοιοῦτον διενενόηντο, ῥᾴστην μὲν τὴν διάβασιν, βεβαίαν δὲ τὴν ὑποδοχήν. For the chronology, D. Kennedy, *Britannia* 14 (1983), 186–8.

but a flimsy pretext.[136] The subsequent generous treatment which
Antiochus and his sons enjoyed at Rome is additional proof of this. It
has been argued that there was a real danger that Commagene would
transfer its loyalty to the Parthians, because of religious and cultural
affinity.[137] Josephus did not think so. There is no point in speculating
about the affair. Josephus presumably repeats the story as told in
Rome. The result is clear: Samosata became a legionary base. It may be
noted that Commagene had already been incorporated for a short time
by Tiberius, from AD 17 till the reign of Caligula. The motives then were
equally vague. At the same time King Archelaus of Cappadocia was
accused of 'rebellious conduct'.[138] Personal spite of the emperor is
alleged. Tacitus, however, adds that with the revenues from Commagene the one per cent tax could be lightened and was in fact fixed
at a·half per cent. Commagene may on both occasions have been
annexed, at least partly, because annexation was profitable. It is
possible, but there is no evidence to prove this, that Emesa was
annexed at the same time.[139]

The reorganization of the eastern frontier, including the annexation
of Commagene most probably represents an effort to apply lessons
learnt from the failure of the attempts to conquer Armenia by Paetus
and Corbulo under Nero. In 58 Corbulo when campaigning in
Armenia had his supplies brought from Trapezus on the Black Sea over
mountains occupied by Roman troops.[140] In 69 Trapezus proved to be
vulnerable, being attacked during the rebellion of Anicetus in Pontus—
'a famous old city, founded by the Greeks at the end of the Pontic coast.
The local garrison was destroyed, an auxiliary cohort of the king, which
had been granted Roman citizenship. Although they were armed and
organized as a Roman unit, they retained the negligence and laxness of
the Greeks. Anicetus also set the fleet on fire.'[141]

In 62 logistics were a serious problem in Cappadocia.[142] '(Caesennius) Paetus . . . before he had sufficiently prepared his winter-camps or
provided for his corn supply, hurried his army across the Taurus in
order to recapture Tigranocerta, as he claimed, and to ravage regions
which Corbulo had left intact.' This was a senseless campaign, according to Tacitus, as it had to be interrupted because of a lack of food.

---

[136] Syme, *CAH* xi. 139.   [137] E. Dabrowa, *Syria* 58 (1981), 198.

[138] Tacitus, *Ann.* ii 42; Dio lvii 3–7.

[139] Cf. R. D. Sullivan, *ANRW* ii. 8, 198–219. Emesa was annexed not before 72 and at the
latest in the reign of Antoninus Pius.

[140] Tacitus, *Ann.* xiii 39. For this route see below, p. 42, n. 149; for Trapezus (Trabzon),
below, p. 48, 50; for the garrison, above, p. 38.

[141] Tacitus, *Hist.* ii 47–9.   [142] Tacitus, *Ann.* xv 8.

Later in 62 Roman troops had to withdraw from Armenia because the Parthians threatened to invade Syria. While Paetus campaigned in Armenia, Corbulo, who commanded the army in Syria, moved troops to the Euphrates, secured the roads into Syria, built a bridge across the Euphrates, and established a bridgehead on the other bank at Zeugma.[143] The aim of all this, according to Tacitus, was to prevent a Parthian attack on Syria, an attack which itself aimed at forcing the Roman army to vacate Armenia. When Paetus' army in Armenia was in desperate trouble, Corbulo marched with part of his army from Zeugma to bring assistance.[144] He 'took the shortest route, which at the same time did not lack supplies, through the land of Commagene, then through Cappadocia and thence to Armenia'. Later Corbulo, in the words of Tacitus, said that a further campaign in Armenia was impossible because Syria might be threatened by the Parthians.[145] The war ended without the Romans achieving their central aim: the securing of Armenia. Corbulo gave up his positions across the Euphrates, and the Parthians withdrew from Armenia which remained unoccupied by either party.

Improving communications in Syria and Cappadocia and moving part of the Roman army closer to the frontier enhanced the weight of Roman diplomacy toward Armenia and Parthia. It also would be helpful in a future expedition. The troops were moved *in spem magis quam ob formidinem*. In particular, the importance of lateral communication is clear from Tacitus' account. Supplies had been brought to the army in Armenia through Trapezus. Reinforcements marched from Zeugma through Commagene and Cappadocia. Syria had proved to be vulnerable to Parthian moves when the Roman army was campaigning in Armenia. The obvious response was a reorganization that entailed forward movement to stations which were good bases for an attack and, at the same time, allowed safe and quick lateral movement. These measures may be compared with the preparations for Nero's Armenian war: the emperor ordered levies to be held; allies were to deliver troops for the invasion; the legions were moved towards Armenia and bridges thrown over the Euphrates.[146] The forward movement of bases in the East appears to resemble a pattern which has been observed in Upper Germany,[147] where the advance of bases under Vespasian was followed, in the eighties, by Domitian's war against the Chatti, 83–(?)85, which led to the occupation of territory east of the Rhine.[148] When

---

[143] *Ann.* xv 3, 9.   [144] *Ann.* xv 12.   [145] *Ann.* xv 17.   [146] *Ann.* xiii 7.
[147] Syme, *CAH* xi. 158–61; Schönberger, *JRS* 59 (1969), 155–64.
[148] Syme, 162–8; Schönberger, 158.

Trajan invaded Armenia in 114 his advanced bases were Melitene and Satala, the legionary bases established by the Flavians.

J. Crow has observed that there is no good evidence to show that the Euphrates line represents a defence system, and he tends towards the view that it is a road linking stations on major east–west roads. He suggests that internal security rather than frontier defence may have been an important function of the system.[149]

Following the annexation of Mesopotamia as a Roman province two legions were stationed in the province, one certainly at Singara, the other probably at Rhesaena.[150] Evidence, now lost, has been found which shows that Roman units were based right on the Tigris, just below Mosul.[151] These may have been connected with the cohort which was based for some time in the third century at Hatra further south.[152]

The North-East

The evidence for a Roman presence farther north, in the Caucasus, needs to be discussed at some length, for several reasons.[153] First,

[149] J. Crow, *DRBC*, 87 f. In an earlier paper a different interpretation was presented: J. G. Crow and D. H. French, in *Roman Frontier Studies 1979*, ed. W. S. Hanson and L. J. F. Keppie (1980), 903–9—'hypothetical defence systems' (907–9). For frontier roads between Melitene and Samosata, D. French, *AFRBA*, 71–101. For the Nikopolis–Satala–Erzurum road, A. Bryer and D. Winfield, *The Byzantine Monuments and Topography of the Pontos* i (1985), 24–37. For the road from Trapezus (Trabzon) to Satala, ibid. 48–52. See also J. Wagner, 'Die Römer an Euphrat und Tigris', *Antike Welt*, Sondernummer 1985; *DE* iv. 1307–19.

[150] For Singara see the tombstone of the veteran of I Parthica 'a legion which is in Singara of Mesopotamia on the river Tigris', *ILS* 9477; J. Reynolds and M. Speidel, *Epigraphica Anatolica* 5 (1985), 31–5. For the site see also the references below, ch. V. III Parthica is attested at Bezabde in the fourth century. Its base in the third century is not known with certainty, but coins of Rhesaena bear the legend *L III P* which is probably an indication that the legion was stationed in the area, as shown by J. C. Mann, *Legionary Recruitment and Veteran Settlement During the Principate* (1983), 43. For the coins, K. O. Castellin, *The Coinage of Rhesaena in Mesopotamia*, Num. Notes and Monographs 108 (1946), 14 f. and 45 f. Kennedy, *Antichthon* (forthcoming), assumes that the coins refer to a veteran colony and thinks Nisibis the likely base for the legion III Parthica. The latter paper contains a full discussion of the garrison of Mesopotamia in the late Antonine and early Severan period. Singara and Bezabde were included in the territory which Rome lost to Persia in 363.

[151] D. Kennedy, *ZPE* 73 (1988) 101–3, discusses a stone found by D. Oates which was said to have borne an image or an eagle in relief and, below, the words *occuli* (sic) *legionum*. D. Oates, *Studies in the Ancient History of Northern Iraq* (1968), 77, has argued that Mosul was the site of *Ad Flumen Tigrem* of the Peutinger Map.

[152] See below, ch. III.

[153] Survey by D. M. Lang, 'Iran, Armenia and Georgia', *Cambridge History of Iran*, iii. 1 (1983), 505–36, bibliography in vol. iii. 2. 1310–12. For Iberia (Georgia), W. E. D. Allen, *A History of the Georgian People* (1932); D. M. Lang, *The Georgians* (1966). For the history of Armenia, R. Grousset, *Histoire de l'Arménie des origines à 1071* (1947); N. Adontz, *Armenia in the Period of Justinian* (trans. N. G. Garsoïan, 1970). For the Albanians, Movses Daskhurantsi, *The History of the Caucasian Albanians*, trans. C. J. F. Dowsett (1961).

exaggerated claims are sometimes made regarding the Roman entrenchment in the region, and it will be useful to see the importance of the region in perspective. Second, on the Pontic coast there was a real and well-attested presence which must be discussed. Third, during the later empire the area played a significant role in the conflict between Rome and Persia. Developments in both the early and the later empire are better understood when both are considered.

There was contact as early as Pompey's eastern campaign. Various peoples south of the Caucasus became nominal clients.[154] In 37/6 BC Armenia was forced to become an ally, and the Iberians and Albanians were defeated.[155] Strabo, writing in the reign of Augustus, considered the Albanians and Iberians good subjects as long as they were properly supervised, though when neglected they tended to make trouble.[156] He describes Colchis, Iberia, and Albania as rich and fertile lands which could provide a very good livelihood.[157] That would be reason enough to attract a Roman campaign. Under Tiberius there was effective diplomacy. The Romans induced Iberia and Albania to attack Parthia with the participation of Sarmatians but without active support from the Roman army.[158] When the Parthian king advanced against Iberia the Alani invaded Parthia from over the Caucasus. In the second century, too, the Iberians used the Alani for their own purposes south of the Caucasus.

We hear of abortive plans for a Caucasian expedition under Nero in 66–7. A new legion was enrolled, and troops were concentrated—but actually used for the suppression of the revolt of Vindex.[159] Detachments from the German, British, and Balkan armies were on their way, in the words of Tacitus, to the 'claustra Caspiarum et bellum quod in Albanos parabat'. The target and the geography are uncertain, for this would mean the Darial (Krestovy, Juari) pass, the route which crosses the central Caucasus, east of the Kazbek, through the river valleys of the Terek and the Aragvi. In recent history this was called the Georgian Military Road, from Ordzhonikidze (Vladikavkaz) to Tbilisi (Tiflis).

[154] Mommsen, iii. 130–4. The previous history of the region and Pompey's campaign in the area are discussed by E. L. Wheeler, *Flavius Arrianus: A Political and Military Biography* (Dissertation, Duke University 1977), ch. II.

[155] Dio xlix 24.   [156] vi 4. 2 (288); see also xi 1. 6 (491).   [157] xi 2. 19 (499).

[158] Tacitus, *Ann.* vi 31–6. The Darial pass was used. Cf. Debevoise, 158 f.

[159] Pliny, *NH* vi 15. 40; Suetonius, *Nero* 19; Tac. *Hist.* i 6. 9; Dio lxiii 8. 1–2 (iii 72–3). Discussion by B. W. Henderson, *The Life and Principate of the Emperor Nero* (1903), 226–8, with notes on p. 480; W. Schur, *Die Orientpolitik des Kaisers Nero*, Klio, Beiheft 15/2 (1923), 62–111; J. G. C. Anderson, *CAH* x. 776; 880–4; A. B. Bosworth, *Antichthon* 10 (1976), 73 f; M. Griffin, *Nero, the End of a Dynasty* (1984), 228 f.; D. Braund, *DRBE*, 38–49; Keppie, ibid., 419. I have not seen J. Kolendo in *Neronia 1977* (1982), 23–30. For the recruitment of the legion I Italica, Mann, 54.

It is beautifully described in Lermontov's *Hero of our Times*, a difficult route, but not impossible to cross. *Albanos* on the other hand, fits the defile past Derbent on the shore of the Caspian sea, farther east, the easier route.[160] Pliny attempts to explain where the expedition was supposed to be going in a passage which itself contains obvious geographical errors.[161] It is therefore impossible to say what was the purpose of the intended expedition. We cannot be certain that those who planned it had a very clear idea where they were going, let alone that we ourselves can gain one on the basis of the remarks of Pliny or Tacitus.[162] We should not exclude the possibility that Nero's generals intended to cross the Darial pass. It is indeed a difficult route, but not worse than others which were under permanent Roman control.[163] Nor do we know how difficult Roman planners thought it was. It is, however, obvious that control of the Caucasus would serve no purpose for the defence of Syria, but might be useful in moves against Armenia and, particularly, Media. The plan was obviously expansionist in intention rather than defensive.[164] Less clear is the meaning of reports of plans for an Ethiopian campaign.[165]

Under the Flavians, in the 70s, these interests were pursued on a less grandiose scale. Pliny mentions forts at Absarus and Dioscurias on the Black Sea coast.[166] An inscription of AD 75 records Roman assistance in the restoration of a fort at Harmozica, 14 km from Tbilisi (formerly Tiflis).[167] The site is significant. This is the old capital of Georgia, which 'covered all the middle and lower Kura and was the key to eastern Transcaucasia as far as the Caspian'.[168] A centurion is mentioned under Domitian in an inscription found at the foot of the Apsheronsky peninsula on the Caspian coast, not far from Baku.[169]

---

[160] *Hist.* i 6. 9. This should not be corrected to *Alanos*, for one must allow for the possibility that Tacitus was confused or meant something we do not understand. See the critical apparatus of Fisher's edition. For Nero's endeavours in war and foreign policy in general, see now Griffin, 230–4. For extensive discussion of Nero's aim and the relevant sources, see Wheeler, 117–23.

[161] *NH* vi 15. 40.   [162] See also below, p. 404.

[163] So I gather from personal observation. Extensive description in F. Dubois de Montpéreux, *Voyage autour de Caucase* iv (1840), 227 ff., 292 f.; for the military geography of the region, W. E. D. Allen and P. Muratoff, *Caucasian Battlefields* (1953), 3 ff.; and cf. C. Burney and D. M. Lang, *The Peoples of the Hills: Ancient Ararat and Caucasus* (1971), 2 ff.

[164] On the background of Roman interest in the region, D. Braund, *DRBE*, 31–49.

[165] Cf. *CAH* x. 778–80.

[166] *NH* vi 12, 14. For Absarus and Sebastopolis see also below, p. 48.

[167] *SEG* xx 112; see also *SEG* xvi 781. Harmozica = Armazi-c'ixe (the castle of Armaz), one of the forts dominating Mtskheta at the confluence of the Aragvi and the Kura. For the excavations at Mtskheta, the ancient capital of Georgia, see the brief summary of A. L. Mongait, *Archaeology in the U.S.S.R.* (1961), 220–3; also D. M. Lang, *The Georgians* (1966), 82.

[168] Allen and Muratoff, 9.

[169] *AE* 1951. 263, said to have been found at Bejouk Dagh, 70 km. south of Baku:

These two inscriptions show that Roman troops were occasionally dispatched to an area which otherwise remained on the fringes of the empire. Bosworth, indeed, concludes that the Flavians had entrenched their power in the Caucasus.[170] But the distance from the Black Sea to the Caspian is about 600 kilometres; when the Romans really entrenched their power in an area as large as this they left more than two inscriptions.[171] Nero had been prepared to interfere there on a massive scale and no doubt intended to achieve such an entrenchment. The Flavians, on the other hand, extended Roman influence in the area without investing too much.[172] There are similar questions regarding the interpretation of the Roman presence in the desert of Arabia.[173]

There is indeed evidence of more substantial numbers of troops on the south-eastern coast of the Black Sea under Hadrian: five (auxiliary) cohorts were stationed at Absarus, according to Arrian (*Peripl.* 11. 2), attested also in an inscription from Hadrian's reign.[174] The remains of a fort measuring 194 × 245 metres are visible but have not been excavated.[175] It may be best to assume that these stations saw to the security of the coast and ports and kept an eye on Roman clients immediately to the East. There had been a revolt in Pontus in 69,[176] and the area was troubled by piracy.[177] The most important means of communication along the southern and eastern Pontic coast has always

'Imp(eratore) Domitiano Caesare Aug(usto) Germanic(o) L. Ilius Maximus (centurio) leg(ionis) XII Ful(minatae).' It is a remarkable discovery but cannot be construed as evidence of a permanently held position in the area.

[170] *Antichthon*, 75; *HSCP* 81 (1977), 226–8. Reference to the area is perhaps also made by Statius, *Silv.* 4. 4. 63 f.: 'metuendaque portae limina Caspiacae'. See also H. Halfmann, *Epigraphica Anatolica* 8 (1986), 39–50.

[171] However, Dr Kennedy points out to me that the evidence from Cappadocia is so far rather meagre as well.

[172] Cf. Syme, *Athenaeum*, 282. Suetonius, *Vesp.* 8. 4, says that legions were stationed in Cappadocia 'propter adsiduos barbarorum incursus'. As we do not hear elsewhere of 'continuous barbarian incursions' the statement may perhaps be taken with a grain of salt.

[173] See below, p. 122–31. For a survey of the evidence regarding those years on the Upper Euphrates, J. Crow, *DRBE*, 80 f. It appears that very little is, in fact, known.

[174] *ILS* 2660: an early Hadrianic dedication to a 'praeposit. numeror. tendentium in Ponto Absaro'. For the remains, V. A. Lefkinadze, *Drevnei Historij* (1969)/2, 75–93. Cf. M. Speidel, *AFRBA*, 17, argues that the garrison of Absarus consisted of auxiliaries and cites *Ch. Lat.* xi 477.

[175] Dr Kennedy observes that this is a large fort: 4.7 ha./11.7 acres, about a quarter of a legionary fortress. The appearance, with projecting towers, is better suited to a later date. Mitford, *ANRW*, 1192, n. 52, finds both the date and the position suspect and suggests a medieval date.

[176] Tacitus, *Hist.* iii 47–8.

[177] Brigandage on the east coast of the Black Sea is mentioned in sources throughout antiquity: Strabo xi 2. 12 (495 f.); Josephus, *BJ* ii 16. 1 (366 f.); Tacitus, *Hist.* iii 47; Zosimus i 32; Procopius, *de Aed.* iii 6. 2. F. Cumont, *Anatolian Studies Presented to W. M. Ramsay*, 109–227, points out that the Romans had problems with piracy in the Black Sea and banditry in Cappadocia. This threatened economic life and logistics in times of war. See also Cumont, below, n. 205; Bosworth, *Antichthon*, 67; *HSCP*, 228 f. Cf. Syme, *Athenaeum*, 276 f.

been the sea, for the coast road crosses numerous valley torrents and the mountains leave no space for a reliable road.[178] 'From Phasis', says Strabo, 'people go to Amisus and Sinope by sea . . . because the shores are soft and because of the outlets of the rivers.'[179] Even now the coast road along the western slopes of the Caucasus is often blocked by landslides. According to modern maps there exists no road along the coast where the delta of the Phasis (Rioni) flows into the sea. In the nineteenth century the remains of a fort were visible at Phasis, then malarial and surrounded by swamps.[180] I am told that Gagra, further northwards on the coast is still marshy. The ancient remains at Phasis have now disappeared. Strabo describes it as a market centre of the Colchi, 'which is protected on one side by the river, on another by a lake, on the third by the sea'.[181] Arrian is the only good source on this area in the second century. His remarks on the army post at Phasis, which he visited in AD 131/2, are therefore worth citing in full:

The guard post there, where four hundred picked soldiers are stationed, was in my opinion very strong because of the nature of the terrain, and very suitable for the protection of those sailing in the area. . . . In a word, everything is organized in such a way as to discourage any of the savages from approaching it; and there is no danger that those on guard in it will be put under siege. Since the harbour needed to be secure for ships, and the surrounding territory inhabited by veteran soldiers and other people engaged in trade had to be made safe, I decided to build, starting from the second ditch which surrounds the wall, another ditch down to the river; this will protect the harbour and the homes outside the wall.[182]

Arrian's provisions for defence were necessary because Phasis was an isolated spot: as is well-known, forts in long-established provinces were not organized for defence in this period. For comparison it is instructive to cite the comments of Dubois de Montpéreux, who visited the site early in the nineteenth century: 'Poti will always be of primary importance, both for military and commercial reasons, for it com-

---

[178] A. Bryer and D. Winfield, *The Byzantine Monuments and the Topography of the Pontos*, i (1985), 18 f. for references to travellers who found progress along the coast by land difficult. Their ch. II deals with the road-system in the area.

[179] xi 2. 17 (498) with interesting information on the economy and peoples of the region. According to Procopius, *Bell.* ii 15. 4–5, 28. 28, all trade between Lazica (Colchis) and Roman Asia Minor was transported by ship along the coast.

[180] For Phasis, Dubois de Montpéreux, i (1839), 65 f. and Atlas, pl. xviii; below, n. 183. Dr Kennedy doubts whether these are the remains of a Roman fort. They were very large—about 200 paces square, i.e. 4 ha./9.9 acres and with very large circular projecting towers. That would definitely make it too big for Arrian's 400 men. See also D. B. Campbell, *BJb* 186 (1986), 125 f., discussing evidence of the use of artillery by auxiliaries.

[181] xi 2. 17 (498).

[182] *Periplus* 9, 3. Cf. Campbell, 3 f., whose translation is reproduced here.

mands the entrance to the river.' In his day a sand-bar blocked the river mouth and, as already noted, the site had become malarial.[183]

Another point is brought out very clearly by Dubois: the importance of the site did not lie in its connection with Tbilisi in eastern Georgia or the passes across the Caucasus. The river Phasis (Rioni) could be negotiated easily as far as it flows through the plain. But in the mountains it flows 'between two walls of rock and does not always leave enough space . . . a road and twenty bridges carried the traveller twenty times from one bank of the river to the other. Now that the twenty bridges are destroyed one crosses the river Phasis twenty times by ferry.'[184] Two fortresses manned by Colchians were sufficient to guard the border with Iberia.[185] Strabo says the Phasis was navigated as far as the fortress of Sarapana and from there people travelled by land to the river Cyrus (Kura) by a wagon road in four days, through narrow defiles over one hundred and twenty bridges'.[186] That is not an invasion route the Romans would seriously have had to worry about. In a work on the modern history of the region it is observed that 'the natural line of division between a power controlling the Ponto-Anatolian area and the Caspian-Iranian region has always been the Suram ridge and the main chain of the Zagros running in a general direction south-south-east'.[187] In other words, this is a natural dividing line between two major states, and it may be noted that it was to serve in this capacity in the Byzantine period as well.

There are indeed a number of passes across the Caucasus which afford direct communication with Colchis (Lazica).[188] These, however, could be used only for a few months in summer, and the passage of an army across these routes was very difficult. The passes normally could be held by modest garrisons of local troops. For the later period Procopius says that this was normally done by the Colchians who were 'subject to the Romans without paying tribute'.[189] Their king was

---

[183] Dubois de Montpéreux, iii. 77 f.

[184] Ibid. ii. 71 f. The best map available to me, the 1:500.000 Tactical Pilotage Chart, shows that there exists now a single-track railroad through the river valley.

[185] Procopius, *Bell.* viii 13. 15–20; cf. i 22. 16–18. Procopius emphasizes that they were traditionally manned for the Romans by the Lazi (Colchians).

[186] xi 3. 4 (500).   [187] Allen and Muratoff, 8.

[188] Dubois de Montpéreux, ii. 77 f.; iv. 293, 298. The Klukhor pass links Dioscurias (Sukhumi) with the Kuban valley. This is the best route. The most recent maps available to me do not mark it as a road practicable for cars. The Mamison (Imeretian Military Road), via the Malusonski pass, west of the Kazbek, links the Valley of the Ardon with the Rioni. Allen and Muratoff, 6 note: 'There are some seventy other tracks and paths across the main chain, some of which are only suitable for pack transport and others for men marching in a single file. In many cases they are blocked by snow except for two or three months a year.'

[189] *Bell.* ii 15. 2–5.

formally nominated by Rome, and their duty was to keep the Huns
from crossing the Caucasus into Roman territory. However, the
important routes, as already noted, were Derbent and Darial. These
had to be guarded by a stronger force and played a role in the
relationship between the peoples of the region and in that between
Rome and Parthia/Persia.[190]

Arrian's report on his inspection tour generally gives special attention to ports and the navigability of rivers.[191] He mentions that
Hadrian was responsible for the construction of a harbour at
Trapezus.[192] The forts on the Pontic coast face the sea and are directed
towards it. They are placed at distances which vary between 58 and 70
kilometres, one day's sailing.[193] No Roman installations such as towers
or little forts have been found in between. It would be interesting to
know more about the duties of the Pontic fleet and its stations.[194]

When the Alani, during their raid south of the Caucasus,
approached Armenia, or even Cappadocia, Arrian, as governor of
Cappadocia, himself interfered with his army.[195] However, the Pontic
coast will not have been on their route because, as observed above, the
coast-road was hardly practicable.[196] In any case, the brief account of
these events given by Cassius Dio shows that the Pontic coast was not
the target of the Alani:[197] Pharasmanes, the Iberian king, had invited
them to attack his enemies, Albania to the east and Media to the south-
east. This is the second time we hear of an occasion when the Iberians
invite the Alani to attack their own neighbours south of the Caucasus.

---

[190] See below, ch. V, p. 262 f.

[191] Harbours: *Periplus* 3. 1; 4. 1. The navigability of rivers: 8. 1; 10. 1.

[192] 16. 6.

[193] As observed by Lefkinadze. Two other forts are known on this coast. For Sebastopolis
(Dioscurias, modern Sukhumi) Lefkinadze, 82–4, fig. 6 f. Part of this has been excavated and is
said to date to the second–third centuries, but no finds have been published. In a suburb a tower
was apparently excavated with coin-finds from Commodus to Severus. For Pityus (Pizunda),
Lefkinadze, 85 f., fig. 8. It has been excavated and is said (it is not clear on what basis) to date to
the second and third centuries. Some three or four kilometres further north-west a wall and a
tower were excavated, producing coins from the second to the sixth centuries and a stamped tile.
See also M. P. Speidel, *SMR* iii (1986), 657–60. Speidel assumes that the Roman troops on the
Black Sea coast controlled the hinterland as far as the Darial Pass and speaks of 'the Caucasus
frontier'.

[194] For the fleet in the Black Sea, cf. C. G. Starr, *The Roman Imperial Navy* (1960), 125–9; D.
Kienast, *Untersuchungen zu den Kriegsflotten der römischen Kaiserzeit* (1966), 116–19.

[195] Dio lxix 15. 1. In the *Acies contra Alanos* Arrian describes his marching and battle orders for
the intended campaign. Bosworth, *HSCP*, 217–55, and Syme, *Athenaeum*, 273–83, for this affair
and for Hadrian's relationship with the kingdoms of the area.

[196] M. Speidel, *SMR* iii, 658, argues that Arrian operated out of Absarus on the Pontic coast
towards Iberia.

[197] Dio lxix 15 (iii 235); cf. Marie-Louise Chaumont, *Recherches sur l'histoire d'Armenie de
l'avènement des Sassanides à la conversion du royaume* (1969), 9 f.

Moreover, it shows that the Alani moved through the central Caucasus and Georgia, making for the south-east. When their movements began to affect Armenia and Cappadocia, Parthian and Roman action put an end to the Alanian expedition.

Pharasmanes was later warmly received in Rome by Antoninus.[198] The affair gives us a glimpse of Roman attitudes towards the vassal states in the north-east in this period, but it cannot be used to interpret the meaning of the Roman presence on the Pontic coast. Another glimpse of the position of the leadership in Iberia is provided by a bilingual epitaph of a princess, inscribed in Greek and Aramaic, which shows that the viceroy bore an Iranian title (*pitiakhsh*, satrap), and yet was a member of the local aristocracy.[199] The ancient capital of Iberia appears to have had the same international ambience as its nineteenth-century successor Tiflis with its German and Russian settlements and a native quarter inhabited by Persians, Tatars, and Cherkessians.[200]

In the third century indeed the Roman stations on the Euxine coast were attacked by invaders, but these came by boat.[201] This is a remarkable episode. As the Goths were no sailors they forced the Bosporans to provide them with convoys for their raids to the east and south coast of the Euxine, an indication that the voyage over land was not practicable.[202] The Boranes, called 'Scyths' by Zosimus, first attacked Pityus, 'which was surrounded by a very strong wall and had an excellent harbour', and were repelled. This was the northernmost

---

[198] Dio lxx 2. For Pharasmanes, C. Toumanoff, *Studies in Christian Caucasian History* (1963), 101 f.

[199] G. V. Tsereteli, 'Armazskaya bilingva', *Izvestiya Instituta Yazkya i Material'noi Kul'tury* 13 (Tbilisi, 1942), which I have not seen. The following translation is cited by Lang, *Cambridge History of Iran* iii. 1. 515: 'I am Serapita, daughter of Zevakh the younger, *pitiakhsh* of Farsman the king, and wife of Iodmangan the victorious, winner of many conquests, master of the court of Ksefarnug, the great king of the Iberians, and son of Agrippa, master of the court of King Farsman. Woe, woe, for the sake of her who was not of full age, whose years were not completed, and so good and beautiful that no one was like her in excellence; and she died at the age of twenty-one.' For further discussion see Toumanoff, 155 f., 260 f.

[200] A beautiful description of Tolstoy's visit may be found in Henri Troyat, *Tolstoï* (1965), part II, ch. 1.

[201] Zosimus i 32 (the only source). The date, *c*. 254, is not quite certain, cf. Kettenhofen, 64 f., 90 ff.

[202] J. O. Maenchen-Helfen, *The World of the Huns* (1973), 75, plausibly interprets *Cod. Theod.* 40. 24 as aimed at preventing the Huns from repeating these methods. In 419 Asclepiades, the bishop of Chersonese on the Crimea, petitioned the emperor for clemency towards 'those who have betrayed to the barbarians the art of ship building which was hitherto unknown to them'. The petition was granted, but capital punishment was made mandatory in future cases. The barbarians in the region were local Goths and Huns. As argued by Maenchen, it is likely that the imperial authorities wanted to prevent the Huns from obtaining ships for raids along the coast. For similar reasons *Cod. Theod.* vii 16. 3 (18 September 420) forbids the export of goods in ships. As noted below, in ch. II, the Huns invaded the eastern provinces once, by the Dariel pass across the Caucasus.

Roman post on the eastern Euxine; Arrian mentions it, but not as the site of a garrison.[203] A second attempt succeeded. They then proceeded to lay siege to Trapezus. Zosimus relates that the city was taken although it was surrounded by a double wall and occupied by a very strong garrison. The soldiers were drunk and did not stand guard.[204]

From this discussion of Roman activity in the north-east several conclusions may be drawn. First, there was a permanent occupation of a series of fleet stations on the Black Sea coast. These guarded the shipping route along the coast, which was of special importance because the land route was difficult. The Roman presence here had nothing to do with the passes across the Caucasus or with defence against barbarian invaders. Iberia was of marginal interest in this period, although it could be counted as a vassal state and there is at least one inscription which attests Roman military activity in the capital. If the Alani from over the Caucasus threatened to invade Roman territory its defence was the responsibility of the governor of Cappadocia. The region was not involved in the conflict between Rome and Parthia. In Chapter V we shall return to this region, which became an issue of greater importance in the wars between Byzantium and Persia than had been the case in the early empire. This again was the result of the presence of a formidable foe north of the Caucasus, the Huns, which required an active military presence in Iberia.

Conclusions

Cumont, it seems, was the first to interpret the Flavian reorganization as a reaction to events in the sixties.[205] However, this approach has by no means been generally accepted. It is more common to see the Flavian activity in the East as defensive in nature.[206] This is important, for the assumption that Vespasian wanted 'secure boundaries' itself again justifies another assumption, namely that the existing

---

[203] *Periplus* 18. 1. For remains at Pityus, Lefkinadze, 87.

[204] i 33.

[205] F. Cumont, *Académie royale de Belgique, Bulletin de la classe des lettres* (1905), 197–227. Cumont emphasizes the importance of road-building in the Flavian period. Bosworth, *Antichthon*, 63–78, sees the Flavian reorganization of the north-east frontier as designed to encircle Armenia. Cf. Syme, *Athenaeum*, 272–83, esp. 275: 'to keep [Armenia] under control legions stood at Melitene and Satala, the strategic bases for an invasion'. Cf. also Syme's earlier observations in *CAH* xi. 139 ff.

[206] J. G. C. Anderson, *CAH* x. 780: Vespasian 'realized that what the empire needed was, not enlargement, but consolidation and defence. . . .' Luttwak, 57 f., takes for granted that the Flavian strategy was planned for defence and not for conquest. For the Euphrates frontier in Cappadocia, Mitford, *JRS*, 160–75; *SMR* ii (1977), 501–509; *ANRW*, 1168 ff.

boundaries were not secure enough. Hence a strategy of defence required another offensive under Trajan. In the words of Luttwak:

Anatolia now had an organized frontier, but with only two legions in Cappadocia and only three in Syria itself, it could not be a safe frontier. If Parthian forces could assemble freely in Armenia they might strike with greater forces either due west or due south at their choosing, and to the south was Syria, a core province of the Empire. Both strategic necessity and personal ambition required war.[207]

Several observations may be made. First, this scenario is wholly imaginary: Persia several times invaded Syria, but never through Armenia. Second, these arguments are not found in any ancient source: they are formulated by modern students and represent a twentieth-century attempt to reconcile what was in fact a policy of expansion with a strategy thought by modern scholars to be defensive. The real reason, according to Dio, was the emperor's longing for glory. Dio does not lend any support to the theory that there was any other reason for the campaign.[208] Finally, and most important, it is assumed as a matter of course that both the Flavians and Trajans wanted to establish secure boundaries and considered Parthia dangerous. The alternative view recognizes that Romans considered expansion desirable if it could be attained at reasonable cost. Vespasian witnessed the failure of Nero's eastern policy. It is perfectly reasonable to assume both that Vespasian wanted to prepare for a successful conquest of Armenia in future and that Trajan thought he could proceed from there. Trajan, after all, reached the Persian Gulf. No Roman ever claimed that this was necessary for the defence of Antioch on the Orontes.[209]

There is no information, so far, that would allow us to distinguish between Hadrian's organization following the withdrawal from Mesopotamia and that of the Flavians before Trajan's conquest.[210] The important difference was the lasting occupation of Transjordan and the reinforcement of the garrison in Judaea, both discussed below. The results of the campaign of Avidius Cassius in the sixties of the second century are not quite clear, apart from the fact that Dura-Europos

---

[207] 54.

[208] lxviii 17. 1 (iii 204).

[209] K.-H. Ziegler, *Die Beziehungen zwischen Rom und dem Partherreich: Ein Beitrag zur Geschichte des Völkerrechts* (1964), 2 f., considers the relationship between Rome and Parthia in the first and second centuries AD to have been generally peaceful in nature, interrupted only by the Trajanic war.

[210] For the Parthian organization of the region early in Hadrian's reign see Parchment no. x, a contract of loan of AD 121, published by M. I. Rostovtzeff and C. Bradford Welles, *The Excavations at Dura Europos: Preliminary Report of the Second Season, October 1928–April 1929*, ed. P. V. C. Baur and M. I. Rostovtzeff (1931), 201–16.

became a garrison town.[211] Auxiliaries were based also on the Euphrates.[212] Steps were indeed taken towards the incorporation of Armenia as a province. A city named Kainepolis, modern Echmiadzin, was (re?)founded 28 kilometres from Artaxata (modern Artashat), itself near Yerevan, the ancient capital of Urartu.[213] At Echmiadzin the presence of a garrison, a vexillation of XV Apollinaris, is attested through inscriptions of AD 175/6 and 184/5.[214] Near Artaxata itself two military inscriptions have been found.[215] A milestone of Commodus was found some 30 km. south-west of Kainepolis on a road which will have linked it with Cappadocia.[216] Some 28 kilometres east of Yerevan is the site of Garni, ancient Gorneae, with a city-wall, a remarkable classicizing temple, and a palace, the find-spot of a Greek inscription which mentions Tiridates, future king of Armenia.[217]

The consequences of the Severan conquest of Northern Mesopotamia are discussed below in Chapter V. Another subject reserved for further discussion is the function of army units in towns. For the present it should be mentioned that the evidence discussed above is mostly derived from urban centres. Below, in Chapter III it will be seen that this is true also for Judaea and Arabia. This is clearly a familiar pattern in the eastern provinces, and the implications must be considered.

To sum up, Rome had long-standing ambitions to acquire parts of the Persian empire and frequently made attempts to realize them. On the other hand, it is not clear that either the Parthians or the Sassanians actively desired or attempted to conquer permanently regions west of the Euphrates. Persia, however, never accepted a permanent presence of Rome east of the Euphrates. Roman ideology was not constant, and there were periods when it was held desirable to conquer and annex only what was profitable to acquire. We can derive that much from opinions expressed in literature. A survey of Rome's Persian wars shows that Rome usually was the attacker, and the distribution of troops from the Flavian period onward indicates that the Roman army

[211] *Excavations at Dura Europos: Final Report* v. 1. 22–46. D. Kennedy, *Antichthon* (forthcoming) emphasizes that there must have been more troops based east of the Euphrates than can now be identified with certainty. The Severan conquest, then, was to some extent anticipated by the actions of Avidius Cassius.

[212] See J.-P. Rey-Coquais, *JRS* 68 (1978), 69.

[213] Dio lxxi 3. 2 (iii 247 f). The capture by Lucius Verus is mentioned by Fronto, *ep. ad Verum* ii 1. Echmiadzin is the successor of the Armenian capital Vagharshapat.

[214] *ILS* 9117 (poor reading) and 394 (AD 184–5); cf. *DE* iv 1322 f.

[215] *AE* 1968. 510 f.   [216] *CIL* iii 13527a.

[217] In the reign of Claudius a Roman cohort had been stationed there (Tacitus, *Ann.* xii 45. 3). For the site of Garni, Mongait, 214 f.; C. Burney and D. M. Lang, 250–2.

in the East, in so far as it was organized for large-scale warfare, was prepared for further advance, not for defence, at least until the Byzantine period. Major campaigns took place sporadically, at intervals of fifty years or more.[218] The periods of major warfare were: 65–36 BC; AD 52–63; 112–17; 163–5; 194–217. The intervals are almost ninety, fifty, almost fifty, and thirty years. Most soldiers never took part in major expeditions, but that should not influence our judgement of the Roman aims in the area.

---

[218] Cf. the observations of J. C. Mann, *ANRW* ii. 1 (1974), 512: 'Although usually maintained at a reasonable pitch of efficiency they (sc. the troops) were in fact unemployed, a great machine virtually rusting away.' The army in peacetime is of course the subject of R. MacMullen, *Soldier and Civilian*.

II

CONSOLIDATION AND INTERNAL UNREST

> Consequently he [Varus] did not keep his legions together as was
> proper in a hostile country, but distributed many of the soldiers to
> helpless communities, which asked for them for the alleged
> purpose of guarding various points, arresting robbers or escorting
> provision trains.[1]

THIS chapter will consider the functions normally fulfilled by armies of
occupation, those connected with initial consolidation and with the
organization and policing of an area which no longer resisted Roman
rule.[2] The Roman army was trained to fight full-scale battles, but most
soldiers were only occasionally engaged in major wars. It need not be
supposed that there was always tension at the frontier of the empire
when there is no evidence for it. Hence the suggestion, in Chapter IX,
that barriers like those in southern Germany had no military
significance.

In the last century and the present one it would be natural for
scholars in Western Europe to assume that the Roman army in Europe
existed first and foremost to defend a clearly defined frontier against a
foreign enemy. Even today, while Europe has enjoyed peace for over
forty years, armies face each other across elaborate frontier systems,
doing nothing but preparing for full-scale hostilities.

A modern West European army is not normally involved in internal
police-duties or the occupation of neighbouring lands, but that is what
part of the Roman army did most of the time. We have little information on the extent to which Roman government in the provinces was
based on force or on the degree of consent to Roman rule there.
However, more attention should be given to these problems than is
usual in modern literature, which as a result of the bias of our sources
focuses mainly on major outbreaks of violence, both internally and

---

[1] Dio lvi 19. 1 f. (ii 532): Οὔτ᾽ οὖν τὰ στρατεύματα, ὥσπερ εἰκὸς ἦν ἐν πολεμίᾳ, συνεῖχε, καὶ ἀπ᾽
αὐτῶν συχνοὺς αἰτοῦσι τοῖς ἀδυνάτοις ὡς καὶ ἐπὶ φυλακῇ χωρίων τινῶν ἢ καὶ λῃστῶν συλλήψεσι
παραπομπαῖς τέ τισι τῶν ἐπιτηδείων διέδωκεν.
[2] See in general R. MacMullen, *Soldier and Civilian in the Later Roman Empire* (1963).

externally. It is generally assumed as a matter of course that there was relative peace and quiet in the interior and that there was a continuous state of hostility towards the people across the imperial border, which therefore had to be defended. In Chapter I we considered relations with the people across the border, the Persians. We turn now to the question of internal peace and quiet—or, to put it another way, the extent of unrest towards the margins and in the interiors of the Roman provinces of the East.

Chapter II will be concerned with the internal problems that the Romans faced in Syria, Arabia, and Judaea. Chapter III will deal with the Roman army of the principate and will attempt to describe its organization in terms of the conclusions reached in Chapter II; Chapter IV will do the same for the army of the later empire. The advantage of this arrangement is that it avoids confusing historical information on the security situation in the provinces with inferences on the aims of the Roman army drawn from a combination of literary and archaeological information. While there is historical information available on the subject of the present chapter, Chapters III and IV will depend largely on inference. That is to say, in those chapters we shall be considering to what extent there is evidence of a widespread distribution of military units in the interior. Where distribution is widespread we may legitimately infer that the troops served as an internal security force, even if we have no literary evidence of resistance to Roman rule.

The arrangement of this chapter—on Syria, Arabia, and Judaea—is partly geographical and partly chronological. The aim is, first, to show the specific forms of resistance encountered in the period during and after the annexation of the territories and their organization as Roman provinces, and then to survey the information on different forms of internal unrest that continued to exist after the initial consolidation. These varied from minor robberies to major revolts.

The latter will not be treated here systematically. They are best known from Judaea and the Jews, where, it is usually agreed, Rome encountered an unparalleled scale of continuous opposition. The present chapter will not discuss the full-scale wars between Rome and the Jews, but some attention will be given to evidence of unrest in periods of relative quiet and, in particular, in the centuries following the Revolt of Bar Kokhba, which was the last organized Jewish effort to regain independence. It is natural to assume that only major outbreaks of violence would be recorded in Roman sources, since they are basically uninterested in the state of affairs in the Roman provinces, an assumption easily confirmed by the brevity of the mention in these sources of, for instance, the Bar Kokhba war, which all agree to have been a major outbreak of violence. Any evidence of minor forms of unrest which somehow has survived in the sources must therefore be taken seriously.

We shall have to see also to what extent there was unrest in other areas and among other peoples, even if this did not take the form of resistance to Roman rule as such. There are indeed large areas where there is no evidence of unrest or of a widespread distribution of military units, as in much of Spain, Britain, Pannonia, Sicily, and Greece. Here we may assume that, once Roman rule was consolidated, there was a comparatively easy acceptance of the empire and its institutions. On the other hand, where there is evidence of internal unrest we may legitimately consider the possibility that the army was there to serve as an internal security force.

CONSOLIDATION

Peacetime activities of the army are not usually described in ancient sources, unless there is a specific reason. In AD 47 Corbulo re-subdued the Frisians, received hostages, settled them in a restricted area, 'imposed a senate, magistrates, laws, and established a garrison in a fort so that they would not shake off their submission . . .'[3] This is a specific reference to the function of the troops as forces of occupation, although these facts are mentioned not as interesting in themselves, but because Claudius subsequently ordered Corbulo to withdraw the troops. Similarly Dio's account of Varus' disaster in AD 9, cited at the head of this chapter, is of interest as a description of the routine of consolidation, even though the reason for its appearance in the source is the disaster which followed. Our sources do not usually describe daily life in the provinces: only when something went totally wrong do we get some information of the process of consolidation.

Dio describes Varus as engaged in the second of the two stages, the organization of Germany as if it no longer resisted Roman rule. Modern students often claim that Varus' defeat was the result of his inexperience as a general. He was, so it is claimed, a lawyer.[4] Whether or

---

[3] Tacitus, *Ann.* xi 19: 'datis obsidibus consedit apud agros a Corbulone descriptos: idem senatum, magistratus, leges imposuit. ac ne iussa exuerent praesidium immunivit. .'

[4] The judgement is based on Velleius ii 117. 2: 'Vir ingenio mitis, moribus quietus . . . otio magis castrorum quam bellicae adsuetus militiae.' See e.g. G. Webster, *The Roman Imperial Army*

not the distinction is generally applicable, in the case of Varus it is certainly incorrect. When governor of Syria, he successfully marched with two legions and auxiliaries through the countryside of Samaria in time of war.[5] This was, in a different way, as treacherous a country as the forests of Germany. Varus had, at the time of his defeat, more experience in the field than Vespasian had when Nero sent him to Judaea. (This is no proof of Vespasian's superior insight, for Judaea was already in revolt at the time, and Vespasian knew that a legion had almost been lost there.) As for the alleged 'mild character and quiet disposition' of Varus, according to Josephus there was 'fire and killing everywhere' in Samaria, and Varus crucified two thousand considered guilty of rebellion. All this was standard practice in the suppression of rebellions, described with approval by Tacitus, for instance, in his account of the revolt of Boudicca. A premature end to the 'destruction by fire and sword' is termed 'lame inaction under the honourable name of peace'.[6] As every ancient author knew, there were various stages in the incorporation of foreign peoples. Differences of opinion existed only regarding the appropriate application of one method or the other. The destruction of the economic base of the enemy was standard practice with the Romans as with other peoples. It made it impossible for the losers to continue a regular war, although, of course, it could lead to increased economic banditry among peoples who had nothing to lose. That would not bother an army which merely came to win a war (or a battle), but it would be a disadvantage for Rome when it permanently occupied a region.

The disaster in Germany was not the result of tactical mistakes made by the commander, but of fundamental errors of judgement as regards the situation in newly conquered territory.[7] As in Illyria in AD 6 and in Britain at the time of Boudicca's revolt, the Romans did not anticipate a revolt led by a strong leader. After the great rebellion in Illyria had been suppressed in AD 9, seven legions were stationed in Moesia, Pannonia, and Dalmatia. As pointed out by Syme, the stations they occupied demonstrate that they were not intended to fight on the Danube frontier, but to keep the peoples of Bosnia and Thrace under control.[8] Similarly, a legion was dispatched to occupy the base at

---

(1969), 52; C. M. Wells, *The German Policy of Augustus* (1972), 238 f., recognizes that he was made a scapegoat.

[5] Josephus, *Ant.* xvii 10. 9 (289–90); *BJ* ii 5. 1 (68–70). For an archaeological survey of the area, S. Dar, *Landscape and Pattern*, 2 vols. (1986).

[6] *Ann.* xiv 38 f.

[7] This is, in fact, the judgement of Velleius ii 117. 3–4 and of Florus, ii 33 f., as well as Dio.

[8] R. Syme, *Actes colloque Strasbourg, 1985* (1987), 146.

Nijmegen in Germania Inferior from *c*.70 as a response to the Batavian revolt in 69.[9]

Revolts frequently broke out at the time of incorporation of a people in a Roman province.[10] 'Provinces are harder to retain than to create.'[11] Other such rebellions were those of the Thracians in 26, the Frisians in 28, the Batavi in 69, and that through which Trajan lost Mesopotamia.[12] The causes, when mentioned in the sources, are usually excessive demands made upon the provincials for money, men, or goods, combined with maladministration by local officials. Curiously, the Romans invariably seem to have been surprised by these rebellions. Even Caesar confesses that he had not foreseen the revolt of Vercingetorix, but unlike Varus in Germany he had kept his legions together. It must be admitted, however, that we do not know how many rebellions failed to materialize because they were anticipated by prudent governors.[13]

Cicero's *Pro Fonteio* provides some insights into the demands made in the late republic upon provincials in Gaul, part of which had been incorporated fairly recently. It is an important source, as the oration was meant to clear Fonteius of charges of maladministration and Cicero's description of the state of affairs in the province may therefore be taken as that of a healthy administration, according to contemporary norms. Gaul was 'crowded with traders, full of Roman citizens. No Gaul does any business without the involvement of a Roman citizen, no coin changes hands which is not recorded in Roman books.'[14] There had been long and bitter wars till recently. Lands and towns had been confiscated and farmers evicted. Large numbers of cavalry had been conscripted for the wars in Spain 'so that they [the Gauls] would always obey the Roman people'[15], and these troops had to be paid for by the Gauls.[16] Huge quantities of corn were demanded for the troops in Spain, an early reference to *annona militaris*. These are counted as achievements.[17] The governor who was responsible for these acts was

---

[9] References in Bogaers and Rüger, *Der niedergermanische Limes* (1974), 76–9.

[10] S. L. Dyson, 'Native Revolt Patterns in the Roman Empire', *ANRW* ii 3. 158–61; also Isaac, *SCI* 7 (1983–4), 68–76. For the Illyrian revolt, Syme, *CAH* x 369–73; E. Koerstermann, *Hermes* 81 (1953), 345–768; J. J. Wilkes, *Dalmatia* (1969), 68–77.

[11] Florus ii 30, on the Germans who 'victi magis quam domiti erant'.

[12] For Trajan's formation of Armenia, Mesopotamia, and Assyria as Roman provinces, F. A. Lepper, *Trajan's Parthian War* (1948); A. Maricq, *Syria* 36 (1959), 254 ff. For a summary of the evidence, J. W. Eadie, *The Breviarium of Festus* (1976), 139 f. For the revolt, Lepper; R. P. Longden in *CAH* xi 250; E. M. Smallwood, *The Jews under Roman Rule* (²1981), 418–20.

[13] See P. A. Brunt on charges of maladministration under the early principate, *Historia* 10 (1961), 189–227.

[14] Cicero, *Pro Fonteio* 5. 11.   [15] 5. 13.

[16] 'magnas pecunias ad eorum stipendium.'   [17] 6. 14: 'Is qui gessit . . .'

supported by the colonists at Narbo Martius, Rome's ally Massilia, and the Roman citizens in the province, the evidence against him furnished by Gauls.

Usually, however, we hear very little of the process of consolidation, and yet it was an essential stage in the incorporation of all newly subjected regions. We have every reason to assume that it was a brutal and humiliating process in which the army was actively involved, or so it appears from Tacitus' description of the rebellion of Boudicca.[18] The Germans rebelled against Varus when they 'experienced laws more savage than arms'.[19]

Part of the process of consolidation of a province was the recruitment into the Roman army of able-bodied men. As already noted, Cicero commended his client Fonteius for recruiting numerous Gauls 'so that they would obey the Roman people forever'. This is more often mentioned by historians when it was the cause of, or an important motive for, rebellion. Until the reign of Tiberius the Thracians served under their own officers and only in neighbouring lands. They revolted in 26 when it was decided to incorporate the Thracian forces as regular units which would serve in the Roman army under Roman officers in all parts of the Empire.[20] The revolt of Boudicca in Britain had several causes, but one reason was resentment at the conscription of Britons into the *auxilia*.[21] Until 69 the Batavians themselves raised the troops Rome required, and these served under their own officers. In return for these contingents they enjoyed fiscal immunity. The revolt of Civilis broke out when a new levy was conducted in a brutal manner by Roman officers.[22] These are three instances when the method led to a crisis. It is obvious that normally there was resentment but not the complex of circumstances which led to actual revolt. The obvious advantage for the Romans of recruitment was that it withdrew precisely those elements which were most likely to rebel or resort to brigandage in newly conquered territory. Moreover, these men could be used to suppress such movements in other areas. For instance, the units of Dromedarii recruited originally from Arabia and numbering some 5,000 men could patrol desert routes and protect travellers and

---

[18] Sources: Tacitus, *Ann.* xiv 29–39; *Agricola* 15–16. 2; Dio lxii 1–12 (Xiphilinus). The revolt: G. Webster, *Boudicca, the British Revolt against Rome AD 60* (1978); S. Frere, *Britannia* (²1978), 104–8; P. Salway, *Roman Britain* (1981), 100–23. Evaluation of the sources: R. Syme, *Tacitus* (1958), 762–6.

[19] Florus ii 32.

[20] Tacitus, *Ann.* iv 46; cf. K. Kraft, *Zur Rekrutierung der Alen und Cohorten an Rhein und Donau* (1951), 35 ff.; P. A. Brunt, *SCI* 1 (1974), 106.

[21] Tacitus, *Agricola* 15. 3. Cf. Brunt, *SCI*, 107.

[22] Tacitus, *Hist.* iv 14; cf. Brunt, *Latomus* 19 (1960), 494 ff.; *SCI*, 106 f.

caravans.[23] They appear on graffiti between Madai'in Salih and al-Ula.[24] A veteran of such a unit appears on a text from the southern Leja (Trachonitis).[25] The Ituraeans were greatly esteemed as archers. There were at least six or seven cohorts and one *ala Ituraeorum*.[26]

Lebanon

In 63 BC at the time of Pompey's eastern campaign several regions suffered from brigandage. One people well known for their bellicose nature was the Ituraeans who lived in the Lebanon mountains and the Beqa' Valley. Strabo in his description of the Lebanon writes:

Now all the mountainous parts are held by Ituraeans and Arabians, all of whom are robbers, but the people in the plains are farmers; and when the latter are harassed by the robbers at different times they require different kinds of help. These robbers use strongholds as bases of operation; those, for example, who hold Libanus possess, high up on the mountain, Sinna and Borrama and other fortresses like them, and down below, Botrys and Gigartus and the caves by the sea and the castle that was erected on Theuprosopon. Pompey destroyed these places; and from them the robbers overran both Byblus and the city that comes next after Byblus, I mean the city Berytus, which lie between Sidon and Theuprosopon.[27]

In modern times similar raiding has occurred in the same region.[28] While it is possible that Pompey thoroughly secured the coast and with it the coast road which linked Egypt with northern Syria, the interior clearly was not pacified in a single campaign. On the contrary, the sort of destruction caused by a passing army is likely to have damaged the economy of the area, and that would increase rather than diminish banditry. Under Augustus veterans were settled in one or two colonies at Berytus and Heliopolis. It is generally accepted that these settle-

---

[23] These are not listed by Cichorius, *RE* iv, s.v. cohors, 324 f. as recruited in Arabia, but cf. G. L. Cheesman, *The Auxilia of the Roman Imperial Army* (1914), 182; *CIL* xvi no. 106.

[24] See below, p. 127.

[25] *ILS* 2541; cf. H. Seyrig, *Syria* 22 (1941), 234 f.; Speidel, *ANRW* ii 8. 704.

[26] Cf. Schürer, *The History of the Jewish People in the Age of Jesus Christ*, ed. G. Vermes and F. Millar, i (1973), 562, 570; M. M. Roxan, *RMD*, i, nos. 9, 53; Isaac, 'Military Diplomata and Extraordinary Levies for Campaigns', in W. Eck and H. Wolff (eds.), *Heer and Integrationspolitik: Die römischen Militärdiplome als historische Quelle* (1986), 259–61. Archers from Trachonitis served in Herod's army: Josephus, *BJ* ii 4. 2 (58).

[27] xvi 2. 18 (756); trans. H. L. Jones, Loeb.

[28] See e.g. the Great Britain Admiralty *Handbook of Syria (including Palestine)* (1920), 229–31. For the history of Ituraea, Schürer, i, Appendix I, 561–73; also W. Schottroff, *ZDPV* 98 (1982), 130–45; F. Peters, *JAOS* 97 (1977), 263–75. See further A. Kasher, *Cathedra* 33 (1984), 18–41, on the relationship between Jews and Ituraeans (in Hebrew); S. Dar, ibid. 42–50, on Ituraean(?) sanctuaries found in the region of Mt. Hermon (in Hebrew).

ments were to act as garrisons and assist in holding the Lebanon tribes in check; in Chapter VII, however, I shall argue that this theory rests on a basic misunderstanding of the nature of such colonies in general, and of the situation in Lebanon in particular.

Veteran colonies could be no more than a focus of loyalty and stability near a hostile area and a base of operations for the army-units on active duty.[29] They can never have fulfilled a significant role in the military consolidation, let alone in the defence of newly conquered territory. Moreover, the Roman authorities never practised large-scale settlement in the eastern provinces. Inscriptions set up by serving soldiers at Heliopolis suggest the presence of an army unit in the area. A famous inscription records a campaign against the Ituraeans in AD 6, well after the establishment of the veteran settlements at Berytus and Heliopolis.[30] It would be wrong to assume that the existence of one such inscription implies that only one expedition was sent against the Ituraeans. We must allow for the possibility that many more were undertaken.

Mountainous territory inhabited by accomplished guerrilla fighters determined to resist a foreign power, can be permanently occupied only by an army which is constantly prepared to interfere, regularly patrols the countryside, visits every village, and protects its own communications. Only a permanent presence in the area, not a passing army can effectively control such brigandage. Strabo, in fact, implies as much since, apart from his reference to Pompey, he speaks in the present. He does not pretend that Pompey or the settlement of veterans in Berytus and the Beqa‘ Valley solved the problems. More than five centuries later Procopius described similar problems with the Tzani, a people living in the Antitaurus mountains.[31] They raided among those settled in the lowlands and lived from their plunder, since their own land was too unproductive. An agreement to pay them a subsidy on condition that they would keep the peace was ineffective. In set battles with the Roman army they invariably lost, but their bases in the mountains were beyond the reach of the Roman forces. An effective policy, we are told, was the enrolment of the men into the Roman army. A suitable

[29] See below, ch. VII, for settlements planned by the authorities in Ottoman Palestine for similar purposes.

[30] *CIL* iii 6687. Serving soldiers at Heliopolis: *IGLS* vi 2711–12, 2714, 2789, 2848. The nearest legionary base was at Raphanaea. The inscription reminds one of *ILS* 740, a text of the mid fourth century from Isauria, another region which suffered from endemic banditry. It mentions a 'castellum diu ante a latronibus possessum et provinciis perniciosum' that had been occupied and garrisoned with Roman troops. It is obvious that this represented merely one move in a long war fought in the region.

[31] *Hist.* i 15. 19–25.

case for comparison is the gradual annexation of the Caucasus by Russia. This went on intermittently from the early eighteenth century till the middle of the nineteenth. Georgia, south of the Caucasus, was incorporated in 1801, but a fierce war with the mountaineers, notably the Circassian tribes, continued for another sixty years. Here it can be seen how a Russian penetration of the plain and larger centres near the mountains could coexist with a nagging state of war in the mountains.[32] In the Lebanon, it may be assumed, the Romans at first gained control of the cities on the coast and the inland Beqaʿ valley. The road from Berytus to Damascus would have required special security measures. Pacification of the mountains will have been a matter of time and could only have been carried out by the regular army.

Trachonitis

Further eastward, on the other hand, where there were similar problems, Strabo claims that the Roman army had taken effective measures. The lava plateau between Damascus and Bostra, modern El Leja (= 'a refuge', a place in which to hide), was, in antiquity, called Trachonitis.[33] Strabo has the following to say:

And then, towards the parts inhabited promiscuously by Arabians and Ituraeans, are mountains hard to pass, in which there are deep-mouthed caves, one of which can admit as many as four thousand people in times of incursions, such as are made against the Damasceni from many places. For the most part, indeed, the barbarians have been robbing the merchants from Arabia Felix, but this is less the case now that the band of robbers under Zenodorus has been broken up through the good government established by the Romans and through the security established by the Roman soldiers that are kept in Syria.[34]

In 23 BC Augustus gave Trachonitis, Batanaea (Bashan), and Auranitis (Hauran) to Herod. His task was to suppress the robber bands in Trachonitis, which had operated in Damascene with the

---

[32] M. Lermontov gives graphic descriptions of this in *A Hero of Our Time*: society from Moscow and Petersburg would visit the mineral springs at Pyatigorsk in the northern Caucasus while sentries were posted all around to protect them against Circassians.

[33] Geography: Schürer, i 336–8; air photographs: A. Poidebard, *Syria* 9 (1928), 114–23. Cf. F. Peters, *JAOS* 97 (1977), 263–75. See now *Hauran I: Recherches archéologiques sur la Syrie du sud à l'époque hellénistique et romaine*, ed. J.-M. Dentzer (1985). Note also the older works: J. G. Wetzstein, *Reisebericht über Hauran und die Trachonen* (1860); M. von Oppenheim, *Vom Mittelmeer zum Persischen Golf*, i–ii (1899/1900), 87–108; H. C. Butler et al., *The Publications of an American Archaeological Expedition to Syria, 1899–1900* (1903–14); *The Publications of the Princeton University Archaeological Expeditions to Syria in 1904–5 and 1909* (1907–43).

[34] xvi 2. 20 (756); trans. H. L. Jones, Loeb.

support of Zenodorus the Tetrarch.[35] The latter received a share of the profit, according to Josephus:

It was not easy to restrain people who had made brigandage a habit and had no other means of making a living, since they had neither city nor field of their own but only underground shelters and caves, where they lived together with their cattle. They had also managed to collect supplies of water and of food beforehand, and so were able to hold out for a very long time in their hidden retreats. Moreover, the entrances [to their caves] were narrow, and only one person at a time could enter, while the interiors were incredibly large and constructed to provide plenty of room, and the ground above their dwellings was not high but almost level with the [surrounding] surface. The whole place consisted of rocks that were rugged and difficult of access unless one used a path with a guide leading the way, for not even these paths were straight, but had many turns and windings.[36]

These two passages from what are obviously independent sources agree and supplement each other. Strabo and Josephus both record that the major problem was that the territory of Damascus and the roads there suffered from bandits; both tell us that the bandits hid in caves. These caves have been identified by archaeologists working in the region.[37] In Israel numerous artificial caves have been found in recent years, clearly used as hiding places in the Roman period. A story told by Ammianus may provide indirect evidence that in the fourth century, in the area of Apamea, bandits also hid in caves. These were the so-called 'Maratocupreni'. The first element of the name almost certainly refers to caves.[38] Strabo makes it clear that the banditry was of special concern to the Romans because not only the rural population around Damascus, but also traders were attacked. This shows that, in the time of Strabo, traders from southern Arabia travelled to southern Syria rather than the ports of Alexandria and Gaza. There are not many indications in ancient literature that the Roman army actively protected commerce. Josephus, on the other hand, insists on the economic cause of brigandage.

A graphic description of the region early this century may be cited here:

The passes, fissures, and caverns in this black and desolate region are so inaccessible that the Bedouin robbers by which El-Leja has been infested for centuries, continue to find secure refuge from the law ... At only a few points

---

[35] Josephus, *Ant* xv 10. 1 (343–8); *BJ* i 20. 4 (398–400). For Zenodorus, Schürer, i, 565 f.
[36] *Ant.* xv 10. 1 (346 f.).   [37] F. Villeneuve, in Dentzer, 73.
[38] Syriac *mᶜarta*, Hebrew *meᶜarah*, Arabic *magharat* = cave, cf. I. Shahîd, *Byzantium and the Arabs in the Fourth Century* (1984), 172 n. 127. The second part of the name has no obvious meaning.

are the rocky borders penetrable and, there, the tracks are hewn out of the rock. The secrets of internal communication are carefully guarded by the inhabitants. Tracks over and around deep fissures or through narrow passes and confused masses of fallen or upheaved rocks, can only be followed in daylight with the help of local guides whose knowledge is confined to particular localities.[39]

Wetzstein, who knew the area in the mid-fifties of the nineteenth century tells that the Turkish authorities never dared to act against the inhabitants of the region, no matter how much the villagers around Damascus suffered from their depredations. He notes that they could be controlled only by a permanent garrison in their land. The caves were famous in his time as well.[40] We may note the expression 'a robbers' cave', used as a matter of course in the New Testament.[41]

Again we find here brigands hiding in caves and, as in Josephus, the need for a guide to lead the way. According to Josephus, Herod pacified the region, but fourteen years later the inhabitants rebelled. Herod had prevented them from practising banditry and forced them to till the soil and live quietly. This they did not want to do and—even had they been willing—the land was too poor, so they again attacked their neighbours. Herod's army took action, and some of the robbers fled to Arabia. There they were provided with a base of operations against Judaea (i.e. Galilee) and Coele-Syria (i.e. the territory of Damascus). Herod first attacked the home base of the bandits in Trachonitis, which was ineffective, since they had a base of operations on Nabataean territory, where 'they numbered about a thousand'.[42] Herod attacked them there and destroyed their base, which led to conflict between him and the Nabataeans. In a further effort to suppress banditry Herod settled 3,000 Idumaeans, his own countrymen, in Trachonitis. All this got him into difficulties with Augustus, by whom he was reprimanded. After this both the inhabitants of Trachonitis and the Nabataeans resorted to brigandage and attacked the Idumaean settlers.

Herod obviously failed to gain control of Trachonitis, for afterwards he planted Jewish settlers at Bathyra in Batanaea.[43] The settlement in itself was successful.[44] The presence of Jewish settlers is attested by

---

[39] *Handbook of Syria*, 562 f.

[40] *Reisebericht*, 34–9. For further literature on the region in the nineteenth century, Dentzer, 400 n. 64.

[41] Matt. 21: 13 σπήλαιον λῃστῶν.

[42] Josephus, *Ant.* xvi 9. 1–2 (271–85).

[43] *Ant.* xvii 2. 1 (23–30). It is perhaps to be identified with Basire, east of as-Sanamein (Aere): R. Dussaud, *Topographie de la Syrie antique et médiévale* (1927), 331; Schürer, ii 14 n.; Th. Bauzou, in Dentzer, 150 and map opp. p. 139.

[44] See below, p. 330.

carvings found at Nawa,[45] which is a site on the road Damascus–Der'a–
Capitolias–Gadara–Scythopolis used by Jewish travellers to and from
Babylonia.[46] Josephus says that they were to serve as a buffer between
Trachonitis and Galilee.[47] This implies that Herod had given up
attempts permanently to subdue the population of Trachonitis itself.

Another indication of Herod's failure here is the inscription set up at
Canatha on the slopes of Jebel Druze, south-east of Trachonitis, which,
in the reign of one of the two Agrippas, mentions people who hide in
holes like animals.[48]

The region retained its bad name. The elder Pliny, writing before AD
79, says of the Arabs in general that an equal part of them were engaged
in trade or lived by brigandage.[49] The *Epitome de Caesaribus* calls the
father of the emperor Philip 'a most notable leader of brigands'.[50] This
refers to the early third century and it is relevant here, for Philip was
born in a town near Trachonitis, refounded by him as Philippopolis.[51]
There is no need to believe the statement, but it may be taken as an
expression of the continued notoriety of this region in antiquity.

A Roman road with watchtowers and blockhouses through
Trachonitis is evidence of Roman army organization. It was constructed in the second century (milestones of Commodus, Septimius
Severus, and Diocletian).[52] It should also be noted that Bostra, a
legionary base, was less than forty kilometres away from the southern
edge of Trachonitis. However, the Roman army organization in the
area will be discussed below, in Chapter III.

I have discussed this region at length because there are relatively good
sources containing relevant information. The ancient sources make it
clear that this was a poor region which did not allow of profitable
cultivation and that the very factors which contributed to its poverty
made it a shelter for brigands. This had consequences, not only for the

---

[45] Cf. Schürer, i 338, n. 3; ii 14, n. 46. For Nava and other sites in the region, F. Villeneuve, in Dentzer, 63–136.

[46] The road is mentioned in the *Itinerarium Antonini*, 196 f., ap. *Itineraria Romana*, ed. O. Cuntz (1929), p. 21.

[47] *Ant.* xvii 2. 1–2 (23–31).

[48] *OGIS* 424; *IGR* iii 1223; Waddington, no. 2329, with extensive comments. The inscription may in fact originate from nearby Si'.

[49] *NH* vi 32 (162).

[50] 28. 4: 'is Philippus humillimo ortus loco fuit, patre nobilissimo latronum ductore.'

[51] Cf. *RE* x, s.v. Iulius (Philippus), 386, 755 ff.; xix, x.v. Philippopolis (2), 2263; A. Spijkerman, *The Coins of the Decapolis and Provincia Arabia* (1978), 258–61; G. W. Bowersock, *Roman Arabia* (1983), 123–7; I. Shahîd, *Rome and the Arabs* (1984) extensively discusses the emperor Philip.

[52] A. Poidebard, *Syria* 9 (1928), 114–23 (air photographs); M. Dunand, *Mem. Ac. Inscr.* 13. 2 (1930), 521–57; Bauzou, in Dentzer, 139–141; pls. i*b*–iii*a*.

region itself, but also for neighbouring, fertile lands which suffered depredations. Since important trade-routes passed through and near by, international trade also suffered from this insecurity. At first Augustus gave his client Herod instructions to solve the problem. Indeed, this seems precisely the sort of problem which client kings were supposed to solve, but in this case the result was armed conflict with another client. We have here, in other words, an example of how the system failed to function. These were the sort of local problems, usually not mentioned in literary sources, that might convince the Romans that it was preferable to annex a region. Eventually the Roman army took the matter in hand. However, problems like these are never solved for good. The factors which caused instability—poverty and inaccessibility—do not change. We learn that Samaritan rebels fled to Trachonitis as late as the sixth century.[53]

The information we gain regarding banditry in Trachonitis is important, because the situation there had nothing to do with the specifically Jewish resistance to Roman rule in Judaea. Its causes were social and economic, and ideology played no role here. Yet we know of this only thanks to the diligence of two good sources, Strabo and Josephus. These two authors describe the problems of consolidation of Roman rule in Lebanon and Trachonitis. However, the possibility must be considered that there was banditry in Trachonitis in other periods of antiquity when there was no author interested in writing about it. If the phenomenon occurred also in later periods this was no longer a matter of consolidation, but a problem of long-term internal security.

Judaea

Several sources accuse the Jews of brigandage before the Roman conquest. Josephus represents Hyrcanus as accusing Aristobulus before Pompey of instigating raids against neighbouring peoples and acts of piracy at sea.[54] Strabo tells us:

the tyrannies [sc. of the Hasmonaeans] were the cause of brigandage, for some rebelled and harassed the countryside, both their own and neighbouring lands, while others collaborated with the rulers and seized the possessions of others and subdued much of Syria and Phoenicia.[55]

---

[53] See below, p. 90.   [54] *Ant.* xiv 3. 2 (43).
[55] xvi 2. 28 (758): . . . ἐκ δὲ τῶν τυραννίδων τὰ λῃστήρια. οἱ μὲν γὰρ ἀφιστάμενοι τὴν χώραν ἐκάκουν καὶ αὐτὴν καὶ τὴν γειτνιῶσαν, οἱ δὲ συμπράττοντες τοῖς ἄρχουσι καθήρπαζον τὰ ἀλλότρια καὶ τῆς Συρίας κατεστρέφοντο καὶ τῆς Φοινίκης πολλήν.

Again, in his description of the coast of Sharon from Joppe to Carmel Strabo says that 'the ports of robbers clearly are merely robbers' dens'.[56] Similar accusations are found in the *Historia Philippica* and in Justinus' *epitome* of Pompeius Trogus,[57] where it is stated that the Jews and the Arabs harassed Syria by brigandage. It is difficult to say whether this refers only to the Hasmonaean conquests of territory outside Judaea proper, or also to armed clashes or raids of which we possess no written record.

Statements like these must be distinguished from the information on banditry in Trachonitis. Accusations of Jewish state-sponsored brigandage, like those levelled by Strabo against Zenodorus and by Josephus against the Nabataeans, may not be true. Their intention was to justify armed intervention by a third party. The alleged purpose of Pompey's eastern campaign was the suppression of piracy, and accusations of robbery and piracy clearly served as justification for the subjugation of various peoples.[58]

Conclusions

It is often claimed that the Roman army, while engaged in a war of conquest, would construct a fortified boundary in order to defend newly conquered lands against attack from outside.[59] This is a notion which could appeal only to those thinking in terms of trench warfare. In the previous pages it has been argued that the reality was completely different. Following an initial campaign of conquest there was a period of consolidation, annexation, and organization which could be difficult and protracted. These were not activities likely to attract the attention of ancient historians, and our information is therefore inadequate. We hear of occasional revolts, the result of gross errors of judgement or crude misbehaviour toward the subjugated peoples. Thanks to Josephus and Strabo we know a little more about some areas in the east. Generally speaking, however, we must assume that this was a phase in which armed forces were involved in various activities, many of them less beneficial than some of our sources would have it.

---

[56] xvi 2. 28 (758). See also 2. 40 (761), where the fortresses of the Hasmonaeans are described in similar terms.

[57] *Historiae Philippicae*, prologus, L. xxxix, and Justinus (Pompeius Trogus) xi 2. 4; for comments, M. Stern, *Greek and Latin Authors on Jews and Judaism*, i (1974), nos. 138 f., p. 343.

[58] See e.g. Appian, *Mithradaticus Liber*, 114 (ed. Mendelssohn, 556 f).

[59] For instance during the campaigns in Germany. See Isaac, *JRS* 78 (1988), 125–47.

INTERNAL UNREST

When a subject people no longer actively resisted Roman rule it was the responsibility of the army to maintain internal security. What has been said above about the process of consolidation among newly conquered peoples is not, of course, to suggest that every province was peaceful once the initial stages of incorporation were concluded. In the last third of the first century there were various kinds of trouble, for instance 'disturbances in Illyricum, Gaul of doubtful loyalty, Britain completely subjected and immediately abandoned'.[60] These were all regions which had long been Roman provinces, and the difficulties were not caused by foreign invaders. Under Hadrian there was trouble in Bosnia, and during the Danubian wars of Marcus Aurelius there was an insurrection by bandits on the border of Macedonia and Thrace.[61] Further east Isauria suffered from endemic banditry; from the third century onward the area became a permanent problem.[62] It is important to realize that all such troubles required intervention from the Roman army. The possibility must be considered that there were forms of unrest in the Roman empire which had nothing to do with resistance to Roman rule as such, but must be described as social troubles with no specifically ethnic or ideological roots. First, however, it has to be seen what evidence we have of threats caused to the security of the provinces by nomads living in the desert.

Nomad Tribes Not a Source of Trouble before the Fourth Century

In other discussions of security problems in the eastern provinces it is usually assumed that there were two basic tasks which the army had to perform: to defend the entire area against the Persian army, and to prevent nomad raids, incursions, and invasions.[63] It is taken for granted that the Roman imperial army, as soon as it occupied the area,

---

[60] Tacitus, *Hist.* i 2: 'turbatum Illyricum, Galliae nutantes, perdomita Britannia et statim omissa.'

[61] As observed by Syme, *Actes*, Vitrasius Flamininus (*suff.* 122) was as governor of Moesia Superior also commander of the army of the province of Dalmatia. For the rebellion under Marcus see *AE* 1956. 124.

[62] Syme, *Actes*.

[63] A. Alt., *ZDPV* 58 (1935), 37, 43–51; F.-M. Abel, *Géographie de la Palestine* ([3]1967), 178–84, 187–91. For the Negev in this respect, M. Avi-Yonah, *The Holy Land* ([2]1977), 119 f.; M. Gichon (below, n. 76). For Arabia, E. W. Gray, *Proc. Afr. Class. Ass.* 12 (1973), 27; M. Speidel, *ANRW*, 688. S. T. Parker, *Romans and Saracens* (1986), 6–9, offers a different view, which accounts for the need to defend Arabia against hostile penetration but recognizes that there was no military barrier against nomadic tribes.

had to prevent an imminent invasion and conquest—and in fact it succeeded in doing so until the seventh century. The army of the principate is believed to have successfully withstood very serious pressure and to have safeguarded the security of provinces which a weakened Byzantine army later lost altogether. We must ask, however, whether this could be an unjustified and anachronistic projection into the past of a historical reality which belongs to the seventh century and not to an earlier period. In an earlier paper I supported the view that Bedouin tribes did not cause serious trouble before the fourth century.[64] The army, I suggested, was there primarily to guarantee the security of the roads.[65] For the sake of clarity these arguments are repeated here and somewhat expanded. If they are accepted as valid for the eastern frontier it is possible that, *mutatis mutandis*, a similar analysis should be considered for some other frontier area.

All over North Africa and in the Near East, wherever the settled regions adjoined the desert, the Romans faced the phenomena of nomadic pastoralism and transhumance. Many modern scholars tend to view these in terms of the late nineteenth and early twentieth century, when the Bedouin caused serious upheavals in the territories of the Ottoman empire, itself the successor to the Mamluk empire which had not kept the Bedouin under control either.[66] From the numerous travellers' accounts of this period it is clear that there was a state of almost total lawlessness in Palestine due to, among other things, the weakness of Ottoman military force, the lack of a firm policy, and the sparseness of the sedentary population. It is assumed that this model would be applicable to the situation under Roman rule, which is less well known.

Modern students are further constantly aware of the upheavals in the seventh century, when much of the Near East and North Africa was indeed conquered by a movement which had its origins in the Arabian peninsula. Roman historians indeed know of actual pressure on the

---

[64] As regards southern Palestine this was first argued in two important papers by P. Mayerson, *Proc. American Philosophical Society* 107 (1963), 160–72, esp. 165 ff.; *TAPA* 94 (1964), 155–99, esp. 168; 188 ff. For the wider area an extensive discussion along these lines will be published by D. F. Graf, 'Rome and the Saracens: Reassessing the Nomadic Menace', *Colloque International sur L'Arabie préislamique et son environnement historique et culturel*, Strasbourg, June 1987 (forthcoming).

[65] *HSCP* 88 (1984), 171–203, esp. 173 f.; a revised version appeared in Hebrew in *Cathedra* 39 (1986), 3–36.

[66] See e.g. F. E. Peters, *JNES* 37 (1978), 315–26, referring to J. Wetzstein, *Reisebericht über Hauran und die Trachonen* (1860), 2; G. Schumacher, *Across the Jordan*, 103 f.; A. Musil, *Arabia Deserta* (1927), 353, 408: J. Porter, *Five Years in Damascus*, ii (1855), 69. For the role of the Bedouin in Palestine in the sixteenth and seventeenth century, M. Sharon in M. Ma'oz, *Studies on Palestine during the Ottoman Period* (1975), 11–30. For efforts, hardly successful, to improve the situation between 1840 and 1861, M. Ma'oz, *Ottoman Reform in Syria and Palestine* (1968), ch. IX.

fringes of several parts of the empire from the later second century onwards. All these concepts taken together have created an image of a Roman 'frontier' in the East under constant pressure from the nomads, and thus in constant need of military preparedness to prevent the collapse of a threatened empire. We may legitimately question whether these various models really should be applied when considering the Near East before the Islamic conquest.

In studying the Roman empire we are faced with an organization which cannot be compared without qualification with the Ottoman empire, neither is the social and economic situation in the desert or at the edge of it necessarily comparable. The Romans may have been capable of more effective or more ruthless military action to avoid trouble, with the help, for instance, of their own units of mounted camel riders. Patterns of transhumance and nomadism may vary between periods, and it is not necessarily true that the Saudi Arabian peninsula has served throughout human history as some sort of a kettle under steam producing nomadic pressure on the settled lands.[67] There is no evidence of overpopulation in Arabia in antiquity.[68] The region did not have the climate or resources for excess population to survive in the first place.

We know very little about the ancient Bedouin, and comparisons with the nomadic pastoralists of a more recent past may well lead to distorted views, for much of the nineteenth-century literature on the subject is coloured with romanticism and represents the Bedouin as they saw themselves.[69] Their way of life was essentially an adjustment of peoples without modern technology to life in a region with scarce water resources in summer. Minor climatic variations, and political and economic factors in the settled regions can drastically influence the life of the Bedouin and thus their behaviour as well.

[67] The best studies of Bedouin tribes in the late nineteenth century known to me are those of A. Musil, *The Manners and Customs of the Rwala Bedouins* (1928); even more interesting are the occasional observations found in other works, notably his *Arabia Petraea: a Topographical Itinerary* (1928). Another classic work is C. M. Doughty, *Travels in Arabia Deserta* (1888). Modern literature on Bedouin and nomads is, of course, very extensive, and I do not claim to have done more than random reading. Works which I have consulted and found to be relevant are: T. Ashkenazi, *Tribus semi-nomades de la Palestine du Nord* (1938); E. Marx, *Bedouin of the Negev* (1967); T. Asad, *The Kababish Arabs: Power, Authority and consent in a nomadic tribe (1970)*; W. Weissleder (ed.), *The Nomadic Alternative: Modes and Models of Interaction in the African-Asian Deserts and Steppes* (1978); F. Donner, *The Early Islamic Conquests* (1981), ch. I on state and society in pre-Islamic Arabia. Some additional bibliography may also be found in the paper by E. B. Banning, *BASOR* 261 (1986), 25–50.

[68] As pointed out by Donner, 268. He cites a complaint by 'Umar that he had difficulties in finding enough men to conscript into the armies during the third phase of the Islamic conquests, an indication that overpopulation was no problem.

[69] See the arguments by E. Marx, *The Nomadic Alternative*, 41–74, esp. 46.

It has even been argued that a basic change in social structure among the Arabs took place as a result of a process which began with the Roman occupation of the Nabataean kingdom.[70] In addition to the Nabataean kingdom there existed various principalities in southern and eastern Arabia: Qataban, Saba', Gerrha, and others. In southern Babylonia there was the principality of Charakene (Mesene).[71] In the north the city-state of Palmyra could also be seen as belonging to the same system: a chain of towns and principalities linked by a network of caravan routes which allowed a certain prosperity and stability to exist in the region as a whole. The Nabataean kingdom was dissolved by Rome, and the various states in the peninsula also came to an end. The kingdom of Mesene was taken over by the Parthians, apparently in the middle of the second century.[72] Palmyra was destroyed in the second half of the third century. All this would then have resulted in the desertion of caravan routes, a decline in economic prosperity, and a resulting transition of part of the population from settled life to nomadism. It is perhaps questionable whether we know enough about patterns of trade in antiquity to accept such a theory with confidence, but there can be no doubt that the role of the two major powers in the area affected nomadic groups everywhere in the region, perhaps more in the Syrian desert than in southern Arabia. Some of the consequences become clear only in the fourth century: the presence of Rome, and her aggressive policy towards other powers in the region, resulted in the appearance of confederacies which were a far more significant factor than the Arabs of earlier centuries had ever been.

There is no reason to go to great lengths in order to deny the obvious conclusion that the one major factor contributing to the upheaval of the Islamic conquest was the rise of Islam itself.[73]

It is not the aim of the present chapter to argue in favour of this theory or any other concerning the social and economic history of pre-Islamic Arabia. It will, however, be useful to consider alternatives to the assumption of perpetual nomadic pressure on the Roman provinces. A possibility which ought to be seriously considered is that a strong central government would create a form of stability that would

---

[70] W. Caskel speaks of 'The Bedouinization of Arabia' in G. E. von Grunebaum (ed.), *Studies in Islamic Cultural History*, Memoirs of the American Anthropological Association 76 (1954), 36–46.

[71] For Mesene, Oppenheimer et al., *Babylonia Judaica in the Talmudic Period* (1983), 241–56.

[72] As appears from the newly discovered inscription on a statue of Hercules taken to the Parthian capital with the spoils from Mesene: W. I. Al-Salihi, *Sumer* 43 (1984), 219–29, esp. 223–5; G. W. Bowersock, *Colloque international, l'Arabie préislamique et son environnement historique et culturel, Strasbourg, 24–27 juin, 1987*, proceedings forthcoming.

[73] This is one of the basic themes in Donner's work.

enable various modest forms of police action in the desert to maintain security at an acceptable level.[74] Camel raiding, customary among the Bedouin till recent times, would not have bothered the Roman authorities, since it did not affect the settled regions.[75] Transhumance need not entail aggressive behaviour among those who practise it. However, it will be best to consider the evidence.

Even those who assume that the primary function of the Roman army in the eastern provinces was the protection of the settled lands against invading nomads will admit that not a single source mentions serious difficulties caused by nomadic tribes before the Byzantine period.[76] This is significant, for information on Judaea is exceptionally rich as compared with other Roman provinces. Josephus is the only historian of antiquity who provides an account of the transformation of an independent kingdom into a Roman province, stage by stage. Talmudic and early Christian sources cannot be read as historiography, but they certainly contain information on major contemporary troubles. Nomad raids are nowhere mentioned.

Many undated graffiti have been found in Sinai, in the Negev, and in the desert regions of Transjordan. Most informative are those produced by the so-called Safaitic tribes.[77] They prove the presence of pastoralists moving annually from the Hauran to the desert and back. However, the texts are hard to interpret and harder still to date. The graffiti as such cannot be taken as evidence of great pressure on the Roman provinces, unless one starts from the preconception that there

[74] E. B. Banning, *BASOR* 261 (1986), 25–50, argues for a state of relatively peaceful relations between nomads and sedentary population in Transjordan; criticized by S. T. Parker, *BASOR* 265 (1987), 35–51, with a reply by Banning, ibid. 51–4, and cf. P. C. Salzman (ed.) *When Nomads Settle* (1980). See also A. Musil, cited below, p. 217. For North Africa, M. Euzennat, *Bull. archéologique du CTHS* ns 19B (1985), 161–7, on the relationship between the Roman military occupation (progressive in the desert) and cultivation, sedentarization, and absorption of the *gentes externae* by stages ('pénétration par osmose').

[75] On camel raiding in recent history, L. E. Sweet, in *Peoples and Cultures of the Middle East*, ed. L. E. Sweet (1970), 265–89.

[76] See various articles by M. Gichon, cited in the Bibliography. He concludes from parallels in other periods that the primary task of the military installations in the Negev was the protection of the settled areas of Judaea against nomad raids and invasions, besides other functions such as the protection of trade and supervision of traffic. Most recently in *Roman Frontier Studies 1979*, ed. W. S. Hanson and L. J. F. Keppie (1980), 843–64. For the relationship between Rome and the nomads, F. E. Peters, *JNES* 37 (1978), 315–326; M. Sartre, *Trois études sur l'Arabie romaine et byzantine* (1982), ch. 3; Bowersock, *Roman Arabia, passim*; Shahîd, *Rome and the Arabs*; *Byzantium and the Arabs in the Fourth Century*.

[77] G. L. Harding, *Al-Abhath* 22 (1969), 3–25; D. F. Graf, *BASOR* 229 (1978), 1–26 with bibliography F. V. Winnett and G. Lankaster Harding, *Inscriptions from Fifty Safaitic Cairns* (1978); M. Sartre, *Syria* 59 (1982), 77–91; H. I. MacAdam, *Studies in the History of the Roman Province of Arabia* (1986), 101–46; Graf, *Colloque International sur L'Arabie préislamique et son environnement historique et culturel*, Strasbourg, June 1987 (forthcoming).

was such pressure. The Romans are mentioned regularly. A few of the inscriptions even mention raids and fighting with the Romans, presumably in the first three centuries AD.[78] However, they present these conflicts from the perspective of tribesmen, which was quite different from that of the Romans. We cannot know whether more than minor camel raids and retaliatory measures were involved. We must distinguish between Roman police activities among transhumant pastoralists in the desert and military action to defend a province against invasion or massive infiltration.

The Thamudic graffiti in the central and southern regions of Arabia do not mention the Romans at all.[79] This is important, for it is from there that pressure is thought to have been particularly heavy and constant. A famous bilingual text shows that, in the reign of Marcus Aurelius, the Thamudians formed a confederation which recognized the authority of the Roman emperor and the governor of the province of Arabia.[80] It originates from Ruwwafa, an important shrine and meeting place on a major trade route.

A number of references relating to the third century may be discarded. The *Historia Augusta* attributes a remark to Niger addressing troops after their defeat by Saracens. The troops complained, 'We get no wine, we cannot fight.' Niger replied, 'Shame on you, for your victors drink water.'[81] This looks like early evidence of pre-Islamic abstention from alcohol.[82] However, it is not evidence of Saracen aggression. The *Historia Augusta* must be mistrusted particularly when it attempts to be witty, and nowhere more so than when we are faced with ethnic slurs. The same source reports that Macrinus bravely and successfully campaigned in Arabia Felix.[83] It is not clear whether the author knew this was untrue; he may genuinely have been confused, like Herodian when he reports an expedition by Severus to Arabia Felix (instead of Adiabene).[84] According to the Latin Panegyrics Diocletian fought the Saracens.[85] Nothing further is known, but whatever happened presumably took place in northern Mesopotamia and may have been connected with his Persian war.[86] Another well-known inscription

[78] Graf, *BASOR*, 5 f., and his forthcoming paper cited in the previous note.
[79] J. Beaucamp, 'Rawwafa et les Thamoudéens', *SDB* ix (1979), 1467–75.
[80] G. W. Bowersock, *Le monde grec: Hommages à Claire Préaux* (1975), 512–22; Graf, *BASOR*, 9–12; Sartre, *Trois études*, 27–29; Beaucamp, *SDB*.
[81] SHA, *Niger* 7. 8.
[82] A dedication of AD 132 mentions the god Shaiʿ al-Qaum who does not drink wine (*CIS* ii 1973).
[83] SHA, *Macrinus* 12. 6.   [84] Herodian iii 9. 3, with Whittaker's comments ad loc.
[85] *Panegyrici Latini* 11 [3], 5, 4.
[86] T. D. Barnes, *The New Empire of Diocletian and Constantine* (1982), 51, in his reconstruction of

of 328 from Namara refers to a 'lord of the Arabs'.[87] It is a difficult text which has been variously interpreted, but Imru'l-quais seems to have been a loyal vassal of the Romans.

All this is not to deny that there were tribal movements and that the Romans took care in monitoring and controlling them. These, however, were activities of an army in peacetime. They were internal police actions—and internal should be emphasized. There is no evidence of great pressure before the Byzantine period or of a threat of instability in the interior of the provinces. There is no indication that exceptional or large-scale measures were required or were taken.

The first real crisis caused by Bedouin tribes we know of was the revolt of Queen Mavia in 378.[88] The first author to describe Saracens as a nuisance is Ammianus,[89] but he describes them only as raiders, not as an invading force. A tribal chief mentioned by Ammianus, an ally of the Persians engaged in irregular warfare, 'had long harassed our frontier districts with great ferocity'.[90] This, however, was part of the confrontation between Rome and Persia in Mesopotamia.

During the following two and a half centuries several nomad incursions are mentioned. There was a major invasion by Huns from across the Caucasus in 395–7.[91] They came over the Darial pass while the Roman army was absent in Italy. Armenia, Cappadocia, and Syria were affected. They came as far as Edessa and Antioch. Rumours held that greed attracted them towards Jerusalem. Antioch and Tyre worried about their defences.[92] Jerome and his friends sought refuge on

the chronology of the reign, allows a month or two at most, in May and June of 290 for Diocletian's campaign against the Saracens. That would suffice for a limited police action. See also W. Ensslin, *Zur Ostpolitik des Kaisers Diokletian* (1942), 15 f., who comments that it will not have been an important war.

[87] For recent discussion and further bibliography, Sartre, *Trois études*, 136–9; Bowersock, *Roman Arabia*, ch. 10, pp. 138–42; Shahîd, *Byzantium and the Arabs*, 32–53; J. A. Bellamy, *JAOS* 105 (1985), 31–48, with a revised reading.

[88] Rufinus, *HE* ii 6 (*PL* xxi, col. 515); Socrates, *HE* iv 36 (*PG* lxvi 553, 556); Sozomen, *HE* vi 38 (*GCS* 50); Theodoret, *HE* iv 23 (*GCS* 44). Cf. G. W. Bowersock, *Studien zur antiken Sozialgeschichte: Festschrift F. Vittinghoff*, ed. W. Eck, H. Galsterer, and H. Wolff (1980), 477–95; P. Mayerson, *IEJ* 30 (1980), 123 f.; Sartre, *Trois études*, 140–4; Shahîd, *Byzantium and the Arabs*, ch. IV.

[89] See especially xxii 5. 1–2 and, on this, John Matthews, *The Roman Empire of Ammianus* (1989). See also Shahîd, *Byzantium and the Arabs*, ch. VII.

[90] xxiv 2. 4: 'Malechus Podosacis nomine, phylarchus Saracenorum Assanitarum, famosi nominis latro, omni saevitia per nostros limites diu grassatus.' See also Shahîd, *Byzantium and the Arabs*, 119–23.

[91] J. O. Maenchen-Helfen, *The World of the Huns* (1973), 51–9, with extensive references. The main sources are Claudian, *In Ruf.* ii 26–35; Jerome, *Ep.* 60. 16; Socrates, *HE* vi 1; Philostorgius xi 8.

[92] As well as several other cities. Jerome, loc. cit.: 'ecce tibi anno praeterito ex ultimis Caucasi rupibus inmixti in nos non Arabiae, sed septentrionis lupi, tantas brevi provincias percucurrerunt . . . obsessa Antiochia et urbes reliquae, quas Halys, Cydnus, Orontes, Eufratesque praeterfluunt. Tracti greges captivorum, Arabia, Phoenix, Palaestina, Aegyptus timore captivae.'

ships. The Persian part of Mesopotamia was overrun as well. The Huns reached Ctesiphon but did not take it. Remarkable distances were covered by the Huns in a single campaign. They carried off many young people, presumably as slaves, though according to Theodoret some people joined their ranks voluntarily—an interesting piece of information.[93]

In a letter, written about 400, Jerome tells of sudden incursions of Isaurians. They ravaged Phoenicia and Galilee, and threatened Palestine. The walls of Jerusalem were strengthened.[94] The Isaurians raided large areas of the Near East in these years; in Asia Minor, and particularly in Cappadocia and Armenia, their presence lasted almost two years. These events formed the culmination of separatist tendencies in Isauria which, in the course of the fourth century, marked a gradual change from endemic banditry to full-scale guerrilla war.[95] Hence the governor of Isauria had, from the second half of the fourth century onwards, special military powers, with a strong garrison,[96] in the words of Ammianus, 'based in many neighbouring towns and forts'.[97] Elsewhere Ammianus speaks of 'the soldiers who guard Isauria from every side' even in his own time.[98] A law of 382 almost certainly shows the existence of a *dux et praeses Isauriae*.[99] Thus Isauria was treated as a military region. The term *limes* is not attested, which is not surprising since it indicates a 'frontier district'. That, Isauria was not,

---

[93] Theodoret, *Commentary on Ezekiel* 38: 10–12 (*PG* lxxxi 1204) and cf. the comments of Maenchen-Helfen, 57 f. On defection to the 'barbarians' and indifference to the disintegration of the Roman empire in the Byzantine period see G. E. M. de Ste. Croix, *The Class Struggle in the Ancient Greek World* (1981), 474–88.

[94] *Ep.* 114. 1: 'Isaurorum repentina eruptio: Phoenicis Galilaeaeque vastitas: terror Palaestinae, praecipue urbs Hierosolymae: et nequaquam librorum sed murorum extructio.' Cf. J. Rougé, *REA* 68 (1966), 282–315, esp. 298 f., and in general E. Demougeot, *De l'unité à la division de l'empire romain* (1951).

[95] For a full discussion see Rougé; for Isaurian raids in the middle of the fourth century, Ammianus xiv 2, xix 13. See also the *Expositio Totius Mundi* 45: 'Isauria, quae viros fortes habere dicitur, et latrocinia aliquando facere conati sunt, magis vero et adversarii Romanorum esse voluerunt, sed non potuerunt invictum nomen vincere.' The text was published perhaps in 359.

[96] *Not. Dig. Or.* xxix 6: he was a *comes rei militaris* and, according to some MSS, also *praeses*, cf. Rougé, 304 ff. He is placed above ordinary governors and *duces*. See also H. Hellenkemper, *SMR* iii 625–34.

[97] xiv 2. 5: '. . . milites per municipia plurima, quae isdem conterminant, dispositos et castella . . .'

[98] xiv 2. 13: 'militibus omne latus Isauriae defendentibus.' Rolfe, in the Loeb edn., translates: 'the troops that defend the whole frontier of Isauria'. This is quoted with approval by Rougé, 307, but it is better to avoid the term 'frontier' when it is not obviously applicable.

[99] *Cod. Theod.* ix 27. 3 = *Cod. Just.* ix 27. 1. The text mentions a *dux et praeses Sardiniae*, but no such *dux* could be mentioned in a law issued by Theodosius, cf. Rougé, 296 f. A *dux Isauriae* is listed in the *Not. Dig. Or.* xxix 18 under the same heading as the relevant *comes*, which may represent a conflation of two different stages of organization. Note also the inscription from Diocaesarea which mentions a governor and *dux*: *MAMA* iii (1931), p. 71, no. 73.

and the use of the term in the modern literature is only confusing.[100] Isauria was a region in the middle of the empire over which the Romans had lost control and an army was needed to keep the problem localized. In the reign of Anastasius the Isaurians again caused trouble. They 'appointed a tyrant for themselves' and raided the neighbouring provinces before being defeated.[101]

For the moment it will suffice to note that these disturbances were caused by a people which had inhabited a Roman province for four centuries and had nothing to do with Arabia or Bedouins. The latter, naturally, is true of the Huns as well, who caused far greater havoc in the west than in the East. Jerome describes some other major incursions in about 410,[102] but these again did not originate outside the empire: it has been shown that they were migrations of Berbers from Cyrene, caused by the activities of Honorius and Stilicho in North Africa.[103]

The period of crisis at the end of the fourth and the beginning of the fifth century is a large subject which cannot be discussed here.[104] Any troubles in these years must be seen against the background of the crisis which hit the empire as a whole. It is, however, important to note that the eastern 'frontier provinces' suffered from full-scale nomad attacks which did not have their origin in the south-east. They came rather from totally unexpected quarters and, in the case of the Berbers, were caused by Roman devastations which forced the tribes to leave their own homeland.

Several sources mention troubles under Anastasius I, apparently in 499.[105] Palestine suffered a raid in 502.[106] After 528 the Lakhmid chief

---

[100] SHA, *Tyr. trig.* 26, uses the term but, as shown in *JRS* 78 (1988), 127 ff., the passage is usually misunderstood. If anything may be learnt from it, it shows that Isauria was *not* a frontier district. Isauria, it says, was defended by nature, not by men.

[101] Zachariah of Mitylene, *Chronicle* vii 2.

[102] *Ep.* 126. 2, written in 412 (*PL* xxii 1086; *CSEL* lvi 144; ed. Labourt, vol. vii, 134–6): '. . . sic Aegypti limitem, Palaestinae, Phoenices, Syriae percurrit ad instar torrentis cuncta secum trahens, ut vix manus eorum misericordia Christi potuerimus evadere.'

[103] D. Roques, 'Synésios de Cyrène et les migrations Berbères vers l'Orient (398–413)', *CRAI* (1983), 660–77. I owe this reference to D. F. Graf, who discusses the affair in a forthcoming paper, to appear in the proceedings of the *Colloque International sur L'Arabie préislamique et son environnement historique et culturel*, Strasbourg, June 1987. The key sources are John Cassian, *Collationes* i (SC 42), 117 f.; Jerome, *Ep.* 126. 2. Jerome, in fact, describes their movements: 'the frontier districts of Egypt, Palestine, Phoenicia, Syria . . .' In other words, they moved from Egypt to Palestine and thence farther northwards.

[104] But see Demougeot and Maenchen-Helfen, opp. citt.

[105] Theophanes, A.M. 5990, ed. de Boor, 141; Evagrius, *Historia Ecclesiastica* iii 35; *Vita Abramii*, ap. Schwartz, *Kyrillos von Skythopolis* (1939), 244; John of Nikiu, *Chronicle*, ch. 89 (trans. R. H. Charles, 1916), 338. For the date, E. Stein, *Histoire du Bas-Empire* ii (1949), 91 n. 4.

[106] Theophanes, A.M. 5994, de Boor 143; Nonnosus, *FHG* iv 179; *V. Euthym*, ap. Schwartz, 67 f.; cf. Stein, 92 and n. 1; I. Kawar, *Der Islam* 33 (1958), 145–8; Sartre, *Trois études*, 159 f.

Al-Mundhir, an ally of the Persians made two of his most destructive inroads.[107] These, however, seem not to have reached southern Syria, Arabia, and Palestine.[108]

To conclude this section, it can safely be maintained that we have no evidence whatever of a serious threat to the security of Palestine and Arabia before the end of the fourth century. Even then the reports of occasional disturbances do not add up to a picture of recurrent or even frequent threats to the security of the province from outside the territory controlled by the Roman army.

Banditry in Judaea

There clearly existed regions where resistance to the Roman authorities was endemic for considerable periods, even if this was not resistance of an ideological, national, or religious character. This is not always sufficiently appreciated. In such areas the army had to provide internal security, in the first place to protect itself and uphold Roman authority. The payment of taxes and the safety of Roman troops clearly had priority. The security of private citizens was of secondary importance, as is indicated by Dio in the passage quoted at the beginning of this chapter.

In Judaea and Arabia there is much evidence of internal problems. For some periods the sources regarding Judaea-Palestine are relatively good compared with those for other provinces. Banditry was a problem in periods other than those well-known through Josephus' work during which various forms of it were endemic. There are two points to be considered. First, it is undoubtedly true that Jewish resistance to Roman rule was *sui generis* in its motives and fierceness. It cannot be said that signs of unrest in Judaea may be taken as indicative of the state of affairs in other provinces. Second, it is equally true that we have more information on Judaea than on many other provinces of the Roman empire because the literary sources are so much better. This remains true also after the period which Josephus describes, for Talmudic sources provide a wealth of information even though they are difficult to interpret, and much can be learnt from the early Christian authors. When we can discover forms of social and economic unrest in Judaea that are not immediately related to specifically Jewish forms of resistance to Roman rule, it may be suggested as a hypothesis that such

---

[107] Procopius, *Bell.* i 17. 29 ff.; Malalas, 423 f. Cf. I. Kawar, *JAOS* 77 (1957), 79–87.

[108] Reports of disturbances early in the sixth century are probably unconnected with the activities of al-Mundhir.

problems may have existed elsewhere as well. We cannot know that this
was so, because for most areas we simply do not have the kind of sources
which would record such phenomena.

Before AD 66

We have seen that the Roman army was faced with the problem of
banditry in Lebanon and southern Syria. According to our sources
banditry was endemic in mountainous and inaccessible areas where the
population could not or would not maintain itself at subsistence level
by means of agriculture. Judaea, and particularly Galilee, were
relatively rich countries, but there, as will be seen in this section,
banditry of a different kind undermined security. It is not the aim of this
book to offer a social history of Judaea under Roman rule. It is,
however, necessary to discuss the problems facing the Roman authorities in this province since an explanation is required as to why banditry
was far more intractable in Judaea than in the neighbouring provinces.

Thanks mainly to Josephus, we have a good deal of information on
unrest in Judaea from Herod's death till the outbreak of the First
Jewish Revolt. But our information derives almost exclusively from this
source, and Josephus is extremely hostile toward the resistance;
moreover, for the early part of the century, he relies on a hostile source.
It is questionable whether the information available allows of a social
analysis of the various groups of rebels, their motives and aspirations.
Much has been written on the subject, and the present study will do no
more than briefly indicate certain patterns.[109]

As noted above (p. 62 f.), it was Herod's task as client king to suppress banditry. His first act as governor of Galilee in 47–46 BC was an
attack on a bandit leader Ezekias, who harassed Tyrian villages. Many
of Ezekias' followers were killed, the Syrians were satisfied, and so was
the governor of Syria, Sextus Julius Caesar,[110] though Herod was called
to account before the sanhedrin in Jerusalem because he had killed
Jews. We have no further information on Ezekias and his followers, but
it is significant that his son Judas was one of the first zealots and many
of his descendants were active in the resistance to Rome before and

---

[109] Schürer i 382 f.; ii 598–606; S. Applebaum, *JRS* 61 (1971), 159; M. Hengel, *Die Zeloten*
(1961); R. Horsley, *Journal for the Study of Judaism* 10 (1979), 37–63; id., *Catholic Biblical Quarterly* 43
(1981), 409–32; D. M. Rhoads, *Israel in Revolution: 6–74 C.E.* (1976); Tessa Rajak, *Josephus* (1983);
and an important study by M. Goodman, *The Ruling Class of Judaea: The Origins of the Jewish Revolt
against Rome A.D. 66–70* (1987). Note the article on banditry in the Roman empire by B. D. Shaw,
Past and Present 105 (1984), 3–52, and the very well-known book on banditry in recent periods, E. J.
Hobsbawm, *Bandits* (²1985).

[110] Josephus, *Ant.* xiv 9. 2 (159); *BJ* i 10. 5 (204).

during the First Revolt, all of them called *leistai* by Josephus. The last was Eleazar ben Yair, commander of the defendants of Masada. The manner in which Josephus describes these men and their followers leaves no doubt that the primary motive for their resistance to Rome was religious commitment.[111]

In 38 BC Herod led a campaign against what Josephus calls bandits in caves near Arbela in Galilee. There is no information on the nature of their activities.[112] However, an old man who killed his family and jumped down the cliff himself, 'submitting to death rather than slavery', was apparently motivated in his struggle by ideology rather than economic misery. Martyrdom and suicide while resisting the foreign tyrant go back at least to 2 Maccabees; in that work much space is taken up by stories of those willing to suffer torture and death rather than eat pork.[113] Judas' army consisted of 'men willing to die for the laws and their country'.[114] Not only martyrdom, but at least one case of suicide is described in bloody detail as an edifying example,[115] the declared motive being 'death is preferable to indignity'. Furthermore, we have here an early reference to the belief in resurrection after death, held later by the Pharisees.

The militants are described by Josephus sometimes with admiration, more often with animosity. They have 'an invincible passion for liberty and take God for their only leader and lord'.[116] Their willingness to die for their way of life was an integral part of their ideology, connected with a belief in recompense in the world to come.[117] Josephus does not hide the fact that he was expected by his comrades to commit suicide rather than surrender at Jotapata.[118] The speech of Eleazar ben Yair, commander of the defendants of Masada, is Josephus' own classic statement of their determination 'neither to serve the Romans nor any other save God'.[119]

[111] For Judas, the son of Ezekias, who was active between 4 BC and AD 9, see *Ant.* xvii 10. 5 (271–2); xviii 1. 1 (4–11); *BJ* ii 4. 1 (56); 8. 1 (117–18); cf. Hengel, 336–40, 343 f. James and Simon, the sons of Judas, were crucified in the governorship of Tiberius Alexander, AD 46?–8: *Ant.* xx 5. 2 (102); cf. *Acts* 5: 37 and the comments in Schürer, i 381 f. A relative, Menahem, was one of the leaders early in the First Revolt: *BJ* ii 17. 9 (447). Cf. Schürer, i 382 n., 441, ii 600–2; Applebaum, *JRS*, 159; Hengel, 219–22. See now the extensive discussion and different approach in Goodman, ch. 4, 'Problems Facing the Ruling Class: Religious Ideology'.

[112] Josephus, *Ant.* xiv 15. 4 (415 f.); 15. 5 (420–30); *BJ* i 16. 2 (304–5); 16. 4 (309–13). For the location of the caves, Schürer, i 282 n. 6.

[113] 2 Macc. 68: 18–31; 7.

[114] 8: 21: . . . καὶ ἑτοίμους ὑπὲρ τῶν νόμων καὶ τῆς πατρίδος ἀποθνῄσκειν.

[115] 14: 37–46.   [116] *Ant.* xviii 1. 6 (23).

[117] *BJ* ii 33. 1 (650); cf. *Ant.* xvii 6. 1 (152); *BJ* i 16. 2 (311); cf. *Ant.* xiv 15. 5 (429 f.), etc.

[118] *BJ* iii 8. 4 (355 ff.).

[119] *BJ* vii 8. 6 (323 ff.). πάλαι διεγνωκότας ἡμᾶς, ἄνδρες ἀγαθοί, μήτε Ῥωμαίοις μήτ' ἄλλῳ τινὶ δουλεύειν ἢ θεῷ . . .

As noted, our information is scanty and coloured by the hostility of our sources. There is no basis here for distinguishing between social and revolutionary banditry, if such a distinction ought to be made, but it is clear that Judaea, from Herod's rise to power until the outbreak of the First Jewish Revolt, saw the emergence of groups refusing to accept the order Rome generally imposed on clients and new provinces. Whenever the sources speak of bandits or murderers the possibility exists that these are not merely economic or anti-social elements, but Jews motivated by ideology and religion. Gentile authors leave no doubt that the First Jewish Revolt was caused by the combination of Jewish religious passion and Roman maladministration.[120] This is not to deny that various elements of social and economic struggle can be recognized in Josephus' description.[121] On the contrary, Josephus' work is an extremely important source of information on the social and economic tension which could be engendered by the incorporation of a country into the empire. These, however, are the very elements which one would expect him to emphasize. One of the aims of his work is to bring out the necessity of his apostasy from the resistance movement, and he does this by describing the war as a gradual take-over of this movement by lowly rabble. His readers would approve of the Romans crushing a revolt by rancorous peasants rather than one motivated by a refusal to live under foreign occupation. One must therefore take very seriously those statements and expressions in his work which refer to religious passion or ideological conviction and also those which describe Roman maladministration.

The modern discussion of these matters has something in common with the arguments about the causes of the Islamic conquest. Here too modern sceptical scholars have tended to discount the importance of the religious factor behind the successful expansionist drive of a people which had been rather marginal before, and stress has been laid upon over-population and economic factors. More recently however, there has to some extent been a return to the view that the new religion of Islam was a decisive element in the movement which destroyed Sassanid Persia and took over many key provinces from the Byzantine empire.[122]

In this connection it is to be noted that there are instances of popular support for, or collaboration with, brigands. The Barabbas released

---

[120] Cf. Tacitus, *Hist.* v 12. 2: 'ex diversitate morum crebra bella.'

[121] P. A. Brunt, 'Josephus on Social Conflicts in Roman Judaea', *Klio* 59 (1977), 149–53; M. Goodman, *The Ruling Class of Judaea.*

[122] F. Donner, *The Early Islamic Conquests* (1981).

upon popular request at the time of Jesus' trial was, according to Mark, 'among the rebels who had committed murder in the insurrection'.[123] John calls him a bandit.[124] Around the middle of the century there was serious trouble between Jews and Samaritans. 'The masses . . . took up arms and invited the assistance of Eleazar ben Dinai—he was a brigand who for many years had had his home in the mountains.'[125] Eleazar is also known from Talmudic sources. He is said to have inspired so many murders that the regular sacrifice of atonement for an unknown murderer was discontinued. He began to be called Ben Harazḥan, son of the murderer.[126] However, elsewhere in Talmudic literature he is described as 'one who prematurely tried to free the Jews'.[127] Here we have one and the same man seen from the perspective of a local, non-Roman source, as either a murderer or a premature freedom fighter. It shows that, even at the stage when these sources were composed, there were differences of opinion regarding those who practised armed resistance to Rome.

The Romans held the local population collectively responsible for guerrilla attacks in the countryside, and responded with savage retaliation.[128] When a Roman company was attacked near Emmaus the town was burned at the orders of Varus.[129] In 4 BC the arsenal of the royal palace at Sepphoris in Galilee was attacked and the arms stored there were seized; Varus burned the city and reduced the inhabitants to slavery.[130] On the road from Emmaus to Jerusalem a slave of the emperor was once attacked and robbed; the governor Cumanus then sent troops to the neighbouring villages to bring the inhabitants to him and reprimanded them because they had let the bandits escape.[131] From an incident reported by Josephus it is clear that the villages were searched in a manner that could easily lead to violence. This was in fact standard procedure established by law, as formulated by Ulpian at a later date on the duties of the proconsul: 'He must besides pursuing temple robbers, kidnappers and thieves, mete out to each of them the punishment he deserves and chastise people sheltering them; without them a robber cannot hide for very long.'[132]

---

[123] 15: 7; cf. Luke 23: 18 f.   [124] 18: 40; cf. Hengel, 344–8.
[125] *Ant.* xx 6. 1 (121 ff.); *BJ* ii 12. 4 (235 ff.).
[126] m. Sotah 9. 9; cf. Sifre on Deuteronomy ccv, ed. Finkelstein, 240.
[127] Midrash Rabbah on Song of Songs 2: 18. For Ben Dinai cf. Hengel, 356 ff.
[128] Destruction 'by fire and sword' was standard practice, see below, ch. IX.
[129] *Ant.* xvii 10. 9 (291); *BJ* ii 5. 1 (71).   [130] *BJ* ii 5. 1 (68); *Ant.* xvii 10. 9 (289).
[131] *Ant.* xx 5. 4 (113 ff.); *BJ* ii 12. 2 (228).
[132] *Digest* i 18. 13, praef.: 'nam et sacrilegos latrones plagiaros fures conquirere debet et prout quisque deliquerit, in eum animadvertere, receptoresque eorum coercere, sine quibus latro diutius latere non potest.'

As a commander of the Jewish insurgents in Galilee Josephus himself incorporated into his army 4,500 so-called brigands which he then proceeds to call mercenaries because he paid them: '. . . seeing it would be impossible to disarm them, [he] persuaded the people to pay them as mercenaries, remarking that it was better to give them a small sum voluntarily than to submit to raids upon their property'.[133] However, he notes that these were the troops in whom he placed most confidence.[134] It is clear also that these were ideologically motivated bandits. They might rob anyone, but they would never support the Romans.[135]

It is typical of their attitude toward the empire that Talmudic sources regularly describe representatives of the Roman government as bandits (*listim*). Many sources describe tax collectors and customs officials in such terms.[136] The Roman occupation is described as a direct cause of instability and banditry. In the words of R. Aha: 'Where the empire takes over government, with it appear bands and bands of *listim*.'[137] It is not quite clear whether the implication is that Roman rule causes impoverishment and hence banditry among the population, or whether Roman officials and tax collectors are bandits. Josephus recognized the connection between maladministration and the breakdown of security. In 39/40 Jewish leaders asked the governor of Syria to point out to Caligula 'that, since the land was unsown, there would be a harvest of banditry because the requirements of tribute could not be met'. In other words, banditry could be the result of poverty and oppressive taxation. Yet the occasion for this statement was a conflict about a purely religious affair which almost led to revolt. Elsewhere Josephus says that famine strengthened the zealots.[138]

In his description of the pre-history of the Jewish war Josephus brings out very lucidly the manner in which extremism on all sides reinforces the dynamics of conflict by acts of provocation. The seizure by the procurator Florus of funds from the temple, the subsequent behaviour of Roman troops in Jerusalem, that of the gentiles in Caesarea, and that of the zealots on the Jewish side all contain elements of provocation intended to elicit violent reactions which would lead to

---

[133] *Vita* 14 (77 f.); cf. *BJ* ii 20. 7 (581 f.) where Josephus refers to these men's habitual theft, banditry, and robbery.

[134] *BJ*. ii 20. 7 (583).

[135] *Vita* 22 (104–11) and 40 (200) for collaboration between bandits and various Jewish groups.

[136] tos. Bava Mezi'a viii 25; tos. Shevu'oth ii 14; Y. Bava Mezi'a vi 11a; b. Shevu'oth 39a; Sifra 8, ed. Weiss 101c; Sifre on Deuteronomy 1, ed. Finkelstein, 6.

[137] Leviticus Rabbah ix 8, ed. Margulies, 196, and parallels.

[138] *Ant.* xviii 1. 1 (8); cf. Hengel, 352.

war. These are the characteristics of a conflict between ideologies rather than groups which are socially disaffected. The Jewish war thus had different origins from those anti-Roman rebellions by disgruntled provincials which caught at least the Romans unaware: those in Illyria, Germany, Thrace, and Britain.

The remarks by Josephus cited above show again that social and economic factors could reinforce banditry and insecurity in Judaea as elsewhere, but this does not justify a denial of the obvious conclusion, that resistance to Roman rule was particularly fierce in Judaea, because of the single feature which distinguished the Jews from other peoples, namely their religious attitudes. Whether one sympathizes with these or not, their importance has to be recognized. Otherwise it cannot be understood why Judaea was the only small interior province where almost 10,000 troops were stationed after 70, and almost 20,000 in the second century.

AD 70–132

There is good evidence to show that banditry did not come to an end with the suppression of the First Jewish Revolt. A Talmudic source relating to the second century tells of the arrest of a member of a band of *listim* (bandits) in Cappadocia.[139] Before he was executed he made a last request: 'Go to the wife of Shimon ben Cahana and tell her that I killed him as he entered the town of Lydda'. Shimon ben Cahana was a pupil of R. Eliezer ben Hyrcanus (*c.*100–130), who taught at Lydda, and a teacher of Raban Simeon ben Gamaliel (*c.*140–170).[140] This establishes the chronology: Shimon ben Cahana belongs to the period between the First Revolt and the Revolt of Bar Kokhba. The sources are discussing when a confession of murder may serve as evidence to allow the widow of the victim to remarry. The murderer of Shimon ben Cahana, by his declaration, saw to it that his victim's wife was legally declared a widow and could remarry. This is peculiar behaviour for the murderer of a well-known scholar and can be explained satisfactorily only by the assumption that this was a case of political murder.

Another well-known scholar in the same period was R. Hanania ben Teradion, one of the wealthiest men in Galilee and treasurer of a fund for the poor. His son first joined a band of *listim* and then proceeded to

---

[139] tos. Yevamot iv 5; cf. the parallel passages: y. Yevamot ii 4b; b. Yevamoth 25b. The Yerushalmi says he was arrested in Caesarea in Cappadocia; the Bavli mentions Magiza, i.e. Mazaca. L. Robert, *Études anatoliennes* (1937), 90–110, in a discussion of banditry and police forces in Asia Minor, expresses the opinion that banditry there was less frequent in the first and second centuries AD than before or afterwards.

[140] Cf. tos. Parah xii 6.

betray them.[141] This was discovered, and he was killed by his former comrades. After three days they gave his body up for burial out of respect for the father. However, instead of praising him his father, mother, and sister vehemently cursed the son. The father R. Hanania was executed by the Romans after the Revolt of Bar Kokhba.[142] It is obvious that the son would not have joined a band of robbers for economic reasons, nor would one expect simple bandits to have particular respect for a wealthy scholar, as shown by the return of the body. The behaviour of the family can be explained only by the assumptions that the term *listim* here stands for 'guerrilla fighters' and that the scholar and the fighters supported a common cause.

A third source describes *listim* who met with pupils of R. Akiba making for the south on their way to Acco. They travelled together for a while, and when they separated the bandits expressed their admiration for R. Akiba and his pupils.[143] 'Happy are Rabbi Akiba and his disciples, for no evil person has ever done them harm.' This again is evidence of a relation of respect and even warmth between a distinguished scholar and 'bandits'. Again the scholar was one of the leaders of the revolt of Bar Kokhba, and the obvious explanation is that the 'bandits' fought the Romans rather than the Jews.

To the same period belongs the case of some Galileans about whom there was a rumour that they had killed a man. They fled to Lydda and there appealed to R. Tarphon to hide them. R. Tarphon, influential in the years before the Bar Kokhba revolt, did not help them, but he did not betray them either.[144] Two points are significant: first, the fact that the murderers thought an influential sage might be prepared to assist; second, the circumstance that R. Tarphon did not hand over the murderers to the authorities. It is likely that this murder also was a political execution.

In recent years remarkable material evidence of the methods used by the guerrilla fighters in Judaea has been found in the form of numerous subterranean hiding-places.[145] Most of these are in ancient settlements,

[141] Lamentations Rabbah iii 6; cf. ed. Buber, 128, and the parallel source Semahot xii 13, ed. Higger, 199 f. For R. Hanania as treasurer of a fund for the poor see e.g. b. Bava Batra 10b.
[142] For his execution as a leader in the revolt, b. 'Avodah Zarah 17b–18a.
[143] b. 'Avodah Zarah 25b. These sources were first interpreted as referring to guerrilla fighters by G. Alon, *The Jews in their Land in the Talmudic Age* ii (1984, trans. G. Levi), 570–2; cf. B. Isaac and I. Roll, *Latomus* 38 (1979), 64 n.
[144] b. Niddah 61a. Cf. Alon, loc. cit.
[145] B. Isaac and A. Oppenheimer, *JJS* 36 (1985), 42–4, with references; A. Kloner, *Biblical Archaeologist* 46 (1983), 210–21. The evidence has now been published fully in a book with copious illustrations, A. Kloner and Y. Tepper, *The Hiding Complexes in the Judean Shephelah* (1987, in Hebrew). Even if the historical conclusions reached by the authors will not convince everybody,

their entrances masked by cisterns or other innocent-looking cavities in the rock. They are rock-cut caves, linked by horizontal passages and vertical shafts connecting different levels. Many are well provided with ventilation-shafts, water tanks, store-rooms, and niches for lamps. Most have been found in the western and south-western foothills of Judaea, but a number have now been discovered in Lower Galilee. They are difficult to date, for virtually all have been emptied of numismatic material by robbers of antiquities. Although some can be dated with certainty to the period of Bar Kokhba there is no clear evidence that they all belong to this period as has been claimed by some explorers. It must be said, however, that they correspond in a remarkable manner to the description given by Cassius Dio of the hiding-places of Bar Kokhba and his men.[146] As has been seen above, natural caves frequently served as hiding-places for bandits and rebels in various areas of Lebanon, Syria, and Judaea; but the phenomenon now encountered in Judaea is different, because we are not faced with natural caves, but with elaborate rock-cut installations found in settlements. They were clearly made by a village population which used them in a form of guerrilla warfare.

After Bar Kokhba

Jewish sources give the impression that banditry was endemic in the second century and afterward. As always, Talmudic sources rarely provide us with straightforward pronouncements which allow of unambiguous conclusions. It is not uncommon for each source to be analysed in isolation and interpreted in a different manner, but this ignores the historical reality which the sources, taken together, indicate in outline.[147]

A source of the second century envisages the case of a *nazirite* (who is not allowed to shave) being shaved by *listim*.[148] That seems an absurd thing to do, and it is not clear why anyone would want to do it, but it certainly would not be the work of ordinary robbers. To the same period belongs the rule concerning payment of ransom for a wife taken captive. If she was imprisoned by the authorities, the husband was not

---

the material presented offers a fascinating insight into the nature of resistance to the authorities organized in scores of underground installations.

[146] lxix 12. 1 (3). Recently Mr Yuval Shaḥar and Mr Yigael Tepper have found a hoard of coins of the First Jewish Revolt in one of the caves which they discovered. I am grateful for their information.

[147] P. Schäfer, *Der Bar Kokhba Aufstand* (1981), follows J. Neusner in his method of analysis of the sources. He seems to suggest that the revolt broke out without any cause at all. He is followed by M. Mor, *DRBE*, 586 f.

[148] m. Nazir 6. 3; cf. Sifre on Numbers 25, ed. Horowitz, 31.

obliged to pay ransom; if she was taken by *listim* he was.[149] The reason for this distinction was that a wife in the hands of the authorities might have consented to having sexual relations with her captors; if she was the prisoner of *listim* there was no such risk. The assumption implicit here says much about the sort of people *listim* are taken to be.

It is generally assumed that Judaea essentially became a quiet province in the later second century. The evidence on *listim* in Talmudic sources, however, relates to the third century as well. In the third century R. Jose bei R. Bun predicted that *listim* would occupy the throne of Israel 'in the fourth generation'.[150] The source is ostensibly discussing the biblical period, but there is no reason to assume that R. Jose here refers to a tradition from biblical times. The statement reflects the realities of his own time, marked by anarchy and various forms of banditry.

Another source of the early third century reminds one of the episode concerning the murderers who appealed to R. Tarphon. Here a conspirator, sought by the authorities, at first actually was hidden by R. Joshua ben Levi (head of the study house in Lydda, 220–50), but when the town was threatened as a result the rabbi handed him over to the authorities. According to tradition this angered Heaven.[151] Another source of that period discusses wives of *listim* and *listim* who are condemned to death. The point at issue is whether sexual relations between them are still permitted.[152] It is significant that there is no indication here of any condemnation of the bandits as such; as in the discussion about the payment of ransom for captive women described above, the question which determines the ruling is how wives were likely to behave when they were in the hands of Roman soldiers and officials. The same source goes on to discuss similar problems as regards women taken either by the Roman authorities or by 'another power like *listim*'. The assumption apparently is that only in the first case were women likely to have been violated.[153] The point here is the difference in the standard of behaviour implicitly attributed to Romans and to *listim*. It is assumed, without any need for an explanation, that the bandits would not touch the women. It is therefore likely that these were not common robbers.

There are many more references to *listim* in Talmudic sources, too numerous to list fully. For example, they appear twelve times in the Mishnah, seventeen times in the Tosephta, twenty times in the

---

[149]   tos. Ketubot 4. 5; cf. b. Ketubot 51b.   [150]   y. Horayot iii 7c.

[151]   y. Terumot viii 46b; cf. Genesis Rabbah xciv 9, ed. Theodor-Albeck, 1184 f.

[152]   y. Ketubot ii 26d. The ruling is ascribed to R. Johanan, head of the sanhedrin in the middle of the third century.

[153]   The ruling is ascribed to R. Judah Nesi'ah, who was patriarch in the same period.

Jerusalem Talmud, and forty times in the Babylonian Talmud.[154] Often they cannot be dated accurately, and it is not always possible to determine whether the examples reflect historical reality or purely academic dispute. Even where this is not in doubt it is not always clear whether the *listim* in question were regular robbers or, when they were not, whether they were part of the imperial establishment or belonged to its enemies. Since the Roman authorities were not considered a legitimate government by the Jews, any representative of the occupying forces could be called a bandit by the Jews. The term might be applied to anyone who used force to achieve his aims, whether on behalf of the Romans or in the struggle against them. The sources discussed above as well as the great number of other references to bandits in Talmudic sources leave no doubt that guerrilla fighting, terrorism, and ordinary brigandage were endemic in Judaea throughout the second and third centuries. Obviously the period of major Jewish wars had come to an end with the suppression of the Bar Kokhba revolt, and there is no reason to deny that Palaestina, as a Roman province, was relatively calm. When there is evidence of endemic banditry after the period of major wars several questions may be asked. First, was Palestine at all times more restless than other provinces? Second, were other provinces less peaceful than we think? In favour of the second possibility it can be said that for most other provinces no evidence exists comparable to that found in the Talmudic sources, and it is possible that Greek and Latin literature and epigraphy, less concerned with daily life in the provinces, ignore a good deal of lawlessness which actually existed, apart from notorious areas such as Isauria. Palestine, at any rate, may never have become an entirely peaceful region, even though there were no major wars after the Bar Kokhba revolt. This is clear from various Talmudic sources that speak of banditry as a permanent feature of life in Palestine. Thus we read that R. Yannai (*flor.* 220–50) would leave a will with his family when going to an inn (i.e. on a journey).[155] Highwaymen who kill and rob are mentioned frequently.[156] Marauders entered the towns, as illustrated in the following passage, which refers to Caesarea in the mid third century:[157]

R. Abbahu went to Caesarea and stayed with a certain person, and he seated a

---

[154] Banditry in Palestine in the third and fourth century as reflected in Talmudic sources is discussed by D. Sperber, *JESHO* 14 (1971), 237–42.

[155] y. Berakhot ivd, cited by Sperber, 238.

[156] See the source cited in ch. VI, p. 282; also Genesis Rabba lxxx 2, ed. Theodor-Albeck, 953: '. . . like *listim* who sit along the road and kill people and take their money'; Midrash Psalms 26. 12; ed. Buber, 253; and cf. Sperber, 238.

[157] Pesikta de Rav Kahana, ed. Mandelbaum, 175–6; cf. y. Terumot viii 46a.

dog next to him. 'Do I deserve such a shame?' asked R. Abbahu (to be seated next to a dog). [His host] answered him: 'Sir, I owe a great deal to this dog. [For] once *shabaya* (literally: captors = marauders) entered the city and one of them came and wished to rape that man's (i.e. my) wife. He (the dog) jumped up and bit off his genitals . . .'[158]

There are a few passages in classical sources that give a similar impression of strife and turmoil. In an account by Ammianus of the emperor Marcus Aurelius travelling through Palestine on his way to Egypt the Jews are described in terms that seem to refer to civil unrest:

For Marcus, when he was passing through Palestine on his way to Egypt, being frequently disgusted with the malodorous and rebellious Jews, is reported to have cried with sorrow: 'O Marcomanni, O Quadi, O Sarmatians, at last I have found a people more unruly than you.'[159]

We should note that Ammianus cites this remark of Marcus Aurelius only because Julian happened to misquote Marcus. It is an example of a random piece of information which is nevertheless quite significant. The same can be said of the following item in the work of Cassius Dio.

In the reign of Severus, according to Dio, a remarkable event took place:

While Severus was very proud of his achievements (in the East), as if he had surpassed all people in insight and courage . . . a certain bandit named Claudius was overrunning Judaea and Syria and was therefore being chased with great ardour. And once he came to Severus with some cavalry, as if he were a tribune, and greeted him and embraced him, and he was not found out then nor caught afterwards.[160]

These were mounted bandits, and there is no reason to believe that they were Jews. More important, the affair resembles that also recounted by Dio regarding the Italian bandit Bulla.[161] Dio tells the story of Claudius with relish, as evidence that Severus was engaged in futile foreign wars

---

[158] Translation and notes by Sperber, 239 f. As observed by Sperber, in this and similar cases it cannot be determined whether the marauders are plain bandits or soldiers on a rampage. The same is true for another passage in the same work: Pesikta Shuva 18, ed. Mandelbaum, 377, cited and translated by Sperber, 240.

[159] xxii 5. 5: 'Ille enim cum Palaestinam transiret, Aegyptum petens, Iudaeorum fetentium et tumultuantium saepe taedio percitus, dolenter dicitur exclamasse: "O Marcomanni o Quadi o Sarmatae, tandem alios vobis in‹qui›etores inveni."' Cf. the commentary in Stern, ii 606. The translation cited is that of J. C. Rolfe, Loeb. The reading 'in‹qui›etores' is uncertain; alternatives are 'inertiores' or 'ineptiores'.

[160] lxxv 2. 4. The story should not be linked with a vague and untrustworthy note in the *Historia Augusta* regarding a Jewish triumph of Caracalla, SHA, *Septimius Severus* 16. 7, or with an equally obscure phrase in Jerome's chronicle on the year 197: 'Iudaicum et Samariticum bellum motum' (*Chronica*, ed. Helm, 211). Cf. the comments by Stern, ii 623 f., and see also B. D. Shaw, *Past and Present* 105 (1984), 43 (where it is unfortunately assumed that Septimius Severus was governor of Syria before his proclamation as emperor).

[161] lxxvi 10. Cf. Shaw, 46–9.

while he could not control banditry at home, right under his nose. Similarly, the story of Bulla is told because Severus was persecuting senators instead of guaranteeing peace and quiet in Italy. Dio's point is that misdirected imperial policy ignored elementary problems at home, and he conveys it by telling Robin Hood-type stories. In other words, we happen to know of these events because a senator disliked imperial policy at the time; we need not therefore conclude that there was no banditry at other times. In fact, the Severan period is usually considered a time of relatively good relations between the Jews in Judaea and the imperial authorities.[162]

Palaestina in the Byzantine Period

Major Disturbances

There may have been disturbances under Constantine, and there certainly was trouble in 351–2, although the scale is by no means clear.[163] In 418 the Jews are again said to have been rebellious. It may be noted that a number of anti-Jewish measures were enacted by law in 415.[164] The man who suppressed the troubles in 418 became consul next year.[165]

In 484 the Samaritans revolted.[166] The *dux Palaestinae*, assisted by a λῃστοδιώκτης, suppressed the revolt. The leader of the rebellion, Ioustasa, is called a 'chief bandit' in the sources. Neither term is remarkable, as it was—and is—common for governments to describe rebels as bandits. It is, however, remarkable that the Samaritans are said to have crowned the leader. If true this might indicate that there

---

[162] Alon, ii, ch. XII.

[163] Events in the reign of Constantine: John Chrysostom, *Adv. Judaeos* v 11 (*PG* xlviii 900); Cedrenus, ed. Bonn, i 499; Syriac chronicle of 848, *CSCO* (SS) iv ii; the last two of these depend on John Chrysostom. Cf. M. Avi-Yonah, *The Jews of Palestine* (1976), 173 f. Trouble in 351: Stern, 500 f., sources and bibliography. For a different, sceptical view of the events in 351, S. Lieberman, *JQR* 36 (1946), 337–41; J. Geiger, *SCI* 5 (1979–80), 250–7. For a critical view of the reports on a revolt under Constantine, Geiger, 257 n. 29. For a recent discussion see G. Stemberger, *Juden und Christen im Heiligen Land* (1987), ch. VI.

[164] *Cod. Theod.* 16.8.22 (20 October 415); cf. comments by A. Linder, *Roman Imperial Legislation on the Jews* (1983, in Hebrew), 194–7.

[165] For the revolt in 418, Marcellinus Comes, *Chronicon ad a. 418*, ed. Th. Mommsen, *Monumenta Germaniae Historica* (1894). The revolt was suppressed by the Goth Plinta. The chronicle has 'deletus est', but the text must be corrupt since the same source lists him as consul for 419 as pointed out by O. Seeck, *Geschichte des Untergangs der antiken Welt* vi (1920–21), 484, n. 1. In that year many Palestinian cities and settlements were destroyed by an earthquake. The chronicle may wish to suggest that there was a connection with the revolt in the previous year.

[166] *Chronicon Paschale*, ed. Dindorf, 603–4; Procopius, *De aed.* v 7. 5–9; Malalas xv 5. 53–4 (Dindorf 382). Cf. *RE* xiv 2395, s.v. Mauropappos (Ensslin); J. A. Montgomery, *The Samaritans* (1907), 111–13; M. Avi-Yonah, *Eretz Israel* 4 (1956), 127–32 (in Hebrew).

were messianic elements and motives at play. Procopius emphasizes
the religious background to the conflict. In the reign of Zeno
Samaritans attacked Christians in Neapolis. Zeno retaliated by con-
verting the Samaritan holy mountain, Mt. Gerizim near Neapolis, into
a Christian place of worship and installing a garrison in Neapolis.
There was continued unrest in Neapolis in the reign of Anastasius
(491–518).[167]

In 529/30 a dangerous Samaritan insurrection broke out, a reaction
to Justinian's order to destroy all their synagogues.[168] It was suppressed by the army, assisted by an Arab chieftain with the title of phylarch.
There was massive slaughter of Samaritans, particularly in the area of
Neapolis. This led to a reorganization of the provincial government,
decreed in Justinian's *novella* 103 of AD 536. The rank of the governor
was raised to that of a proconsul and he had authority over First and
Second Palestine—Third Palestine is not mentioned, presumably
because there were no Samaritans there. The *novella* repeatedly stresses
the need to suppress turmoil, particularly in the cities. Religious strife is
singled out. The proconsul has command over a number of troops,
independently of the *dux* and may ask for more if they are needed.
Novella 102 of the same year concerns the province of Arabia, where a
moderator is appointed. While the main source of trouble there seems to
have been malpractice in the levying of taxes by the troops under the
dux, mention is also made of turmoil and sedition in Bostra.[169]

In 556 Samaritans and Jews are again said to have rebelled in
Caesarea.[170] Between 565 and 578 Christians complained about
Samaritan aggression in churches at the foot of Mt. Carmel.[171] Again
the religious background of these troubles is obvious. The information
is sketchy, and we cannot know the scale of the unrest.

Most important, the disturbances described in this section and the
next, although located in Palestine, have no longer any connection with
specifically Jewish resistance to the authorities. These were troubles

---

[167] *De aed.* v 7. 10–14.
[168] Malalas, 445–7; *Historia Miscella* xvi (*PL* xcv 981); Cyrillus of Scythopolis, *Vita S. Sabae*, 70,
ed. E. Schwartz, *Kyrillos von Skythopolis*, Texte und Untersuchungen 49/2 (1939), 172; Eutychius,
Ann. 160–7 (*PG* cxi 1071 f.); also Procopius, *Anecdota* xi 24–9; *De aed.* v 7. 17. Cf. Stein, ii 287 f.;
Montgomery, 114–17; Avi-Yonah, *Eretz Israel*; Sartre, *Trois études*, 168–70.
[169] As already noted (p. 66), rebellious Samaritans fled to Trachonitis and it is not impossible
that the *novella* refers to trouble caused by the arrival of these refugees in a wild region not far from
Bostra.
[170] Theophanes, A.M. 6048, ed. de Boor, 230; Malalas, 487; *Historia Miscella* xvi (*PL* xcv 991);
Michel le Syrien, ed. and trans. Chabot, ii 262.
[171] See Hardouin, *Acta Conc.* (Nicaea 787) iv 290; cf. Montgomery, 121 f.; Avi-Yonah, *Eretz
Israel*, 132.

which could, in principle, have taken place in any province of the empire.

Banditry

It is clear then, that there were major disturbances in Palestine in the Byzantine period. There is a good deal of evidence to suggest that between 300 and 600 there was constant tension with recurrent large-scale troubles between the various groups of the population, mostly on religious grounds; at least, that is the stated cause. It is impossible to verify whether other factors, besides religious issues, played a role. It is very likely, however, that while clashes between religious groups alone are mentioned in the sources, there was a good deal of enmity about which we know nothing, but which required occasional military intervention.

A notoriously dangerous road led from Jerusalem to Jericho. Luke 10: 30: 'A man was on his way from Jerusalem down to Jericho when he fell in with robbers, who stripped him, beat him, and went off leaving him half dead.' The location is traditionally identified with Qala'at ed Damm–Ma'ale Adumim. Jerome mentions highwaymen on the Jerusalem–Jericho road in his translation of Eusebius' *Onomasticon of Biblical Place-names*.[172] In the entry on 'Adommim', where Eusebius only mentions the presence of a garrison, Jerome adds comments in which he refers to the place-name (*adumim* is red in Hebrew). Jerome says the place is called red because of the blood shed by robbers, hence 'the fort with soldiers located there for the protection of travellers'.[173] It might be argued that Jerome merely alludes to Luke's robbers and that there was, in his time, no problem of banditry there, but the fort is real and can still be seen. The *Notitia* records a 'cohors prima salutaria, inter Aeliam et Hierichunta'.[174] It must be noted that immediately east of Jerusalem the road enters the arid zone. Jericho itself is an oasis.

Early in the fifth century monks were killed in a raid in the Judaean desert near Teqoa.[175] Under Anastasius (491–518) a settlement of sedentary Bedouin, Christianized by Euthymius, was attacked by

---

[172] E. Klostermann (ed.), *Eusebius, das Onomastikon der Biblischen Ortsnamen* (1904, repr. 1966), 25. 9 ff.

[173] *Ep.* 108. 12: 'et locum Adomim, quod interpretatur sanguinum, quia multus in eo sanguis crebris latronum fundebatur incursibus.'

[174] *Not. Dig. Or.* xxxiv 48.

[175] John Cassian, *Collatio* vi 1 (ed. Petschenig [1886], 153; *PG* xlix 645a; *CSEL* xiii 2. This passage and others cited in the following notes were first systematically discussed by A. A. Vasiliev, 'Notes on Some Episodes Concerning the Relations between the Arabs and the Byzantine Empire from the Fourth to the Sixth Century', *DOP* 9/10 (1956), 306–16.

nomads. It was then transferred to a place closer to Jerusalem, where it was attacked again. It seems that the sources tend to overdramatize such events. At any rate, the community still existed and had bishops in 536 and 556. The raids presumably were carried out by tribes of transhumant nomads.[176]

In 531 Saba asked Justinian to construct and maintain a fort with soldiers in this area to protect the lavras that he had founded against Saracen incursions.[177] Justinian instructed Summus, the *dux Palaestinae*, to transfer to Saba the necessary funds for the construction of a fort and to make available a unit of soldiers who were to be fed at public cost.[178] The funds were indeed transferred after Saba's death in 532. However, his successor Melitas gave the money to the Archbishop Peter, who distributed the money to various monasteries. 'And thus the construction of the fort was prevented.'[179] There are two points to be made. First, the monasteries themselves failed to construct the fort, which suggests that they did not feel seriously threatened. Second, these were again communities in the desert, and we cannot deduce from these stories that the densely populated parts of Palestine suffered similar depredations.

Later in the sixth century John Moschus tells various stories of monks who, by their piety, could immobilize Saracen robbers.[180] Their significance for the present discussion is in showing that it was normal for nomad bandits to be present in the region north-east of Jerusalem, where John Moschus lived from 568 till 579. These were not nomadic invaders crossing into the province from outside; they lived in the desert area between the Judaean Mountains and the River Jordan, and made it unsafe. The military installations east of the Jordan did not prevent their presence—for the simple reason that they were not meant to do so.[181] Nor is there any suggestion that the Roman army did much

---

[176] Cyril of Scythopolis, *Vita Euthymii*, 46, ed. Schwartz, 67 f. There is no evidence that the second attack was carried out by al-Mundhir in 529 as suggested by Raymond Génier, *Vie de Saint Euthyme le Grand* (1909), 116, and P. Henri Charles, *Le Christianisme des Arabes Nomades sur le limes* (1936), 46. For the bishops see Charles. See also Abel, 273; Sartre, *Trois études*, 149–53.

[177] *Vita S. Sabae* 72, ed. Schwartz, 175.

[178] Ibid., 73, ed. Schwartz, 178. The fact that the *dux* was involved is significant for the definition of his responsibilities.

[179] Ibid. 83, ed. Schwartz, 188.

[180] *Pratum spirituale*, *PG* lxxxvii 3. 2851–3112; see ch. 99. Ch. 133: Saracens from the region of Clysma who wanted to attack a monk in Sinai. Ch. 155: a Saracen chief in the time of Mauritius who made mischief in the region of the Arnon (Mujib) and its tributary the Aidonas (Heidan), i.e. east of the Dead Sea. Chapter 166: a robber turned monk who eventually was judged at Lydda.

[181] According to Parker, *Romans and Saracens* (1986), 135, the epigraphic and archaeological evidence 'confirms the picture drawn from the literary sources that the fortified frontier was at its height in [the fourth century]'. In the time of John Moschus most of the installations investigated by Parker had indeed been abandoned.

to interfere at a local level. Only Saba's personal intervention at court had some effect, and when Saba died it all came to nothing.

West of Jerusalem Christian, Samaritan, and Jewish bandits infested the area of Emmaus-Nicopolis, according to John Moschus.[182] The point of the story, as told by Moschus, is not the presence of bandits which was not remarkable in itself, but the collaboration of bandits of different persuasions. This is a rare reference to banditry in the densely populated parts of the country. The question is: why is there little information on brigands in the settled lands? Was it more frequent in the second half of the sixth century when Moschus wrote? This is possible. It is also possible that this impression is mainly the result of the nature of our sources. John Moschus wrote about topics of specific religious interest and in particular about monks in the desert. The only legitimate conclusion to be drawn is that there is at least one passage which attests banditry west of Jerusalem in the sixth century.

A week before the capture of Jerusalem in 614 'Ismaelites' attacked and destroyed the lavra of Saba in the desert, according to the description of one of the monks who escaped.[183]

A similar pattern can be recognized at the edge of the settled area near Gaza. According to Jerome the desert of Gaza was full of robbers in the early fourth century.[184] Again it is to be noted that according to all students this is the period when the Northern Negev was well-provided with forts and that these seem not to have prevented small-scale banditry by Bedouin in the desert beyond Gaza, a major city. However, no particular weight should be attached to the fact that the events described by Jerome occurred near Gaza. Jerome wrote about this region because Hilarion happened to have lived there. It is clear that there were bandits there in that particular period, but they may have been elsewhere as well.

Moving farther into the desert, there too we find evidence of small-scale banditry. The story of Nilus and his son Theodolus gives a vivid picture of incursions and banditry in Sinai and the Negev in the late fourth century and of agreements made by small communities with Bedouin sheikhs for protection.[185] Justinian, who was willing to help

---

[182] *Pratum spirituale*, ch. 95 (*PG* lxxxvii 3. 3032).

[183] Antiochus Monachus, *Ep. ad Eustathium*, *PG* lxxxix 1423; see further references in Vasiliev, 311 n. 21.

[184] *Vita Hilarionis* 3–4 (*PL* xxiii 31); note the story of Hilarion's confrontation with robbers near Gaza: ibid. 12 (*PL* xxiii 34).

[185] Nilus, *Narrationes*, iv (*PG* lxxix 589–693). The historicity of the source has been doubted, but, as argued by P. Mayerson, *Proc. Am. Philos. Soc.* 107 (1963), 160–72; *JARCE* 12 (1975), 51–74, it is likely that the setting is historically true.

Saba in the Judaean desert, undertook a similar project in Sinai. In the fourth century the pilgrim Egeria found a group of monks living unprotected near the traditional site of the burning bush.[186] In 373 Saracens are reported to have attacked hermits living there. Most of the evidence regarding Bedouin attacks in Sinai is found in sources of uncertain reliability. However, they may well give a realistic impression of the dangers of monastic life in the Sinai desert.[187]

In the reign of Justinian a new church and fortress were built to defend the monks against Bedouin raids.[188] Procopius curiously misinterprets the purpose of this project:

At the foot of the mountain this Emperor built a very strong fortress and provided it with a very substantial garrison to prevent the barbarian Saracens from using this land, which is, as I said, uninhabited, as a base from which they might secretly invade the lands of Palestine.[189]

Procopius did not know that the site of the monastery was determined by the tradition concerning the burning bush, nor does he mention the harassment of hermits there by nomads. The building was not a 'very strong fortress'.[190] He was unaware of the existence of various monastic centres in the region.[191] These, however, are not very serious errors. They are evidence of a lack of information, but Procopius here is right in his attribution of the work to Justinian.[192]

[186] *Itinerarium Egeriae* i 1 ff. Z. Rubin, 'Sinai in the Itinerarium Egeriae' (forthcoming) points out that the pilgrim received a military escort during her journey *into* Egypt, presumably for protection against local bandits and highwaymen rather than Saracens.

[187] *Ammonii Monachi Relatio*, published text available only in F. Combefis, *Illustrium Christi martyrum lecti triumphi* (Paris, 1660). I am grateful to Z. Rubin for a photograph of the text. The source goes on to describe an attack by Blemmyes, who had sailed from Ethiopia on a stolen ship, upon the monastery at Raithou, somewhere on the west coast of Sinai. Translation of a Syriac version: A. Lewis Smith, *The Forty Martyrs of the Sinai Desert*, Horae Semiticae ix (1912). In the collection of the monastery of St Catherine is a beautiful eighteenth-century icon depicting the forty martyrs, reproduced in G. Gerster, *Sinai, Land der Offenbarung* (1970), 132. For various assessments see R. Devreesse, 49 (1940), 216–20; P. Mayerson, *The Bible World: Essays in Honor of Cyrus H. Gordon* (1980), 133–48; Shahîd, *Byzantium and the Arabs*, 297–319; Z. Rubin, 'Sinai in the Itinerarium Egeriae' (forthcoming). For Nilus, *Narrationes*, see above, n. 185.

[188] Eutychius, *Annales*, PG cxi 1071 f.; Vasiliev, 308, n. 5 refers to the Arabic original which I have not seen: 'Eutychii Patriarchae Alexandrini Annales', *CSCO*, ser. 3, vi. 1, ed. L. Cheikho (Beirut–Paris, 1906) 202.9. 22–204. 1. 3. For a discussion of the relative merits of Procopius and Eutychius, P. Mayerson, *BASOR* 230 (1978), 33–8.

[189] *De aed.* v 8. 9: ἐς δὲ τοῦ ὄρους τὸν πρόποδα καὶ φρούριον ἐχυρώτατον ὁ βασιλεὺς οὗτος ᾠκοδομήσατο, φυλακτήριόν τε στρατιωτῶν ἀξιολογώτατον κατεστήσατο, ὡς μὴ ἐνθένδε Σαρακηνοὶ ἔχοιεν ἅτε τῆς χώρας ἐρήμου οὔσης, ᾗπέρ μοι εἴρηται, ἐσβάλλειν ὡς λαθραιότατα ἐς τὰ ἐπὶ Παλαιστίνης χωρία.

[190] For the sixth-century remains, G. H. Forsyth, *DOP* 22 (1968), 3–19, plates; G. H. Forsyth and K. Weitzmann, *The Monastery of Saint Catherine at Mount Sinai* (1973). The relative weakness of the site and the walls is emphasized. For the monastery, also Y. Tsafrir, *IEJ* 28 (1978), 218–29. See also the inscription published by I. Ševčenko, *DOP* 20 (1966), 258; re-discussed by P. Mayerson, *DOP* 30 (1976), 375–9.

[191] For an archaeological survey, I. Finkelstein, *DOP* 39 (1985), 39–75.

[192] The date is confirmed by an inscription, I. Ševčenko, *DOP*, 262, no. 5, with photograph.

There is significance, on the other hand, in the erroneous statement that it was built for border defence, while it obviously was merely a fortified monastery. It is nowhere stated that soldiers were based in the monastery. It lies at the end of a narrow ravine and would not be on the route of anyone intending to invade Palestine. This is the first instance known to me of a historian confusing installations meant for internal security with those defending the border. It illustrates that even in antiquity such misunderstandings could arise and that Procopius in particular must be read with caution on such matters.

In about 563 the monastery was attacked, but the abbot successfully beat off the attack.[193] It looks as if the building of the fortress was intended to give the monks the means to defend themselves; one cannot expect that the imperial authorities would have spent huge resources on the maintenance of strict security in a remote area of Sinai.

Later, in 570, a pilgrim—whose account is incorrectly ascribed to Antoninus Placentinus—travelled to the monastery of St Catherine. He describes the town of Pharan as walled. It was inadequately(?) defended by a militia of 800(?) horsemen.[194] The pilgrim mentions several hostels in the Negev, but Saracens are referred to only in Sinai. At the time of the pilgrimage the Arabs were celebrating a festival that precluded trading and raiding, so the pilgrims could safely travel through Sinai. When they returned from Mt. Sinai, the festival was over and they took a different route back.[195] No mention is made of any military protection for the travellers. The same is true for the traders mentioned in P. Colt 89 of the same period, who paid a sum of three *solidi* 'to the Arab escort who took us to the Holy Mountain'.[196] As noted there, the amount is considerable, more than half the price of a camel. Even so, the escort seems not to have protected the group adequately, as a camel was taken by Saracens, the *bani al-Udayyid*.[197]

The situation in the frontier zone in Mesopotamia in the sixth

---

[193] Evagrius v 6 (*PG* lxxxvi bis, 2804).

[194] Ps.-Antoninus Placentinus, 40 (*CCSL* clxxv 149 f.), and cf. the discussion by Rubin (forthcoming). For the militia of Pharan (represented as an effective force) see also the Ammonius narrative which tells how a force of 600 select archers from Pharan routed the Blemmyes after their attack on the monastery at Raithou. Jerome, in his translation of Eusebius' *Onomasticon*, ed. Klostermann, 173, gave the name 'Faran' to the entire region: 'Choreb mons dei in regione Madiam iuxta montem Sina super Arabiam in deserto, cui iungitur mons et desertum Saracenorum, quod vocatur Faran.' For a discussion of the position of Pharan, L. I. Conrad, '*Kai elabon ten heran*: Aspects of the early Muslim conquests in southern Palestine', a paper read at the Fourth Colloquium on From Jahiliyya to Islam, July 1987, Jerusalem (forthcoming). For the *Itinerarium* see also the discussion by Shahîd, *Byzantium and the Arabs*, 319–24.

[195] Ps.-Antoninus Placentinus, 39 (*CCSL* clxxv 149). Cf. Mayerson, *TAPA*, 185–8.

[196] C. Kraemer, *Excavations at Nessana: 3. The Non-Literary Papyri* (1958), 11. 22 f.

[197] Ibid. l. 35.

century is vividly described by J. B. Segal,[198] who refers to local, Syriac sources. The frontier was 'closed' in time of war. That, however, could mean no more than that the passage of large companies of men was made impossible. 'Between the villagers living on either side there was constant and friendly intercourse.' Moreover, with the help of Bedouin friends anyone could move in and out of Persia by taking the desert route. Only merchants were forced to travel along the main road, for away from the road on both sides of the border travellers were robbed and carried into slavery by the Bedouin, who 'had not come to fight, but in search of booty'. Segal refers to sources which describe collaboration between the Persian and Byzantine armies, between 485 and 491 and in 575/6, to suppress these activities, but to little effect.[199] Even the main road was not always safe. 'The desert is near the road. There Saracens without permanent homes wander everywhere.'[200] Malchus was kidnapped by nomads and employed as a shepherd. Another typical story is that of Eutherius, born in Armenia of free parents, kidnapped by hostile tribesmen, gelded, and sold to Roman traders.[201]

In the Babylonian Talmud there are interesting descriptions to be found of life with nomads in the vicinity on the other side of the border. 'In the town [of Nehardea on the Euphrates] which was close to the border, they [the nomads] did not come with any intention of taking lives but merely straw and stubble, but the people are permitted to go forth with their weapons and desecrate the Sabbath on their account.'[202] E. B. Banning argues that there may have existed a form of relatively peaceful coexistence between pastoral nomads and settled peasant farmers in the Roman and Byzantine periods.[203] He makes the point, among others, that after the harvest the pastoralist may feed his stock from the otherwise useless stubble.[204] This is quite possible. Indeed, in recent times the flocks of the Negev Bedouin used to pass through the harvested fields of their owners early in the summer and from these to continue westward to the stubble fields of the villages.[205]

Elsewhere we read 'the rabbis taught that a man should not raise a dog unless it is chained, but if he raises it in a border town, he ties it up by day and releases it by night.'[206] Nehardea was not a strongly fortified

---

[198] *PBA* 41 (1955), 127 f., 133.

[199] Cf. Chabot, *Synodicon Orientale* 526 f., 529; John of Ephesus, *Ecclesiastical History* ii 6. 12.

[200] Jerome, *Vita Malchi* 4 (*PL* xxiii 58). See also Palladius, *The Book of Paradise or Garden of the Holy Fathers* (trans. E. Wallis Budge, 1904) ii, ch. 15; Segal, 127 n. 6, also refers to the Chronicle of Arbela, now known to be spurious; cf. J.-M. Fiey, *L'Orient Syrien* 12 (1967), 265–302.

[201] Ammianus xvi 7. 5.   [202] b. 'Eruvin 45a. Nehardea: Oppenheimer, 276–93.

[203] *BASOR* 261 (1986), 25–50.   [204] Op. cit. 29, with references.

[205] E. Marx, in *The Nomadic Alternative*, ed. W. Weissleder (1978), 54.

[206] b. Bava Qamma 83a.

town: 'Rav 'Anan was asked: is it necessary to lock [the gate to an alley] or not? He replied: come and see the gates of Nehardea which are half buried in the ground . . .'[207] One gets the impression that the Bedouin were merely the perpetrators of petty crimes, since a dog and sword were sufficient to keep them away. They certainly did not threaten the economic stability or social security of the townsmen and villagers, and no ancient empire would trouble to keep its forces under arms to combat thieves of straw and stubble. For a modern parallel we may again have recourse to Musil: 'The Bedouins creep around the railway stations under cover of night, they fling themselves upon the soldiers, rob them of their arms and ammunition, and vanish before the victims recover from their surprise.'[208] There are sources which mention the (Persian) army coming to Nehardea, but this may have been in action against the Romans.[209] These matters are not, of course, immediately relevant for the Roman empire, but they are good illustrations of life at the edge of the desert.

A town even closer to the border was Pumbedita: 'Those Arabs who came to Pumbedita and seized lands of people, the owners came to Abbaye. They said to him: Will the master see our deed and write another deed besides it, so that if one is seized, we hold one in our hands.'[210] Yet relations were not wholly bad at all times: '. . . She'azraq the Arab donated a lamp to the synagogue of Rav Judah . . .'[211] And the army which appears in Pumbedita may, again, have been on its way to the frontier of the empire.[212]

Banditry in Syria

Libanius is our main source of information about robbers in the Syrian countryside.[213] After the riots of AD 387 in Antioch many of the fugitives are reported to have been killed by brigands.[214] Again, after the disastrous earthquake of 526, survivors fleeing the city were robbed by country people, who also entered the city and pillaged the ruins.[215]

---

[207] b. 'Eruvin 6b. See also Ta'anit 20b which speaks of 'that dilapidated wall in Nehardea'.

[208] A. Musil, *The Northern Hegaz* (1926), 9.

[209] b. 'Avodah Zarah 70b; 'Eruvin 34b; text, translation, and comments may be found in Oppenheimer, 277, 289.

[210] b. Bava Batra 168b. Pumbedita: Oppenheimer, 351–68.

[211] b. 'Arakhin 6b.

[212] For troops in Pumbedita see the sources cited in Oppenheimer, 357.

[213] J. H. W. G. Liebeschuetz, *Antioch: City and Imperial Administration in the Later Roman Empire* (1972), 121. The index to the major work of G. Downey, *A History of Antioch in Syria from Seleucus to the Arab Conquest* (1961), contains no reference to bandits or robbery or any related term.

[214] Libanius, *Or.* xix 57; xxiii 18; xxxiv 7.   [215] Malalas 419–21.

A band of outlaws regularly imposed taxes on herdsmen responsible for race horses.[216] A notorious affair is related by Ammianus as well as Libanius.[217] The inhabitants of an entire village which had turned to banditry dressed up as officials of the treasury, invaded a town, and attacked a prosperous house of one of the notable citizens 'as if he had been proscribed and condemned to death'. The village was annihilated by the army. The story reminds us somewhat of the bandit Claudius who masqueraded as a military tribune and saluted the emperor. Such stories naturally receive attention because the victims belonged to the upper class who were usually well-protected: the villagers who robbed a rich man were exterminated by the army. The information in Libanius is precious in that it refers occasionally to common and lower-class people suffering from banditry, a fact which would be of no interest to most ancient authors. Yet it is important to note at least the possibility that there existed forms of socially selective banditry. In the Dutch East Indies there were, right till the end of the colonial period, areas which were declared to be infested with banditry. Colonial civil servants could live and move around in such districts with perfect safety, for the victims were local people, particularly Chinese merchants. The authorities were incapable of suppressing banditry as such, but they could and would protect their own representatives. It is possible that similar patterns existed in the Roman empire; not that colonial civil servants are to be compared with the Roman upper class; the point is that banditry and countermeasures may be directed at limited and vulnerable segments of society. This is the counterpart to 'Robin Hoodism': bandits who do not rob the rich and give to the poor, but make socially weak groups their target. It is less attractive and more common. More important still, there is the general truth, insufficiently realized in modern western countries, that advanced and orderly societies may survive and even thrive while yet suffering from various endemic forms of insecurity.

The point is borne out by items of information such as that regarding the herdsmen who had to pay protection money.[218] Libanius frequently alludes to banditry as a persistent problem, taken for granted for instance in such phrases as 'those who have nothing do not fear

---

[216] *Or.* xxvii 4.

[217] Libanius, *Or.* xlviii 36; Ammianus, xxviii 2. 11–14. For their name 'Maratocupreni' see above, p. 63.

[218] Liebeschuetz, 121 f., considers it significant that Libanius was confident that his letters would reach their destination. Apart from the possibility, already mentioned, that bandits would hesitate to attack representatives of the higher classes it is conceivable that men of Libanius' class had means of protecting themselves on the highways with armed guards which others could not afford.

bandits'[219] or 'malefactors make travel by night precarious'.[220] Bandits are spread all over the countryside, men 'who enjoy doing evil and have lived in this way for a long time'.[221] Libanius speaks of 'bandits who block the roads with murders they commit' and of measures taken to ensure the safety of travellers.[222]

There is no reason to believe that banditry in Syria was a phenomenon of the fourth century in particular. We just happen to be informed of it in this period because of the existence of sources that contain relevant information.

CONCLUSIONS

This chapter has considered the internal problems that the Roman army faced in various areas, in two distinct stages of occupation. After the initial conquest of an area there was a period of consolidation of which not much is known from literary or other sources. It is mentioned mainly when things went wrong—from the Roman point of view, that is. It was clearly a harsh process that often led to various forms of resistance: open revolt and warfare, sometimes successful, more often effectively suppressed, or guerrilla warfare. The latter is best known from Judaea where it was ideologically motivated.

Once Roman rule was firmly entrenched internal security could be more of a problem than is often realized. It is commonly assumed that in the East pressure on the settled areas from nomads living in the arid zone was a major problem. But the sources lend no support to this assumption. There is, in fact, no evidence that nomads exerted great pressure before the Islamic conquest in the seventh century. Neither is it certainly true that nomadism and transhumance represented a major security problem to the Roman authorities within the settled area. In Judaea, however, there is evidence of ideologically motivated banditry throughout the first and second century. In the Byzantine period there were several revolts by Jews and Samaritans, a response apparently to discriminatory laws enacted by the Christian authorities. This was not resistance to Roman rule as such, but protest by religious communities within the empire against imperial policy.

[219] *Or.* ii 32: οὐδεὶς γὰρ φόβος ἀπὸ λῃστῶν τῷ γε οὐδὲν ἔχοντι.

[220] *Or.* l 26.

[221] *Or.* xxiii 18, cited above (n. 214) in connection with the riots in 387.

[222] *Or.* lxviii 35. This passage immediately precedes the reference to the bandits who masqueraded as treasury officials already cited, the latter being exceptional behaviour in contrast to the normal practice of robbery on the roads.

While it is clear that there was internal tension in Palestine, there is very little evidence to show that there were long-term problems caused by infiltration by nomads in the settled areas. What happened in the steppe and the desert where the Bedouin actually lived is another matter. There they occasionally attacked monastic centres in the desert or pilgrims travelling in remote areas. Given the nature of our sources it is only to be expected that such incidents would be dramatized; but clearly one cannot draw wide-ranging conclusions from the failure of a government in antiquity to protect hermits who chose to live in uninhabited areas.

It is, however, a fact that nomads are mentioned more often in the sources of the fourth century and afterward than in the previous period. At the same time the areas on the fringes of the desert were more intensely cultivated and inhabited. Nomads, villagers, and townspeople inhabited the same space to a greater extent than ever before, as argued below, and this certainly required active intervention. The present chapter has described the problems which the army faced in the provinces which it occupied. The next discusses the army in its role as a force of occupation and as an internal police force.

III

THE ARMY OF THE PRINCIPATE: AN ARMY OF OCCUPATION

THE last chapter was concerned with the internal situation in Judaea, Arabia, and Southern Syria. Various forms of unrest, banditry, and resistance were described in an effort to identify the problems of security which the Romans faced in this area. The information was derived from literary sources. Through the perspective thus gained we shall now attempt to describe the organization and aims of the Roman forces in the area. These can be traced only, if at all, if we reach a partial understanding of the local security situation and critically combine various sources, literature, epigraphy, and material remains, even though these do not allow of an easy synthesis. At all times the possibility of changes in the security situation and, hence, of the aims of the army in the area, must be allowed for. An effort is made to offer an analysis of all relevant information, leaving aside ambiguous or uncertain material; and at the same time there is some discussion of the methodology of combining historical and archaeological information. Chapter III deals with the army of the principate, Chapter IV with that of the later empire.

The assumption will be that, if we have evidence of both internal unrest and a widespread distribution of military inscriptions attesting long-term presence, then the troops in the area clearly served as an internal security force. If this is accepted it may further be considered whether a widespread military presence in the interior in other regions, even without firm literary evidence of local unrest, can be interpreted as an indication that these troops too served as an army of occupation or an internal police force. This would be of particular interest for areas and periods about which ancient literature has little to tell. It is not the aim of these chapters to suggest that the army everywhere served as an internal police force, but it will be emphasized that the importance of this function is often ignored.

Security of Communications

Every army of conquest must keep roads and other means of communication safe—for itself, in the first place, if it wants to maintain itself in conquered territory, and for the population as a whole, to ensure its own authority and the prosperity of the subject people. This is true for the Roman army, both in the West and in the East. Long ago Sir Ian Richmond noted the close association of important military bases in the western provinces with river ports:

With the exception of Léon, all legionary fortresses of the Trajanic age in Europe were situated upon great rivers, not only because those rivers formed natural frontiers, but, as the British examples show, because water-transport offered a readily accepted alternative to road traffic, especially in the carriage of heavy goods, and a more rapid conveyance for armies on campaign.[1]

In the east, for instance, Septimius Severus' army marched to Babylonia along the Euphrates accompanied by a fleet in 198.[2] In more recent years this association has been confirmed once again by the discovery, at the auxiliary fort of Zwammerdam, of a quay with well-preserved ships in the ancient river-bed,[3] and of a military harbour at Velzen on the North Sea.[4] The military importance of river communications is clearly demonstrated by three projects carried out by the troops in Germany. When in Germany Drusus 'sailed the northern Ocean' and constructed canals beyond the Rhine.[5] As governor of Lower Germany Corbulo suppressed piracy on the coast of Gaul in AD 47 by bringing ships down the Rhine.[6] After his retreat from Frisia he kept his troops busy digging a canal linking the Rhine with the Maas, 'so that the uncertain dangers of the Ocean could be avoided' (by the fleet). There is no reason to assume that this was intended to benefit the civilian population.[7] Finally, in 58, L. Vetus, legate of Upper Germany, ordered a canal to be dug linking the Moselle with the Saône,

[1] Sir Ian Richmond, *Trajan's Army on Trajan's Column* (²1982), 33: fortress depicted in close association with a river port; 38: towers along a river. Cf. C. M. Wells, *The German Policy of Augustus* (1972), 24 f.

[2] J. Hasebroek, *Untersuchungen zur Geschichte des Kaisers Septimius Severus* (1921), 111 f.

[3] M. D. de Weerd and J. K. Haalebos, *Spiegel Historiael* 8 (1973), 366–97; M. D. de Weerd, *Westerheem* 25 (1976), 129–37; J. K. Haalebos, *Zwammerdam–Nigrum Pullum* (1977), 41–6. Landing-stages at Vechten: J. E. Bogaers and C. B. Rüger, *Der Niedergermanische Limes* (1974), 62–5; at Vetera, 106–8; Wells, 108 with n. 3.

[4] J.-M. A. W. Morel, *SMR* iii (1986), 200–12.

[5] Suetonius, *Claud.* 2.

[6] Tacitus, *Ann.* xi 18. 2. The fleet was also used in the region by Tiberius (Velleius ii 106. 2–3) and Germanicus (*Ann.* i 45. 3; 60. 3; ii 6. 2).

[7] *Ann.* xi 20. 2. Archaeological remains: J. H. F. Bloemers, *Rijswijk (Z.H.), 'De Bult'*, i 91.

which would make it possible to convey troops from the Mediterranean to the North Sea all the way by boat.[8]

The province of Germania Inferior was one of the less urbanized regions of the empire. It is, however, a fact too little emphasized that most of the towns that developed lay precisely on the river which also linked the military bases in the province. This includes the two colonies in the province, Colonia Ulpia Traiana (Xanten) and Colonia Agrippinensium (Cologne) and the *municipium* Noviomagus (Nijmegen).[9] Forum Hadriani/Municipium Canninefatium (Voorburg) lay on Corbulo's canal linking the Rhine with the Maas.[10] Later three more urban centres developed: Traiectum (Utrecht), the site of a river crossing, Maastricht, the site of a crossing of the Maas,[11] and Tongeren. Only the last mentioned lay on a major crossroads and not on a river. The colonies were founded as such by the Romans, while the *municipium* of Noviomagus developed near a legionary base. That urbanization, in so far as it developed in the province, is found along waterways can only mean that these served as a social and economic link.

It is easy to confuse lines of communication provided with forts for the protection of military traffic with lines of forts intended to prevent enemy movements across them. For instance, it is now recognized that the so-called Odenwald *limes* (from Wörth to the middle Neckar) was in fact a military road.[12] The same will be true of its continuation southward, the 'Neckar *limes*'.

The army was stationed along major waterways and strategic roads as much for its own traffic as in order to control the movements of subject peoples. Roads and rivers are better interpreted as links than as barriers. Two other factors would have determined the distribution of Roman forces: (a) the availability of local supplies; (b) the distribution and the attitudes of the civilian population. There is at present insufficient information about agriculture in the Roman and Byzantine east to discuss the former. The latter, however, will be dealt with in this chapter.

---

[8] *Ann.* xiii 53. Cf. *Panegyrici Latini* vi (vii) 13, where the Rhine is described as full of armed ships which allow Roman troops to cross over against the enemy. See also SHA, *Firmus*, etc. 15. 1.

[9] The two colonies: C. B. Rüger, *Germania Inferior* (1968), 76–86; Noviomagus: ibid. 88–92; J. E. Bogaers, *BJb* 172 (1972), 310 ff.

[10] Forum Hadriani: Rüger, 92 f.; Bogaers, *BJb* 164 (1964), 45–52; *BJb* 172 (1972), 318–26.

[11] Excavations at Maastricht have indicated that there was a bridge and military base here from the time of Augustus; J. H. F. Bloemers, *BROB* 23 (1973), 238–42.

[12] H. Schönberger, *JRS* 59 (1969), 161. It continued southward along the river. Schönberger comments: 'The *limes* on the Neckar was not a frontier in the strict sense, but rather a strategic line, which incidentally took advantage of the river communications.' The road between these forts ran partly to the west and partly to the east of the river. Description of the installations along this line: D. Baatz, *Der römische Limes* (1974), 153–76.

JUDAEA

Archaeological and Epigraphic Evidence

The manner in which the Roman army secured its communications is
fairly well known in the province of Judaea, thanks to a combination of
abundant remains, relatively extensive exploration, and the availability of literary sources which supply relevant information. The last
chapter discussed at length the internal security problems that the
Roman army faced in this province during many centuries of occupation. In such circumstances security of communications and troop
movements in the province required particular attention. Cestius
Gallus almost lost a legion while marching through difficult terrain.
That happened in a time of war. But even in periods of relative quiet
smaller units faced the danger of guerrilla attack when moving from
one place to another.

During the troubles in Judaea before the Jewish revolt a company of
Roman troops was attacked on the highway from Emmaus while
conveying corn and arms to the forces occupying Jerusalem,[13] and the
centurion and forty men were killed. Thanks to a survey that has been
made of this road and of others in the area in the course of the past few
years we now know a little more about security measures along the
roads.[14] The evidence consists of archaeological remains and inscriptions, and conclusions based on this sort of evidence are interpretative
and inferential: we can never tell with certainty what an army unit was
doing from the simple fact that it was based on a certain spot. However,
if there is substantial evidence regarding the size of units and their
disposition, we can form hypotheses. For current purposes only long-
term presence is relevant, and Josephus' information on the arrangements made in the course of the Jewish War is not discussed here.
While many of the inscriptions cited are undated it is safe to assume
that monumental inscriptions recording the names and numbers of
units are likely to derive from permanent structures where the units will
have spent some time. What we know of the distribution of troops in the
vicinity of Jerusalem allows of the description of a pattern. Most of the
evidence derives from sites on the main roads leading from Jerusalem to
the North, South, West, and East.

Something must first be said about Jerusalem itself. Before the

---

[13] Josephus, *BJ* ii. 4. 3 (63).

[14] A full report will be published shortly by M. Fischer, B. Isaac, and I. Roll, as *Roman Roads in Judaea* ii. For the sites see below, Appendix I.

destruction of the Second Temple in AD 70 any occupying power in
Judaea had to base a strong garrison there because it was the one
important city of Judaea with a substantial population, the cult centre
of Judaism, and a focus of pilgrimage for Jews wherever they lived.[15]
The reason for this was historical only. It is not an important site
strategically; it does not command major strategic routes or substantial
resources. It is, in fact, hard to reach, lying as it does off the main routes
in the coastal plain and in mountains that are hard to cross. Roads lead
to Jerusalem because people want to go there, not because it is a natural
halting place or caravan city. Jerusalem owes its eminence to the fact
that King David made it his capital.[16] This was a political decision, the
town being conveniently situated between Judaea and Israel and
belonging to neither. The choice resembles that of Washington DC as
capital of the United States. Once David had established his capital
there, rather than at Hebron, Solomon chose it for his Temple, and this
determined the centrality of Jerusalem for the Jewish people and hence
for Moslems and Christians, from the tenth century BC till the twentieth
AD. For the Romans before Constantine Jerusalem had no importance
as such. The seat of the governor was established at Caesarea, the main
city on the coast, which had an excellent harbour.[17] Jerusalem had to
be guarded, however.[18] After the destruction of the Temple the city was
left in ruins, either as a matter of political convenience or out of lack of
interest. But even then the site had to be guarded and became a
legionary headquarters from necessity rather than choice.

Another general remark must be made. The strength of the permanent garrison in Judaea is not quite certain. Before 67 there were
certainly three thousand men (one *ala* and five quingenary cohorts?)
and, if we may trust Acts, at least two other units, a *cohors Italica* and a
cohors Augusta, were also based in the province at some stage.[19] The

---

[15] The fame of Jerusalem is clearly brought out in Greek and Latin sources of the period
discussed by M. Stern, *Jerusalem in the Second Temple Period, Abraham Schalit Memorial Volume*, ed. A.
Oppenheimer, U. Rappaport, M. Stern (1980), 257–70 (in Hebrew). For a comprehensive survey
of the history of the city, J. Simons, *Jerusalem in the Old Testament* (1952).

[16] For the history of Jerusalem as a capital, A. Alt, 'Jerusalems Aufstieg', in *Kleine Schriften zur
Geschichte des Volkes Israel* (1959) iii. 243.

[17] Tacitus, *Hist.* ii 78: 'Iudaeae caput'.

[18] For the garrison of Jerusalem before the First Jewish Revolt, see below, ch. VI.

[19] Acts 10: 1; 27: 1. Cf. M. P. Speidel, *Ancient Society* 13–14 (1982–3), 233–40, who suggests
identifying the Italian cohort with the II Italica c.R. mentioned on a gravestone from Carnuntum,
CIL iii 13483a (*ILS* 9169). For the Augustan cohort he refers to an inscription which shows that a
unit of that name served in the army of Agrippa II: M. Dunand, *Le musée de Soueida, Inscriptions et
monuments figurés* (1934), no. 168; see also *SEG* vii 1100; *OGIS* 412. For the army of Herod, I.
Shatzman, *Milet* (Everyman's University, Studies in Jewish History and Culture, in Hebrew) i
(1983), 75–98; for that of Herod and Agrippa II, M. H. Gracey, *DRBE*, 311–18, with reservations
regarding the identification of the Augustan cohort in the *Acts* with that of Agrippa II. Josephus,

evidence from diplomas may sometimes merely indicate a minimum strength. They normally record the number of units with men who were receiving their privileges after 25 years. It is therefore always possible that some units have been omitted from the list for a province, simply because there were no men who qualified at a particular time. After 70, we know of six units in Judaea, about 5,000 auxiliaries, listed on the diploma of 86.[20] Tacitus says that normally the number of auxiliaries equals that of legionaries but that need not be true for every province or for other periods.[21] However, as we saw in Chapter I, it appears to be approximately true for Cappadocia and Syria.

While there may be evidence of the transfer of auxiliary units on several occasions thereafter it is not known what effect these had on the total strength of the garrison.[22] It is clear that the legionary force was doubled under Hadrian at the latest, but how many auxiliary units were added on that occasion is not known.[23] The diploma of 139, issued four years after the end of the Bar Kokhba war, shows a considerable increase: three *alae* and twelve cohorts, two of them military, which would be a total strength, on paper, of 8,500 men against the approximately 10,000 of the two legions.[24] It is therefore quite possible that there are a few unrecorded units, three or four at most. On a document from Dura-Europos of AD 232 a *cohors XII Palaestinorum* is mentioned.[25] If Kennedy's suggestion, cited in Chapter I, is correct this may have been the twelfth cohort in the garrison of the province of Palaestina at the time of the formation of the unit.[26] However, we do not know when this occurred.[27] It is possible that the diploma of 186 shows that a reduction had taken place by that time.[28] This lists two *alae* and seven cohorts, two of them milliary,[29] i.e. one *ala* and five cohorts less, which makes a total of about 5,500 auxiliaries, some 3,000 less than in 139, some 500 more than in 86.

---

referring to AD 66, mentions *two* distinct prefects of cavalry battalions in Judaea: *BJ* ii 14. 5 (291); iii 2. 1 (12).

[20] *CIL* xvi 33. On the army in Judaea from 70 to 132, M. Mor, *DRBE*, 575–602.

[21] *Ann.* iv 5. 6.

[22] R. Mellor, *The J. Paul Getty Museum Journal* 6–7 (1978–9), 173–84, esp. 182 f. on *RMD* 3; H.-G. Pflaum, *Syria* 44 (1967), 339–62, esp. 356 on *RMD* 9.

[23] B. Isaac and I. Roll, *Latomus* 38 (1979), 54–66. W. Eck, *Bull. Am. Soc. Papyr.* 21 (1984), 55–67, has argued that the reinforcement of the army in Judaea and its transformation into a consular province took place under Trajan.

[24] *CIL* xvi 87.

[25] P. Dura no. 30, full references below, n. 243.

[26] If it was assigned to Palaestina after formation.

[27] Above, p. 37; Kennedy, *ZPE* 53 (1983), 214–16.

[28] *RMD* 69, improving on an inferior reading by B. Lifshitz, *Latomus* 35 (1976), 117 ff.

[29] Discussion by C. N. Reeves in his publication of *RMD* 60: *ZPE* 33 (1979), 117–23.

The evidence on army sites in Judaea is rather fragmentary and is therefore collected in Appendix I below. The best information derives from the Jerusalem–Joppe (Jaffa) roads. There is evidence of substantial units stationed at Giv'at Ram, Abu Ghosh, Emmaus (Nicopolis), and possibly at Kubab. Four smaller towers have been excavated along these roads. It is interesting to note that these towers date to the period before the Jewish war and to the Byzantine period. Precisely in the years when Judaea was occupied by a large army of one and, subsequently, two legions they were not used. It seems clear that modest towers and blockhouses were part of the system by which the roads were policed when Jerusalem was the Jewish capital and focus of pilgrimage, and that a similar system was set up again when Christian pilgrims travelled *en masse* to Jerusalem in the Byzantine period.

In the mountains of Judaea, south of Jerusalem, several ancient roads have been traced. Some of these were protected by a system of watch-towers, blockhouses, and small forts once thought to be Roman. However, excavation has proved them to be of Byzantine date.[30] In this area too, therefore, the system by which entire roads were kept under constant observation does not belong to the Roman period. In the period of massive military presence in the province larger units apparently were kept together and occupied a limited number of essential towns and sites, where there is still evidence of engineering activity concerning the water-supply and bathing facilities.

The Romans in Judaea, it seems, intended to avoid the mistakes attributed to Varus in Germany by Dio: 'He did not keep his legions together as was proper in a hostile country, but distributed many of the soldiers to helpless communities, which asked for them for the alleged purpose of guarding various points, arresting robbers or escorting provision trains.'

The Road-System

So far only military sites on roads have been discussed. Since security of movement was of major concern to the Roman army it is obvious that the road-system itself had to be developed. There is indeed much evidence of Roman road-building in Judaea. The physical remains of Roman roads and bridges can be seen in many parts of modern Israel, even after years of intensive urbanization and development of the

---

[30] So far only a brief report has been published: Y. Hirschfeld, *Qadmoniot* 12 (1979), 78–84 (in Hebrew). Three watchtowers along the ascent from the 'Aravah to Mampsis proved to date to the late third to early fourth century: R. Cohen, *Arch. Newsletter* 83 (1983), 65–7 (in Hebrew).

countryside. The number of milestones is, for a small area, very large.
It can in fact be said that the remains of the road-system reflect the size
of the army in the province better than those of other military works.
This is not the place for a full discussion of the system and its
development. Various publications have appeared that describe elements in outline or detail, and more is to follow in future.[31]

Four subjects are to be discussed, two of them in this chapter and two
in Chapter VI: (*a*) the chronological development of the system. (*b*) the
relationship between military sites in the province and the road-
system. (*c*) the significance of milestone-texts as instruments of
imperial administration and propaganda. (*d*) the imposition of
responsibility for the maintenance of the system on local authorities.

The chronological development of the system

Some preliminary remarks must be made. Any reconstruction of the
chronological development of the system depends on the dates of
milestones. There is no other source. We must ask, therefore, whether
the erection of dated milestones reflects the actual development of the
road-system. It is conceivable that the Roman authorities decided to
set up milestones long after they had seen to the development of the
road-system itself. Roads can exist without markers, after all.[32] In
Judaea and Arabia there are Roman roads without milestones. Even
when milestones actually state that they mark the construction of a
road it is still possible to argue that this is not true, except in those cases
where the construction followed immediately upon the annexation of
the region as a province, as happened in Arabia (see below). Even
there, however, the road in question existed as a caravan-route long
before the arrival of the Romans, even though the milestones claim that
a 'new road was opened up'. In Britain the first milestone inscriptions
date to Hadrian's reign; yet it is well known that roads were constructed earlier than that.[33] A difficulty in establishing the practical use of
milestones is that the word *milliaria* came to be used for 'miles' even
where there is no question of the existence of actual markers. Pliny, for
instance, uses it in measuring distances in southern Babylonia where of
course there were no Roman milestones.[34] Thus, in the well-known

---

[31] Isaac and Roll, *Roman Roads in Judaea*, i (1982), with references there; also *JRS* 66 (1976), 15–
19; Isaac, *PEQ* 110 (1978), 47–60; I. Roll and E. Ayalon, *PEQ* 118 (1986), 113–34; *Roman Roads in
Judaea*, ii, forthcoming.

[32] M. Dunand, *Mém. Ac. des Inscriptions et Belles-Lettres* 13 (1933), 552, goes so far as to state: 'On
sait que les voies stratégiques n'étaient pas, le plus souvent, jalonnées par des miliaires'.

[33] J. P. Sedgley, *The Roman Milestones of Britain* (1975), 2; and below, ch. VI.

[34] *NH* vi 30. 122. Eusebius, in his *Onomasticon*, and Jerome in the translation use the term where
there were no roads.

inscription regarding *angaria* in Phrygia it is hard to be sure that actual milestones are referred to rather than simply miles.[35]

Judaea and other eastern provinces, unlike Britain, had a road-system of sorts before the arrival of the Romans. Major armies had marched through the country ever since the Egyptians fought the Hittites. Alexander had followed the coast road; and Pompey clearly was able to use the existing road-system. In 4 BC Quinctilius Varus marched to Jerusalem through the countryside of Samaria with two legions and auxiliary troops; he too must have used existing roads.[36] So what in actual fact was the Roman contribution? There were three different forms of activity:

(*a*) The construction of entirely new roads. This was done in difficult terrain where major engineering was required such as only the Roman army could accomplish: clearing away stretches of forest-land or the construction of a foundation for a road in marshy areas. There are several such roads in Judaea.[37]

(*b*) Technical improvement of existing roads in accordance with Roman standards. This was the usual procedure in the hill country or mountainous areas where topography dictated the alignment of the roads.

(*c*) The development of organization, as opposed to the mere physical improvement of the pavement. This entailed the erection of milestones, the maintenance of road-stations and other facilities and, along part of the roads, the organization of the imperial post.[38]

Only the third form of activity is firmly dated by milestone inscriptions, where these are available. It is, however, a very significant stage and one that can often be shown to represent an intensification of Roman military involvement in the province. The Roman army had engineers who would construct or improve roads when necessary,[39] though extensive organization was, for obvious reasons, not undertaken in an active war-zone. Military road-building following a war is attested in Illyricum where a network of military roads was built after the war of AD 6–9 by legions controlling native labour.[40] Note in particular the

---

[35] For the inscription see below, p. 292.

[36] Josephus, *BJ* ii 5. 1 (66–76); *Ant.* xvii 10. 9 (286–92).

[37] e.g. the Roman road from Antipatris to Caesarea, explored by S. Dar and S. Applebaum, *PEQ* 105 (1973), 91–9; and that from Legio to Scythopolis.

[38] T. Pekáry, *Untersuchungen zu den römischen Reichsstrassen* (1968), with excursus on the *cursus publicus*, 173–5 containing bibliography which appeared after the publication of H.-G. Pflaum, '*Essai sur le cursus publicus sous le haut-empire romain*', *Mémoires présentés par divers savants à l'Académie des Inscriptions et Belles-Lettres* 14 (1940), 189–391.

[39] Josephus, *BJ* iii 7. 3 (141 f.); 6. 2 (118); see also v 2. 1 (47).

[40] J. J. Wilkes, *Dalmatia* (1969), Appendix iv, 452–5.

plaque which reads: 'item viam Gabinianam ab Salonis Andetrium aperuit et munit per leg. VII.'[41] Here we find a road reconstructed soon after AD 9 being named after a proconsul of 48–7 BC. It may be inferred that this year represented the first stage of Roman activity on this road. In the case of Judaea all this will be clear from a brief survey of the chronology of milestone texts and their geographical distribution. It may be added that the evidence from Judaea is relevant because it is extensive. Most of the milestones come in series, but there are a few cases of single milestones representing a specific year.

Under Claudius there were dangerous troubles between Jews and Samaritans, which were investigated on the spot by Ummidius Quadratus, governor of Syria, and led to the dismissal of the prefect of Judaea in about 52. Rebellion continued under Felix, the next prefect.[42] Veterans of four legions were settled in a new colony at Ptolemais-Acco, in Syria but bordering on Judaea.[43] Next, the coast road from Antioch to Ptolemais was constructed and marked with milestones 'from Antioch to the new Colony of Ptolemais'. These are dated AD 56. The connection between these events is clear, and so is the military nature of the project, even though this is not stated in ancient sources. Ten years later, in 66, Cestius Gallus marched to Judaea along this road, and in 67 Vespasian took the same route, using Ptolemais as his base of operations against Lower Galilee. This was the first Roman road marked by milestones in Syria. It was a project undertaken because of security problems in Judaea.

In AD 69 M. Ulpius Traianus, commander of the legion X Fretensis, is mentioned on a milestone of the Scythopolis–Legio road. As explained elsewhere, the construction of this road, part of a major strategic route, facilitated communication between the legionary win-ter-quarters at Caesarea and Scythopolis. The road probably con-tinued to Pella and Gerasa.[44] It was built in a period when the army had nothing else to do. So far this milestone has remained a unique specimen, one of the few not belonging to a series.

There are no milestones bearing Flavian or Trajanic dates in Judaea. This is remarkable, for there are Flavian milestones in Cappadocia and Syria, and in Arabia Trajan constructed his major road from the north

---

[41] *CIL* iii 3200 (cf. 10158) and cf. Wilkes, 452 f.

[42] Schürer, i (1973), 458–60, 462 ff.

[43] On the colony see below, p. 322. Mount Carmel, south of Ptolemais, marked the boundary between Syria and Palaestina; cf. Eusebius, *Onomasticon*, 118. 8–9.

[44] Milestones of 112 discovered between Pella and Gerasa mention restoration of the road; cf. P. Thomsen, *ZDPV* 40 (1917), nos. 215, 216, 218a, 220; S. Mittmann, *Beiträge zur Siedlungsgeschichte des nördlichen Ostjordanlandes* (1970), 157 f.

to the south of the new province. It has often been assumed that the First Jewish Revolt was followed by substantial work of this nature, but there is no evidence of this, and the conclusion seems to be that Flavian interests were focused on the more important province of Syria, while the reign of Trajan was marked by activity in the new province of Arabia.

In Judaea at least twelve roads were first marked by milestones under Hadrian, all dated to the years 120 and 129/30, well before the outbreak of the revolt of Bar Kokhba. The series of 129/30 is contemporary with the emperor's visit to Judaea.[45] This shows increased Roman activity in the province. It could be argued that the milestones do not necessarily represent more than a propaganda campaign in preparation for the imperial visit. But two factors suggest that more was involved. First, we know of extensive construction accompanying or following the emperor's journeys elsewhere (Hadrian's Wall, for instance). Second, there is evidence of other forms of special activity in Judaea itself. The garrison was doubled and, according to Cassius Dio, the decision was taken to found the Roman colony of Aelia Capitolina at Jerusalem.

The milestones of AD 162 are by far the most extensive series attested in Judaea. In Arabia, too, milestones were set up with identical texts. It is obvious that there was a connection with the Parthian campaign of Lucius Verus which started in the winter of 161/2.[46] This does not contradict what has been said above: no milestones were set up at times of war *inside* the province. Another such series found in several provinces reflects preparations for Severus Alexander's Persian campaign, in 231–3.

We may safely conclude that the chronology of milestone inscriptions in Judaea proves that the system was originally organized by the military authorities for their own use.

The relationship between civil settlements, military sites, and the road-system in the province

Milestones in Judaea are found almost exclusively in the heavily

---

[45] In a forthcoming paper Mrs Alla Stein has shown that a significant proportion of the Hadrianic milestones all over the empire coincide with the emperor's journeys.

[46] H. I. MacAdam, *Studies in the History of the Roman Province of Arabia: the Northern Sector* (1986), 91, thinks this conclusion is 'making much of coincidence'. But there clearly are significant patterns in the dates of Roman milestones—e.g. above, n. 45. With regard to those note, first, the extraordinary number of stones of this year in the region and, second, the fact that milestones of Marcus Aurelius are extremely rare elsewhere.

populated parts of the country which rebelled against Roman rule and had to be kept in check by the local garrison. The most striking example is the Scythopolis–Jericho road. The first seven miles of this road run through the fertile Valley of Beth Shean, and every mile-station is represented by several inscribed stones. After seven miles the road reaches the fort at Tel Shalem, and thereafter enters the arid Jordan Valley; here it can hardly be traced and there are no milestones. Yet it was a Roman road, marked on the Peutinger Table. In the Negev milestones are very rare; in fact, not a single inscribed stone has been found in this part of the country. This coincides with a total absence of military inscriptions of the second and third centuries. Again, no inscribed milestones have been found on the Jerusalem–Jericho road, which runs through the desert, although all the other roads to Jerusalem have produced some. The road through the desert from Gaza on the Mediterranean to Aela (Aqaba, Elath), attested by Strabo and Pliny, has not yielded any milestones.[47] These facts are all the more significant because it is in the settled lands that milestones are re-used or destroyed. Desert conditions are obviously more favourable for the preservation of the stones. Below it will be seen that the same phenomenon may be observed in other provinces.

We should note also the absence, so far, of recorded roads in Galilee north of the Ptolemais–Tiberias road. This was an area without cities.

The *capita viarum* form another source of information. In Judaea distances are counted from cities—territories are ignored. In a few cases, however, such as that of the legionary base at Capercotna-Legio, it is certain, and in others likely, that a military site served as a *caput viae*. Furthermore, as discussed below, cities often *were* military bases.

Finally, there are hardly any milestones in the settled area of Judaea of the Tetrarchs and their successors. This coincides with the demilitarization of the province in this period. In Syria and Arabia, on the other hand, where the army was not withdrawn but reorganized there are many inscriptions.[48]

In Judaea, following the First Jewish war, the units or substantial vexillations of legions apparently were kept together, as was proper in a hostile country. The army guarded towns and roads for its own use and kept the local population under control. Under Hadrian a strengthened garrison reorganized the road-system. It is possible that the army took over more of the regular police duties as active hostility diminished over

---

[47] Strabo xvi 2. 30 (759); Pliny, *NH* v 12. 65. For the roads leading from Gaza, C. Glucker, *The City of Gaza in the Roman and Byzantine Periods* (1987), 26–30.
[48] See below.

the years, as was certainly the case in other provinces.[49] This was in particular the function of the *stationarii*, who served as road police and suppressed banditry.[50] They served also as frontier guards,[51] and manned the tollhouses. Other duties included the exaction of taxes and the maintenance of the imperial post.[52] In Egypt the *stationarii* are well attested in the later second century.[53] In addition there were *skopelarioi*, civilians upon whom guard duty was imposed as a corvée. They were based at *skopeloi*, small forts along the roads discussed below.[54] There is no evidence that the Roman army in Judaea was engaged in frontier defence or the struggle with nomads.

The development of the Roman road-system and its lay-out have been described extensively because this is the best preserved element of the military organization in Judaea. The surviving evidence shows that security of communication was of primary concern to the military command. As noted, two other basic factors would have determined the distribution of military sites where there was no external enemy, as in Judaea: (*a*) the availability of supplies and (*b*) the distribution and attitudes of the civilian population. Little can be said about the former. As regards the latter, Appendix I clearly shows that military installations are often found in or near towns which also formed the nodal points of the road-system. The next section will show that there is good evidence of the Roman army policing the Jewish towns in Judaea.

A Comparison: Road-Security in the Ottoman Period

On the whole our information on the reality of the Roman occupation is not abundant. The problem is that the archaeological and epigraphical material on which we mostly depend for proof of the presence of certain types of army-units in certain places does not tell us anything about the nature of their activities. Talmudic sources offer some help, because

[49] R. MacMullen, *Soldier and Civilian*, 50–55. A Byzantine text describes the duties of *limitanei* in Cyrene (*SEG* ix 356, para. 11; 14). They were mostly police and guard duties: controlling movement through the frontier districts.

[50] L. Robert, *Études Anatoliennes* (1937), 98 f., 285; *Revue de Philologie* 16 (1943), 111 ff.; cf. G. Lopuszanski, *L'antiquité classique* 20 (1951), 5–46, esp. 28–44, for evidence which shows that these units were active at times of persecution of Christians.

[51] e.g. Ammianus xiv 3. 2, for which see below, p. 235, n. 92; xviii 5. 3.

[52] MacMullen, 57–60. For *burgi* manned by *burgarii* along the roads see below.

[53] R. Bagnall, *The Florida Ostraka: Documents from the Roman Army in Upper Egypt* (1976), esp. 25 ff.; *JARCE* 14 (1977), 67–86, esp. 70 f.

[54] Bagnall, *Ostraka*, 25. The recorded names of *skopelarioi* are all Egyptian. They were commanded by *dekanoi*. See N. Lewis, *Inventory of Compulsory Services*, Am. Stud. Papyrology 3 (1968), for various forms of compulsory guard duty in Egypt. For these watch towers see also below, Chapter IV.

they give us an impression of daily life in the period. Comparison with other periods may clarify matters, if used with great caution.

In the Ottoman period Palestine suffered numerous social and economic ills, internal strife, almost incessant rebellion, and acts of brigandage by Bedouin.[55] One of the major problems was the deterioration of road-security as a result of brigandage, since this affected both caravan trade between Egypt and Syria and Muslim pilgrimage to Jerusalem and Hebron.[56] In one attempt to improve the situation Bedouin chiefs were made heads of districts and given responsibility for the safety of the roads passing through their territory. But this did not work, as the chiefs themselves kept attacking travellers.[57] At important sites in uninhabited areas new villages were established so as to protect travellers against attacks.[58] Elsewhere road-stations were constructed, for instance at 'Uyun at Tujjar near Mount Tabor in 1581. This site, 'through which [many] merchants pass, is a meeting place of rebellious Bedouins and other trouble-makers and highway robbers. They descend on the roads of the Muslims who are making a pilgrimage to Jerusalem and Hebron and other Egyptian merchants . . . If a caravanserai (ḥan) with a tower[59] on each of its four sides [corners] is built . . . and ten men stationed in each [of those] tower[s], the said place will become inhabited and cultivated.'[60] A fortress which could hold 'ten fortress soldiers and thirty horsemen' was indeed built (and attacked several times during and after the construction).[61] A market was held there.[62] The fortress soldiers remained on the spot to stand guard; the horsemen could be dispatched to extend assistance elsewhere.[63] The weakness of this system lay in the fact that the

---

[55] U. Heyd, *Ottoman Documents on Palestine 1552–1615* (1960), 40–4. For the period of attempted reforms, from 1840 till 1861, M. Ma'oz, *Ottoman Reform in Syria and Palestine* (1968).

[56] Heyd, 87, document 41* of 1567, the complaint of a woman named Fatima: 'When I went with my son on a pilgrimage to Jerusalem, rebellious Bedouins suddenly attacked [us] on our return journey, plundered my luggage and took my son prisoner. They demanded a price [as ransom].'

[57] Heyd, 91 and document 52, n. 10.

[58] Heyd, 91. See e.g. document 55 on the site of el 'Arish (on the main coast road) where 'the Bedouins constantly attack pilgrims and merchant caravans'. People were to be settled at this place 'which has agricultural possibilities'. This is standard practice in such circumstances. Compare the efforts to settle *gentiles* in insecure border regions in Africa in the fourth century (*Cod. Theod.* vii 4. 30 [409]), or Prince Gorchakov's memorandum of 1864 (cited above, p. 19), 335: 'It was essential that the line of forts thus completed should be placed in a fertile country not only in order to ensure supplies, but to facilitate regular colonisation which alone can give an occupied country a future of stability and prosperity, or attract neighbouring tribes to civilised life.' For the function of Roman veteran colonies, described in similar terms, see below, ch. VII.

[59] The Turkish word is *burc*!   [60] Heyd, 110 ff., document 62*.

[61] Heyd, 113, n. 18.   [62] Heyd, 114 f., document 64.

[63] e.g. Heyd, document 58: horsemen went out to meet the caravan of Mecca pilgrims.

numerical strength in these stations fell below that originally envisaged. The fortress near Mount Tabor, for instance, in 1660 had a complement of 28 instead of 40 men.[64] Besides, unreliable elements were often enrolled.

Talmudic Sources

Talmudic sources give a lively impression of the manner in which Roman army units carried out internal police duties among the Jewish population. In this section I cite some examples.

A *midrash* on Deuteronomy 32: 14 characterizes those who represent Roman authority in the province as greedy oppressors:

'And he ate the produce of my field': these are four kingdoms; 'and he made him suck honey out of the rock and oil out of the flinty rock': these are the oppressors who have taken hold of the land of Israel and it is as hard to receive a farthing from them as from a rock, but tomorrow Israel inherits their property and they will enjoy it as oil and honey. 'Curds from the herd': these are their consulars and governors; 'fat of lambs': these are their tribunes; 'and rams': these are their centurions; 'herds of Bashan': these are *beneficiarii* who take away (food) from between the teeth (of those who eat); 'and goats': these are their senators; 'with the finest of the wheat': these are their *matronae*.[65]

'[When] a patrol of gentiles enter a city in times of peace open wine-jars are forbidden, closed ones are allowed. [When it happens] in times of war both are allowed because there is no time for libation.'[66] The significance of this second-century source is not so much in the distinction between patrols in times of war and peace, which seems to be made in order to establish a point of academic interest. What does reflect the reality of the times is the reference to patrols interfering in daily life as a matter of course.[67]

Another mishnah discusses the establishment of Shabbat limits (*Eruv*) from two opposite locations when gentile (soldiers?) are likely to come and one does not know from what direction. This would allow people to flee as far as possible without desecrating the Sabbath.[68]

---

[64] Heyd, Appendix iii. In the province of Aleppo forts were constructed with good results, see Ma'oz, ch. IX.

[65] Sifre Deuteronomy, cccxviii, ed. Finkelstein, 359 f.

[66] m. 'Avodah Zarah v 6.

[67] For comparison note a discussion in the Babylonian Talmud regarding wine casks which had been opened by troops passing through Nehardea in Babylonia. This would probably not have been the Roman army but it shows the reality of life with an army presence in town: b. 'Avodah Zarah 70b. Cf. Oppenheimer, *Babylonia Judaica*, source 5 and pp. 289 f.

[68] 'Eruvin iii 5. In the Dictionary of M. Jastrow the relevant explanation of *Eruv* is as follows: '*Erub, a symbolical act by which the legal fiction of community or continuity is established*, e.g. (a) with ref. to

Again, relating to the same period, a passage in the tosephta discusses the rule that on festivals no food may be prepared for gentiles and dogs. Shimeon Hatemani was asked why he had not appeared in the study-house on the eve of a holiday. He explained, 'A patrol of gentiles came into town and they (the townspeople) were afraid that they (the soldiers) might harm them and therefore we prepared them a calf and we fed them and gave them to drink and rubbed them with oil so that they would not harm the townspeople.'[69]

It is well-known that the relationship between the Roman authorities and the Jews in Judaea improved considerably during the half-century which followed the Bar Kokhba war. Yet various talmudic sources of the third century show that one should not overstate this. For instance R. Isaac is quoted as saying: 'There is no festival without a patrol coming to Sepphoris. And R. Hanina said: there is no festival without the 'Hegemon' (the governor) or the *comes* or the holder of the *zemora* (an official who cannot be identified with certainty) coming to Tiberias.'[70]

There is at least a hint that soldiers may have acted as secret service men: 'The government sent two soldiers [*sarditia'ot*] and told them: "Go and behave like Jews and see what their *torah* is like". They went to Rabban Gamaliel at Usha . . .'[71]

In the days of Rabbi Joshua ben Levi, a third-century sage, the following episode is reported to have taken place: ''Ulla the son of Qoshev (Qosher [= conspirator]) was wanted by the government. He fled and went to Rabbi Joshua ben Levi in Lydda. They came and surrounded the city. They told them: If you do not give him up we will destroy the city. Rabbi Joshua ben Levi went to him and persuaded him and delivered him to them. Elijah of blessed memory used to appear to him and [now] did not appear. He fasted a few days and he appeared to him. He said to him: Do I appear to traitors? And he said: Did I not follow the law of the Mishnah? And he said: But is this the Mishnah of the pious?'[72] Lydda was in this period a town with a considerable Jewish population, perhaps a majority. The moral of the case is that R. Joshua ben Levi acted against the spirit of Jewish law—

Sabbath limits: a person deposits, before the Sabbath (or the Holy Day), certain eatables to remain in their place over the next day, by which act he transfers his abode to that place, and his movements on the Sabbath are measured from it as the centre.

[69] tos. Betzah ii 6.   [70] b. Shabbat 145b.

[71] Sifre Deuteronomy 344, ed. Finkelstein, p. 401; cf. y. Bava Qamma iii 4b; b. Bava Qamma 38a. The two parallels do not mention Usha. Cf. G. Alon, *Jews in their Land*, ii 463 f.

[72] y. Terumot viii 46b; cf. Genesis Rabbah xciv, ed. Theodor-Albeck, pp. 1184 f. In y. Codex Vatican, 'Ulla bar Qosher is mentioned (instead of bar Qoshev in the standard edition). Thus we can trace the connection between the deeds of a man and his name or byname (see L. Ginzberg, *Seridei ha-Yerushalmi*, p. 366).

though not against the letter—in persuading a man sought by the Romans to give himself up. The episode illustrates the Roman preparedness to be utterly ruthless, even in the third century, and the degree to which fundamental loyalty bound the Jews together when a man was wanted by the Romans for a political offence.

The subject of discussion, in another source of the second century, is the status of a priest's wife who tells that she was embraced, though not quite raped, by a soldier.[73] This clearly was an individual case. But priests' wives were considered unclean collectively and as a matter of principle when soldiers entered a town in large numbers. The language of the source does not make it clear whether a siege is referred to, or a massive search for resistance fighters.[74] Roughly a century later the status of a woman who managed to escape under similar circumstances is discussed.[75]

While it is clear that legal discussions can often be rather academic in nature, these passages certainly reflect the reality of life under Roman rule in Judaea, a reality of intensive army interference which takes brutality as a matter of course. It is also significant that they date from both the second and the third centuries, when Judaea was no longer openly rebellious.

There may have been exceptions. In the tosephta we find a curious statement: 'To a gentile who comes to extinguish a fire (on Shabbat) one should not say "extinguish and do not extinguish."' And then we are told:

Once it happened that there was a fire in the yard of Joseph ben Simai from Shiḥin (a village in Galilee, near Sepphoris). And the men from the 'castra in Sepphoris' came to extinguish (the fire), but he would not let them and a cloud descended from heaven and extinguished. The sages said: that was unnecessary, even though he sent, after the Shabbat, a 'sela' to each of the men and fifty dinarii to the *hipparchos* who dispatched them.[76]

Even so one cannot really maintain that this shows us the better face of the Roman army, for a parallel source adds that the man, Joseph ben Simai, was the 'apotropos', or procurator, of a king, presumably Agrippa.[77] He may have been an excessively pious Jew, but he would nevertheless qualify for special treatment on the part of the Roman forces.

The Talmudic sources repeatedly refer to the activities of the army in towns. We know that army units were permanently stationed in many

---

[73] y. Nedarim 11. 42d.   [74] m. Ketubot ii 9.   [75] y. Ketubot ii 26d.

[76] tos. Shabbat xiii 9; y. Shabbat xvi 15d; y. Yoma viii 45b; b. Shabbat 125a.

[77] b. Shabbat 121a; cf. b. Sukkah 27a, where the same man is mentioned as having two wives, one in Tiberias and another in Sepphoris.

urban centres: Emmaus-Nicopolis, Hebron, Neapolis, Samaria, and possibly Eleutheropolis-Beth Govrin. Emmaus is an excellent example of the dual function which military installations can have in periods of relative calm and in wartime.[78] The town is situated at the spot where the main road from the coastal plain enters the hill country, and history shows its strategic importance. We have seen above (p. 104) how Jewish resistance fighters attacked a Roman company in the immediate neighbourhood; it was the scene of one of Judas Maccabaeus' victories;[79] and there was a Seleucid fort nearby, on a site which was moreover the scene of active fighting in the Bar Kokhba war.[80] As explained below, it became the base of the legion V Macedonica in the First Jewish Revolt, and inscriptions suggest that the legion stayed there for some time, being thereafter apparently replaced by an auxiliary cohort. There were certainly soldiers in Caesarea, this being the provincial capital and seat of the governor. There were always troops in Jerusalem, both before and after 70.[81] The presence of the Roman army, notably of legionary vexillations, *in* towns is characteristic of the urbanized eastern provinces and was not common in the West. It involved a complicated social relationship, of which more will be said in Chapter VI below.

ARABIA AND SOUTHERN SYRIA

Arabia

We have no way of establishing the size of the Roman army in the province of Arabia in the second century. There is no military diploma, and the information regarding the auxiliary forces derives from papyri and inscriptions.[82] So far we know of two *alae* and six cohorts, one of them *milliaria*. That would give a total of some 4,500 auxiliaries, fewer than the legionaries, but our list may be incomplete. In the second century the paper strength of the army in the province was therefore at least 10,000 men, which is still less than half the number of soldiers in Judaea under Hadrian and afterwards.

For Arabia there is no literary evidence to help us understand what

[78] Full treatment in H. Vincent and F.-M. Abel, *Emmaüs, sa basilique et son histoire* (1932). Report on recent excavations of a Roman bath house: M. Gichon, *IEJ* 29 (1979), 101–10.

[79] 1 Macc. 4: 1–25.

[80] M. Gichon, *Cathedra* 26 (1982), 30–42 (in Hebrew).

[81] For the evidence see below, ch. VI and Appendix I.

[82] M. P. Speidel, *ANRW* ii 8. 699 f.

the army was doing there, such as we have in the case of Judaea. Apart from occasional scraps in Roman literature, the only materials available are archaeological remains and inscriptions. That, as emphasized throughout this book, is a very dubious basis for conclusions about the functions which the troops fulfilled. It leaves us with an inevitably incomplete impression of the distribution and identity of units, and of what problems the army faced or whom the troops were supposed to control. But even so we can reach some tentative conclusions about Roman priorities in the area, notably for the second century. We shall find that modern students lay far more emphasis on control of the desert than the Roman authorities themselves appear to have done in this period. As I argued in Chapter II, there is no evidence that nomads were a serious problem for the Romans. Neither was the army in Arabia defending a frontier against external threat.

We do not know the reasons for the annexation of the Nabataean kingdom as the province of Arabia by Trajan in 106. It need not surprise us that there is no evidence of serious trouble in the area.[83] Strabo makes it clear that vassal kingdoms were considered already part of the empire,[84] and the formal reason for incorporation as a province might simply be disloyalty or the end of the line of the royal family. For instance, Commagene was annexed on a pretext of disloyalty; the real reason may have been the desire to establish a legionary base. Caracalla annexed Osrhoene after centuries as a loyal vassal upon what seems to be a feeble excuse.[85] Trajan had eastern ambitions. That could have been a motive. Judaea was annexed because Herod's successor was not satisfactory, but we know nothing concrete of the successor to Rabbel II. Rude behaviour or bad grammar may have been the reason for Trajan's decision. The Romans did not agonize about the annexation of a client kingdom. How much would we know about the annexation of Judaea if Josephus had been a proper zealot and committed suicide at Jotapata? Client kingdoms were part of the empire, and their kings did not rule by right but by special consent which could be withdrawn at any moment.[86]

What we do know is easily summed up. One legion was stationed at Bostra in the extreme north of the province, and a road was constructed

---

[83] G. W. Bowersock, *Roman Arabia* (1983), ch. vi. For a different view, J. E. Eadie, in *The Craft of the Ancient Historian: Essays in Honor of Chester G. Starr* (1985), 407–23.

[84] vi 4. 2 (288).

[85] Dio, lxxvii 12. 1, says Abgar, King of Edessa, ostensibly forced his subjects to assume a Roman way of life, but in fact indulged in tyrannic power. Caracalla then imprisoned him in a treacherous manner.

[86] P. A. Brunt in P. D. A. Garnsey and C. R. Whittaker (eds.), *Imperialism in the Ancient World* (1978), 168–70.

from Bostra to the Red Sea. Its construction is recorded on milestones
of 111 and 114:

[Trajan's titulature in the nominative] redacta in formam provinciae Arabia
viam novam a finibus Syriae usque ad mare Rubrum aperuit et stravit per C.
Claudium Severum leg. Aug. pr.pr.[87]

The text emphasizes the connection between the annexation and the
construction of the road. The milestones date the completion of the
project, not its beginning, but it may be assumed that construction
began immediately after the annexation in 106. A well-known papyrus
of March 107 refers to soldiers cutting building stones not far from
Petra.[88] This shows that the army was constructing something at the
time, and it was probably the road.[89] We may infer too that the
governor, who was also commander of the legion, was present in person
and that, at the time of writing, the headquarters of the legion were
about to be transferred to Bostra.[90]

The road from Bostra to the Red Sea was on an old caravan route, in
use by the Nabataeans and before.[91] To assume that it became part of a
line of defence under Trajan involves assuming also that as a Roman
road its function was radically different from its use before and after
Roman rule. It makes better sense to compare its function—without
pressing the parallel too far—with that of a similar project of the
Turkish government: the Hejaz railway. The Ottoman railway system
consisted of two main branches: (1) a west–east link which connected
Constantinople with Mosul and was planned to be carried further
towards Baghdad. (2) A north–south link branching off the former line
at Aleppo. The intention had been to extend it as far as Yemen, but it
never reached beyond Medina. Even so it linked Damascus, Der'a, and
Ma'an with northern Syria and with the Arabian provinces of the
Turkish empire. This project demonstrates the basic fact that any
power which wants to control the Near East from the Bosporus to the
Euphrates or the Persian Gulf must face the immense difficulty of
holding together a large area where communications are drawn out and
vulnerable. Since the Ottoman solution, like that of the Romans,
followed the dictates of topography it is not surprising that the two

---

[87] e.g. *CIL* iii 14176. 2–3. All milestones known by 1917 are listed in P. Thomsen's article,
ZDPV 40 (1917), 1 ff., map 1. For information on the construction of the road to be derived from
the milestones, Pekáry, 140–2.

[88] P. Mich. 465–6; text, translation and discussion also in Speidel, *ANRW*, 691 f.

[89] As observed by Pekáry, 141.

[90] The identity of the legion which first occupied Arabia is not certain. Speidel, *ANRW*, 691–4;
D. Kennedy, *HSCP* 84 (1980), 283–309.

[91] 'Aperuit' does not necessarily indicate that the road as such is new, cf. above, p. 109 f.

systems should resemble one another. The Roman system, however, contained an additional major artery: the coast road linking Egypt with northern Syria. In the later nineteenth century the Turks had less need of such a branch because they had lost Egypt, but there was an offshoot of the railway system in Palestine.

The only natural and logical way, then, of looking at the Trajanic road is to see it as a link between southern Syria and the northern part of the Arabian peninsula. To describe it as a line of defence is speculative and implausible. Those who wish to speculate could claim that it would be far more characteristic of Roman behaviour if the construction of the road was conceived as the first stage of renewed action in the general direction of southern Arabia.[92] However, it is equally possible that even Trajan realized that the Arabian peninsula was unsuitable terrain for Roman expansion.

Most of the Trajanic road can be traced. This has to some extent obscured the fact that very few milestones have been found south of Petra, only two of them bearing inscriptions.[93] This resembles the situation in the desert region west of the Jordan and, it seems, in Syria. We may note in passing that no milestones have been published from the roads in the eastern desert in Egypt, although these were constructed and organized in the first and second centuries.

At least one new road was constructed under Hadrian, in 120—from Gerasa via Adra'a to Bostra.[94] The existing road from Caesarea on the coast to Scythopolis and Gerasa (see above) was repaired, the section

[92] Trajan identified with Alexander and claimed that he had surpassed him (Dio lxviii 30; 30, 1). Alexander had cherished unfulfilled Arabian ambitions (Arrian, *An.* vii 19, 5 f.). I can think of only one occasion when the route was used by an army of conquest, namely Lawrence's unconventional move against 'Aqaba. Because he realized that it would be impossible to proceed northwards into Transjordan against an enemy holding the road itself, he made a detour from the Hejaz to Ma'an and thence followed the road southwards to 'Aqaba. Palestine has often been conquered from the south-west, from the north, and from the north-east, but never, to my knowledge, from the south-east.

[93] See the map in Thomsen's study, *ZDPV* 40, nos. 174 a–c and 175: two mile-stations. No. 175a has an inscription dated 111. For four more mile-stations, near Queira, on one of which an inscription of Trajan was found, see A. Alt, *ZDPV* 59 (1936), 92–111. To my knowledge not a single stone has so far been found south of Wadi Yutm. While conceding that what is said here is true in general Dr Kennedy notes that the following groups of milestones are to be found in the desert areas of Arabia: (1) several milestones south of Petra (Stein) and between that site and Petra (the Humema survey); (2) a series north of Azraq; (3) others on the section of the Trajanic road which runs from west of Umm el-Jimal to Thugrat al-Jubb.

[94] Report on the section Gerasa–Adraa (Der'a) by S. Mittmann, *ZDPV* 80 (1964), 113 ff. = *ADAJ* 11 (1966), 65 ff.; cf. B. Isaac and I. Roll, *Latomus* 38 (1979), 54–66, esp. 61 f. The section Adraa–Bostra has not so far produced any milestones but only a building inscription recording the construction of a bridge at at-Tayyibeh, dated 163/4. Cf. T. Bauzou in *Hauran i*, *Recherches archéologiques sur la Syrie du sud a l'époque hellenistique et romaine*, ed. J.-M. Dentzer (1985), 151 and map (fig. 1). There is no doubt that the section Adraa–Bostra was already part of the road in Hadrian's time, as the milestones count the distance from Bostra.

Gerasa–Scythopolis in 112 and that from Scythopolis westward in 129. It appears that, under Hadrian, a legion was based at Legio-Caparcotna, and these roads were intended to provide an organized link with the legion at Bostra.[95]

The Disposition of the Army

Although it is clear that a Trajanic road was constructed down to the Red Sea there is almost no evidence of a military presence there in this period, let alone of a system of 'defence in depth'.[96] The absence of evidence is so striking that an archaeologist has recently wondered whether Hadrian abandoned Arabia.[97] In fact, the dates of the installations along the road south of Petra have not been established with any certainty. There are no military inscriptions that unambiguously identify units as permanently based in the southern part of Arabia before Diocletian. The sites that may have been occupied were stations along the main road. These are approximately twenty kilometres apart, that is, almost a day's march, and such a distance is appropriate for road-stations rather than a system of defence. What kind of troops were based there, if any, before the fourth century is not known. There may have been just enough forces to secure the safety of the road down to Aela.[98] This is not to deny that, even in the second century, there may have been more troops in this sector than we now know. However, even if Udruh should prove to have been a substantial fort early in the second century that would not significantly alter the pattern.

The recent publication of the results of work carried out east of the Dead Sea strengthens this impression.[99] In his report on a survey of what he calls 'the *Limes* Zone' Frank L. Koucky concludes that in the Nabataean period 'there is no place apart from er-Rāma for the concentration of a large military force in the surveyed region. . . .'[100]

---

[95]   For other roads linking Bostra with Scythopolis, Isaac and Roll, *Latomus*, 62, n. 44; Bauzou, ·loc. cit.

[96]   See the results of the explorations by D. Graf, *BASOR* 229 (1978), 1–26; *ADAJ* 23 (1979), 121–7; *The Word of the Lord Shall Go Forth: Essays in Honor of David Noel Freedman in Celebration of his Sixtieth Birthday* (1983), ed. C. L. Meyers and M. O'Connor, 647–64; *Damaszener Mitteilungen* (forthcoming). S. Thomas Parker, *Romans and Saracens* (1986), esp. 6–8, describes the Trajanic road as part of a fortified frontier or *limes*.

[97]   J. Lander, *DRBE*, 447–53. For a critical review of the archaeological evidence, Eadie, *DRBE*, 245–8. A. Killick, who excavated at Udruh, has concluded that this was a Trajanic fortress: *Levant* 15 (1983), 110–31. We shall have to wait for further information. For the results of Parker's survey see *Romans and Saracens*, 87–113, 126; and S. T. Parker (ed.), *The Roman Frontier in Central Jordan: Interim Report on the Limes Arabicus Project, 1980–1985*, i–ii (1987).

[98]   For additional arguments in the case of al-Khaldi (Praetorio) see below, ch. IV.

[99]   See the publications by Parker, above, n. 97.

[100]   In Parker, *Roman Frontier*, 64–79, esp. 65 f.

More sites were occupied in the Nabataean period (first century BC to first century AD) than any other. In that period there was a relatively dense population, living in small towns, villages, and farmsteads.[101] A marked decline occurred in the second–third century, followed by an increase in settlement in the subsequent period. Farther east, that is, east of the Desert Highway, results were somewhat different.[102] Here the major periods were Chalcolithic/EB and Nabataean/Early Roman. There was no significant evidence from the Roman and Byzantine periods.

In other words, in this region there is no indication that the Roman annexation resulted in the establishment of any 'frontier-system' or elaborate military organization. The only clear evidence of provincial organization is still the construction of one major trunk road. The conclusion that the annexation was followed by a decline in settlement is interesting, as this is a pattern observed during the same period in various parts of Judaea. There one could think in terms of the aftermath of the First Jewish Revolt, but that is irrelevant east of the Dead Sea. Conclusions are premature, but it is possible that we have here an indication of the expulsion of population groups, as attested in the north and north-west.

As matters stand at present, then, it seems that there was very little Roman military presence in the desert parts of the Roman province of Arabia before Septimius Severus. The present state of our knowledge can be summed up briefly.

The location of the fortress of the legion at Bostra has now been identified in the north of the town near a perennial spring. On air photographs a large rectangular enclosure is clearly visible. This measures 463 × 363 metres (16.8 ha.), which is appropriate for a full-size legion. Stretches of wall, towers, a gate, and stamped legionary bricks have been observed.[103] Moreover, the numerous inscriptions of the legion III Cyrenaica there, as well as the coinage of the city, definitely confirm its presence.[104] None of the interior buildings have been identified. Yet it is a step forward that we now have some impression of the physical relationship between a legionary base and a

---

[101] Op. cit. 78.

[102] V. A. Clark, 'The Desert Survey', op. cit. 107–63.

[103] S. Mougdad identified the location: *Felix Ravenna* 111–12 (1976), 65–81; R. Brulet, *Berytus* 32 (1984), 175–9 and fig. 1 (stamped bricks); M. Sartre, *Bostra, des origines à l'Islam* (1985), pl. 1; the best aerial photograph may be found in A. Segal, *J. Soc. Architectural Historians* 40 (1981), 111, fig. 7. and see now D. Kennedy and D. N. Riley, *Rome's Desert Frontier in the East from the Air* (1990), 124 f.

[104] For the inscriptions, M. Sartre, *IGLS* xiii 1; for the coinage, A. Kindler, *The Coinage of Bostra* (1983); see also Sartre, *Bostra, des origines à l'Islam* (1985), pl. 1.

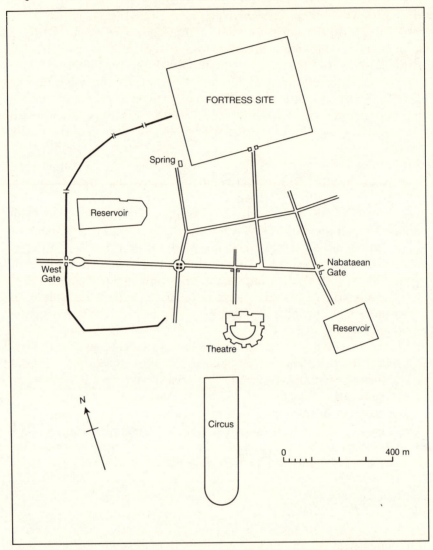

FIG. I. Bostra, with the site of the legionary fortress

town, given the absence of information on similar establishments
elsewhere in the East.

Otherwise we are entirely dependent on the evidence of inscriptions.
A series found at Gerasa gives the impression that there was a unit
based in or near the city from the first century onwards.[105] A Hadrianic

[105] Three inscriptions referring to the *ala I Augusta Thracum*: C. B. Welles, in C. Kraeling,
Gerasa: City of the Decapolis, 446 f., nos. 199–201; cf. Kennedy, *HSCP* 84 (1980), 288, n. 14.

inscription mentions VI Ferrata.[106] Several mention III Cyrenaica.[107] A vexillation of VI Ferrata occurs on a fragmentary inscription from Salt.[108]

New evidence from the Babatha archive shows that a cavalry commander (ἔπαρχος ἱππέων) was based at Rabbatmoba, the capital of Moab, in AD 127. Nothing is known of the unit under his command, but it is likely to have been an *ala*.[109]

An *eques* of III Cyrenaica was buried at Petra, probably early in the second century,[110] and one of the *cohors I Augusta Thracum* at Mampsis (Kurnub) in the Negev, probably in the beginning of the second century.[111] An undated epitaph of a soldier of III Cyrenaica has been found in Wadi Tuwweiba near Elath.[112]

The *Periplus Maris Erythraei*, 19, describes Leuke Kome (the White Village) as a 'port and garrison, from which there is a road to Petra, which is subject to Malichas, king of the Nabataeans. It serves as a market-town for the small vessels sent there from Arabia.' A duty of twenty-five per cent was charged by a customs officer, and the place was guarded by a centurion (*hekatontarches*) with troops, presumably Nabataeans.[113]

It is important to distinguish between firm evidence of long-term presence in the form of a building inscription or a series of inscriptions on the one hand and, on the other, single epitaphs which do not prove more than that a soldier died somewhere. South of Philadelphia (Amman) there is evidence of regular army-activity so far only between Mada'in Salih and al Ula, as noted below. This is not to suggest that

---

[106] Welles, 435, no. 171; cf. Kennedy, *HSCP*, 299.

[107] Welles, nos. 23, 211, 213; cf. 219.

[108] Kennedy, *HSCP*, 299 f., figs. 2 a–b. For the find-spot, *IGLJ* ii 3. Military tombstones from Salt: ibid., nos. 30, 34, and 38. See also two inscriptions from Madaba referring to centurions of III Cyrenaica: ibid., no. 117; P.-L. Gatier, *Liber Annuus* 37 (1987), 365–7.

[109] P. Yadin, 16.

[110] C.-M. Bennett and D. Kennedy, *Levant* 10 (1978), 163–5; cf. Kennedy, *HSCP*, 292 f. A triumphal arch with inscription in honour of Trajan, AD 114, was erected at Petra, see G. W. Bowersock, *JRS* 72 (1982), 198; *Roman Arabia*, 84 with n. 28.

[111] A. Negev, *IEJ* 17 (1967), 46–55; J. Mann, *IEJ* 19 (1969), 211–14; cf. Speidel, *ANRW*, 710. Negev states that he also found a tombstone of a centurion who served in III Cyr. and II Traiana Fortis (*ANRW* ii 8. 645, 658). I have seen no photograph or published text of this inscription.

[112] *AE* 1972. 671; 1936. 131; cf. E. D. Kollmann, *IEJ* 22 (1972), 145 f.; Speidel, *ANRW*, 694 f.

[113] Mommsen, *Römische Geschichte* (1856), 479 with n. 30, followed by S. J. De Laet, *Portorium* (1949), 306 ff., assumed that they were Roman; Bowersock, *Roman Arabia*, 70 f., argues that they were Nabataean. J. Teixidor, *Un port romain du désert* (1984), 43 f., has argued that the centurion was a Roman officer. The site of Leuke Kome is still uncertain. See L. Kirwan, *Studies in the History of Arabia*, ii, *Pre-Islamic Arabia* (King Saud University, Riyadh, 1984), 55–61, inaccessible to me; id., reviewing Huntingford, *GJ* 147 (1981) 80–5. For the physical evidence from Aynunah which Kirwan prefers, M. Ingraham et al., *Atlal* 5, 59–80.

there were no soldiers at all in the south, but it cannot be ignored that evidence, though copious in the north, is missing in the south.

This is all the more significant because there is convincing evidence of Roman activity in the desert from Septimius Severus onward. It comes, however, not from the southern part of the province, but from the north-east, east of the line Bostra–Philadelphia:[114]

(*a*) Two inscriptions recording the establishment of a new fort, built by a vexillation of III Cyrenaica at Qasr el 'Uweinid near Azraq.

(*b*) Milestones north of Azraq.

(*c*) At Azraq itself, the remains of a military installation, visible on an air photograph. It has the familiar playing-card shape and rounded corners of pre-fourth-century forts. Dr Kennedy notes that it may not have been a permanent fort.

(*d*) At Qasr el-Hallabat an inscription of about 212 records the construction of a *castellum novum* by soldiers of four auxiliary cohorts. This is a post on a road connecting the main Trajanic road with Azraq.[115]

An inscription set up by a centurion of III Cyrenaica shows that the Roman army reached Jawf near the southern end of the Wadi Sirhan.[116] Such a text gives no indication how frequently or for how long the army came to the place. But if permanently occupied army posts were established in this area the intention will have been to secure and control the important route through Wadi Sirhan.[117] At the same time we must recognize that the siting of permanent army installations in such areas is to a large extent dictated by logistics, the availability of sufficient water and the ability of units to feed themselves.

A famous bilingual inscription from Ruwwafa shows that, in the reign of Marcus Aurelius, the Thamudians formed a confederation that recognized the authority of the Roman emperor and the governor of

[114] As shown by D. L. Kennedy, *Roman Frontier Studies 1979* (1980), 879–87. See in general Bowersock, *Roman Arabia* ch. viii, esp. 118–20. For the region, Kennedy, *Archaeological Explorations* (1982), 75–96; 107–13; 124 f.; S. Gregory and D. L. Kennedy (eds.), *Aurel Stein's Limes Report* (1985), 250 ff. D. L. Kennedy and H. I. MacAdam, *ZPE* 65 (1986), 231–6, for an inscription found on the top of a peak 4.5 km. SW of Umm el Qottein which mentions a vexillation of III Cyr. (construction of a watchtower?); also, at Umm el Qottein itself, one that mentions the coh. I[II] Aug. Thr. Eq.

[115] Kennedy, *Archaeological Explorations*, 39, no. 3; for the fort and its environs see pp. 17–68. See also below, ch. IV, p. 169.

[116] Kennedy, *Archaeological Explorations*, 190, no. 39; Bowersock, *Roman Arabia*, 98 with n. 26 and pl. 14.

[117] Bowersock, *Roman Arabia*, 118 f., and cf. N. Glueck, *BASOR* 96 (1944), 7–17. For the site of Jawf, A. Musil, *Arabia Deserta*, 531 f.; and see above, Introduction, p. 13. Musil describes Jawf as a centre of trade caravans where three large commercial routes converged. It was an important oasis on the route from Kufa in Mesopotamia to Damascus, and the Bedouin held an annual fair there.

Arabia.[118] An inscription on a statue base of the same year in honour of the two emperors was found on a site 120 kilometres north-east of Palmyra. The editor has pointed out that both inscriptions coincide with the Parthian expedition of Lucius Verus.[119] Farther southward there is (undated) evidence of a Roman desert patrol. Roman units were engaged in protecting the security of caravans moving along the trade route in the Hejaz.[120] Graffiti show the presence of an *ala Gaetuloreum* at Hegra (Mada'in Salih), and farther south, along the road to Dedan (al-'Ula), record the names of soldiers of an *ala Dromedariorum*.[121] For those who are clearly Roman the onomastic material suggests a date of the late second or early third century. The establishment of the desert patrol would then coincide with expansion of the army into the desert elsewhere under Severus. It is impossible to say for how long these units operated in the region.

Trajan established a fleet in the Red Sea (*in Mari Rubro*). This may have been either the Persian Gulf or the sea still called by that name.[122] If it were the former the fleet would have ceased to exist under Hadrian.

The route east of the Trajanic road was only partly organized as a Roman road with milestones, but there are forts of the Byzantine period along it. There were, in the latter period, two parallel north–south roads, both provided with military stations. It is, again, questionable

---

[118] D. F. Graf and M. O'Connor, *Byzantine Studies* 4 (1977), 52–66; G. W. Bowersock in *Le monde grec: Hommages à Claire Préaux* (1975), 513–22; *Roman Arabia*, 96 f.; M. Sartre, *Trois études sur l'Arabie romaine et byzantine* (1982), 27–9; I. Shahîd, *Rome and the Arabs* (1984), ch. ix. D. F. Graf discusses the inscription further in a forthcoming paper, 'Qura 'Arabiyya and Provincia Arabia'. See also below, ch. V.

[119] G. W. Bowersock, *Chiron* 6 (1976), 349–55.

[120] H. Seyrig, *Syria* 22 (1941), 218–23 = *Antiquités Syriennes* iii (1946), 162–7, discussing inscriptions found between Mada'in Salih and al-'Ula. Cf. M. Sartre, *Trois études*, 30–33. Add to the evidence discussed by Seyrig the inscription of a painter of III Cyr. (AE 1974. 662); cf. Bowersock, *Roman Arabia*, 96, n. 19. D. F. Graf reinterprets the texts from the Hijaz and their significance (in his forthcoming paper, above, n. 118). On Mada'in Salih see also J. Bowsher, *DRBE*, 23–9.

[121] Graf (forthcoming) has re-read part of the inscriptions and come to the conclusion that some refer to Nabataean guardsmen before the annexation. He also reconsiders the inscriptions attributed to *beneficiarii*. There is not, at present, solid evidence of the presence of *beneficiarii* in the area.

[122] Eutropius viii 3. 2; Festus xx, cf. comm. Eadie, p. 139 f. The names 'Erythra thalassa' and 'Rubrum mare' are used indiscriminately for the Red Sea, the Indian Ocean, and the Persian Gulf, cf. S. E. Sidebotham, *Roman Economic Policy in the Erythra Thalassa* (1986), Appendix A, 182–6. In Mesopotamia Trajan levied customs, according to Fronto, *principia historiae* 15–17 (Haines, p. 214): 'quom praesens Traianus Euphrati et Tigridis portoria equorum et camelorum tribularet . . .' On the Red Sea he will have maintained the old customs station at Leuce Kome (above, p. 125). Leuke Kome was, in Strabo's time an *emporium* with a fort controlling the road to Petra (xvi 4. 23 [78]). In the Byzantine period there was a custom house on the island of Iotabe (also unidentified). See F.-M. Abel, *RB* 47 (1938), 512 ff.; *IGLS* xiii 9046 with comments. Whatever the reasons for Trajan's eastern expansion, he did not ignore the possibilities of financial gain.

whether anything is gained by describing this as a system of 'defence in depth'.[123] Recent publications tend to ignore the existence of an ancient route east of the Trajanic road. Some modern maps indicate only the eastern road from Udhruh in the south, where it branches off to the north-east, as far as Wadi Hasa northward. This is the stretch of road marked by milestones.[124] Although I have not seen the area I do not hesitate to state that the road continued northward for several reasons: (*a*) As noted several times in this study, some Roman or Byzantine roads are well attested even though they are not marked by milestones.[125] In the Byzantine period no milestones were set up, so no road constructed or organized after Constantine has milestones.

(*b*) The stretch of eastern road as marked on modern maps leads nowhere. It makes no sense if it does not continue.

(*c*) Brünnow and Domaszewski clearly mark the continuation of the road. Parts of it are described as certain, others as uncertain, but that does not affect the issue.[126] There must have been a road here, because there are forts. Brünnow and Domaszewski, who imagined they had discovered here the 'outer *limes*', an outer line of forts designed to prevent barbarian incursions, realized that such a system cannot exist without roads. But in truth the roads were not laid out for the benefit of the forts: they were, on the contrary, the *raison d'être* of the forts. In this connection it is worth remembering that this road runs parallel to, or is identical with, a very old caravan route, the Darb el-Haj. This, in turn, runs parallel to, and west of the Turkish railway line. The forts along it will have served to keep the route as well as the area secure. Any hypothesis on the significance of military works in an area must be based on an understanding of communications. Mapping and dating forts without considering the road-network is an unstructured procedure which cannot lead to an understanding of the system.

The 'Aravah and the Negev

The theory that there was a double line of defence in the Wadi Araba, the broad and arid valley which stretches from the southern tip of the Dead Sea to the Red Sea, a line supposedly marked by Diocletianic

---

[123] See J. C. Mann in his review of Luttwak, *JRS* 69 (1979), 175–83, esp. 180.

[124] Thomsen, *ZDPV* 40 (1917), nos. 177–84.

[125] See also Isaac, *HSCP* 88 (1984), 191, n. 103.

[126] R. Brünnow and A. v. Domaszewski, *Die Provincia Arabia* (1904–9). See Brünnow's map in vol. i (Tafel xl) and maps 2 and 3 in the same volume. There is a good description in F.-M. Abel, *Géographie de la Palestine*, ii (³1967), 229 and map x. See also Gregory and Kennedy, 349 f. and the folding map in part ii. The Roman road system in the Petra-Sadaqa area is insufficiently clear. These matters are now being clarified by David Graf in a survey of the roads in the area.

castella,[127] has been altogether disproved by archaeological explorations.[128] There is, however, information from unpublished excavations that proves the existence of a number of stations on roads crossing the 'Aravah from east to west.[129]

There is no consensus on the period when the Roman army first established a permanent organization in the Negev. S. Applebaum and M. Gichon argued in a series of articles that there was a Flavian system which, in fact, continued an earlier, similar one.[130] This view has been challenged by I. Shatzman who is not persuaded that there was a Roman military organization in the Negev before Diocletian.[131] The controversy can be solved only by full publication of excavated sites. For the present it must be noted that there are no literary sources or epigraphic material from the Negev attesting the presence of specific units before the fourth century.[132]

Two Roman roads crossed the northern Negev:

(1) The Petra–Gaza road. In the past it was claimed that the installations along this road were unoccupied after the first century, but excavation has shown that the towers and stations along the road continued to be occupied throughout the Roman imperial period.[133] Extensive excavations have been carried out at the important road station in the 'Aravah usually called Mo'ah (Moyet 'Awad), one of the '*limes*' stations tentatively identified by A. Alt.[134] The plans of three buildings have been published. A small structure of about 20 × 16 m. dates from the first century AD. Another building, usually described as a 'fort', dates from the late first and early second century, which makes it a Nabataean rather than a Roman installation.[135] It measures about

---

[127] The first survey of the area was carried out by F. von Frank, *ZDPV* 57 (1934), 191–280. A. Alt, *ZDPV* 58 (1935), 25, interpreting his finds in combination with literary sources, believed that they represented parts of a double line of defence.

[128] The first to point out that no such system existed was B. Rothenberg, *Roman Frontier Studies, 1967*, ed. S. Applebaum (1971), 160 ff.; *Tsephunot Negev* (Archaeology in the Negev and the 'Aravah, 1967, in Hebrew), ch. 6. Rothenberg made a thorough exploration of the entire western part of the valley. D. Graf briefly visited a number of sites in the eastern part and found no evidence of occupation after the Nabataean period (oral information).

[129] References in M. Gichon, *Roman Frontier Studies, 1979* (1980), 850–2; R. Cohen, *Biblical Archaeologist* 45 (1982), 240–7; *Qadmoniot* 20 (1987), 26–30 (in Hebrew). For the site of Yotvetah, see below, p. 188.

[130] S. Applebaum, *Zion* 27 (1962), 1–10 (Hebrew); Gichon, *Roman Frontier Studies 1979*, 843–64, with references to his numerous previous articles.

[131] I. Shatzman, *American Journal of Ancient History* 8 (1983), 130–60.

[132] Except for the tombstone(s) at Mampsis already mentioned.

[133] A. Negev, *PEQ* 98 (1966), 89–98, claimed that the road was not used after the first century. For a brief report on the excavations, R. Cohen, *Biblical Archaeologist*.

[134] Cohen, *Qadmoniot* 20.

[135] In Cohen, *Qadmoniot* 20, the captions on p. 278 have been misplaced, exchanging the 'fort' and the caravanserai.

17 × 17 m. and has eleven rooms round a courtyard of 8 × 7 m. The excavations brought to light an olive press and several mills. There is no justification for calling this a fort: neither the plan of the building, nor the finds in it provide clear evidence of military use. The largest structure, referred to as 'caravanserai', measures 40 m. square. This was in use from the third–second century BC till the third century AD. Rooms are arranged against the exterior wall around an open courtyard. Traces of a bath were noted. These are clearly the remains of a substantial halting place on the road, in use throughout the Hellenistic period and well into the third century AD. It is quite possible, and even likely, that there was a police force there, but so far there is no clear evidence of this. The site must clearly be considered part of the facilities for transport in antiquity, but provides no evidence whatever with regard to Roman military organization in the Negev.

Part of this road was marked with anepigraphic milestones.[136] The major town on it was Oboda (Avdat), where the largest Roman fort in the Negev is to be found (100 × 100 m.). This looks like a fourth-century fort, but unpublished excavations are said to have produced material of the first and second centuries.[137]

(2) The road, parallel to (1), from Mampsis (Kurnub) to Phaeno and thence to the Trajanic road. At Mampsis a military epitaph was found, as noted above. The road is marked by a few anepigraphic milestones. Since all inscribed milestones in the eastern provinces are dated between the mid first century and the early fourth we may assume that the uninscribed stones date to the same period. A road-station in the oasis of Hatzevah in the 'Aravah has now been dated by excavation to the first and second centuries.[138]

The site of the Iron Age fort of H. 'Uzza has been under excavation during several seasons. It is now clear that it was reoccupied in the Hellenistic period and again from the first to the third century. It lay on an ancient track, identified with the biblical 'way of Edom' (2 Kings 3: 8; 20), along which the kings of Israel and Judah went to fight the

---

[136] Z. Meshel and Y. Tsafrir, *PEQ* 106 (1974), 103–18; 107 (1975), 3–21, and discussion by Isaac, *Roman Frontier Studies 1979* (1980), 889–901; both were published before excavation reliably dated the road-installations.

[137] For the most recent excavations, R. Cohen, *Qadmoniot* 13 (1980), 44 f. (in Hebrew); also A. Negev, *ANRW* ii 8. 624; Cohen, *Biblical Archaeologist*, 244–6.

[138] A. Musil, *Arabia Petraea*, ii (1907), 112; 207 f. with plan; B. Rothenberg, *Tsephunot Negev*, 123–5; *Roman Frontier Studies 1967* (1971), 216 f. The excavations were carried out by R. Cohen; for a brief notice see *Hadashot Arkheologiyot* 44 (1972), 36–8. No further information has been made available. Note also a report on a road around the south end of the Dead Sea, ascending to Charakmoba over the south ridge of the Wadi 'Isal: L. Jacobs, *ADAJ* 27 (1983), 245–74. The results of the survey of the sites connected with the road seem to point to a somewhat later date, perhaps fourth century.

Edomites (2 Sam. 8: 13).[139] The size and nature of the Roman structure are not clear. It has not been identified, and nothing is known of the identity of the occupants. It is likely, however, that further excavation will uncover more Roman sites in the region.

Conclusions

As in Judaea, the best evidence for the presence of army units comes not from the desert or sparsely settled parts but from the towns: Bostra, Gerasa, Madaba (?), Petra, Mampsis (Kurnub). This agrees with the pattern observed elsewhere in the East and will be further discussed below.

Several roads were constructed or laid out in the arid parts of the province, including the Negev. The scarcity of milestones everywhere in the desert is remarkable. There is no unambiguous evidence so far of posts permanently occupied by the Roman army in the second century, although inscriptions found at various spots indicate that Roman soldiers had passed there. At some stage the Roman army organized a desert patrol in the northern Hejaz, perhaps also in Wadi Sirhan. This, however, is not likely to have occurred before the reign of Septimius Severus. Unambiguous evidence of permanent army presence is found in the settled, northern part of the province, particularly in several cities. The first certain movement of the army into the desert of north-east Jordan can be observed in the Severan period. This will have been connected with the security of the caravan route through Wadi Sirhan.

In the previous chapter it was argued that there is no evidence, in the centuries following the annexation of Arabia, of frontier trouble, nomad invasions, or pressure on the settled areas of the province. It can now be concluded that the Roman army was, in this period, not organized for frontier defence. It did not take up permanent stations in the desert, but established itself in the cities of the Decapolis and in Bostra. The annexation of Arabia was, at first, an expansion of the Roman organization in southern Syria and northern Judaea.

This is not to deny the importance of the construction of the *Via Nova Traiana*, which was clearly an essential element in the organization of the province. However, it must be recognized that this was indeed a road, linking the settled parts in the north of the province with Petra and the Hejaz. It was not a fortified frontier, and it was not meant to control the movements of nomads. There is, it is true, no direct evidence of the function of the installations along this road, no

---

[139] For the fort, Y. Beit-Arieh, *Qadmoniot* 19 (1986), 31–40 (in Hebrew); for the (tentative) identification with the biblical route, Y. Aharoni, *IEJ* 8 (1958), 35.

inscriptions that show who occupied the stations or what they were called. But comparison with similar installations elsewhere is instructive. There is good evidence from quite a number of Roman and Byzantine forts to support the view that they can be described better as road-stations or police-posts than as forts belonging to a system of frontier defence.

The slowness of the Roman penetration of the desert should not surprise us. Strabo expresses what will have been a common attitude: 'the Nomads are altogether useless because they have no intercourse with peoples and require watching only; the remaining parts, generally speaking, belong to the Tent-dwellers and Nomads who are exceedingly remote.'[140] A similar attitude can still be found in Procopius, after six centuries of Roman rule in the eastern provinces:

> However, in the country once called Commagene and now Euphratesia, they [the Romans and Persians] do not live close to each other at all. A wholly empty and sterile land forms the boundary between the Romans and the Persians over a great distance, and there is nothing there worth fighting for. Both, however, have built forts of sun-dried brick in the desert nearest to the region where they live. These never suffered attack from those nearby, for both peoples lived without antagonism, since they had nothing which the other might want.[141]

Service in the desert will have been considered a heavy and unwelcome burden by the troops, as is clear from documents found in Egypt, which vividly illustrate the problems of boredom and morale, not to mention, at another level, those of supply.[142] This may have made the authorities reluctant to inflict it on them. One solution was to impose such duties as a corvée on civilians, as in the case of *burgarii* and of *skopelarioi* in Egypt, both discussed in the next chapter.

This still leaves us with the question where the Roman army in Arabia is to be sought from Trajan to Septimius Severus. Not, apparently in the south, apart from detachments installed at Petra, Aela, and perhaps a few other places. Dr Kennedy thinks that in the second century, in that part of Arabia which had been the Nabataean kingdom, the forts continued to be occupied by much the same people

---

[140] vi 4. 2 (288): τὸ δ' (sc. τῶν Νομάδων) ἄχρηστον εἰς πᾶν διὰ τὸ ἀκοινώνητον, φυλακῆς δὲ μόνον δεόμενον καὶ τἆλλα δὲ τὰ πολλὰ Σκηνιτῶν καὶ Νομάδων ἐστὶ πόρρω σφόδρα ὄντων.

[141] *De aed.* ii 8. 4–6: ἐν δέ γε τῇ πάλαι μὲν Κομμαγηνῇ χώρᾳ, τανῦν δὲ καλουμένῃ Εὐφρατησίᾳ, οὐδαμῇ ἀλλήλων ἄγχιστα ᾤκηνται. χώρα γὰρ ἔρημος καὶ ἄγονος ὅλως διορίζει ἐπὶ μακρότατον τὰ Ῥωμαίων τε καὶ Περσῶν ὅρια, περιμάχητόν τε οὐδὲν ἔχουσα. ἑκάτεροι μέντοι ἐν ἐρήμῳ ᾗπερ ἄγχιστα γῆς τῆς πρὸς αὐτῶν οἰκουμένης τυγχάνει οὖσα φρούρια παρέργως ᾠκοδομήσαντο ἐκ πλίνθου ὠμῆς· ἅπερ ἐπιβουλῆς οὐδεμιᾶς παρὰ τῶν πέλας ἔτυχε πώποτε, ἀλλ' ἀνεπιφθόνως ἀμφότεροι τῇδε ᾤκησαντο, ἐπεὶ οὐκ εἶχον οὐδὲν ὅτου ἂν καὶ οἱ ἐναντίοι ἐφεῖντο.

[142] Bagnall, 28–31.

as before, units of the Nabataean army, re-equipped and reorganized under Roman officers. These could have been retained in Arabia for some time.[143]

It is to be noted that the Roman presence in the desert has received more attention than is strictly justified in view of its relative unimportance. This is the result of what is, academically speaking, a random factor, namely the survival of archaeological remains. The bulk of the Roman forces in the East clearly were stationed in cities, at least until the fourth century, but the ruins of forts are found mostly in the desert, where the material remains of all periods are so much more visible than in towns which often have remained occupied uninterruptedly from antiquity to modern times. A Roman fort of 20 square metres, where perhaps 50 men were based, is still a landmark in the desert, but a legionary base in town, where thousands of men were serving, is usually obliterated and attested only through a number of inscriptions and references in literary sources. The two striking exceptions are Palmyra and Dura-Europos—both desert towns. The extraordinary visibility of the structures in the desert has resulted in an exaggerated view of their importance.

While there is plenty of evidence to show that the Roman army was based in force in the towns of the province we have no information about what it was doing there. But the fact itself must be considered in combination with the absence of activity in the desert areas. Whatever it was doing must have had more to do with the local, settled population than with nomads in or outside the territory of the province.

Before concluding this part of the chapter something must be said of the strengthening of a number of cities in Arabia in the third century.[144] The programme is best known from a series of inscriptions in Adraa, but texts from Bostra and Soada (Dionysias) show that here too a similar project was realized. It was carried out between 259/60 and 263/4 and resumed from 274/5 till 278/9. It is probably no coincidence that the walls of Tiberias in Galilee were repaired in roughly the same period.[145] Unlike the towns in Arabia, however, Tiberias received no support from the state.

[143] I am grateful to Dr Kennedy for suggestions along these lines. He is developing this theme in a joint paper with David Graf.

[144] Texts assembled and discussed by H.-G. Pflaum, *Syria* 29 (1952), 307–30; add *IGLS* xiii 1 no. 9105 from Bostra. Bostra: M. Sartre, *Bostra, des origines à l'Islam* (1985), 88–90. See also *IGLS* xxi 179 from Dhiban (AD 245–6) recording the construction of a tower by order of the provincial governor.

[145] b. Bava Batra vii b–viii a, cited by D. Sperber, *JESHO* 14 (1971), 241 f. In the case of Tiberias R. Johanan is mentioned, in that of Sepphoris R. Judah Nesiah. This fixes the events between 250 and 280. See below, ch. VIII, for a translation of the source.

The question is against whom the cities were to be defended. Against the Persians, who had devastated many cities of Syria and Asia Minor? Against Palmyra, the rising power in Syria? Or against nomadic tribes?[146] In the previous chapter it was argued that there is no evidence of a nomadic threat in this period. It is a truism that people apply the lessons learnt in the last war in their preparations for the next: the Persians had ravaged scores of cities in the East and nobody could be certain that they would not invade again and move to the south-west instead of the north-west.[147] Palmyra threatened Roman power rather than the cities of the east. In several ways the project foreshadows the fortification of Mesopotamian cities by Diocletian and his successors. It stems from the assumption that the countryside cannot be defended against an invading power; and it further assumes that the citizens themselves will defend their city in case of need. The latter is clear from the role played by the local militia in constructing and manning sections of the fortifications.[148] The provincial authorities organized, financed, and supervised the construction, but it was not carried out by or for the army.

Southern Syria

In Chapter I it was argued that the army in Syria was organized to support a policy of expansion into Mesopotamia and Armenia. While this is true for units on the Euphrates in northern Syria, something must be said in this chapter of the troops in southern Syria. The main legionary base was that at Raphanaea, an important crossroads at the foot of the Alawite Mountains.[149] Troops of this legion must have been responsible for security in the mountains of Lebanon, though there is no evidence to confirm this; Trachonitis and the very serious problems in policing this area were described in Chapter II. A Roman road was constructed through the area, linking Bostra with Damascus. It appears on the Peutinger Table (Chanata–Aenos, i.e. Phaena) and was explored by Poidebard (from the air) and Dunand.[150] All along the most difficult section of this road, between Phaena and Aerita, there

---

[146] Pflaum, 322 f., does not believe fear of the Persians played a role, because they had not reached Arabia in their attack. He does not consider the Palmyrene threat decisive either because the fortifications were completed after Aurelian had defeated Palmyra. Bowersock, *Roman Arabia*, 131, sees a connection with both the Persian invasion and the rising power of Palmyra.

[147] For dubious and undated evidence regarding Persian attacks in the region of Bostra see Sartre, *Bostra*, 89 f.

[148] As shown by Pflaum, esp. 318.   [149] See above, p. 39.

[150] A. Poidebard, *Syria* 9 (1928), 114; M. Dunand, *Mém. Ac. des Inscriptions et Belles-Lettres* 13.2 (1930), 521–57. See also T. Bauzou, *Hauran*, i, 139 and fig. 1.; pls. i b–iii a.

were watchtowers at a quarter-of-an-hour or half-an-hour's distance. While obviously Roman they were, according to Dunand, still used in his time as observation posts by the local Bedouins. They could have been signal towers.[151] Two inscriptions found in a little sanctuary on the road mention the legion IV Scythica, one of them set up by a centurion of the legion, the other a dedication made by a *beneficiarius* during the governorship of Avidius Cassius (166–75).[152] Milestones record the restoration of this road under Commodus from Phaena (Mismiyeh) to Aerita (Ahire).

Phaena was the most important centre at the north-west edge of Trachonitis,[153] and a series of military inscriptions found there indicates the presence of a substantial garrison. At least three centurions of III Gallica (based at Raphanaea) are mentioned on four inscriptions, two of them dated to the reign of Marcus Aurelius.[154] Two centurions of XVI Flavia Firma occur on four inscriptions, one of the two men again from the time of Marcus Aurelius or Commodus.[155] Another inscription mentions a military tribune.[156] They were all serving soldiers, so it is likely that they were on duty in the area. This impression is confirmed by the fact that one of the centurions appears also on an inscription from Aerita on the same road, the only settlement in the heart of Trachonitis with a good source of water.[157] This man also appears on a similar inscription from Nela in Hauran (AD 171), where three more such inscriptions have been found.[158] Another was found at al-Kafr in Auranitis.[159] At Shaqqa (Maximianopolis, Saccaia, Eaccaia), Bashan,

---

[151] For a discussion of towers see the next chapter.

[152] Dunand, 536–40.   [153] MacAdam, *Studies*, 54–7.

[154] Waddington, no. 2525 (*IGR* iii 1113): M. Aurelius and Lucius Verus in combination with Avidius Cassius as governor; no. 2528 (*IGR* iii 1114), also of the reign of M. Aurelius, as appears from no. 2438 from Aerita and no. 2221 from Nela in Auranitis, where the same centurion is mentioned; no. 2536. A. H. M. Jones, *JRS* 21 (1931), 268, concluded from these inscriptions that Trachonitis and northern Auranitis were treated as a single administrative area placed in the charge of a centurion. The evidence regarding military officers is more likely to be a record of military activity than of administrative organization, especially as we know Trachonitis to have been an area of chronic banditry. It must be noted that most of these inscriptions belong to a relatively short period.

[155] Waddington, nos. 2531–2 (*IGR* iii 1121–2), both undated, but the same officer, Petusius Eudemus, is mentioned on an inscription dated 177–9 from Shahba which afterwards became Philippopolis, ibid. no. 2071 (*IGR* iii 1195), and on another with the same date from al-Kafr in Hauran (*IGR* iii 1290). The inscriptions which mention L. Aurelius Maximus (nos. 2526–78) may be somewhat later.

[156] Waddington, no. 2533 (*IGR* iii 1132): Severus Askaion, χειλίαρχος.

[157] T. Aurelius Quirinalius (no. 2528 from Phaena and no. 2438 from Aerita). The latter inscription was set up by T. Cl. Magnus, a veteran, from Aerita.

[158] Waddington, no. 2212 (*IGR* iii 1261). Also from Nela: Waddington, no. 2213 (*IGR* iii 1262); *IGR* iii 1296, for an improved reading of which see MacAdam, *Studies*, 92 f.; Waddington, no. 2214, read by MacAdam, 93–5 in combination with *AAES* no. 381.

[159] *IGR* iii 1290. For Petusius Eudemus, see also above, n. 155.

a centurion set up a statue for the *Tyche Megale* of this village in his own name and that of his children. He was not a veteran and may therefore have been the local commander.[160] If he was, the inscription shows a certain degree of social integration. The date is 238. IV Scythica is found also at Canatha and at the village of Rimet Hazim, both near the road.[161] Another centurion of XVI Flavia Firma supervised repair work on the Damascus–Abila–Heliopolis road in 163–5.[162] At Phaena an inn was built for the use of soldiers to spare the inhabitants the nuisance of compulsory billeting.[163]

Another centurion of XVI Flavia occurs on an inscription at Aere from the reign of Commodus.[164] Aere (as Sanamein) lies near and east of the Damascus–Nawa–Capitolias–Gadara–Scythopolis road, and from this road a branch led westward to Tiberias via Capernaum. Two Roman watchtowers measuring 6×6 metres have been found on this branch, sited at mile-stations with milestones *in situ*. One of them has been excavated by Mr Zvi Ma'oz of the Department of Antiquities of Israel, who has kindly informed me that he found in it coins of Commodus and Elagabalus. A similar phenomenon, watchtowers placed near mile-stations, was observed by Mr T. Bauzou in a survey of the Bostra–Mafraq–Gerasa road. The milestones there are dated 214.[165]

All these items together leave no doubt that legionary centurions were responsible for the organization of road-security in southern Syria, particularly in the difficult area of Trachonitis and its vicinity.[166] Centurions as commanders of small garrisons are well attested.[167] In the winter of 67–8 Vespasian placed garrisons commanded by decurions in villages and by centurions in towns in Judaea.[168] One of these is almost certainly honoured on an inscription from Ascalon.[169]

---

[160] M. Sartre, *Syria* 61 (1984), 49–61 (*AE* 1984. 921 bis): Juvenalius Proclus, son of Taurinus. His wife Sonomathe was of local origin. For the village see Waddington, comments on his no. 2136.

[161] Cagnat, *IGR* iii 1230, from Canatha; Waddington, no. 2407 (*IGR* iii 1242) from Rimet Hazim, mentioning a centurion of the legion.

[162] *CIL* iii 199–201 from Abila in Wadi Barada.

[163] Waddington, no. 2524; *OGIS* 609, and cf. S. Hill, *DOP* 29 (1975), 347–9, pls. 1–6 on a building which since the nineteenth century, but without good reason, has been identified with this inn (incorrectly referred to as *praetorium*). For compulsory billeting, below, p. 297.

[164] Waddington, nos. 2413 f. (*IGR* iii 1128).

[165] I am grateful to Mr Ma'oz and Mr Bauzou for their information.

[166] A. H. M. Jones, *JRS*, 268; 54–7; Appendix 1, 91–6.

[167] e.g. a centurion 'responsible for the peace in the area' at Antioch in Pisidia: J. F. Gilliam, *Bull. Am. Soc. Papyr.* 2 (1965), 65–73 = *Roman Army Papers* (1986), 281–7, esp. 281.

[168] Josephus, *BJ* iv 8. 1 (442). These were of course temporary garrisons.

[169] *SEG* i 552; *AE* 1923, 83, set up by the council and people of the city for Aulus Instuleius Tenax, centurion of X Fretensis. This officer is mentioned as *primipilaris* of XII Fulm. on *CIL* iii 30

In 124 a centurion is attested as commander of an auxiliary detachment at Ein Gedi.[170] We have no information on the nature of their duties there, but the centurion was engaged in lending money to a local man.[171] Ein Gedi was not a frontier settlement. It was an oasis on the Dead Sea, of considerable economic importance because of its famous balsam and palm trees, which were imperial property.[172] In the gospels we hear of a centurion based at Capernaum.[173] In 127 an equestrian cavalry officer was based at Rabbatmoba, the capital of Moab in Arabia,[174] where he was involved in receiving census declarations. It is of interest that this officer was engaged in administrative duties in a town, only two decades after the organization of the province. We should also note that his attestation was translated from the Latin.[175]

The social hierarchy in general, and the position of centurions, in the cities of the Roman provinces is nowhere better illustrated than in the following Talmudic source:[176]

It is like a man who stands up in the market place and defies the *bouleutes*. Those who heard him said to him: 'You utter fool, you defy the *bouleutes*?' What if he wanted to beat you or tear your clothes, or throw you in prison, what could you do to him? Or if he were a *qitron* [centurion], who is greater than him, how much more so! Or if he were a *hapatqas* [*hypatikos*, governor] who is greater than the two of them, how much more so!

Below, in Chapter VI, we shall see to what extent common townspeople in Antioch were helpless before the military. The present passage shows how the average Jewish townsman in Judaea envisaged the social balance around and above him. The other element to be noted is the natural assumption of an immediate threat of physical violence towards social inferiors in the face of defiant behaviour. Another passage further refines our insight in the provincial hierarchy:[177]

. . . like a *qitron* [centurion] who has completed his time in the army and he did

---

of AD 65. Note also Aurelius Marcellinus, centurion of X Fretensis, buried by his spouse at Tiberias (*IGR* iii 1204).

[170] Lewis, *Documents*, no. 11.

[171] The editor concludes from the text that there is a concealed usurious squeeze exerted upon the borrower, op. cit., 41.

[172] References in Schürer, *History*, ii 194, n. 40.   [173] Matt. 8: 5–9; Luke 7: 2.

[174] P. Yadin 16. *Bullae* of Rabbatmoba and Charakmoba have been found at Mampsis: A. Negev, *IEJ* 19 (1969), 89–106. For two centurions attested at Madaba, above, n. 108.

[175] The role of centurions at the time of the annexation of the kingdom of the Iceni in Britain is brought out by Tacitus. Roman power was exercised, or rather abused, by centurions and (the procurator's) slaves—*Ann.* xiv 31: 'quod contra vertit, adeo ut regnum per centuriones, domus per servos velut capta vastarentur.'

[176] Sifre Deuteronomy, cccix, ed. Finkelstein, 348.

[177] Sifre Numbers, cxxxi, ed. Horovitz, 169.

not serve his *plomopilon* (*primuspilus*), but he ran away. The king sent for him
and they brought him back and sentenced him to be beheaded. And when he
was about to be killed the king said: 'fill [his bag] with a measure of gold dinars
and show it to him' and they said: 'if you had done like your friends you would
have received your measure of gold dinars and kept your life. Now you have
lost your life and lost your money . . .'

The tradition shows a clear appreciation of the differences in status
within the army. A centurion might be vastly more powerful than a
bouleutes, but he had to serve his *primuspilus*. It may be noted that there
were two such officers in Judaea in the second and third centuries.

It is remarkable to what extent the evidence from southern Syria
focuses on the reigns of Marcus Aurelius and Commodus. The army
perhaps did not continue these activities far into the third century when
the local population may have been made responsible for police-duties
of this kind.[178] As usual the Roman authorities used supplementary
methods to ensure the security of the region, notably the enlistment of
local men as soldiers.[179] In fourth-century Egypt, however, it is clear
that troops were engaged in police duties and the collection of regular
taxes as well as *annona militaris*, combining all these activities with
looting, robbery, and violent behaviour.[180]

There is evidence also of auxiliary units based in other parts of
southern Syria, notably in the region of Damascus and on the
Damascus–Palmyra road.[181] Auxiliary troops were based at Palmyra
after the Parthian campaign of Lucius Verus.[182] A *cohors II Thracum
Syriaca* was stationed on the road from Palmyra to the Euphrates.[183]

North-east of Damascus, on the road to Emesa, an inscription was
found (at Khan Kosseir) among the ruins of a Roman site. It appears to
mention Septimius Severus and a governor of Syria Coele and reads:
'Hoc proesidium (*sic?*) construxit in securitatem publicam et
Scaenitarum Arabum terrorem'.[184] The site was far from any frontier
zone, but Damascus lay on the edge of the vast interior steppe of Syria,

---

[178] Note that, already in the time of Marcus Aurelius, the city of Abila had to pay for the repair
of the Roman road, carried out by the army, above, n. 162. See further below, ch. VI, for such
duties.

[179] For local recruitment in Trachonitis, MacAdam, *Studies*, 79–84.

[180] H. I. Bell et al., *The Abinnaeus Archive* (1962), no. 9, pp. 50 f.; no. 12, pp. 54 f. (police duties);
nos. 13–15, pp. 55–60 (collection of taxes); no. 26, pp. 73–5; 29, pp. 178 f. (*annona*); nos. 27, pp.
75 f.; no. 28, pp. 76 f. (violence and hooliganism).

[181] For evidence of auxiliary units in bases along other roads in southern Syria, J.-P. Rey-
Coquais, *JRS* 68 (1978), 68.

[182] References in Rey-Coquais, *JRS*, 68 f. with n. 337. For Palmyra see the second part of this
chapter.

[183] Ibid., n. 338.

[184] *CIL* iii 128; cf. Rey-Coquais, *JRS*, 66 with n. 300; 70 with n. 356. The reading is not certain.

and nomads were therefore part of the life of the area. The city was always an important one, thanks to its strategic location and regional economic importance.[185] It stood on several major overland routes, among them the highway from Anatolia to Arabia. Khan Kosseir lies on this road, and we may record it as another example of a police-station on a major road intended to protect the safety of travellers and commerce and perhaps serving also as the local centre of administration.[186]

As in Judaea and Arabia, the garrisons were often based in cities.[187] Cyrrhus and Zeugma had been cities since Hellenistic times.[188] Samosata was an old royal capital and appears to have received city status at the time of its annexation, when it also became the site of legionary headquarters.[189] On the other hand, the settlements near the legionary bases of Raphanaea and, in Cappadocia, Melitene and Satala seem to have owed their rise to being garrison towns.[190] We have no archaeological information on any of these camps. For the third century, however, there is numismatic evidence of the army's presence in towns. Coins minted at Tyre in the reign of Septimius Severus probably show that there was a vexillation of III Gallica based there.[191] The same legion is mentioned on coins of Sidon from the reign of Elagabalus.[192] VI Ferrata appears on coins of Damascus (Otacilia, wife of the emperor Philip, 244–9);[193] so does III Gallica (Trebonianus Gallus and Volusianus, 251–3).[194] None of these cities has produced any earlier evidence of the presence of an army unit and we cannot know, of course, how long the units remained there. There is comparable material from Neapolis in Judaea.

---

[185] N. Elisséeff, 'Dimashk', *Encyclopaedia of Islam*, new edn., ii 277.

[186] For other stations on this road, *DE* iv, s.v. 'Limes', 1353 f.

[187] For the legionary bases in Syria and Cappadocia see above, ch. I. The fact that troops were frequently based in cities in the eastern provinces is not generally recognized; see, e.g. R. W. Davies, *ANRW* ii 1. 322, who states that this was only the case where trouble was likely to break out, as in Alexandria, Jerusalem, Caesarea, and Byzantium.

[188] A. H. M. Jones, *The Cities of the Eastern Roman Provinces* (²1971), 241–4. Zeugma: J. Wagner, *Seleukia am Euphrat–Zeugma*, Beiträge zum Tübinger Atlas des Vorderen Orients (1976); ii (1977), 517–39. Cyrrhus: E. Frézouls in *ANRW* ii 8. 164–97, esp. 182 f.

[189] The era of Samosata dates from 71 and it issued coins as Flavia Samosata from Hadrian onward; W. Wroth, *BMC Galatia, etc.*, 117 ff.

[190] Raphanaea: Jones, *Cities*, 267; Melitene: ibid. 179. Josephus, *BJ* vii 1. 3 (18), still described it as a district rather than a town. Procopius, *De aed.* iii 4. 15–18, ascribes its development to the presence of the legion; cf. D. Magie, *Roman Rule in Asia Minor* (1950), 1436, 1464. Satala: Magie, 1436, 1465.

[191] G. F. Hill, *BMC Phoenicia*, 269. As noted also in ch. VIII, in this period such evidence cannot be taken as referring to the settlement of veterans in the city, a practice which is not attested after the reign of Hadrian.

[192] Ibid. cxi f.   [193] *BMC Galatia etc.*, 286, no. 25.

[194] H. Cohen, *Médailles impériales* (1930), 257, no. 174, and 284, no. 177.

Conclusions

As will be emphasized in Chapter VI, it was undesirable in every respect to keep military units on active duty in the interior and in cities. It was clearly preferable, when it could be done, to leave the maintenance of order to the cities. We may therefore assume that evidence of army units in the interior, when it occurs, shows that there was an urgent need to keep soldiers there. We cannot escape the conclusion that the Roman army was engaged in internal police duties in many parts of Syria in various periods. This clearly was the case in Isauria, notorious for its brigandage.[195] But we might also suppose that the units attested as serving in the interior would have been kept there for as short a period as possible. This would explain why the inscriptions regarding centurions in towns in southern Syria all seem to date from roughly the same period.

PALMYRA, DURA-EUROPOS, AND THE SYRIAN DESERT

In the second part of this chapter an area will be discussed where the Roman military presence had a dual function. It was a region of vital importance in the confrontation between Rome and Parthia—and as such might have been treated in Chapter I. In peacetime, however, it was of equal interest for economic reasons. These are the desert parts of Syria and Mesopotamia. The routes that crossed the region were used by the armies of the two empires in wartime and by traders and civilians in periods of quiet. The region contains a number of major sites, such as Palmyra and Dura-Europos, which have been explored with great success and are central to many of the themes of this book. They are considered here in some detail in an attempt to define the character of the Roman military presence in the region. The first question to be asked is whether we are faced with a 'system of defence', a frontier system. If this is not the case it must then be seen whether these were military stations intended to serve other purposes in times of major conflict, or whether the troops served as a 'desert police'. Another matter of interest is the organization of military units in the towns of Palmyra and Dura, because nowhere else do we gain such full information on units based in eastern towns. They may therefore be

---

[195] R. Syme, *Actes du colloque organisé à Strasbourg (novembre 1985)*, ed. E. Frézouls (1987), 144 f.; Hopwood, *DRBE*.

used as examples of how military units were organized when based in an urban environment.

Palmyra

A subject of much debate has been the formal status of Palmyra in the empire.[196] The question is of more than merely administrative interest, since the answer will indicate to what extent the Romans were directly involved in controlling the routes through the desert. To decide the matter we must be certain what we mean by inclusion in the empire. As argued throughout this book, being part of the empire could be interpreted in a flexible manner. It was not a legal concept and need entail no more than the mutual recognition of ultimate Roman authority, unlike incorporation into a province, which was indeed a formal act with consequences in various fields. But it was quite possible for Rome to forego the exercise of sovereignty while still claiming that a state was part of the empire. We must distinguish between the inclusion of Palmyra in the empire and its incorporation into the province of Syria. As regards the latter, we shall consider what were the actual consequences.[197]

In 41 BC Antony sent a raiding party of horsemen to Palmyra under the pretext that the Palmyrenes, 'living as they did on the border between the two peoples, manoeuvred between the two sides; for, being traders, they bring from Persia Indian and Arab commerce and sell it in the Roman empire'.[198] The people of Palmyra did not await the Roman plunderers, but took their property across the Euphrates, preparing to defend themselves there.[199] Appian adds that the Parthians considered the Roman raid an act of war.[200] We may note that Appian, writing in the middle of the second century, uses the present tense in his description of the Palmyrenes as traders between Persia, India, and Rome. When Antony sent his raiders, the city's wealth will have

---

[196] H. Seyrig, *Syria* 22 (1941), 155–74 (= *Antiquités syriennes* iii [1946], 142–61); A. Piganiol, *Revue Historique* 195 (1945), 10–29; I. Richmond, *JRS* 53 (1963), 43–54; G. W. Bowersock, *JRS* 63 (1973), 133–40; J.-P. Rey-Coquais, *JRS* 68 (1978), 51; J. F. Matthews, *JRS* 74 (1984), 157–80. On Palmyra see now J. Teixidor, *Un Port romain du désert: Palmyre* (1984).

[197] Matthews, 157–80, esp. 161 f., argues that it is clear that Palmyra was part of the hegemonial structure of the Roman empire from the time of Tiberius, but it is not quite certain when it was legally made a city of the province of Syria.

[198] Appian, *BC* v 1. 9: . . . ὅτι Ῥωμαίων καὶ Παρθναίων ὄντες ἐφόριοι ἐς ἑκατέρους ἐπιδεξίως εἶχον (ἔμποροι γὰρ ὄντες κομίζουσι μὲν ἐκ Περσῶν τὰ Ἰνδικὰ ἢ Ἀράβια, διατίθενται δ᾽ ἐν τῇ Ῥωμαίων) . . .

[199] Matthews, 161, rightly pointed out that nothing should be deduced regarding the state of the walls of Palmyra at the time.

[200] *BC* v 1. 10.

consisted of bullion, coinage, and livestock; and the Palmyrene response to the Roman attack was still that of nomads facing a force of superior strength. On the other hand, in Appian's days Palmyra's wealth clearly was no longer as movable. It had become a splendid city.

Recognition of Roman sovereignty is not necessarily expressed in the inscription on the base of a statue in honour of Tiberius, AD 14–19, dedicated by a legate of the legion X Fretensis.[201] After all, we know that there was a temple of the *Augusti* at Vologesias,[202] and surely that cannot be taken to imply that the Parthians considered themselves part of the Roman empire. The imperial statue at Palmyra need prove no more than that a commander of a Roman legion paid a visit to Palmyra. Another inscription records in Aramaic a mission performed at the orders of Germanicus, who visited Syria in AD 18.[203] Mesene and the king of Emesa are mentioned here. It is an intriguing document, a record of Roman interests in the East, but not an indication of direct control over Palmyra. The limits of the territory of Palmyra to the west were established by a Syrian governor between AD 11 and 178.[204] This in itself does not prove that Palmyra, like its neighbour to the west, Apamea, had become a city of the province of Syria in every respect. This will be clear, for instance, from the boundary stone of 195 delimiting the border between Osrhoene and the kingdom of Abgarus. The former was a province, the latter a dependent state.[205] It cannot be denied that the tax law of Palmyra contains phrases which imply direct Roman intervention in the affairs of the city.[206] Yet such intervention may well have been sporadic in this period. After Germanicus' visit to Syria many years may have passed before a high Roman official visited the town again.

Pliny wrote of Palmyra that it 'is a city with an outstanding location, a rich land, and pleasant springs. A vast sand desert surrounds its fields everywhere and nature has, as it were, isolated it from other lands, so that it has preserved its own fortune between the two greatest empires of the Romans and the Parthians and, as soon as there is discord, is

---

[201] H. Seyrig, *Syria* 13 (1932), 274; *AE* 1933. 204: '[Dr]uso Caesari, Ti Caesari, divi Aug. f., Augusto, divi Iuli nepoti; Ge[rmanico Caesari] | imperatoribus posuit | [Min]ucius T. f., Hor. Rufus legatus leg. X Fretensis.'

[202] R. Mouterde, *Syria* 12 (1931), 105–15; *SEG* vii 135.

[203] J. Cantineau, *Syria* 12 (1931), 139–41, no. 18: '. . . .] who is also called Alexandros | . . .]Palmyrene, because he carried out . . .? | before(?) and Germanicus sent him | . . . .]of Maishan, and to Orabzes | . . . . . | Samsigeram, Supreme King.' Other cities also retained mementos of Germanicus' eastern journey. Thus there are three cities which received the name Germanica and declared Germanicus their founder, for instance Ptolemais-Acco in Syria (see below, p. 322 and B. V. Head, *Historia Numorum* (²1911), 511).

[204] D. Schlumberger, *Syria* 20 (1939), 43–73; *AE* 1939. 178f.

[205] J. Wagner in *AFRBA*, 113f; *AE* 1984. 919.   [206] Matthews, 178f.

always the focus of attention of both sides.'[207] This is probably best seen as a literary *topos*, based more on a rather vague perception of an oasis somewhere in the desert between Syria and Mesopotamia than on any precise information.[208] However, the exploitation of the Palmyrene countryside, indicated by Pliny, has been confirmed by archaeological exploration.[209] It is a reminder that no ancient city could live on trade alone.[210] In the seventies a road was laid out linking the settled region of Syria with the Euphrates via Palmyra.[211] The road gave the Romans access to the Euphrates—it was used by one of the three army groups which invaded Mesopotamia under Severus Alexander.[212] At the same time it was an important physical link connecting the city with the province of Syria and with Mesopotamia.

Incorporation into a Roman province normally had military, financial, and judicial aspects. The military aspect often involved the presence of a Roman garrison and the obligation to furnish recruits to the Roman army. There is no reason to assume that either was the case in Palmyra in the first century AD.[213] Neither is there at present any evidence to show that it was a *civitas stipendiaria* in the first century or a *civitas libera* in the second.[214] We ought to be wary of attaching too great weight to random bits of information of a purely formal character, such as the existence of a tribe named Claudias,[215] or the statement that Palmyra was renamed Hadrianopolis or Hadriana.[216] Purely formal re-foundation was so common under Hadrian, as will be argued in Chapter VIII, that we cannot deduce from this that any meaningful change in status took place. However, by the middle of the second century there was an auxiliary *ala* based at Palmyra, the commander being honoured by the city in various ways.[217] It was later replaced by a

[207] *NH* v 21. 88.

[208] As argued by E. Will, *Syria* 62 (1985), 263–9.

[209] D. Schlumberger, *La Palmyrène du Nord-Ouest* (1951). Cf. Josephus, *Ant.* viii 6. 1 (154): 'Nowhere in that country is there water, but in that place only are springs and pits to be found.'

[210] Cf. Matthews, 162.

[211] As shown by the milestone mentioned above, p. 34.

[212] Herodian vi 5. 2; *IGR* iii 1033, attesting the emperor's presence at Palmyra.

[213] It is possible, but not at all certain, that *OGIS* 629, 103–6, shows there was a Roman unit at Palmyra in the first century.

[214] As argued by Seyrig, *Syria* 22, 164 f. and 171 f. For scepticism see Rey-Coquais, *JRS*, and J. C. Mann, Appendix II in M. M. Roxan, *RMD 1978–1984*, 218.

[215] *CIS* ii 4122.

[216] Stephanus of Byzantium, s.v.; on the tax law, 1 (b), the city is named Hadriana Tadmor.

[217] C. Vibius Celer, commander of the local *ala I Ulpia singul(arium)* was honoured at Palmyra and made a citizen and *synedros*: H. Seyrig, *Syria* 14, 152–68 (*AE* 1933. 207). He was procurator of Arabia in the early years of Pius, cf. E. Birley, *Roman Britain and the Roman Army* (1953), 146 f.; H.-G. Pflaum, *Carrières*, no. 155. A later inscription, *AE* 1933. 208, honours Iulius Iulianus, prefect of the *ala Herculana*, whose career is known from *ILS* 1327. He became praetorian prefect under Commodus; cf. Birley, 148 f.; Pflaum, no. 180.

partly mounted cohort.[218] At this stage there were no regular
Palmyrene units in the Roman army. Palmyrene archers did serve in
the army from the reign of Trajan; four military diplomas record
citizenship granted to such men.[219] It has been argued that these were
first recruited for an extraordinary six-year period at the start of
Trajan's Parthian war.[220] Even though Palmyrene archers continued
to serve, no regular auxiliary *ala* or *cohors* existed until the early third
century or somewhat earlier, when the *cohors XX Palmyrenorum* appears
to have been formed.[221] At that time Palmyra was elevated to colonial
status.[222] This brings us again to the reign of Severus as the period of
increased Roman involvement in the desert. We may note, however,
that the Palmyrene cohort is the only unit of that name known so far;
and it was based at Dura, where archers of the Palmyrene militia had
been stationed earlier. The cohort, therefore, served in a familiar
capacity. It would be of interest to know whether the soldiers were
commanded by Palmyrene officers, like the Batavians and Thracians in
the first century.[223]

We know that the Palmyrenes very successfully established themselves as middlemen organizing the trade between Rome and Parthia
and beyond. This appears from a series of explicit documents which
give us an impression of the way the system worked.[224] It was based on
a network of trade-stations in important Mesopotamian centres—
Babylon, Vologesias, Mesene[225]—and it extended to Egypt, as appears

---

[218] Several third-century inscriptions attest the presence at Palmyra of the *coh. I Fl(avia)
Chalc(idenorum) Equit(ata)*: M. Gawlikowski, *Palmyre*, viii. 125, no. 40, pl. cv, 239; a later inscription: ibid. 126, no. 41; an inscription of 244–7: Seyrig, *Syria* 14, 166. It is of some interest that
inscriptions of this unit were found in secondary use in the fourth-century *principia*, an indication, perhaps, that this part of the city had served in such a capacity well before Diocletian
established there the legionary headquarters.

[219] *CIL* xvi 68 and *RMD* 17 (29 June 120) and *RMD* 27–8 (126).

[220] Mann, *RMD*, 217–19.

[221] Mann plausibly argues that the cohort was simply the old Palmyrene unit which had been
stationed at Dura and was transformed into a Roman unit when Syria was split into two
provinces, as a result of which Palmyra and Dura found themselves in two different provinces.

[222] Mann, *RMD*, 219. Colonial status is mentioned in the *Digest* L 15. 1 (Ulpian): 'Est et
Palmyrena civitas in Provincia Phoenice prope barbaras gentes et nationes collocata'. The
context implies that the town had the *ius Italicum*, and the phrase itself suggests no more than
that Palmyra was situated in the desert, a region inhabited by nomads. D. Schlumberger,
Bulletin d'Études Orientales 9 (1942–43), 54–82 analyses the Roman personal names attested at
Palmyra.

[223] C. Bradford Welles, R. O. Fink and J. F. Gilliam, *The Excavations at Dura-Europos, Final
Report* v, part i, *The Parchments and Papyri* (1959), 22–46, esp. 26 ff. on the cohort. The known
names of commanding officers do not tell us anything (see list, ibid. 28). But those of several
centurions are Semitic (list, ibid. 29 f.): Mocimus, Malchus, Zebidas, etc.

[224] M. Rostovtzeff, *Mélanges Gustav Glotz*, ii (1932), 739–811; E. Will, *Syria* 34 (1957), 262–77;
M. Gawlikowski, *Syria* 60 (1983), 53–68; Matthews, *JRS*, 164–9; Teixidor.

[225] Oppenheimer, *Babylonia Judaica*: Babylon, 44–62, esp. 58; Vologesias, 456–61, esp. 458;

from inscriptions set up by Palmyrene merchants who made donations at Coptos.[226] The responsibility for the safety of caravans on their trip through the desert and beyond was accepted by individual Palmyrenes who often accompanied the caravans in person. They had the knowledge, the connections, and the means to protect the caravans against raiders; a number of inscriptions thank them for their help in times of danger. One specifically expresses gratitude to Ogleos son of Makkaios for 'the continuous expeditions he raised against the nomads . . . always providing safety for the merchants and caravans on every occasion on which he was their leader'.[227] We cannot judge how serious the risk was on the part of the Palmyrenes. No dedications were made after expeditions that came to an unhappy end.

Under Ottoman rule Bedouin tribes regularly acted as 'protectors' along specific caravan routes.[228] They received a subvention and protected the caravans on their territory. The following Bedouin poem is cited by A. Musil:

They will come to Farhan's father, that tormentor of the wounded,
In a struggle of riders, when one vanquishes and the other is vanquished,
To the protector of loads, freighted for al-Mzêrîb,
When the redcaps fix the day of complaints.
Say: 'O Hmûd! he surely will reward thee with cuffs and kicks,
And, if victorious, will tread on thee as on a slipper.
Thou must know what it means for thee to be far from the chief and what to be
    near him. . .'[229]

Musil comments:

Abu Farhân was a nickname of Muhammad eben Smejr, the chief of the Weld 'Ali tribe, his eldest son being Farhân. The poet calls him . . . a torment to the wounded, because the wounds caused by his blows were slow in healing. The Weld 'Ali had undertaken to transport half of the supplies destined for Mecca and al-Medina as well as half of the pilgrims from al-Mzêrib, south of Damascus, to Medâjen Sâleh, or al-Hegr. Muhammad eben Smejr guaranteed to the Turkish officials, who from their red tarbushes were called . . .

Mesene, 241–56, esp. 251–3. See also 442–5. At least one man from Palmyra left his traces in Wadi Sirhan. The inscription is the work of a soldier or a member of a caravan: J. Starcky, in F. V. Winnett and W. L. Reed, *Ancient Records from North Africa* (1970), 161 f. (undated).

[226] *OGIS* 639; J. Bingen, *CE* 59 (1984), 355–8 (*AE* 1984. 925). Palmyrene *naukleroi* of the Red Sea made donations at Coptos which shows that trade was maintained over sea via Mesene. J. P. Rey-Coquais, *JRS* 68 (1978), 55 with n. 143; Teixidor, 43.

[227] H. Ingholt, *Syria* 13 (1932), 289–92 (*SEG* vii 139). See also C. Dunant, *Mus. Helv.* 13 (1956), 216–25; and cf. J. and L. Robert, *BE* 1958. 506.

[228] N. N. Lewis, *Nomads and Settlers in Syria and Jordan 1800–1980* (1987), 7–9. In times of diminishing trade the tribes would often be tempted to raid the caravans instead of protecting them, which would then contribute to further decline.

[229] A. Musil, *The Manners and Customs of the Rwala Bedouins* (1928), 582.

redcaps, not only the safety of the transport but also its punctual delivery . . . For failing to keep to the time agreed on or for despoiling the caravan Muhammad was liable to prosecution by the Turkish officials. He was therefore dependent on them, as if he were their slave. The second half of the transport and the pilgrims were convoyed by the Beni Sahr as far as Ma'ân, from this place by the Beni 'Atijje to Tebûk, and thence by the Beli to Medâjen Sâleh.[230]

It will be clear that this caravan followed the pilgrim road in Transjordan. Otherwise it may serve as a vivid illustration of the complexities and risks involved in such endeavours.

However, the essence of the matter was that the Palmyrenes were in a position to do for the Romans and Parthians what these could hardly do for themselves. The reality of life in the desert is best illustrated by another reference to Musil. When travelling in eastern Sinai in 1897 he was held up by Salem, sheikh of the Kederat Bedouin.

After half an hour we saw Salem returning with the others. What had happened or would happen? The brave Sallâm el-Barâsi was a friend and relative of the sheikh of the 'Ateje whose protection we enjoyed. He therefore declared our case to be his own and explained to the furious Salem what strife he could expect if he would rob us of our possessions. Salem had no fear at all of the authorities in Gaza, but with Sallâm and his clan, let alone with the sheikh of the 'Ateje, he wanted no conflict. So in the end he returned to us our horses, arms and part of our belongings.[231]

The dependence of the Turkish authority on Bedouin support is best illustrated by the fact that they paid fees on a fixed scale to the Bedouin tribes encamped along the Pilgrim route so that they would protect the pilgrims on their way to Mecca.[232]

The Palmyrene merchants had at their disposal a network of trading colonies, and a working relationship with the nomads and semi-nomads that allowed them to pass through the desert without being attacked; if there were an emergency they were capable of defending the caravan under their protection. All this required connections, experience, and knowledge which the Romans did not have and could not acquire for themselves. The Palmyrenes performed a unique function for the Romans, and they did it so well that they acquired immense riches. Palmyra produced six known senators, more than any city in Syria proper, apart from Antioch, and eight or nine equestrian officers (all of them in the second century). The next largest number was six

---

[230] Ibid. 581.

[231] A. Musil, *Arabia Petraea*, ii (1907), 186.

[232] A. Musil, *The Northern Heǧaz* (1926), 9. The construction of the railway changed the situation.

from Berytus.[233] As regards *equites*, however, it is possible that Palmyrenes are, relatively speaking, over-represented because more inscriptions have been preserved in the ruins of this desert town than in other near eastern cities which have been occupied without interruption.[234]

There has been speculation that the rise of Sassanian Persia and the conquest of Mesene—now known to have been carried out by Parthia in the mid-second century—unfavourably influenced Palmyra's position in the international trade. It can only be said that the increased military power of the city in the third century, a period of political and economic disorder, does not bear this out.

All this should make it clear that Palmyra could never have been—and never was—an ordinary provincial town, whatever its formal status. Moreover, in addition to the various activities already discussed, there was yet another, more specifically military duty which Palmyra carried out for the Romans. There is now good evidence of Palmyrene troops posted at various stations along the Euphrates. The clearest indication that Palmyra never became a regular provincial town is the extraordinary rise to military power of the city in the third century, to be discussed in Chapter V. A subject which has not even been mentioned, because it lies outside the scope of this book, is the matter of languages. Palmyra is unique among the cities of the Roman province of Syria in its retention of its own language, besides Greek, on official as well as private inscriptions.[235]

Mesopotamia

Interesting discoveries have been made, in recent years, at Kifrin and Bijan, two forts on the Middle Euphrates in the area of Ana, below Dura. They appear to have been occupied from Severan times till the middle of the third century.[236] Kifrin may be the Beccufrayn mentioned as an outpost in several papyri from Dura-Europos.[237]

---

[233] Senators: G. W. Bowersock, *Atti del colloquio internazionale AIEGL su Epigrafia e ordine senatorio, Roma 1981, Tituli* 5 (1982), 651–68. Equestrian officers: H. Devijver, *DRBE*, 183.

[234] As observed by Dr David Kennedy. [235] F. Millar, *JJS* 38 (1987), 155 f.

[236] Bijan: M. Gawlikowski, *Archiv für Orientforschung* 29/30 (1983/4), 207; *Sumer* 42 (1985), 15–26. Kifrin: A. Invernizzi, *DRBE*, 357–81; id., *Mesopotamia* 21 (1986), 53–84; F. A. Pennacchietti, ibid. 85–95. Other sites of interest in this area are Telbis and, in particular, Ana (Anatha), but no information has as yet been made available on the excavations there: *Iraq* 45 (1983), 202 f.; 47 (1985), 215 f. Ana: A. Oppenheimer with B. Isaac and M. Lecker, *Babylonia Judaica in the Talmudic Period* (1983), 26–9; D. L. Kennedy, *Iraq* 48 (1986), 103 f.; Kennedy and A. Northedge, in A. Northledge, *Excavations at Ana* (1988), 6–8; Kennedy and Riley, 114 f. Telbis is to be identified with 'Talbus' mentioned in the Talmud: b. Yoma 10a, cf. Oppenheimer, 445 f.

[237] P. Dura 46, 100, 101.

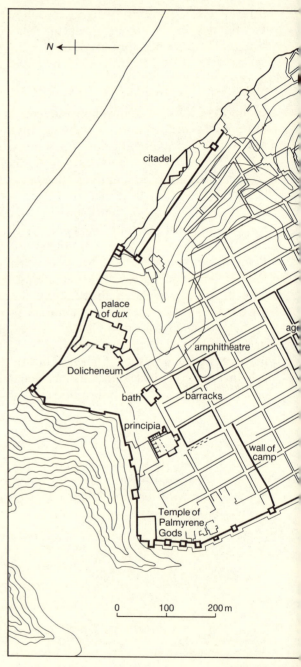

N

citadel

palace
of *dux*

Dolicheneum

amphitheatre

bath

barracks

principia

ag

wall of
camp

Temple of
Palmyrene
Gods

0   100   200 m

FIG. 2. Dura-Europ

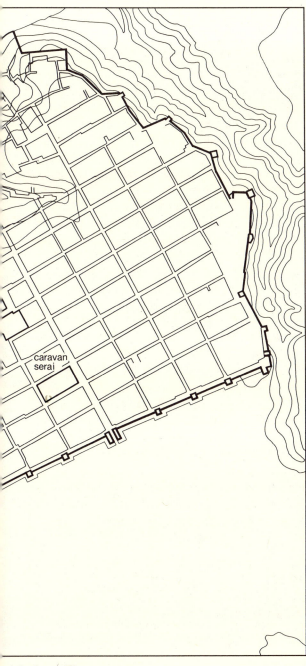

caravan
serai

with the military camp

The excavator of Kifrin considers these forts part of a *'limes* system': 'the Ana corridor actually received a new defensive structure. Advancing the border meant creating a new *limes* line . . .' I would suggest that these posts are better interpreted as stations controlling a vital section of the trade routes between Roman Syria and Persia.[238] The arguments put forward at the beginning of this chapter (above, p. 102) about the function of the river Rhine in Lower Germany may be applied here as well, with the difference that the Euphrates, unlike the Rhine, provided one of the most important trade routes of antiquity.

Sir Aurel Stein observes in his discussion of Ertaje (Biblada?), another site on the Euphrates: 'It was natural enough that the permanence of local conditions should have caused the Roman post of the time of Septimius Severus to be set up in the same place which had before served for a watch station on the Parthian highroad. . . . Its naturally strong position made it (i.e. Biblada) very suitable for keeping watch on the traffic following the route on the left bank of the river.' So far so good. But Stein proceeds: 'But when Biblada was chosen for a Roman frontier post provision had to be made for a fort more in keeping with the established system of defensive organization on Rome's borders.' There is an obvious contradiction between Stein's personal observations on the nature of the site through the ages and his *a priori* assumption that, as a Roman fort, it had an altogether different function in an imaginary established system of defensive organization.

The garrison of these posts, like that of Dura-Europos, very probably consisted of Palmyrene troops.[239] Appian, in his description of the empire, clearly implies that the Palmyrene sphere of activity extended as far as the Euphrates: '. . . and the region from the sea to the Euphrates river, that is to say Palmyra and the sand-desert of the Palmyrenes extends as far as the Euphrates.'[240] More important, there is good epigraphic evidence to show that Palmyra secured the caravan route from Palmyra to Hit on the Euphrates with her own troops serving under their own commanders. These were based at several stations on the Euphrates beyond Dura, notably at Ana and Gamla.[241]

---

[238] *Sir Aurel Stein's Limes Report*, ed. S. Gregory and D. Kennedy (1985), 187; pp. 145–182 of Stein's *limes* report deal with the sites on the Euphrates (comments on pp. 403–8).

[239] Gawlikowski, in his report on the excavations at Bijan (above, n. 236), is uncertain whether it was occupied by a Roman or a Palmyrene garrison. He notes, however, that some inscribed pottery fragments carry letters in Palmyrene, Latin, and a local script closely related to the Hatra inscriptions. He suggests therefore that the troops will have been recruited locally, partly in Palmyra. I see no reason to deny the obvious possibility that these were, in fact, Palmyrene troops.

[240] *Praef.* 2.

[241] *CIS* ii 3973 from Palmyra is a dedication by a Nabataean cavalryman, Obaidô son of

As early as AD 54 a dedication was set up by an association (of merchants) at Dura 'to Aphlad, god of the village of Anath on the Euphrates'.[242] It is uncertain when, if ever, there was a long-term military presence by Roman troops below Dura. Documents from Dura record a Roman unit stationed in 227 on the lower Khabur, further north; there was another not far away in 232.[243] The documents mention several places as Roman military posts.[244] Those in the region which can be identified are north of Dura.[245]

The fact that Palmyrene archers were stationed at Dura-Europos while it was nominally under Parthian control[246] is consistent with Pliny's description of Palmyra's position between the two empires. The unit was still there in AD 168 and 170/1 after the Romans had taken possession of Dura (in 165). Under Commodus a regular Roman unit is attested there.[247] Various legionary detachments are found at Dura during the reign of Caracalla and probably afterwards as well, but the unit permanently there, first attested in AD 208, was again a Palmyrene cohort, a milliary unit.[248] It was organized as a regular Roman unit with *dromedarii* attached to the centuries of infantry as was suitable in the region. The local commander at Dura was the *dux ripae*, a title which reminds one of the *praefecti ripae fluminis Euphratensis*,[249] *Danuvii* in Pannonia[250] and Moesia,[251] and *Rheni*.[252] These probably were military

Anamô, who served at Hîrta and in the camp at Ana (AD 132); J. Cantineau, *Syria* 14 (1933), 178–80. For the site of the road–station, Umm es-Selabith, Kennedy and Riley, 92 f. An inscription, perhaps of 188, mentions a cavalryman of the detachment of Ana and of Gamla (presumably = Gmeyla, a site 4 km. from Ana according to Cantineau): C. Dunant, *Le sanctuaire de Baalshamin* (1971), iii. 65, no. 51: ZB' BR MQY' DY 'QYM LH PRSY' B'BR['] | DY GML' W'N'. A fragmentary Palmyrene inscription of 225, found on the site of a road-station, mentions a *strategos* at Ana and Gamla, cf. Cantineau, 178–80. See the recent discussion of these and related inscriptions by Matthews, *JRS*, 168 f.; D. L. Kennedy, *Iraq* 48. For the Palmyra–Hit road see Stein's *limes* report (Gregory and Kennedy, 183–237). For Ana see also A. Northedge, *Sumer* 39 (1983), 235–9, with a survey of the classical and Islamic sources.

[242] Ann Perkins, *The Art of Dura-Europos* (1973), 77–9, pl. 31 (no text given); cited by Kennedy, *Iraq* 48.

[243] *Dura-Europos, Final Report*, v, part i, 26: the *cohors III Augusta Thracum* was stationed on the lower Khabur (no. 26), and a marriage contract of a soldier of the *cohors XII Palaestinorum* was deposited in Dura (no. 30). [244] Ibid., pp. 40, 44.

[245] Appadana, at the mouth of the Khabur; Birtha, at or near Zenobia. Unidentified are Castellum Arabum, Chafer Avira, and Magdala. Becchufrayn may be Kifrin, above, n. 236.

[246] Ibid. 24, n. 3.

[247] A *cohors II Ulpia Equitata*, ibid. 24, n. 5.

[248] The *cohors XX Palmyrenorum*; for its history, ibid. 26–38. For the vexillation see most recently *AE* 1984. 921.

[249] *ILS* 2709.

[250] *ILS* 2737.

[251] *AE* 1926. 80.

[252] Tacitus, *Hist.* iv 55, 64, cf. 26: 'dispositae per omnem ripam stationes quae Germanos vado arcerent'. The *praefecti* are discussed by J. F. Gilliam, *TAPhA* 72 (1941), 157–75. He compares them with other *praefecti*, those in command of the *ora maritima* in Mauretania (*CIL* xi

officers with a local, territorial command rather than one over a specific unit; moreover, the examples given all seem to entail combined activity on land and at sea or on the river. The same would have been true of the *dux ripae* attested at Dura-Europos before the middle of the third century. Gilliam points out that, unlike the later *duces*, this officer was subordinate to the governor of Syria. The Romans lost control of these stations by the mid-third century, as shown by the *Res Gestae Divi Saporis* which mentions among other things the capture of Anatha (i.e. Ana).

The excavations at Dura provide very valuable insights into the physical organization of an army unit in a previously existing town: the northern section was taken over and separated from the civilian part by a strong mud-brick wall.[253] Major structures include a *principia* of classic shape, an amphitheatre, baths, and the houses of the commander and the *dux ripae*.[254]

Hatra

Hatra lies some 50 kilometres west of ancient Assur and approximately 80 kilometres south-west of modern Mosul, 4 kilometres west of Wadi Tharthar.[255] It owed its prominence to its position as a caravan city on an important trade route connecting Seleucia-Ctesiphon with Singara and Nisibis.[256] This was the line of retreat followed by Jovian's army in 363. The route here had to leave the Tigris bend and pass on to desert land, according to Ammianus, 'because the land near the river was rough and difficult'.[257] Further west, however, 'there stretches a perfectly open valley plain as far as Hatra. With its flat surface, plentiful desert grazing, and a number of drinking wells this ground is particularly suited for caravan traffic with camels, though not for a large force.'[258]

5744); the *ora Pontica* (Pliny, *Ep.* x 21; 86a) and the *Baliorum insulae* (*ILS* 9196). To the evidence in Gilliam's paper add *AE* 1968. 321: a *praefectus ad ripam* (sc. *Rheni*) under Claudius and Nero.

[253] Cf. C. Hopkins, *The Discovery of Dura-Europos* (1979), 225.

[254] C. Hopkins and H. T. Rowell, *The Praetorium, Excavations at Dura-Europos, Prel. Report 5th Season of Work* (1934); *9th Season of Work*, i (1944), map at end of vol.; R. Fellmann, *Mélanges d'histoire ancienne et d'archéologie offerts à Paul Collart* (1976), 173–91, esp. 187–9.

[255] Excavations at Hatra; W. Andrae, *Handbuch der Archäologie* i (1936), 746; id., *Hatra, nach Aufnahmen von Mitgliedern der Expedition der Deutschen Orient-Gesellschaft* i, WVDOG 9 (1908); ii, WVDOG 21 (1912); *RE* vii, col. 2516 f. (M. Streck); H. J. W. Drijvers, *ANRW* ii 8 (1978), 804–13 (bibliography). For more recent explorations see the brief reports published in the current issues of *Sumer*. The fullest publication known to me is F. Safar and M. A. Mustafa, *Hatra, the City of the Sun God* (1974, Arabic). For a ballista from Hatra see D. Baatz, *Sumer* 33 (1977), 141 ff.

[256] Sir Aurel Stein, *JRAS* (1941), 299–316 = Gregory and Kennedy, ch. 2, with folding map at the end of vol. ii.

[257] xxv 78. 14. Cf. Stein, 303 f.

[258] Stein, loc. cit.

The soil provides grazing for camels but cannot be cultivated for lack of water. An inscription shows that caravans from Mesene passed through Hatra: 'Prayer to our Lord, to our Lady and to the sons of our Lords, to Sharon, to Baalshamin and to Atarate for (those) who come here from Mesene.'[259]

Herzfeld notes that two inscriptions of the twelfth century record the existence at Hatra of a caravanserai.[260] Andrae states that the caravan route from Baghdad to Mosul passed Hatra in his time. Other routes led from Hatra to Mejaddin, Der, and Ana. The route from Hatra to the Euphrates is indicated on the Peutinger Table.[261] These routes caused no problems for travellers who took care to maintain good relations with the nomads.[262]

What we know of the history of Hatra is derived from classical sources, Arab legends, and numerous inscriptions discovered in recent years.[263] Dio's first mention of Hatra is in connection with the Mesopotamian revolt of 116–17 against the new Roman occupation. Its participation is interesting. It may be another indication that patterns of trade were seriously disturbed by Trajan's conquest or, more likely, evidence of resistance to alien western domination and a closer control than Parthia had ever sought to exert.[264] Trajan failed to capture Hatra, 'although it was neither large nor prosperous'. Dio points out that the region has insufficient water, timber, and fodder for a large besieging army.[265] Some time between 197 and 199 Severus again attempted to take Hatra, since it had supported his rival Niger, according to Herodian.[266] Dio says that Severus twice tried to capture the town because it 'enjoyed great fame, containing as it did, a vast number of offerings to the Sun-god as well as vast sums of money'.[267] In this account Severus' motives are the desire for glory and pure avarice; if there were stategic considerations Dio ignores them. The difference between Dio's descriptions of Hatra in Trajan's time and when besieged by Severus has been emphasized and interpreted as proof that Hatra's growth was mainly in the second century.[268] Dio's remarks,

[259] A. Caquot, *Syria* 30 (1953), 235, no. 29: BGN MRN | WMRTN W BR M(RYN) | WSHRW W B'SM(YN) | W'TRT' 'L (MN) | DL'WL MHK' | BMSN.

[260] E. Herzfeld, *ZDMG* 68 (1914), 655–76, esp. 676.

[261] For the road system, L. Dillemann, *Haute Mésopotamie orientale et pays adjacents* (1962), 75 f.

[262] Andrae, *Hatra*, i 1; ii 4–5.

[263] Inscriptions: Drijvers, *ANRW* ii 8. 813–28. Arab legends: Hertzfeld, 657–9 and references in Drijvers, 816, n. 47.

[264] The latter is a suggestion by Dr David Kennedy.

[265] lxviii 31.   [266] iii 9. 3.

[267] lxxvi 12. 2: δόξα τε γὰρ τοῦ χωρίου ὡς καὶ πάμπολλα τά τε ἄλλα χρήματα καὶ τοῦ Ἡλίου ἀναθήματα ἔχοντος μεγάλη ἦν . . .

[268] Andrae, *Hatra* ii 1–2; Drijvers, 818.

however, are misunderstood if interpreted out of context. Moreover, there seem to be no clearly distinguishable stages in the development of the city.[269]

Dio states that Ardashir I also unsuccessfully attacked Hatra.[270] Three Latin inscriptions show that it was occupied by Roman troops by 238, and that the unit which formed the garrison was the *cohors IX Maurorum Gordiana*.[271] Before the discovery of these inscriptions Sir Aurel Stein had already shown that the highway from Nisibis to Hatra was marked by a series of structures south of the Sinjar range.[272] Maricq has plausibly argued that these date from the reign of Severus Alexander.[273] The Roman presence at Hatra is further attested by two unidentified portrait heads.[274] The Sassanian capture of Hatra is now firmly dated by the Greek Mani Codex to 240/1.[275]

What can be said of the reasons for imperial interest in the possession of Hatra? The only ancient opinion we have is Dio's view that Severus was motivated by the desire for glory and by avarice. For Trajan the reason is not far to seek. He intended to incorporate all of Mesopotamia, and it is only natural that he would not leave a crucial halting place undisturbed if it was hostile. If we are not satisfied with Dio's explanation the following line of thought suggests itself. Neither Severus nor Severus Alexander seriously attempted to occupy Babylonia permanently, but Severus extensively campaigned there,

---

[269] Herzfeld, 668, and Maricq, *Syria* 32 (1955), 268 n. 2 = *Classica et Orientalia*, 14.

[270] lxxx 3. 2; cf. Drijvers, 818 n. 56.

[271] D. Oates, *Sumer* 11 (1955), 39–43; A. Maricq, *Syria* 34 (1957), 288–96 = *Classica et Orientalia*, 17–25; *AE* 1958. 238. (*a*) An inscribed altar (AD 235): 'd(onum) d(edit) non(is) | iunis Seve|ro et Quin|tiano co(n)s(ulibus).' (*b*) Inscribed on a statue-base: 'Deo Soli Invicto | Q. Petr(onius) Quintianus | trib(unus) mil(itum) leg(ionis) I Part(hicae), | trib(unus) coh(ortis IX Maur(orum) | Gordianae | votum re|ligioni lo|ci posuit.' (*c*) Inscribed on the base of a statue of Hercules, as read by Maricq: 'Erculi Sanct(o) | pro salute domini nostri Au[g(usti) Q.] | Petronius Qu[in]|tianus, dom(o) [Nico]|midia, trib(unus) mil(itum) | leg(ionis) I P(arthicae), trib(unus) coh(ortis) IX | Gordianae, genio coh(ortis).' The commander of the unit who set up (*b*) and (*c*) had previously been tribune of the legion I Parthica. This was misunderstood by Oates, followed by Maricq, 290 = 19, and Drijvers, 825, who assume that the cohort of Mauri was part of the legion I Parthica. This, impossible in itself, is in no way suggested by the inscriptions.

[272] Stein, 307–313 with map on p. 301, corrected by Maricq, *Syria* 34, 293 = 22. For criticism of Stein's views on the Roman military organization of the area see L. Dillemann, *Haute Mésopotamie orientale et pays adjacents* (1962), 201–2, 208.

[273] Maricq, 292–5 = 21–4: a milestone of 231/2 shows that the road from Carrhae and Callinicum to Singara received attention at the time of Alexander's Persian campaign.

[274] J. M. C. Toynbee, *Sumer* 26 (1970), 231–5; *JRS* 62 (1972), 106–10; A. Invernizzi, *Mesopotamia* 21 (1986), 21–50, with further references in n. 2. There is no agreement on the identification.

[275] P. Colon. 4780: A. Henrichs and L. Koenen, *ZPE* 5 (1970), 120, 125–32; cf. X. Loriot, *ANRW* ii 2. 760–2; Drijvers, 827. The codex says that Mani received his second revelation on 23 April 240, the year in which Ardashir took Hatra and Shapur I was crowned.

whatever his reasons, and Alexander intended to do the same.[276] In wartime Hatra was a crucial halting-place for an army marching from Singara to Ctesiphon and back. In times of peace its possession was of great economic advantage. The Roman cohort which occupied the town for a brief period can never have been intended to halt a Persian invasion of Roman Mesopotamia. Nor is there any indication that its base was part of a 'system'. It was a modest unit asserting Roman control over an isolated and advanced desert post.

From this brief review of the evidence concerning the Roman military presence beyond the Khabur two conclusions may be drawn. First, the officer in command at Dura was responsible for movements on the river and along it. His title may be seen as an expression of the restricted nature of Roman involvement. Regular Roman units are to be found in this region only in the later second century and the first half of the third, and much of the evidence may relate to sporadic rather than permanent presence. This fits the observations made elsewhere that the Roman army in the East kept away from the desert until the reign of Septimius Severus and only expanded its presence in stages.

Roman control was exercised through Palmyra, at least from 165. This did not just take the form of protection of caravans, well-known through inscriptions from Palmyra; there was also a permanent occupation of key sites by regular military units, organized to conform to Roman standards. The existence of these units, rather than an informal desert police, made possible Palmyra's sudden rise to military independence between the 250s and the 270s. This development can only be understood in the framework of the period. It also shows by inference the central position occupied by Palmyra even in the preceding period.

The position of Hatra may have resembled that of Palmyra as a halting place in the desert, but with the important difference that neither Hatra nor Parthia would accept Roman control over this town as easily as Palmyra.

Roman rule in the region never entailed territorial control, but meant occupation of important sites along trade routes. Hatra was lost in 240/1, and Dura could not be kept much longer. With the destruction of Palmyra Rome demolished the means to oversee and regulate movements in the region beyond the province of Mesopotamia. The forces manning Diocletian's fort at Palmyra could not replace the Palmyrenes in the Orient. They were there only to guard the most important oasis between Damascus and the Euphrates. The wars of the

[276] For Severus' campaign see above, ch. I; for that of Alexander see Herodian vi 5. 1–2.

third century left all three centres in ruins. We have no way of knowing what were the consequences for the trade between the two empires.

We see again how flexible the Romans were in their organization of the frontier, in the second and third century no less than in the period of the Republic. They were not bound by fixed geographical limits, nor by firm or frozen administrative and legal concepts.

CONCLUSIONS

In Chapter II it could be shown that the provinces of Arabia and Judaea were not, before the fourth century, faced with very intense pressure from nomads, and even in the Byzantine period there is no evidence that this would have been a cause of genuine anxiety on the part of the authorities. In Judaea, on the other hand, there is evidence of serious trouble and violence which did require intervention, long after the suppression of the last major Jewish revolt against Roman rule. In many ways this is a unique case in Roman history, because elsewhere there is so little information on the non-Roman population of the provinces or those living just outside the province. It is clear also that Jewish resistance to Roman rule was determined by religious and ideological attitudes absent among other peoples. Yet the occasional evidence of social and economic unrest among the other elements of the population cannot be ignored.

The present chapter has considered the evidence regarding the organization of the Roman army in these two provinces, in southern Syria before the fourth century, and in parts of the Syrian desert and northern Mesopotamia. Our information is fragmentary. Given the scarcity of fully published excavations, we have gone on the principle that only epigraphical evidence should be used in an attempt at reconstructing the distribution of army units.

This may seem unjustified when there is so much archaeological material in both provinces. Yet there are good reasons for a restricted use of the archaeological information. First, the material consists almost exclusively of sites surveyed without excavation. The literature on these surveys is copious and easily accessible, but difficulties of interpretation have caused controversy on essential matters in both provinces. As long as there is no consensus on elementary points, notably the periods of occupation of entire areas by the Roman army, it is better not to rely on such information for a general reconstruction of developments. At the time of writing there are no fully published excavation reports of sites occupied before the Byzantine period. Archaeological surveys carried out without excavation do not produce totally reliable information on the dates of sites, as archaeologists themselves are the first to admit. Even if there was no controversy it would be premature to rely on this sort of information.[277] Second, the epigraphical evidence, which is reliable as far as it goes, shows a fairly consistent pattern in Judaea and Arabia. It is essential, in the interpretation of inscriptions, to distinguish between texts that attest a long-term presence and those that do not. Isolated documents produced by individuals or units in action or on patrol should not be interpreted as proving the existence of a permanent base in the vicinity. The same is true for inscriptions recording work carried out by legionary vexillations. Finally, it is one of the dilemmas of archaeological exploration that it appears to be extremely difficult to determine the function of a building, even if it has been dated and a plan can be drawn (which in desert areas is sometimes possible without excavation)—whereas one line of an inscription might make clear what the buildings were used for. The Arabian fort of Qasr Beshir, discussed below is a case in point.

It has been shown that the army has not left any record in the form of written documents in the desert areas earlier than the reign of Severus. This includes the desert in Transjordan, south of Petra. Here there are enough milestone texts to show that the army constructed the main road to the Red Sea, but even so milestones in this area are very rare. On the other hand, there is evidence of army presence in the settled areas of both provinces. Vexillations of legions and auxiliary units were established in and near cities and on key sites along the Roman road system. Evidence of legionary vexillations based in or near towns in the eastern provinces gradually accumulates and now appears to form a pattern. There seems, therefore, to be a fundamental difference in the deployment of units, particularly of legions, in the eastern frontier provinces as compared with those in the north and west. More information is needed, but it can now be said that many legionary detachments were permanently stationed near urban centres, away from the legionary headquarters, a phenomenon not encountered along the Rhine and Danube or in Britain.

The army in Arabia appears at first to have been an extension of the army in southern Syria, separately organized, in the urbanized

---

[277] Witness the case of the Petra–Gaza road. All the archaeologists who had just picked up pottery on the sites along the road agreed that it was not used after the first century. After several sites have been excavated they now agree that the road installations continued to be used throughout the second century.

Decapolis and in the north and central part of the former Nabataean kingdom. In southern Syria there is good evidence that legionary centurions were responsible for the organization and maintenance of road-security in the period of Marcus Aurelius and Commodus. The army in Judaea was also kept together in larger units and based in the regions which caused the major security problems: the towns, the area around Jerusalem, the main roads. There is little information on army units in Galilee, but that may be coincidence and no conclusions should be drawn from the absence of such evidence.[278] However, it is a significant fact that the best evidence of army presence in all provinces comes from towns. This will be further discussed in Chapter VI, below.

The road-system was organized more or less in one stage, in Arabia under Trajan and in Judaea under Hadrian. Thereafter milestones were set up at the initiative of the central government on special occasions. There is little to show routine maintenance, at least in so far as the milestone texts may serve as a record. Milestones, like army-units of the period, are found almost exclusively in the settled areas. While there is no doubt that Roman roads existed elsewhere the milestones were set up first and foremost between cities. The reasons for this are discussed below in Chapter VI.

Further north the pattern varies a little. Trajan attempted in vain to conquer Hatra, an important halting place in the desert. The various stages which bound Palmyra closer to Rome are hard to trace, but it is clear that the expedition against Parthia under Marcus Aurelius and Lucius Verus resulted in closer supervision of the Euphrates, with a unit occupying Dura. It is clear, however, that throughout the region the reign of Severus brought decisive changes involving increased Roman presence and organization.

While scepticism as regards the validity of conclusions based on archaeological material is necessary, one must be equally wary of over-confidence in the handling of inscriptions. Notably it is dangerous to draw conclusions from negative evidence, the absence of material. As far as it goes, the information gathered is totally consistent, the pattern is logical. The Roman army spent no time on certain activities which modern states consider elementary duties toward their citizens. Its primary function was to promote the security of Roman rule rather than the peace of the inhabitants of the provinces. Yet it is clear that the epigraphical evidence is limited in what it can tell us. It tells us, at best, what the distribution of the armed forces was at a specific date. Even if

---

[278] Note, for instance, the random information on a centurion at Capernaum: Matt. 8: 5–9; Luke 7: 2.

we had complete epigraphic information on the Roman army we should not know what the units were supposed to be doing or were planning to do. One can only speculate, which is no bad thing as long as one realizes that one is merely speculating.

Modern army intelligence does not usually tell us anything about enemy plans. For Roman historians, too, the most serious difficulty is that they know almost nothing about the enemies of the Romans. Here epigraphy does not help, of course. The enemies appear in occasional descriptions (by Roman historians) of battles; otherwise they remain shadows. Can one know what the aim of an army of occupation was if one knows virtually nothing of the occupied? Modern studies often turn the enemy into marionettes, or anonymous arrows on maps of frontier zones that merely record known Roman army camps. Those who studied the Roman army-sites in the nineteenth century naturally assumed that they served the same purpose as the forts of their own time, which did indeed form lines confronting an enemy across the border. For Roman forts they could not, or did not, attempt to conceive of a different pattern. The result is over-preoccupation with defence in general, and with frontier defence in particular. Hence the emphasis, in this and other chapters, on the need to consider the multitude of functions that fort-like buildings may have performed. They may have been police-posts, administrative centres, toll-stations, or hostels—all of which similar buildings elsewhere (Egypt) and in other periods (the Ottoman road-stations) are known to have been. Even where there was no active resistance to Roman rule the military installations may have served to impress the physical power of Roman authority on provincials.

We know nothing of the enemies—if there were any—of Roman troops in Arabia and in the western part of Syria, but in Judaea, at least, something is known. Josephus gives an impression of the climate of hostility in the century and a quarter from Pompey to AD 66. Talmudic sources give a glimpse of the army at work in the second century and afterward. In Judaea, at least, it can be shown that the local population was being policed by the Roman army.

At the beginning of this chapter it was argued that a widespread distribution of military inscriptions in the interior of a province may be interpreted as an indication that the troops served as an internal security force, even if there is no literary evidence of active resistance to Roman rule. In Arabia and those parts of Syria which were far from the frontier it may be concluded that extensive Roman presence represents a force which served to keep parts of the provinces themselves under control. It is in keeping with this elementary truth that the epigraphical and archaeological material gives a consistent impression that the army's role was to protect the rulers rather than the ruled.

IV

THE ARMY OF THE FOURTH CENTURY

THIS chapter will continue the theme of Chapter III. The relevant information on army organization will be analysed in an attempt to gain a better understanding of the function of the troops. During the late third and early fourth centuries, in the reigns of the tetrarchs and of Constantine, a major reorganization is known to have taken place. We shall have to consider both the nature of the reform and the change in the distribution of the troops in the east, notably the increased army presence in the desert. Numerous relatively small installations can be dated to this period. Their function will be discussed. The interpretation proposed, like other opinions expressed in this book is closely connected with the interpretation of the concept '*limes*' proposed in a recent paper and briefly restated in Chapter IX.[1] It is argued that *limes* nowhere means 'defended frontier' and never denotes any physical form of military organization. For the period under discussion, the fourth century, it can easily be shown that *limes* is an administrative concept. It means 'frontier district' and refers to an area under the military (as distinct from the civil) command of a *dux limitis*. This has important consequences for our understanding of the military organization in districts called *limites*, as attested in the provinces of Palaestina and Arabia. If a *limes* is not a defended frontier it is no longer necessary to interpret the military installations in such an area as connected with frontier defence and we are free to consider other hypotheses.

The Nature of the Evidence

For the period of Diocletian and afterwards we have three categories of information. Two of these are literary: the *Notitia Dignitatum*, which gives us information of a formal nature on the command structure and

---

[1] B. Isaac, *JRS* 78 (1988), 125–47.

about the distribution of army units at various undefined dates; and scattered references to military affairs in other works. The third consists of the material remains of forts and roads, sometimes datable with the help of inscriptions. In using this information we have to take into account the deficiencies of each source. The *Notitia* is full of information, but it is a bureaucratic list. The use of literary sources like Malalas or Zosimus as quarries without understanding their limitations—the one may be naive and uninformed, the other disingenuous—may lead to erroneous conclusions. The remains of military installations are of great interest, but it is a mistake to assume that one can easily understand why a particular site was chosen for a fort. In the first place, it is usually assumed that the military authorities selected the best possible sites for their installations, whatever their aims. Anyone with experience of armies and other bureaucracies knows that numerous factors regularly prevent the best possible decision from being taken, and this includes the selection of sites for permanent bases. But even if sites were chosen in a purely rational manner, military installations do not usually provide an explanation of why they were there in the first place—particularly if one does not know anything about enemy forces in the area or the native population to be kept under control. Furthermore, permanent army bases always change their function in the course of time.

The Reforms of Diocletian and Constantine

There are scattered references in literary sources to reforms made by Diocletian and Constantine. For example, Ammianus says in an incompletely preserved passage that Diocletian fortified Circesium when he organized the 'inner *limites*' near the borders with the barbarians as a response to the Persian raids into Syria.[2] It is not clear what was the nature of the reform apart from the fortification of one city. Malalas, in a poorly formulated statement, tells us that Diocletian built forts in the frontier districts from Egypt to the Persian frontier.[3] They were manned by border troops on guard duty under the command of *duces*.[4] *Stelae* were erected in honour of the emperor and Caesar;

---

[2] Ammianus, xxiii 5.1–2.

[3] *Chron.* xii (Dindorf, p. 308).

[4] A statement made by John Lydus, *de magistratibus* ii 11 (ed. Bekker, pp. 175 f.) suggests that this was an institution of Constantine. See on this passage J. C. Mann, *CBA Research Report 18: The Saxon Shore*, ed. D. E. Johnson (London, 1977), 12 and n. 8. Professor Mann translates: 'On the frontiers from Egypt as far as the borders of Persia, Diocletian built forts establishing in them frontier troops; and, choosing *duces*, he stationed one in each province within the ring of forts, with

this is plausibly taken as a reference to milestones, which have in fact
been found. There is, however, no other evidence to show that *duces*
were in command of the territorial army in all the frontier districts
before Constantine. Zosimus says that Diocletian made the empire
impenetrable to barbarians by stationing troops in cities, *castella* and
towers in the frontier zones,[5] but that Constantine demolished this
system by withdrawing the troops from the frontier to cities in the
interior which did not need them.[6]

All these statements are rather vague. They do not tell us more than
that Diocletian was responsible for the construction and manning of
military installations in the frontier areas. Zosimus clearly exaggerates
the merits of Diocletian's work—the frontier never was impenetrable—
and he is hostile toward Constantine and must therefore be mistrusted.
His words are echoed by the equally false statement of Procopius on
Justinian's work: 'But, to speak briefly, he has made impregnable at the
present time all the places which previously lay exposed to assailants.
And as a result of this, Mesopotamia is manifestly inaccessible to the
Persian nation.'[7] Diocletian's activities may have had a substantial
impact, but the fact is that in the East there had always been garrisons
in cities and there were troops in border towns before Diocletian and
after Constantine.[8]

Roads and Military Installations

Van Berchem has convincingly shown that, in Syria, Diocletian's
organization may be recognized in the *strata Diocletiana*, a road from
north-east Arabia and Damascus to Palmyra and the Euphrates, with
its installations. These in turn are listed with their units in the *Notitia*.
He further observed that another road from Damascus to Palmyra
which runs parallel to it and north of the Rawaq ridge is part of the
same system. This road and its installations are less well-known, but
there is at least one interesting inscription from H. el Abyad.[9] In

large numbers of men as a mobile reserve. And he set up inscriptions to the Augustus and the
Caesar on the frontier of Syria.'

[5] ii 34. 1.

[6] Aurelius Victor, *liber de Caesaribus* 41. 12, and John Lydus, *de mag.* ii 11, ed. Bekker, 176 f.,
mention army reform under Constantine, but do not add anything helpful.

[7] *De aed.* ii 4. 21, trans. H. B. Dewing, Loeb.

[8] Zosimus' statement is untrue for the West as well; see e.g. the building activity on the Rhine
under Constantine: J. E. Bogaers and C. Rüger, *Der Niedergermanische Limes* (1974), 20 f. However,
we do not know the state of the army in the East after the third-century crisis and before Diocletian
took things in hand. His policy may have seemed an impressive innovation at the time.

[9] For this road, briefly, A. Poidebard, *La trace de Rome dans le désert de Syrie* (1934), 40 f.

Arabia, as in Syria, numerous milestones are found on roads mostly constructed earlier.[10] In Syria-Palaestina only one Diocletianic milestone has been found on the Legio–Scythopolis road, the strategic route linking the coastal plain with the north-east.

So far five forts in the entire region are firmly dated by tetrarchic inscriptions:

(1) Qasr Beshir, north-east of Lejjun, on the eastern route in Arabia, dated by an inscription of 293–305.

(2) Deir el Kahf, on the *Strata Diocletiana*, north of Azraq, dated by an inscription of 306.[11]

(3) An inscription from Palmyra, AD 293–303, records the construction of a '*castra*' there.[12]

(4) An inscription dated 293–305 was found among rubble near the gate of the fort of Yotvetah in the southern ʿAravah (ad Dianam of the Peutinger Table, Ar. Ghadhyan).

(5) An inscription from el Qantara on the coast-road near the Egyptian border dated to 288.[13]

Archaeological evidence suggests that many more forts were established in these years, but for the present it will suffice to cite only the epigraphic evidence.[14] That is not sufficient to justify attributing all the fourth-century forts and major troop transfers in the region to these years, but it certainly proves that there was a good deal of activity in the arid zone where previously there seems to have been less of a permanent Roman presence.

The pattern is simple. Apart from Lejjun (Betthoro of the *Notitia*),[15] the legionary bases are all found along the major roads, and many of them are still based in towns: Aela,[16] Udruh (not identifiable in the

[10] For a summary, Isaac and Roll, *Milestones in Judaea* i. 94 f. New tetrarchic milestones have been found in the desert area south and south-east of Bostra, at Hallabat, D. L. Kennedy, *Archaeological Explorations* (1982), 162; on the road from Umm el Jemal to Umm el Qottein (dated 293–305), S. T. Parker, *ZPE* 62 (1986), 256–8. An important road-inscription from Azraq has recently been rediscovered and published, S. Gregory and D. L. Kennedy, *Sir Aurel Stein's Limes Report* (1985), 416 f. See also D. L. Kennedy and H. I. MacAdam, *ZPE* 65 (1986), 231–6, for a milestone on the Bostra–Quttein road.

[11] H. C. Butler et al., *The Publications of the Princeton University Archaeological Expeditions to Syria in 1904–5 and 1909*, iii A 2 (1910), no. 228, 126 f. For the fort see also the observations by S. T. Parker, *Romans and Saracens* (1986), 21–4.

[12] *CIL* iii 133.

[13] *CIL* iii 13578. To the list of Diocletianic forts may now perhaps be added that at Aela, below, n. 16.

[14] Parker, *Romans and Saracens*, 135–43, assigns numerous forts in Arabia to the reign of Diocletian.

[15] From the available maps and publications I have not been able to form a clear idea of the original function of this large fort. Dr Kennedy informs me that he cannot explain it either, agriculture being limited in the area and the villages modest and few in number.

[16] The site of Aela is now under excavation. Some results have been described in D. Whitcomb,

Notitia), Bostra, Danaba (probably on the road from Damascus to Palmyra), Palmyra itself, Oresa, Sura, and finally at Circesium on the Euphrates.[17] The old road-system from the Red Sea to the Euphrates was strengthened. The legions in Judaea and Raphanaea near the coast were withdrawn, and so were those along the Euphrates where this river had ceased to be the border in northern Syria.

The tetrarchic *castra* at Palmyra, the base of the legion I Illyricorum, has been excavated.[18] The *principia*, apparently established in a former sanctuary, is one of the best preserved anywhere, and the quarter where it is situated is clearly separated from the rest of the town by a wall. The construction was, apparently, contemporary with the erection of the fourth-century town wall. The remains, now lost, of a military camp were seen outside the wall at the time of the construction of the modern village in the 1930's.[19] The position of the legion there is not really comparable with that of military units based in cities, for Palmyra in this period was no longer the flourishing trade centre it had been until the time of Zenobia. The best comparison might be with Jerusalem, where a legion was permanently based following the destruction of the city as the Jewish capital. However, unlike the Jews in AD 70, it is not very likely

Aqaba, 'Port of Palestine on the China Sea' (1988). The site is north of the Old Town with its late medieval castle. The excavator dates the fort which he found to the Early Islamic period, but amongst the building material was found a fragmentary Latin inscription (Tetrarchic or House of Constantine). The outlines of the camp very much resemble those of Lejjun but it is half size, if the plan published is correct. Twenty minutes NE of Aqaba Musil saw a field of ruins still called 'Ila', of which he wrote (*Arabia Petraea* (1907), i, 259f.): 'Das Klima ist sehr ungesund, weil die Westwinde keinen Zugang haben; das Wasser ist schlecht. Zu jener Zeit bestand die dortige Bestazung aus 220 Soldaten, von denen jedoch zwei Drittel fieberkrank waren.' The Roman garrison may have been better organized. Nelson Glueck found remains of at least one church of the Byzantine period; cf. 'Explorations in Eastern Palestine', ii, *AASOR* 15 (1935), 47; iii, *AASOR* 18–19 (1939), 1 ff. A Greek grave inscription dated 555 was published by M. Schwabe, *HTR* 64 (1953), 49–55. For discussion of the military organization of Southern Palestine, Y. Tsafrir, *IEJ* 36 (1986), 77–86.

[17] *Not. Dig. Or.* xxxv 24. For all these sites see again the references in the *DE* s.v. *limes*. Oresa is probably to be identified with Taybe, cf. D. Kennedy and Riley, 136f.: as observed by the authors, the fort there is rather small, estimated at 2.25 ha./5.6 acres, about half the size of Lejjun, Udruh, and Palmyra. For Circesium, A. Oppenheimer *Babylonia Judaica* (1983), 378–82. In the first and second centuries AD it was known as the village of Phalga or Phaliga. In AD 121 there was a Parthian frontier fort here commanded by a *phrourarchos*, M. I. Rostovtzeff and C. Bradford Welles, parchment no. X 11. 3–6, *The Excavations at Dura-Europos: Preliminary Report of the Second Season, October 1928–April 1929*, ed. P. V. C. Baur and M. I. Rostovtzeff (1931), 201–15.

[18] K. Michałowski, *Palmyre, fouilles polonaises 1961* (1963); id., *Palmyre v, fouilles polonaises 1964* (1966); M. Gawlikowski, *Le temple Palmyrénien* (1973); id., *AA* 83 (1968), 289–304; R. Fellmann, *Mélanges d'histoire ancienne et d'archéologie offerts à P. Collart* (1976), 178–91; M. Gawlikowski, *Palmyre viii, Les principia de Dioclétien: Temple des Enseignes* (1984).

[19] See the inscriptions of the *coh. I Fl. Chalc. Equit.*: *IGLS* vii 4016 and Gawlikowski, *Palmyre* viii, pp. 125 f., nos. 40 and 41; Seyrig, *Syria* 14 (1933), 166.

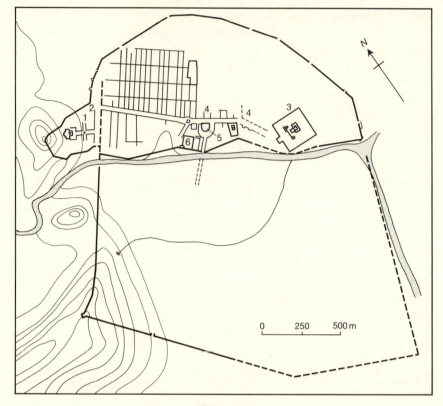

FIG. 3. Palmyra: plan

1 Military quarter
2 Wall between military quarter and rest of town
3 Temple of Bel
4 Grand Colonnade
5 Theatre
6 Agora

that the Palmyrenes were thought to constitute a threat to Roman control after their defeat by Aurelian. Palmyra, even after it ceased to function as a trade centre with a substantial population, still retained its importance as an oasis and as the nodal point of roads in the Syrian desert. It is therefore better to see this as one of the major stations on the line from Damascus to Sura than as a legion controlling the old town. While the *principia* is known very well the remainder of the base is not very clearly defined. No barracks have been excavated. According to Procopius Justinian strengthened Palmyra, and Malalas states that he made it a base of *limitanei*.[20]

Danaba superseded the fortress at Raphanaea. Samosata and

[20] Procopius, *de aed.* ii 11. 10–12, unaware of the city's past, thought it had always been a fortress built to prevent Saracen raids. Malalas, 425 f., relates that this was the place where David

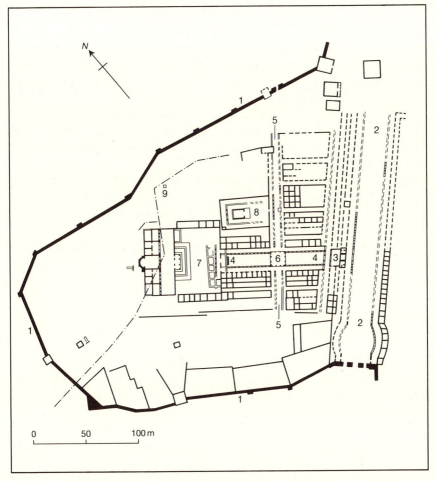

FIG. 4. Palmyra: the military quarter

1 Tetrarchic wall	4 Via Praetoria	7 Principia
2 Transverse Colonnade	5 Via Principalis	8 Temple of Allat
3 Porta Praetoria	6 Tetrapylon	9 Source

Zeugma were replaced as legionary bases by Oresa and Sura at an unknown date. Oresa (Taybe) lies on a hill on the Palmyra–Sura road at a crossroads with an east–west road.[21] Udruh is listed together with

defeated Goliath; hence Solomon founded the town, also for the defence of Jerusalem. Such passages show the extent to which these authors were ignorant of the history of cities, as well as their lack of insight in military geography.

[21] For Oresa, Waddington, no. 2631 (a civilian inscription of AD 134); for the site, Poidebard, *Trace de Rome*, 79 and pl. lxxi.

other places of Palaestina Tertia on a Byzantine administrative inscription from Beer Sheva.[22] The *Chronicon Paschale* mentions 'the eastern *limes* from Arabia and Palaestina to the *castrum* of Circesium', implying that this formed the end of the line of fortresses.[23] The *Chronicon* here tells a curious story about the emperor Decius who introduced lions in the area against Saracens.[24]

Other legions were based at nodal points of the road-system in Mesopotamia, at Singara and, perhaps, Bezabde.[25] With the loss of territory to the Persians in 363 these were withdrawn to Cepha and Constantina.[26]

Further north along the Euphrates the old stations of Melitene, Satala, and Trapezus were legionary bases.[27] These lay along the strategic north-south route from the Black Sea to Northern Syria. Melitene and Satala had also been legionary bases before Diocletian. At Trapezus the new legion I Pontica was stationed in the tetrarchic period.[28] It was an important port where troops of dubious efficacy had been based before, with disastrous results.[29] Aela on the Red Sea and Trapezus were comparable localities, garrisoned ports at the end of a road. The importance of Trapezus had been seen at the time of Corbulo's campaign, when the Roman army received supplies over sea through Trapezus and thence over land.[30] Aela, however, may have been more important as a caravan station than as a port. Sailing in the gulf is difficult: 'Anchorages are few, and most of them are exposed to southerly winds. Native shipping makes little use of the gulf, partly because the coast is barren and desolate, with very few inhabitants, but mainly because the northerly winds which prevail for the greater part of the year raise considerable swells.'[31] It may be noted that Aela twice

[22] C. Clermont-Ganneau, *RB* NS 3 (1906), 412–32, esp. 417–19; Alt, *Inschriften*, no. 2, p. 8; and cf. above, n. 17. Another inscription mentions a site which may be Betthoro (Lejjun), but there are other possibilities, Alt, no. 3, pp. 10 f. These inscriptions are undated, but similar texts from Arabia and Cyrenaica are of the reign of Anastasius. For the site of Danaba, probably on the road from Damascus to Palmyra, *RE* iv 2083 f.; *DE* ii 1463.
[23] *Chronicon Paschale* 504 f. (Dindorf).
[24] Ammianus, xviii 7. 5, also has peculiar information about lions along the Euphrates.
[25] Singara had been a legionary base since the annexation of Mesopotamia by Septimius Severus. At that time the other base was probably at or near Rhesaena. It has been suggested that Bezabde was a legionary base on the evidence of Ammianus, xx 7, 1, but this is quite uncertain.
[26] *Not. Dig. Or.* xxxvi 29 and 30.   [27] *Not. Dig. Or.* xxxviii 13, 14, 16.
[28] *CIL* iii 6746. For Trapezus, *DE* iv 1310 f. A. Bryer and D. Winfield, *The Byzantine Monuments and the Topography of the Pontos* i (1985), 179–250 and ii, pls. 105–192.
[29] For the Pontic stations see also below, ch. V.
[30] Tacitus, *Ann.* xiii 39. 1.
[31] Geographical Handbook series, *Western Arabia and the Red Sea*, June 1946, Naval Intelligence Division, 91. A ship which had sailed from Aela to Ethiopia is mentioned in the *Ammonii Monachi Relativo*, ed. Combefis, pp. 107 f.

played a role in a campaign of conquest: it served as springboard for the Islamic conquest of Palestine; and the capture of Aqaba was a key element in Lawrence's campaign in the First World War. In both cases the actual conquest of Palestine took place from the south-west.

In Arabia an inscription recently rediscovered at Azraq shows that the route from Bostra through Wadi Sirhan to Jawf was somehow organized by the army under Diocletian.[32] It contains the interesting phrase 'praetensione colligata mil(itibus) suis ex leg(ione) III Kyr(enaica)'. This seems to mean that a connection was formed between the legionary base at Bostra and an outpost,[33] evidence that the route was kept under control at the time.[34]

The legions in this period were smaller than before, but in the eastern provinces at least, the fourth-century reforms may have made little difference since they were usually split up in vexillations long before Diocletian, as noted in Chapter III.[35] The change was in the command structure rather than the number of men in each unit. Basically following the old system the most important units were stationed on the strategic north-south route from the Black Sea to the Red Sea and between Damascus and the Euphrates. This allowed both lateral and eastward movement wherever required. Ammianus' account makes it quite clear that the legions were still, in the fourth century, the backbone of the army.[36] Auxiliary units, also reduced in size, were stationed along the routes in the arid zone, east of the *via Traiana*, in the 'Aravah north of Elath, along the *Strata Diocletiana*, and elsewhere.

[32] Kennedy and MacAdam, *ZPE* 60 (1985), 97–108; suggestions for an improved reading and discussion by M. Speidel, *Historia* 36 (1987), 213–21. See also Kennedy and MacAdam, *ZPE* 65, 231–6. Speidel's reading: '[D.n. Diocletiano ---- | ------]| per mil(ites) fortiss(imos) suos | legg(ionum) XI Kl(audiae) et VII Kl(audiae) | et I Ital(icae) et IIII Fl(aviae) et | I Ill(yricorum), praetensione | colligata mil(itibus) suis ex | leg(ione) III Kyr(enaica). A Bostra | Basianis m(ilia) p(assuum) LXVI et | a Basienis Amat(a) LXX | et ab Amata Dumata | m(ilia) p(assuum) CCVIII.'

[33] Speidel, *Historia*, 219 f. The inscription is of the same general type as the famous republican milestone from the *via Appia*, *CIL* i² 638. For the unique term *praetensio*, presumably a synonym of *praetentura* which in the fourth century indicated an outpost, cf. Ammianus xiv 3. 2; xxv 4. 11; xxxi 8. 5, and see discussion by J. Šašel, *Museum Helveticum* 31 (1974), 225–9.

[34] As concluded by Speidel, who goes too far, it seems, when he speaks of 'the frontier strategy of *praetensione colligare*'.

[35] For the occupation of Lejjun, J. Lander and S. T. Parker, *Byzantinische Forschungen* 9 (1982), 185–210. They note that the fortress measures 240 by 190 m. (4.6 ha.), between 20–25% of a full-sized legionary *castra*. It may therefore have held 1,500 men. See in general R. P. Duncan-Jones, *Chiron* 8 (1978), 541–60, for the strength of army units in this period. As early as the reign of Hadrian, the *cohors milliaria* based at Hebron had been split up. In Judaea and Arabia there are numerous inscriptions that refer to vexillations, an indication that the legions were not permanently based in one fortress.

[36] Ammianus always refers to legions when he gives information on units that participated in battles, e.g. xx 6. 8: Singara defended by two legions with local troops.

As observed by Professor Mann, 'the keynote of Diocletian's army reforms was consolidation rather than innovation. By the time that he abdicated, in 305, the frontier system of the principate could still be discerned, strengthened and intensified but not essentially altered.'[37] It follows that we must be very cautious in ascribing a new strategy—about which we know, in fact, nothing—to these years. For the army of the late empire the same must be said as for the early empire: we only confuse the issues by introducing vague or incorrect concepts, in particular the popular notions of 'defence in depth' and of the 'Bewegungsheer', the 'mobile army'. The latter term somehow conveys the impression that the army was in constant motion, an army of Flying Dutchmen on land. Worse, it suggests by contrast that the army of the early empire was static. This it clearly was not, although each unit had its permanent base.[38] In the late empire it is better to speak of a field army and of territorial troops.

The objections to the notion of a 'grand strategy' apply equally to the concept of 'defence in depth'. These terms suggest that the Romans were capable of realizing in practice what they could not verbally define: no evidence of a Roman strategy of defence in depth is found in any explicit ancient statement. The concept of 'defence in depth' interprets as a defensive system a complex of physical remains that may have served other purposes. We must beware of imposing on inadequate evidence an interpretation that seems attractive only because of our limited knowledge. In the East the same is true, it seems, regarding the interpretation of remains in the Negev and in Transjordan: we do not know enough about the development of settlement and relationships with the nomads to formulate definite conclusions.

In discussing the military occupation of Transjordan two sources are frequently cited. Eusebius says of the Arnon (Wadi Mujib) 'that it is

---

[37] Mann, *CBA*, 11.

[38] The term 'Bewegungsheer' was introduced by A. Alföldi, *Der Untergang der Römerherrschaft in Panonien*, i (1924), 89, and appears in the title of D. Hofmann, *Das spätrömische Bewegungsheer und die Notitia Dignitatum*, Epigraphische Studien 78 (1969). Note the clarification on p. 1: 'Seit der Herrschaft des Kaisers Augustus, der zu einer rein defensiven Militärpolitik überging, war die römische Reichsarmee . . . so gut wie ausschliesslich auf die Grenzen des Imperiums verteilt.' Various peoples, such as the Britons, the Dacians, and the Parthians would have been surprised at the first statement. That the armies were concentrated on the border is true only for part of northern Europe. In the East six out of ten legions were based far from the border and, as argued above, many detachments may permanently have been outposted. In the late empire the legions were moved closer to the border. At all times parts of the army were transferred, if necessary, and kept in the field when this was thought desirable. A random example: in 218 the army in Syria was kept in tents throughout the winter 'in spite of apparent peaceful conditions' (Dio lxxviii 28. 2 [iii 436]; Herodian v 6).

guarded everywhere by army posts because it is a fearful place'.[39] Ammianus describes Arabia as follows:

Bordering on this region (sc. Palestine) is Arabia, which on the other side adjoins the (land of the) Nabataeans, a country which offers an abundant variety of goods and is full of strong fortresses and castles which the ancient inhabitants with careful vigilance built in appropriate and well-secured ravines to repel raids of the neighbouring peoples.[40]

Eusebius merely notes that there were many forts guarding the Arnon because it is a terrifying place. This nobody would deny, but it does not tell us anything about strategy, defence in depth, or defence of any other kind. What it shows is that this was a difficult area that had to be policed thoroughly because of the presence of bandits.

Ammianus cannot be interpreted as referring to the Arabia of his days. His description of the East in this chapter is a mixture of 'geographic rhetoric' and ancient history. The reference to Nabataeans is anachronistic.[41] No ruler after Trajan is mentioned, and the Arabian forts are said to have been constructed by the 'ancient inhabitants'. His statement has therefore no contemporary value—but it has been used out of context by historians of the Roman provinces.

Nor is there any valid reason to describe as a system of defence in depth the remains farther north, notably the *strata Diocletiana*. Though usually interpreted as a fortified line, it might equally well, or better, be described as a military road linking southern Syria with the Euphrates. The same is true of the heavily manned frontier in Cappadocia, which, to my knowledge, was rarely crossed by any enemy force. In the late empire, as before, troops were based there in order to permit optimal movement, lateral and into Armenia.[42]

---

[39] *Onomasticon* (ed. Klostermann) 10. 15 ff.: Ἀρνών . . . δείκνυται δὲ εἰς ἔτι νῦν τόπος φαραγγώδης σφόδρα χαλεπὸς ὁ Ἀρνωνᾶς ὀνομαζόμενος, παρατείνων ἐπὶ τὰ βόρεια τῆς Ἀρεοπόλεως, ἐν ᾧ καὶ φρούρια πανταχόθεν φυλάττει στρατιωτικὰ διὰ τὸ φοβερὸν τοῦ τόπου.

[40] xiv 8. 13: 'Huic Arabia est conserta, ex alio latere Nabataeis contigua, opima varietate commerciorum, castrisque oppleta validis et castellis, quae ad repellendos gentium vicinarum excursus sollicitudo pervigil veterum per opportunos saltus erexit et cautos.'

[41] It may indicate, however, that Ammianus speaks in the present passage only of the Arabia of his own times, which did not include the southern part of the old province. The cities he mentions are in the Arabia of his own day.

[42] It is remarkable that Poidebard himself describes the sites he explored as stations along a road system without recognizing their actual functions. 'Les étapes de la route sont jalonnées par de postes plus importants situés à xxx mp (45 km.) environ de distance. Les étapes moindres ou postes intermédiaires sont à distance de x ou xx mp (15 ou 30 km.) ... Le relevé fait au cours de nos recherches établit que c'était la règle général des étapes romaines sur tout le limes romain de Syrie: étapes de xxx mp (45 km.) correspondant au étapes actuelles des caravanes chamelières (50 km. environ).' (*Trace de Rome*, 368 f.)

The Function of the Smaller Installations

Arabia

The fort of Qasr Beshir is identified by an inscription of AD 293/305:[43] '[Diocletian, Maximian, Constantius, Valerius in the ablative] castra praetorii Mobeni a fundamentis Aurelius Asclepiades praeses provinciae Arabiae perfici curavit.[44] This can only mean that we have here a fortified *praetorium*.[45] (It has been remarked that 'Mobeni' shows that the name Moab was still current in the area.[46]) The meaning of the term *praetorium* is well-known. In the early principate at the latest it lost its military associations and became a term for a residence of a provincial governor in town or along a Roman road.[47] In this sense it is used in Greek in the New Testament for the former royal palaces in Jerusalem[48] and in Caesarea.[49] *Praetoria* soon came to be used by governors on official journeys, where they would dispense justice and maintain contact with the inhabitants of the provinces. This is obvious from fourth-century legal texts, for instance: 'The *praetoria* of judges and houses used for judicial purposes ought to have been appropriated to public ownership and use.'[50]

[43] For the chronology, T. D. Barnes, *The New Empire of Diocletian and Constantine* (1982), 4. For the building, S. T. Parker (ed.), *The Roman Frontier in Central Jordan* (1987), 457–95, Kennedy and Riley, 176–8.   [44] *CIL* iii 14149.

[45] Brünnow and Domaszewski, *Die Provincia Arabia*, ii (1905), 49–59, esp. 58 f., and Musil, *Arabia Petraea*, i 57, convinced that they were faced with a fort which formed part of a system of defence, tried to explain away their difficulty by conjecturing that an early *praetorium* had been replaced by the extant building. Parker, *Romans and Saracens*, 54 f., rightly points out that the language of the inscription proves that this was a new building. Indeed his investigations have revealed no traces of an earlier one. Other scholars had no difficulty in accepting the inscription as it stands, e.g. H. Vincent, *RB* (1898), 436: 'La désignation de *praetorium* dans le texte de l'entrée caractérise ce château'. Cf. R. Cagnat, *l'Armée romaine d'Afrique* (1912), 578 n. 7: 'Ce mot paraît désigner en ce cas, non pas un établissement militaire, mais un gîte d'étape comme on en construisait le long des grandes routes pour servir d'abri aux officiers et aux fonctionnaires en voyage.' The identification of what may have been stables in the building would suit such a structure perfectly well, cf. V. A. Clark, *The Roman Frontier in Central Jordan* (1987), 476, 493. Mrs Shelagh Gregory, in a discussion of the structure in a draft of her Ph.D. thesis, notes that there would have been stabling for 69 horses, which would suit a garrisoned road-station better than a purely military fort, the garrison or the commander of which would in any case presumably have been mentioned in the inscription. However, according to Mrs Gregory, the manger recesses may also be explained as cupboards.

[46] Vincent, 436.

[47] Mommsen, *Hermes* 35 (1900), 437–42 = *Ges. Schr.* vi 128–33; H.-G. Pflaum, 'Essai sur le cursus publicus', 222 f. See further *RE* xii 2537; M. Rostovtzeff et al., *Preliminary Report of the Excavations at Dura-Europos, Ninth Season* iii (1952), 83–94; R. Egger, *Öst. Ak. Wien*, Phil.-hist. Kl. S.-b. 250 (1966), no. 4; T. Pekáry, *Untersuchungen zu den römischen Reichsstrassen* (1968), 10, 164 f.; R. MacMullen, *Athenaeum* 54 (1976), 26–36. See also S. Mitchell, *Anatolian Stud.* 28 (1978), 93–6, esp. 95.

[48] Matt. 27: 27; Mark 15: 16; John 18: 28, 33, 19: 9.

[49] Acts 23: 35: 'Herod's praetorium.'

[50] *Cod. Theod.* xv 1.8 (2 December 362): 'Oportuit praetoria judicum et domos judiciarias

A law of 17 January 400 decrees that all judges should keep away from *praetoria* when the civil governor is in residence.[51] Another, of 23 November 407, decrees that civil governors may lodge in *palatia* in cities far from the public highway, if there is no *praetorium*.[52]

The connection with Roman military roads is particularly clear in an inscription of AD 61 from Thrace: 'tabernas et praetoria per vias militares fieri iussit per Ti. Iulium Iustum proc(uratorem) provinciae Thrac(iae).'[53] In the course of time buildings like these came to be guarded and administered by soldiers and were fortified.[54] In desert areas where nomad raids and banditry were endemic that was clearly a necessity. Several place-names derive from the term *praetorium*.[55] Many *praetoria* were renovated or first constructed in the period of the tetrarchs.[56]

The inscription identifying Qasr Beshir as a *praetorium* also shows that the term *castra* does not by itself define the purpose of a structure.[57] It is used in combination with another term, in this case *praetorium*, which specifies the building's actual function. Moreover, in the Latin of this period *castra* does not necessarily have a military meaning, but can simply mean 'halting-place' or camp.[58] This has implications for other buildings named *castra*.

There were not many *praetoria* in the provinces, and these were either in cities or along main roads. Once we have recognized that Beshir was a *praetorium*, we can see the significance of the fact that it lay on a main road, as indicated on Brünnow and Domaszewski's maps (but not on maps in any modern studies). This is the road through the desert, east of the Trajanic road. Only a few milestones have been found on it, and those are all south of Wadi Hasa.[59] But where a *praetorium* is found on a road, we may expect the full organization of the *cursus publicus*, which

publico iuri adque usui vindicari.' Cf. xv 1. 35 (396): 'Quidquid de palatiis aut praetoriis iudicum aut horreis aut stabulis et receptaculis animalium publicorum ruina labsum fuerit id rectorum facultatibus reparari praecipimus . . .'

[51] *Cod. Theod.* vii 8. 6: 'Cunctos iudices scire volumus a praetoriis ordinariorum iudicum his praesentibus abstinendum.'

[52] *Cod. Theod.* vii 10. 2: 'Ordinarii iudices in remotis ab aggere publico civitatibus, si praetoria non sint, metu legis adempto, quae de palatiis lata est, in aedibus, et etiamsi palati nomine nuncupantur, commanendi habeant facultatem.' This is an amendment to vii 10. 1 of 10 July 405 where it is stated that no one may lodge in *palatia*.

[53] *CIL* iii 6123 (14207. 34). For a *praetorium* built in Aenos, on the Thracian coast, in the fifth or sixth century, I. Kaygusuz, *Epigraphica Anatolica* 8 (1986), 67.

[54] Pflaum, 'Essai', 354–62.   [55] *RE* xxii 1634–9.

[56] References in MacMullen, *Athenaeum*, n. 33.

[57] The genitive following 'castra' is to be considered a regular explicative.

[58] e.g. Jerome, who uses 'castra' to translate Greek 'stathmos': Eusebius, *Onomastikon*, ed. Klostermann, 145, 1–2. Note the *castra* mentioned in the inscription from Coptus.

[59] Apart from Thomsen, *ZDPV* 40 (1917), no. 176, east of Lejjun.

included *stationes, mansiones,* and *mutationes,* familiar from the *Itineraria* in East and West.[60] It is conceivable that a *praetorium* which lay in such an isolated spot as Qasr Beshir was not as restricted in its use as those near cities. We may guess that it also served as a fortified road-station for passing troops.

The police stations along Roman roads were called *praesidia* (Greek: *phrouria*).[61] They are found all over the empire and not necessarily in frontier districts.[62] A πραισίδιον at Ein Gedi is mentioned in P. Yadin 11, one of the documents of the Babatha archive. It is described as situated on a street or road in the village and flanked on two sides by the soldiers' quarters (σκηναί).[63] It was manned by soldiers of the *cohors I milliaria Thracum* and commanded by a centurion.[64]

At Qasr el-Uweinid the following inscription has been found, recording the construction of a Severan police-station with a bath: 'Castellum et ⟨s⟩ praesidium | Severianum. Vexillatio leg(ionis) III Cyrenic(ae) (*sic*)| baln(eum) Mucia[no] et | Fab[ian]o [co](n)s(ulibus) | extruxit.'[65] *Aquae* are also familiar as road-installations in many parts of the empire.[66] The first stage from Aela on the road to Petra is marked on

---

[60] Pflaum, 'Essai', ch. vii, 'l'organisation des relais de la poste romaine'; Pekáry, *Untersuchungen,* 164–7. Many places bear the name 'Praetorio', D. Cuntz, *Itineraria romana* (1929), index s.v. A building west of the legionary base of Lejjun has been tentatively described as a *mansio,* P. Crawford, in Parker, *The Roman Frontier in Central Jordan,* 385–97.

[61] It goes without saying that *praesidium* can refer to any sort of garrison. I certainly do not want to argue that every fort called a *praesidium* was a police station along a road. It is, however, clear that 'police station' was a very specific meaning that occurs frequently. When used in connection with Greek cities *phrourion* has a different meaning; J. et L. Robert, *BE* 1961, 195 f.: 'c'est un forteresse, indépendante du site d'une ville et plus ou moins développée.' See also L. Robert, *Études Antatoliennes* (1937), 192. When he had re-subdued the Frisians Corbulo established a garrison in a fort ('praesidium immunivit') among them 'ne iussa exuerent' (Tacitus, *Ann.* xi 19).

[62] e.g. in the Eastern Desert in Egypt: *IGR* i 1142; Pliny, *NH* vi 26. 103. The Egyptian Red Sea coast was organized as a separate district under a *praefectus praesidiorum et montis Berenicis, CIL* ix 3083. For a *hydreuma* and *praesidium* constructed at the order of the prefect, D. Meredith, *CE* 29 (1954), 284 f. The commander of a *praesidium* was a *curator praesidii,* R. S. Bagnall, *The Florida Ostraka* (1976), 6. 1 with comments on p. 24. Four place-names 'Praesidio' occur in the *Itinerarium Antonini,* none in a frontier zone; Cuntz, index x.v.: Corsica, Hispania Baetica, Tarraconensis (two).

[63] Lewis, *Documents,* no. 11. For the use of σκηναί as soldiers' housing (not temporary tents) Professor Lewis refers to the *Archiv für Papyrusforschung* 33 (1987), 15 n. 5. At the time of writing this publication was not yet accessible to me, but Professor Lewis kindly informs me that the essential citations are Preisigke, *Wörterbuch,* s.v. 1; Photius and Hesychius, s.v.; Polybius xii 8. 4; xxxi 14. 2.

[64] See above, ch. III.

[65] AD 201; for the reading, Kennedy, *Explorations,* 125, no. 20. For the site, Kennedy and Riley, 159–61. The authors are sceptical of this being the site of a *balneum,* and suspect that the inscription originates from Azraq Shishan, where there are extensive pools today. See also the discussion by J. Lander, *Roman Stone Fortifications* (1984), 136.

[66] Cuntz, index s.v.; for baths on the Peutinger Table, A. and M. Levi, *Itineraria Picta* (1967) 65, 113, 170.

the Peutinger Table as *Praesidio*, identified with al-Khaldi.[67] Another place named Praesidium is to be sought south of the Dead Sea. This is mentioned in the *Notitia* and in the fragmentary edict from Beer Sheva, and it appears on the Madaba Map.[68]

The term *praesidia* is used in Talmudic literature for guard posts along the roads to Jerusalem.[69] The sources refer to an earlier period, but they do so in the language of their own times, which shows that the Latin term was so widely used that it had become part of the daily language.

It is clear that any of the buildings along the *via nova Traiana* and the eastern road might be identified with such structures. One important building (Qasr Beshir) has been unambiguously identified as an administrative centre rather than an installation connected with frontier-defence; and two other sites (Praesidio and Uweinid) have been described as installations of a kind that could be connected with the organization of the road-system in non-military provinces anywhere in the empire. It is therefore no longer possible to assume as a matter of course that other unidentified structures were all part of a system of frontier defence. Such a system, moreover, is not explicitly mentioned in any ancient source, for the term *limes*, as shown elsewhere, has no military connotations.[70]

Another inscription from Arabia may be cited to support the view that many structures are connected with road-organization and police duties: it commemorates work on the water supply for an *agrario statio* along the Roman road from Bostra to Azraq:

Vincentius, who was acting as *protector* . . ., observing that many of the *agrarienses* had been ambushed and killed by the Saracens while fetching water for themselves, laid out and constructed a reservoir for the water.[71]

---

[67] Cf. *Not. Dig. Or.* xxxiv 41 (under the *dux Palaestinae*): 'cohors quarta Frygum, Praesidio'. For the site, Gregory and Kennedy, 314, 432; Parker, *Romans and Saracens*, 108 f.

[68] *Not. Dig. Or.* xxxiv (under the *dux Palaestinae*): 'ala secunda felix Valentiana, apud Praesidium'. The formula shows that the garrison itself is considered distinct from the place named Praesidium. For the edict from Beer Sheva, C. Clermont-Ganneau, *RB*, 414; Alt, *Inschriften*, 8, no. 2. The Madaba Map has 'Prasidin' south of the Dead Sea, east of Mampsis and north of Thamara and Moa. It is usually identified with Ghor el-Feife in the northern Arava; references in M. Avi-Yonah, *Gazetteer of Roman Palestine* (1976), 89.

[69] tos. Ta'anit iv 7; 8: 'Pardesi'ot'; y. Ta'aniot iv 69 c: 'prosdiot'. Cf. discussion and parallels in A. S. Rosenthal, *Yuval Shay*, ed. B. Kurtzweil, (1958), 321 f., who notes that the term is found in Syriac as well (he refers to Lex. Syr. 601a).

[70] See above, n. 1.

[71] 'Cum pervidisset Vincentius protector agens Basie plurimos ex agrariensibus, dum aqua(s) sibi in uso transfererent, insidiatos a Saracenos perisse, receptaculum aqua(rum) ex fundamentis fecit, Optato et Paulino vv cc conss.' J. H. Iliffe, *QDAP* 10 (1942–44), 62–4 (*AE* 1948. 136). For the site, Kennedy, *Explorations*, 184. For the *protectores*, E. Stein, *Histoire du Bas Empire*, i (1949), 80 ff.;

The same official organized the water supply at Azraq, as appears from a recently published inscription.[72] Protecting or denying the water-supply is always essential in controlling transhuming nomads and in the fight against banditry in the desert. If bandits control a well they have a base from which to operate. If the authorities control it the facility is available to travellers and peaceful nomads, while at the same time the bandits are denied a base.[73]

Vegetius advises cities which do not possess a water supply that can be controlled from the walls to build a 'small fort which they call "burgus" between the city and the source and to man it with *ballistae* and archers in order to defend the water against enemies'.[74] According to Procopius the citizens of Cyrrhus in Syria suffered from precisely such a problem. Justinian solved it for them by digging a channel which made the water accessible.[75]

The inscription regarding the *agraria statio* is evidence of such trouble and of countermeasures taken by an official. But it does not prove that the whole road-system in the area served to fight nomads. On the contrary, it shows that the system itself did not keep the nomads away and that local, small-scale measures were taken and sufficed to keep them under control.

Syria

In Syria too there is at least one inscription proving that a military installation along a road served to keep the road itself safe for travellers; it comes from Khan el-Abyad, a road-station on the Damascus–Palmyra road. This is a fourth-century inscription thanking the *dux Foenicis*, 'guardian of the *limes* and the cities' in Latin verse for the construction of a '*castrum*', a *mansio* or *statio*, and for the cultivation of the surrounding land. The *mansio* served as hostel for travellers in the desert.

On a plain totally arid and much feared by travellers because of its great expanse, because of the fate of a neighbour who died from hunger—the worst that can happen—you, *comes*, have provided a fort (*castrum*), perfectly equip-

---

A. H. M. Jones, *The Later Roman Empire* (1964), 636 f. For the *agrariae* stationes, van Berchem, *L'armée de Dioclétien et la reforme constantinienne* (1952), 30 n. 1.

[72] Kennedy and MacAdam, ZPE 60, 49–105, no. 2; ZPE 65, 231 f.

[73] J. F. Jones, 'Researches in the Vicinity of the Median Wall', *Selections from the Records of the Bombay Government*, NS 43 (1857), 238 f., cited in Isaac, *HSCP* 88 (1984), 186 n. 83.

[74] *Epitoma rei militaris* iv 10: 'Quod si ultra ictum teli, in clivo tamen civitatis subiecta sit vena, castellum parvulum, quem burgum vocant, inter civitatem et fontem convenit fabricari ibique ballistas sagittariosque contitui, ut aqua defendatur ab hostibus.' The equivalent in Greek is *phrourion*, cf. J. et L. Robert, *BE* 1961, 195 f.

[75] *De aed.* ii 11. 5–7.

ped, you, Silvinus, most valiant guardian of the *limes*, of the cities, and of the emperors honoured loyally all over the earth. You have prepared the earth so that it is enriched by the heavenly waters, so that it will bow under the yoke of Ceres and Bacchus. Hence, stranger, pursue your journey cheerfully and, having profited from a good deed, sing the praise of a magnanimous judge, brilliant in war and peace who, I pray, will, advanced in rank, build more such forts for the emperors, although it is a difficult task, and will rejoice in children worthy of the deeds of such a father.[76]

The inscription shows that the *dux* built a fort which served as a road station in the desert. No mention is made of nomads and the *dux* is described as the guardian of the *limes* and the cities, in other words, of the urbanized parts and the frontier district.[77]

Several inscriptions attest the construction of military inns in Syria in the sixth century.[78] One from Umm el-Halahil refers to a ξενεών dedicated to St Theodore.[79] This saint was, together with St Longinus, St Sergius, and St George, the patron of soldiers.[80] The site is not far from Ma'an where a φρούριον is mentioned on a Justinianic inscription.[81] At Raphanaea, the base of the legion III Gallica, we find a reference to the μητάτον of St Sergius.[82] An inscription dated 524/5 from Gour (= ?Garion) in Emesene mentions an inn of St Longinus, St Theodore, and St George.[83] Finally, at El-Burj (north of Jebel 'Ala between Hama and Aleppo) an inscription records an inn of the archangel Michael and St Longinus, the centurion. It is of interest that the building in which this inn is established is referred to as a πύργος (*burgus*).[84] In southern Syria inns or rest-houses are a very common feature on inscriptions.[85] These would have served the military whenever there was a demand for hospitality.

[76] *IGLS* v 2704: '[Siccum utiq]ue campum et viantib[u]s satis invisum [ob sp]a[ti]a prolixa, ob vicini mortis eventus, [sort]iti{s} famem, qua non aliud grav[iu]s [ull]um, [c]astrum reddidisti, comes, ornatum sumo decori, Silvine, limitis ur[biu]m[que] fortissimae custos dominorumque fide [c]u[ltoru]m toto per orbe, et lymfis polle[r]e ca[elestibu]s ita parasti Caereris ut iugo Ba[cch]ique posset ‹b›eneri. Hospes, unde laetus itineris perage cursum, et boni potitu[s] actus cum laude caneto [m]agnanimi [iudi]cis [p]ace belloque nitentis, quem p[r]a[e]cor super[o]s altiori [grad]u subnixum tal[i]a dom[i]n[is v]el ardua c[ond]ere [cas]tra, et natis gaude[r]e deco[r]antibus facta parentis.' For the site, *DE* s.v. *limes*, 1359.

[77] For a *praesidium* built in the reign of Severus on a road not far from Damascus 'for the security of the public and the terror of the Scenite Arabs', *CIL* iii 128.

[78] I am grateful to Dr Marlia Mango for information and references.

[79] *IGLS* 1750.

[80] As observed by the editors of the inscription. For the patron saints of the army, A. Poidebard and R. Mouterde, *Analecta Bollandiana* (1949), 114 f.

[81] *IGLS* 1809, the only Justinianic fort inscription in Syria, as noted by Dr Mango.

[82] *IGLS* 1397: 'gîte d'étape comparables à d'autres casernements pour les troupes de passage.'

[83] *IGLS* 2155.   [84] *IGLS* 1610.

[85] H. I. MacAdam, *Berytus* 31 (1983), 103–15, esp. 108; no references are given because they are too numerous.

We may note in passing that a similar inscription from Dionysias (Soada) in Arabia shows that an inn (ξενεών) of St Theodorus was constructed under the authority of the bishop.[86] In Judaea an inscription recently discovered records the construction of an inn (ἐπαντητήριον) near Eleutheropolis (Beth Govrin) by the *Dux Palaestinae*.[87] It is significant that the project was carried out at the command of the *dux* rather than the civilian authorities.

As observed by Waddington, such establishments were constructed and maintained by the cities in order to be spared forced billeting of passing troops.[88] It is to be noted, moreover, that these inns are found in the settled parts of the provinces as well as the isolated areas. Wherever there is an army, troops will continually be travelling.

It is no coincidence that a number of Roman forts continued to exist in the Islamic period as road-stations and hostels.[89] They probably served a similar purpose in the Byzantine period.

Burgi

It seems best to discuss *burgi* in the present chapter, because in the eastern provinces the evidence for them is mostly to be found in inscriptions of the later periods. The small watchtowers along roads in southern Syria and North-West Jordan discussed above are an exception.[90]

Burgi are not novel or characteristic of the army of the fourth century. They are mentioned in references to provinces farther west from the second century onward. The term could in principle indicate any kind of blockhouse and does not in itself denote a specific function. On Trajan's column blockhouses are depicted as established on the

---

[86] Waddington, no. 2327, with note.

[87] Y. Dagan, M. Fischer and Y. Tsafrir, *IEJ* 35 (1985), 28–34. Note also C. Dauphin, *Cathedra* 29 (1983), 29–44 (Hebrew), on the excavations of a church at Dora (Dor) which may have been part of a pilgrim-station.

[88] Note on Waddington, no. 2524 (*OGIS* 609): a letter from the legate to the citizens of Phaena on forced billeting.

[89] The Byzantine system of forts and towers between Damascus and the Euphrates was reconstructed in the eighth century; see Poidebard, *Trace de Rome*, 34 ff. On the Byzantine station at Qasr el Heir reconstructed in the period of the Umayyads see A. Gabriel, *CRAI* 1926, 249 f.; D. Schlumberger, *Syria* 20 (1939), 200 ff. In north-east Jordan several forts were similarly reconstructed: Kennedy, 48 ff.: Azraq; 69–96, esp. 75: Hallabat; 128–32: Ain es Sol, perhaps. For this region, Gregory and Kennedy, ch. 6 with notes. For Qasr Hallabat, Ghazi Bisheh in *Studies in the History and Archaeology of Jordan*, ii (1985), 263–5. The plan of new Umayyad forts and palaces, even where they were built on sites previously unoccupied derived from that of Late Roman forts: cf. K. A. C. Creswell, *PBA* 38 (1952), 89–91; H. Gaube, *Ein Arabischer Palast in Südsyrien: Hirbet al Baida* (1974). In a discussion of the Umayyad occupation of north-east Jordan (*DRBE*, 531–47) H. I. MacAdam stresses that the so-called Umayyad palaces will have been military installations, while observing that most of these were *not* preceded by Roman forts.

[90] See ch. III.

opposite bank of the Danube, where their function must have been to supervise the river-traffic and convey messages along its banks. 'It is worth while to note', writes Richmond, 'that these towers could only be used for look-out purposes or for signalling by getting out on the balcony. They have no side-windows and no effective means of defence except the little palisade around them, which is more in the nature of a boundary. Thus they are entirely for guard-duties and for signalling.'[91]

The term *burgarii* is first encountered in the time of Hadrian.[92] *Burgi* are attested a little later.[93] The erection of *burgi* and *praesidia* under Commodus on the Danube is recorded in the well-known inscriptions discussed by A. Alföldi:[94] a series of building-inscriptions of the year 185 which attest new buildings on the bank of the Danube below Aquincum. These had a military function: they were meant to prevent *latrunculi*, bands of irregulars, from secretly crossing the river.[95] They were thus installations against a low-intensity threat, to use Luttwak's terminology.[96] Alföldi thought they were manned by Illyrian tribesmen who had immigrated into the area rather than by regular troops.

Vegetius with his advice to build *burgi* for the defence of water sources which cannot be controlled from a city wall has been cited above.

Similar installations in a later period are mentioned by the anonymous Byzantine writer on strategy.[97] These towers were located in border areas of active confrontation with an external enemy. By way of illustration we may cite Procopius' description of a *pyrgos* with *phroura* (garrison) at Thannouris:[98]

And there was a certain spot near the larger Thannourios to which the hostile Saracens, after crossing the Aborrhas River, had complete freedom to resort, and making that their headquarters they would scatter through the thick leafy forest and over the mountain which rises there, and then they would descend with impunity upon the Romans who lived in the places round about. But now the emperor Justinian has built a very large tower (*pyrgos*) of hard stone at this

---

[91] *Trajan's Army on Trajan's Column* ([2]1982), 38.   [92] *CIL* iii 13796.

[93] References in *TLL* ii 2249 f.; see also *DE* iv s.v. *limes*, 1089 f.

[94] For further references see also A. Mócsy, *Pannonia and Upper Moesia* (1974), 196 f. In the fourth century the *duces* were made responsible for the repair and construction of such towers in their districts (*limes*) as is shown, for example, by *Cod. Theod.* xv 1. 13 (19 June 364[?]) addressed to the *dux Daciae Ripensis*.

[95] *DE* iv s.v. *latrones*, 460–6; *DE* iii s.v. *latrocinium*, 991 f.; Pfaff, *RE* xii 978–80; Düll and Mickiewitz, *RE* Suppl. vii 1239–44, s.v. Strassenraub.

[96] *The Grand Strategy of the Roman Empire* (1976), 78 f.

[97] H. Köchly and W. Rüstow, *Griechische Kriegsschriftsteller* 2. 2 (1853), 41–209, esp. 60–70.

[98] *De aed.* ii 6. 15 f. Cf. L. Dillemann, *Haute Mésopotamie orientale et pays adjacents: Contribution à la géographie historique de la région, du V⁰ siècle avant l'ère chrétienne au VI⁰ siècle de cette ère* (1962), 77; F. E. Peters, *AAAS* 27–28 (1977–78), 102.

point, in which he has established a very considerable garrison, and thus he
has succeeded completely in checking the inroads of the enemy by devising this
bulwark against them.

Allowing for the exaggerations of the source it is clear that we have
here a description of nomad raids organized perhaps with the support
of the Persians. These were not full-scale invasions but minor hit-and-
run affairs which could be stopped by a small garrison, such as could be
housed in one fairly large tower.

A clear distinction is to be made between such posts and others, also
named *burgi*, in the interior which served to police the countryside and
roads within the empire. The earliest references again derive from
western provinces and the second century.

A series of inscriptions of 152–5 from Thrace record the construction
in city territories of *praesidia*, *burgi*, and *phruri* 'for the protection of the
province of Thrace' by the authorities.[99] It is clear that here the *burgi*
are of intermediate size, the *phruri* being the small towers often
associated with the term *burgi*. This is further evidence that the term
was used in a flexible manner. A Greek inscription of 155 refers only to
πύργοι built by the city of Bizye itself. It would be idle to speculate on
the nature of the insecurity that gave rise to this project. There is no
reason to assume that it had anything to do with foreign invasion or
major threats.[100] Conceivably it was a system organized to protect the
safety of roads in the rural parts of city territories. The famous
inscription recording the foundation of the *emporium* of Pizos in Thrace,
dated 202, shows that the provincials were normally obliged to furnish
burgarii and garrison troops and provision for the imperial postal
service.[101] It is not far-fetched to assume that these *burgarii* manned the
burgi built fifty years before. The general content of the inscription from
Pizos may indicate that we have to think in terms of road-security. It
certainly proves that these installations were manned by local levies
and not by regular troops.

An inscription from Africa from the reign of Commodus (AD 188)
clearly formulates the function of a *burgus* in terms of road-security: '. . .
burgum [Commodianum] s[p]eculatorium inter duas vias ad salutem
commeantium nova tute[l]a c[o]nstitui iussit . . .'[102] Here 'spe-

---

[99] G. Mihailov, *Studi Urbinati* 35 (1961), 42–56; J. S. Johnson in *De Rebus Bellicis*, 69–71.

[100] Mihailov has no doubt that the structures formed part of a line of defence protecting the
province against foreign invasion.

[101] G. Mihailov, *IGBR* iii 2. 1690, pp. 103–20: those who settled at the emporium at Pizos in
Thrace would be granted exemption from the obligation to furnish *burgarii* and garrison troops
and provisions for the imperial postal service.

[102] *CIL* viii 2495.

culatorium' is probably purely descriptive, meaning a *burgus* which could specifically keep an eye on the roads and on travellers.[103]

There are a few inscriptions from the eastern provinces recording the construction of *burgi*, again from the later empire, but their function is not specified. In 348 one was built at Inat southwest of Imtan/Motha,[104] in 371 another at Umm el-Jimal.[105] A Byzantine inscription (sixth-century) from Caesarea in Greek records the construction of a *burgus* under the authority of the *comes*.[106] This building clearly stood in the settled area of the province and will therefore have had a police-function of sorts.[107]

We turn now to literary sources.[108] A Tannaitic source which refers to the second century and is itself probably no later than the early third century shows that there were *burgi* along the coast road north of Ptolemais (Acco):

It happened that Rabban Gamaliel and Rabbi Ilai went from Acco to Keziv (Akhziv, Ecdippa) and he saw a piece of white bread. He said to Tavi his servant: pick up that piece of bread. He saw a gentile and said to him: Mavgai, pick up that piece of bread. Rabbi Ilai ran after him and said to him: Who are you? He answered: I am from the (places of the) *burganin*. And what is your name? He answered: Mavgai is my name . . .[109]

The remainder of the source is not immediately relevant for the present subject. The point emphasized is that Mavgai was a gentile. Lying on the coast, north of Acco, Akhziv (Keziv) was in the province of Syria. This passage is thus in accordance with the archaeological evidence, cited above, which indicates that there were towers along roads in southern Syria in this period, while they have not so far been found in Judaea. Mavgai is a common Syrian name.[110] It is used here as a typical example of a gentile name and indicates that the *burgarii* here were drawn from local levies, as is clear also from other sources

---

[103] As pointed out to me by J. C. Mann, *speculatores* are in this period employed only in judicial functions, i.e. either at the provincial capital, or at *praetoria* away from the capital where the governor held trials while on circuit. They were therefore not likely to man a tower.

[104] Butler, *PAES*, no. 224.   [105] *CIL* iii 88.

[106] M. Schwabe, *Tarbiz* 20 (1950), 273–83 (in Hebrew).

[107] K. Hopwood, *AFRBA*, 173–87, discusses the policing of Rough Cilicia and Isauria with the help among other things of towers.

[108] On *burganin* in Talmudic sources, S. Klein, *Monatsschrift für Geschichte und Wissenschaft des Judentums* 82/ns 64 (1938), 181–6.

[109] tos. Pesahim i 27; cf. y. 'Avodah zarah i 40a; b. 'Eruvin 64b; cf. Lieberman, *Tosefta Kifshutah*, 498 f.

[110] e.g. 'Mabogaios': E. Littmann et al., *Publications of the Princeton Expedition*, iiia, 429, no. 797, 9; C. Clermont-Ganneau, *RAO* 4 (1901), 99–109; Waddington, nos. 2554 f.; *RE* Supp. iv, col. 733 s.v. Hierapolis; *IGLS* vi 2907 (territory of Heliopolis); 'Mabagoni' on a mosaic in south Lebanon: P. Figueras, *Liber Annuus* 35 (1985), 297–302.

mentioned above. The nature of the *burganin* referred to in this source is not immediately clear.

It seems that eventually *burganin* came to indicate any sort of modest permanent structure, for instance: 'Rav said: a settlement which consists of tents, there everybody measures from his tent. [Where] there [are] three huts and three *burganin*, he measures from the perimeter.'[111] The subject of discussion here is the distance one may walk on the Sabbath from various structures. Here *burganin* is not a functional description, but an indication of the character of the building. It is more than a hut, but less than a town house. The usage of the term resembles that of the Arabic 'Qasr' which used to be thought of as connected with the Latin *castellum* or *castra*, but has been shown to refer to any permanent structure built of stone or mud bricks.[112]

The coast road from Acco, further north, appears in another passage where it is stated that one may walk from Tyre to Sidon and from Sepphoris (Diocaesarea) to Tiberias on the Sabbath because there is a continuous line of caves and towers which makes it possible to walk between these towns without violating the Shabbat limits.[113] In a parallel in the Jerusalem Talmud the term *burganin* is used instead of 'towers', which might perhaps show that this term became more common in the fourth century.[114] It is to be noted that, so far, no towers have been discovered along the known stretches of the Sepphoris–Tiberias road. That may not be very significant since it is clear that the term is not necessarily associated with Roman military organization.

A Talmudic source clarifies the use of some such installations along highways:

Rabbi Hanina said: for instance, a caravan was on its way. When it began to darken it came to a burgus. The keeper of the burgus said: 'come inside the burgus, because of the wild beasts and the bandits.' The leader of the caravan said: 'it is not my custom to enter a burgus.' As he went on it became utterly dark and he went back to the keeper of the burgus and he shouted and asked him to open up. The keeper said: 'it is not the custom of the keeper of a burgus to open up at night and it is not the custom of the burgus to admit at such an hour. When I invited you you did not accept and now I cannot open the gate for you.'[115]

---

[111]   y. 'Eruvin v 22c.

[112]   L. I. Conrad, *Al-Abhath, Journal of the Center for Arab and Middle East Studies, Faculty of Arts and Sciences, American University of Beirut* 29 (1981), 7–23.

[113]   tos. 'Eruvin vi 8, referring to R. Shimon bar Yohai (*c.* 140–170).

[114]   y. 'Eruvin v 22b.

[115]   Midrash Psalms x 2, ed. Buber, pp. 92 f., and parallel sources. Cf. Libanius, *Or.* l 26: τήν τε ἐν νυκτὶ πορείαν σφαλερὰν τῶν κακούργων ποιούντων, 'for malefactors make travel by night hazardous. . .'

This shows that such installations served not only as police stations or guard-posts, but also as hostels, although not everybody would welcome an opportunity to pass the night there.[116] Note that an Ottoman document of 1571 states that '. . . it is against the law for fortresses to be opened by night and for men to go in and out . . .'[117]

Here is a further indication that *burgi* were used as guest-houses: 'Rabbi Avin said: as a king who travelled in the desert: enter the first *burgus*, eat there and drink there. He entered the second *burgus*, ate there, drank there and stayed overnight.'[118] It may be assumed that 'a king' here stands for an official. Even if the case is interpreted as wholly imaginary it still reflects a reality in which *burgi* were used for such purposes.

In another passage, Rabban Yohanan ben Zakkai was going up to Emmaus in Judah and is reported to have said to the Jews: 'You were unwilling to repair the roads and the streets leading up to the Temple, so now you have to repair the "burgasin" and the "burganin" leading to the royal cities. And thus it says: "Because you did not serve Heaven. . . therefore you will serve your enemy." '[119] The *burgi* are conceived of as an integral part of the road system linking the cities of the province.

From *Cod. Theod.* vii 14 it appears that *burgarii* were considered of the lowest class and of the same status as mule-drivers and slave workers in the imperial weaving works. The *burgi* were clearly not manned by regular soldiers.

John Chrysostom, writing in the late fourth century, describes the journey to Babylon in his time.[120] There were road stations, towns, and villas along the road. The roads were paved, and the towns maintained groups of armed men, well disciplined under officers of their own, whose sole duty was to guarantee the safety of the road. Every mile there was a building, where guards were stationed at night. Thanks to their vigilance travellers were fully protected against attacks by robbers.

---

[116] For a military inn established in a *pyrgos* see above, p. 177.

[117] Cf. U. Heyd, *Ottoman Documents on Palestine 1552–1615* (1960), document 57 of 1571, pp. 105 f.

[118] Leviticus Rabbah vii 4, ed. Margulies, pp. 158 f.

[119] Mekhilta de Rabbi Ishmael, Bahodesh, i, ed. Horovitz–Rabin, 203 f. Translation of this passage from G. Alon, *The Jews in their Land in the Talmudic Age*, i (1980), trans. G. Levi, 68 f. For an edition and translation of the whole text, J. Z. Lauterbach, *Mekilta de Rabbi Ishmael* (1933). The events described are attributed to Rabban Yohanan ben Zakkai of the first century, but it seems that the end, from 'you were unwilling' onwards reflects third-century reality, the period in which the Mekhilta was edited, as noted below, ch. VI. The installations referred to were not in the desert, since the discussion is clearly situated in the settled area of Judaea and the roads concerned led to the cities there.

[120] *Ad Stagirium* ii 189 f. (*PG* xlvii 457), cited also in *HSCP* 88 (1984), 202 f.

One Talmudic source referring to Babylonia shows that the Jews there knew *burgi* as typical of the roads in Palestine:

Rav Hisda said to Mari son of Rav Huna son of Rav Jeremiah b. Abba: 'They say that you came from Barnesh to Daniel's synagogue on the Sabbath, that was three parasangs away. What do you rely upon, *burganin*? But your father's father said in the name of Rav that there are no *burganin* in Babylonia.' He went out and showed him some (ruined) settlements that were within seventy cubits and a fraction from each other.[121]

Rav Hisda belonged to the third generation of Babylonian Amoraim (290–320).

After devoting so much space to a discussion of the literary and epigraphic evidence for 'blockhouses' we had better sum up our conclusions. From the material cited it is clear, as was to be expected anyway, that there are many different kinds of *burgi* in various periods and with various functions. However, it can be shown that the term *burgus*, or its Aramaic derivate, was used for very specific structures which formed part of the road system and were manned by special troops, usually maintained by the cities in the provinces. These are attested from the second century onward in written sources of the western provinces. In the East one Talmudic source definitely suggests that they existed in southern Syria in the second century, but there is no clear-cut evidence of their presence in Judaea. That may not be decisive, but it is consistent with our findings in Chapter III (above, pp. 111–13).

We turn now to the archaeological evidence. At least two minor road-stations along the roads to Jerusalem existed in the Hellenistic period and were abandoned toward the end of the first century, after the First Jewish Revolt. They were used again in the Byzantine period. In the southern part of Judaea proper, the area south of Jerusalem, various roads have been surveyed which were provided with different kinds of towers and small forts. Before excavation it had been tentatively suggested that these were engineering works carried out during the suppression of the Revolt of Bar Kokhba.[122] Several structures have now been excavated and, according to a preliminary report, they all date to the Byzantine period.[123] The absence of milestones along roads

---

[121] b. 'Eruvin 21a; cf. Oppenheimer, *Babylonia Judaica* 63 f. (text and trans.).

[122] *Judaea, Samaria and the Golan: Archaeological Survey 1967–1968* (1972), ed. M. Kokhavi, 26, and map 3 on p. 27 (in Hebrew).

[123] Y. Hirschfeld, 'A Line of Byzantine Forts along the Eastern Highway of the Hebron Hills', *Qadmoniot* 12 (1979), 78–84 and folding map opposite p. 77 (in Hebrew).

of obviously Roman construction supports this conclusion. There are several roads in this area with installations which require further exploration.[124] As so often the archaeologists who studied these remains wish to interpret them as lines of defence rather than policed roads. There is no need to accept this view. The chronological conclusions, however, fit the pattern described above.

It must be emphasized that most of the archaeological evidence discussed derives from Judaea and southern Syria. From other parts of Syria and from Arabia there is so far insufficient information. It is clear that in southern Syria there were watchtowers along several Roman roads, as noted in Chapter III. Further discoveries may show that *burgi* were quite common in parts of the eastern frontier provinces before the fourth century.

Relevant material is also recorded in the publications of recent surveys in Transjordan, east of the Dead Sea: 'It is possible that the scattered small (Nabataean) towers served a police function allowing protection of tribal lands'. Regarding the Late Roman/Early Byzantine Period it is observed that most of the newly built towers 'were in major wadis at heavily guarded crossings. Pottery collected from the campsites around many Late Roman towers suggests frequent use of these areas from the Chalcolitic period onward. . . . Thus it would seem that these towers were built as part of a plan to guard these campsites and wadi crossings. It suggests that a principal role played by the army was to control movement through this area and protect travelers crossing the region.'[125] A recent examination of Qasr Burqu in the desert of north-east Jordan has led to the conclusion that the nucleus of the site consisted of a watchtower and water reservoir of the third–fourth century. This was later followed by the establishment of a monastery on the site.[126]

Towers were also widely used by civilians in the countryside. 'There was a householder who planted a vineyard, and set a hedge around it, and dug a wine press in it, and built a tower (*pyrgos*) . . .'[127] There are

---

[124] Kokhavi, map 3 on p. 27. The remains of seven watchtowers have been seen along the Roman road from Heshbon to Livias. Pottery of the Roman and Byzantine periods was picked up on the surface, S. D. Waterhouse and R. Ibach, *Andrews University Seminar Studies* 13 (1975), 217–33, esp. 226.

[125] Frank L. Koucky, in S. T. Parker (ed.), *The Roman Frontier in Central Jordan*, 64–79, esp. 66. On pp. 71–5 the forts and towers are usefully considered in terms of caravan travel. See further B. MacDonald, *Échos du monde classique / Classical Views* 28 (1984), 219–34. See now: B. MacDonald, *Wadi El-Hasa Survey* (1988).

[126] H. Gaube, *ADAJ* 19 (1974), 93–100. There is no epigraphical evidence to support these conclusions and so far the site has not been excavated.

[127] Matthew 21: 33; Mark 12: 1. These may describe the reality of Roman times, but cf. Isaiah 5: 2.

hundreds of towers to be seen in the countryside of Samaria.[128] Similar towers, apparently, are found in Transjordan in Wadi el-Hasa.[129] The towers here might have been in use for temporary camps, inhabited by farmers or transhumant shepherds, when their work required extended stays away from their homes. They could be used to live in and for storage space. When located on high spots they would afford a view of the surrounding area, which would be useful for farmers and shepherds even if there was no security problem at all. In Syria watchtowers were erected in many villages, particularly from the fourth century on. They are referred to as *phrouria* in inscriptions.[130] In northern Syria there are numerous towers, some of them isolated, others in settlements or monasteries. Their function varied. Many were clearly watchtowers built by civilians for the surveillance of their fields or villages.[131] Some will have served as summer dwellings or warehouses. These may perhaps be recognized by their small size and the fact that they have only one opening.[132] This shows how terminology and function vary regionally and over the centuries. It is clearly necessary to verify always how terms like these are used.[133]

The Siting and Function of Fourth-Century Forts (Palaestina)

It is a commonplace that forts of the principate were not built on the assumption that they would have to withstand attack. This can be deduced from the absence of strong defences, and from the siting of many of them. Support can be found in Tacitus' well-known comments on the base at Vetera, captured by Batavian rebels:

Part of the base lay on a gently sloping hill, part was accessible on level ground. Augustus had believed that this base would lay siege to Germany and put pressure on it. He did not think it would ever come to such a disaster that they (the Germans) would take the initiative to come and attack our legions. Hence no labour was spent on the site or the defences. Our vigour and our arms seemed enough.[134]

---

[128] Cf. S. Applebaum, S. Dar, and Z. Safrai, *PEQ* 110 (1978), 91–100. For similar structures in Greece, references in S. C. Humphreys, *La Parola del Passato* 22 (1967), 379 n. 15.

[129] MacDonald, *Échos*; E. B. Banning, *BASOR* 261 (1986), 25–50, esp. 35 f., 39; ibid. 265 (1987), 52.

[130] See H. I. MacAdam, *Berytus* 31 (1983), 103–15, esp. 108, where, however, no specific references are cited.

[131] For watchtowers in northern Syria, G. Tchalenko, *Villages antiques de la Syrie du nord*, i (1953), 30–3.

[132] Tchalenko, 30 n. 5.

[133] As a curiosity reference may be made to Magda Révész-Alexander, *Der Turm als Symbol und Erlebnis* (1953), 91 f.: 'Warum hat die römische Baukunst keine Turme?'

[134] Tacitus, *Hist.* iv 23. For the site, Bogaers and Rüger, 106–111.

As Luttwak puts it, 'Nor were the troop bases on the frontiers situated for tactical defense; they were merely set astride lines of communications, with a view to logistics and residential convenience.'[135] These observations are easily confirmed by anyone who visits Roman military sites of this period.

It is then assumed that a drastic change took place under Diocletian. Fourth-century forts were organized for defence, it is claimed, and this found expression in a different construction. Until the end of the third century forts were usually rectangular, of the familiar playing-card shape, with insignificant corner and interval towers and modest walls, lacking wide berms and ditches. All this changed under Diocletian. Forts were now square, had wide berms, thick walls with ramparts, and projecting corner and interval towers. Gates were heavily defended. No longer was there a broad road separating the buildings in the forts from the walls, but barracks were built against the inner face of the walls. Another difference, it is said, can be found in the siting of fortifications. These are now usually built on sites chosen for tactical dominance. Unlike their earlier counterparts, fourth-century forts, it is concluded, were meant to be defensible.[136] At a general level that seems only natural, in a period when warfare was far more often defensive than previously. But Luttwak argues that this change is to be explained in terms of a new strategy, organized in depth:[137] 'the concentrated forces of the principate could deal with the enemy by taking the offensive, but the smaller frontier garrisons of the late empire would often be obliged to resist in place, awaiting the arrival of the provincial, regional or even empire-wide reinforcement.'

There are several arguments against these conclusions. First, as emphasized repeatedly in this book, it is a mistake to attempt to deduce too much from the mere shape of buildings. Function is not necessarily reflected in outward shape. This is especially true for military architecture.[138] Second, it is wrong to associate every military building with battle-field functionality. Every large army has a variety of buildings, only some of which serve as actual fortifications. Third, there is a

---

[135] *Grand Strategy*, 135.

[136] Description in Luttwak, 161–7. Lander, *Roman Stone Fortifications*, reaches the important conclusion that the arrangement whereby barracks were built against the inner face of the walls was merely a matter of size. In the larger forts of the fourth century a road does exist between the walls and the barracks, as in the preceding period.

[137] Luttwak, ch. III, esp. 135 f., 161.

[138] The compendium in Lander shows how difficult it is to reach any independent conclusions on the strength of architecture alone, even if they are based on careful argument and on a compilation of all available material.

tendency, in the study of late Roman buildings, to interpret too many of them in military, as opposed to civilian, terms.

Something will now be said in support of these arguments. This is not a study of fortifications in general, nor is it primarily concerned with fortifications even in the area under consideration, the eastern frontier provinces. Yet it may be useful to record observations made in the small area with which I am tolerably familiar. This can be no basis for generalizations, but it may be mentioned that Luttwak considers the province of Palaestina III (Salutaris) an extreme example of the pattern of defence in depth. This included the Negev and the southern part of the old province of Arabia. 'There, the *limes* did not exist to protect a province, but rather the province existed to sustain the *limes*, which served a broad *regional* function in protecting the southern Levant from nomad attacks.'[139] Accordingly, if the pattern falls apart here this may serve as an argument for reconsidering matters elsewhere. As in the previous chapter only forts dated through inscriptions or excavation will be considered.

Ad Dianam (Yotvetah, Ghadhyan)

The name suggests a road-station near an altar or sanctuary.[140] As noted above, the fort is dated by an inscription to the tetrarchy. It records the establishment of an *ala* named 'Costia' (= Constantianam?) at the site.[141] An *ala Constantiana* is registered in the *Notitia Dignitatum* as serving under the *dux Palaestinae*.[142] It is of interest that we know both the type of the unit based there and the size of the fort, a *quadriburgium* of 39.7 by 39.4 metres. The identification of the site with the Ad Dianam indicated on the Peutinger Table rests on geographical considerations and a definite resemblance between the Arabic and the Latin name. From the excavations carried out by Mr Ze'ev Meshel it appears that the fort was not occupied after the fourth century.[143] This may explain why it is not mentioned in the *Notitia*, where the *ala*

---

[139] Luttwak, 160.

[140] So far no altar or sanctuary has been identified near the site. There is also an *Ad Dianam* in Numidia: *It. Ant.* 21. Cf. *Ad Templum* (ibid. 74. 4); *Ad Herculem* (408, 2); *Ad Aras* (413. 4); *Ad Septem Aras* (419. 2). On names of road-stations, T. Kleberg, *Hôtels, Restaurants et Cabarets dans l'Antiquité Romaine* (1957), 63–73.

[141] I. Roll, *IEJ* 39 (1989), 239–60, with a different interpretation of the inscription, *but* cf. *l'Année Épigraphique*. The inscription reads: 'Perpetuae Paci | Diocletianus Augus(tus) et {Maximianus Augus(tus)} | Constantius et Maximianus | nobilissimi Caesares | alam Costia constituerunt | per providentia Prisci Praesidis.' The name of the province is erased. Left and right of the inscription: 'MVLXX' and 'MVLXL'.

[142] *Not. Dig. Or.* xxxiv 34.

[143] Z. Meshel, *IEJ* 39 (1989), 228–38; for the coins, A. Kindler, ibid., 261–6.

Constantiana is listed as the garrison of Toloha.[144] Yotvetah is the most important of all sites in the western 'Aravah because it has the best water-supply in this otherwise extremely arid region.[145] The remains are visible of an ancient water collecting system called in English 'chains of wells' (*qanat, foggara*); with it were associated sherds of the Persian and Roman periods.[146] A small Turkish police post still stands on the ancient fort. The site lies about 34 kilometres, one day's march in military terms, north of Elath and was, according to the Peutinger Table, the first station on the road to Oboda, Elusa, and thence to Aelia.[147] If there was a road leading to the north through the 'Aravah, Ad Dianam lay at a junction.[148] The Peutinger Table links Ad Dianam also with Praesidio (al-Khalde) on the Trajanic road, but this line has not so far been discovered in the field. The reason for the existence of a fort on this site, even though it lasted less than a century, is obvious. It served as a road-station in an oasis on an important road, perhaps a junction or cross-roads. It policed the oasis and, conversely, it could exist where it did thanks to the water supply. It lies a kilometre south of the earlier remains of the Chalcolithic period and Iron Age I, apparently because the road here made for the mountain pass to the west. As for defensibility, the fort is indeed square and has projecting towers.[149] The walls are 2.45 metres thick and built of sun-dried mudbricks on foundations of rough field stones. No remains of interior buildings have been found. It lies on level ground by the road, in the shelter of a high cliff, which might well have exposed it to the fire of persons standing on top.[150] If defensibility had been a primary factor in the choice of the site, the cliff would have offered various good locations,

---

[144] *Not. Dig. Or.* xxxiv 34. For Toloha, references in Avi-Yonah, *Gazetteer*, 102; add Clermont-Ganneau, *RB* NS 3 (1906), 414, 429.

[145] F. von Frank, *ZDPV* 578 (1934), 240, 250; N. Glueck, *AASOR* 15 (1935), 40; Y. Aharoni, *IEJ* 4 (1954), 12, 14; B. Rothenberg, *Roman Frontier Studies 1967*, ed. S. Applebaum (1971), 218 f.; id., *Tsephunot Negev* (1967), 142–4 and pl. 89. The first description known to me is by Musil, *Arabia Petraea*, ii 254, with figs. 139–40.

[146] M. Evenari et al., *The Negev: The Challenge of a Desert* (²1982), 172–8, with aerial photographs.

[147] For this road, Aharoni, *IEJ* 4, 9–16. As he points out, the distance between Aela and Ad Dianam should be xxvi m. instead of xvi m. as indicated on the map. He describes the road which leads from Yotvetah into the high mountain range to the west and reached Elusa. Rothenberg, *Tsephunot Negev*, describes it as making for the Darb el-Ghaza farther west, but that is not important for the site under discussion.

[148] The existence of such a road is denied by Rothenberg, *Roman Frontier Studies 1987*. If he is right it is hard to account for Eusebius' statement, *Onomasticon* 8. 8 (Klostermann), that Thamara (below, p. 193) was on the road from Mampsis to Aela.

[149] Meshel, *IEJ*, p. 230, fig. 1.; for the remains of a bath with hypocaust, 234–6, with fig. 4.

[150] See the sketch plan of the area in Rothenberg, *Frontier Studies 1967*, 218. All the photographs that show the fort from the west are taken from the cliff.

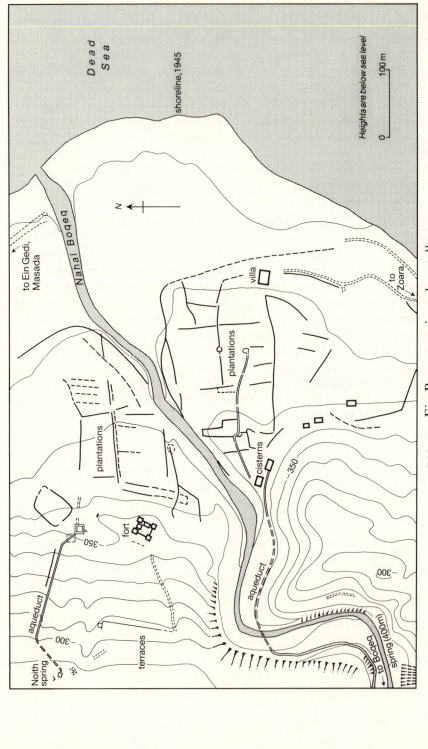

FIG. 5. Ein Boqeq: oasis and castellum

though water would not have been available. Instead it was placed near the road and a spring from which water is still being pumped. A little farther north Rothenberg found a watchtower on the cliff.[151] Similar towers are found on hill tops near other Roman forts, and below more will be said about their function.

This, in other words, was no more built for defensibility than any fort of the principate. It was a road-station and the base of a mounted police force that guarded the oasis and the road. It may have served as the administrative centre for the oasis and its vicinity, but there is no evidence of this. It was not part of any 'system'. The nearest site was Aela, and there was no other fort anywhere in the area.

Ein Boqeq (Qasr Umm Begheq)

This is an oasis with two springs on the Dead Sea shore, about 12 kilometres south of Masada. There are remains of ancient field walls, terraces, and irrigation works. M. Gichon excavated remains of the Herodian period, and a Byzantine fort occupied from the second half of the fourth century until the seventh.[152] A passable track climbs the mountains to the west past another small fort, that of Upper Zohar (see the next section), to gain the plateau of the northern Negev. The site cannot be identified with any place mentioned in ancient sources. The fort is a square building, 20 by 20 metres, with projecting corner towers measuring 6 square metres. The walls are about 1.90 metres thick. Sets of two rooms are built against the inner faces of the eastern and northern walls of the fort. Like Ad Dianam—than which it seems to have been only a little less isolated—it guarded one of the rare fertile and well-watered spots in an arid region, but it did not lie near an important road. It is built on a steep slope and thus exposed to fire from the west. A papyrus fragment of the sixth–seventh century contains a list of debtors and creditors.[153] This may indicate that it served as an administrative centre besides being a small police post guarding the oasis, the road past the Dead Sea, and the track to the west. It is difficult to conceive of the fort as part of a system of defence.

Upper Zohar

This is another small fort of roughly the same size as Ein Boqeq[154] and

---

[151] *Cf. Tsephunot Negev*, 144.

[152] For a brief account, M. Gichon, *Encyclopedia of Archaeological Excavations in the Holy Land*, ii (1976), ed. M. Avi-Yonah, 365–70.

[153] Ibid. 368 f. The papyrus will be published in the forthcoming excavation report.

[154] Preliminary excavation reports by R. P. Harper, *DRBE*, 329–36; *Hadashot Arkheologiyot (Archaeological Newsletter)* 89 (1987), 54.

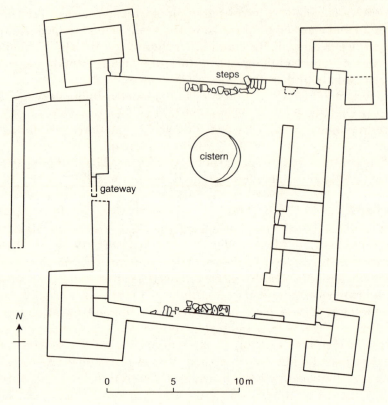

FIG. 6. Upper Zohar fort

very much like it. So it may be contemporary, but the excavations have produced no material that can be securely dated before the fifth century.[155] Evidence was found of Justinianic refurbishment and subsequent occupation. As observed by the excavator, the fort, like the Palestine Police Post some 500 metres uphill to the south-west, will have been in its day the only permanent structure for miles around. The site offers a fine view of the southern Dead Sea and northern 'Aravah. It controlled the track mentioned above which comes up from Ein Boqeq and merges with another coming up from Mezad Zohar.[156] The fort,

---

[155] *DRBE*, 336.

[156] Rothenberg, *Tsephunot Negev*, 110–14, surveyed the eastern part of this track and records several sites which he dates to the Iron Age and the Hellenistic period, although later pottery was also picked up on several sites. He identifies this track with the biblical 'way of Edom' (2 Kings 3: 8, 20), along which the kings of Israel and Judah went to fight the Edomites (2 Sam. 8: 13), cf. Y. Aharoni, *IEJ* 8 (1958), 35. Farther south-west this track passed another fort, H.

therefore, policed one of the secondary routes from the Dead Sea to the northern Negev. Again, that does not justify describing it as part of a system of defence. These two sites are best compared with the isolated British and French police posts in the desert.

Mezad Thamar (Qasr al-Juheiniya, Thamara?)

The identification of this fort with biblical Tamar is uncertain and not essential for the present argument.[157] A 'Thamaro' is mentioned by Ptolemy; and that is the name given on the Peutinger Table to a station on a road that links the Aelia–Elusa road with the Trajanic road in Transjordan. 'Thamara' appears on the Madaba Map, apparently sited between Prasidin (Praesidium, south of the Dead Sea)[158] and Moa (Moye Awad). That would place it in the 'Aravah, but no great weight need to be attached to this argument since the Madaba Map is topographically unreliable. The key source, however, is Eusebius, *Onomasticon*:[159] 'There is also a village Thamara, one day from Mampsis on the road from Hebron to Aela, where there is now a garrison'. There is little doubt that this refers to a site in the 'Aravah, perhaps the one now called Ein Tamar, which is very well watered—there is an extensive palm grove quite near the Dead Sea.[160]

There is or was no village to be seen anywhere near the fort now called Mezad Thamar, and it seems rather unlikely that Eusebius would have referred to 'a village where there is a garrison' if the garrison were fifteen kilometres removed from the village.[161] The fort now called Mezad Thamar therefore has to be considered as unidentified. However, it does lie on an ancient road recognizable by watch-

---

'Uzza, which has been under excavation for several years. It was established in the Iron Age, reoccupied in the Hellenistic period, and again from the 1st to the 3rd cents., Y. Beit-Arieh, *Qadmoniot* 19 (1986), 31–40 (in Hebrew). It has not been identified and nothing is known of the identity of the occupants.

[157] The identification was first proposed by A. Alt, *ZDPV* 58 (1935), 34 f.; it was rejected by Aharoni, *IEJ* 13 (1963), 30–42 and Rothenberg, *Tsephunot Negev*, 162 f.

[158] See above, p. 175.

[159] 8. 8, and Jerome 9. 6 (Klostermann): λέγεται δέ τις Θαμαρὰ κώμη διεστῶσα Μάψις ἡμέρας ὁδόν, ἀπιόντων ἀπὸ Χεβρὼν εἰς Ἀϊλάμ, ἥτις νῦν φρούριόν ἐστι τῶν στρατιωτῶν. Jerome: 'est ed aliud castellum Thamara, unius dei itinere a Mampsis oppido separatum, pergentibus Ailam de Chebron, ubi nunc Romanum praesidium positum est.' *Castellum* is the normal expression for 'village' in Jerome, cf. 23. 22. *Not. Dig. Or.* 34. 46: Thamana is probably another site.

[160] Rothenberg, *Tsephunot Negev*, 162 f., pls. 75 f. For the site and its surroundings, ibid. 114–178; id., *Frontier Studies 1967*, 214, fig. 101. Rothenberg reports seeing a building of 20 × 40 m. with 4th cent. sherds on the surface. Aharoni, *IEJ* 13, 30–9, argued for an identification with 'Ain el Husb, Hatzevah, farther south.

[161] Frank, 259; G. E. Kirk, *PEQ* 70 (1938), 224, who saw the site before modern development had disturbed ancient remains did not see any remains of settlement near the fort. Frank saw ancient tombs *c.* 100 m. from the fort on both sides of the road.

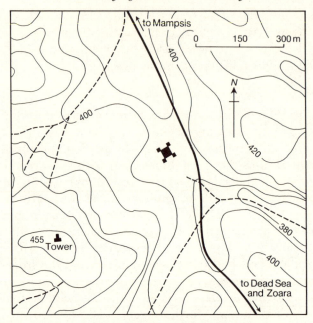

FIG. 7. Mezad Thamar and vicinity

towers and the rock-cut steps which mark the descent into the 'Aravah.[162] One of the towers, Tsafit, here illustrated, has been excavated.

The fort, excavated by M. Gichon,[163] measures 38 × 38 metres. It has four corner towers of 6 × 6 metres, which were added at a later stage.[164] The walls are a little over one metre thick. There are no interval towers nor any flanking the gate. Rooms are built against the inner face of the four walls of the fort. In the middle of the open court is an open cistern measuring 10 × 10 × 3.80 metres. The fort was occupied till the Islamic conquest. It lies on the lowest spot in a narrow valley, the worst place conceivable for defence. The reason for the location is that water could be collected here; in the 1930s two further reservoirs were seen outside the fort.[165] Watchtowers resembling the one seen near Ad Dianam were established on the surrounding hills.

---

[162] Rothenberg, *Tsephunot Negev*, 165 f. Tsafit tower was excavated, M. Gichon, *Saalburg Jahrbuch* 31 (1974), 16–40. The remains of the road were first reported by Kirk, 225 f.

[163] See M. Gichon, *Saalburg Jahrbuch* 33 (1976), 80–94; *Encyclopedia of Archaeological Excavations in the Holy Land*, iv, ed. M. Avi-Yonah and E. Stern (1978), 1148–52.

[164] Frank, who discovered the fort, had already noted this (258). For similar observations at Qasr el-Hallabat, Kennedy, *Explorations*, 26 f. .

[165] Frank, 279 f.; Kirk, 223; Gichon, *Saalburg Jahrbuch* 33, 90. One reservoir of 14 × 6 m. was

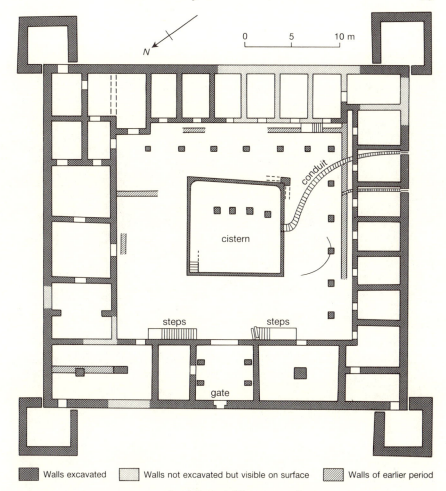

FIG. 8. Mezad Thamar: plan

Here again, we see that defensibility was not a factor in the choice of the site. The fort was originally built without corner towers and these are therefore not an essential feature. It would seem that it was a road-station controlling water-supply. This is true for three out of the four sites discussed. Apart from Upper Zohar they were all sited in disregard of defensibility and they controlled water-supply along a desert road.

seen against the west wall and another, measuring 12 × 6 m., at a distance of 300 m. to the south.

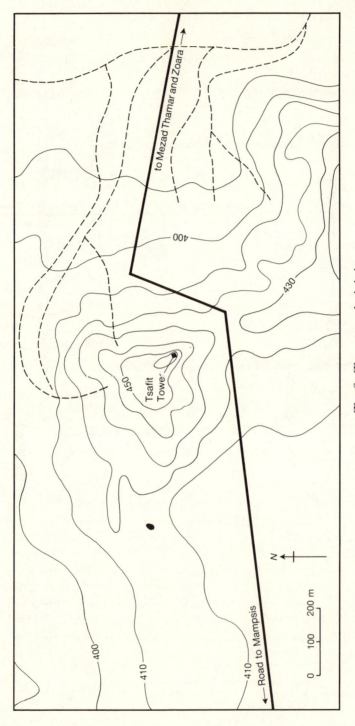

FIG. 9. Tsafit Tower and vicinity

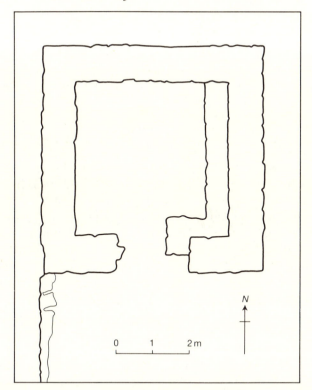

FIG. 10. Tsafit Tower: plan

I have no means of checking in person whether any of these observations apply to installations in Jordan and Syria, but it seems that they do. For instance, Parker writes about al-Khalde (Praesidium):

Situated at an elevation of 740 m., the fort and a smaller ruined structure occupy a wash between the steep wall of the gorge and a detached outcrop. Defensibility of the site is poor because it is dominated by the surrounding heights. But observers stationed atop the isolated outcrop could have obtained a much better view of the wadi. Stein noted the remains of a water channel that led from a nearby spring and emptied into several cisterns both within and without the fort . . . During the mandate the military cleaned out six large cisterns roofed by arches and slabs. . . .[166]

The same appears to be true of the legionary base at Lejjun in Jordan. Parker has the following to say of the advantages of the site: (1) It lies at the eastern edge of the region suitable for dry farming. (2) It

---

[166] Parker, *Romans and Saracens*, 108 f. I am grateful for excellent photographs sent to me by Professor David Graf.

has a copious spring, the best water source in the area. (3) It lies on the only good east–west route across the deep Wadi ed-Dabba connecting, in Roman times, the *via nova Traiana* with the desert route.[167] Elsewhere, however, he observes that 'the fortress . . . is in a tactically vulnerable position. The fortress is dominated by the heights to the west along both sides of the Wadi Lejjun.'[168]

The Function of Roman Installations: Further Arguments

These arguments can be clarified by reference to crusader castles.[169] These are always sited as well as constructed for defensibility. They are found on elevated positions which rendered them tactically strong. Where they are exposed to attack on level ground they are often surrounded by deep moats. They brought the art of fortification to an unparalleled level. Unlike the late Roman and Byzantine forts they were planned as independent logistic units in which the garrison could live for extended periods without requiring supplies from outside. They contained store-rooms and large cisterns. We know that, unlike the military installations of the Roman and Byzantine periods, some of these were indeed besieged and were well equipped to hold and repel at least small bands of invaders. The type which most resembles the *quadriburgia* of the fourth century and later is the so-called *castrum*.[170] Unlike the more heavily defended spur-castle these were not impregnable strongholds designed to withstand long sieges. They were defended bases for a garrison that would seek out the enemy and fight in the open field. In the past all crusader forts were usually assumed to be part of a system of frontier defence. A more modern view is that, particularly in the case of the *castra*, their function was far more diverse. Many changed their purpose over time. Some, like the forts around Ashkelon, were purpose-built to hold offensive garrisons and tighten

---

[167] Parker, *Roman Frontier*, 187.

[168] Ibid. 445, with map on p. 188 and aerial photographs. Parker says that the contemporary structure of Fityan made up for this deficiency, but for one who has never seen the site it is hard to understand what tactical advantage the legion would have derived from support based at a distance of more than a kilometre on the other side of a deep ravine. The main reason for the choice of the site might well be the presence of a good water supply. But, as noted above, it is not clear why there was a strong base here at all.

[169] R. C. Smail, *Crusading Warfare (1097–1193)* (1956), ch. VII, 204–44; M. Benvenisti, *The Crusaders in the Holy Land* (1970), Part 4, 273–339. I am grateful to Dr Paul Hyams for information and instruction.

[170] Smail, 228–33; Benvenisti, 280–2. There is no agreement to what extent the crusaders were influenced by Byzantine forts when they built their *castra*, and this is not important for the present discussion.

pressure on an enemy centre.[171] Others, like Belvoir, were built to hold positions of strategic importance. At least one is specifically said to have been planned to protect pilgrims to Jerusalem against attacks by bandits.[172] 'They served as residences, as administrative centres, as barracks, and as police posts. Above all, they were centres of authority. The commander of a castle and its garrison was master of the surrounding district and had means at his disposal to meet any challenge to his authority.'[173] It is not suggested that the comparison of crusader castles with Roman and Byzantine forts in itself would decide anything. The argument is simply that if even crusader castles had diverse functions and were not built exclusively for defence, this will be true *a fortiori* of the Roman and Byzantine structures which were hardly—or not at all—designed to withstand hostile attack.

It may also be helpful, in seeking to clarify the function of the fourth-century structures in Syria, Arabia, and Palestine, to compare them with the installations in Egypt's eastern desert.[174] One of these, Der el-'Atrash, is illustrated below (Fig. 14). They are dateable with certainty to the first and early second centuries,[175] and we must bear in mind that what follows is a comparison of Egyptian installations of the principate with fourth-century forts in the Eastern region. The Egyptian installations went out of use in the later Roman empire, while no comparable structures of the earlier period have as yet been found in the East. But we are concerned here only with typology and siting. The fourth-century structures in Syria, Arabia, and Palestine are similar in layout and construction to the earlier structures in Egypt. Yet in Egypt it is clear that there can have been no question of frontier defence. These roads were nowhere near a frontier, but linked the Nile with the Red Sea. Moreover, we have evidence from Pliny, as well as from a series of

---

[171] William of Tyre xiv 22 (RHC Occ. i. 638 f.) describes the function of those forts in precisely these terms.

[172] William of Tyre xiv 8 (RHC Occ. i. 617).

[173] Smail, 60 f.

[174] D. Meredith, *Tabula Imperii Romani, Coptos* (1958). See S. E. Sidebotham, *Roman Economic Policy in the Erythra Thalassa, 30 BC–AD 217* (1986), 48–67; G. W. Murray, *JEA* 11 (1925), 138–50 for the literary sources and archaeological remains; D. Meredith and L. A. Tregenza, *Bull. Faculty of Arts, Fouad I University* 11 (1949), 1–30; D. Meredith, *JEA* 38 (1952), 94–111; id., *CE* 28 (1953), 126–41. For the graffiti along the roads, A. Bernand, *De Koptos à Kosseir* (1972). For the garrison under Augustus and Tiberius, M. P. Speidel, *SMR* ii 511–15. See also *DE* s.v. *limes*, 1376/7 f.; J. C. Colvin and M. Reddé, *CRAI* (1986), 177–91.

[175] The dating rests on literary and epigraphical sources and has not yet been confirmed by thorough archaeological exploration. The installations at Mons Claudianus are now under excavation, and Dr V. Maxfield informs me that the first results seem to bear out the traditional date. The circumstance that some of these structures do not look like Roman forts of the principate merely reinforces the argument that their function was a different one.

inscriptions, to identify these installations as watering stations, halting-places, and guard posts. Pliny describes the road from Coptus in the Thebaid to Berenice as part of the shortest and safest route to India:[176]

From Coptus one travels on camels, stations (*mansiones*) being organized for the water supply: the first is called Hydreuma, 32 miles; the second is in the mountains, one day's journey; the third is again called Hydreuma, at 85 miles from Coptus; the next is in the mountains; then one comes to the Hydreuma of Apollo, 184 miles from Coptus; another station in the mountains; then one comes to New Hydreuma, 236 miles from Coptus. There is also another station, Old Hydreuma, named Trogodyticum, where an outposted garrison is stationed in a caravanserai which offers accommodation for two thousand travellers, at 7 miles from New Hydreuma. Next one arrives at the town of Berenice, a port on the Red Sea, 257 miles from Coptus.

An inscription from Coptus records work carried out by soldiers for the construction of cisterns at road-stations on this road and the road to Myos Hormos, probably under Augustus or Tiberius, certainly before 105:

Per eosdem, qui supra scripti sunt, lacci aedificati et dedicati sunt Apollonos hydreuma . . . Compasi . . . Berenicide . . . Myoshormi . . . castram [sic!] aedificaverunt et refecerunt.[177]

One of the roads, from Coptus to Leukos Limen, was further marked out by a system of intervisible beacons and signal towers.[178] Ostraka refer to the towers along the road as 'upper' and 'lower' guard posts.[179] These are small solid watchtowers, respectively on the mountains and on the lower slopes along the wadi-system. They are square, between 2 and 2.5 metres high and have no interior space. Three suggestions have been put forward with regard to their function:[180]

(*a*) They served to signal the nearby *hydreumata* of approaching caravans or marauding nomads so that measures could be taken for the reception of the caravans or the defence against attack.

(*b*) They served to signal Coptos when the merchant ships arrived at Leukos Limen.

---

[176] *NH* vi 26. 101–3; the road appears also on the *Itinerarium Antonini*, ed. Cuntz, 23; cf. Sidebotham, *Economic Policy*, 60 f.; Bernand, op. cit.; Murray, 143 f.

[177] D. Kennedy, *JEA* 71 (1985), 156–69, an improved reading of *CIL* iii 6627 = *ILS* 2483, corrected under *CIL* iii 14147; see also *CIL* iii 6123. For discussion, Sidebotham, *Economic Policy*, 65.

[178] Murray, 139, 145 f., pl. xv, 2; Sidebotham, *Economic Policy*, 64, pls. 7 and 8.

[179] R. S. Bagnall, *CE* 57 (1982), 125–8; also R. Coles, *ZPE* 39 (1980), 126–31, and the Amsterdam Ostraka, *Studia Amstelodamensia* ix (1976). For the information on such installations derived from ostraka, above, ch. III.

[180] Bagnall, *CE*. (1) is due to S. Sidebotham, (2) to D. Whitcomb and J. H. Johnson, and (3) to R. Bagnall.

(*c*) They were for local police work: signals could be sent back and forth between the towers on the mountains to those in the valley about small security problems. Small groups of bandits or marauders could be conveniently seen from above and handled from below.

Whatever their function, it must be kept in mind that they were manned by *skopelarioi*, civilians upon whom guard duty was imposed as a corvée and who could not have performed any tasks that demanded the skills of professional troops. In favour of (*c*) it may be recalled that the fourth-century forts in the Negev were also situated on low-lying sites, while modest watchtowers are found on the hill tops along the roads.

Hadrian constructed a road linking his foundation at Antinoe with Myos Hormos.[181] An inscription records that he 'opened up a new Hadrianic road from Berenice to Antinoe along the Red Sea, over safe and level terrain, and provided with *hydreumata, stathmoi, and phrouria*' (the Greek equivalent of *lacci, stationes,* and *praesidia*). As already noted, there are no milestones along these roads, although their identity as Roman roads is very well attested. They served without doubt as commercial links between the Red Sea and the Nile.[182] The interpretation of the structures along them is relevant for other areas where the evidence is ambiguous, since they look exactly like the installations along other desert roads.

By way of illustration let us compare descriptions of the stations in Egypt and of one of the Arabian forts. First, the stations in Egypt:

The stations along the roads, although varying considerably in details, conform to a general type—a rectangular caravanserai with substantial rubble walls and flanking towers at the angles and at either side of the gateway, which was often of dressed stone . . . Small rooms for the garrison and the travellers crowded the interior, but in the centre was usually a well and an open space for animals.[183]

Then Qasr Beshir in Jordan:

The water supply of the garrison was provided by a large external reservoir, several exterior cisterns, and two cisterns within the fort. . . . The plan of the fort forms a nearly square rectangle . . . with four outset angle towers. . . . Two outset, rectangular interval towers flank the main gate in the southwest wall. . . The interior of the fort consists of a large courtyard surrounded by ranges of

---

[181] *IGR* i 1142; *OGIS* 701, of 25 February 137. The text reminds one of the milestones of Trajan's road in Arabia. Cf. Sidebotham, *Economic Policy*, 61.

[182] e.g. Pliny, *NH* v 11. 60: 'Coptos Indicarum Arabicarumque mercium Nilo proximum emporium.' See in general Sidebotham, *Economic Policy*.

[183] Murray, 140; cf. Sidebotham, *Economic Policy*, 63: 'The *hydreumata* . . . resembled Roman military camps. . .', and the description that follows.

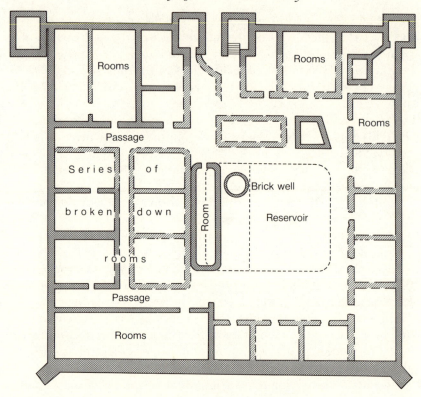

FIG. 11. Der al-ʿAtrash: plan

rooms against the enclosure wall. Apparent mangers are built into the walls of several ground floor rooms, suggesting these served as stables.[184]

It has been seen that this building was not in fact a fort but a *praetorium*, a roadside residence for the governor.

   The similarity between some of the Egyptian *hydreumata* and sites like Mezad Thamar is remarkable in many respects. They are square structures with corner towers. Rooms are often built against the inner face of the fort walls. A large water reservoir occupies much of the interior space. Like Mezad Thamar, the Egyptian stations occupy low-lying spots where water is collected. Watchtowers are found on hill-tops.[185] Mezad Thamar is even less well defended than some of the

---

[184] Parker, *Romans and Saracens*, 54. I have omitted many details of importance in the description of this particular installation. For this structure, above, pp. 172–4.

[185] e.g. Sidebotham, *Economic Policy*, pl. 7: Wekalat el-Liteima on the Coptus–Leukos Limen (Quseir) road, showing a fortified *hydreuma* and excavated reservoir or well below in the wadi, and a watchtower on top of a hill.

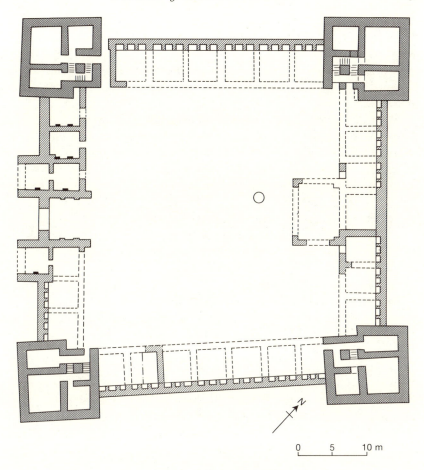

FIG. 12. Qasr Beshir

Egyptian road-stations, for it has no interval towers and an undefended gateway.

To conclude the comparison with the Egyptian installations, since the Egyptian examples date from the first and second centuries and those in Palestine and Arabia from the third and fourth, it seems that this sort of organization is not characteristic of any single period or region, but dictated by what Roman or Byzantine builders found convenient. Allowing for considerable variations in size and execution, there is yet nothing in the plan of such buildings that permits us to define them as purely military, purely civilian, or a combination of the two. As regards the road-system and installations in Egypt, it is clear that the army was responsible for construction and maintenance.[186] In the case of Qasr Beshir in Arabia we are fortunate in that a building inscription of 293–305 actually identifies its precise function. In any event, it is significant that buildings may look like heavily defended forts while, at the same time, they are sited without any regards for defensibility.

Too often scholars describe as defensive installations any Roman site which is not obviously civilian in character. An exception may be mentioned here: Sir Aurel Stein's reflections on the function of a large defended structure amongst the remains in the Wadi as-Swab on the Palmyra–Hit road. These were discovered by Poidebard and studied again by Stein, who disagreed with Poidebard's assumption that they were defensive installations. The analogy with a modern halting-place in the desert led him to suggest that this could have been an ancient road-station.[187] Stein reached this conclusion because the structure manifestly could not have been a defensive installation. However, at other sites when the impossibility is not evident, he too interprets ancient sites without hesitation as elements in a line of defence.

There is nothing new in the misinterpretation of road-stations in this manner. There are several instances in Procopius. He says that Palmyra was built to prevent Saracen raids into Syria.[188] He describes Sergiopolis (Resapha) merely as a fortified church.[189] But on the Peutinger Table, Resapha appears as a road-station on the Palmyra–Sura road, and in the *Notitia* as the garrison of the *equites promoti indigenae*.[190] He totally misunderstands the function of the monastery of Saint Catherine at the foot of Mount Sinai, which he thinks was fortified in order to prevent Saracens from invading Palestine.[191]

---

[186] Sidebotham, *Economic Policy*, 64–7.

[187] Gregory and Kennedy, 217 f.   [188] *De aed.* ii 11. 10–12.

[189] ii 9. 3. For this site, A. Poidebard and P. Mouterde, *Le limes de Chalcis* (1945), 131–4; on its position as a roadstation, 131, 134. See now M. Mackensen, *Resafa*, i (1984), full publication of a structure outside the walls, and T. Ulbert, *Resafa*, ii, *Die Basilika des heiligen Kreuzes in Resafa-Sergiupolis* (1986). The pottery dates mostly from the fifth century. Note also the Greek building-inscription recording the dedication of the Church of the Holy Cross by Abraamios, bishop of Sergioupolis in 559 (cf. J. and L. Robert, *BE* 1978, 521) and the Greek graffiti published by C. Römer, pp. 171–7. On the importance of this site in the Byzantine period see below, ch. V.

[190] *Not. Dig. Or.* xxxiii 27.

[191] Ibid. v 8. 9. Cf. P. Mayerson, *BASOR* 230 (1978), 33–8. Averil Cameron, *Procopius* (1985), 96 f., argues that Procopius was in fact correct: the monastery did not indeed prevent raids into Palestine, but it had 'the effect of deterring razzias that were the predominating method of attack in that region by its strong statement of Byzantine authority'. If that were its purpose the site chosen would make it a singularly futile exercise. Sinai in general, and southern Sinai in particular, has always been sparsely populated. In 1917 the entire population of Sinai numbered no more than 7,000: Geographical Handbook Series, *Western Arabia and the Red Sea*, ed. K. Mason (Naval Intelligence Division, ²1946), 366. Even in southern Sinai it is hard to think of any spot

On the other hand it is relevant to note that in the West there are parallel cases of roads provided with chains of guard posts in the late Roman period, and these, too, have sometimes been described incorrectly as *limites*, for instance the road from Boulogne via Tournai, Tongeren, and Maastricht to Cologne.[192]

Even where we are not faced with road-stations meant to provide services to civilian or military travellers, it is essential to distinguish between defence against invasion or large-scale raiding and the police activities maintained by any power that aims at controlling desert areas. It is the latter which many of the late Roman and Byzantine forts in the desert are obviously equipped for. They are confidently placed on poorly defensible sites, blocking roads and passages, controlling and using wells and other sources of water, an essential element in preventing banditry—though they could, of course, function also as bases for patrols and centres of administration.

The description of road-stations used by pilgrims who travelled to Mount Sinai may be of some assistance. The *Itinerarium Egeriae* describes a journey, made in 383, from Jerusalem to Mount Sinai and back by way of Clysma (Suez) and Pelusium and the coast road of Sinai.[193] While travelling in Sinai she was protected by Saracen tribes centred at Pharan.[194] When she entered Egypt at Clysma (Suez) she found a functioning chain of *mansiones* which served as halting-places and bases for soldiers and officers who escorted the travellers as far as the next station: 'From Clysma and the Red Sea it is four desert staging-posts before you reach the city Arabia [probably = Phacusa, Faqus], and the desert is of a kind where they have to have quarters at each staging-post for soldiers and their officers, who escorted us from one fort to the next.'[195] Note the dual function of the *mansiones*. As the pilgrims reached

more isolated than that occupied by the monastery. It is difficult to reach even by the few almost waterless tracks that cross the region. The only target of any razzia in the area could have been pilgrims. There is no obvious reason to go to great trouble in order to deny the obvious fact that Procopius had no idea where the monastery was in Sinai—even though he came from Caesarea. If the Byzantine government had wanted to make a statement of authority the only rational site for it would have been the settlement of Pharan.

[192] H. Schönberger, *JRS* 59 (1969), 183, with fig. 23, and 179: 'The road, although protected by small military forts and *burgi*, was not a frontier line. Elsewhere, roads in the late Roman period were similarly protected.' Schönberger mentions the Constantinian or, more likely, Valentinianic 'Ausonius road' between Trier, Bingen, and Mainz, and the road from Augsburg to Kempten and Bregenz.

[193] For the date, P. Devos, *Analecta Bollandiana* 85 (1967), 165–94.

[194] As observed by Z. Rubin, 'Sinai in the Itinerarium Egeriae' Atti del convegno . . . 1987, 176–91. I have not seen P. Maraval, *Égérie, Journal de voyage* (1982) and *Lieux Saints et pélerinages d'Orient, histoire et géographie des origines à la conquête arabe* (1985).

[195] *Itinerarium Egeriae* ix 2 (*CCSL* clxxv 47): 'Sunt ergo a Clesma, id est a mare Rubro, usque ad Arabiam civitatem mansiones quattuor per heremo sic tamen per heremum, ut cata

the public road in the heart of Egypt there was no need for their protection any more and the soldiers were dismissed.[196] In the fourth century *mansiones* and *xenodochia* were built and kept up by the authorities. We hear of a bishop of Antioch initiating such activities in 350.[197] The emperor Constantius is said to have spent much money on the church, the orphans, and *xenodochia*.[198] The empress Eudoxia gave funds for a hospice to be built in Gaza, where pilgrims received three days of free lodgings.[199]

Many installations performed several functions at once. The account of a journey to Mount Sinai in 570 ascribed to Antoninus Placentinus mentions three *xenodochia*, two of them being forts that contained churches as well as *xenodochia*, the third a *castellum modicum, infra se xenodochium*.[200] In Arabia several forts contain churches.[201] In Syria churches are found in many forts.[202] It is quite possible that some of these too would be described as *castella* containing a *xenodochium* and church, being, in fact, installations with various functions. However, in the fifth and sixth centuries a fort with a purely military function could also include a church.

In this connection the acropoleis of Oboda (Avdat) and Nessana should be mentioned. These apparently attained their present form in

mansiones monasteria sint cum militibus et prepositis, qui nos deducebant semper de castro ad castrum.' Trans. J. Wilkinson, *Egeria's Travels to the Holy Land* (1981), 101; for the identification of Arabia see his p. 216.

[196] Op. cit., ix 3, *CCSL* clxxv 49: 'Nos autem inde iam remisimus milites, qui nobis pro disciplina Romana auxilia prebuerant, quamdiu per loca suspecta ambulaveramus; iam autem, quoniam agger publicum erat per Egyptum . . . et ideo non fuit necesse vexare milites.'

[197] *Chronicon Paschale*, AD 350, ed. Dindorf, 535 f. For Christian hostels, H. Leclerq, *Dictionnaire d'archéologie Chrétienne et de liturgie*, vi 2. 2748–70, s.v. hopitaux, hospices, hôtelleries.

[198] *Chron. Pasch.* AD 360, ed. Dindorf, 545.

[199] Mark the Deacon, *Vita Porphyrii* 53, ed. Grégoire et Kugener, 44; cf. Carol A. M. Glucker, *The City of Gaza in the Roman and Byzantine Periods* (1987), 97. For the doubtful origin of Eudoxia's wealth see below, p. 365.

[200] Antoninus Placentinus 35, *CCSL* clxxv 146 f: twenty miles from Elusa was the 'castrum in quo est xenodochius sancti Georgi, in quo habent quasi refugium transeuntes vel heremitae stipendia'. The reference to St George shows that it was a military inn (see above, p. 177). P. Mayerson, *Proc. Am. Phil. Soc.* 107 (1963), 170, has argued that this was the fort of Nessana. id. 41, *CCSL* xxv 150: '. . . castellum modicum, qui vocatur Surandala; nihil habet intus praeter ecclesiam cum presbytero suo et duo xenodochia propter transeuntes.'

[201] Deir el-Kahf: H. C. Butler, *Ancient Architecture in Syria, Publications of the Princeton Archaeological Expedition to Syria*, ii A 2 *Southern Hauran* (1909), 146, fig. 127; reproduced by Parker, *Romans and Saracens* 23, fig. 6. Qasr el-Ba'iq: Butler, 82, fig. 61, reproduced by Parker, 25, fig. 78. Chapel built on to 'the barracks' at Umm el-Jemal: Parker, 28, fig. 9. For the *principia* at Udruh, A. Killick, *Levant* 15 (1983), 110–31, esp. 121, 125. For the church probably *c.* 500 in the legionary base of Lejjun, R. Schick, in Parker, *Roman Frontier*, 353–77.

[202] Butler, ii A 3., *Umm idj-Djimal* (1913), 171; examples from Androna, Stabl 'Antar, and il-Habat, all dated 556–8: ibid., ii.B; Mouterde and Poidebard, 174 f. and inscriptions nos. 56–60 on p. 217 (Androna and Stabl 'Antar). For a photograph, J. Wagner, *Antike Welt*, Sondernummer (1985), 66.

the Byzantine period.[203] They are both divided into two parts, one half being occupied by a church (two at Oboda) and additional rooms, the other by an oblong fort. The latter contained a cistern and chapel in Oboda, and a series of rooms built against two of the walls at Nessana. Papyri from Nessana show that a *numerus Theodosiacus*, a camel-mounted cavalry unit, was based there in the fifth century. It is usually assumed that these forts are instances of centralized planning with no consideration of local needs. Woolley and Lawrence write: 'The forts there are of Justinian's plan and most probably his work, but only a bureaucratic pedant could have imposed on a desert such incongruous defences, which seem intended rather to complete a theory than to meet a local need.'[204] It would be more correct to say that the work does not suit modern preconceptions of Byzantine organization. Both towns lay on important routes through the desert. They were both provided with churches, a monastery, a fort and, presumably, a *xenodochium*. The structures may have had various other functions unknown to us. In particular they are likely to have been an assertion of government authority in the region. The cavalry unit at Nessana will have policed the wider area. These were not troops likely to be engaged in local defence. The fact that forts were built is not remarkable in itself. The Roman army had always built permanent quarters for itself.

It may legitimately be asked why many civilian or half-military buildings were made to look like forts in the fourth century and after. The answer may be that many buildings were in fact built by military units, since there was no easily available civilian building force and army building was cheap—there were no labour costs.[205] Another factor may be that the authority of the state was identified with military power. Any building that represented this authority was therefore made to look like a military installation. Imposing architecture naturally took the form of fortifications and was a means of conveying the power of Rome, even where there was no expectation that the fortifications would have to withstand attack. This is merely a way of arguing that the massive fourth-century structures were raised in the same spirit which in an earlier period led to the construction of the

---

[203] For Nessana, H. D. Colt et al., *Excavations at Nessana* i (1962). For the date, C. J. Kraemer, *Nessana: Non-literary Papyri* iii (1958), 16, 22. Colt, i 6, notes that the Nessana fort and the smaller one at Oboda are so alike in plan that they almost certainly were planned at the same time. For plan and photograph of Obodas, Avi Yonah and Stern, *Encyclopedia of Archaeological Excavations in the Holy Land* ii (1976), 347 f. (A. Negev). The fort is there dated to the middle of the sixth century, it is not clear on what grounds.

[204] L. Woolley and T. E. Lawrence, *The Wilderness of Zin* (1914–15), 49; followed by Mayerson, *TAPA* 95 (1964), 185.

[205] As suggested to me by Professor J. C. Mann.

principia at Lambaesis. Diocletian's palace in Split looks like an army camp, but it was no more intended to defend the frontier than are the walls of the Kremlin.

The Limitanei

The first point to be noted is that the term *limitanei* applies to 'soldiers serving in a *limes*, a frontier district'. This follows from the definition of *limes* formulated at the beginning of this chapter. *Limitanei* does not mean farmer soldiers or members of a peasant militia. It is a term that distinguishes the troops commanded by a *dux limitis*, who held a regional command, from the *comitatenses*, the field army. In Palestine, for instance, according to *Novella* 103 of Justinian, the troops under the command of the *dux* included *limitanei*. These could serve anywhere under the command of the *dux* and were not necessarily confined to a specific part of one province. The *dux limitis* of Palestine, for instance, was the military commander of all three provinces so named, and he was responsible for military affairs anywhere in these provinces. Hence *limitanei* can be found anywhere in Palestine, and their duty was not confined to that of defending the frontier. Thus a legal text of AD 409 can refer to the *limitanei* in First, Second, and Third Palestine.[206] First and Second Palestine, of course, were nowhere near a frontier. The Samaritan revolt in 484 was suppressed by the *dux Palaestinae* with a large force (of *limitanei*, that is).[207] Yet another indication that the *dux* was responsible for security throughout the Palestinian region can be found in an episode recorded by Cyril of Scythopolis who reports that the *dux* was ordered to put a garrison in a fort to be built for the protection of monasteries in the Judaean desert (in Palaestina Prima).[208] All this again allows us to consider different hypotheses as regards the function of these troops. This is true for the sixth century as it is for the fourth. Procopius describes the *limitanei* as regular soldiers stationed 'all over the frontier districts (*eschatia*) of the state'.[209]

Finally, if *limitanei* are regular troops and not a farmer militia it follows that the same separation between army and civilians must be postulated as existing from the fourth century onwards as we know to

---

[206] *Cod. Theod.* vii 4. 30; *Cod. Iust.* xii 37. 13: 'Limitanei militis et possessorum utilitate conspecta per primam, secundam ac tertiam Palaestinam huiuscemodi norma processit', etc.

[207] Malalas, 382; *Chronicon Paschale*, 603 f. Procopius, *de aed.* v 7. 8, says that after the revolt a large garrison was placed in the city of Neapolis and smaller one on Mount Gerizim, the centre of Samaritan worship, which had been converted into a church. These soldiers would have been *limitanei* as well.

[208] Cyril of Scythopolis, *vita Sabae*, 73, ed. Schwartz, 178.

[209] *Anecdota* 24. 12 f.

have been applicable in the early empire. In other words, the units listed in the *Notitia* or in the fragments of the edict from Beer Sheva were troops on active service. They may have been recruited locally, and they could own land in a private capacity, which would have the same status as land owned by civilians, but there is no reason to assume that they counted as civilians or were engaged in cultivating the land. They would have been entitled to supplies in kind or money from the local population, as is clear from the edict from Beer Sheva.[210]

These matters are vividly illustrated in the sixth-century papyri from Nessana.[211] This was the base of a camel corps, the Theodosian *numerus*.[212] The unit was certainly based there in 548, was still there in 590, and was perhaps disbanded or transferred shortly afterwards.[213] The soldiers, at least in part local people, owned landed property in the area, but it is significant that when land from the paternal estate of one soldier was transferred to another this was registered at the civilian record office in Elusa.[214] On the other hand, legal business between soldiers was decided by a regular military court in the camp.[215] The discovery of the soldiers' archive, a collection of documents recording personal and financial transactions, shows that, as in the principate, unit headquarters served as a depository for the personal papers of the troops.[216] All this shows that they were regular soldiers subject to military jurisdiction, rather than a militia. As citizens they could possess land subject to civilian authority and had families living with them, which was formally permitted ever since the reign of Septimius Severus. The situation is, in fact, the same as in Ein Gedi, where a centurion lent money to a civilian in the reign of Hadrian on the security of a courtyard in the village.[217] If his debtor had failed he would have become the owner of it. At least one of the papyri shows again that the *limitanei* based in Third Palestine were in fact part of a territorial command which covered all Palestinian provinces, for seven squads are drawn upon to supply men for a mission to Caesarea.[218] One

[210] *Contra* the German translation by A. Alt, *Die griechischen Inschriften der Palaestina Tertia* (1921), no. 2, p. 8, which proceeds from the assumption that the *duces* and *limitanei* were to make payment rather than receive it.

[211] C. J. Kraemer (ed.), *Excavations at Nessana*, iii. *Non-Literary Papyri* (1958).

[212] No. 15 and comments on p. 41 for the identity of the unit. From nos. 35 and 37 it is clear that this was a camel corps.

[213] No. 19 of AD 548, no. 24 of 569, and no. 29 of 590 with comments on pp. 24 and 89. The fact that a 'loyal soldier from the camp at Nessana' is mentioned (in l.3) proves that the unit was still there.

[214] No. 24.   [215] No. 19 of AD 248 with comments on pp. 60 f.

[216] Kraemer, Introduction, p. 5.   [217] See above, p. 137.

[218] No. 37 with comments on p. 22 f.

man was re-routed to Egypt, and another papyrus seems to indicate that two soldiers of the unit lived for a long time in Rhinocorura in the province of Egypt.[219]

In his *Anecdota* Procopius states that the *limitanei* were disbanded by Justinian. This occurs in a lengthy description of harmful measures taken by that emperor:[220]

Since the discussion of the army leads me to it I shall add one further point. The Roman rulers in former times stationed a large force of soldiers everywhere in the frontier districts of the state in order to guard the frontiers of the empire, particularly in the eastern part, checking the incursions of Persians and Saracens. These troops they called *limitanei*. These the emperor Justinian treated in the beginning so carelessly and so miserly that their paymasters were four or five years behind in paying their salaries. When peace was concluded between the Romans and the Persians these wretched men were compelled to donate the salary owed to them for a specific period to the public treasury, on the pretence that they too would profit from the blessings of peace. Later he took away from them the very title of an army without reason. Henceforth the frontiers of the Roman empire remained without guards and the soldiers suddenly had to look to the hands of those accustomed to do good deeds.

This statement has been taken too seriously. In the *Buildings* Procopius himself states that strong garrisons of regular soldiers commanded by *duces* (i.e. *limitanei*) were established at several posts.[221] Procopius has many shortcomings, but he knew the difference between regular troops and a militia.[222] In 528 Justinian ordered the *duces* of Phoenice, Arabia, and Mesopotamia (and the phylarchs) to march against Mundhir and punish him for his murder of Arethas, the Kindite vassal of the Romans.[223] At this stage there was apparently not the slightest doubt that the troops under the command of the *duces* could undertake a difficult campaign far from home. *Limitanei* are mentioned among the troops in Palestine in Justinian's *Novella* 103, dating from 536, which records a reorganization of the government of Palestine following the serious Samaritan revolt which broke out in 530. It emphasizes that a primary task of the troops in the province is the suppression of religious strife. In 541 Belisarius marched against the Persian army with forces that included the *duces* of Lebanon and Phoenice with their troops.[224] They participated in operations in the

---

[219] No. 15.   [220] *Anecdota* 24. 12–14.
[221] *De aed.* iii 3. 14: Artaleson (in Chorzane, south of Erzerum); ii 6. 9: at Circesium; iii 6. 17: at Tzanike.
[222] He describes a peasant militia in *De aed.* iv 2. 15.
[223] Malalas, 434 f.   [224] Procopius, *Bell.* ii 16. 17–19.

Persian part of Mesopotamia. This caused them a good deal of concern, as it meant leaving the provinces for which they were responsible exposed to hostile attack, but Belisarius was unwilling to release them.[225] All this shows that the eastern *limitanei* not only existed in the reign of Justinian but could also function as a fully trained field army.

While there is quite a bit of information on the organization of the *limitanei* and their installations in the various parts of Syria in the fourth century, the state of affairs in the fifth and sixth centuries is insufficiently clear.[226] Since there is good evidence that units were withdrawn from the remote forts in some areas of Palestine the question arises whether the same was true in Syria. At present there is no archaeological material that can help, and the literary evidence is inconclusive. There is, however, at least a suggestion that the units between Damascus and the Euphrates were withdrawn. Towards the middle of the sixth century there was a dispute about grazing lands in the region of Palmyra between nomad chiefs.[227] One of the parties argued that the name of the region, 'Strata' showed that it was part of the Roman empire. That is an obvious reference to the old *strata Diocletiana*, and the very fact that such a dispute could take place is an indication that there was no army presence there. When Khusro besieged Resapha on the Palmyra–Sura road in the sixth century the citizens defended themselves without aid from imperial troops.[228] In the same period nomad raids could be carried out more easily in Syria and Osrhoene than in northern Mesopotamia where the presence of numerous guard posts made raiding very awkward.[229] These guard posts, it may be noted, are hardly known archaeologically. We may therefore conclude that there is a likelihood that at least some of the units in the desert parts of Syria were withdrawn.

The date of the departure or disbandment of the unit at Nessana is of some importance for the question of *limitanei* in Palestine. First, it is firmly attested there after Justinian's death, which is indisputable proof that at least this unit of *limitanei* was unaffected by any measure he might have taken with regard to these troops.[230] Second, there is no indication in the papyri that the departure of the unit very seriously

---

[225] *Bell.* ii 19. 39.

[226] For discussion of the defences of Syria in the sixth century, W. Liebeschuetz, *SMR* ii (1977), 487–99.

[227] Procopius, *Bell.* ii 1. 3 ff. Cf. Liebeschuetz, *SMR* ii 489.

[228] See below, ch. V.

[229] Procopius, *Bell.* i 17. 34, citing the advice given by Mundhir the Lakhmid to the Persian king. For the raids actually carried out, see above ch. II, and below, ch. V.

[230] e.g. Kraemer, *Non-Literary Papyri*, no. 37, of *c.* 560–80, is an account of military camels assigned to the troops, each serving under a *decurio* (δέχαρχος).

affected economic prosperity or the routine of civilian life, as there was a good deal of building activity well into the seventh century.[231] There is, however, archaeological evidence of the abandonment of forts elsewhere. The fort at Yotvetah was abandoned before the end of the fourth century,[232] and in central Transjordan several sites were unoccupied in the sixth century.[233] There appears indeed to have been a reduction of forces in parts of Third Palestine, but this occurred before the reign of Justinian and does not support the statement of Procopius that *limitanei* were disbanded.

In the north-eastern desert parts of Jordan there is no such evidence of withdrawal. An inscription of 529 records restoration of the fort of Hallabat.[234] At several sites in northern Arabia fragments have been found of Anastasius' decree regarding the frontier troops.[235] In the absence of more reliable information it seems therefore best to assume that troops were indeed withdrawn from a number of the remote desert posts established in the period of Diocletian and Constantine. It is possible that this was done in stages, since some forts appear to have been occupied longer than others.[236] However, there is definitely no uniform pattern.[237] More excavation may alter our views. It must also be emphasized that Nessana is the only site at which we know the nature of the occupation. As argued in the next chapter, it is quite possible that the alternative arrangements, involving collaboration with Arab chiefs, that were instituted in the remote parts of Third Palestine worked quite satisfactorily till the Islamic conquest; and we have no reason to believe that this defeat could have been prevented by the troops which occupied the desert in the fourth century. Given the state of our information we can only speculate on these matters. It is possible that the army was over-extended in the fourth century. It is conceivable that more troops were needed elsewhere during and after the costly wars of the sixth century.

Finally, it is perhaps no coincidence that the two main phases of military building activity in the period under consideration are those of Diocletian and Constantine and of Anastasius and Justinian. While we

---

[231] Kraemer, 28 f.   [232] See above, p. 188.

[233] Parker, *Roman Frontier*, summary, 820 f.   [234] Kennedy, *Explorations*, 40.

[235] Sartre, *IGLS* xiii 1, no. 9046, and references on p. 111. Fragments have been found at Bostra and four sites in the north.

[236] As already noted, Yotvetah was abandoned before the end of the fourth century. Parker, loc. cit., lists several sites which were abandoned by *c.* 500: Khirbet el-Fityan, Rujm Beni Yasser, and Qasr Beshir. Other forts, notably Lejjun, were occupied into the sixth century. The unit at Nessana, as observed, did not leave its posts before the end of the sixth century. Upper Zohar, Ein Boqeq, and Mezad Thamar were all three occupied till the Islamic conquest.

[237] For a different view, Parker, *Romans and Saracens*, 151 f.

may not know enough to understand the patterns of military activity it is worth noting that these were also the periods of most intensive warfare between Rome and Persia. It is true that there were several wars after Constantine and before Anastasius that were not accompanied by building activity, but even so it is likely that the two major construction programmes of the late third and sixth centuries were connected with the warfare in those years.

The Army in the Desert: Considerations

In Chapter III it was emphasized how little solid evidence there is of army presence in the desert during the first centuries of Roman rule. Penetration clearly took place in stages. The reign of Severus saw a change in north-east Jordan, and the desert patrol beyond Aila may date to the same period. The last quarter of the third century and the beginning of the fourth marked the establishment of various permanent structures where there is no clear evidence of occupation in the second century. It is far too early to draw maps with any confidence. There can be no doubt, however, that there was some expansion of the Roman presence in the Negev, in southern Jordan, and along the eastern desert road in Jordan. In Syria the same can be seen along the so-called *strata Diocletiana*. The *Notitia Dignitatum* and the fragments of the Beer Sheva edict clearly show the extent of the military occupation of the steppe and desert, even if individual sites cannot always be identified with certainty. It is also clear that, when army presence in the desert increased in the period of the later empire, there was a corresponding reduction of troops in the interior of Palestine and the coastal area of Syria. Legions, reduced in size as they were in this period, were now based in Aela and Lejjun in Transjordan and on the road to the Euphrates in Syria.

So far there is agreement. The function of the troops, however, is a matter of dispute, and this book argues that, in the Byzantine period, the security situation in Mesopotamia and northern Syria was totally different from that in Palestine, Arabia, and southern Syria. Hence the northern region has been discussed separately in Chapter I. The southern region was relatively quiet and unthreatened, as is argued in Chapter II. The gradual military expansion into the remote parts of these provinces, therefore, need not be explained in terms of defence of the settled lands against invading nomads. In the present chapter I have tried to show that the troops were not in fact organized for such a task. As evidence for this I have cited a few inscriptions which show that some forts did not have the function commonly attributed to them; analysed a small number of dated forts; drawn a comparison with known halting-places in Egypt; and quoted literary evidence that there were stations in the desert functioning as combined garrisons and staging-posts.

If it is accepted that Roman and Byzantine organization in the desert represented policing and road-security rather than defence, several questions may be asked. Was the increased Roman presence here a response to increased trouble caused by nomads or is it an indication that the authorities had begun to accept responsibility where previously they had not done so? If the latter is the case, did the security situation improve because of increased Roman intervention or did the increased Roman presence actually cause a deterioration of the situation by engendering tensions which did not exist before, so that further intervention was required? This is a phenomenon observed among Bedouin in recent history: 'When the rulers or neighbours exerted constant military or administrative pressure on any group of tribes they compelled it to organize within a larger framework and brought about the development of an aggressive leadership.' Such an organization would not be capable of fighting, for instance, the Ottoman forces in a full-scale battle, but it could resist small punitive actions.[238] However, this explanation for the formation of political associations is not generally accepted; and when sociologists and anthropologists do not agree about such matters in recent times, there is obviously very little chance of obtaining certainty about them in antiquity. In any event it is likely that, whenever a strong central government develops, the Bedouin will resent and resist its interference and its attempts to regulate and change their way of life while they merely want to be left alone.[239]

It is clear that anyone who travelled through desert and steppe would require protection against attacks by Bedouin. That was true for every period in antiquity. The organizing of this protection, as the Nabataean kingdom, Palmyra, and the authorities in Egypt found, could be a source of great wealth. It is therefore quite possible that the

---

[238] E. Marx in W. Weissleder (ed.), *The Nomadic Alternative: Modes and Models of Interaction in the African-Asian Deserts and Steppes* (1978), 52. Marx gives as example the Rwala which, in the nineteenth century, found themselves under pressure in the Wadi Sirhan between the Ottoman kingdom and that of Ibn Rashid.

[239] Shortly before the Sinai was returned by Israel to Egypt I asked a Bedouin which government he preferred. He replied: 'The best government in the world is no government. And if there has to be a government you want one that does not cheat, does not impose taxes, does not take our lands, and asks for no permits.'

traces of a Roman army presence in the steppe and desert areas of the Middle East represent steps taken by the authorities to safeguard all forms of traffic and profit financially in the same manner as the Nabataeans and Palmyrenes did in their time. It is not necessary to believe that this was a response to increased trouble caused by nomads.

An essential factor that cannot be evaluated till more work is done and work already carried out has been fully published is the increase in settlement in the Byzantine period. It is quite clear that Palestine, including the north-western Negev, was more densely populated in the Byzantine period, particularly in the fifth and sixth centuries, than in any period of history before the twentieth century. In the Negev there are the cities of Oboda, Mampsis, Elusa, and Nessana, as well as many smaller settlements and traces of occupation on many other sites,[240] though these are confined to the north-western and central area; in the eastern and southern parts military sites must be seen as connected with the road system rather than local settlement.

While it is clear that it took place during the Byzantine period, not enough is yet known about the chronology of the development of the settlement pattern to make possible a correlation with increased army presence. Moreover, it is not a local phenomenon, but can be observed also in other parts of Palestine. It is not even necessarily confined to the Roman empire. In Babylonia, notably in the Diyala plains, a parallel development took place. There it has been shown that the Sassanian period witnessed a spectacular growth in settlement beyond the level already attained in the Parthian period. Ctesiphon 'embraced a larger area within its walls than the total area of the 130 known sites in the entire basin during the Isin-Larsa period, the apogee of earlier anti-quity'. This development took place on the east bank of the river, not on the west bank, perhaps because the former suffered far less than the latter from the destructive activity of passing Roman troops.[241] So we are faced with a phenomenon that can be traced throughout the Middle East. To explain it requires a better understanding of ancient social history than we now have.

One factor that may be mentioned here, for whatever it is worth, is the remarkable prosperity of Mecca as a trade centre in the sixth

---

[240] For Elusa, Y. Dan, *IEJ* 32 (1982), 134–7; P. Mayerson, *IEJ* 33 (1983), 247–53; *Encyclopedia of Archaeological Excavations in the Holy Land*, ii 359 f. For Oboda and Nessana, above, pp. 206 f. P. Mayerson conjectures that the prosperity and the expansion of settlement in the Negev in this period was due to pilgrimage: *Cathedra* 45 (1987), 19–40 (in Hebrew). For ancient agriculture in the region, M. Evenari et al., *The Negev: The Challenge of a Desert* (²1982), 95–119, 179–219.
[241] R. McC. Adams, *Land Behind Baghdad* (1965), 71–3.

century.[242] The reasons for this are not altogether understood, but it may be connected with interruptions of trade through Mesopotamia resulting from the wars between Rome and Persia.[243] However this may be, it clearly implies that Arabian trade with the Byzantine empire flourished at the time, and with it the trade route through the Negev.

The increased military presence in the desert could, as suggested, be an indication that the authorities had begun to accept responsibility where previously they had not done so. But it is also possible, although we know nothing about this, that improved security in the steppe or semi-desert country together with the expansion of settlement in these areas were sufficient in themselves to cause friction and conflict between the settled population supported by the army and the nomads who lived there.[244] The urbanization of the northern Negev in the Byzantine period obviously must have interfered with previously existing patterns of nomadic pastoralism, although we do not know in what way. Clearly the settling of the land and the opening of the water resources both near the cities and along the main roads restricted the movements of the nomads and perhaps reduced their pastures.

We need to know more about settlement patterns in the regions concerned.[245] In this connection the regional explorations at Humayma in Jordan, a military site and civilian settlement, are of interest. A preliminary report notes that all the Romano-Byzantine sites in the region were associated with the Trajanic road, unlike the earlier Nabataean sites which were more widely distributed and situated on high ground and hills. At the site of Humayma itself Roman installations and a civilian settlement existed side by side.[246]

Recently it has been argued that the archaeological remains in Wādi el-Hasa may be interpreted as evidence of relatively peaceful coexist-

[242] I. Kawar, *Arabica* 3 (1956), 187–92; F. McG. Donner, *The Early Islamic Conquests* (1981), 51 f. with references in n. 1.

[243] Procopius, *Bell.* i 20. 9, 11–12, says that Justinian proposed that the Aethiopians should act as middlemen in the silk trade so as to circumvent Persia. This was impossible, as the Persians controlled all the ports of contact with the Indians. But it shows that the notion existed.

[244] This was the pattern, for instance in South Africa, as described above, p. 27.

[245] For the towns in the Negev see the relevant entries in *Encyclopedia of Archaeological Excavations in he Holy Land*; A. Negev, *ANRW* ii 8, 520–686, esp. 620–63; and in general Y. Dan, *The City in Eretz-Israel during the Late Roman and Byzantine Periods* (1984, in Hebrew).

[246] W. Eadie, *ADAJ* 28 (1984), 211–24; J. P. Oleson, *Echos du Monde Classique* 28/NS 3 (1984), 235–44; see also J. W. Eadie and J. P. Oleson, *BASOR* 262 (1986), 49–76; Kennedy and Riley, 146–8. At Umm el Jimal investigations have revealed an unwalled settlement of the Nabataean and Roman periods and a Byzantine city with a small *castellum* beside a reservoir. The city continued into the Umayyad period; B. de Vries, *DRBE* i 227–41; Kennedy and Riley, 183–5. As part of the project at Udruh several other sites are investigated, see A. C. Killick, *DRBE* i 431–6, with references. For other surveys in Transjordan, J. M. Miller, *BASOR* 234 (1979), 43–52; B. MacDonald, *BASOR* 245 (1982), 35–52; S. Hart, *Levant* 18 (1986), 51–8.

ence rather than perpetual conflict.[247] Even in the period of lax control when Musil travelled through the region there was little conflict.[248]

No wandering Bedouin tribe would think of trying to force a passage across Wadi el-Hasa [that is, from the south to the north], for the passes of el-'Akkuza and Ksuba on the right bank of the wadi can be defended very easily, with stones even. Nor would the tribes which practice agriculture north of the wadi ever allow the passage of a wandering Bedouin tribe in spring or early summer. They are pleased, however, when the Bedouins wander around at the edge of the desert because they can sell, i.e. exchange a lot. This I was told by Hajel.

Musil, in other words, explains that there existed a pattern of trans-humance between the 'Aravah and the desert in Transjordan which was peaceful because the topography made it physically impossible for the Bedouin to penetrate the settled lands north of Wadi el-Hasa.[249] As long as the Bedouin stayed away from their fields before the harvest, the farmers found them a useful element because goods could be exchanged. In Chapter II it has been noted that Bedouin might peacefully let their flocks move on to the stubble fields of the villages. The parallel does not in itself prove anything, but it is to be noted that movements were dictated and limited by topography at all times. Under Ottoman rule Bedouin tribes sometimes developed trading and political relationships with Syrian cities.[250]

It has been pointed out that, in the economic sphere, nomads, semi-nomads, and the sedentary population of Arabia were interdependent at all times.[251] The former depended on the latter for many essential goods which they could never produce themselves, such as various foodstuffs, cloth, and metal products. They sold some of their livestock and related products, served as guides and guards for caravans, and exacted protection money. Moreover, there existed many social and religious ties between the various groups.[252] All this is not to suggest that life was peaceful and pleasant in the region, but that a *modus vivendi* may have existed, good enough for the Roman authorities to refrain from interfering on a massive scale.

It is possible that Roman policy resulted in an entirely different situation from that observed in the Ottoman empire, as a survey

---

[247] E. B. Banning, *BASOR* 261 (1986), 25–50; criticized by S. T. Parker, *BASOR* 265 (1987), 35–51, followed by a reply by Banning, 52–4. See also E. B. Banning and I. Koehler-Rollefson, *ZDPV* 102 (1986), 152–70.

[248] Musil, *Arabia Petraea*, ii 15.

[249] Cf. Banning, *BASOR* 261, 43; and on patterns of transhumance in the region, G. L. Harris, *Jordan: Its People, Its Society, Its Culture* (1958), 51–3.

[250] N. N. Lewis, *Nomads and Settlers in Syria and Jordan, 1800–1900* (1987), 6 f.

[251] Donner, 26 f., with references in n. 32.   [252] Donner, 27 f.

carried out in the desert area east of the Dead Sea has found no significant evidence of the Roman and Byzantine periods. The stages of intensive settlement here seemed to be Chalcolithic/EB and Nabataean/Early Roman. That could indicate that the Roman occupation brought with it an end to settlement in the region without a subsequent revival in the later period.[253] In contrast to these conclusions for the desert, there appears to have been a revival of settlement in the fertile region, between the desert and the Dead Sea, in the fourth century, as well as in other non-desert regions.[254] These conclusions are based only on surface surveys and can therefore be taken as no more than promising hypotheses. In Judaea and the Negev it is clear that the Byzantine period saw unprecedented expansion over large areas, always an indication of prosperity and security, especially when the settlements are numerous and small.

All this should not obscure the fact that the army continued to police the more densely settled areas as well. In Chapter III something was said of the banditry and more serious troubles known to have occurred in Palestine in the later period. In Chapter VI more will be said of the role of the army as a police force in cities. During the later Roman empire, however, the main area of confrontation was still that between Rome/Byzantium and Persia; and this is where most of the troops were engaged.

[253] V. A. Clark, in Parker, *Roman Frontier*, 107–63.
[254] Frank L. Koucky, in Parker, *Roman Frontier*, 78.

V

ENEMIES AND ALLIES
AFTER SEPTIMIUS SEVERUS

THE conquest of northern Mesopotamia by the Roman empire at the end of the second century had many consequences, notably an increase in tension which resulted in a century of intensive warfare. The Parthian dynasty was succeeded by the Sassanids, a development which was accompanied by changes in religion, government, and society in Persia. In the middle of the third century, for the first time in almost three hundred years, the eastern Roman provinces were overrun by enemy forces. It is not intended to recount the history of the relationship between Rome and Persia during the centuries following the Roman expansion east of the Euphrates in the second century, but to describe changes that occurred between the third and sixth centuries.

The conflict between Rome and Persia had a different character in this period for several reasons. First, the relative strength of the two rival empires and the construction of heavily fortified cities in Mesopotamia made it harder for either side to make lasting conquests.

Second, there was the increased involvement of the local population. This was not altogether a new phenomenon: Trajan's conquests were lost through a revolt of the newly conquered peoples; neither he nor Septimius Severus could overcome the resistance of the people of Hatra. Yet it would be correct to describe the wars between Rome and Parthia in the first and second centuries as a series of campaigns involving only the armies of the two empires, which was not at all the case in the later wars, when both the population of the fortified cities and the 'Saracen' allies played a major role.[1]

Third, the arrival of the Huns in the region north of the Caucasus in

---

[1] The term 'Saracens' will be used here to designate the nomads in the eastern frontier provinces irrespective of ethnic or linguistic affiliation. This is how ancient sources such as Ammianus seem to use the expression (see e.g. Ammianus xiv 4; xxii 15, 3; xxiii 6, 13). In ancient sources such as the Talmud 'Arabs' often refers to people with a nomadic way of life, rather than a linguistic or ethnic group, but in order to avoid confusion I use this term only for 'speakers of Arabic' while I do not use the term 'Bedouin' when referring to pre-Islamic history.

the fourth century significantly increased pressure on the two empires from those quarters. In the period of the principate measures had occasionally been taken to prevent incursions from across the Caucasus, for instance when Arrian mobilized against the Alani, but there was no regular or serious pressure such as developed in the later period, when the need for constant vigilance became in itself a factor of importance in the struggle between the two empires.

While we shall be considering further the aims of the two empires in their relationship and the causes of their conflict, there are four subjects that deserve special treatment: (*a*) the brief supremacy of Palmyra in the East, (*b*) the importance of the Caucasus region in the struggle between the two empires, (*c*) the role of the Saracen (nomad) allies of the two states, and (*d*) that of the fortified cities in the frontier zone. At the end of the chapter an attempt is made to define the causes of the continuing conflict between the two empires under the altered circumstances of the Byzantine period.

Palmyrene Independence

The sudden rise of Palmyra took place after Shapur's devastating invasions into Roman territory and the defeat and capture of Valerian in 259/60.[2] These were important events which had great impact. They have been variously assessed, the major question being with whose support Palmyra could have risen to such power or, in other words, what forces enabled a local dynasty to detach the eastern provinces from the empire even for a short period. Clarification of these matters requires consideration of the kind of empire the rulers of Palmyra thought they were seizing. First, the facts must be reviewed. This will entail careful consideration of the titles granted to, and assumed by, Odenathus of Palmyra and the members of his family, not as a subject of interest in itself, but as a reflection of the image which the new rulers of the Roman east wanted to project.

Odenathus collected an army, attacked Shapur on his way back near Carrhae, and managed to inflict serious losses.[3] In 261 Odenathus supported Gallienus against two pretenders, defeating them at Emesa.[4]

[2] J. G. Février, *Essai sur l'histoire politique et économique de Palmyre* (1931), 81 ff. For the chronology, D. Schlumberger, 9 (1942–3), 35–50; G. Lopuszanski, *Cahiers de l'Institut d'études Polonaises en Belgique* 9 (1951); T. Pekáry, *Historia* 11 (1962), 123 ff.; *PIR*² L 258; A. Alföldi, *Berytus* 4 (1937), 53 ff. (= *Studien zur Geschichte der Weltkrise des 3.Jahrhunderts* (1967), 138 ff.).
[3] Festus xxiii; Jerome, *Chron.* 221 (Helm); SHA, *Tyr. Trig.* 15; Malalas 297; Syncellus 716 (Bonn).
[4] Zonaras xii 24; SHA, *Gallienus* 3, 4; Petrus Patricius, *FHG* iv 195 (Dio, ed. Boissevain iii 744); cf. A. Alföldi, *Berytus* 5 (1938), 47.

He was then entrusted with the command of the Roman armies in the East.[5] Having strengthened his forces of Roman and Palmyrene troops with levies from Syria,[6] he opened a counter-attack in 262, regaining Carrhae and Nisibis and all of Roman Mesopotamia. As a result Gallienus took the title *Persicus Maximus* in 263.[7] In the course of the next few years Odenathus moved into Persian Mesopotamia and reached Ctesiphon, perhaps more than once.[8] After this victory he probably called himself *restitutor totius Orientis*.[9] He had become *vir consularis* by 258[10] and assumed, in addition, the title 'King of Kings' (*mlk mlk'*) in his capacity as ruler of Palmyra.[11] The same title appears on a Greek dedication to Sep[timius Herodi]anus, presumably the son of Odenathus, also named Hairan.[12] This inscription explicitly links the acquisition of kingship with a victory over the Persians on the Orontes. The evidence regarding these titles derives from Palmyrene inscriptions, and we cannot be certain which were formally bestowed by the Roman emperor, although it is hardly likely that Odenathus would have assumed the title *vir consularis* as early as 258 without permission. It has been assumed that he also received the titles *imperator* and *dux Romanorum*,[13] but these are not attested in ancient sources.

Allowing for various uncertain elements we are still faced with a series of unprecedented events: a local dignitary of a city of the empire

[5] Zosimus i 39. 1. See also SHA, *Gallienus* 10. 1: 'Odaenathus rex Palmyrenorum obtinuit totius Orientis imperium . . .'; *Tyr. Trig.* 15. 1–2; cf. Syncellus 716 (Bonn).

[6] Festus xxiii: 'Sub Gallieno Mesopotamia invasa etiam Syriam sibi Persae coeperant vindicare, nisi quod turpe dictu est, Odenathus, decurio Palmyrenus, collecta Syrorum agrestium manu acriter restitisset et fusis aliquotiens Persis non modum nostrum limitem defendisset, sed etiam ad Ctesiphontem Romani ultor imperii, quod mirum dictu est, penetrasset.' See also the parallel passage, ed. Eadie, 91 f.

[7] *CIL* viii 22765; *ILS* 8923.

[8] Festus, loc. cit.; SHA, *Tyr. Trig.* 15. 1–4; *Gallienus* 10; Eutropius 9, 10; Jerome, *ann.* 266, p. 221 (Helm); Orosius vii 22. 12. Zosimus, i 39. 1–2, says that Odenathus besieged Ctesiphon twice. The same is implied by Syncellus, 712. Cf. Février, 86–9.

[9] *CIS* ii 3946: 'mtqnn' dy mdnh' klh' = *restitutor* (or just ruler) rather than *corrector* as argued by J. Cantineau, *J. Asiatique* 222 (1933), 217, against Février, 97–9. There is no indication that this particular title was recognized by the Roman authorities. The last man to proclaim himself *restit(utor) Orientis* had been Valerian, as is seen on the reverse of coinage of 256, cf. Alföldi, *Berytus* 4, 46 and pl. xi, 7–10 (*Studien*, 130 f.). For the titles of Odenathus see further Schlumberger, *BEO*, 35 f.

[10] *IGR* iii 1031; Waddington, no. 2602; J. Cantineau, *Inventare des inscriptions de Palmyre* iii, no. 17.

[11] Cantineau, *Inventaire* iii, no. 19, recording the dedication of a statue in 271, after Odenathus' death, by the supreme commander of Palmyrene troops, Septimius Zabda, and the general Septimius Zabbai. The former is mentioned by Zosimus, i 51. 1.

[12] Cantineau, *Inventaire* iii 3. See also below, for a dedication to Septimius Hairan, senator and 'exarch' of Palmyra, dated AD 251.

[13] Alföldi, *Studien zur Geschichte der Weltkrise*, 193 with n. 97. These were the titles which Vabalathus claimed when he succeeded his father, and Alföldi assumes that at that stage Vabalathus would have been satisfied with the titulature of Odenathus. See also Février, 99 f.

routed an invading Persian army, defeated two pretenders to the throne, became formally commander of the troops in the Roman East, carried the war into enemy territory, and obtained the highest title the empire could bestow on any man who did not belong to the imperial house.

Odenathus and his son Herodianus were murdered at Emesa (in 266/7) and were succeeded by another son Vabalathus.[14] There is a confused report which may suggest that the murder was instigated by a Roman governor.[15] There is accordingly some cause for suspicion that the Roman emperor or one of his representatives betrayed a benefactor of the empire in an ugly manner.

Vabalathus assumed the titles *corrector totius Orientis*,[16] and 'King of Kings'. In 270 he appears as *v(ir) c(larissimus), consul, dux Romanorum*, and *imperator*. Again it is not clear which were granted by Rome and which were assumed without permission. In any event, these titles, particularly the first and the last, reflect claims to imperial rank: Only emperors could accumulate such a series of titles, and no emperor would willingly bestow them on anyone but an associate. The evidence is reliable, deriving from Alexandrian coins and milestones in Syria, Judaea, and Arabia.[17] The latter are clearly connected with the Palmyrene expedition to Egypt in 269–70. It was undertaken by a substantial army consisting of Palmyrene, Syrian, and barbarian (Nomad?) troops.[18] It passed through Arabia and appears to have met with resistance from the local legion III Cyrenaica.[19]

---

[14] Zosimus i 39. 2. However, according to Syncellus 716 f. (Bonn), he was killed in Cappadocia at the time of a Gothic invasion.

[15] The governor was perhaps Cocceius Rufinus, attested as legate of Arabia in this period. Petrus Patricius, frs. 166, 168 (Dio, ed. Boissevain, iii 744 = Müller, *FHG* iv 195); John of Antioch, fr. 152 (*FHG* iv 599) cf. Alföldi, *CAH* xii, 176 f. Malalas, 298 f., says that Odenathus was murdered by Gallienus and adds that Zenobia invaded Arabia to avenge the murder of her husband. For Cocceius Rufinus, M. Sartre, *Trois études sur l'Arabie romaine et byzantine* (1982), 56; 93.

[16] *CIS* ii 3971: 'pnrtṭ' dy mdnh klh (cf. Greek ἐπανορθωτής). Cf. Février, 111–14; F. Millar, *JRS* 61 (1971), 9 f. with n. 109.

[17] For the evidence from Egypt, P. J. Parsons, *CE* 42 (1967), 397; cf. BMC Alexandria, 309, no. 2387. For the milestones (in Greek) from Syria, on the Palmyra–Emesa road, Waddington, comments on no. 2610 and no. 2628; cf. H. Seyrig, *Mélanges Michałowski*, 659 ff. For the milestones from Arabia and Judaea see below. For the chronology, Millar, *JRS*, 9.

[18] Zosimus i 44: 70,000 men; cf. SHA, *Claud.* 11. 1–2. H. Seyrig, *Syria* 31 (1954), 214–17, has published an inscription which probably originated from the Hauran and mentions numerous people killed in Egypt. Zosimus' reference to 'barbarian' troops does not justify the assumption that the Romans were faced with a 'native revolt' in the East. If such a thing had been possible in this period we would probably have had more information.

[19] Malalas, 299, says Zenobia invaded Arabia to avenge the death of her husband and defeated 'Trassos, the *dux* of Arabia' and his army. H. Seyrig, *Syria* 22 (1941), 46 (*IGLS* xiii 1, no. 9107), from Bostra, records the reconstruction of the temple of Jupiter Hammon which had been

The Latin milestone inscriptions are an interesting record of the supremacy of Palmyrene troops in the area. Along the Trajanic road in Arabia two series have been identified, an earlier one which omits the title Augustus, but also ignores any other emperor,[20] and a later one which gives Vabalathus the full titulature of an Augustus with the victory-titles often assumed by Roman emperors.[21] In Judaea, two stones have been found north of Scythopolis which again omit the title of Augustus, but do not mention any other ruler.[22] The conquest of Egypt and Alexandria is well attested.[23] There was strong support for the Palmyrenes there.[24]

The extension of Palmyrene supremacy to northern Syria, and to Antioch in particular, belongs to the same period and may have followed the Egyptian campaign.[25] At Antioch too there was support for the Palmyrenes.[26] Zenobia assumed the title of Augusta, and that of Augustus for her son Vabalathus, only after the death of Claudius II, presumably in 272.[27] We cannot know whether in practice it made any difference in their position when they did so, since the Egyptian expedition had already been an irrevocable step making reconciliation with the emperor impossible. The widest extent of Palmyrene supremacy is not quite clear, but it is said that at the time of Aurelian's accession they were in control of Asia Minor east of Ankara and were planning to move westwards.[28] The events ending in the defeat of the Palmyrene forces by Aurelian in 272 do not concern us here.[29] It is of

destroyed 'a Pa[l]myrenis hostibu[s]'. Jupiter Hammon was the tutelary deity of the legion, cf. A. Kindler, *The Coinage of Bostra* (1983), 92 f.

[20] T. Bauzou, *DRBE*, 1–8. Two stones on the Bostra–Philadelphia road: 'L(ucius) Iulius Aureli[us Septi]mius [Va]ballath[us Ath]enodorus Co(n)s(ul) [Impe]rator dux [R]omanorum.' Mr Bauzou kindly informs me that he has discovered yet another unpublished inscription of Vabalathus.

[21] P. Thomsen, *ZDPV* 40 (1917), 38, no. 73 b; 44, no. 96 b.; Bauzou, *DRBE*, 2. Three stones: 'Im. Caesari L. Iulio Aurelio Septimio Vaballatho Athenodoro Persico Maximo Arabico Maximo Adiabenico Maximo Pio Felici Invicto Au(gusto).'

[22] 'Vaballatho | Athenodoro | VC Regi Cons | Imp Duc Roma | norum', unpublished.

[23] Alföldi, *Studien*, 207–9; Millar, *JRS*.

[24] According to Zosimus i 44. 1–2.

[25] As shown by Millar, *JRS*. The literary sources are not very clear about this, but a late occupation of Syria is implied by Eutropius ix 13. 2; Orosius vii 23. 4; Festus xxiv.

[26] See below, p. 271.

[27] In August 271 Zenobia is not yet named Augusta on an inscription from Palmyra: Cantineau, *Inventaire* iii, no. 20 (*OGIS* 648), dedicated by the same officers mentioned above, n. 11. The coinage of Antioch uses the title Augustus only in the spring of 272: see Schlumberger, *BEO*; H. Seyrig, *Mélanges*, 659. Millar, *JRS*, 9 n. 99, cites an ostracon, *O. Mich.* 1006 of May/June 271 which describes both Aurelian and Athenodorus as *Augusti*. See further *IGR* iii 1065 (from the comments on Waddington, no. 2611) and *OGIS* 647: a milestone from the coast road in Syria found near Byblos; note the milestones from Arabia mentioned above.

[28] Zosimus i 50. 1.

[29] See G. Downey, *TAPA* 81 (1950), 57–68; id., *A History of Antioch* (1961), 266–9.

interest, however, to see what can be said about the nature of the forces that enabled the dynasts of Palmyra to obtain such power over such a wide area.

The character of Palmyrene rule has been variously interpreted, in both ancient sources and in modern literature. In the former it is often impossible to separate fact from gossip. Of Odenathus, for instance, we are told that he first made overtures towards Shapur and only when these were rebuffed did he turn against the Persians to become the saviour of the Orient.[30] Another source, however, claims that Gallienus betrayed the Roman state while Postumus in the West and Odenathus in the East saved the empire.[31]

In the modern literature Palmyra is often represented as embodying native, eastern, or local elements as opposed to Roman, western forces.[32] This is, for instance, the point of view of Alföldi:

It was most fortunate for Rome that Palmyra could find no support against her in Persia. It was not only the senseless folly of Shapur or the adroit diplomacy of Gallienus, not even the entanglements of the last years that compelled the Queen to fight out the battle for the East in a Roman setting and under Roman forms. Not that the strength of Iranian influence in this environment need be denied. Odenathus, it is clear, was regarded as a pure barbarian, not only by the Roman commanders who were active in the East, but by the Syrians of Emesa themselves.[33]

Statements such as these will not be found with regard to that other separatist entity, the Gallic empire founded by a Roman general in the same period. They must be reconsidered in the light of what little we know about the nature of Palmyrene supremacy and the support for it in the East. This book is not concerned with the nature of Aramaic-Greek culture in the East and its possible influence on regional attitudes towards the Roman empire. That is an important subject of great complexity. But in the present discussion we can only refer to unambiguous statements of social identity. Despite the risk of being misled by purely formal declarations and claims we can learn a good deal about the political and social nature of Palmyrene society by considering the kind of dignities asserted there.

Something has already been said of the status of Palmyra in the

---

[30] Petrus Patricius, fr. 10, *FHG* iv 187.

[31] Eutropius ix 11. 1: 'Ita Gallieno rem publicam deserente Romanum imperium in Occidente per Postumum, per Odenathum in Oriente servatum est.' Cf. Festus xxiii.

[32] See on this Millar, *JRS*. Bowersock, *Roman Arabia* (1983), 129–37, discusses the relationship between Palmyra and Arab tribes on the basis of later, Arabic sources which I cannot evaluate.

[33] *CAH* xii. 178.

empire (above, Chapter III). In the third century the city produced a number of senators, presumably all from the same family.[34] The members of this family proudly refer to themselves as Roman senators in bilingual inscriptions that have all the familiar characteristics of such texts in the eastern Roman provinces.[35] They apparently received the citizenship when the city became a Roman colony in the early third century, which is very late as compared with other provincial towns, both in the West and the East, where the local aristocracy was often co-opted into the Roman hierarchy fairly soon after the incorporation of such towns into the provincial organization. There are, for instance, many Syrian senators of the second century from other cities.[36] This contrast shows that the status of Palmyra before Septimius Severus was not comparable with that of other important provincial towns.

There is no lack of equestrian officers in the second century.[37] They served in the positions for which Palmyrene soldiers were particularly suitable, in units of archers, in the desert, and in units of camel riders. The existence of equestrian officers from Palmyra cannot be construed as a symptom of Palmyrene incorporation in the social fabric of the imperial upper class, but only as the result of the military integration of Palmyrene troops in the Roman imperial army.

An important change in the status of Palmyra is marked by the grant of colonial rank. On that occasion the regular constitution of such cities was adopted, and from 224 till 262 several administrators of the city are referred to as *strategoi*, the Greek equivalent of Latin *duoviri*, in both Greek and Palmyrene texts.[38] One of these, Julius Aurelius Zenobios,

[34] The first recorded was Septimius Odenathus, son of Hairan, father of the great Odenathus, who probably acquired senatorial rank in the reign of Philippus: *CIS* ii 4202; Waddington, no. 2621 (hence *IGR* iii 1034). Cf. Bowersock, *Atti del colloquio internazionale AIEGL su Epigrafia e ordine senatorio, Roma 1981*, *Tituli* 5 (1982), 651–68. For the family and career of Odenathus see M. Gawlikowski, *Syria* 62 (1985), 251–61.

[35] Another senator was Septimius Hairan, son of Odenathus, 'exarch' of Palmyra, perhaps identical with the Herodianus reported to have been killed at the same time as his father: *CIS* ii 3944; Cantineau, *Inventaire* iii, no. 16, cf. D. Schlumberger, *BEO* 9, 35–8; Gawlikowski, *Syria* 62, 254, no. 4, and 255, no. 20: a dedication to Septi[mius Herodi]anus, King of Kings.

[36] See the list in Bowersock, *Atti*.

[37] For the equestrian officers from Palmyra, H. Devijver, *DRBE*, 183. Note also Septimius Vorodes, mentioned below; Aurelius Vorodes, *hippikos* and *bouleutes*, AD 258–9 (Cantineau, *Inventaire* iii, no. 12); Julius 'Ogga, *eques*, AD 259 (ibid., no. 15); Marcus Ulpius Malchus, an officer who had completed the *tria militia* (Cantineau, *Inventaire* ix, no. 24); Julius Aurelius Salmes, one of those who honoured Septimius Vorodes and who was an *eques* himself (Cantineau, iii, no. 6 = Waddington, no. 2609).

[38] Cantineau, *Inventaire* iii, nos. 14 f. = Waddington no. 2601; – 5: Julius Aurelius 'Ogga, also named Seleucos, already mentioned because of his equestrian status; Cantineau, iii, no. 22 = Waddington, no. 2598: for Julius Aurelius Zabdilah, who was responsible for the reception of Severus Alexander and his troops (AD 242–3); Cantineau, iii, no. 5 = Waddington, no. 2597. The Palmyrene texts use the same title in transcription.

also named Zabdilas, probably was the father of Zenobia. Another,
Septimius Vorodes, was caravan leader as well, *iuridicus*, and procurator with the rank of *ducenarius*.[39] The designation of such men, and in
particular of Odenathus and Vabalathus, as 'sheiks' belongs entirely to
the modern literature; there is no indication that they would have
called themselves Arabs, in the sense that they would have felt that this
identified them more accurately than other descriptions. The ancient
sources call them Palmyrene[40] and never refer to them as barbarians.[41]
Odenathus 'had been considered worthy of honours by the emperors
because of his ancestors'.[42] The Palmyrene language, of course, was a
variant of Arabic, but the city was officially bilingual in the third
century. Yet this was exceptional in itself. In Bostra, which was a
normal, modest provincial capital and military base, nothing but
Greek and Latin was used on inscriptions. Emesa, Palmyra's western
neighbour, has produced exclusively Greek inscriptions. Zenobia, it is
true, associated with Greek literary figures,[43] but Greek culture may
have affected only a small section of the population. Considering the
fact that Vabalathus was styled *Arabicus Maximus* it cannot even be
maintained that the Palmyrenes consciously dissociated themselves
from their own people.

When the rulers of Palmyra called themselves kings as well as
Roman senators this was an innovation. Palmyra had never had a king,
as far as is known, and had formally been part of the province of Syria
for a long time. There is no evidence at all for the assertion, sometimes
made, that the family had been dynasts at Palmyra for many generations. Till the sixties of the third century the city was administered by
strategoi (*duoviri*), and the titles, granted or assumed, that the dynasts
bore in the years of their military supremacy all emphasize continuity
in the framework of the Roman state: senatorial rank, the consulship,
military leadership. When Vabalathus finally assumed the titles of an
emperor he was merely following the same pattern as any other Roman

---

[39] Waddington, nos. 2606–10; Cantineau, *Inventare* iii, 6–11.

[40] e.g. Zosimus, i 39. 1 and *passim*; Festus xxiii: *decurio Palmyrenus*; SHA, *Gallienus* 10. 1; *Tyr. Trig.* 15. 1–2; *Valerian* 4. 2.

[41] At Zosimus i 45. 1 Palmyrenes and barbarians occur in the same sentence as clearly distinct groups. Only Malalas, 298 f., calls them Saracen barbarians, but he was not even aware that they were Palmyrenes. The inscription from Bostra (above, no. 20) refers to the Palmyrenes as 'hostes'. *Digest* L 15. 1 (Ulpian) describes Palmyra as a Roman colony situated near bar-barian peoples, but not as barbarian itself: 'Est et Palmyrena civitas in Provincia Phoenice prope barbaras gentes et nationes collocata.'

[42] Zosimus i 39. 1.

[43] Millar, *JRS*, and the references in his nn. 56 f. Longinus withdrew to Zenobia's court, and in Egypt Zenobia identified herself with Cleopatra.

ruler or usurper of the period.[44] The Palmyrenes' means of proclaiming their supremacy were the traditional ones: milestone inscriptions and coinage. While those in Syria are in Greek the milestone inscriptions in Arabia and Judaea are in Latin, the normal language of milestone inscriptions. This is not to suggest that Vabalathus as Augustus was no different from other emperors or usurpers. What made him different was not his origin—there had been an Arab emperor a few decades before—but the local character of his power base, the fact that he represented one particular town which always had been a marginal element in the empire. It was a unique event, unparalleled before and afterwards, presumably because Palmyra was unique.

This brings us to the next subject: the base of support for Palmyra in the East. It seems best to admit that we have, in fact, no information. In Egypt there was strong support for the Palmyrene expedition, which happened to occur in a period of serious civil disturbances in the province as a whole and in Alexandria in particular.[45] At Antioch as well there was support for Palmyra.[46] The existence of milestone inscriptions in Latin almost certainly indicates support among the troops in Judaea and Arabia. We know that Odenathus had received the command over Roman forces in the region, and it is possible that these remained loyal to Zenobia and Vaballathus after his murder. If this was the case it could be explained by a possible widespread feeling in the East that this was not a position for a foreign or barbarian king, but for commanders who had proved their effectiveness in a time of emergency. The Roman officers and troops who lent their support to them may have felt that this act was no different from all the other occasions when regional usurpers were supported by their troops.

It is, in fact, known that a few years before somewhat similar events occurred further west. The usurper Uranius Antoninus, known only from coinage, is almost certainly to be identified with Sampsigeramus, priest of the sun-god of Emesa, who succeeded in halting the Persians in 253 near the city.[47] This is confirmed by the fact that Shapur's own record of his conquests shows that he failed to reach Emesa, although he took Arethusa immediately to the north. The attempt at usurpation was suppressed by Valerian when he reached the East. There are insufficient facts to determine the nature of this movement. There were

---

[44] See the milestone texts above, nn. 20–2.
[45] Zosimus i 44. For the disturbances see Alföldi, *Studien*, 187, 207 f.
[46] Zosimus i 51. 3.
[47] H. R. Baldus, *Uranius Antoninus, Münzprägung und Geschichte* (1971), combining the evidence from coinage with the garbled information in Malalas 296 f. (Bonn).

several persons of the name Sampsigeramus among the priests of Emesa and the name of the usurper was L. Julius Aurelius Sulpicius Severus Uranius Antoninus. That is an indication that he belonged to the family that had earlier produced the usurper Elagabalus. There was a good deal of emphasis on origin in Elagabalus' unusual insistence on his association with the local god of his home town.[48] On the other hand the successful action against the Persian army is hard to explain without assuming there was more than local backing. As in the case of Palmyra afterwards, support from parts of the Syrian army is likely.

What then can we learn from the peculiar episode of brief supremacy as an imperial capital? First, it shows what extraordinary power and influence could be derived from the control of a crucial road-station— for that is what Palmyra represented. It profited from the movement of goods and armies and, through its own armed forces which were adapted to desert conditions, gained both riches and military power. Second, it can be seen that Roman generals did not hesitate to destroy that entire structure when it suited them to do so in a power struggle in the East. The flourishing 'caravan city' was replaced by a Roman military base that could do no more than ensure Roman control over the oasis.

Third, it is obvious that Odenathus and his family gained power in the east despite ethnic and cultural factors which might have played a role, but did not. Palmyra had always remained marginal. Its leading citizens were not integrated into the imperial upper class until the third century, and administratively it never became an ordinary provincial town. Yet in the midst of a crisis the authority of its leaders was accepted by numerous people in Egypt, Syria, and other provinces, apparently because considerations of ethnic identity and all that came with it were thought irrelevant. For a while the rulers of Palmyra were accepted as pretenders to the imperial throne, like so many generals who gained power with the aid of their troops. The Palmyrenes were destroyed by another general not because they were 'barbarians', but for the same reason as Pompey and Antony. Finally, a century afterwards Odenathus was still remembered with gratitude in Antioch as one 'whose name shook the Persians and, being victorious everywhere, saved the cities and their territories . . .'[49]

---

[48] Cf. F. Millar, *JJS* 38 (1987), 157 f. See also A. von Domaszewski, *Arch. f. Rel.wiss.* 11 (1908), 223–42.

[49] Libanius, *ep.* 1006, ed. Foerster, vol. xi, p. 135, mentioning a descendant of Odenathus; cf. no. 1078, Foerster xi, p. 195. Cf. P. Petit, *Libanius et la vie municipale* (1955), 184. See also the positive description in the otherwise defective SHA, *Tyr. Trig.* 15–17.

The North-East

During the principate, the period discussed in Chapter I, the north-east was an area of minor interest, apart from the fleet stations on the eastern Black Sea coast held by Roman garrisons.[50] The various peoples south of the Caucasus were vassals of the Romans. Invasion over the Caucasus passes was clearly not a real danger to the security of the Roman provinces. These passes were easily defended, and this was a task undertaken by the local peoples.

There are several regions of interest: first, Iberia (the eastern part of modern Georgia), which afforded one of the two best routes to the north over the Darial pass; second, the western part with its stations on the coast, and the hinterland whence a few difficult passes gave access to the north. A third region, Albania in the east (roughly = Azerbaijan) with the best route past Derbent on the Caspian, will not concern us here. The Albanians were allies of the Persians in the fourth century and afterwards throughout the Byzantine period.[51] Armenia was less of a cause of hostilities than it had been during the principate and will be mentioned briefly.

In Iberia, the Roman position was insecure. Shapur I claimed that he was king of '. . . Armenia, Iberia, Machelonia, Albania (Balasagan) as far as the Caucasus and the Gates of Albania and the whole Mt. Pressouar [Elbruz]'.[52] Iberia changed hands frequently: with the conclusion of the peace of Nisibis in 297 the Persians recognized Roman sovereignty in Armenia and Iberia.[53] In 361 the kings of Armenia and Iberia were bribed by the Romans in order to keep them loyal.[54] In 369 the Roman vassal in Iberia was deposed,[55] and the country was then divided between a Roman and a Persian vassal.[56] It is clear, therefore, that the fourth century represented a weakening of the Roman position in the north-east. This was a factor of far greater consequence then than it would have been in the earlier period.

In the fourth century control over the Caucasus passes assumed an importance it had never had before, because of the appearance of new

[50] For bibliography see ch. I.

[51] Ammianus xviii 6. 22; xix 2. 3; Procopius adds that they were Christians: i 12. 2; also Zacharias Rhetor xii 7, p. 254. Cf. M.-L. Chaumont, *Historia* 22 (1973), 664 ff.

[52] *Res Gestae Divi Saporis*, A. Maricq, *Syria* 35 (1958), 295–360, esp. 305 f. Following the defeat and death of Gordian III the emperor Philip ceded suzerain rights over Armenia. Cf. Chaumont, *Historia*.

[53] Petrus Patricius, fr. 14, Müller, *FHG* iv 189.

[54] Ammianus xxi 6. 8.

[55] Ammianus xxvii 12. 4.   [56] Ibid. 16 f.

peoples in the area to the north: the Huns.[57] Their first penetration of Persian territory in the mid-fourth century would not have troubled the Romans, but by the end of the century there was cause for serious worry. In 394 Theodosius withdrew his troops from the east.[58] The Huns then penetrated into Persia, Melitene, and Syria as far as Cilicia.[59] In the same period they invaded through the Darial pass and Armenia.[60] In 441 there was trouble with various invaders, including Huns.[61]

In the fifth century the Persians demanded Roman cooperation and financial support in guarding the Darial pass.[62] In the sixth century Anastasius lost a chance to gain control over this pass, which was the most convenient route for the Huns if they wanted to invade across the Caucasus, but one which could be blocked with relative ease.[63] The commander of the frontier fortress, a Persian ally, offered to hand over the structure and with it control over the pass. This was seen at least by some people as a splendid opportunity, offered at a time when Persia faced serious difficulties, both internal and external. Anastasius, however, concluded that it would be impossible to maintain a Roman garrison on the spot. This was perhaps a reasonable decision, despite Procopius' strictures. It would have been impossible to maintain a garrison in the Caucasus without securing supplies and communications, and that in turn would have been impossible without an elaborate military organization and the cooperation of the peoples in the hinterland. After the division of Armenia between Rome and Persia

---

[57] See in general J. O. Maenchen-Helfen, *The World of the Huns: Studies in their History and Culture*, ed. M. Knight (1973).

[58] He thought he could rely on his alliance with Persia and withdrew his troops to use them against the usurpers Maximus and Eugenius: Claudian, *in Ruf.* ii 156–8, 104–19.

[59] Philostratus xi 8; Claud. *in Ruf.* ii 36; 28–35.

[60] Jerome, *ep.* 60. 16.

[61] Marcellinus Comes, *Chronica minora*, ed. Mommsen, ii 80: 'Persae, Saraceni, Tzanni, Isauri finibus suis egressi Romanorum sola vastaverunt. Missi sunt contra hos Anatolius et Aspar magistri militiae pacemque cum his unius anni fecerunt.'

[62] Priscus fr. 31, Müller, *FHG* iv 105 (AD 464); see also fr. 37, p. 107, which describes the deflection of an invasion in 466 by the Persian garrison stationed near the pass. This was followed by renewed demands for either soldiers or financial support which were turned down again by the Romans. See further John Lydus, *de mag.* 52 f., ed. Bandy, 215: Rome agreed to participate in the defence of the Caspian Gates in a peace treaty. Z. Rubin, *DRBE*, 683, argues that this was the treaty of 441–2. It is clear that both Priscus and John Lydus refer to the Darial pass when they speak of the Caspian Gates and the fortress of 'Iouroeipaach' or 'Biraparach', for John Lydus, 52, says it is most accessible from Artaxata, and that is definitely true for the Darial pass but not for Derbent. In 53 he says the Caspian Gates are accurately described by Arrian in his history of the Alans and in Book VIII of his 'Parthian Wars' and this again can only refer to the Darial pass. There is considerable confusion in various modern works, but for straightforward discussion see *RE* iii 1, col. 489 s.v. Biriparach (Tomaschek); xi, col. 58 s.v. Kaukasiai Pylai (Mittelhaus).

[63] Procopius, *Bell.* i 10. 4–12.

Iberia inevitably belonged to the sphere of influence of Persia, since there was a good road between the northern capital of Armenia (Artaxata near modern Yerevan) and the capital of Iberia (Harmozica, near modern Tbilisi).[64]

War in such an area is difficult:

[It] has essentially the character of a mountain war: battles for saddles and defiles followed by attacks on fortified localities commanding main alleys of communication along river valleys. Transport and supply difficulties impose the use of relatively small forces accustomed to the rigours of climate in the highlands. The experience of former wars shows that when the commanding saddles have been lost fortified localities can sustain long sieges owing to the difficulty of transporting heavy artillery and the supplies necessary to the support of a siege force.[65]

In the nineteenth century Russian troops spent decades fighting in the Caucasus. As already noted in Chapter I, the region of Tbilisi is more naturally controlled by a power based in Persia than one in Anatolia. Anastasius probably knew better than Procopius what was involved in controlling the Darial pass.[66] The Persians then took possession of the fortress.

A Byzantine effort to regain influence in Iberia in this period came to nothing.[67] The issue of control over the pass came up in negotiations in 530 and in the treaty of 532. The Persians at first demanded either support in maintaining the garrison there or the dismantling of the fortifications of the Mesopotamian border town of Dara.[68] In the treaty Rome agreed to pay a large sum to Persia. Persia, for its part, would maintain the garrisons at the Caspian Gates (the Darial pass), while Rome kept its fortifications at Dara intact.[69] At the time of his invasion of Syria, in 540, Khusro again made financial demands in return for the existing arrangements at the pass and at Dara.[70] In the treaty of 562 it was stipulated that the Persians would guard the pass and prevent incursions into Byzantine territory, in return for subsidies to be paid by the Byzantine authorities.[71]

[64] Indicated on the Peutinger Table.

[65] W. E. D. Allen and P. Muratoff, *Caucasian Battlefields: A History of the Wars on the Turco-Caucasian Border* (1953), 7.

[66] John Lydus, *de mag.* 52, ed. Bandy, 212, offers a different view: Iberia is naturally controlled by the power established at Artaxata in Armenia Major. As a result the Persians were closer to the Darial pass and had no choice but to guard it. They did not have the means to carry the extra burden and therefore demanded Roman financial support.

[67] Procopius *Bell.* i 12. 2 ff.; ii 15. 6; ii 28. 20 f.   [68] Procopius, *Bell.* i 16. 7.

[69] *Bell.* i 21. 3–5, 18. This was 'the endless peace'. Rome gave up two forts in Persarmenia, and Persia withdrew from Lazica—for the moment.

[70] *Bell.* ii 10. 21–4.

[71] Menander Protector, fr. 11, Müller, *FHG* iv 206–17, esp. 208; 212. See below.

Essentially then the Byzantine authorities depended on Persia to watch the two major passes between the Black Sea and the Caspian and to keep the Hunnish invaders at a distance. The Persians could do this and were prepared to do it because they had the same interest in keeping the Huns out as the Romans. Since the Romans did not contribute troops the Persians demanded financial support for the maintenance of the garrison guarding the Darial pass. This demand was one of the major recurring causes of conflict between the two empires, as will be seen below.

The Roman position in the region further west, Colchis, which Procopius calls Lazica, appears to have been stable till the reign of Justinian.[72] The Lazi, says Procopius, were vassals of the Romans without paying tribute or being subject to direct Roman rule.[73] Their king was formally nominated by the Roman emperor, and otherwise their only responsibility was to guard the Caucasus passes issuing into their territory and to prevent Hunnish invasions through their territory.[74] These Huns, it may be noted, were also kept friendly by Roman subsidies.[75] The Colchians did not supply the Roman army with auxiliaries, nor were Roman troops stationed in their land. Byzantine interest in the area was limited: they maintained a number of coastal stations but made no demands from the local population as long as it guarded the passes.

In the sixth century this state of affairs no longer applied. Various intrigues, the details of which are not immediately relevant, led to direct Byzantine rule in the area and Persian claims that it be handed over to them. In the sixth-century wars between Byzantium and Persia Colchis was turned into a theatre of war as Persia became actively interested in expelling the Romans from the region.[76] It is quite possible that this was partly the result of the circumstance that it was a region where substantial gains seemed relatively easy, while in Mesopotamia every inch of movement could be achieved only by exhausting sieges of strongly fortified towns.[77] However, that is speculation.

Procopius says there were three reasons for the Persian interest in the

---

[72] For a survey of the wars in Lazica, J. B. Bury, *History of the Later Roman Empire* (1958), ii 113–19.

[73] *Bell.* ii 15. 1 ff.

[74] For these passes see above, p. 47 and n. 188. They were routes of minor importance as compared with the Darial and Derbent passes.

[75] Procopius, *Bell.* ii 10. 23. On subsidies paid by the Romans, Maenchen-Haelfen, 180–6.

[76] Extensive descriptions by Procopius in *Bell.* i and ii, continued in viii.

[77] The struggle between Persia and Byzantium for influence in southern Arabia will not be discussed here; for bibliography, R. N. Frye, *The History of Ancient Iran* (1984), 328 n. 105.

country. First, it would strengthen the Persian hold on Iberia to the east, where revolt was not unlikely. Second, Persia would no longer be threatened by Hunnish raids which might be turned against Roman territory. Third, it would be a convenient base of operations against Roman Asia Minor.[78] At the same time, Procopius stresses that Khusro had no illusions about the reliability of the local population and that there were no economic reasons for the interest. It was a poor region with a primitive economy. Whether that was true or not, we may assume that this reflects contemporary perceptions of the reasons for the Persian ambitions there.[79]

In the fourth century the Roman army maintained its presence at several stations on the eastern Black Sea shore. Zosimus mentions 'garrisons near the Phasis [Rioni]'.[80] The *Notitia Dignitatum* lists a series of garrisons from Trapezus to Pityus.[81] In 396 an ex-general of Theodosius, Abundantius, was banished to Pityus 'where he had a lack of everything'.[82] In 407 John Chrysostom was sent there.[83]

Procopius tells that two of the garrisons on the Euxine, Rhizus and Sebastopolis, were restored by Justinian,[84] the latter having been previously dismantled, together with Pityus, out of fear that the Persians might take them over. In Lazica, south of the Phasis, several passes are said to have been secured, and Justinian fortified Petra (Tsikhis-dziri, north of modern Batumi) in that region.[85] As the result of Roman losses in the area all these positions had to be evacuated,[86] and Petra became the Persian base in the region. The war in Colchis dragged on for years. The treaty of 562 stipulated that the Persians would return Lazica to the Romans.[87] A *novella* dating perhaps to 578–82 mentions *annona* to be delivered for ships in the region of the Lazi,

---

[78] *Bell.* ii 28. 18–23. Frye, 323, thinks Khusro's interference in Lazica was connected with an ambition to control the trade of the silk route to China.

[79] According to Strabo, xi 2. 19 (499), Colchis was fertile and prosperous. It is of course possible that the economy had deteriorated during the half millennium between Strabo and Procopius.

[80] ii 33. 1: ἄχρι Τραπεζοῦντος καὶ τῶν παρὰ τὸν Φᾶσιν φρουρίων . . .

[81] *Not. Dig. Or.* xxxviii 15 ff. Cf. *DE* s.v. *limes*, 1311–13; van Berchem, *L'armée de Dioclétien et la réforme Constantinienne* (1952), 31 f.

[82] Jerome, *ep.* lx 16: 'Abundantius egens Pityunte exulat.'

[83] Palladius, *Dialogus de vita S. Johannis Chrysostomi*, xi 37 f. (*PG* xlvii 5–82); cf. Sozomenos viii 28.

[84] *De aed.* iii 6. 3–7.

[85] Procopius, loc. cit. The site is reported to have been excavated: D. M. Lang, *Cambridge History of Iran* iii 1. 521.

[86] Procopius, *Bell.* viii 4. 4–6.

[87] Menander Protector, fr. 11, Müller, *FHG* iv 208. Cf. *Nov. Iust.* 28, which describes Pityus and Sebastopolis as forts rather than towns. In Lazica there are the towns of Petra, Archaeopolis, and Rhodopolis, as well as a number of *phrouria* acquired from the Persians.

Bosporus and Chersonesus.[88] That shows Byzantium to have been in effective control of the eastern Black Sea coast in this period.

Events in this area have been considered at some length because the clashes between the two major powers in the region represented a development characteristic of the age. It was a consequence of the fact that real movement had become impossible in Mesopotamia and of the danger posed by the peoples north of the mountain chain. The latter is particularly relevant to one of the central themes of this book: the defensive value of military installations on the frontier. Here, in the Caucasus, the sources clearly spell out that forts blocking mountain passes were in fact essential in preventing nomad invasions, not at all times, but in the period following the arrival of the Huns in the fourth century. It was an exceptional situation, due to the fact that a few difficult passes formed the only practicable routes over the Caucasus, between the Black Sea and the Caspian. This is clearly recognized by the ancient authors, who elsewhere tend to ignore the defensive function of military bases. It became a central issue in the friction between the two major empires. A policy of neglect or nonchalance on the part of an emperor is severely criticized, as we see in the case of Anastasius and the Darial pass. The alternative view, that he realistically assessed the cost and the means at his disposal, is not represented in ancient sources. There clearly was an awareness of the crucial importance of these routes for the security of the empire, and yet Byzantium failed to secure control of them. Since this was either dangerous or led to increasing Persian demands for subsidies it is best to assume that Byzantium simply did not have the means to control these passes.

Armenia had been one of the major causes of conflict from the first century BC onwards. In the fourth century Shapur II sought to re-establish control over Armenia and northern Mesopotamia. This came to an end with Julian's campaign and the ensuing treaty. At an uncertain date after Julian's expedition into Mesopotamia (363) Armenia was divided between the Romans and Persians.[89] Although as a consequence Rome lost its grip on Iberia, the measure solved for the time being one of the most serious difficulties between the two powers and afforded a period of relatively peaceful relations. However, when hostilities were renewed the two parts of Armenia were as much

---

[88] *Nov. Inst.* clxiii 2. For the history of Georgia in the late sixth and early seventh century, Lang, *Cambridge Hist. Iran* iii 1. 522–4.

[89] For the most recent discussion, R. C. Blockley, *Historia* 36 (1987), 222–34, with references in n. 1.

involved as any other area of contact. The war under Anastasius (502–6) began with a Persian invasion in that region, and so did that under Justinian. In the Byzantine period Armenia was no longer a primary focus of warfare, as it had been during the principate, but it remained a theatre of war because of its geographical position.

Nomad Allies

The first point to be noted is the relative prominence of these peoples in the later period compared with that of the principate. During the first three centuries, even in local or regional sources, such as Josephus or Talmudic literature, they are mentioned only incidentally as exotic barbarians.[90] From the fourth century onwards every author who discusses the eastern wars or every source of a local nature—whether or not aware of the eventual success of the Islamic conquest—refers to the Saracens as a factor of importance. It is worth observing that, by the time of the conquest, Arab forces had had centuries of experience of warfare as allies of the two empires.

Byzantium and Persia each encouraged their respective allies to attack the territory of the other power. Here again it was Mesopotamia that suffered most from the combination of raids and warfare between the great powers.[91] Ammianus, discussing the early stages of the eastern war in the year 356, says that the Persians applied a new technique: instead of the usual set battles they now practised raids and guerrilla warfare.[92] The carrying off of property and cattle was the speciality of their Saracen allies *ad furta bellorum appositi*.[93] The object of such raids will have been to thrust as far inside enemy territory as was

---

[90] e.g. the passage cited below, ch. VI, on Rabban Yohanan ben Zakkai going up to Emmaus in Judaea: Mekhilta de Rabbi Ishmael, Bahodesh, i, ed. Horovitz–Rabin, 203 f. In the New Testament Arabs are mentioned once, at Acts 2: 11.

[91] The Romans and Persians were not the last to use such methods. Later the Mamluk governors, in constant strife amongst themselves, incited the Bedouin to attack each other's territory. See M. Sharon, 'The Political Role of the Bedouins in Palestine in the Sixteenth and Seventeenth Century' in M. Ma'oz (ed.) *Studies on Palestine During the Ottoman Period* (1975), 15.

[92] Ammianus xvi 9. 1: 'At Persae in oriente per furta et latrocinia potius quam (ut solebant antea) per concursatorias pugnas hominum praedas agitabant et pecorum.' Ammianus uses the same terminology for the tactics of the Isaurian bandits (xix 13. 1; cf. xiv 2). Sometimes the Persians were successful, sometimes the Roman army caught up with them. Referring to the year 354 Ammianus, xiv 3. 2, says that all of Mesopotamia suffered frequent attacks and was therefore guarded by *praetenturis et stationibus agrariis*.

[93] xxiii 3. 8; xxxi 16. 4: 'Saracenorum cuneus . . . ad furta magis expeditionalium rerum, quam ad concursatorias habilis pugnas.' For Ammianus and the Saracens, John Matthews, *Roman Empire*; also I. Shahîd, *Byzantium and the Arabs in the Fourth Century* (1984), 82–6, 107–24. For the Persian allies, C. E. Bosworth, 'Iran and the Arabs Before Islam', *Cambridge Hist. Iran* iii 2. 593–612.

possible without endangering one's retreat and, while there, to do as much damage as possible. Successful raids were intended to discredit the authorities with the local population; the discredit was the measure of their attackers' success. Ammianus, however, seems to have had his doubts as to the effectiveness of this innovation. He found the Saracens desirable neither as allies nor as enemies.[94] This reminds one of the judgement of Joshua the Stylite on the war between Persia and Rome under Anastasius: '. . . to the Arabs on both sides this war was a source of much profit and they wrought their will upon both kingdoms.'[95] Joshua gives extensive descriptions of the nature and effects of such warfare.[96]

It is hard to judge whether the new military policy really was useless from a strategic point of view. Both parties adhered to it for centuries, and it cannot be denied that this was the sort of operation that the nomads were qualified to carry out. In the words of an expert:

Our largest available resources were the tribesmen, men quite unused to formal warfare, whose assets were movement, endurance, individual intelligence, knowledge of the country, courage. We must impose the longest possible defence on the Turks (this being the most materially expensive form of war) by extending our own front to its maximum. Tactically we must develop a highly mobile, highly equipped type of army, of the smallest size, and use it successively at distributed points of the Turkish line, to make the Turks reinforce their occupying posts beyond the economic minimum of twenty men.[97]

The pre-Islamic nomads did not engage in siege warfare. When they attacked rural settlements they refrained from attacking the settlements themselves, but turned on anything of value outside the fortified quarters, burning or trampling crops, destroying palm groves and fruit trees, filling wells, and destroying water systems.[98] Desert conditions can be used as a weapon by anybody who knows how to exploit them. Pliny, writing about Cyrenaica, says that until recently it had been impossible for Roman troops to march to the land of the Garamantes, because 'bandits of that people filled the wells with sand—for one who

---

[94] xiv 4. 1: 'Saraceni tamen nec amici nobis nec hostes optandi . . .'

[95] 79 (*The Chronicle, Composed in Syriac, AD 507*, text and trans. W. Wright, 1882).

[96] 57 and 79 for descriptions of this kind of attack practised by the Arab allies of both the Romans and the Persians in coordination with the movements of the main armies.

[97] T. E. Lawrence, cited by B. H. Liddell Hart, *T. E. Lawrence: In Arabia and After* (1934, repr. London 1965), 177.

[98] See P. Mayerson, *Transactions and Proceedings of the American Philological Association* 95 (1964), 180–4; L. I. Conrad, *Al-Abhath: Journal of the Center for Arab and Middle East Studies, Faculty of Arts and Sciences, American University of Beirut* 29 (1981), 7–23; F. Donner, *The Early Islamic Conquests* (1981), 29 f.

is aided by familiarity with the country they need not be dug deep'.[99]
However, Musil explains how a similar weapon could be used against
the Bedouin themselves on a long-distance raid: in discussing Hâled's
march from Anbar to Palmyra (500 km.) through the territory of his
enemies he notes: 'All they would have had to do was to poison two
watering places in the desert with naphtha, locusts, or dead animals,
and Hâled could scarcely have saved his corps from dying of thirst.'[100]
When the nomads fought for themselves the outcome would normally
be that they received payments made in cash or goods and would then
refrain from destruction. When they were raiding on behalf of an
imperial power that would not be the case.

But against towns or in set battles the nomads were ineffective at all
times.[101] This is repeatedly stated by Ammianus,[102] and it is obvious
from the tactics of Khusro in the sixth century. When about to storm a
city-wall he placed his Saracens behind the other troops, so as not to
participate in the assault, but to catch refugees afterwards.[103] When
used in a manner appropriate to their skills the Saracens could be very
effective: they once saved Constantinople.

Ammianus was clearly right in his observation that the systematic
use of Saracen raiders by both parties was an innovation of the fourth
century. He himself saw the destructive effects on the countryside in the
Near East. But contact between the Romans and the nomads and semi-
nomads in the Near East was not in itself an innovation: it had existed
since the extension of the empire to the Syrian region. In December 51
BC there was a false suspicion that Cassius had let loose a horde of Arabs
into his province.[104] Why he was suspected of having done so is
irrelevant. What we learn from the passage is that Arabs were already
known as raiders at the time.

Diodorus, writing about the fourth century BC in the period of Caesar
and Augustus, gives a fairly extensive description of the 'Arabs' (i.e. the

---

[99] Pliny, *NH* v 5. 38.

[100] A. Musil, *The Middle Euphrates*, 303. Shapur (I or II?) is said to have filled wells with sand
against the Arabs: T. Nöldeke, *Tabari* (1879), 56.

[101] See the last note. The relevance of these observations for the Roman and Byzantine
periods is confirmed by statements made by Ammianus, xxv 6. 8, and Procopius, *Bell.* ii 19. 12,
both frequently cited.

[102] See above, and note the description of the tactics employed by the Saracens in xxv 1. 3:
avoiding contact with the main body of Roman infantry.

[103] Procopius, *Bell.* ii 27. 30.

[104] Cicero, *ad fam.* iii 8. 10: 'Sed de Parthorum transitu nuntii varios sermones excitarunt . . .
A te litterae non venerunt et, nisi Deiotari subsecutae essent, in eam opinionem Cassius
veni‹eb›at, quae diripuisset et Arabas in provinciam immisisse eosque Parthos esse senatui
renuntiasse.'

nomads).[105] Strabo says something of the relationship in the Augustan period:

While the Euphrates and the other bank of it constitute the boundary of the Parthian empire, the lands on this bank are held by the Romans and the Arab chiefs (phylarchs) as far as Babylonia, some of them being allies of the Romans whose neighbours they are; the Scenite (tent-dwelling) nomads near the river rather less so, those farther away and near Arabia Felix more so.[106]

This is the first description of phylarchs, nomad chiefs, as allies of the Romans.[107] There are several Greek inscriptions erected by nomad chiefs to show that they formally recognized Roman authority.[108] The earliest known was set up in Batanaea in honour of King Agrippa by the son of Chares, commander(?) of the Augustan (?) cohort and *strategos* (?) of the nomads.[109] Another inscription from Batanaea is a tombstone of 'Hadrian, also named Soaidos (son of?) Malechos, ethnarch, *strategos* of the nomads'.[110] These two nomad chiefs were clearly vassals of some sort of the Romans. Such a relationship is brought out again in an inscription from Tarba in which soldiers recruited from among the nomads honour a governor.[111] Particularly important is the bilingual inscription, in Greek and Nabataean, found almost 200 kilometres south-east of Aela, at Ruwwafa in the Hejaz.[112] It records the building of a temple by the people (or the confederation) of the Thamud in honour of Marcus Aurelius and Lucius Verus, under the auspices of the governor Claudius Modestus (legate of Arabia, 167–

---

[105] xix 94. 2–95. 2.

[106] xvi 1. 28 (748): Ὅριον δ᾽ ἐστὶ τῆς Παρθυαίων ἀρχῆς ὁ Εὐφράτης καὶ ἡ περαία·τὰ δ᾽ ἐντὸς ἔχουσι Ῥωμαῖοι καὶ τῶν Ἀράβων οἱ φύλαρχοι μέχρι Βαβυλωνίας, οἱ μὲν μᾶλλον ἐκείνοις, οἱ δὲ τοῖς Ῥωμαίοις προσέχοντες, οἷσπερ καὶ πλησιόχωροί εἰσιν ἧττον μὲν Σκηνῖται οἱ νομάδες οἱ τῷ ποταμῷ πλησίον, μᾶλλον δ᾽ οἱ ἀπωθεν καὶ πρὸς τῇ εὐδαίμονι Ἀραβίᾳ.

[107] Cf. Festus, *Breviarium* 14, ed. Eadie, 56 f.: '. . . sub Lucio Lucullo . . . Phylarchi Saracenorum in Osrhoena cessere superati.' This is clearly later terminology.

[108] Discussed by M. Sartre, *Trois études*, 123–8. For an earlier list and historical survey, R. Devreesse, *RB* 51 (1942), 263–307.

[109] Waddington, no. 2112 from El-Hit; cf. *OGIS* 421; *IGR* iii 1126: Ἐπὶ βασιλέω[ς μεγάλου Μάρκου Ἰου]|λίου Ἀγρίππα[, ἔτους . . . ὁ δεῖνα]| Χάρητος ἔπα[ρχος ---]| σπείρης Αὐ[γούστης? καὶ στρατηγὸ]ς νομάδων ---| ης καὶ Χαλ ----

[110] Waddington, no. 2196: Ἀδριανοῦ τοῦ καὶ Σοαίδου Μαλέχου ἐθνάρχου, στρατηγοῦ νομάδων, τὸ μνημῖον, ἐτῶν κη΄. The title of *ethnarch* is not very common and denotes a somewhat higher rank than that of *tetrarch*, if indeed it was a title granted by the Romans; cf. Schürer, *History* i 333–4 n.; Sartre, *Trois études*, 125.

[111] Waddington, no. 2203: Τὸν δεῖνα πρεσ]β(ευτὴν) Σεβ(αστοῦ) ἀντιστρά(τηγον) οἱ ἀπὸ ἔθνους νομάδων, ἀγνείας χάριν.

[112] First published by J. T. Milik in a paper by P. J. Parr, G. L. Harding, and J. E. Dayton, *BIAL* 10 (1972), 54–7. For discussion, D. F. Graf and M. O'Connor, *Byzantine Studies* 4 (1977), 52–66; Graf, *BASOR* 229 (1978), 9–12; J. Beaucamp, *SDB* 9 (1979), 1467–75; G. W. Bowersock, *Le monde grec: Hommages à Claire Préaux* (1975), 513–22; Sartre, *Trois études*, 27–9; Bowersock, *Roman Arabia*, 96 f.; Graf, in his forthcoming paper on Qura 'Arabiyya and Provincia Arabia.

9). The Nabataean text mentions his predecessor Antistius Adventus (166–7),[113] as having made peace, presumably in an intertribal dispute.

The inscription is evidence of the activity of the governor of Arabia well beyond the provincial boundary.[114] It shows that the Roman empire had allies which recognized its suzerainty without themselves forming part of the provincial administrative structure, a relationship often, but apparently without justification, thought to belong to the Byzantine period. It may further provide evidence of the existence of a nomad confederation such as were formed from time to time in the pre-Islamic period.[115]

In the third century a comparable status was occupied by the Tanukh whose homeland was apparently in the north-east of the Arabian peninsula.[116] They are said to have been in conflict with Zenobia of Palmyra, and their relationship with Rome is attested through a bilingual inscription from Umm al-jimal, in the north-east of the province of Arabia. It mentions a teacher of Gadimathos (Jadhima), King of the Thanouenoi,[117] a figure also mentioned in the Arabic tradition.

Another well-known inscription of 328 refers to a 'lord of the Arabs'.[118] Found at Namara, north-east of the Jebel Druz, it is written in Nabataean characters, the oldest document in classical Arabic. It is a difficult text which has been variously interpreted. Imru'l-qais is also attested in the Arabic sources and was apparently related to the newly

---

[113] For the dates of these governors, Sartre, *Trois études*, 84.

[114] I agree with the interpretation of D. Graf in his forthcoming article mentioned above. Other aspects of significance are the use of Nabataean in one of the texts and the designation of the Thamud as *ethnos* or *šrkt* which may indicate a confederation. For the Thamud and other Arab peoples in the region see also the earlier survey in R. Dussaud, *La pénétration des Arabes en Syrie avant l'Islam* (1955), ch. V.

[115] E. A. Knauf, *Ismael* (1985), has argued that the Ismaelites were a 'protobedouinic' confederation encompassing tribes all over northern Arabia, with their cultic and political centre at Duma.

[116] Most of the evidence regarding this people is found in Arabic literature with which I am not familiar. See Sartre, *Trois études*, 134–6; Bowersock, *Roman Arabia*, 132–4.

[117] E. Littmann, *PAES* iv.A, no. 41, with comments; cf. Sartre, *Trois études*, 134 with n. 50.

[118] For recent discussion and further bibliography, Sartre, *Trois études*, 136–9; Bowersock, *Roman Arabia*, 138–42; I. Shahîd, *Byzantium*, 32–53; J. A. Bellamy, *JAOS* 105 (1985), 31–48, with a revised reading. I cite Bellamy's translation as given on p. 46: 'This is the funerary monument of Imru'u l-Qays, son of 'Amr, king of the Arabs; and(?) his title of honour was Master of Asad and Madhij. And he subdued the Asadis, and they were overwhelmed together with their kings, and he put to flight Maʿdʿhij thereafter, and came driving them into the gates of Najrān, the city of Shammar, and he subdued Maʿadd, and he dealt gently with the nobles of the tribes, and appointed them viceroys, and they became phylarchs for the Romans. And no king has equalled his achievements. Thereafter he died in the year 223, on the 7th day of Kaslūl. Oh, the good fortune of those who were his friends!'

established Lakhmid dynasty of Hira who themselves also belonged to the confederation of the Tanukh, according to the Arab traditions.[119] It is hard to judge his actual power on the strength of the grandiose language of the text.[120] We do not know the real significance of the term *mlk* at the time. Ammianus apparently uses it (*malechus*) in referring to a tribal chief (see below). The king of Hatra was called '*mlk*' of Arabia'.[121] The inscription and the sources, however, betray activity over a wide territory, in the central and southern Arabian peninsula, and on the Persian Gulf. The find-spot of the inscription as well as its contents show that Imru'l-qais was a loyal ally of the Romans.[122]

Despite their increased importance in the fourth century and after, our information about such allies is still fragmentary. The allies of Persia were the Lakhmid dynasty who resided at Hira.[123] There was a unit of Persian troops there. The Lakhmids had wide influence in the peninsula. They made agreements with powerful chiefs to supply troops for the Lakhmid army to keep the caravan routes safe, and levied taxes where they could. Another important group were the clans of Kinda originating from the central and northern parts of the peninsula.[124] They were the Lakhmids' most serious rivals and at one stage managed to dislodge them for three years from their capital. In the second half of the sixth century the Lakhmids lost much influence, and their key position came to an end early in the seventh century, a short period before the collapse of the Sasanian empire itself.

The confederates of the Romans were at first the Tanukh in the desert west of the Euphrates.[125] Towards the end of the fourth century they were superseded by the Salih who covered a wide territory in the Syrian and Mesopotamian desert.[126] The latter were supplanted by the Ghassanids towards the end of the fifth century.[127]

---

[119] The earliest reference to a Lakhmid ruler occurs in the Persian inscription at Paikuli from the reign of Narseh (293–302): recent translation in Frye, *History of Ancient Iran* (1984), appendix 5, pp. 375–78 with references to editions on p. 375.

[120] Cf. the reservations of R. E. Brünnow and A. v. Domaszewski, *Die Provincia Arabia* iii (1909), 283 f.

[121] MLK' DY 'RB, cf. B. Aggoula, *Syria* 63 (1986), 353–74.

[122] Shahîd, *Byzantium*, 46: a client-king, not genuinely independent. See also the other inscriptions from Namara, Waddington, nos. 2265–85, many of them set up by Roman troops.

[123] T. Nöldeke, *Geschichte der Perser und Araber zur Zeit der Sasaniden* (1879); G. Rothstein, *Die Dynastie der Lahmiden in al-Hîra* (1899); Devreesse, *RB* 51, 263–307; Bosworth, *Cambridge Hist. Iran* iii 1. 593–612; esp. 597–609.

[124] G. Olinder, *The Kings of Kinda* (1927). The record of the role they played before they extended their activities northwards goes back to the end of the fifth century. Bosworth, loc. cit.

[125] Above, p. 239. Shahîd, *Byzantium*, 465–76.

[126] Sartre, *Trois études*, 146 ff.; Shahîd, *Byzantium*.

[127] T. Nöldeke, 'Die Ghassanischen Fürsten aus dem Hause Gafnas', *Abhandlungen der königlichen preussischen Akademie der Wissenschaften zu Berlin* (1887); I. Kawar (Shahîd), *JAOS* 77

One of the first important figures among the nomad allies to be mentioned by name was 'Malechus [the King] named Podosaces, phylarch of the Assanitic Saracens, an infamous bandit, who had long raided our border districts with every kind of cruelty'.[128] From the fourth century onwards nomad tribes were incorporated into the military organization of the Near East in roles that exploited their particular capabilities to the full. Their use as raiders against the enemy became a regular feature in an offensive, complementary to the activities of the main army of either empire, as in the Persian campaign of 356, mentioned above, and as in that of 363, when Podosaces acted in such a capacity.

It was also the Persian policy in 531, when Saracen allies made the vulnerable parts of Euphratesia (formerly Commagene) their target instead of the strongly defended region of northern Mesopotamia.[129] Across the Tigris there were defences in place as early as the fourth century. Ammianus saw them during the Roman retreat in 363: 'dykes which artificially raised the height of the river banks in order to prevent Saracen incursions into Assyria'.[130] The existence of means to counter such raids shows that they were a persistent problem.[131] When Belisarius invaded Persia in 541 similar raiding missions into Assyria were entrusted to the Byzantine phylarch and client king;[132] and likewise, in the seventh century the Persian invasion of Byzantine territory was accompanied by Saracen raids.[133] Saracen tactics were effective in 378 when they served in the Roman army against the

---

(1957), 79–87; *Arabica* 5 (1958), 145–58; *Der Islam* 33 (1958), 145–58; F. E. Peters, *AAAS* 27–28 (1977–8), 97–113; Sartre, *Trois études*, 155 f. Zeev Rubin notes that Amorcesos already belonged to this movement.

[128] Ammianus xxiv 2. 4: 'Malechus Podosacis nomine, phylarchus Saracenorum Assanitarum, famosi nominis latro, omni saevitia per nostros limites diu grassatus . . .' Cf. Sartre, *Trois études*, 139 f.; Shahîd, *Byzantium*, 119–23.

[129] Procopius, *Bell.* i 17 f., esp. 17. 34 ff. This was not a novel idea, as Procopius thought, for it had been attempted by the Persian general Nohodares in 354: Ammianus xiv 3. On that occasion the plan was thwarted by betrayal. When Kavad did not succeed in subduing Amida in 502 he sent the Lakhmids under Nu'man into Osrhoene where the farmers were in the fields harvesting. Numerous prisoners and cattle were carried off: Joshua Stylites, 50 and 51. In the fifth and early sixth century Saracen raids are mentioned on several occasions: under Theodosius II (Theophanes, ed. de Boor, 85), Zeno (ibid. 120), Anastasius (ibid. 143), and Justinus (ibid. 171).

[130] xxv 6. 8.

[131] Cf. S. Lieu, *DRBE*, 487–90, citing the *Acta Archelai* which I have not seen, as illustrating raids across the border in the early fourth century.

[132] Procopius, *Bell.* ii 16. 15; 19. 12–18, 26–28. I. Kawar (Shahîd) has shown that the accusations of treachery levelled by Procopius against Arethas are false: *Byzantinische Zeitschrift* 50 (1957), 39–67; 362–82; *Byzantion* 41 (1971), 313–38.

[133] Theophanes, *Chron.* AM 6104 (AD 611), ed. de Boor, p. 300; Michael the Syrian, *Chron.*, ed. Chabot, ii 401.

Goths.[134] The Ghassanids under Arethas took part in a pitched battle at Callinicum in 531.[135] Another task for which the Saracens were eminently qualified was scouting and spying.[136]

In times of war the phylarchs frequently acted independently. The most notorious of all raiding nomad chiefs was Mundhir the Lakhmid, who for years 'plundered the whole east' while Byzantine counter-measures were never really effective, according to Procopius.[137] After the five-year treaty concluded by Rome and Persia in 545 Arethas the Ghassanid, the Roman ally, and Mundhir, the ally of the Persians, 'waged war against each other without Roman or Persian support'.[138] During negotiations between Byzantium and Persia in 550 the Persian ambassador accused the Romans of violating the truce, asserting that the Saracen confederates of the Romans had attacked their federate chief in times of peace.[139] In 563 Arethas complained in Constantinople about attacks carried out by his Lakhmid enemies.[140]

Attacks by nomads on the settled population were by no means the exclusive result of decisions on the part of the major powers. The nomads were easy to encourage, but hard to control.

The Ṭamūrāyē too, who dwell in the land of the Persians, when they saw that nothing was given to them by him rebelled against him (i.e. Kavād, the king of Persia). They placed their trust in the lofty mountains amid which they dwelt, and used to come down and spoil and plunder the villages around them, and (rob) the merchants, both foreigners and natives of the place and go up again.[141]

Such pressures increased particularly in times of drought. There are not many sources that explicitly describe such a situation, but we have a letter written in 484 by the bishop of Nisibis to the Nestorian patriarch.[142] In this case a complicating factor was that the problems

---

[134] Zosimus iv 22: a conventional description of swift cavalry avoiding the main body of the enemy troops and killing isolated individuals (cf. Paschoud (ed.), *Zosime*, ii (1979), pp. 378 f., n. 145). Ammianus, xxxi 16. 6, vividly describes their demoralizing effect on the enemy when the Goths attacked Constantinople after the battle of Adrianople. Sozomenos, *HE* vi 38, says Mavia was responsible for sending Saracen reinforcements after concluding peace with the Romans. That would be typical of the obligations of such an ally. See also Theophanes, *Chron.* AM 5870, ed. de Boor, 65. On Mavia see most recently Z. Rubin, *Cathedra* 47 (1988), 25–49 (in Hebrew).

[135] Procopius, *Bell.* i 18. 35–7; Malalas, *Chron.* 464. For the false charge of treachery, see Kawar, above, n. 127.

[136] e.g. Procopius, *Bell.* i 17. 35; ii 19. 16. Cf. I. Kawar, *Arabica* 3 (1956), 196 f.; Lieu, *DRBE*, 491.

[137] *Bell.* i 17. 29–48; ii 1.　　　　[138] *Bell.* ii 28. 12–14.

[139] Procopius, *Bell.* viii 11. 10.

[140] Theophanes, AM 6056, ed. de Boor, p. 240.

[141] Joshua Stylites 22.

[142] Cited by J.-B. Chabot, *Synodicon Orientale* (1902), 532 f. and thence by F. Nau, *Les Arabes Chrétiens de Mésopotamie et de Syrie* (1933), 13–15. For banditry in general see above, ch. II.

occurred in the frontier area. The Persian governor of Nisibis was held responsible for the acts of the Arabs who ravaged villages across the border, but he was incapable of keeping them under control.[143] In the treaty between Rome and Persia of AD 562 it was specifically stated that the Saracens on both sides of the border would be bound by the agreement.[144] That was another way of saying that the two parties to the treaty took it upon themselves to keep their own allies under control. Although the letter just cited is the only explicit mention of nomad raids across the border it must be noted that for this region there are frequent references of a general nature to attacks by nomads and to military structures to counter them.

Participation in full-scale campaigns clearly was not the most important task of the phylarchs. Essentially they had four functions:

(i) The one already mentioned: they carried out raids against the rural population in enemy territory.

(ii) They defended their own civilians against raids by the other empire's Saracen allies.

(iii) They protected the settled population in the provinces against nomad raids in general.

(iv) Occasionally they assisted the territorial army in internal police duties.

The second and third functions were no less important than the first. 'For these peoples are invincible by any other than themselves because of the swiftness of their horses. When surrounded they cannot be caught and they outstrip their enemies when retreating.'[145] In an episode often cited, Arethas the Kindite, a Roman phylarch, quarrelled in 528 with the *dux* of Palestine and had to flee into the inner desert, where he was killed by Mundhir, the Persian phylarch.[146] Justinian then ordered the *duces* of Phoenice, Arabia, and Mesopotamia and their phylarchs to punish Mundhir. The latter withdrew deeper into the desert, 'where no Roman ever came'. The Romans and their allies then raided his camp, took many captives, camels, and other animals, freed Roman captives, and burnt four Persian forts. This was a combined operation in which *limitanei* and several phylarchs collaborated. In other cases, when the sources mention action undertaken against

---

[143] See also Marcellinus, [Auctarium] an. 536 (ed. Mommsen, p. 105): 'Ipso namque anno ob nimiam siccitatem pastura in Persida denegata, circiter quindecim milia Saracenorum ab Alamundaro cum Chabo et Hesido fylarchis limitem Eufratesiae ingressa ubi Batras dux eos partim blanditiis, partim districtione pacifica fovit et inhiantes bellare repressit.'

[144] See below.

[145] Evagrius, *HE* 20.

[146] Malalas, 434 f.; Theophanes, AM 6021, ed. de Boor, p. 178.

Persian phylarchs, it is not always clear whether these were joint operations of the Roman army with Arab allies or not.[147]

Eventually the phylarchs became a regular part of the Byzantine provincial organization. A law of Justinian ratifying the appointment of a 'moderator' with enhanced power over the province of Arabia defines the authority of this official with regard to the *dux*, the phylarch, the offices of the sacred patrimony, and others.[148] There is at least one hint of social integration: a case of intermarriage between the family of a phylarch and a Byzantine official.[149] This reminds one of the report that the daughter of Mavia, the Saracen rebel queen, married the Roman commander Victor.[150]

The services rendered by the Arab confederates could take many forms. A remarkable case is the '*strata* dispute'. In 540 Khusro asked Mundhir to provide him with a pretext for a breach of the treaty with Byzantium, and Mundhir then picked a quarrel with Arethas the Ghassanid about pasturage south of Palmyra.[151] In the end Khusro started a war for different reasons, but the story as told by Procopius contains several points of interest. Mundhir claimed he could raid Roman territory without breaking any treaty, since the Saracens were not mentioned in it, a claim which Procopius says was true, as they were not separately mentioned, but always included under the names of the Persians and Romans. It was no doubt because of this that in the treaty of 562 they are specifically mentioned.[152] The second point of interest is Arethas' claim that the land was Roman because of the name '*strata*' applied to it by everybody, a name which derived from the *strata Diocletiana*, the Roman road from southern Syria to Palmyra. This shows that the name familiar to us from the milestones was actually in common use,[153] even among Arab confederates. Apparently the road lent its name to the whole region. This also indicates an awareness, in

---

[147] e.g. in 498 (see below, where no mention of Roman phylarchs is made) or in 503 when the Roman allies marched against Na'aman, according to Joshua Stylites 58 (cf. Sartre, *Trois études*, 161).

[148] *Nov. Iust.* 102.

[149] *IGLS* 297: the marriage of Silvanos, an officer, with the daughter of a phylarch. The inscription was found at Anasartha, 60 km. SE of Aleppo. See also nos. 281, 288, 292.

[150] Rejected by Mayerson, *IEJ* 30 (1980), 128; I. Shahîd, *Rome and the Arabs* (1984), 159 ff.; accepted by Rubin, *Cathedra*, 28. An inscription from southern Syria, dated 425, records the dedication of a church by a woman named Mavia: *AE* 1947. 193. Another Mavia, the son (or daughter?) of Qais the Kindite, a phylarch of Byzantium, was sent as a hostage to the court of Justinian under the terms of a treaty: Nonnosus, *FHG* iv 179.

[151] Procopius, *Bell.* ii 1.

[152] Menander Protector, *FHG* iv 208 ff.

[153] Malalas, 308, says 'stelae' were erected for the emperor (Diocletian) and for Caesar in the *limes* of Syria, an obvious reference to the milestones along the *strata Diocletiana*.

the mid sixth century, that such a road was a typically Roman structure. Finally, as already observed in the previous chapter, the whole story conveys the impression that there were no longer any Roman troops based in the region around Palmyra.

The *casus belli* adopted by Khusro instead of the '*strata* dispute' was another quarrel involving Mundhir. Khusro accused Justinian of attempting to persuade Mundhir by promises of large sums of money to join the Romans. He also claimed that Justinian had attempted to induce Huns to invade Persia. Whether these accusations were true or not, it is important to note that such steps could in principle be construed as *casus belli*.

The third of the phylarchs' functions was obviously connected with the second. The Romans paid subsidies to various nomad chiefs for giving protection. It is impossible to say when this became customary, but in 363 Julian's army found Saracens beyond the Tigris hostile 'because Julian had forbidden to give them subsidies and numerous presents, as in the past',[154] so it clearly had become customary by this time. A *novella* of 443 warns the *duces* that they have no right to remove and seize any part of the subsistence granted to the Saracen allies and other tribes.[155] This shows that such allies received a subsistence allowance through the *duces*, similar to that of the *limitanei*, and it appears that there were the familiar problems of corruption and theft by senior officials. Procopius represents Khusro as saying that the Romans made an annual payment in gold to some of the Huns and to the Saracens, not as if they were subjects paying tribute, but as a fee for guarding their land against harm at all times.[156]

This is not to suggest that Byzantium made such payments willingly. When Justin II decided to follow Julian's example and end the payment of protection money to Arab chiefs raids on Byzantine territory were resumed.[157] On the Persian side there was a similar reluctance to accept their obligations towards the Saracen allies: Khusro II deposed the last Lakhmid vassal in 602, and this resulted in a loss of authority over the nomads of northern Arabia.[158]

Persecuted individuals regularly sought haven in enemy territory.[159]

---

[154] Ammianus xxv 6. 10.

[155] *Nov. Theod.* xxiv 2 (12 Sept. 443): 'De Saracenorum vero foederatorum aliarumque gentium annonariis alimentis nullam penitus eos decarpendi aliquid vel auferendi licentiam habere concedimus.'

[156] Procopius, *Bell.* ii 10. 23.

[157] He also halted subsidies to Persia, which resulted in renewal of the war.

[158] See Bosworth, *Cambridge Hist. Iran* iii 2. 607–9.

[159] N. Garsoïan, *Cambridge Hist. Iran* iii 1. 571, 573. Under Valens Persia offered asylum to pro-Nicaean Christians expelled by Arians: cf. Lieu, *DRBE*, 492.

Migrations of the various nomad clans naturally cannot be traced with any accuracy, but there is at least some evidence of large-scale movements between the two empires. It is no coincidence that the information is found in a local source.[160] In 420 Aspebetos (a Persian title: *spahbadh*), chief of an Arab clan which belonged to the Persian sphere of influence, went over to the Romans and settled in Roman territory with the permission of the regional commander. It is very likely that such immigration and settlement occurred more often than we know.[161] Unlike that of small numbers of individuals the reception of this massive migration was considered a hostile act by the Persian king.

Aspebetos was accepted as ally and made 'phylarch of the Roman confederates in Arabia'. This seems to be a title of a higher rank than that granted to previous phylarchs since it implies authority over all clans in (the province of?) Arabia. The clan converted to Christianity,[162] and settled in a camp (*parembole*) in Palestine, with Aspebetos, renamed Petrus, as their bishop.[163] This is remarkable: a nomad chief who was recognized by the Byzantine authorities as a sort of 'super-phylarch', not only converted to Christianity, like many other allies, but also chose to be appointed bishop himself. This shows the extent to which that position carried authority in the Byzantine empire, something which is obvious also from the description of sieges, where they played a central role in the defence of their cities. It is further apparent in the story of Mavia's rebellion, where the appointment of a bishop is also an event of crucial importance. The indispensable role played by the bishops is nowhere better illustrated than in the description of the building of Dara, undertaken at the behest of Anastasius' generals by the bishop of Amida with funds provided by the emperor.[164] At an even higher level the bishops were used regularly as plenipotentiaries by both sides. Thus they maintained contacts with communities lying on both sides of the border.[165]

---

[160] Cyril of Scythopolis, *vita Euthymii*, ed. Schwartz, 18 f. See also Socrates, *HE* vii 18, *PG* lxvii 774–8. Cf. Sartre, *Trois études*, 149–53; Rubin, *DRBE*, 680 f.

[161] G. E. M. de Ste. Croix, *The Class Struggle in the Ancient Greek World* (²1983), appendix iii, 509–18, on the settlement of 'barbarians' within the Roman empire. The present case is not mentioned. Arab immigrants who settled in the empire in the same period are also mentioned in *Nov. Theod.* ii 24 (12 Sept. 443).

[162] Cyril 20 f. For the Christian Arabs in the province of Arabia, R. Devreesse, *RB* 51 (1942), 110–46. For the Christians in the Persian empire, J. Labourt, *Le Christianisme dans l'empire Perse sous la dynastie Sassanide* (1904); J. M. Fiey, *Assyrie chrétienne*, 3 vols. (1965–8); id., *Communautés syriaques en Iran et Irak des origines à nos jours* (CSCO 54, 1977); J. P. Asmussen, *Cambridge Hist. Iran* iii 2. 924–48 and bibliography on 1355–7.

[163] Cyril 25.   [164] Zachariah of Mitylene, *Chron.* vii 6.

[165] See Garsoïan, *Cambridge Hist. Iran* iii 1. 573 with n. 1.

In the mid sixth century a descendant of Aspebetos was 'phylarch of the Saracens in that region'.[166] Here then is a case which allows us to follow the migration of nomad confederates of Persia to the Byzantine region, their integration in the Byzantine provincial organization, conversion, and sedentarization.

With their sedentarization such Arabs became more vulnerable to raids by nomads or semi-nomads. We hear of attacks on them in the reign of Anastasius.[167] In Chapter II it was seen that there were many such minor disturbances in the desert and at the edge of it. This will serve to remind us that the measures taken by the Byzantine government to ensure peace and security would never have resulted in the degree of control a modern state would be expected to provide. Remote or inadequately supported communities had to find their own *modus vivendi*. An example is the walled town of Pharan in Sinai. An account written about 400 describes how the council made representations to a local chief for having violated an agreement with the town that apparently entailed the payment of protection money.[168] In 570 it is described as inadequately(?) defended by a militia of 800 horsemen.[169] From both instances it is clear that the Pharanites had to find their own solutions for the protection of their community, without the support of the central government.

The role of the phylarchs in a regional context is best illustrated by the Iotabe affair.[170] An Arab chief named Amorcesos (Imru'l-qais, not to be confused with the earlier person of that name, buried at Namara) moved from a region under Persian control to the Roman frontier zone,[171] where he carried out raids against Persian subjects. He gained control of the island of Iotabe and expelled the Roman customs officials, levying the duties himself.[172] He also acquired a number of villages in the region. Following negotiations he was granted the status of phylarch and was confirmed in his possession of Iotabe. As in the case, first of Mavia, then of Aspebetos, conversion to Christianity was an integral part of the agreement.[173]

[166] Cyril 18.
[167] Cyril 67.
[168] Nilus, *narrationes*, *PG* lxxix, col. 661. Cf. P. Mayerson, *Proc. Am. Phil. Soc.* 107 (1963), 162.
[169] Ps.-Antoninus Placentinus 40, *CCSL* clxxv 149 f.
[170] F.-M. Abel, *RB* 47 (1938), 510–37. The location of Iotabe is unknown. Those who confidently state that it is to be identified with the island of Tiran at the entrance to the Gulf of Elath/Aqaba ignore the conclusions reached by numerous archaeologists who have been unable to find any ancient remains on the island.
[171] Malchus Philadelphensis, fr. 1, Müller, *FHG* iv 112 f.
[172] Cf. Sartre, *IGLS* xiii 1, no. 9046, with comments on pp. 116 f.
[173] Note also the conversion of the phylarch Zokomos: Sozomenos, *HE* vi 38, and cf. Sartre, *Trois études*, 144–6; Rubin, *Cathedra*, 35–8.

In 498 action was taken by the Byzantine government.[174] As part of a campaign to subdue and expel groups of nomads in the several provinces, the island of Iotabe was recaptured by the *dux* of Palestine.[175] The interest of the Iotabe episode lies in the fact that this again was a place on the periphery of the empire which the Byzantine authorities sometimes managed to hold and sometimes had to leave to others, if possible through some sort of agreement that preserved peaceful relations.

Another chief in the same general area about whom we know a little more is Abokharabos (Abūkarib), Justinian's phylarch in Palestine.[176] This man gave the emperor palm groves beyond the provincial boundary as a present, 'and he guarded the land against harm at all times'.[177] He was feared both by the barbarians who were his subjects and by the enemy. Here again we have a chief whose authority covered an area partly in the province proper and partly outside: his responsibility for the protection of Roman citizens against nomad raids clearly implies activity beyond the borders of the province, since one cannot police nomads in a static manner. Theophanes, in a notice referring to the years 633–4, reports that Arab tribes received a modest subsidy for guarding the entrances (*stomia*) of the desert in the region of Sinai.[178]

The fourth task, assisting in internal police duties, is attested in at least one case in 529/30, when the phylarch of Palestine intervened in the suppression of the Samaritan revolt.[179] His identity is less important for the present discussion than his interference in such an affair in the interior of Palestine. In the last stage of the revolt he captured twenty thousand young people who had fled to Trachonitis and sold them 'in the Persian and Indian regions'.[180] This again illustrates the mobility of these allies.

Perhaps the most remarkable feature in all the information presented above is the degree to which the relationship with the nomads made it impossible to distinguish between subjects and foreigners. The

---

[174] Theophanes, AM 5990, ed. de Boor, pp. 140 f.

[175] Theophanes, AM 5990, ed. de Boor, p. 141; Evagrius iii 36. Cf. Sartre, *Trois études*, 156. A quarter of a century afterwards the island is mentioned as one of the places that provided ships for the war against the king of Himyar: *Life of Saint Arethas*, ed. Boissonade, which I have not seen. See Abel, *RB* 47, 528 f.; Sartre, *IGLS* xiii 1 p. 116 n. 4. Iotabe provided 7 ships, Aila 15, Clysma 20. Iotabe is mentioned once again in a speech of 535–6 by Choricius of Gaza. The *dux* Palaestinae, we are told, expelled Jews who had occupied the island from the Arabian peninsula: Choricius Gazaeus, *Laud. Arat. et Steph.* 66 f., ed. Foerster and Richtsteig, 65 f.

[176] Procopius, *Bell.* i 19. 8–13; cf. Kawar, *JAOS* 77 (1957), 85–7; Sartre, *Trois études*, 169 ff.

[177] Probably the oases of Tabūk and Taymā'.

[178] Theophanes, AM 6123–4, ed. de Boor, i 335. Cf. P. Mayerson, *TAPA*, 156–60.

[179] Malalas 445–7.

[180] Malalas 447.

phylarchs were confederates who recognized the authority of the emperor. At times of major wars they carried out special missions, often independently of the regular army or alongside it. They fought for Rome against various enemies, kept their own peoples under control, suppressed rebellious provincials. They possessed territory inside and outside the provinces, but also acted within the provinces, in collaboration with the military authorities. Yet their people were nomads and as a consequence ther position was never static or stable. They moved into and out of the provinces. A phylarch who had assisted in suppressing a revolt inside a province could sell his captives in Persian territory. Much appears to have depended on the personality and power of the individual chiefs, a feature which seems to have been characteristic of the later Bedouin tribes as well. The authority granted by the authorities in Constantinople to the individual phylarchs seems to have varied: Aspebetos, for example, seems to have had a senior position. The Imru'l-qais who was buried at Namara in 328 was able to claim that he had 'dealt gently with the nobles of the tribes [whom he had subdued in Arabia], and appointed them viceroys, and they became phylarchs for the Romans'. After the successes of Mundhir against Roman territory Justinian gave his own phylarch Arethas the Ghassanid authority over the other phylarchs.[181] The conclusion particularly relevant for this book is the futility of any effort to draw a political or military boundary line for the empire in this period.

Finally it is noteworthy how the peculiar characteristics of these peoples as fighters suited the nature of warfare between Rome and Persia in these centuries. They were masters at raiding and plundering, which became a key element in the wars between the two empires in the third century and afterwards, though a costly and destructive form of warfare that never brought a lasting success to either party. As already argued, this is a reflection of a (partial) change in war aims in the period. After Julian's failure to follow in the footsteps of Alexander the wars between Byzantium and Persia became in themselves mere raiding expeditions. It is impossible to claim for either side that there was any other rational plan determining the nature of the hostilities.

Mesopotamia

As argued in Chapter I, the chronology of the Persian wars shows that those in the third and fourth centuries were due in large measure to the

---

[181] Procopius, *Bell.* i 17. 45–7; Theophanes, ed. de Boor, 240; cf. Kawar, *JAOS* 75 (1955), 205–16; Sartre, *Trois études*, 170–2.

fact that the Persians did not accept the Roman presence east of the Euphrates. Before the seventh century the Persians reached Antioch only twice, the Romans southern Mesopotamia again and again.[182]

In Mesopotamia even more than elsewhere the imperial authorities and the army made the citizens bear the burdens of military organization.[183] It was the area of the most direct confrontation between the Roman and the Persian empire. In 359 the Persians were advised to 'give up the dangerous sieges of frontier cities (in Mesopotamia), and to break through across the Euphrates and invade provinces which in all the previous wars (except in the time of Gallienus) had been untouched and had become prosperous in the long period of peace'.[184] Thus Ammianus brings out the elementary truth that Syria and Cappadocia rarely suffered foreign invasions or raids, while Mesopotamia was attacked very frequently and also served as base for the Roman army in its actions against Persia. This is true both for the period before the treaty of 363 and afterwards, for even when neither party succeeded in effecting substantial changes of the frontier there were frequent hostilities and occasional large-scale wars in this part of the East.

In the sixth century al Mundhir gave the same advice to the Persian king Kavaḍ:

The cities of Mesopotamia and of the land called Osroene, as they are nearest your borders, are stronger than all the others and full of soldiers as never before, so that if we go there the battle will not be safe. However, in the land beyond the Euphrates and in neighbouring Syria there is no fortified city nor an army worth mentioning.[185]

It has been pointed out that the partition of Mesopotamia divided a people which formed to a certain extent a homogeneous unit with a common language and shared historical traditions.[186] This was

[182] For a survey, W. Eilers, *Cambridge Hist. Iran* iii 1. 481–504; bibliography in iii 2. 1308–10. Add A. Oppenheimer et al., *Babylonia Judaica* (1983).

[183] The cities themselves were responsible for the maintenance and manning of road stations, according to John Chrysostom, *ad Stagirium* ii 189f. (*PG* lx 457). See also the words ascribed to Johanan ben Zakai, quoted above. J. B. Segal, *PBA* 41 (1955), 114f., cites sources that describe a bishop building bridges and roads in Mesopotamia. Others repaired town-walls. For the military sites in Mesopotamia, *DE* s.v. *limes*, iv 1325–36. As noted above, this article fails to distinguish between cities which were garrisoned and sites thought to be exclusively military in nature. For the manner in which the confrontation between the two empires affected civilians in the frontier zone, Lieu, *DRBE*, 475–505.

[184] Ammianus xviii 6. 3: 'posthabitis perniciosis obsidiis perrumperetur Euphrates . . .'

[185] Procopius, *Bell.* i 17. 34: Μεσοποταμίας γὰρ καὶ τῆς Ὀσροηνῆς καλουμένης χώρας, ἅτε τῶν σῶν ὁρίων ἄγχιστα οὔσης, αἵ τε πόλεις ὀχυρώταταί εἰσι πασῶν μάλιστα καὶ στρατιωτῶν πλῆθος οἶον οὐ πώποτε πρότερον τανῦν ἔχουσιν, ὥστε ἡμῖν αὐτόσε ἰοῦσιν οὐκ ἐν τῷ ἀσφαλεῖ τὰ τῆς ἀγωνίας γενήσεται, ἐν μέντοι τῇ χώρᾳ, ἣ ἐκτὸς Εὐφράτου ποταμοῦ τυγχάνει οὖσα, καὶ τῇ ταύτης ἐχομένῃ Συρίᾳ οὔτε πόλεως ὀχύρωμα οὔτε στράτευμα λόγου ἄξιόν ἐστι.

[186] Segal, *PBA*, 109–41. For similar observations on Armenia, Mommsen, *Römische Geschichte* v 356f.

recognized by Dio in his criticism of Severus' conquest of Mesopotamia, when he said that the empire now had reached peoples who were closer to the Medes and the Parthians than to the Romans and that the Romans were therefore fighting other peoples' wars. The conquest and annexation of part of this area brought about a state of permanent conflict between Rome and Persia. Neither party was satisfied with the status quo. The result is lucidly described by Procopius:

The other boundaries of the Romans and the Persians are generally as follows: the territories of the two peoples are contiguous. They march from their own territory and fight each other or resolve their differences, as people do whenever they share a border while differing in customs and constitution. However, in the old Commagene, now called Euphratesia they live nowhere near each other. For they are separated by the desert.[187]

In another passage, also cited elsewhere in this book, Procopius describes Chorzane in Armenia (the district of modern Kighi), an area through which the border ran, before Justinian 'fortified all of that remote frontier district':[188]

There was no marked frontier. The subjects of both peoples had no fear of each other and were not suspicious of attack, but they intermarried and held joint markets. Whenever the king of either empire orders the generals to march against the others they always find the neighbouring people unguarded. For the lands, while being close to each other are densely populated and yet there was no fort on either side from ancient times.

Justinian then converted a town in the region into 'an unconquerable fort', stationed there a *dux* with regular troops, 'and thus fortified that whole frontier district'. We are not told what happened to the intermarriages and the joint markets.

Roman and Byzantine rule in the East beyond Anatolia lasted seven centuries. The border remained more or less static for one extended period, during the two and a half centuries following the Byzantine loss of Nisibis in 363.[189] In this period there were no major changes because neither power succeeded in effecting any in the many wars that were actually fought. These again were fewer in number than during most of the other centuries, probably because both powers were exhausted by the struggle with invaders from the north in the late fourth and early fifth centuries.

---

[187] *De aed.* ii 8. 3 f.
[188] *De aed.* iii 3. 9–14.
[189] Ammianus xxv 8. 13–9. 2 for the surrender of Nisibis. Before 363 Nisibis frequently changed hands. It was, in the words of the Babylonian Talmud, Qidushin 72a, one of the cities which Rome 'sometimes swallows and sometimes spits out'. For the city, Oppenheimer, 319–34.

The Fortified Cities

The fortified cities were the primary issue in the wars between the two empires, and they had to bear the brunt of the warfare. The fall of any of these to the enemy was a major blow, as is illustrated by Ammianus' description of the surrender of Nisibis in 363. Justin II is said to have lost his mental balance at the fall and capture of Dara. Yet the citizens had to defend themselves often without support from the Roman army.[190] Take, for instance, Ammianus' description of the site of Singara.[191] It was chosen as a legionary base after the annexation of the region by Septimius Severus and lost to Persia in 363, together with Nisibis and Bezabde.[192] It was a convenient place for learning of sudden enemy movements, but the site was such that it could not be provided with adequate support and so it had been captured repeatedly with the loss of its defenders. The citizens themselves were also responsible for the defence of Amida during the siege of 502, as described by Procopius, Joshua the Stylite, and Zachariah of Mitylene.[193] The anonymous Byzantine treatise on strategy takes it for granted that signal towers on the frontier served to warn the civilian population of the approach of enemy forces so that they should have time to flee.[194] The first function of frontier guard posts ($\phi\varrho o\acute{v}\varrho\iota a$), it tells us, is to provide information on enemy movements and to serve as bases for exploratory excursions across the border.[195] Consistently with Ammianus' comments on the site of Singara, it recommends that no great masses of people should gather in such locations. Otherwise the enemy will be tempted to lay siege to them, for they are hard to reach for the Roman troops while the enemy can easily withdraw.[196]

Zenobia is a good example of an isolated position. It was fortified by Justinian 'because it occupies a position far away from any neighbour and will therefore be always in danger because there happen to be no Romans nearby who would offer support'.[197]

---

[190] For Syriac sources, Segal, *PBA*, 113.
[191] xx 6. 9.   [192] See chs. I, IV, and VIII.
[193] Procopius, *Bell.* i 7. 1 ff.; Joshua Stylites 50 and 51; Zachariah of Mitylene, *Chronicle* vii 3–5.
[194] H. Köchly and W. Rüstow, *Griechische Kriegsschriftsteller* ii. 2 (1853), 64.
[195] On the gathering of information by embassies se A. D. Lee in *DRBE*, 455–61.
[196] Köchly and Rustow, 66.
[197] Procopius, *de aed.* ii 8. 15: . . . ἐπεὶ ἐν χώρῳ ἐπὶ μακρότατον ἀγείτονι οὖσαν καὶ διὰ τοῦτο μὲν ἐν κινδύνοις ἀεὶ ἐσομένην, ἐπικουρίας δὲ τυχεῖν Ῥωμαίων πλησιοχώρων οὐκ ὄντων αὐτῇ οὐκ ἂν δυναμένην . . . J. Lauffray, *Halabiyya-Zenobia, place forte du limes oriental et la Haute-Mésopotamie au vi ͤ siècle*, i (1983), esp. ch. VIII, for the date of the walls, which is uncertain. No remains can be assigned with any certainty to the times of Palmyra's ascendancy.

All this substantiates Dio's implication that the Roman lines were too far extended and those of the Persians shorter than before the annexation of northern Mesopotamia. The system was organized on the principle that the citizens could hold out against a siege by a substantial force until the regular army arrived on the spot. Even where there were regular army units 'native' troops assisted in the defence of the cities.[198] Procopius vividly describes the situation of many cities at the time of Khusro I's invasion of Syria. 'All the Romans, officers and soldiers would not even consider facing the enemy or blocking his advance, but they garrisoned their forts, each as best he could, and thought it sufficient to guard these and save themselves.'[199] The local leadership was taken over by the bishops, as Procopius' account makes abundantly clear—yet another indication of the central role they played in this period.

In these circumstances reliance on the citizens for the defence of their cities may instead have been an effective system. Procopius gives remarkable examples of the resilience of many city populations under siege. The citizens of Sergiopolis, for instance, saved their city with 200 soldiers against Khusro's 6,000.[200] The notion that a citizens' militia cannot possibly fight effectively belongs to the period of the development of standing professional armies in Europe. But even in our times of massive fire power it has been shown that local militias can be very effective in defending their own homes. This was demonstrated in Israel's War of Independence and again in the Lebanon War of 1982. 'The real war in South Lebanon was not fought by the Fatah's semi-regular forces [which collapsed at the approach of the Israeli army] but by the homeguards in the refugee camps. It was a static, tenacious battle fought in built-up areas cut through by narrow alleyways that barely accommodated a vehicle . . .'[201] The reason was given by the chief of military intelligence before the war broke out: 'You can flee from an outpost, but it is not so easy to get up and run when you are in a city, and especially not in a refugee camp, where there are families—old people and children. They will fight in these places; these are the vital centres of their lives.'[202]

All this, including the description of built-up areas, will have been

---

[198] e.g. Ammianus xviii 9. 3: '(Amida) Cuius oppidi praesidio erat semper Quinta Parthica legio destinata, cum indigenarum turma non contemnenda.' xx 6. 1: '(Singara) Tuebantur autem hanc civitatem legiones duae (prima Flavia primaque Parthica), et indigenae plures cum auxilio equitum, illic ob repentinum malum clausorum.'

[199] *Bell.* ii 20. 19.   [200] *Bell.* ii 20. 11–15.

[201] Ze'ev Schiff and Ehud Ya'ari, *Israel's Lebanon War* ([2]1986), 137.

[202] Ibid. 137 f.

even more true of the ancient cities, which were both surrounded by strong walls and faced only with armies without fire-arms. The best description of a city defended by untrained—or half-trained—civilians against a professional army is, of course, Josephus' account of the siege of Jerusalem. It is important to realize that there was indeed a people's militia in the Byzantine empire; but it was composed, not of *limitanei* as is so often assumed, but of townspeople.

The very fact that the Mesopotamian cities were fortified on a massive scale implies that Diocletian and his successors gave up any notion of protecting the countryside against major raids. In case of a massive threat the army could march quickly to the front, and the peasants would seek refuge in the cities but their possessions would be destroyed. However, even this system did not always work in the way it was supposed to, as is clear to any reader of Procopius.[203] The regular army might fail to intervene, and the cities were often ill prepared for a siege.

Ammianus gives an impressive description of the Roman preparations ('scorched earth') for the Persian invasion of 359: the peasants were forced to move to fortified places, Carrhae was abandoned as being indefensible, and the plain was set on fire 'so that from the very banks of the Tigris as far as the Euphrates no green was visible'.[204] According to Ammianus the very purpose of the fortification of Amida by Constantius was to serve as a refuge for the peasants.[205] In the words of a would-be traitor to the Roman cause from Amida: 'Roman soldiers . . . are wandering about this area in small groups and maltreat the miserable peasants. . . .'[206] Often the cities were left to fend for themselves or surrender. All this must have had a serious impact on the social and economic life of the area.

The city fortresses became ever more important in the wars between Rome and Persia. They had various functions:

(*a*) As refuges for the army. According to several sources one of the reasons for the foundation of Dara (in 505–6) on Roman territory near the frontier opposite Nisibis was that it could serve as a refuge for the army when it met a stronger enemy force. Joshua Stylites states that the proposal to found a city on the border was made by the generals, who claimed that the troops suffered many casualties because the nearest

---

[203] e.g. *Bell.* i 21. 4–9: the siege of Martyropolis. The wall was easy to storm; supplies and engines of war were insufficient; a Byzantine relief force did not dare to intervene.

[204] xviii 78. 3: 'ut ad usque Euphraten ab ipsis marginibus Tigridis nihil viride cernetur.'

[205] xviii 9. 1.

[206] Procopius, *Bell.* i 9. 7: . . . καὶ γάρ που ἐς τὰ ταύτῃ χωρία κατ' ὀλίγους περιόντες (sc. στρατιῶται ῾Ρωμαῖοι) τοὺς οἰκτροὺς ἀγροίκους βιάζονται.

bases were Tella and Amida.[207] In 527 a Roman attempt to capture
Nisibis failed, and the army withdrew; the cavalry (but not the
infantry) succeeded in reaching Dara.[208]

(*b*) As staging posts for campaigns. Nisibis served as the Persian
supply base.[209] Dara was built to serve the Romans in a similar
capacity against Nisibis.[210]

(*c*) As armouries. Zachariah in his description of the foundation of
Dara emphasizes this function.[211]

(*d*) As customs posts. Nisibis functioned as one for both powers in
various periods.[212]

(*e*) As bases for troops whose function was to protect the local
population against nomad raids.[213] It is not clear how effective their
defence was against large-scale raids in wartime, but it may well have
been forceful enough to make an impact against smaller raids in
peacetime.

(*f*) As refuges for the population in times of major campaigns, as noted
above.

The fortified cities together with the road-system in Mesopotamia
and Syria have often been described as elements of a system of defence.
As argued repeatedly in this book, many works confuse roads with
fortified frontiers. With regard to Mesopotamia the situation is even
more confused since there is no agreement as to the actual alignment of
the frontier in various periods. Poidebard in his monumental work
sought the '*limes*' along the rivers Khabur and Jaghjagh.[214] His
identification of the sites he photographed as Roman and Byzantine
limes-forts was based on no evidence at all. Many were in fact old
settlements going back to Assyrian times. They had previously been
surveyed without prejudice by Sarre and Herzfeld, who did not observe

[207] 90. Similarly Zachariah, *HE* xi (PG lxxxv 1162): 'Hunc imperatorem rogabant ut urbem
aliquamprope montem fabricari mandaret, quae exercitui perfugium esset et statio, armorum
officina, et regionis Arabicae praesidium adversus Persas latrones atque Ismaelitas: porro
Daram . . . aedificandam muniendamve suadebant.' Also Michael the Syrian, ix 8 (trans. J.-B.
Chabot (1899), ii 1, p. 159). The reliability of Procopius' information on Dara and its fortifications is the subject of two recent papers: B. Croke and J. Crow, *JRS* 73 (1983), 143–59, and M.
Whitby, *DRBE*, 737–83. Cf. Whitby, *DRBE*, 717–35 for a general paper on Procopius and the
development of Roman defences in Upper Mesopotamia.

[208] Zachariah, *HE* ix 1.

[209] Procopius, *Bell.* i 10. 14, 17. 25; Zachariah, *HE* ix 3.

[210] Zachariah, *HE* vii 6.

[211] Zachariah, loc. cit.

[212] Nisibis after Diocletian: Petrus Patricius, *FHG* iv 189, no. 14. According to a law of 408/9:
Cod. Inst. iv 63. 4 (together with Callinicum and Artaxata). Nisibis and Dara according to the
treaty of 562: Menander Protector, ed. Bekker and Niebuhr, 360 f., ed. de Boor, 180.

[213] See above on Thannouris and on Dara (n. 207).

[214] *La trace de Rome dans le désert de Syrie* (1934).

a Roman frontier along these lines.[215] A recent survey of the middle Khabur has clearly brought out the variety of periods of occupation of these sites.[216] Oates observed that the sites 'lie on one of the most important highways of the Near East and, given favourable conditions, have at times achieved a prosperity and assumed a cultural importance out of proportion to their size'.[217]

Apart from the fortified cities very few genuine Roman forts have so far actually been found and described in this area. Those that are known, Ain Sinu, Tell Brak, and Tell Bali, are 'all three on important highways and well supplied with water'.[218] Of Sergiopolis (Resapha), south of Sura on the Euphrates, Sarre and Herzfeld observed that the existence of a settlement on this barren site can only be explained by its location on an important caravan route.[219] An inscription shows that a modest building north of the town served as *praetorium* for the Ghassanids. At the time of the annual pilgrimage of Saint Sergius they came up from their centre in the region east and south of Mount Hermon and resided there, together with numerous Arab pilgrims. It served as the Christian version of one of the traditional cultic and political centres of a confederation of nomad tribes, like Duma and Ruwwafa in earlier periods, but it was of far wider importance. It was there that Khusro II dedicated gifts bearing Greek inscriptions at the imperial shrine in gratitude for the Byzantine help he had received in his struggle for the throne.[220] Nicephorium-Callinicum (ar-Raqqa), 'a strongly fortified

---

[215] F. Sarre & E. Herzfeld, *Archäologische Reise im Euphrat-und Tigris-Gebiet*, i (1911), 172 ff. For the Khabur Valley, p. 175; 189 ff.: 'Es ist voller Ruinenhügel, in einer Dichtigkeit, wie wir sie bisher nur in der Ebene östlich Aleppo beobachtet hatten.' For later researches in this area, M. E. L. Mallowan, *Iraq* 9 (1947); he counted at least five hundred ancient settlements (11). In the Balih Valley (*Iraq* 8 (1946), 111–59) he saw scores of ancient settlements; like the Khabur, he observes, this was a natural line of movement (112). But there is nothing in his published material to justify his conclusion (122) that after Julian this was a fortified line.

[216] Only a preliminary report of a few pages has been available to me: J.-Y. Monchambert, *Annales Archéologiques Arabes Syriennes* 33 (1983), 233–7, esp. the tables on 235 f.

[217] D. Oates, *Studies in the Ancient History of Northern Iraq* (1968), 9. For a survey of the various opinions on the actual alignment of the *'limes'* in Mesopotamia, iv 1327 f.

[218] *Studies*, 90. Oates discusses at length the plan of the fort at Ain Sinu and its possible functions, but has not been able to reach any firm conclusions. For the Roman (or Palmyrene) forts on the Middle Euphrates now under excavation see above, p. 147.

[219] Sarre & Herzfeld, i 136–41; cf. for the remains ibid. ii 1–45, and see now W. Karnapp, *Die Stadtmauer von Resafa in Syrien* (1976). For the publications on this site see also above, p. 204, n. 189. This caravan route, it may be noted, was one of Poidebard's *'limites'*. Sarre and Herzfeld, on the other hand, describe a road-system in the region and do not refer to any system of defence. For an ancient source describing a journey *along the road* from Barbalissos via Sura and Tetrapyrgia to Resapha, see the 'Martyrium SS Sergii et Bacchi', *PG* cxv 1017, 1025, 1027. Sura is described as a *phrourion*, Resapha once as a *polis* and once as a *phrourion*. Resapha served as *praetorium* of the Ghassanids, according to a well-known inscription: J. Sauvaget, *Byzantion* 14 (1939), 115–30.

[220] Evagrius vi 21, ed. Bidez and Parmentier, 235 f. Cf. P. Peeters, *Analecta Bollandiana* 65 (1947), 5–56. Nonnosus, *FGH* iv 179, mentions bi-annual meetings of Saracens.

town and very prosperous trade centre',[221] at the confluence of Balikh and Euphrates, served as base of the *equites promoti Illyriciani*.[222]

An interesting excavated site is that of Dibsi Faraj (ancient Athis?) on the Euphrates, some 60 kilometres west of Surà.[223] Here a fort was grafted on to an existing civilian settlement. The fort was created in the late third century by the addition of a major enceinte and a *principia*, and was reconstructed in the sixth century. The excavator assumes that it was not permanently garrisoned, but contained facilities that could be used by the field army when necessary. It would thus have served a similar purpose to that of the fortified towns, but on a smaller scale. An alternative possibility is that, like the great fortified cities, it served as a refuge for the rural population in times of war.

The non-existence of any fortified line in Mesopotamia, against the assumptions of Chapot and Poidebard, was clearly seen by Dillemann.[224] The very fact that there exists no agreement on the line of the frontier in this area proves its irrelevance as a military concept. For the pre-Diocletianic period Dillemann observed that the military foci of the area were the cities, Nisibis and others. On the later period he is less lucid, mainly because like others, he misunderstood the meaning of the term *limes* attested in ancient sources.[225] As argued above for the forts in Arabia, local security and safety of communications are the most likely objects of known forts in the countryside. Ammianus says that all districts of Mesopotamia were guarded by *praetenturae* and *stationes agrariae* because of frequent disturbances.[226] Several sources refer to Justinian's forts west of Balad Sinjar, notably Thannouris.[227] According to Procopius they were intended to check Saracen raids across the Khabur upon the population living in the countryside.

The most obvious argument against the assumption that there was a 'fortified frontier' in the east apart from the fortified cities is the fact that

---

[221] Ammianus xxiii 3. 7.

[222] *Not. Dig. Or.* xxxv 16. See also Procopius, *de aed.* ii 7. 17: Justinian restored the walls. For the site see M. al-Khalaf and K. Kohlmeyer, *Damaszener Mitteilungen* 2 (1985), 132–62.

[223] R. P. Harper, with an appendix by T. J. Wilkinson, *DOP* 29 (1975), 319–38; R. P. Harper, *SMR* ii 453–60; *Actes du colloque de Strassbourg 1977*, ed. J. C. Margueron (1980), 327–48.

[224] L. Dillemann, *Haute Mésopotamie orientale et pays adjacents* (1962), 198–203: 'les plus fortes densités de postes y correspondent à des besoins de sécurité et non de défense militaire.'

[225] Ibid. 212–26. Dillemann concluded that after Diocletian forts were still sited along the main roads and the rivers, but he is not very clear about the nature of the system.

[226] xiv 3. 2.

[227] Procopius, *de aed.* ii 6. 15 f.; Zachariah of Mitylene, *Syriac Chronicle*, ix 2, trans. F. J. Hamilton and E. W. Brooks (1899), 222 f.: 'During the lifetime of Justin (should be: Justinian) the king who had learned that Thannuris was a convenient place for a city to be built as a place of refuge in the desert, and for a military force to be stationed to protect 'Arab against the marauding bands of Saracens . . .'

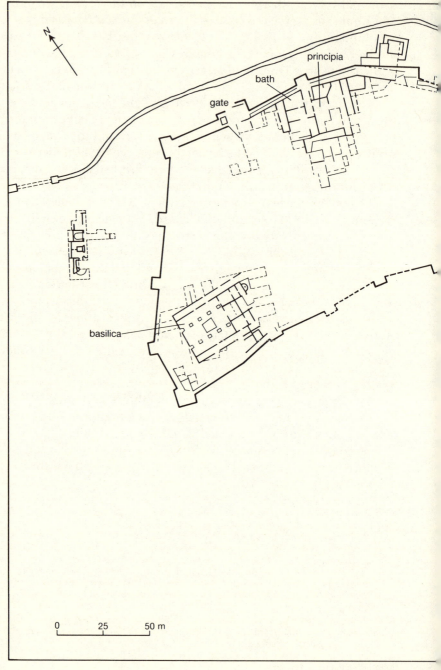

FIG. 13. Dibsi Far:

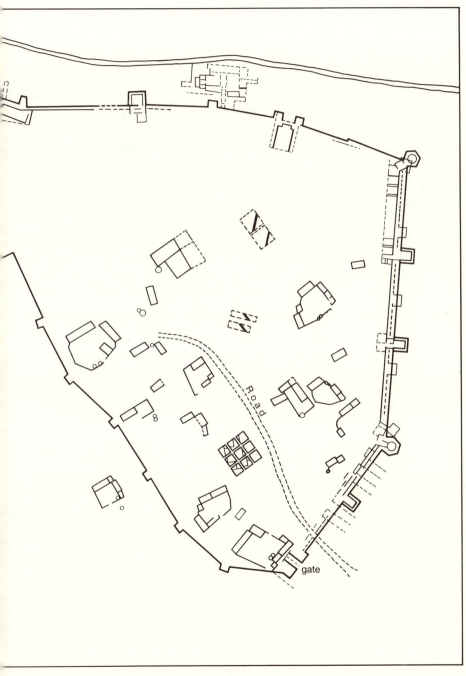

Road

gate

e defences

it does not play any role in Ammianus' and Procopius' accounts of the major Persian wars. (The exceptions which prove the rule are the cases of the Caucasus passes, where a single fort could bar the way of the Huns and those in the pass between Colchis and Iberia.) The most superficial perusal of their works shows that in Mesopotamia these wars were fought for cities, not for lines of defence. It is true that literary sources refer to guard posts policing the border. They served to prevent minor nomadic raids and existed, apparently, besides the major fortifications which played such an important role in the major wars. But archaeological fieldwork in the region has not yet provided an impression of the outline of the system of guard posts, let alone a description in detail. The situation in Mesopotamia developed as a result of the peculiar relationship between Rome and Persia. It was characteristic of this area and not of others; moreover, it developed slowly, and not as the result of a set of decisions made by a single emperor.[228] Wherever Roman frontiers are studied regional differences must be acknowledged before general policies can be recognized.

Byzantium and Persia

So far three spheres of conflict have been described in some detail: the North-East, the role of the nomad allies, and Mesopotamia with its fortified cities. It remains to be seen whether we can now place the conflict in perspective.

The best starting point is the treaty of 562 of which a relatively full text is extant.[229] The Persians were to withdraw from Lazica (Colchis).[230] The peace would apply to the whole East, including Armenia and Lazica. Byzantium would pay the Persians a yearly sum of 30,000 *solidi* in gold, with two instalments of respectively seven and three years' payments in advance.[231] The treaty was concluded for fifty years.

---

[228] Croke and Crow, 143–59, use the example of Dara to show that Justinian's building activity in the East is overemphasized by Procopius, and that much that is attributed to him is actually due to Anastasius. Their conclusions were anticipated for several projects by other scholars. Sarre and Herzfeld, i 138, point out that Resapha was called Anastasiopolis (Georgius Cyprius, 883) and had a garrison according to the *Notitia*; they assume that Justinian merely restored the walls and built some cisterns. Dillemann, 105, reached similar conclusions for Rhabdium, and Oates, *Studies*, 106, for Singara. The value and veracity of Procopius' information is defended by M. Whitby, *DRBE*, 717–83.

[229] Menander Protector, fr. 11, Müller, *FHG* iv 208 ff. Cf. I. Kawar, *Arabica* 3 (1956), 181–213; Z. Rubin, *DRBE*, 684 f.; E. Winter, *Münstersche Beiträge zur antiken Handelsgeschichte* 6 (1987), 46–74.

[230] *FHG* iv 208.

[231] = 416⅔ lbs. of gold. See on this Rubin, *DRBE*, 684 ff.

The text as cited by Menander Protector contains the following clauses:[232]

(*a*) The Persians will not allow Huns, Alani, or other barbarians to pass through the Caspian gates (the Darial pass) and invade Roman territory. The Romans will not invade Persian territory.

(*b*) The Saracen allies of both parties are bound by the treaty and may not attack the other state.

(*c*) Merchants must import their wares through the traditionally appointed toll-stations.

(*d*) Ambassadors and envoys of both parties on official journeys are entitled to the use of the *cursus publicus* in both states and their possessions may not be taxed.

(*e*) Saracen and other barbarian merchants are not allowed to use unknown and little used routes, but must pass through Nisibis and Dara and with formal permission only. If they trespass they will do so under pain of punishment.

(*f*) Wartime refugees and deserters may return to their own state unharmed. Henceforth neither state will accept and admit refugees or emigrants.

(*g*) Neither state will fortify installations near the border.

(*h*) Clients or allies and their territory are not to be attacked.

(*i*) The number of troops at Dara may not exceed that required to guard the place, and the commander of the troops in the east may not reside there, so that there will be no attacks on Persia.

(*j*) Both states accept responsibility for violence or injuries perpetrated by their own cities or individuals against the other.

A separate agreement guaranteed freedom for the Christians in the Persian empire to practise their religion.[233]

This treaty shows the conditions under which both rulers felt they could live with each other in peace after years of bloody warfare. Taking the treaty point by point we can see that virtually all the clauses refer to issues which had been of real concern.

First, the issue of Byzantine payments to Persia. This had come up again and again. Joshua Stylites mentions that such payments were also part of the fifth-century agreements:[234]

Further there was a treaty between the Greeks and the Persians that if they had need of one another when carrying on war with any nation, they should help

---

[232] *FHG* iv 212 f.

[233] *FHG* iv 213.

[234] Joshua Stylites 8, trans. Wright, p. 7. On the importance of subsidies see in particular Rubin, *DRBE*; on the present passage see his n. 17.

one another by giving three hundred able-bodied men, with their arms and horses, or three hundred staters in lieu of each man, according to the wish of the party that had need. . . But the kings of the Persians have been sending ambassadors and receiving money for their needs; but it was not in the way of tribute that they took it as many thought.

Elsewhere he says: 'Even in our days Pêrôz, the king of the Persians because of the wars that he had with the Kûshânayê or Huns, very often received money from the Greeks, not however demanding it as tribute . . .'[235] Joshua could see the Persian point of view very well. King Valash (484–8) 'was a humble man and fond of peace. He found nothing in the Persian treasury, and his land was laid waste and depopulated by the Huns.' Zeno turned down his request for money.[236] Valash 'because he had no money to maintain his troops was despised ·in their eyes'. He was deposed and replaced by Kavad, who presented Zeno's successor Anastasius with an ultimatum which again was refused.[237] This is merely one of the episodes which resulted in the first of the long wars of the sixth and seventh century.

The argument that the payments were not a form of tribute re-occurs later: when in 540 Khusro demanded payment, he emphasized that it was not tribute, but compensation for Persian services rendered in guarding the Caspian Gates.[238] These payments were to be compared with those made to Huns and Saracens, not as taxes, but in exchange for the protection of Roman lands.[239] When concluding a truce in 551 the Romans preferred to pay the whole amount at once rather than in annual instalments so that they would not appear to be paying tribute each year.[240]

---

[235] Op. cit. 9.

[236] Joshua Stylites, 18, trans. Wright, 12.

[237] Ibid. 19 f., trans. Wright, 13 f. Another source on the wars under Anastasius is Zachariah of Mitylene, esp. books vii and ix, ed. and trans. E. W. Brooks, *CSCO, Scriptores Syri*, iii/vi; English translation: *The Syriac Chronicle Known as That of Zachariah of Mitylene*, trans. F. J. Hamilton and E. W. Brooks (1899).

[238] Procopius, *Bell*. ii 10. 21–4. The same connection is found in the chronicle of Michael the Syrian: J. B. Chabot, ed. and trans. *Chronique de Michel le Syrien* (1899), ii 178 (trans.): Kavad demanded money from Justinian for the expenses of the Persian army guarding the Gates against the Huns. When the request was turned down he sent nomad tribes into the lands of the Romans who caused damage and took captives. 'Mundhir the Taiyaya' ravaged the whole frontier region from Balikh to Khabur. The Romans organized similar expeditions into Persian territory.

[239] There could be other demands: in 545 Khusro demanded money and a certain physician in exchange for a truce: Procopius, *Bell*. ii 28. 7 f. Royal physicians at Ctesiphon usually were Christians, many of them imperial envoys. Cf. N. Garsoïan, *Cambridge Hist. Iran*, iii 1. 571 with n. 1; Lieu, *DRBE*, 491 f.

[240] Procopius, *Bell*. viii 15. 2. However, some oriental sources represent the Persians as claiming they received tribute from Rome, Rubin, *DRBE*, 686 f.

Further comments on the subsequent clauses:

(*a*) The importance of the Caspian Gates (the Darial pass) has been mentioned above. Its defence became an issue of crucial importance with the arrival of the Huns north of the Caucasus. Rome took no active steps to undertake it, and Persia considered this a justification for demands of subsidies.

(*b*) As already noted, in 550 Persian ambassadors accused the Romans of violating the truce because Arethas and his confederates attacked Mundhir, or so they alleged. This may be taken as an acknowledgment that both powers were responsible for the behaviour of their allies. And yet during the '*strata* dispute' Mundhir claimed he was not bound by the existing treaty between Rome and Persia. It was therefore logical that the next treaty would attempt to clarify the issue. As a result we see Arethas complaining in Constantinople about attacks by the Lakhmid chief.[241] He considered it an affair that ought to be handled by the authorities in the capital and the Persians in accordance with the treaty.

(*c, d, e*) The provisions regarding customs duties, envoys, and smuggling are merely the traditional means by which states would regulate their relations in peacetime. In 297 it was agreed that Nisibis—still in Roman hands—would be the centre of commercial exchange.[242] A law of 408/9 prescribes that merchants may hold markets only at the places agreed upon, namely at Nisibis, Callinicum, and Artaxata.[243]

(*f*) One of the fifth-century treaties between Rome and Persia included a provision that neither party would accept rebellious Saracen allies of the other state.[244] The fifth century produced two notorious phylarchs who changed sides from Persia to Rome: Aspebetos and Amorcesos, both mentioned above. More recently Khusro had claimed that Justinian made attempts to bribe Mundhir into joining the Romans.[245] Whether true or not, in principle it was considered a breach of treaty. It would therefore make sense for the two sides to guarantee that they would refrain from admitting such immigrants.

(*g*) The significance of the fortified cities in the frontier zone needs no further clarification. In 441–2 it was agreed that neither side would

---

[241] See on this clause the extensive discussion by Kawar, *Arabica* 3 (1956), 197 f.

[242] Petrus Patricius, fr. 14, Müller, *FHG* iv 189.

[243] *Cod. Iust.* iv 63. 4: the reason given is the prevention of spying: 'ne alieni regni, quod non convenit, scrutentur arcana'.

[244] Malchus Philadelphensis, fr. 1, Müller, *FHG* iv 112 f. Rubin, *Mediterranean Historical Review* 1 (1986), 34, argues that the treaty referred to is that of 422.

[245] Procopius, *Bell.* ii 1. 12 f.

strengthen installations near the frontier.[246] The Persians still considered this rule to apply in the sixth century.[247]

(*h*) The extension of the treaty to clients and allies was essential, for Persia had made strenuous efforts to conquer Lazica, a Byzantine vassal state. The Arab allies, Mundhir and Arethas, had fought each other without Roman or Persian support.[248] Under the new clause Byzantium and Persia both assumed responsibility for the behaviour of their allies and promised to refrain from attacking them themselves.

(*i*) The crucial importance of Dara as a military base and an object of prestige is clear. The arrangement of 562 represented a compromise: the fortifications of Dara remained intact and in Roman hands, but they were to be largely demilitarized.

The position of the Christians in the Persian empire, the subject of the final clause in the treaty of 562, is a large topic which cannot be discussed here. There are many factors involved: the varying degrees of religious freedom in Persia, Roman interference and missionary activities which were considered insufferable by Persia, occasional attempts to exploit the dual loyalty of those Christians.[249] The agreement of 562 aimed at defusing the potential for conflict.

The Last Years

The treaty of 562 clearly shows how the two states thought the most pressing issues could be resolved. It is also clear that these were the issues which in various combinations served as *casus belli*. That does not mean, of course, that any of these or their combination represent the ultimate cause of the conflict between the two empires. On the contrary, the war continued and even escalated later in the sixth century.[250] Hostilities were renewed with the accession of Justin II, who withheld the yearly payment to Persia and supported an Armenian uprising in 572. The first of these acts was a constant ingredient in the events that led to wars in the Byzantine period, the second common to many wars between Rome and its eastern neighbour. The last half-century of Byzantine and Persian confrontation was marked by an escalation of hostilities and by violent fluctuations in the balance of power. At the end of the sixth century (591) Byzantine

---

[246] *Bell.* i 2. 15. For the chronology, Rubin, *DRBE*, 682, with n. 12.
[247] *Bell.* i 10. 16; cf. 16. 7.
[248] *Bell.* ii 18. 12–14.
[249] For bibliography, above, n. 162; Lieu, *DRBE*, 481–6.
[250] For summary and bibliography, Frye, 334–9 and n. 120.

troops entered the Persian capital.[251] Not long before the Islamic conquest most of the Diocese of Oriens, Cilicia, and Egypt were temporarily occupied by Persia, and a counter-offensive then again brought Byzantine troops to the Persian capital. Yet these campaigns failed to produce any fundamental change, except the weakening of the two states. The Persian conquest of the Orient, like that in the first century BC, was made possible by a civil war.[252] As usual, the warfare was accompanied by large-scale havoc caused by nomad raids.[253]

Conclusion

Summing up we must say that it is hard to point to any single cause of conflict between the two empires. It is a truism that this was a confrontation about power and money. The relationship between the two empires can only be seen in full perspective if contemporary events elsewhere are taken into account: Rome's wars in the north and west, Persia's troubles in the east.[254] The ancient sources often indicate that these affairs were of influence. Where they do not, chronological patterns may be suggestive. Only a few general observations may be made here.

For centuries after Pompey's annexation of Syria there existed a notion in Rome that the Persian empire could be destroyed. Julian may still have thought so, but there is no evidence that the later Byzantine rulers dreamt of emulating Alexander. Nor is there any indication that the Persian kings of this period were more expansionist than their Parthian predecessors. Julian once claimed that the Persians wanted to conquer all of Syria.[255] In fact at the time they only laid siege to Nisibis.

Byzantine military policy in the east gives an impression of much rhetoric and no strategy. There existed a notion that the two empires together should preserve order among mankind, but it is expressed only twice—by Persians.[256] There were occasional friendly exchanges.

---

[251] The events may be reconstructed from the works of Theophylactus Simocatta and Theophanes.

[252] As in earlier centuries, there were substantial segments of the population that had no cause for loyalty towards Constantinople: the Monophysites, the Samaritans, and the Jews. They accordingly favoured Persia. M. Avi-Yonah, *Geschichte der Juden im Zeitalter des Talmud* (1962), 257–74. See, for instance, Michael the Syrian, *Chronique*, ed. and trans. J.-B. Chabot (1901), ii. 400 f. xi 1 (AD 593): 'Les Juifs à cause de leur haine pour les chrétiens, achetaient ceux-ci (i.e. those in Jerusalem) aux Perses, à vil prix, et les mettaient à mort.'

[253] Michael the Syrian, op. cit., 403 (same year).

[254] For a preliminary outline, Z. Rubin, *Mediterranean Hist. Review*, 13–61.

[255] Julian, *Or.* i, 27 A. See also 17 C ff. for the Persian wars and Julian's view of them.

[256] Petrus Patricius, fr. 13, Müller, *FHG* iv 188: Persian ambassadors, late third century;

Upon his death the emperor Arcadius entrusted his infant son to the guardianship of the Persian monarch, and the young prince was duly adopted and protected by the Persian.[257] Yet it does not appear that the concept of collaboration and coexistence was accepted by Rome. A century later Kavad I asked for a return of this generosity, but Justin I refused to adopt the Persian king's favourite son.[258]

The wars concentrated on plunder and, if possible, the capture of a city in northern Mesopotamia. In this region the two states fought for tactical advantage. Rome might have lost its emulators of Alexander, but even so it refused to withdraw from those areas that brought it into immediate physical contact with Persia. Hence there was the permanent disadvantage to Byzantium of having to defend northern Mesopotamia, a region which favoured Persia in the matter of food depots, supply lines, and garrison towns. At the same time Byzantium refused to accept either military or financial responsibility for defence against invaders from the north-east as a permanent obligation. There is no evidence of an active policy of improving the military position in the east. From the time of the army reorganization in the early fourth century discussed in Chapter IV, till the age of Justinian, in the mid sixth century, there was no drastic review of military policy in the region.[259]

It is in fact obscure what the strategic aim of the Byzantine rulers was in fighting Persia, other than limited conquests or an advantage in the matter of subsidies. In the case of Persia, however, successful military campaigns had significant social, political, and economic consequences, as they were often followed by the foundation of new cities, populated with captives.[260] Transfer of populations after military victory and conquest had been an old near-eastern practice. It has been argued that the foundation of new cities by the Sasanid monarchs served the special purpose of consolidating royal power at the expense of the nobility.[261] That is possible. However, even in the absence of

Theophylact Simocatta iii 18. 6 ff.: Khusro II, three centuries later. The language used is strikingly similar: the two empires are as two eyes illuminating the world together. This must have been a *topos*.

[257] Procopius, *Bell.* i 2.7–10.

[258] *Bell.* i 11.6–22.

[259] As observed by E. Demougeot, *De l'unité à la division de l'empire romain 395–410* (1951), 504 nn. 54 ff. About 400 Damascus became the capital of Phoenicia Libanensis: Honigmann, *RE* s.v. Syria, 1699–1701; Eisfeldt, s.v. Phoinikia, *RE* 1940. About 368 Tyre became the capital of Phoenicia Paralia. After 426 Coele Syria was sub-divided into two provinces: I with Antioch as capital, II with Apamea. However, all this concerns administrative organization.

[260] See Adams, *Land Behind Baghdad: A History of Settlement on the Diyala Plains* (1962), 69 f.; Lieu, *DRBE*, 475–505.

[261] Adams, loc. cit. Gundaisabur (Be Lapat) was founded by Shapur I and settled with

statistics it is clear that the warfare between the two states cannot be explained as a consequence of rational and calculated considerations.

Greed or financial difficulties rather than ideology were the chief motivation in many of the wars. Hence the disputes about subsidies for Persia's garrisons in the north. Hence the plundering campaigns such as that of Khusro in the forties of the sixth century. It is likely that both empires had too many troubles with the tribal movements in the north for either to consider seriously destroying its rival, but that is speculation. We do not know whether either of them believed that its existence was threatened from those quarters.

The main characteristics of the wars of these centuries are the following:

(*a*) At the centre, an essential function was performed by the fortified cities and their citizens in Mesopotamia. Here the front had hardened to such an extent that there was no longer any real movement between 363 and the seventh century. A major role was played by the townspeople themselves. When Persia attacked, they rather than the field army bore the brunt of the fighting. All this was unknown in the period of the principate, which rarely saw major sieges as the focus of a campaign.[262]

(*b*) At the periphery the two empires fought over the remote region of the north-east where unprecedented emphasis lay on the defence of the mountain passes which might be used by invading Huns. The strategic value of a pass was, as it were, that of a tap: those who controlled it could release a flow of Hunnish invaders. Once these had crossed the pass, however, it was impossible to direct their movements. They could attack both empires. So the value of controlling the Caucasus passes was very limited as a means of blackmail against the other empire. To control the pass was a necessity to prevent disaster, but in itself it was unproductive. It was a situation without precedent in the early empire. At that time 'barbarians' were not kept out by blocking passes, but by attacking them in their homeland. The two best routes across the Caucasus, however, lay clearly beyond the reach of the Byzantine troops and in the Persian sphere of influence. Byzantium had to leave their control to Persia.

Roman captives taken in the battle of 259–260: Oppenheimer, 86–90. Other cities founded after this event were Sadsabur in Mesene and Bishapur in Fars: cf. Lieu, *DRBE*, 477–9. Buzurg-Sabur ('Ukbara) was founded by either Shapur I or II: cf. Oppenheimer, 452–6. Shapur II founded Eranshahr-Shapur in Khuzistan (Susiana): Oppenheimer, 77. Ve Antioch was founded by Khusro I following his successful raids in Byzantine territory.

[262] The sieges of Hatra by Trajan and Septimius Severus are exceptional. The siege of Jerusalem in 70 is another exception, but its value in the war was essentially different: the capture of the city effectively ended the Jewish revolt.

(*c*) Also at the periphery there were the Saracen confederates based at the edge of the desert. The nature of their activities makes it impossible to define a military border in the Byzantine period, just as it was impossible to mark such a border in the period of the principate. In peacetime the confederates played a rather important and constructive role in policing the edge of the desert. In wartime, however, they campaigned in their own manner with largely negative results: they caused economic destruction and suffering, but there is no indication that their masters derived a decisive strategic advantage from these activities. Finally, there is no evidence at all that either power thought a serious danger threatened from the south. They certainly had an interest in southern Arabia and Ethiopia, but it was mainly for commercial reasons. There was no obvious reason to fear destruction by the Arabs, as no one could predict the rise of Islam. In the end it was a wholly unexpected war of ideas and religion that brought down the existing order.

VI

ARMY AND CIVILIANS IN THE EAST

THE Roman army in the East, unlike that in the West and North, was frequently based in cities. The evidence of permanent garrisons in towns has been listed above, but the function of the troops in towns and the effect of their presence there was not discussed. That would not have been out of place in chapters which attempt to describe the army as a force of occupation instead of frontier-defence. However, in the present chapter an attempt is made to describe what we know about the relationship between army and civilians in cities in the East. It is not an attempt to replace any part of R. MacMullen's *Soldier and Civilian.*[1] It aims to clarify various aspects of this relationship that result from the peculiarities of army organization in the eastern frontier-provinces. Three subjects are discussed: the army in cities, the army and taxation, and propaganda.

THE ARMY IN CITIES

Tacitus writing about Corbulo's army says:

. . . his legions had been transferred from Syria, and having become slack because of a long peace they found it very hard to bear the duties of an army camp. There is no doubt that there were in the army veterans who had never been on piquet or guard duty, who found the wall and ditch remarkable sights, men without helmets or breast plates, elegant and wealthy, who had served in towns.[2]

Fronto also considers the effect of the amenities of Antioch on army discipline to have been pernicious:
The army you took over was demoralized with luxury and immorality and prolonged idleness. The soldiers at Antioch were wont to spend their time

---

[1] For military oppression of civilians see also J. B. Campbell, *The Emperor and the Roman Army* (1984), 246–54.
[2] *Ann.* xiii 35.

clapping actors, and were more often found in the nearest café-garden than in the ranks.[3]

A similar view is represented in a spurious letter attributed by the *Historia Augusta* to Marcus Aurelius:

I have put Avidius Cassius in command of the Syrian legions, which are corrupted by luxury and which live according to the life style of Daphne.[4]

This source clearly conveys a common knowledge that there were army units based in Antioch and its vicinity in the period of the author of the Historia Augusta.[5] However, the ever-recurring assertion that soldiers in cities, especially eastern cities, are idle and become demoralized may well be regarded as a literary 'topos'. As observed above, the sort of complaints about army discipline voiced by Tacitus and Fronto are clearly some of the standard arguments put forward against an inactive frontier policy in the East.[6] Service will indeed have been comfortable for the soldiers who served in towns, but they would hardly have been based there in the first place if this had not been necessary. The evidence of an army presence is reasonably good for three cities: Antioch, Jerusalem before 66, and Alexandria.

Antioch

We may reasonably assume that there always was a substantial garrison in Antioch. We do not have epigraphic evidence of a large military force in the town, and only in the 390s is there explicit reference in a literary source to a permanent garrison.[7] But an absence of evidence does not necessarily prove anything. Antioch was the seat of the governor, who had a substantial force of *singulares*,[8] and the presence of soldiers in the city is implied by all the literary sources cited above. In a speech attributed by Herodian to Septimius Severus at the time of the latter's bid for power it is said of the troops in Syria that they

---

[3] Fronto, *ad Verum imp.* ii 1 (128 Naber = ii 148 Haines). For Fronto on Hadrian and the Roman army, R. W. Davies, *Latomus* 27 (1968), 75–95. Cf. Mommsen, *Römische Geschichte* v 448 f.; B. Isaac, *Talanta* 12–13 (1980–1), 34 f.

[4] SHA, *Avidius Cassius* 5. 5.

[5] Similarly SHA *Severus Alexander* 52 f.

[6] Above, p. 23 f.

[7] P. Petit, *Libanius et la vie municipale à Antioche au IVe siècle après J.-C.* (1955), 187, and J. H. W. G. Liebeschuetz, *Antioch: City and Imperial Administration in the Later Roman Empire* (1972), 116–18, assume that there was no substantial army presence there before this period. The evidence for 390 consists of one reference in Libanius, *Or.* xlvi 13. It is better not to argue from silence regarding other periods for which the sources are so much scarcer.

[8] It is a matter of chance that there is evidence of these only at Dura and Heliopolis. Cf. M. Speidel, *Guards of the Roman Provinces* (1978), 8 f., 13 f., 103 ff.

'are satisfied to remain there and consider their daily life in luxury a benefit which they derive from the empire unstable as it still is. Witty and sophisticated jests, that is what the Syrians are good at, especially those in Antioch.'[9] It is not necessary to believe that Severus actually said this or, if he said it, that it was true, but the story definitely reflects awareness of the fact that the troops in Syria were based in cities, of which Antioch was the most important. There obviously existed a popular conviction, not necessarily unfounded, that these troops lacked discipline. We may add that there is now evidence that there also was a militia of citizens from Antioch.[10]

There were good reasons to keep forces in Antioch. It was the scene of strife between Jews and gentiles in the first century and again in the Byzantine period.[11] In 175 the city became one of the centres of the revolt of Avidius Cassius. In 194 it served as base for Pescennius Niger and supported him with enthusiasm.[12] In 260 the Persians were brought in by a member of the city council, Mareades;[13] there are reports that he had the support of part of the population.[14] Shortly afterwards many citizens of Antioch supported Zenobia of Palmyra in her attempt to establish a separate eastern empire.[15]

The *Expositio Totius Mundi*, a document published perhaps in 359, considers Antioch an important army base, but that may have been due to the presence of an expeditionary force against Persia.[16] In AD 387 a

---

[9] Herodian ii 10. 6 f.: . . . ἀγαπητῶς ἐκεῖ μένοντες, καὶ τὴν ἐφήμερον τρυφὴν κέρδος τῆς οὔπω βεβαίας ἀρχῆς νομίζουσιν. ἐπὶ μὲν γὰρ τὸ χαριέντως καὶ μετὰ παιδιᾶς ἀποσκῶψαι ἐπιτήδειοι Σύροι, καὶ μάλιστα οἱ τὴν Ἀντιόχειαν οἰκοῦντες . . .

[10] This almost certainly follows from the occurrence of 'milites legionum . . . item cohortium (viginti), [item?] Antiochensium . . .' on a milestone of 75, according to the revised reading in *BJb* 185 (1985), 85 ff.

[11] For the former, E. Schürer, *The History of the Jewish People in the Age of Jesus Christ*, iii 1, ed. G. Vermes, F. Millar and M. Goodman (1986), 13, n. 23; for the latter, G. Downey, *A History of Antioch in Syria* (1961), 426–33, 497–9, 505 f. For other cities with a substantial Jewish population, Schürer, iii 14, and vol. ii, ed. G. Vermes, F. Millar, and M. Black (1978), paragraph 23.

[12] Downey, 238 f. The SHA, *Hadrian* 14. 1, contains a bogus story about conflict between Hadrian and the city, clearly influenced by later events, cf. R. Syme, *Historia Augusta Papers* (1983), 180–9. G. W. Bowersock, *Bonner Historia-Augusta-Colloquium 1982/1983* (1985), 75–88, has argued that there is an element of truth in the passage in that it appears to reflect the grant of the status of *metropolis* to Damascus and Tyre in addition to Antioch, a measure which diminished the status of Antioch as sole city of that rank in Syria.

[13] Ammianus xxiii 5. 3; also Malalas, Dindorf, p. 295 f.; Anon. cont. Dio, fr. 1, Müller, *FHG* iv 192. See Downey, 254–9, with further sources on p. 255 n. 103; cf. S. Lieu, *DRBE*, 476 f.

[14] Petrus Patricius, fr. i, *FHG* iv 192.

[15] Zosimus, i 51. 3, relates that the pro-Palmyrene group prepared to flee the city when Aurelian took it in 272 and refrained from doing so when the emperor issued an edict of amnesty.

[16] 27: '. . . Laodicia, quae suscipiens omne negotium et emittens Antiochiae magnifice adiuvit et ‹exercitui›' (Rougé's reading); 28: Constantius constructed the new port of Seleucia for the use of the town and the army. War with Persia and an imperial army in the East are mentioned ibid. 36.

brief insurrection broke out in protest against increased taxation,[17] and was suppressed by a unit of archers reinforced with other troops by the *comes Orientis*.[18] In the seventies of the fifth century there were troubles between monophysite and orthodox factions at Antioch.[19] In 484 Illus, the *magister militum per Orientem*, who had been based at Antioch since 481/2, made an attempt at usurpation, which was suppressed by the emperor Zeno.[20] He had found support amongst both pagans and the orthodox in the city. Towards the end of this century there were factional and anti-Jewish disorders at Antioch.[21] These broke out again under Anastasius in 507.[22] On both occasions the *comes* suppressed the troubles. Under Justin there was a change of religious policy in favour of orthodoxy, and this caused serious disorders at Antioch, which was a centre of monophysite activity. They were accompanied by fighting between the blue and green factions between 520 and 526.[23] Despite attempts to suppress them they broke out again in 529, the year of the great Samaritan revolt in Palestine.[24] Finally there are sensational and conflicting reports of factional fighting under Phocas (AD 602–10).[25]

These occasions are merely the ones we happen to hear of in random items of information. They should be regarded as representative of the sort of tensions engendered in ancient society by urbanization on this scale. They are clear evidence of the importance of Antioch as one of the capitals of the eastern empire, and it can safely be assumed that there were army units in town and nearby to ensure control, just as there were army units in Rome and Alexandria.

While their main objection to service in cities was the bad influence it had on military discipline, classical sources do not deny that it was a misfortune for a city to be garrisoned. Aristides claims that the cities of the empire were free of troops, except for a few very large ones which required a garrison, and compares this situation with the sufferings of the cities of the Athenian empire.[26] It is a pronouncement which was, in his own time, true only for part of the empire and not for the eastern frontier provinces.

---

[17] For the sources see Downey, 426–31; cf. Liebeschuetz, *Antioch*, 124.

[18] Libanius, *Or.* xix 34–6. According to Libanius the *comes* arrived himself and brought in reinforcements only when he heard that archers had engaged the rebels. This shows that there were troops in or very near the city which could be moved to the scene of trouble at a moment's notice. See also *Or.* xxii 9.

[19] Downey, 484–90.   [20] See Downey, 490–6.

[21] Malalas 389 f., 392 f. Cf. Downey, 497–9, 504.

[22] Malalas 395–8; cf. Downey, 504–7.

[23] Downey, 515–19.

[24] Malalas 448 f.   [25] Cf. Downey, 572–4.

[26] Aristides, *Roman Oration* 67; cf. 52.

Zosimus criticizes Constantine for imposing garrisons on cities, a decision which was a misfortune for the cities and weakened the frontier, or so he says.[27] In 303 there was a mutiny by five hundred soldiers employed in deepening the mouth of the harbour at Seleucia Pieria. The troops were so busy that they had to prepare their food during the night and thus suffered from lack of sleep.[28] Libanius describes the following incident:

a soldier provokes a market trader, mocking him and goading him, and then he lays hands on him, pulling him and dragging him about. Then he too perhaps is touched, but apparently the actions are not comparable: such men may not raise voice or hand against the soldier, and so this man, who is bound to suffer is seized and finds himself at headquarters and buys exemption from being beaten to death. Every day much is thus sown and harvested, minor matters compared with the following: the emoluments of office . . .[29]

Libanius also describes in detail a protection racket which was organized by the army based in the countryside around Antioch. According to him, the peasants refused to pay their rent, shook off the established rural order, and turned into bandits through the influence of the soldiers billeted among them.[30] The local guardsmen took no notice and did not attempt to resist the soldiers when they supported the peasants.[31] Elsewhere we read that lower-class civilians were helpless in the face of maltreatment by soldiers.[32] Even so the common soldiers were not very well off. Libanius repeatedly claims that the higher officers did well for themselves while the common soldiers were pauperized and starving.[33] 'I know that I have complained on behalf of the soldiers as well as the councillors and rightly so, for they starve and shiver from cold and have not a penny, thanks to the "justice" of their colonels and generals, who make them utterly miserable and enrich themselves.'[34] The officers kept the pay of the men and the money intended for the fodder of the horses. The soldiers received inadequate

[27] ii 34. For this statement see also above, p. 163.

[28] Libanius, *Or.* xi 158–62; xix 45 f.; xx 18–20; also Eusebius, *HE* viii 6. 8; cf. Downey, 330 n. 55. The affair was not important as such and is recounted by Libanius because of Diocletian's fierce reaction and unfair punishment—according to Libanius—of leading citizens of Seleucia and Antioch. There was a far more dangerous mutiny of the troops in the East under Maurice, in 588, but this touched Antioch only indirectly, Downey, 567–9.

[29] *Or.* xlvii 33; for the interpretation of this passage see ed. Reiske, ii 522 n. 37; Liebeschuetz, 115 with n. 4.

[30] *De Patrociniis, Or.* xlvii 4 f.

[31] Ibid. 6. It has been suggested that the *magister militum* was involved in the affair. See L. Harmand, *Libanius, Discours sur les patronages* (1955); Liebeschuetz, 201–8.

[32] *Or.* xlvii 6.

[33] *Or.* xlvii 32.

[34] *Or.* ii 37.

rations which they had to share with their families.[35] As a result, says Libanius, the army had seriously deteriorated as a fighting force.

The suffering caused by compulsory billeting of troops, the natural result of the presence of army units in cities, is discussed below.

Whatever the size of the permanent garrison at Antioch in different periods, the city became truly militarized only at times of Persian campaigns. According to the *Historia Augusta* the mutiny of the army at the time of Severus Alexander's Persian campaign was the result of disciplinary action against troops who misbehaved at the baths of Daphne near Antioch.[36] Whether the story is true or not, it is significant that the author thought it might be credible in the eyes of his readers. The presence of an expeditionary force in Syria about 333 coincided with and undoubtedly was the cause of a severe famine which was especially bad in Antioch and Cyrrhus and their territories.[37] Another famine was probably caused by the demands made by an army which was to set out for Persia in 354, under Gallus Caesar,[38] and yet another occurred in 360 during the preparations for the Persian war.[39]

Antioch usually served as headquarters and rear base during Parthian and Persian wars, and in such periods the city was often an imperial residence. The many occasions when this happened are listed in Appendix II. Indeed, during the three decades from 190 to 220 this led on several occasions to the city becoming the centre and focus of the struggle for the imperial throne.[40] Herodian reports that Caracalla and Geta proposed to divide the empire. The latter, who would receive the East, declared that he would move the eastern senators to his capital, either Antioch or Alexandria.[41] Whatever the truth of the report, the concept was realistic in social terms, given the actual developments in the fourth century, and it is noteworthy that there was no doubt that the

---

[35] Libanius, who has a high regard for the Roman army of the past, specifically mentions that soldiers in those days remained unmarried. As we know, soldiers could not legally marry till the reign of Severus, but they did in fact live with women and had children. Hence military diplomas.

[36] SHA, *Severus Alexander* 53.

[37] The connection between these two events was seen by Downey, 354, with references in n. 160.

[38] Downey, 365, who notes that the sources are not very good and drought may have been another cause of the shortages.

[39] Libanius, *Or.* xi 177 f.; Julian, *Misopogon* 370 B; Socrates, *HE* iii 17 (*PG* lxvii 424); cf. Downey, 383. Ammianus, xxii 12. 6, describes Julian's excessive zeal in offering, sometimes a hundred oxen at once. Almost every day, he says, soldiers, drunk and over-fed, were carried from the temples to their billets.

[40] Between AD 202 and 222 tetradrachms of Caracalla, Macrinus, and Elagabal were issued at Antioch, cf. A. R. Bellinger, *The Syrian Tetradrachms of Caracalla and Macrinus* (1940), 21–9. Bellinger has supposed that those of 214–17 were intended to finance the Parthian war.

[41] iv 3. 5–9.

eastern empire would have a senate like the one in Rome.[42] This illustrates the standing Antioch and Alexandria had obtained by the third century as imperial centres in the eastern provinces. The *Expositio Totius Mundi*, referring to the mid fourth century describes Antioch as 'the royal city, good in every respect, where the lord of the world resides'.[43]

The episode of Palmyrene supremacy in the East has been discussed in the previous chapter. Unlike Palmyra Antioch did not in itself enjoy any position of power; it could never have acted independently as Palmyra did in the third century. No one could rule the eastern provinces without controlling Antioch, but the citizens of Antioch had no military power of their own. Palmyra's influence extended to Antioch, it seems, from 270 till 272, supported by a considerable pro-Palmyrene party in the city.[44] When Aurelian marched against the Palmyrenes, Zenobia and her general Zabdas chose to make a first stand at Antioch, and their defeat here determined the loss of their hold on Syria.[45] This no doubt is to be explained by the fact that the city was the first major centre to be passed by anyone on the way from Anatolia to western Syria—a fact that accounts, not only for its importance to Zenobia, but also of course to a large extent for its prominence as a city throughout antiquity.

From 333 till the death of Valens in 378 Antioch served virtually without interruption as military headquarters in the East. For part of this time it was also the residence of an eastern Augustus or Caesar and hence the capital of the eastern empire. It is interesting to note that the establishment of the capital of the empire at Constantinople, between Europe and Asia, did nothing to diminish the importance of Antioch as a centre in the eastern provinces.

During the later empire Antioch was one of several important cities of the East where imperial armouries were located, the others being Damascus, Edessa, Caesarea in Cappadocia, Nicomedia and Sardis.[46]

---

[42] As observed by Fergus Millar, *A Study of Cassius Dio* (1964), 187f.

[43] 23: 'Est ergo Antiochia prima, civitas regalis et bona in omnibus, ubi et dominus orbis terrarum sedet.' See also 36, where it is said that the eastern provinces are supported with grain from Alexandria 'propter exercitum imperatoris et bellum Persarum'.

[44] For the evidence on the situation at Antioch in the 260's see F. Millar, *JRS* 61 (1971), 8–10.

[45] Zosimus i 50f. Cf. Downey, 266–9.

[46] *Not Dig. Or.* xi 18ff.: 'Fabricae infrascriptae: Orientis V: Scutaria et armorum, Damasci. Scutaria et armorum, Antiochiae. Clibanaria, Antiochiae. Scutaria et armamentaria, Edesa. Hastaria Irenopolitana Ciliciae: Ponticae tres: Clibanaria, Caesarea Cappadociae. Scutaria et armorum, Nicomediae. Clibanaria, Nicomediae. Asianae una: Scutaria et armorum, Sardis Lydiae.' Malalas, 307, says the armouries at Antioch, Edessa, and Damascus were founded by Diocletian. A detail reported by Ammianus, xiv 7. 18, shows that the presence of such installations could become a factor of some significance in times of instability: *tribuni fabricarum* were said

During the Persian wars in the reign of Justinian, Antioch served as the military headquarters and communications centre of the Roman commander from 528 till 561. This was a period of frequent earthquakes which increased the suffering caused by the war. For the first time since the third century Antioch and its territory now suffered from enemy raids, by Al Mundhir, in 523 and 529. These were followed by the disastrous capture and sack of the city by the Persians in 540.[47]

Even if it is assumed that there was a permanent garrison at Antioch from the moment it became the capital of the Roman province, it is clear that the town grew only gradually into an imperial governmental and military centre. During the first three centuries of Rome's hegemony Antioch was the seat of the governor of Syria Coele, but thereafter it became the permanent residence of the three major officials in the East: the *comes Orientis*, the *consularis Syriae* and the *magister militum per Orientem*, the latter almost certainly from the fourth century onwards.[48] The *comes* was a civilian official, but on several occasions he appears to have been carrying out military operations. As noted above, at least three times he suppressed disorders with troops under his command. The *magister militum* appears in the work of Libanius as a sinister figure who manages to extort great sums in kind and money,[49] who maintained and supported the protection racket against which Libanius protested,[50] and appropriated the stores of the public post for his own profit.[51]

Antioch was one of the great cities of the empire, strategically located, a city of culture and the arts. The fact that it also became a centre of administration and, at times, a military command centre was the cause of great misery for its inhabitants. Occasional munificence was not enough to compensate for the rapaciousness of the soldiers and the greed of officials—as emphasized below and in Chapter VIII. Even when there was no war bringing an emperor to the city social relations appear to have been tense, with frequent outbreaks of factional dis-

---

to have promised the delivery of arms if a rebellion was organized in the days of Gallus Caesar. See also *Cod. Theod.* x 22. 1, which compares the rate of production of helmets in the factories at Constantinople and Antioch in AD 374. That at Antioch was higher. Antioch was in those years the headquarters for Valens' Persian war.

[47] Malalas 479 f.; Procopius, *Bell.* ii 8 ff.

[48] For the *comes Orientis* and the *consularis Syriae*, Liebeschuetz, 110–14; for the *magister militum* in the time of Libanius, ibid. 114–16; for his residence at Antioch in the fifth century, Downey, 454 f., 494 f., 625 f.

[49] *Or.* xlvii 33.

[50] *Or.* xlvii 13.

[51] *Or.* xlvi 20; cf. Liebeschuetz, 115 f., who notes that references to this official are surprisingly rare in the work of Libanius.

orders. There will have been far more of this than we know from our haphazard information.

Alexandria

A perhaps spurious story told by Suetonius may serve to illustrate the prominence of Alexandria under the principate. There were rumours among the population of Rome that Julius Caesar 'planned to move to Alexandria or Ilium, take the wealth of the empire with him, exhaust Italy by levies, and leave the care of the city to his friends'.[52] Whatever the truth of the matter, it is interesting to note that Alexandria could be a candidate for such speculations, while the choice of Ilium shows that, long before the transformation of Byzantium into Constantinople, this was seen as an area from which the empire could conceivably be ruled. Unlike Ilium, however, Alexandria was a major city, of the same order as Antioch in Syria.

Alexandria, as far from the frontier as any place in Egypt can be, had two legions. In AD 38 bloody pogroms took place, carried out by the Alexandrian mob, but instigated by the emperor Gaius and his governor Flaccus.[53] According to Philo the latter could have suppressed the riots in an hour.[54] He used his troops to search Jewish homes for arms in a degrading manner.[55] Josephus relates that the troops there were used to suppress fighting between Jews and Greeks at the time of the First Jewish Revolt.[56] He also cites Agrippa II as exclaiming in his well-known speech to the Jews, '. . . what a centre for revolt (Egypt) has in Alexandria . . .!', and also, 'two legions stationed in the city curb this far-reaching Egypt and the proud nobility of Macedon'.[57] Agrippa's speech is tendentious rhetoric. Yet the description of the provinces and their armies is significant: throughout his survey of the empire it is taken for granted that the function of the provincial armies was to control the local inhabitants. Frontier defence is not even mentioned, apart from a vague allusion to the Germans across the Rhine.

[52] *Divus Iulius* 79. 3: 'Quin etiam varia fama percrebruit migraturum Alexandream vel Ilium, translatis simul opibus imperii exhaustaque Italia dilectibus et procuratione urbis amicis permissa . . .'
[53] Philo, *Legatio* 18–20 (120–37); *In Flaccum* 68 (36) ff.; cf. Schürer, i, 389–91.
[54] *Legatio* 20 (132).
[55] *In Flaccum* 11 (86–91).
[56] *BJ* ii 18. 8 (494–8).
[57] *BJ* ii 16. 4 (385): . . . καίτοι πηλίκον ἀποστάσεως κέντρον ἔχουσα τὴν Ἀλεξάνδρειαν πλήθους τε ἀνδρῶν ἕνεκα καὶ πλούτου . . . δύο δ' ἐγκαθήμενα τῇ πόλει τάγματα τὴν βαθεῖαν Αἴγυπτον ἅμα τῇ Μακεδόνων εὐγενείᾳ χαλινοῖ. Aristides, *Roman Oration* 67, indubitably refers to Alexandria, among others, when he speaks of very large cities that required a garrison.

The *Acts of the Pagan Martyrs* contain a series of episodes in the first and second centuries which leave no doubt that there was a bitterly hostile attitude toward the Roman authorities in Alexandria.[58] The surrounding countryside could also be a source of trouble, as is clear from the events in the 170s when the *fellahin* of the Delta defeated a Roman legion and almost captured Alexandria itself.[59] A soldier named Claudius Terentianus wrote in the second century to his father: 'For you know that we are working very hard now, in view of the fact that we are suppressing the uproar and anarchy of the city.'[60]

In 215 an imperial visit to Alexandria resulted in a massacre, the cause of which is not clearly explained in the various sources.[61] According to Dio, after the massacre cross-walls and guards were established in the city.[62] The *Historia Augusta* describes a soldier causing a mutiny at Alexandria under Gallienus. The mob attacked the house of the *dux*, according to the source.[63] Another rebellion is said to have occurred under Diocletian who harshly suppressed it in person.[64] The *Expositio Totius Mundi* writes in about 350:

You will consequently find that this is a city which imposes its will on governors; the people of Alexandria alone quickly rise up in rebellion; for governors enter this city fearfully and in terror, afraid of the justice of the people, for they do not hesitate to throw fire and stones at offending governors.[65]

Ammianus, in the second half of the fourth century, still notes that Alexandria was for a long time seriously troubled by internal conflict, notably in 272 under Aurelian.[66] Socrates, explaining that the Alexandrians are more fond of *staseis* than the peoples of other cities, gives an account of strife which resulted in the banishment of Jews from the city early in the fifth century.[67] There were further riots in Alexandria in

---

[58] H. Musurillo, *The Acts of the Pagan Martyrs, Acta Alexandrinorum* (1954), with commentary.

[59] Dio lxxii 4, containing the usual accusation of cannibalism.

[60] P. Mich. iii (Oxford, 1951), no. 477, inv. 5399, l. 28–30: οἶδες γὰρ ὅτι κοπιῶμεν ἄρτι δ[ιό]τ[ει] κα[θαιροῦμε]ν τ[ὸ]ν θόρυβον καὶ ἀκαταστασίαν τῆς πόλ[εως. In the comments (p. 61) it is noted that the correspondence of Terentianus with his father is assigned on palaeographic grounds to the early part of the second century, but the reference to the disturbance seems much too casual to link it to the difficult years of the Jewish War under Trajan. It is therefore taken as one of the riots that periodically occurred in the city.

[61] Millar, *Cassius Dio*, 156–8, for the evidence and discussion.

[62] lxxvii 23. 3 (401).

[63] SHA, *Tyr. Trig.* 22. There was no *dux* in Alexandria in this period.

[64] Malalas 308 f.; Eutropius ix 24 [15]; Orosius vii 25 and cf. Eusebius *Chron.* ad an. ccxcii.

[65] 28, ed. Rougé, p. 174: 'Iam et civitatem iudicibus bene regentem invenies; in contemptum se ‹facile movet› solus populus Alexandriae: iudices enim in illa civitate cum timore et tremore intrant, populi iustitiam timentes; ad eos enim ignis et lapidum emissio ad peccantes iudices not tardat.'

[66] xxii 16. 15; Eusebius, *HE* vii 21. 1; 22. 1.   [67] *HE* vii 13 (ed. Hussey, 753–7).

455: 'the soldiers killed the Alexandrians without pity.'[68] In a fragment from the *History* of Priscus Panites we have a graphic description of a riot in these years which again shows the population attacking magistrates.[69] Soldiers who were dispatched to suppress the unrest were attacked with stones, fled to the old temple of Serapis, and were besieged and burned alive in the building. Two thousand troops were then sent as reinforcement. On that occasion the governor managed to calm the population.

Jerusalem

In Jerusalem, before 67, auxiliary forces were quartered in two camps. At least one cohort was permanently present in the city;[70] its commander is described as tribune, χιλίαρχος or φρούραρχος,[71] and it was partly mounted.[72] The barracks were in the courtyard of the fortress Antonia, north of the Temple.[73] This fortress, built by the Hasmonaeans and strengthened by Herod, commanded the Temple Mount and the eastern part of the city.[74] In the words of Josephus, 'For if the temple lay as a fortress over the city, Antonia dominated the Temple, and the occupants of that post were the guards of all three.'[75] These troops carried out police duties in town and on the Temple Mount: '. . . a body of men in arms invariably mounts guard at the feasts, to prevent disorders arising from such a concourse of people.'[76] The *Acts of the Apostles* describes at length how these troops were used in town as a police force and for riot control in times of unrest.[77]

---

[68] Michael the Syrian ix 1 (trans. J.-B. Chabot (1899), ii 1, p. 126 f.); see also viii 2 (Chabot, p. 11 f.).

[69] Priscus fr. 22 from Evagrius, *HE* ii 5, Müller, *FHG* iv 101.

[70] Josephus, *BJ* v 5. 8 (244). See also B. Isaac, in *SMR* iii, *Vorträge des 13. Internationalen Limeskongresses, Aalen 1983* (1986), 635–640. Recently D. B. Campbell, *BJb* 186 (1986), 117–32, esp. 122–5 has discussed the evidence for the possession of artillery by auxiliary units in Jerusalem..

[71] The χιλίαρχος is referred to in John 18: 12; Acts 21: 31; he is called φρούραρχος by Josephus, *Ant.* xv 11. 1 (408); xviii 4. 3 (93); cf. Schürer, i 366.

[72] Paul was conveyed from Jerusalem to Caesarea by 200 soldiers, 70 cavalry, and 200 light-armed soldiers: Acts 23: 23.

[73] For the barracks, Acts 21: 34. Josephus mentions the garrison in Antonia, *BJ* ii 17. 7 (430), and says that it was quartered in the courtyard of the fortress.

[74] For the most extensive description, Josephus, *BJ* v 5. 8 (238–46). For the remains, Soeur Marie-Aline de Sion, *La Forteresse Antonia à Jérusalem et la question du Prétoire* (Jerusalem, 1956); L. H. Vincent and A. M. Stève, *Jérusalem de l'Ancient Testament* (1954), 193–221; J. Simons, *Jerusalem in the Old Testament* (1952), 325–28, 374–81, 413–17, 429–35; P. Benoit, *HTR* 64 (1971), 135–67.

[75] *BJ* v 5. 8 (245), trans. Thackeray, Loeb: φρούριον γὰρ ἐπέκειτο τῇ πόλει μὲν τὸ ἱερόν, τῷ ἱερῷ δ' ἡ Ἀντωνία, κατὰ δὲ ταύτην οἱ τῶν τριῶν φύλακες ἦσαν. Cf. *BJ* ii 15. 5 (328–31).

[76] *BJ* ii 12. 1 (224): . . . ἔνοπλοι δ' ἀεὶ τὰς ἑορτὰς παραφυλάττουσιν, ὡς μή τι νεωτερίζοι τὸ πλῆθος ἠθροισμένον . . .

[77] Acts 21: 31–6.

The western part of Jerusalem was dominated by Herod's palace, which was also built as a fortress: 'and the upper town had its own fortress: Herod's palace.'[78] After the annexation of Judaea as a province this fortress was taken over by the Roman authorities. As in the Antonia, there was an army camp in the courtyard.[79] The structure has always remained in use as a fortress, gradually altered and rebuilt, but one tower of Herod's palace still stands.[80] After the First Jewish Revolt the headquarters of the legion X Fretensis were established in the western part of the city, perhaps near these towers.[81] During the Parthian war of Trajan it was temporarily replaced by a vexillation of III Cyrenaica.[82] X Fretensis retained its base in town until it was transferred to Aela on the Red Sea sometime in the second half of the third century, perhaps under Diocletian. The *Notitia* mentions a unit of *equites Mauri Illyriciani* as based in Aelia.[83]

Similar but smaller forts stood in various towns and on strategic sites in the countryside where they served among other things as treasuries and armouries, which made them targets in periods of tension and civil unrest.[84] In such times the garrison in Jerusalem was reinforced. Pilate once transferred his army to winter quarters there.[85] Florus brought up to Jerusalem first one cohort[86] and then two others.[87] He subsequently left one of the latter as garrison in the city.[88] When needed, legions were brought from Syria, and at least once a legion was left as garrison in Jerusalem.[89] This was encamped, like the smaller units, in the Antonia fortress, on the Temple Mount and in the Royal Palace in the western part of the city.[90]

---

[78] *BJ* v 5. 8 (246): . . . καὶ τῆς ἄνω δὲ πόλεως ἴδιον φρούριον ἦν τὰ Ἡρώδου βασίλεια. For a description, v 4. 3 (161–83). For a description of a siege of the palace, *BJ* ii 3. 1 (44)–4 (51–4); *Ant.* xvii 10. 1 (253); *BJ* ii 17. 7 (431)–8 (440).

[79] *BJ* ii 17. 8 (440).

[80] For the archaeological remains, Vincent and Stève, 222–32, pls. 55–60; Simons, 265–71; C. N. Johns, *QDAP* 14 (1950), 121–90; *PEQ* 72 (1940), 36–58; R. Amiran and A. Eitan, *IEJ* 20 (1970), 9–17; 22 (1972), 50 f.

[81] See above, p. 105, and below, Appendix I.

[82] *CIL* 13587 (*ILS* 4393) of AD 116/17, a dedication to Jupiter Sarapis now lost.

[83] *Not. Dig. O.* xxxiv 21.

[84] Treasuries: Josephus, *Ant.* xvii 9. 3 (222 f.); 10. 1 (253). The royal palace at Sepphoris served as an armoury: xvii 10. 5 (271).

[85] *Ant.* xviii 3. 1 (55).

[86] *BJ* ii 14. 6 (296); cf. 15. 6 (332).

[87] *BJ* ii 15. 3 (318 ff.).

[88] *BJ* ii 15. 6 (332).

[89] By Quinctilius Varus after Herod's death: *Ant.* xvii 10. 1 (251); *BJ* ii 3. 1 (40); *Ant.* xvii 11. 1 (299); *BJ* ii 5. 3 (79).

[90] *BJ* ii 3. 1 (44); *Ant.* xvii 10. 2 (255).

Conclusion

Generally the archaeological evidence regarding the presence of army units in eastern cities has not increased very much in recent years. However, the number of inscriptions is now quite substantial.[91] The excavations at Dura-Europos and Palmyra are still unique in the information they provide about garrisons quartered in cities in the third century.[92] But there is some new information from Umm el Jimal,[93] and the location of the legionary base at Bostra is now better defined.[94]

In Chapters I and III we saw how much of the evidence regarding army units in the eastern provinces derives from cities. It consists mostly of plain inscriptions which merely record the name of a unit and do not tell us what the units were actually doing in these places.[95] They do, however, help to establish that in these provinces the army was often based in urban centres. This is true of the fourth-century army no less than of that of the early principate: even when the army expanded its activity into the arid zone the legionary bases were almost all in towns. The exceptions are Lejjun and Udruh in Transjordan.

Another pattern, common in western provinces, but less frequent in the east, although a number of cases are attested, was the development of towns around legionary bases established on non-urban sites. The cases known to me are Raphanaea in Syria, Melitene and Satala in Cappadocia, and the camp of the legion VI Ferrata in Judaea. The process is very well described by Procopius in his comments on Melitene:

There was in antiquity a certain place in Lesser Armenia, as it is called, not far from the Euphrates River, in which a unit of Roman soldiers was posted. The town was Melitene, and the unit was called a 'legion'. In that place the Romans in former times had built a stronghold in the form of a square, on level

---

[91] See above, ch. III. II Parthica was certainly at Apamea in 217–18 and 231–3: *AE* 1971. 469.

[92] Cf. M. I. Rostovtzeff (ed.), *The Excavations of Dura* (1934) (report on the fifth season, 1931–2), 201 ff; T. Wiegand, *Palmyra* (1932), 85–106, pls. 9–10, 45–54; D. van Berchem, *Syria* 31 (1954), 257 ff.; R. Fellmann, 'Le camp de Dioclétien à Palmyre', *Mélanges P. Collart* (1976), 178–91; M. Gawlikowsky, *Palmyre viii, les principia de Dioclétien* (1984).

[93] B. de Vries, *DRBE*, 227–41. Also S. T. Parker, *Romans and Saracens* (1986), 26–9. A plan of a Roman(?) castellum in Damascus appears in C. Watzinger and K. Wulzinger, *Damaskus, die antike Stadt* (1921), 54–6, pl. iii. For scepticism, A. Poidebard, *La trace de Rome dans le désert de Syrie* (1934), 54, with reference to Sauvaget. For many of these sites, references in *DE* s.v. *limes*.

[94] See above, p. 124, fig. 1.

[95] The opposite is the case in P. Yadin no. 16 of AD 127, which attests a cavalry prefect at Rabbatmoba as involved in the registration of the census for the district. His unit is not mentioned.

ground, which served adequately as barracks for the soldiers and provided a place where they could deposit their standards. Later on, by decision of the Roman emperor Trajan, the place received the rank of a city and became the metropolis of the province. And as time went on, the city of Melitene became large and populous. But since the people were no longer able to live inside the fortifications (for the place was restricted in size, as I have said) they settled in the adjoining plain, and here their shrines have been erected and the residences of the magistrates and their market-place, and all the other places for the sale of goods, and all the streets and stoas and baths and theatres of the city, and whatever else contributes to the embellishment of a great city. In this way it came about that Melitene was for the most part unwalled. Accordingly the Emperor Anastasius undertook to surround the whole of it with a wall . . .[96]

We may, perhaps, question whether Procopius is right in assuming that the civilians lived within the perimeter of the legionary fort. The fact that he calls it small may indicate that only a part of the legion was stationed there, but perhaps this point must not be pressed. Otherwise this is an excellent description of a process that can usually be traced only through archaeology. It is significant that here too the town developed in the immediate vicinity of the fort, not at some distance from it, and without any form of separation such as we find in the western provinces.[97]

TAXATION AND THE ROMAN ARMY

In Talmudic literature we find the following statement:

Rabbi Levi said: whoever takes a palm-branch unlawfully acquired may be compared with a bandit who sat on a crossroads and robbed those who passed by. And once a soldier who collected 'demosia' (i.e. public taxes) in that district passed him and he rose and took everything he had collected.[98]

The passage is instructive in two ways. It reminds us of the frequency of banditry in the Roman empire, even where the Roman army was present; and it represents the Roman army as engaged in collecting taxes even while it failed to guarantee the elementary security of the state. The taxes concerned, moreover, were not the specifically military levies such as *annona militaris*. Evidence of this kind is singularly

---

[96] *De aed.* iii 4. 15–19, trans. H. B. Dewing, Loeb, with minor modifications.

[97] For the army in cities generally, R. MacMullen, *Soldier and Civilian in the Later Roman Empire* (1963), 77–85. MacMullen assumes that the lodging of army units began to take shape only in the 3rd cent. (p. 79). It is now clear that it always was a feature of the army in the East.

[98] Leviticus Rabbah xxx 6, ed. Margulies, 702; cf. Tanhuma Emor xviii; Tanhuma Buber Leviticus, p. 99; Midrash Aggada ii, ed. Buber, 56.

valuable because it gives an honest impression of the way in which some of the inhabitants of one of the eastern provinces saw the institutions of the empire. The information cited in most modern works on these matters derives almost exclusively from legal texts and inscriptions, in other words, from documents produced by or for the authorities. Talmudic sources, on the other hand, express the view of the provincials in a hardly censored form. In the following pages only those forms of taxation will be discussed that were levied for the army itself. Other taxes were common to all provinces of the empire and are therefore not a subject for special treatment in a work about the Roman army in the East. Generally speaking, it is hard to distinguish between excessive taxation and plain robbery by soldiers. As we read in the Gospel according to Luke:

Tax collectors also came to be baptized, and said to him, 'Teacher, what shall we do?' And he said to them, 'Collect no more than is appointed you.' Soldiers also asked him, 'And we, what shall we do?' And he said to them, 'Rob no one by violence or by false accusation, and be content with your wages.'[99]

The implication, of course, is that misbehaviour was the norm with such people.

The burden of Roman taxation is occasionally noted in Talmudic literature.[100] Where the sources can be dated there appears to be a direct correlation between the level of taxation and the relations of the Jews with the authorities. The burden seems to have been felt as particularly heavy during the third-century crisis. A colourful description of this may be found in the words of Resh Laqish, one of the leaders of the Palestinian *amoraim* in this period.

Rabbi Yohanan said likewise: Let him come (i.e. the messiah), and let me not see him. Resh Laqish said to him: Why so? Shall we say, because it is written: 'As if a man did flee from a lion, and a bear met him; or went into the house, and leaned his hand on the wall, and a serpent bit him' (Amos 5: 19). Come and I shall show you an example from our own time. When a man goes out into the field and he meets a bailiff it is as if he met a lion. When he enters town and he meets a tax collector it is as if he met a bear. When he enters his house and finds his sons and daughters suffering from hunger it is as if he was bitten by a serpent.[101]

Naturally the burden of taxation was increased after rebellions— already times of prevailing hardship. This is taken as a matter of course in Cicero's *Pro Fonteio*: among the Gauls recently subdued lands were

---

[99] Luke 3: 12–14.
[100] For taxation in Talmudic literature, M. Hadas-Lebel, *REJ* 143 (1984), 5–29.
[101] b. Sanhedrin 98b.

confiscated; large numbers of troops were conscripted for the war in Spain, and their pay was made a charge on their countrymen; corn was demanded for the troops in Spain.[102] In Judaea this could go so far as to threaten the very existence of the Jews as a people in their land. This is illustrated by the rules regarding the Sabbatical year (Shevi'it). In the period after the Bar Kokhba revolt *halakhah* was established as follows:

Those are unfit (to serve as witnesses): Anyone who grinds in a pot, who lends money on interest, who lets doves fly, who trades in Seventh Year produce. Rabbi Shimeon said: In the past they used to call them 'gatherers of Seventh Year produce'. But when the *anasim* (extortioners) multiplied they changed that and called them 'traffickers in Seventh Year produce'.[103]

In normal years the Roman authorities would exempt Jews from taxes on harvest in the Sabbatical year.[104] But in the period of persecutions after the Bar Kokhba revolt this exemption was apparently cancelled. Against this background R. Shimeon bar Yohai determined that, in view of the great number of 'extortioners', apparently the tax collectors for the authorities, those who gather produce in the Sabbatical year would no longer be included in the list of men unfit to testify and they would remain *persona grata* in their community. In other words it was permitted *de facto* to gather harvest in the Sabbatical year in order to transfer it to the tax-collectors.

Generally the *halakhot* and *taqanot* of the generation after the Bar Kokhba revolt formed a continuation of those established by the leadership in the period after the First Jewish Revolt, and thus we find that laws enacted after the First Revolt were expanded and elaborated after the Second Revolt. However, the *halakhot* regarding the Sabbatical year were strengthened after the destruction of the temple, for these were the only significant religious precepts regarding the produce of the soil that were not basically connected with the Temple. The observation of these precepts would help in preserving the continuity of Judaism after the destruction of Jerusalem and in the absence of the Temple. In the Yavneh period, therefore, the local authorities in villages and towns were organized to supervise the scrupulous observance of commandments regarding the Sabbatical year.[105]

---

[102] *Pro Fonteio* 5. 13.
[103] m. Sanhedrin iii 3; cf. tos. Sanhedrin v 2.
[104] See e.g. Julius Caesar's edict cited by Josephus, *Ant.* xiv 10. 6 (202–6).
[105] See S. Safrai, 'The Commands regarding Shevi'it in practice after the Destruction of the Temple', *Tarbiz* 35 (1966), 310–20.

Annona Militaris

A further relaxation of the rules regarding Shevi'it was also connected with an increased burden of taxation, namely the wide and uncontrolled levying of the military subsistence allowance, *annona* (the Hebrew term is 'arnona'), in the period of crisis in the third century.[106] By way of clarification of the mishnah discussed above it is said in the Babylonian Talmud: 'When the extortioners multiplied, and what are they? (collectors of) *annona*, as Rabbi Yannai declares: go and sow your seed (even) in the Sabbatical year because of the *annona*.'[107] Rabbi Yannai, one of the major Palestinian *amoraim* of the first generation (220–50), here seems to be calling for the cultivation of the land in the Sabbatical year because of the insufferable burden of the *annona*. It is true that in the parallel source in the Jerusalem Talmud Rabbi Yannai's ordinance appears to be formulated in a more restricted sense, which allows only the initial ploughing in the Sabbatical year.[108] It is not clear, however, how, according to this version, the problem of *annona* in the Sabbatical year would be solved, and it appears that in this case we may prefer the version of the ordinance in the Babylonian Talmud. But the Jerusalem Talmud here adds a distinction which is interesting in its reflection of the way in which the Jews in Palestine perceived Roman taxation. It is asked whether work in the Sabbatical year can be included in the phrase 'he will be killed rather than violate the law of the Torah'. The answer is then given that this approach does not apply in the present case, for 'the intention is not to persecute, but to collect *annona*'.[109] The Talmud, therefore, distinguishes here between 'times of persecution', which involved oppressive and persecuting enactments, and the increased taxation during the crisis of the third century, which did not aim at persecution. At the same time there were

[106] For the *annona militaris*, D. van Berchem, 'L'annone militaire dans l'Empire Romain au IIIe siècle', *Mem. Soc. Nat. Antiq. France* 8/108 (1937), 117–202. For the *annona* in Egypt, M. Rostovtzeff, *Roman Empire*, 483–5, 721 n. 45, where references are given to exactions of camels, hides, palm wood for spears, cows, calves, goats, hay, and wine for the soldiers. Two very important documents of AD 298 and 300 deal almost exclusively with *annona* and military supplies: T. C. Skeat, *Papyri from Panopolis in the Chester Beatty Library, Dublin* (1964). For the exaction of *annona* elsewhere, Rostovtzeff, 743 n. 42. For epigraphical evidence regarding the various levies mentioned in this chapter see also F. F. Abbott and A. C. Johnson, *Municipal Administration in the Roman Empire* (1926), nos. 139 (for which see now Mihailov, *IGBR* iv 2236, pp. 197–229) and nos. 141–3; and references in *IGBR* iv 207 f. and iii p. 121 and no. 1960.

[107] b. Sanhedrin 26 a.

[108] y. Sanhedrin iii 21b. See Safrai, *Tarbiz*, 39 f.; Y. Feliks, 'Go and sow your seed in the Sabbatical year because of *Arnona*', *Sinai* 73 (1973), 235–49 (both in Hebrew).

[109] y. Sanhedrin, loc. cit. The same is said as regards the permission to bake on the Sabbath in the days of the rebellion under Gallus, below, p. 290.

people who continued to insist on keeping the commandment regarding the Sabbatical year despite the increased exaction of the military subsistence allowance, as we learn from the words of Rabbi Isaac of the same period: 'and he (who keeps the commandment of Shevi'it) sees his field uncultivated and his vineyard uncultivated and (yet he) gives *annona* and keeps quiet, do you know a greater hero than this?'[110]

Talmudic literature, in particular amoraic literature, usually mentions *annona* together with *tributum capitis*.[111] This apparently reflects the process which originated in the period of crisis in the third century whereby the *annona* became a regular tax instead of an extraordinary one. Another development of the collection of the *annona* is to be found in the variety of commodities exacted. Tannaitic sources (roughly first and second century) mention *annona* in connection with animals and dough.[112] But a source that apparently reflects the period of the *amoraim* (third–fourth centuries) also mentions foodstuffs, wine, and clothing while emphasizing the Romans' demand to deliver the best:

Thus is it written in Deuteronomy by Moses our Teacher: 'They shall be a sign and a portent to you and your descendants forever, because you did not serve the Lord your God with joy and with a glad heart for all your blessings. Then in hunger and thirst, in nakedness and extreme want, you shall serve your enemies whom the Lord will send against you' (Deut. 28: 46–8). How 'in hunger'? While a person is eager to eat even barley bread and he cannot find it, foreign nations demand of him fine bread and choice meat. How 'in thirst'? When a man desires to drink even a drop of vinegar or a drop of beer and he cannot find it, foreign nations demand of him the finest wine in the world. How 'in nakedness'? When a man is eager to wear even a garment of (coarse) wool or linen and he cannot find it, foreign nations demand of him silk garments and *kulk* from all lands.[113]

A ruling of Rabbi Judah Hanassi establishes that payment of *annona*, like that of other taxes, has precedence over other obligations affecting a man's property.[114] This ruling reflects the better economic conditions as well as the improved relationship with the authorities in the days of Rabbi Judah Hanassi (late second and early third centuries). *Halakhah*, we see again, takes for granted that part of the produce had to be

---

[110] Leviticus Rabbah i 1, ed. Margulies, 4, and parallel sources.

[111] This is the case in most of the relevant passages in the Jerusalem Talmud. See y. Ketubot xiii 35d and parallel sources; y. Shevi'it iv 35b and parallel sources; y. Peah i 15b and parallel sources.

[112] For instance tos. Hallah i 4 (dough); tos. Bekhorot ii 2 (animals).

[113] Avot de-Rabbi Nathan, version A, xx, ed. Schechter, p. 71. *Annona* is not explicitly mentioned in the source, but it is very likely that this was meant. Cf. G. Alon, *The Jews in their Land in the Talmudic Age*, i (1980), 67. For *kulk*, S. Lieberman, *JQR* 36 (1946), 345 n. 114: 'cloth made of the down found at the roots of goats' hair'.

[114] y. Ketubot x 34a.

delivered to the army: 'When a man leases a field from a Samaritan he keeps apart tithes and gives him his due, he keeps apart tithes and pays the treasury, he keeps apart tithes and pays the centurion.'[115] Another *halakhah* shows that the burden of *annona* later in the third century caused people to flee and evade taxation which was then imposed on others: 'Rabbi Joshua ben Levi said: In no case must he reimburse him except in the case of *annona* and *tributum capitis*.'[116]

It is perhaps worth noting that originally all requisitioned supplies were supposed to be paid for, as shown for instance in the *Verrines* of Cicero, where it is asserted that the corn requisitioned in Sicily for the use of the governor is paid for at a generous rate. The development of the abuse of the system cannot be traced in detail. It is described by Cicero.[117] In discussing the government of Britain Tacitus refers to it as a burden that requires no explanation;[118] it can only be alleviated, not eradicated. In the end Diocletian converted requisition into a tax in kind, with no pretence of payment.

Two chapters in the Theodosian Code are concerned with these levies: xi 1, on taxes in kind and tribute ('de annona et tributis'), and vii 4, on the issue of military subsistence allowances ('de erogatione militaris annonae'). Wine was part of the *annona*,[119] and a separate heading is concerned with military clothing imposed as a levy.[120] Many of the texts are concerned with a problem to which the Talmudic sources do not allude, namely abuses by the military of the alternative of receiving a sum of money instead of a subsistence allowance in kind.[121] The fragments of imperial edicts from Beer Sheva are relevant here:[122] their purpose may well have been to publish the cash equivalents of supplies in kind to be paid as *annona* by the various communities listed, in an attempt to protect civilians against greed on the part of bureaucrats and soldiers.[123] This interpretation is supported by a legal text:

In view of the interests of soldiers of the frontier districts and of landowners in First, Second, and Third Palestine a ruling has been issued that, when taxes

---

[115] tos. Demai vi 3. Cf. D. Sperber, *Latomus* 28 (1969), 186–9. S. Lieberman, *Tosefta Kifshutah*, ad loc., p. 265, explains the word 'qitron' as *actarius* or *actuarius*, the quartermaster of a unit who issues rations to the troops. The dictionaries assume it stands for centurion, and this is likely to be the correct rendering, cf. *Dig.* xiii 7. 43. 1, cited below, p. 292.

[116] y. Ketubot xiii 35d and parallel sources.   [117] *Verr.* ii 3. 163–203.

[118] *Agricola* 19. 3: 'frumenti et tributorum exactionem aequalitate munerum mollire . . .'

[119] vii 4. 6; 25. Also straw (vii 4. 9).

[120] vii 6, *de militari veste.*   [121] vii 4. 12; 18; 20–2.

[122] A. Alt, *Die griechischen Inschriften der Palästina Tertia westlich der 'Araba* (1921), nos. 1–4, pp. 4–8; cf. Ch. Clermont-Ganneau, *Recueil d'archéologie orientale*, v (1902), 13–147 and other publications listed by Alt. See also P. Mayerson, *ZPE* 684 (1986), 141–8.

[123] Alt, p. 5, may have missed the point in his translation: '[Es sollen ihre Abgaben entrichten

have been paid at a fixed rate, exaction of payment in kind shall be suspended. But the office of the *dux* under the name of the garrisons at Versaminum and Moenonium attempts to nullify this salutary statute . . .[124]

We should note in passing that the *limitanei milites* referred to are not farmer-soldiers, but simply 'soldiers serving in a frontier command', as opposed to those in the field army. For the discussion of the meaning of the term *limes* it is of interest to see that there were such soldiers not only in Third Palestine, which included the Negev and the desert of Southern Jordan, but also in First and Second Palestine which were nowhere near any kind of frontier. Even if it is accepted that the term *limes* meant no more than 'frontier district' no part of First or Second Palestine could even have been so designated. We must therefore assume that the *limitanei milites* referred to are a specific category of soldiers under the command of the *dux* who had as the area of his command the three provinces of Palestine. Their designation as *limitanei milites* in this text must have had an administrative meaning; these soldiers were not necessarily ever stationed in an area described as *limes*.[125] They could, in other words, have served anywhere in Palestine, and the law cited above would have applied to all three provinces of Palestine.

The text provides clear evidence of malpractice in the levying of taxes for the provision of supplies to the army. The contrast between *pretia* and *species* is essential: if assessments are paid in money, no exactions in kind are permissible. It is repeated later in the text (*specierum exactio* v. *adaeratio statuta*) and, despite the opening words of our quotation, is clearly in the interest of the landowners, not the soldiers. This is in itself a fourth-century development. In a papyrus of AD 298 from Panopolis in Egypt it is noted that collectors of military supplies had accepted

die . . . der] jeweiligen Duces, sowie die treuergebenen unter[stellten] Grenzsoldaten [und die übrigen Steuerpflichti]gen Jahr für Jahr in folgender Weise. . . . The [??] of the *duces* and the soldiers were to receive payment, not to pay others. Similar texts from the reign of Anastasius were found in Arabia, E. Littmann et al., *Publications of the Princeton University Archaeological Expedition to Syria, in 1904–1905* iii, *Greek and Latin Inscriptions*, A2 (Leiden, 1910), p. 33, frs. 15–19; *IGLS* XIII 1 no. 9046; J. Marcillet-Jaubert, *ADAJ* 24 (1980), 122 f.; D. L. Kennedy, *Archaeological Explorations on the Roman Frontier in North-East Jordan* (1982), 44–8: a text concerned with the payment of penalties by officials which makes reference to, among others, 'those in charge in the *limes* of Palaestina and of Euphratensis' (i.e. Commagene). For the relevance of these inscriptions as regards the meaning of the term *limitanei* see Isaac, *JRS* 78 (1988), 125–47.

[124] *Cod. Theod.* vii 4. 30 (23 Mar. 409) = *Cod. Iust.* xii 37. 13: 'Limitanei militis et possessorum utilitate conspecta per primam, secundam ac tertiam Palaestinam huiuscemodi norma processit, ut pretiorum certa taxatione depensa speciorum inte[r]mittatur exactio. Sed ducianum officium Versamini et Moenoni castri nomine salutaria st[a]tuta conatur evertere', etc.

[125] R. Grosse, *Römische Militärgeschichte von Gallienus bis zum Beginn der byzantinischen Themenverfassung* (1920), 66, had already pointed out that some of the *limitanei*, such as those in Isauria and Upper Egypt, were not stationed in frontier zones.

money in lieu of meat, which was forbidden at that time.[126] But in the period between the date of the papyrus (298) and the law under discussion (409) it had become the usual practice to demand payment of *annona* in money instead of in kind. It is clear what happened: originally the army was entitled to receive various supplies in kind. It then found it profitable to demand money instead of the supplies. Efforts on the part of the authorities to prevent such demands from being made remained ineffective, and laws were therefore enacted to prevent extortionary sums being demanded. The law of 409 deals with cases where payment was being exacted both in money and in kind. In 298 it is further mentioned that the collectors had taken quantities of goods many times greater than those laid down in the regulations; barley and chaff had also been demanded in larger measures than the authorized ones. Such practices had, in AD 28, led to the revolt of the Frisii. Their tribute consisted of cow hides for the use of the military,[127] but a greedy *primipilaris* had established hides of *uri* (wild cattle) as the standard of measurement instead of the hides of the smaller domestic cows of the Frisians themselves.

Finally it appears that there were also disputes about the use of pastures owned by private persons (at Antioch) or of public lands (at Apamea) by animals belonging to the army.[128]

Justinian's *novellae* 102 and 103 of AD 536, particularly the former, emphasize that taxes may be collected only by the newly appointed governors of senior rank, and explicitly forbid the military to engage in these matters. From the text it is clear that the collection of taxes by the *duces* had led to extortion and subsequent unrest, and the transfer of the levying of taxes back to the civilian authorities was an attempt to improve the lot of the civilian population and suppress corruption. We cannot know, of course, what was the effect of the measures taken in 536. In mid-fourth-century Egypt it had been common for army units to be engaged in the collection of taxes, both *annona* and regular duties. While the *exactor* was responsible for the delivery, the soldiers actually collected the taxes.[129] This frequently caused friction between the civilian and military authorities, it seems.[130] The soldiers are accused of looting and robbery of cattle, violent behaviour during the collection of

---

[126] Skeat, 1. 229 ff.

[127] Tacitus, *Ann.* iv 72–4.

[128] *Cod. Theod.* vii 7. 3 (11 Mar. 398).

[129] H. I. Bell et al., *The Abinnaeus Archive* (1962), no. 13, pp. 55–8. For the collection of *annona*, no. 26, pp. 73–5; no. 29, pp. 78 f.

[130] There is plenty of evidence from the Abinnaeus archives: nos. 13–15, pp. 55–60; nos. 26; 29. Admittedly, these represent a brief period in a single district.

taxes,[131] and drunkenness combined with brutality.[132] It is to be remembered that the same troops performed police duties in the region.[133]

The obligations of *annona* were naturally hard and likely to cause friction, particularly in times of stress between the Jews and the authorities. To the period of the alleged rebellion under Gallus (mid fourth century) belong testimonies of sages who allowed the Jews to bake on Sabbath in the days of Ursicinus, the general of Gallus, and to bake leavened bread on Passover in the days of 'Proqla' (Proculus?), perhaps one of the latter's officers.[134]

It was not only wars or rebellions that caused an increased demand for extraordinary military supplies. Another type of calamity was an imperial visit to the province. In his 'Embassy to Gaius' Philo gives a lively impression of the organization needed for an intended imperial visit to Egypt. The emperor would travel by boat while spending every night on shore.

It would be necessary therefore to have fodder for the beasts and a vast stock of food got ready in all the cities of Syria, particularly on the coast. For a huge crowd would come both by sea and by land, drawn not only from Rome itself and Italy, but also from the successive provinces right up to Syria, a crowd composed partly of persons of high rank, partly of soldiers, infantry and cavalry and marines, while the multitude of servants would be not less than the military. Supplies were needed calculated not merely for absolute necessities but for the excessive expenditure which Gaius demanded.[135]

We happen to have confirmation that Philo does not exaggerate. The papyrus of 298 is largely concerned with the preparations for the forthcoming visit of Diocletian to Egypt.[136] These preparations consist principally of arrangements for provisioning the troops accompanying the emperor. Particularly instructive is a lengthy list of appointments of officials responsible for the collection and distribution of a special *annona* for these troops. There is a good deal in the papyrus about the various foodstuffs demanded: lentils, meat, chaff, bread, barley, and wheat. Wine was to be commandeered.[137] An entire bakery was to be made ready, with provision for the bakers who would work there, so that the military supplies might be continuously maintained.[138]

---

[131] No. 27, pp. 75 f.   [132] No. 28, pp. 76 f.

[133] No. 9, pp. 50 f.; no. 12, pp. 54 f.; no. 42, pp. 96 f.

[134] y. Betzah i, 60c; y. Sanhedrin iii, 21b. Cf. Lieberman, *JQR*. 352.

[135] *Legatio* 33 (251 f.), trans. F. H. Colson, Loeb.

[136] Skeat, no. 1. Note also the record of expropriations in money and goods in anticipation of Hadrian's visit to Egypt in AD 130: P. Sijpestijn, *Historia* 18 (1969), 109–18.

[137] Skeat, no. 1. 205 ff.   [138] 334 ff., 374 ff.

Animals were to be supplied for the sacrifices due to take place.[139] More than food was involved: a complaint is registered that the hides supplied for the strengthening of the gates and posterns of two forts were nibbled by mice and mutilated.[140] Craftsmen and skilled workmen were to be sought out everywhere for the manufacture of helmets and breastplates and greaves.[141] A smith required for work in the arsenal was to be taken into custody and sent under escort together with his tools.[142] For the court itself there was a superintendent of bedding at the various halting places.[143] For the use of the imperial post on the Nile skiffs with their crews were to be made available.[144] Here we are, in fact, faced with another kind of extraordinary levy, *angaria*, which is discussed in the next section. All this gives us an impression of the disaster which struck a province each time an emperor made a visit. Even worse, of course, was the passing of an emperor with a full army, on the way to Mesopotamia, a frequent event in the eastern provinces.[145]

A series of legal texts is concerned with the transportation of provisions for the army.[146] It appears that the provincials were responsible for the transport and delivery of *annona*: 'Taxes in kind will be transported to the *limes* in accordance with the site and proximity of the landholdings. This order will be carried out without difficulty, if the registrars may be prevented by fear of the customary torture from their usual fraudulent practices.'[147] This brings us to the next extraordinary form of taxation to be discussed.

Angaria

'The exaction of supplementary post-horses has annihilated the estate of many men and fed the avarice of some.'[148] *Angaria* (requisition of transport) is mentioned in the Gospels[149] and was another form of

---

[139] 381 ff. [140] 385 ff. [141] 342 ff.

[142] 211. [143] 256 ff. [144] 254 ff.

[145] The *Expositio Totius Mundi* 36, published perhaps in 359, states that Egypt supported the eastern provinces with grain 'propter exercitum imperatoris et bellum Persarum'.

[146] This form of liturgy is attested in Egypt, see Rostovtzeff, *Roman Empire* 484 f.; 743 f. n. 44, citing B. Grenfell, *P. Oxy.* 1412. 14, note on *P. Oxy.* 1261: a declaration concerning the transport of produce for troops at Babylon as a liturgy. It is, however, not clear whether the produce itself was exacted as *annona*. In general, F. Oertel, *Die Liturgie* (1917), esp. 88–94 for *angareia* in Egypt; and see now N. Lewis, *Inventory of Compulsory Services in Ptolemaic and Roman Egypt*, revised edn., 1975 (American Studies in Papyrology, iii), s.v. 'transport'.

[147] *Cod. Theod.* xi 1. 11; see also xi 1. 21, 37; vii 4. 15 (*Cod. Iust.* xii 37. 4).

[148] *Cod Theod.* viii 5. 7 (3 Aug. 354 [360]): 'Paravedorum exactio patrimonia multorum evertit et pavit avaritiam nonnullorum.'

[149] Matt. 5: 41; 27: 32; Mark 15: 21.

taxation known and current in the Mishnah and the Talmud.[150]
Tannaitic *halakhah* (*halakhah* of the period of the Mishnah, first–second
centuries) establishes: 'When a man hires a donkey and it turns blind
or was taken for *angaria*—he may say (to the owner): here, this is
yours.'[151] A similar ruling may be found in the *Digest* (with reference to
annona):

Titius received a loan from Gaius Seius on the security of some wine skins.
While Seius was keeping the skins in his warehouse a centurion on duty for the
collection of supplies seized them as *annona*. Later they were recovered at the
demand of Gaius Seius, the creditor. My question is whether the debtor,
Titius, or the creditor, Seius, should be held responsible for the damage and
costs resulting from the operations. The answer is that in the case as presented
here there is no one to be held liable for the resulting damage.[152]

As this is attributed to Scaevola, a jurist of the time of Marcus Aurelius,
it is therefore a relatively early reference to *annona militaris*. As well as
the seizure of a donkey for *angaria*, tannaitic *halakhah* also mentions in
similar terms the seizure for *angaria* of a labourer working a field: 'When
a man hires a labourer and he is seized for *angaria*, he may not say to him
(i.e. to the labourer): here this is your (own fault), but he pays him
wages for his work.'[153]

   In the Babylonian Talmud a distinction is made between 'returning
angaria' and '*angaria* which does not return'.[154] That is to say, there are
cases when an animal is taken temporarily for work for the authorities
and there are cases where it is lost for good. The distinction is ascribed
to Rav and Samuel of the first generation of Babylonian *amoraim* (220–
50), who had both lived in Palestine as well, and it is therefore likely
that their words reflect the severity of taxation there in the third-
century crisis. In this source the term is used for the property seized

---

[150] For *angaria*, M. Rostovtzeff, *Klio* 6 (1906), 249–58: R. argues that the Roman authorities
found *angaria* as an existing institution in the eastern part of the empire which they adopted and
expanded after Diocletian; see also id., *Roman Empire*, 381–7. Note in particular an inscription
recording a drawn-out dispute in the 3rd cent. between Phrygian villages concerning the
allocation of *angareia* for the public post: W. H. C. Frend, *JRS* 46 (1956), 46–56. The fullest
treatment is in the publication of an important inscription from Pisidia, S. Mitchell, *JRS* 66
(1976), 106–31. For Egypt, Lewis, *Inventory*, s.v. 'billeting'.

[151] m. Bava Metzi'a vi 3; cf. tos. ibid. vii 7; y. ibid., v 11a; b. ibid., 78b.

[152] Scaevola in *Dig.* xiii 7. 43. 1: 'Titius cum pecuniam mutuam accepit a Gaio Seio sub
pignore culleorum. istos culleos cum Seius in horreo haberet, missus ex officio annonae centurio
culleos ad annonam sustulit ac postea instantia Gaii Seii creditoris reciperati sunt: quaero,
intertrituram, quae ex operis facta est, utrum Titius debitor an Seius creditor adgnoscere
debeat. respondit secundum ea quae proponerentur ob id, quod eo nomine intertrimenti accidis-
set non teneri.'

[153] tos. Bava Metzi'a vii 8.

[154] b. Bava Metzi'a 78b; cf. y. Bava Metzi'a vi 11a.

instead of the obligation to provide it.[155] From Panopolis we have an instruction to 'send off the men who provided the carts and cattle dispatched . . . for the service of the quarries . . . so that they may receive back both their carts and their same cattle'.[156] It is easy to see how carts and cattle might remain unreturned under such circumstances. A fourth-century law prohibits severe mistreatment of animals delivered as *angaria*.[157] That would be another explanation for the cases of 'non-returning *angaria*'. The previous law in the same section states that it is forbidden simply to take away an ox plowing a field.

A case described by Rabbi Aha of the fourth generation of Palestinian *amoraim* (320–50) reflects the reality and arbitrariness of *angaria*:

Rabbi Aha said: it happened that a man sold all his household goods and spent it on wine, the beams of his house and he spent it on wine, and his sons gave him lodging and said: the old man, our father, will die and he will not leave us anything after his death. What shall we do to him? Come, let us ply him with wine and make him drunk and lay him down and take him out and let us say he died and let us lay him in his tomb . . . A few ass drivers passed on their way into that town. They heard there was angaria in town. They said: come, let us unload these goatskins in this tomb and let us flee . . . when he (the old man) woke up from his sleep he saw a wine-skin placed above his head. He opened it and put it in his mouth. He began to drink. When he was sated he began to sing. When his sons came to see what had happened to him and found him sitting with a wineskin in his mouth and drinking they said: Since they gave you (wine to drink) from heaven we do not know what to do with you. Come let us take him (home) and let us make a ruling and a fixed law (*katastasis*). They made an arrangement to take turns and provide their father with wine each for a day.[158]

It is clear that the wine merchants were afraid that their merchandise would be confiscated. That would properly have been called *annona*. It appears, however, that those whose property was confiscated were often forced to transport the goods themselves and that would have been called *angaria* or *prosecutio annonae*.

A source ascribed to the days after the destruction of the second Temple mentions royal taxes, notably *angaria* in the form of various kinds of forced labour for the authorities:

Rabban Yohanan ben Zakkai was going up to Emmaus in Judaea and he saw a girl picking barleycorn out of the excrement of a horse. Said Rabban Yohanan

---

[155] *Angareia* has the same dual meaning in the Phrygian inscription cited above, n. 150.

[156] Skeat, 2. 154. Oertel, 90, distinguishes between 'Zwangsvermietung, Zwangsverkauf', and 'Zwangsgratislieferung'.

[157] *Cod. Theod.* viii 5. 2.

[158] Leviticus Rabbah xii 1, ed. Margulies, pp. 245–7; cf. Esther Rabbah v 1. The term

to his disciples: What girl is this? Said they to him: A Jewish girl. Said he further: And whose is the horse? They answered: It belongs to a nomad (Arab) horseman. Then said Rabban Yohanan to his disciples: All my life have I been reading this verse, and not until now have I realised its full meaning: 'If thou dost not know, O fairest among women (go thy way forth by the footsteps of the flock, and feed thy kids beside the shepherds' tents.' *Song of Songs* 1: 8). You were unwilling to pay the biblically ordained head-tax of 'one beqa per head' (*Exod.* 38: 26), so now you have to pay fifteen shekels under a government of your enemies. You were unwilling to repair the roads and the streets leading up to the Temple, so now you have to repair the 'burgasin' and the 'burganin' leading to the royal cities.[159]

The provincial population was forced to construct roads at least from the late republic onwards, as is clear from a passage in Cicero's *Pro Fonteio*.[160] Inscriptions from Asia Minor tell the same story.[161] In 163–5 the road from Damascus to Heliopolis through Wadi Barada was repaired by the army, but the town of Abilene paid for the work.[162] In Chapter I an inscription was mentioned which records the construction of a hydraulic water installation at Aine on the Euphrates. The work

katastasis (κατάστασις) is a *hapax legomenon* and therefore enhances the impression of authenticity of the source.

[159] Mekhilta de-Rabbi Ishmael, Bahodesh, i, ed. Horovitz-Rabin, pp. 203 f. Translation of this passage taken from Alon, 68 f. For an edition and translation of the whole text, J. Z. Lauterbach, *Mekilta de Rabbi Ishmael* (1933). In the Oxford MS Rabban Yohanan goes up to 'Maus in Judaea' which refers, apparently, to Emmaus. This is preferable to 'Ma'on in Judaea', found in other versions. The entire saying in the Mekhilta is attributed to Rabban Yohanan ben Zakkai, leader of the people in Yavneh after the destruction of the Temple in 70. The beginning of the passage and the quotation from the Song of Songs have the appearance of an authentic description of the state of affairs after the failure of the First Revolt. This impression is strengthened by the fact that a unit of '*Petraei*' is attested at Emmaus: AE 1924. 132; below, Appendix I, p. 429. But the continuation, 'You were unwilling to pay . . .', is an addition by the editor of the Mekhilta which refers to the reality of a later period, apparently the third-century period of crisis in the empire. Proof may be found in the fact that this part is missing in all parallel sources: tos. Ketubot v 10; Sifre Deuteronomy 305, ed. Finkelstein, p. 325, where another addition is found; y. Ketubot v 30b–c; b. Ketubot 67a; Lamentations Rabbah i 48; Pesikta Rabbati xxix–xxx, ed. Friedmann, p. 140a. Cf. E. E. Urbach, 'The Jews in their Land in the Tannaitic Period', *Behinot Beviqoret Hasifrut* 4 (1953), 70 (in Hebrew).

[160] 8. 17 f. Cf. T. Pekáry, *Untersuchungen zu den römischen Reichsstrassen* (1968), 115 f. Fonteius is accused of accepting bribes for exemption from the duty to construct or repair roads. From this it follows that such duties were the rule. See Pekáry, 91–119, for extensive discussion of financial matters and Roman roads.

[161] Inscriptions from Thrace and Asia Minor show that local labour was used for road construction, see L. Robert, *Hellenica* i 90–2; *Opera minora* i 298–300; J. and L. Robert, *Fouilles d'Amyzon* (1983), 30–2. Note in particular *OGIS* 519 f., 1251; Frend, *JRS* 46 ff. Cf. *Digest* xlix 18. 4. 1, where no immunity is granted to veterans as regards road construction and *angaria*.

[162] *CIL* iii 199: (M. Aurelius and Lucius Verus) 'viam fluminis vi abruptam interciso monte restituerunt per Iul(ium) Verum leg(atum) pr(o) pr(aetore) provinc(iae) Syr(iae) et amicum suum impendiis Abilenorum.' *CIL* iii 200–1: 'Pro salute Imp(eratorum) Aug(ustorum) Ant[o]nini et Veri M(arcus) Volusius Maximus (centurio) leg(ionis) XVI F(laviae) F(irmae) qui oper(i) institit v(otum) s(olvit).' Both inscriptions are engraved in the rock twice, at both ends of a rock-cut passage.

was carried out by a legionary vexillation, but it was paid for by a local community. In Judaea there are various indications that milestones were set up by local communities[163]—for example, the giving of the distance 'from the city' rather than 'from Scythopolis' or the repeated occurrence of anomalous abbreviations near one city. The change to an indication of distance in Greek from the nearest city instead of one in Latin from a point much farther away also clearly reflects this procedure.[164] Fourth-century laws in the Theodosian code list the construction and maintenance of roads and bridges among the extraordinary services demanded from every person, save those who were exempted, of course.[165] From Egypt in particular there is good evidence of compulsory police duties.[166]

There is also evidence of personal *angaria*, for instance an account of Rabbi Ze'ira, of the third generation of Palestinian *amoraim* (280–320), who was seized for *angaria*, namely the transportation of myrtle to the 'palatin' (*palatium*).[167] The *palatium* concerned was not necessarily an imperial residence, for the term probably came to be used for any official halting-place.[168] Their function was thus close to that of *praetoria*, as appears from two legal texts which first attempt to prevent the use of *palatia* by officials, and then allow it in the case of cities far from the public highway, where there were no *praetoria*.[169] Since it is clear from legal sources and papyri that landowners could be required personally to deliver payments in kind to stations of the *cursus publicus* there can be no doubt that the account of Rabbi Ze'ira reflects reality. 'No landholder will be required to furnish *mansiones* or to deliver payments in kind at great distances, apart from *annona* for the *limitanei*, but the entire journey and the necessity of it will be taken into account.'[170] The wording of this law is clearly flexible. It may be noted

---

[163] See B. Isaac and I. Roll, *Roman Roads in Judaea*, i (1982), 76, 93 f.

[164] Notably on the coast road from Antioch to Ptolemais: R. G. Goodchild, *Berytus* 9 (1948), 91 ff.; also on the roads from Caesarea to Scythopolis and from Legio to Diocaesarea: Isaac and Roll, 66 f., 84 n. 27.

[165] *Cod. Theod.* xi 16. 10 (13 Mar. 362); 15 (9 Dec. 382); 18 (5 July 390). The *Digest*, L 4. 1, lists road-construction among the duties imposed on persons rather than on their *patrimonium*.

[166] See above, ch. III; Oertel, 263–86.

[167] y. Berakhot i, 2d. Cf. the 'prosecutiones' referred to in *Cod. Theod.* xvi 8. 2.

[168] As pointed out by F. Millar, *The Emperor in the Roman World* (1977), 41 f. For *palatia*, R. MacMullen, *Athenaeum* 54 (1976), 26–36, esp. 33 ff., who points out that many were constructed by the tetrarchs and after 325. In the present source, however, there is at least a suggestion that an imperial palace is meant, for in the sequel it is said that people might be prepared to pay merely to see it.

[169] *Cod. Theod.* vii 10. 1 (10 July 405); 2 (23 Nov. 407). Cf. xv 1. 35 (396): governors must repair 'quidquid de palatiis aut praetoriis iudicum aut horreis aut stabulis et receptaculis animalium publicorum ruina labsum fuerit'. For further evidence see Millar, loc. cit. (n. 168).

[170] *Cod. Theod.* xi 1. 21: 'Nemo possessorum ad instruendas mansiones vel conferendas species

that two laws enacted in AD 330 exempted all synagogue officials from various *munera*, including *prosecutiones (angaria)*.[171]

In Roman legal sources the term *angaria* is used not for transport duty as such, but for the animals exacted. Similarly, *parangariae* are supplementary transport animals, and *paraveredi* supplementary posthorses.[172] The term for 'transport duty' is *translatio*. Animals were, in fact, taken for two distinct purposes. One was the imperial post, called *vehiculatio* and later *cursus publicus*. Animals were confiscated for this organization, and supervising the stations of the post was among the personal services demanded from the provincials.[173] As is well-known, the post was an extremely heavy burden, and it was constantly abused by those who had a chance to do so. The other was 'transport duty', which was the obligation to convey goods for the use of the authorities and the army. It may be useful here to cite a law that lists the frequent extraordinary services demanded from provincials:[174] baking bread, burning lime, contributions of timber, of horses and wagons for the post, the construction and maintenance of public buildings and of roads and bridges. To a special category, because the ordinary exemptions did not apply, belonged the transport of military food-supplies and the delivery of charcoal for minting money or arms manufacture. A law of 10 July 375 (applying to Africa) stresses that 'military clothing must be transported all the way to the bases of the soldiers. For the soldiers must not be taken away from their posts even for a short distance.'[175]

Libanius devoted an entire speech, 'For the peasants about *angareia*', to the casual requisitioning of services by the *comes*, resident at Antioch, who forced the peasants to use their own asses for the transport of rubble from the city.[176] From the section on public works in the Theodosian code it is clear that the provincial governors, who in the fourth century were responsible for the construction of public buildings in cities, would normally employ local workers.[177] The term *angareia*

excepta limitaneorum annona longius delegatur, sed omnis itineris ac necessitatis habita ratione.' Cf. *Cod. Iust.* x 16. 8.

[171] *Cod. Theod.* xvi 8. 2 and 4; cf. A. Linder, *Roman Imperial Legislation on the Jews* (in Hebrew, 1983), 96–100.

[172] See e.g. *Cod. Theod.* vi 23. 3–4; viii 5: *de curso publico angariis et parangariis*, passim; xi 16. 18: . . . *paravedorum et parangarium praebitio.*

[173] *Cod. Theod.* viii 5. 36 (27 Feb. 381), stipulating the death penalty for absentees.

[174] *Cod. Theod.* xi 16. 18 (5 July 390).

[175] *Cod. Theod.* viii 5. 33.

[176] *Or.* 1.

[177] xv 1. 5 (27 July 338) which determines that the governor may grant exemptions. Senators may not be forced to provide compulsory services: xv 1. 7 (3 May 361), a rule which shows that all others were included.

does not appear in this connection; construction work was evidently a local imposition, legally distinct from compulsory transport services regulated by imperial decree. That will not have made any difference to the peasants who had to do it. However, it is relevant for the present discussion that this was imposed not by the army, but by the civilian authorities, while being enforced by soldiers. 'Whippings by the soldiers in charge also occur.'[178]

Akhsaniah (hospitium)[179]

The burden of *akhsaniah* (*hospitium*, compulsory billeting) and associated duties is reflected in cases discussed and *halakhot*. The Jerusalem Talmud reports a halakhic discussion on the question whether it is permitted to bribe a quartermaster in charge of the allocation of billets. It is established that 'it is permissible to bribe the quartermaster [the Aramaic word 'parkha' derives from *xenoparchos*] before the Romans (the Roman soldiers) come, but after their arrival it is forbidden'.[180] The reason for this limitation may be that bribes at that stage merely transfer the burden from one man to another. Elsewhere in the Jerusalem Talmud we learn that guests may be removed from an inn which is being cleared for *akhsaniah*. Though there is some evidence that, in contrast, the inhabitants of a private house are not removed upon the arrival of those entitled to billeting,[181] it is nevertheless clear that in practice there were people evicted from private homes: '"And I shall provoke them with those who are not a people" (Deut. 32:21), do not read "belo 'am" (with not a people), but "bilway 'am" (with associates of a people), (I shall provoke them with) those who come from among the nations and kingdoms and expel them from their homes.'[182] The sources distinguish between those who receive billeting to which they are entitled and those who receive it although they are not, and they discuss the principle on which billets are assigned,

---

[178] *Or.* 1. 27.

[179] The Roman empire was by no means unique in the establishment of this institution. In the Ottoman empire peasants often fled rather than go on receiving soldiers on the march or travelling grandees: N. N. Lewis, *Nomads and Settlers in Syria and Jordan, 1800–1980* (1987), 12, with n. 22. For *hospitium militare* see also Daremberg–Saglio, *Dictionnaire*, iii 302 f. (Cagnat).

[180] y. Bava Qamma iii 3c. The Latin term for quartermaster is *mensor*; it occurs in *Cod. Theod.* vii 8. 4, which deals with cases where people delete the names of soldiers written by *mensores* on the doorposts of the houses in which they are to be billeted. Vegetius, ii 7, uses the term *metatores* for those who pick the site of a camp for an army on the march. Presumably both terms originally indicated the same function.

[181] y. 'Eruvin vi 23c.

[182] Sifre Deuteronomy cccxx, ed. Finkelstein, p. 367, as interpreted and translated by Lieberman, *JQR*, 355. The text dates probably from the early third century.

whether '*akhsaniah* is distributed *per capita* or according to the number of doors'.[183]

In Chapter IV we saw that, especially in the Byzantine period, many inns were built expressly for the use of the military. If there was space available in an inn soldiers should not be billeted in private homes, according to an inscription from Phaenae in Trachonitis: 'Since you have an inn you are not obliged to receive strangers in your homes'.[184] As usual, this statement shows that the town turned to the authorities because, in practice, the system did not work as it ought to. In southern Syria the 'public guest-house' was a very common feature in villages.[185] It will have served the military whenever *hospitium* was required.

Compulsory billeting did not entail lodging only, but also the supply of food to the soldiers or officials who were billeted in the course of duty. The following case which took place in the Yavneh period, early in the second century, may serve as an illustration:

It happened that Shimeon Hatemani did not go out on the night of the festival to the Study House. the next morning Rabbi Judah ben Bava encountered him and said: Why did you not come to the Study House last night? He answered: I had an opportunity to obey a religious duty (*mitzvah*) and I did it. A patrol of gentiles came into town and they (the townspeople) were afraid that they (the soldiers) might harm them and therefore we prepared them a calf and we fed them and gave them to drink and rubbed them with oil so that they would not harm the townspeople. He (Rabbi Judah) said to him: I am not certain whether you have gained more than you have lost, for they have said that one does not prepare food for gentiles or for dogs on a festival.[186]

In a later period the Bishop of Gaza organized the provision of supplies to soldiers in order to prevent trouble.[187]

A number of alleviations were enacted in the *halakhah* for compulsory billeting. It was permitted to supply food regarded as *demai*, that is, of which it was suspected that the tithes had not been properly set apart: 'One may feed *demai* produce to the poor and to billeted troops.'[188] Similarly it was permitted to supply produce of a Sabbatical year in the case of *hospitium*, while this was forbidden in the case of gentile guests who were not claiming *hospitium*: 'One feeds billeted troops produce of

---

[183] y. 'Eruvin vi 23b; b. Bava Batra 11b. Cf. Lieberman, *JQR*, 354–6.

[184] Waddington, no. 2524 (*OGIS* 609).

[185] H. I. MacAdam, *Berytus* 31 (1983), 108, who notes that references in inscriptions are too numerous to list individually.

[186] tos. Betzah ii 6 (Vienna MS); Mekhilta de-Rabbi Shimeon ben Yohai, Bo 12: 16, ed. Epstein-Melamed, 21; b. Betzah 21a. See also above, p. 116.

[187] Choricius, *Laud Marc.* ii 24 (p. 34).

[188] m. Demai iii 1 and parallels.

the Sabbatical year, but one does not feed a gentile or a hired (day) labourer produce of the Sabbatical year'.[189]

So far the billeting of passing troops. *Hospitium*, however, could also be demanded by individuals who had the right or the muscle to do so.[190] The authorities could, in fact, issue warrants for the use of the postal system, that is, free transportation combined with the right to demand lodging and food.[191]

The earliest law on the subject known to me mentions most of the duties discussed in the present chapter: 'Whether exemption is granted to a person from personal obligations alone, or also from civil obligations, they cannot be excused from *annona*, from *angariae*, from post-horses, or from billeting, or from the provision of a ship, or from the collection of poll-tax, apart from soldiers and veterans.'[192] It is, of course, no accident that those who profited most from the system did not suffer the burden it imposed. This text is attributed to a jurist from the time of Constantine, but he goes on to cite rescripts by Vespasian and Hadrian, which shows that the obligations were to some extent in force by the Flavian period. Teachers, doctors, orators, and philosophers had been granted immunity from billeting.[193]

It hardly needs to be said that there existed further exemptions from the duty to provide billeting. There are a number of laws concerning *hospitium* in the *Codex Theodosianus* under the heading 'de metatis'. They deal with various exemptions granted to senators,[194] synagogues,[195] and others.[196] Ordinary persons quartered receive one third of the

[189] tos. Shevi'it v 21 (Vienna MS); cf. 'those who live with you including *akhsania*' (Sifra Behar i 7, ed. Weiss, 106c; cf. y. Demai iii 23b). The Erfurt MS of the Tosefta reads: 'One does not feed billeted troops produce of the Sabbatical year.' If this reading is accepted a contradiction results between the Tosefta and Sifra, see Alon, 704. It seems, however, that we must prefer the version of the Vienna MS and the standard edition; cf. Lieberman, *Tosefta Kifshutah*, ad loc., 560.

[190] Rules are formulated in *Cod. Thod.* viii 6, *de tractoriis*.

[191] See *Cod. Theod.* viii 5. 2, which insists that such warrants must not be issued indiscriminately.

[192] *Digest* L 4. 18. 29: 'sive autem personalium dumtaxat sive etiam civilium munerum immunitas alicui concedatur, neque ab annona neque ab angariis neque a veredo neque ab hospite recipiendo neque a nave neque capitatione, exceptis militibus et veteranis, excusari possunt' (Arcadius Charisius).

[193] Ibid. 30: 'Magistratis, qui civilium munerum vacationem habent, item grammaticis et oratoribus et medicis et philosophis, ne hospitem reciperent, a principibus fuisse immunitatem indultam et divus Vespasianus et divus Hadrianus rescripserunt.'

[194] vii 8. 1 (3 May 361). Exemption from *angaria* and from *hospitium* is combined in the *Digest* L 15. 2: 'Paulus libro primo sententiarum: Angariorum praestatio et recipiendi hospitis necessitas et militi et liberalium artium professoribus inter cetera remissa sunt.'

[195] vii 8. 2 (*Cod. Iust.* i 9. 4) of 6 May 368 or 370 or 373 confirms the immunity of synagogues as regards *hospitium*. On this law, Linder, 116–18.

[196] vii 8. 3 (16 Sept. 384); 8.

house, the part to be assigned by the owner, *illustrissimi* one half.[197] No food for men or their animals is to be demanded and the journey must be swift and continuous.[198] This law seems to relate only to estates in Africa, but it is clear enough that it attempts to restrict a very common abuse, the daily reality of which is obvious from Talmudic sources. Several laws establish that no oil and wood may be demanded.[199] The fact that the injunction was reiterated three times in less than eighty years shows that these laws had only a limited effect. An interesting letter of Honorius to the troops in Spain mentions *hospitium*.[200] The sense of the document appears to be that troops about to be discharged should move elsewhere and behave in accordance with the rules regarding *hospitium* ('hospitiis obsequamini').[201] The hardship caused by the demands of billeting is well known from inscriptions.[202]

Problems of this kind, however serious, engendered by the presence of a substantial army of occupation are not usually touched upon in classical literature. They are of no interest to a Roman senator or knight. A letter allegedly written by Aurelian gives advice how to keep the soldiers under control, listing many offences which, by implication, were considered common among the troops by the author of the *Historia Augusta*: 'Let no one steal another's chicken or touch his sheep. Let no one carry off grapes or thresh out (another man's) corn, let no one exact oil, salt, timber, and let each man be satisfied with his own allowance . .

let them behave properly in their lodgings, let anyone who starts a brawl be flogged.'[203]

Hospitium is mentioned in legal sources, but these merely reflect attempts to put an end to selected abuses of the system and to regulate by law the numerous exemptions claimed by the upper class. To get an impression of life under occupation one needs sources produced by local subjects of a province. These are missing for the western provinces. For Palestine we can turn to Talmudic sources, and for

[197] vii 8. 5 (6 Feb. 398).

[198] vii 10. 2 (12 June 413).

[199] vii 9. 1 (12 Aug. 340); 2 (11 Oct. 340/361); 3 (29 July 393); mattresses: 4 (10 May 416).

[200] E. Demougeot, *Revue historique de droit français et étranger* 36 (1956), 33 f.; A. H. M. Jones, *The Later Roman Empire* (1964), 1106 n. 44. A new edition has now been published by H. S. Sivan, *ZPE* 61 (1985), 273–87.

[201] This is Sivan's interpretation, 274, 282. Demougeot emends the text and interprets it as imperial permission to demand *hospitium* as the need arose.

[202] See above, n. 106, esp. *IGBR* 2236.

[203] SHA, *Aurelian* 7, 5–7: 'nemo pullum alienum rapiat, ovem nemo contigat. uvam nullus auferat, segetem nemo deterat, oleum, salem, lignum nemo exigat, annona sua contentus sit . . . in hospitiis caste se agant, qui litem fecerit vapulet.'

Mesopotamia a good parallel can be found in *The Chronicle of Joshua the Stylite*:[204]

The common people protest 'The Goths ought not to be billeted upon us, but upon the landed proprietors.' At the request of the grandees the *dux Romanus* gives orders what each of these Goths should receive by the month: an *espâda* of oil per month, 200 pounds of wood, a bed and bedding between each two of them. This causes mutiny and the decision is not realised.[205]

All these taxes and levies by no means replaced the regular taxes that are also mentioned in Talmudic sources, *tributum capitis* and *tributum soli*. It is not certain when the special Jewish tax instituted by Vespasian was abolished.[206] Furthermore, several taxes are mentioned in Talmudic sources which cannot be identified with certainty but may in part be identical with the well-known taxes.[207]

A form of taxation that was originally military in nature but developed into an extraordinary supplementary income tax is the payment of gold crowns.[208] It is mentioned on several occasions in sources connected with the times of Rabbi Judah Hanassi (late second, early third centuries). For instance:

As crown-tax was imposed on the people of Tiberias they came to Rabbi (Judah Hanassi) and said to him: Let the sages pay their share. He refused. They said: (then) we shall run away. He said: do so. Half of them ran away. They remitted half the sum demanded. The remaining half came to Rabbi and said: let the sages pay their share. He refused. They said: we shall run away. He said: do so. They all ran away except one fuller. The money was demanded of him and he ran away. The demand for crown-tax was dropped.[209]

Here, as elsewhere in connection with *aurum coronarium*, Rabbi Judah Hanassi appears as the man responsible for the levyng of the tax: in the case cited he had to decide whether sages had to pay part of the tax; on another occasion he had to determine the responsibility of the local

---

[204] *The Chronicle of Joshua the Stylite, Composed in Syriac* AD *507*, text and trans. by W. Wright (1882), 93.

[205] Cf. 95 (AD 505–6): in preparation for an expedition the army was stationed at Edessa; it was also quartered in villages and convents. Cf. 39, 66, 82, 93–6.

[206] For the Jewish tax, V. Tcherikover, A. Fuks, and M. Stern, *Corpum Papyrorum Judaicorum* (1957–64), i 80–8; ii 111–16, 119–36, 204–8. See also Schürer, *History*, iii 1 122 f.

[207] See e.g. y. Pe'ah i 15b: Rabbi Abba said: (that means) if you give alms out of your own pocket (voluntarily) the Lord blessed be he will protect you against 'pissim', 'zimayot', *tributum capitis*, and *annona*. y. Pe'ah i 16a: the *bouleutai* of Sepphoris had 'tzumut' (a meeting for public work?).

[208] On crown gold in general, *Cod. Theod.* xii 13; Millar, *Emperor* 140–2.

[209] b. Bava Batra 8a. S. Safrai attempts to identify the events with the concessions made by Severus Alexander in 222: *Proceedings of the Sixth World Congress of Jewish Studies*, ii (Jerusalem 1975), 56 f.

authorities in levying it.[210] Another element in this case worthy of notice is the disappearance *en masse* of those who could not pay their taxes. Fleeing the tax collectors was common in Palestine as elsewhere in the third century. It is described in legendary form in several Talmudic sources.[211] An immediate parallel is an inscription from Scaptopara in Thrace which cites a petition from the villagers regarding *hospitium* and the exaction of supplies. They threaten to flee unless an imperial decree granting exemption from these liturgies is upheld.[212] They emphasize the losses in income which the *fiscus* suffered from the disappearance of villagers.

A law of the early fifth century sadly states: 'The necessities of an exhausted treasury require the payment of commutation money for the purchase of recruits and horses.'[213]

Compulsory conscription and the payment of money for exemption from conscription (*tironia, aurum tironicium, adaeratio*), known from a few sources to have existed elsewhere as early as the third century, appear to be mentioned in Talmudic sources, though the term itself is not used here.[214] For instance:

And Tidal king of Goyim (Gen. 14: 1)—that is the wicked kingdom which levies *tironia* from all the nations of the world.[215]

There is a case of a man who conscripted recruits. A man came to conscript someone's son. He said: look at my son, what a fellow, what a hero, how tall he is. His mother too said: look at our son, how tall he is. The other answered: in

---

[210] b. Bava Batra 143a; y. Yoma i 39a. It is of interest that Rabbi Judah Nesi'ah, grandson of Rabbi Judah Hanassi, did not exempt the sages from participation in the costs of building the town wall of Tiberias (b. Bava Batra 7b–8a). This is not so much a change in the image of the Patriarch as a reflection of the changed circumstances in the third-century crisis.

[211] e.g. y. Shevi'it ix 38d (the inhabitants of Caesarea Paneas); cf. Lieberman, *JQR*, 350–2. For Egypt cf. Rostovtzeff, *Roman Empire*, 484 f., 487 f. *P. Oxy.* 1414. 19 ff., cited by Rostovtzeff, forms a good parallel for the Talmudic source cited here.

[212] Mihailov, *IGBR* iv no. 2236, 11. 59–66, 91–3 (AD 238) and cf. his comments on p. 212. Scaptopara was a village which lay between two military bases and possessed warm baths. The governor and the procurator were entitled to hospitality, but many soldiers also demanded it. See also Abbott and Johnson, no. 142: villagers on an imperial estate threaten to seek protection against exactions by taking refuge on private estates. Great landowners were able to protect their tenants better than the emperor.

[213] *Cod. Theod.* xi 18 (15 Feb. 409; 16 Feb. 412).

[214] For compulsory conscription or the '*synteleia tironon*', M. Rostovtzeff, *JRS* 8 (1918), 26–33. There is not much evidence: a persuasive reading of the famous inscription from Pizus in Thrace and an undated inscription from Lydia, which Rostovtzeff assigns to the third century. For the inscription from Pizus, Mihailov, *IGBR* iii, no. 1689, pp. 102–25, esp. l. 61 with comments on p. 120. The troops concerned were not regular forces but served as local policemen and guards. It goes without saying that the Romans always had drawn great numbers of recruits from newly conquered peoples, thus reinforcing their army and weakening the peoples concerned. This is explicitly stated by Cicero, *Pro Fonteio* 5. 13, in the case of newly subdued Gauls.

[215] Genesis Rabbah xli 4, ed. Theodor-Albeck, p. 409 and parallel passages.

your eyes he is a hero and he is tall. I do not know. Let us see whether he is tall. They measured and he proved to be small and was rejected.[216]

From these *midrashim* it is clear that conscription was not unknown, but in themselves they do not prove that it existed in Palestine. A clear indication may be found in the following passage:

In the days of Rabbi Mana, there was a *numerus* in Sepphoris and their (the Sepphoreans') sons were pledged to them (to the *numerus*). When it was time for them to leave, Rabbi Mana declared the law in accordance with Rabbi Immi: He said, I am not in agreement with him but (I have ruled thus) for the sake of the Sepphoreans whose sons will not be forfeited.[217]

Although the term *tironia* is not used the passage shows that the institution as such existed, at least from the days of Rabbi Mana of the fifth generation of Palestinian *amoraim*, that is the second half of the fourth century. It is also clear that, like other provincials, the Jews preferred to pay rather than have their sons conscripted. In the words of Ammianus: 'the provincials are pleased to give gold instead of their bodies, a prospect which has several times endangered the Roman state.'[218]

When Valens in 376 allowed great numbers of Goths to settle in Thrace he was, according to Ammianus, motivated in part by the expectation that the Goths would furnish numerous recruits for the army. This would then allow the government to grant paid exemptions in the provinces:[219] '. . . the good fortune which unexpectedly offered him so many recruits drawn from the ends of the earth. Combining his own with the foreign troops he would have an invincible army. Also, a vast amount of gold would accrue to the treasury instead of the reinforcements sent annually by each province.' This led, in fact, to the disaster at Hadrianopolis. The church historian Socrates (*c.*380–450) accuses Valens of neglecting the recruitment of the army in his eagerness to receive payment instead.[220] The collection of such pay-

---

[216] Aggadat Genesis xl 4, ed. Buber, p. 82. This would have been an unusual case where the parents in fact wanted the son to be accepted for army service.

[217] y. Pesahim iv 31b; trans. S. S. Miller, *Studies in the History and Traditions of Sepphoris* (1984). The halakhic context is that in such a case Rabbi Mana permitted the people of Sepphoris to sell their houses even if they were occupied by tenants.

[218] xix 11. 7, referring to the reign of Constantine: 'aurum quippe gratanter provinciales pro corporibus dabunt, quae spes rem Romanam aliquotiens aggravavit.'

[219] xxxi 4. 4: '. . . fortunam principis . . . quae ex ultimis terris tot tirocinia trahens, ei nec opinanti offerret, ut collatis in unum suis et alienigenis viribus, invictum haberet exercitum, et pro militari supplemento, quod provinciatim annuum pendebatur, thesauris accederet auri cumulus magnus.'

[220] *HE* iv 34 (*PG* lxvii, cols. 553, 556) and cf. Rostovtzeff, *JRS*, 27 f.

ment is listed among the compulsory public services in the fourth century.[221]

It is not to be assumed, however, that compulsory recruitment without paid exemption no longer existed in the fourth century. The Abinnaeus archive (*c.* AD 342) provides an example of a conflict between a local council in Egypt and an army unit which collected recruits.[222] In the later Byzantine period hereditary conscription seems to have been retained only for the *limitanei*, to judge from the absence of references in the sources, including the Justinian Code.[223] In their case (the references derive from Egypt) it seems that service was seen as a privilege rather than an obligation.[224]

PROPAGANDA

In a chapter on the army and civilians it may be of interest to consider certain elements of propaganda which are familiar to every student of the principate. This is not the place to deal with imperial propaganda at a literary level, nor with propaganda in the city of Rome,[225] but only with that to which the inhabitants of the provinces were exposed. This consisted of inscriptions and coinage. Among these I shall concentrate on the most ubiquitous category of inscriptions, those on milestones. It is impossible to estimate the number of inscribed milestones that were originally to be seen along the roads of a province, but the sheer repetitiveness of the texts leads one to ask what was the purpose of the system. For whom were these texts set up?

It cannot be claimed that the milestones were mere utilitarian objects, for their distribution shows curious patterns. In the eastern provinces there are many milestones in the settled regions, but hardly any in the desert, as observed in Chapter III. If they had been set up to meet a practical need this is where they ought to have been. The Roman penetration of the desert began relatively late and intensified under the tetrarchy. Since no milestones were set up after Constantine this may

---

[221] *Cod. Theod.* xi 16. 18 (5 July 390). It is also mentioned in the *Digest*, L 4. 18. 3, together with other personal obligations: the provision of horses or other animals, transport duty, taxation in money, *annona*, or the supply of clothes.

[222] Bell, *The Abinnaeus Archive*, no. 18, pp. 62 f.

[223] See *Cod. Iust.* xii 47. 1. 2; cf. J. F. Haldon, *Recruitment and Conscription in the Byzantine Army, c.550–950* (1979), 20–408.

[224] As observed by Jones, *Later Roman Empire*, i 669 with n. 146.

[225] See in general J. B. Campbell, 120–56, on imperial military honours and the importance of military propaganda; on the period of Septimius Severus, Z. Rubin, *Civil-War Propaganda and Historiography*.

account for their absence along roads that were not constructed until that period. But they are also scarce along roads that were first laid out in the early second century. Almost none are found along the Trajanic road, south of Petra. No inscribed milestones have been found in the arid Jordan Valley along the Scythopolis–Jericho road, south of the military site of Tel Shalem. On the other hand there is a remarkable concentration of stones in certain spots, often as many as five or six of them on any one mile-station. A comparable phenomenon is encountered elsewhere: only one milestone has been found in Scotland, and only three in the non-urbanized eastern part of Anatolia.

The conclusion must be that counting miles was, or became, a secondary issue. If the indication of distance was not the primary motive, the other element, the imperial titulature, must have been important. We must ask then who were the target of this exercise in imperial propaganda. It is easy to assume that it was the inhabitants of the provinces who were supposed to be impressed by the repetitive appearance of the names and titles of the ruler along the highways. This assumption presupposes that the provincial authorities cared what the inhabitants of the provinces thought. Conversely, if it could be proved that this kind of propaganda was aimed at them it would be clear that the authorities did indeed attach importance to the opinion of literate subjects of the provinces.

As a matter of fact, however, it can be shown that, in the eastern provinces at least, the subjects of the provinces were considered irrelevant. The imperial titulature on milestones is invariably in Latin. This part of the milestone-text is bilingual on only one milestone in Judaea (out of about 150).[226] Elsewhere Greek is extremely rare.[227] In Syria I do not know of any instances. In Arabia secondary inscriptions of Julian are occasionally found in Greek.[228] On the other hand, in Judaea, Syria, and Arabia, the indication of distance appears regularly in Greek as well as Latin, or even Greek only from the later second century onward.[229] In the eastern provinces the population spoke Aramaic or another Semitic language and Greek. If texts were written in Latin they were not meant to be read by the provincials, but by the

---

[226] See Isaac and Roll, 73, no. 10.

[227] See e.g. the bilingual stone which marks the construction of the Via Egnatia in the Republican period, perhaps 2nd cent. BC: C. Romiopoulou, *BCH* 98 (1974), 813–16 and figs. 1–2; P. Collart, *BCH* 100 (1976), 182. However, in southern and south-western Asia Minor Greek milestone texts are found, e.g. D. French, *Epigraphica Anatolica* 8 (1986), 86. This was an urbanized area with few troops.

[228] e.g. *CIL* iii 14149. 41 ff.; P. Thomsen, *ZDPV* 40 (1917), 126a 2, etc.; 127a 2, etc.

[229] Isaac, *PEQ* 110 (1978), 57–9.

army. The language of inscriptions is also discussed below, in Chapter VII. Here it will suffice to note that Latin was used on private inscriptions by soldiers and their relatives and by the citizens of Roman veteran colonies, at least until the fourth century. Official inscriptions are in Latin when connected with the imperial authorities and the army. Municipal inscriptions are usually in Greek.

It is therefore clear that those meant to read the imperial titulature on milestones were the army, the most substantial group of users of Latin in these provinces and those by whom and for whom the roads were constructed in the first place. This would be a reasonable assumption, even without conclusive evidence, since the position of the emperor depended on the loyalty of the troops. His popularity with the inhabitants of the provinces, on the other hand, was irrelevant. No elections were held in the empire, and imperial propaganda must therefore be understood against the background of monarchic rule.

But were the soldiers genuinely the target of this kind of propaganda or only ostensibly so? Are these texts to be compared with the slogans proclaiming the beauty of communist rule to Soviet factory workers? There it is not the factory workers who are the target of propaganda, but the party apparatus which must be convinced of the loyalty of the factory management. Similarly it is conceivable that the imperial titulature appeared on milestones to convince the monarch and his entourage of the loyalty of the provincial governor and his army.[230] In support of this hypothesis—it cannot be more—it may be pointed out that, as in Judaea, the first milestone series in Britain and in Pannonia were set up in the reign of Hadrian, who was the first emperor since Claudius to visit Britain,[231] and who apparently visited Pannonia in 118 and 124.[232] We may also note that the governor is often mentioned on milestones while army units appear but rarely.[233] Coups were organized by generals, not by army units. Only in times of severe crisis did the loyalty of individual legions become an issue, as for instance in the war between Severus and Niger.

[230] See Pekáry, *Untersuchungen*, 16–22, 'Zum Dedikationscharakter der Meilensteine'. He goes too far when he asserts that the text on milestones was always checked by the provincial governor and sent to the emperor for approval. See the arguments by I. König, *Chiron* 3 (1973), 419–27. Many of the texts I have seen were edited by persons without an elementary knowledge of Latin grammar and spelling.

[231] For the milestones, R. S. Collingwood and R. P. Wright, *The Roman Inscriptions of Britain*, i (1965), nos. 2244, 2265, 2272, cf. J. P. Sedgley, *The Roman Milestones of Britain* (1975), 2. For Britain under Hadrian, S. Frere, *Britannia* (1967), ch. 7.

[232] For Hadrian's visits, W. Weber, *Untersuchungen zur Geschichte des Kaisers Hadrianus* (1907), 71–6, 153–5. For the earliest milestones, A. Mócsy, *Pannonia and Upper Moesia* (1974), 108 f.; for military construction work under Hadrian, ibid. 104–11.

[233] A recent exception: French, *Epigraphica Anatolica*, 87.

This should not be taken as an indication that the milestones were set up without any accompanying road-construction, for in the three provinces mentioned there is good evidence of major military building projects. The milestones that appear under Hadrian should be seen as declarations of loyalty by the army to an emperor who had an interest in military construction of which road building was an aspect, who travelled much in the provinces, and was fond of declarations of loyalty.

The special character of imperial propaganda as declarations of loyalty on the occasion of imperial visits is interestingly demonstrated by finds at Tel Shalem in the Valley of Beth Shean.[234] As already observed, the milestones on the Scythopolis–Jericho road do not go beyond this military site and the earliest stones date to 129, the year of Hadrian's visit to the area. At the site of the fort itself parts of a splendid bronze statue of the emperor have been found.[235] Fragments of a very large monumental inscription bearing Hadrian's titles were discovered nearby.[236] It is not clear from what kind of building it derives, whether from the main entrance to the camp, the *principia*, or from a triumphal arch, such as was set up for Hadrian at Gerasa in 130.[237]

To sum up, milestones and other similar military inscriptions must be seen as propaganda in an autocratic environment. Often they are not what they seem to be, helpful markers for travellers, but an exercise in political control. In a monarchical system the mechanical repetition of declarations of loyalty is not really meant to persuade the masses to remain loyal. They are signals on the part of commanders to their superiors that the system functions all right. Such signals naturally were expected and demanded by monarchs who would usually not be aware of an attempt at usurpation before it was well under way.

In the provinces with which this book is concerned later series of milestones were set up in connecton with special events: imperial visits, major eastern campaigns, or civil wars that called for declarations of loyalty. The latter will not have entailed actual work carried out. The propaganda element did not change and the milestones show us something of its mechanical character. In editing the text each province followed its own standard. In Syria and Arabia the provincial governor is usually mentioned both before and after the reign of Hadrian, but not on Hadrianic stones. In Judaea, where the first *milliaria* belong to the

---

[234] See Appendix I.

[235] G. Foerster, *Qadmoniot* 7 (1975), 38–40 (in Hebrew); *'Atiqot* 17 (1985), 139–60; *Israel Museum News* 16 (1980), 107–10. For an inscription identifying the unit based there as a vexillation of VI Ferrata, N. Tzori, *IEJ* 21 (1971), 53 f.

[236] Reported so far only in the daily press. I am grateful to Dr G. Foerster for information.

[237] C. H. Kraeling, *Gerasa: City of the Decapolis* (1938), plan IV and inscr. no. 58.

reign of Hadrian, the governor is missing on these and all subsequent series. The absence under Hadrian suggests a common plan for all three provinces. The subsequent omission in Judaea and the return to previous practice elsewhere is best explained as a local variation.[238]

As already observed, milestones are very often found in extraordinary numbers on specific stations, or not at all. This is best explained by the assumption that those responsible simply added stones where they saw some already and disregarded mile-stations where none were visible. This is evidence of a careless, mechanical procedure. Also the stones are very often carelessly cut, and the inscriptions contain numerous mistakes and are produced in a crude hand without traced guidelines, so that the whole inscription is lopsided. There is nothing there to suggest that this is the work of citizens who loved their ruler. They are the symptoms of a system that makes any official suspect who does not produce mechanical declarations of obedience.

A change in the formula of the stones deserves a note: before the reign of Severus the 'republican' elements in the emperor's titulature are never missing.[239] In 198 for the first time the tribunician power is not mentioned, while on later series the military *cognomina* always appear and the tribunician power infrequently. This may be taken to be a reflection of the attitude of the monarch himself and his priorities. The change in emphasis would not have occurred without his permission and it was there for all to see.[240] It is a direct reflection of the words of advice to his sons, attributed to Severus by Cassius Dio: 'Be united, enrich the soldiers, and despise all the others'.[241]

There is no reason to assume there was an elaborate civil service involved. At first the army was responsible—which explains the existence of common features in different provinces. Probably from the time of Septimius Severus onward cities carried out the work, as observed above. Various features of milestones in Judaea suffice to prove this, such as mistakes found in common on stones of different roads in the vicinity of a city.[242] The fact that the indication of distance is given in Greek as well as in Latin, or in Greek only, shows that this part of the text was produced by and for the townspeople.[243] The imperial titulature, however, appeared in Latin as before, since the

---

[238] For the evidence, Isaac, *PEQ* 110 (1978), 56 f. I suspect I over-interpreted the phenomenon in that article.

[239] The exception which confirms the rule: Isaac and Roll, *JRS* 66 (1976), 14; cf. *PEQ*, 52 f.

[240] On the military *cognomina* of the emperor see J. B. Campbell, 128–33.

[241] lxxvi 15. 2: ὁμονοεῖτε, τοὺς στρατιώτας πλουτίζετε, τῶν ἄλλων πάντων καταφρονεῖτε.

[242] Isaac and Roll, *Roman Roads*, i 76, 93 f.

[243] For *capita viarum* on Judaean milestones, Isaac, *PEQ*, 57–9.

cities set up the stones for the benefit of the army. It is possible, though there is no proof of this at all, that the indication of distance on milestones corresponds to the assignation of duties concerning road repair in the period which also saw the institution of the *annona militaris* as a permanent feature, the creation of the *Itineraria*, and the reorganization of the imperial post.[244]

CONCLUSION

We have seen in this chapter that the relation between the army and civilians in the eastern frontier provinces was in many respects different from that in other areas. The permanent presence of army units in cities hardly featured in the western provinces because there was less urbanization there—leaving aside the city of Rome itself, where units were indeed stationed,[245] and a few other centres, such as Carthage, from where corn was shipped to Italy, Pozzuoli and Ostia, where it arrived, and Lyons.[246] The presence of troops in a city was undesirable according to all sources, but it was unavoidable because the population of large cities, often hostile, could not otherwise be kept under control. Yet the very presence of the soldiers engendered serious tensions which occasionally caused rioting and these invariably resulted in massacres. Billeting in cities was bad for discipline—there is no reason to doubt the veracity of the sources on this point—and made it very hard to use such units for service in war; even the attempt to do so could cause a mutiny. It is also clear that the system could and did result in serious corruption, best attested in Libanius' oration on protection rackets, but also detectable in Talmudic sources.

Talmudic sources also give a good impression of the reality of the taxes imposed for the benefit of the troops. They confirm, what was to be expected anyway, that the many laws which attempted to regulate and moderate the demands made upon civilians were not very effective. It is clear that the levies imposed became hard to bear, particularly during the third-century crisis. At that time, even more than before, the

[244] Isaac, *PEQ*, 59; for the connection between road-repair and the imperial post, Pekáry, *Untersuchungen*, 146; for the *annona militaris* and *itineraria*, G. Rickman, *Roman Granaries and Storage Buildings* (1971), ch. viii, esp. 280 f. It is my impression that in Arabia and Judaea the distances were usually counted from one city to the next without change in the middle. In other words: milestones on the road from A to B would count from A till the road reached B on one series. A later series might then count from B all the way to A. However, more evidence is needed. It is hard to verify this, for changes were made on milestones in antiquity.

[245] For a brief survey, L. Keppie, *The Making of the Roman Army* (1984), 153 f.

[246] Ibid. 188 f.

monarchy depended on the support of the army, and all measures to protect the civilians in the military provinces were necessarily futile. There was no authority with the power to impose such measures.

The dependency of the monarchy on the loyalty of the army is, of course, well known. It is, however, strikingly illustrated by the milestones which, in the eastern provinces, were clearly set up for the benefit of the army, at first by the army and later by the local authorities, perhaps as part of the system regulating the various services the civilians were obliged to render officials and army personnel. They were inscribed with proclamations of loyalty toward the emperor in Latin and set up so as to be visible where there were troops to see them, sometimes where an emperor and his court might pass. The latest of such inscriptions date to the reign of Constantine, presumably because in the fourth century the belief in such slogans evaporated.

VII

THE MILITARY FUNCTION OF ROMAN VETERAN COLONIES

IT is clearly of interest to determine what was the function of veteran colonies, what was the motive for their establishment, and what was their share in the transformation of a defeated people into subjects of a Roman province. The economic, social, and cultural aspects often discussed do not concern us here.[1] The impact on Rome and Italy of the removal of numerous citizens and their settlement elsewhere was of course significant, but this is not a topic to be considered in a work which deals with the provinces. And since we are interested specifically in the eastern parts of the empire hopes of 'Romanization' can be disregarded, for this was not an aim that could have been contemplated in earnest by Roman policy-makers in the East. There were not very many such foundations there, but those that existed have been credited with an important military function; and the question for us is whether this is correct. The subject, however, cannot be discussed in isolation, and something will therefore have to be said of Roman colonies in other regions and other periods than those which form the subject proper of this book.

General Characteristics

The veteran colonies of Augustus, we are told in the *Cambridge Ancient History*, represented 'a carefully planned scheme, whereby not only were the claims of the soldiers met but mountainous and wilder regions such as Western Spain or Pisidia could be guarded and held in check.'[2] The veteran colonies established at Berytus and Heliopolis were 'to act as garrisons and assist in holding the Lebanon tribes in check.'[3] This echoes the opinion expressed by A. H. M. Jones in a well-known article where he speaks of the Ituraean country as 'being now securely

---

[1] For Caesar's colonizing, Z. Yavetz, *Julius Caesar and His Public Image* (1983), 143–50.
[2] M. P. Charlesworth, *CAH* x (1934), 120.
[3] J. G. C. Anderson, ibid. 281 f.

garrisoned by two veteran colonies whose combined territory cut it into two.'[4] In a more recent paper J.-P. Rey-Coquais refers to an 'axe de pénétration de la Méditerranée vers la Syrie intérieure, qui coupait en deux les pays ituréens encore dangereusement insoumis.'[5]

E. T. Salmon calls the Augustan colonies 'bulwarks of empire' and gives as examples Augusta Taurinorum and Augusta Praetoria: '. . . strategically placed to control the passes through the western Alps; and they helped Eporedia to keep the recently subjugated tribes of Piedmont in check.'[6]

All these writers envisage the function of the veteran colonies as basically defensive: they were established near but not in mountainous and wilder regions on the frontiers of the empire and defended it against attacks, raids, or invasions by hostile and incompletely subjugated peoples. However, Salmon's claim that mountain passes were controlled by the colonies presumably entails more than just static defence, since one does not control a pass merely by sitting in the plain nearby and watching the mountains from below. Some form of regular patrol or permanent presence along the route is needed.

None of these works attempts to explain how and by what means these veteran colonies would perform such far-reaching strategic functions. Vittinghoff tried to say a little more: 'the veteran colonies were very significant in terms of political power . . . From the time of Sulla retired veterans were usually settled *en bloc* with their tribunes and centurions and thus they formed in the first years of the existence of a new colony a reserve unit that could be called up immediately in case of need.'[7] Bowersock expressed himself in similar terms: 'veteran colonies constituted *ad hoc* garrisons . . . Their function is plain. Once established in the colonies, the veterans were organized and drilled in case their service should one day be needed'.[8] 'The garrison colonies' he concludes, 'represent prophylactic . . . measures.'[9] Luttwak writes:

The colonies were a second instrument of strategic control. . . . Not primarily intended as agencies of Romanization, the colonies were islands of direct

[4] 'The Urbanization of the Ituraean Principality', *JRS* 21 (1931), 267.

[5] *JRS* 68 (1978), 51. All this stands in clear contrast to Mommsen's earlier opinion: 'Die wenigen Kolonien welche hier angelegt worden sind, wie unter Augustus Berytus und wahrscheinlich auch Heliopolis, haben keinen anderen Zweck gehabt als die nach Makedonien geführten, nehmlich die Unterbringung der Veteranen' (*Römische Geschichte*, v 450).

[6] *Roman Colonization under the Republic* (1969), 144. Mommsen clearly distinguished between the military campaign that resulted in the subjugation of the Salassi and the foundation of Augusta Praetoria. For the latter he did not claim more than that it served as a foothold controlling the Little St Bernard pass (v 18); cf. R. A. van Royen, *Talanta* 5 (1973), 66 f.

[7] F. Vittinghoff, *Römische Kolonisation und Bürgerrechtspolitik unter Caesar und Augustus* (1952), 52.

[8] G. W. Bowersock, *Augustus and the Greek World* (1965), 69 f.

[9] Ibid. 71. Similar views are to be found in an article on the function of the colonies of

Roman control in an empire still in part hegemonic . . . Whether located in provincial or client-state territory, the colonies provided secure observation and control bases. Their citizens were, in effect, a ready-made militia of ex-soldiers and soldiers' sons who could defend their home towns in the event of an attack and hold out until imperial forces could arrive on the scene.[10]

The theory put forward by Vittinghoff and Bowersock implies a rather different view from the others we have cited. In this view the veterans were not so much an actual defence force as a strategic reserve to be called up in case of emergency. Their military function, in other words, would remain dormant in peace-time and they would play a military role only in times of war. Also, it was short-lived. As the veterans grew old and died the settlement would cease to be a garrison colony, for the next generation would not be born as veterans. The sons of the veterans might join the army and return after twenty-five years as retired veterans, but that would be a different matter.

In the following pages it will be argued that Roman colonies did not in fact function in the way modern scholars claim: they were not meant to defend the empire at times of large-scale hostilities, and they did not control large areas or tribes or routes beyond their territorial boundaries.

Cicero and Tacitus on Cremona and Placentia

Salmon's description of the colonies founded by Augustus as 'bulwarks of Empire' is clearly an echo of the term *propugnaculum* used by Cicero and Tacitus to describe older citizen colonies, not settled with veterans.[11] Tacitus says of Cremona that it was founded in 218 BC '. . . as a *propugnaculum*, a bulwark against the Cisalpine Gauls or any other force which might cross the Alps'. Cicero states in general: 'Our ancestors . . . established colonies on such suitable sites to ward off danger that they seemed to be not just towns of Italy but bulwarks of Empire.' Unlike many modern authors Cicero was aware that he was using a metaphor.

These statements might indeed seem to be clear evidence that republican colonies were founded in order to defend the empire against attack by foreigners. It must be noted, however, that they were made

---

Augusta Raurica and Julia Equestris in Gaul: K. Kraft, *Jb RGZM* 4 (1957), 82–95. For a dissenting view, J. C. Mann, *Legionary Recruitment and Veteran Settlement during the Principate* (1983), 8. While emphasizing the military character of the settlements he concluded that the founding of the Caesarian and Augustan colonies is to be attributed to the practical necessities of the period, and to economic considerations, rather than to military planning.

[10] E. Luttwak, *The Grand Strategy of the Roman Empire* (1976), 19.
[11] Tacitus, *Hist.* iii 34; Cicero, *de lege agraria*, ii 27. 73.

centuries after the foundations took place. They reflect an attitude, often encountered, that tends to view the expansion of an empire and the consolidation of recent gains as defence of the homeland. Like readers of the modern press, historians should not accept without critical judgement the explanations of foreign conquest given (in a later period) by those with an interest in the process.

In fact, Mommsen has shown that Cremona was by no means a *propugnaculum* in Tacitus' sense. Founded in the territory of the Insubres four years after their defeat at Clastidium in 222 BC,[12] it was clearly established to secure and take advantage of land confiscated from them. When Cremona and her sister colony Placentia were established they were isolated outposts, *propugnacula* only in the sense that their hinterland, the Emilia, was not yet incorporated.[13] The colonies were incapable of defending themselves, let alone protecting the South against invaders, as became clear when the Boii and Insubres, angered by the land confiscations, attacked the new foundations.[14] In 206 ambassadors of the Cremonenses and Placentini complained 'that their territory was being raided and laid waste by neighbouring Gauls and that now they had sparsely peopled cities and land desolated and deserted'. The colonies clearly needed active support from Rome which, however, was not forthcoming until the eighties of the second century.[15]

Cicero uses the term *propugnaculum* again in his *Pro Fonteio*, delivered some time after 70 BC, in referring to Narbo Martius in Gaul.[16] He describes the colony as a 'guard post of the Roman people and a bulwark established against these peoples (i.e. the Gauls)', but the context exposes these phrases as so much hot air. The Gauls in the region had been subdued by the Roman army in a series of strenuous campaigns, followed by confiscations, evictions, compulsory recruit-

[12] Comment on *CIL* V 1, p. 413.

[13] Cf. W. Harris, *War and Imperialism in Republican Rome* (1979), 225, on the foundation of Placentia and Bononia.

[14] Polybius iii 40; Livy xxi 25; xxxi 10; xxxiv 56.

[15] Another outpost founded not for purposes of defence, but to occupy lands hitherto beyond the sphere of Roman control was Aquileia (181 BC): Livy xliii 1. Livy indicates that the main purpose of this venture was the prevention of immigration by peaceful Gauls who did not in fact threaten Roman territory. Another point of interest is the slow development of the colony, which, like Cremona and Aquileia, had to ask for support from Rome (in 171 and 169). Note further the debate on the original purpose of the eight Italian coastal colonies founded in 194 BC. While it has been claimed that they had been founded in anticipation of a possible Syrian invasion, Harris, 221, argues that they were intended to secure and take advantage of land confiscated from Italian supporters of Hannibal.

[16] 5. 13: 'Narbo Martius, colonias nostrorum civium, specula populi Romani ac propugnaculum istis ipsis nationibus oppositum et obiectum . . .'

ment on a large scale, and harsh impositions. The region was so full of Roman citizens that no Gaul could transact any business without the involvement of a Roman citizen. Fonteius was accused of extortion by Gauls, while citizens from Massilia and Narbo and Romans resident in the province acted as witnesses for the defence. Cicero's argument is that the testimony of barbarian Gauls should not be accepted against that of Roman citizens.

Caesar and Augustus

Our argument may be further clarified by considering a number of other colonies, rather arbitrarily selected, of the period of Caesar and Augustus, and afterwards till the reign of Hadrian. First, however, a general observation. Under the republic Rome had no professional standing army, but only a citizens' militia supported by troops from allies and subject states. The citizen colonies were normally exempt from military duty—except in case of extraordinary emergency—presumably because they were responsible for local security.[17] Latin colonies, being formally independent communities, had their own armies.[18] In other words, troops from colonies were not part of the regular levy that made up the Roman army and could not be counted upon except in time of extraordinary need. Under the principate Rome did have a professional standing army, in which the legionaries had to serve twenty-five years. It was not an army of reservists, and veterans were recalled into service only in times of emergency, during civil wars or, for instance, the Illyrian rebellion of AD 6 when Italy was threatened.[19]

The possibility of recalling retired soldiers into service was not therefore an important consideration in the organization of veteran colonies, as has been assumed. After all, soldiers discharged in their forties do not remain recallable for long even today, let alone in the Roman period!

Julia Equestris and Augusta Raurica in Gaul

The function of the Caesarian colonies Julia Equestris (Nyon) and

---

[17] Livy xxvii 38. 5; xxxvi 3. 4–6; cf. the *Lex Ursonensis* 103.

[18] G. Tibiletti, *Athenaeum* 28 (1950), 222–4.

[19] In 43 BC Caesar's veterans were recalled. See L. Keppie, *The Making of the Roman Army, From Republic to Empire* (1984), 118, 121 f.; *Colonisation and Veteran Settlement in Italy, 47–14 BC* (1983), 24 f.; G. Walser, *Der Briefwechsel des L. Munatius Plancus mit Cicero* (1957), nos. vii, xii, xxv. For the Pannonian revolt in AD 6, Velleius ii 110. 1. For the recall of veterans in 69, Tacitus, *Hist* ii 82. 1. For the exemptions specified in the Lex Ursonensis, *CIL* i 2. 594, cf. Cicero, *Phil.* v 19. 53, and see A. N. Sherwin-White, *The Roman Citizenship* ([2]1973), 82 f.

Augusta Raurica (Augst) has been the subject of extensive debate.[20] Together with contemporary Lyons, they have been thought to be key positions guarding the road that linked the Rhine with the Rhône and hence Gaul with Italy.[21] Vittinghoff took this theory one step further and argued that the colonies formed a line defending Italy against Gaul.[22] In Kraft's view these notions are to be rejected on geographical and historical grounds: Raurica and Equestris were sited so as to block the passages from the Swiss plain to Gaul and this would render impossible any recurrence of the Helvetian attempt to migrate into Gaul.

The trouble with all these theories is that they cannot be proved. Neither Germans nor Helvetians invaded Gaul or Italy in the period after the foundation of the colonies, and it is impossible to prove that invasions would have taken place if the colonies had not been there.

Of course we do not know whether the Helvetians were capable—or seemed to be capable—of attempting large-scale migrations after Caesar had defeated them. Kraft's theory springs from the common a priori assumption that the Romans must have been organizing for defence at times when, in fact, they were consolidating recent gains and, presumably, preparing for further advance. Moreover, it fails to take into account the essential difference between major hostilities in a full-scale war and police duties in peace-time. While it is unthinkable that a veteran colony could prevent a whole tribe from migrating, it is conceivable that it could carry out modest police duties on their own territory.[23]

The citizens of Lyons once claimed to be 'a Roman colony and (hence) part of the army'.[24] This, however, was clearly a case of special pleading. The story as told by Tacitus makes it clear that the colonists wanted to exploit their identification with the army in order to engage the support of soldiers against their neighbours who had no colonial

[20] C. Jullian, *Histoire de la Gaule*, v 88 n. 1; F. Stähelin, *Die Schweiz in römischer Zeit* (³1948), 95 f., 102; Vittinghoff, 69; W. Schleiermacher, *Jb RGZM* 2 (1955), 245–52; K. Kraft, *Jb RGZM* 4 (1957), 81–95.

[21] Thus Jullian, Stähelin and Schleiermacher.

[22] 'Die caesarischen Kolonien der Narbonensis und Galliens sperrten in einer verlängerten Mittelmeer – Rhone – Rheinlinie die drei Gallien von Italien ab.' (Vittinghoff, loc. cit.).

[23] As pointed out by van Berchem, that is the implication of the inscription from Equestris which mentions a *praefectus arcendis latrociniis*, an officer in charge of the suppression of brigandage: *CIL* xiii 5010: 'C. Lucconi Cor(nelia) Tetrici, praefecti pro duoviro, duoviri bis flaminis Augusti.' Cf. D. van Berchem, 'Nyon et son "praefectus arcendis latrociniis"', in *Les routes et l'histoire* (1982), 47–53.

[24] Tacitus, *Hist.* i 65. The colony was founded in 43 BC, cf. CIL x 6087. Dio lxvi 50 says this was a grant of colonial status to men whom the Allobroges had driven out of Vienna.

status. Like Aelia Capitolina, discussed below, Lyons was a colony where an army unit was permanently based.[25]

Camulodunum

Next, Camulodunum (Colchester) in Essex. When troops were transferred westward in 49 a veteran colony was founded, according to Tacitus, in order to make it possible for the legion based there among the Trinovantes to be moved to South Wales where it might help in subduing the Silures.[26] The colony was thus founded with a dual purpose: 'as an aid against rebellion and in order to familiarize the allies with their legal duties.'[27] Tacitus states that a strong body of veterans was installed on expropriated land and describes vividly the procedure: the veterans ejected Britons from their homes, confiscated their land, and treated them as slaves. The army—there were apparenty some troops left in the area—supported the veterans. The town was 'the seat of servitude' in the eyes of the Britons, and we are told of their fierce hatred of the veterans. The imperial cult was organized with the forced participation of the provincials, with a temple for the Divine Claudius as its focus, an 'arx aeternae dominationis'.[28]

Yet the town remained unfortified. Eleven years after its foundation it was stormed and taken immediately, except for the temple, which the veterans succeeded in holding for two days.[29] What can be learned from these events? Not, it seems, that there was anything very unusual in the organization of this particular colony. Colonies were hated elsewhere. In a speech that Tacitus puts in the mouth of Arminius, the leader of the Germanic revolt, the essence of Roman provincial rule is expressed by the phrase 'dominos et colonias novas'.[30] The walls of Colonia Agrippinensis (Cologne) are referred to as 'munimenta servitii'.[31]

Camulodunum may have been typical of citizen colonies on captured land; what may have been exceptional was the native revolt that

---

[25] The *cohors XIII Urbana*, afterwards reconstituted as the *cohors I Flavia Urbana*. For the urban cohorts, H. Freis, *Die Cohortes Urbanae = Epigraphische Studien* ii (1967).

[26] *Ann.* xii 32. 4.

[27] Tacitus, loc. cit.: 'subsidium adversus rebelles et imbuendis sociis ad officia legum.' This conforms with John Mann's thesis that veteran colonies were formed on the site of a former legionary base: *Recruitment*, 26, 60.

[28] For the imperial cult at Camulodunum, D. Fishwick, *Britannia* 3 (1972), 164–81; 4 (1973), 264 f.; P. Crummy, *Britannia* 8 (1977), 65–105, esp. 70 f. For the temple of Claudius, P. J. Drury, *Britannia* 15 (1984), 7–50. For the pre-colonial military presence, ibid. pp. 21–4.

[29] *Ann.* xiv 31 f.

[30] *Ann.* i 59. 8. Appian, *BC* v 12-14, describes problems caused by the settlement of veterans in Italy.

[31] Tacitus, *Hist.* iv 64.

destroyed it. Like the Cisalpine colonies two and a half centuries earlier it was incapable of defending itself against determined attack, and it was not organized to withstand one. The army had to protect the colonists.

The Colonies in the East

Berytus and Heliopolis

Now we may turn to Berytus and Heliopolis in Lebanon. The strategic value of the cities is often described in grandiose terms (above, p. 311 f). We know from Strabo and Josephus what the Romans were up against in Lebanon. Strabo goes on to describe how Berytus was razed to the ground and then restored by the Romans as a veteran colony.

Veterans were settled at Berytus in 14 BC by Agrippa.[32] Heliopolis (Baalbek) and the Beqa' valley were apparently assigned to the colony of Berytus down to the reign of Septimius Severus.[33] The Romans were faced with banditry based in the mountains and along the coast. The history of every period, including our own, has shown how difficult it is to solve such problems. The settlement of retired soldiers in the fertile plain would guarantee a loyal and reliable presence there, but at the same time military forces would have to operate in the mountains to fight the bandits in their own territory and to keep the roads safe. This includes the difficult road through the mountains which linked Berytus with the Beqa' valley. Retired soldiers could not possibly do this for any length of time. Strabo, in fact, says that security was established in Syria by the Roman army. He makes no mention of veterans in *this* connection.[34]

A famous inscription originally set up at Berytus honours an equestrian officer who was dispatched by the governor of Syria at the beginning of the first century to destroy a fortress of the Ituraeans in the mountains of the Lebanon.[35] The officer, it may be noted, later became *quaestor, aedilis, duumvir,* and *pontifex* of the colony. This inscription happens to be preserved. There is no reason to believe that it was the only one of its kind. To judge from modern experience, many more expeditions must have been undertaken with a similar purpose.

---

[32] Some veterans were established there at an earlier date, after Actium and before 27 BC: *CIL* iii 14165. 6. For Berytus, E. Schürer, *The History of the Jewish People in the Age of Jesus Christ*, i (1973), 323 n. 150; J. Lauffray, *ANRW* ii 8. 135–63.

[33] References and discussion by J.-P. Rey-Coquais in *IGLS* vi 34 n. 9 and *JRS* 68 (1978), 51 f.

[34] Strabo xvi 2. 20 (756).

[35] *CIL* iii 6687; *ILS* 2683; E. Gabba, *Iscrizioni greche e latine per lo studio della bibbia* (1958), 52–61, pl. 3. The inscription reminds one of *ILS* 740, set up in a later period in Isauria.

Berytus served as base of operations just as the colony at Ptolemais-Acco did in 67.[36] Inscriptions testifying the presence of soldiers on active service at Heliopolis (Baalbek)[37] suggest that there was an army unit on active service in the area. The epigraphic material clearly shows the social and cultural impact of the veteran settlement in both centres and their territory far into the third century. Veterans were settled in and around the cities and in the Beqa' valley, but not in the mountains. These became crown land, as appears from numerous Hadrianic inscriptions referring to imperial forests.[38]

One has the impression that urban and rural development was a slow process. Dated inscriptions are not found in substantial numbers before the second half of the first century, almost a century after the foundation. The road-system in the region is marked by milestones of the second century.

Public inscriptions set up by the town are in Latin, as one would expect in a Roman veteran colony, even in the East.[39] As observed by J. F. Gilliam, despite regional recruitment many men in the legions in the East were either Roman in some degree or at least different in origin from the mass in the provinces in which they served.[40] There are very few inscriptions in Greek and those dated are not earlier than the fourth century.[41] It is of more interest that inscriptions set up by private individuals tend to be in Latin as well. Again this is not surprising when these are serving soldiers,[42] or when serving soldiers are com-memorated;[43] it might well be evidence of the presence of an army unit in the town or in its vicinity. It is, however, clearly significant that Latin is used by civilians in the surrounding territory.[44]

Of special interest is the material from Niha, in the Beqa' Valley, where a series of inscriptions set up by the *Pagus Augustus* in Latin records the existence of a sanctuary of 'the Syrian Goddess of Niha'.[45]

[36] For Prolemais-Acco, below, pp. 322 f.

[37] For Berytus and Heliopolis, see also below, Chapter VIII.

[38] These are fully published and discussed in *IGLS* viii 3.

[39] The published material from Berytus is far less in quantity than that from Heliopolis, but even there inscriptions are in Latin, e.g. J. Lauffray, *Bull. Mus. de Beyrouth* 7 (1944–5), 13–80, esp. 60, 67 f., 77. This is the case even if they are set up by persons bearing Semitic names, e.g. p. 67: 'I.O.M. H(eliopolitano) Ti. Claudius Zmaragdus' and 'I.O.M. Malechia Brudeno'.

[40] *Bull. Am. Soc. Papyrologists* 2 (1965), 65–73 = *Roman Army Papers* (1986), 281–7. esp. 283.

[41] *IGLS* vi, nos. 2740, 2827 f., 2830 f. For a tetrarchic inscription in Latin, *CIL* iii 14165. 7. The latest Latin inscription known to me dates to AD 344 (*ILS* 1234).

[42] e.g. nos. 2711 f., 2714, 2789, 273 f., 2848.

[43] e.g. nos. 2786 f., 2789, 2798.

[44] e.g. nos. 2894, 2904, 2908 f., 2925, 2955.

[45] Nos. 2936, 2942. The inscriptions from Niha are nos. 2928–45. For *pagi*, country districts or communities attached to cities, and *vici*, rural settlements, *RE* xviii 2418–39; R. Chevallier,

The *Pagus Augustus* was apparently an association of Latin-speaking Roman citizens which will have been settled there at the time of the foundation of Berytus as a Roman colony. Here some evidence of social integration may be detected.[46] The sanctuary preserved its indigenous character, and the gods did not receive Greco-Roman names. In contrast to the sanctuary at Heliopolis itself the priests and prophetesses were *peregrini*.[47] On the other hand, there is a dedication in Latin to the god Mifsenus.[48] The personal names found on the inscriptions also show a measure of integration, for instance in the case of C. Claudius Marcellus whose children had Semitic names.[49]

There are many inscriptions showing that citizens of the colony combined army careers with local office. Some of them reached very high positions.[50] Many citizens have names which reflect long-standing citizenship.[51] On the whole purely Latin names with the *tria nomina* for men and *filiatio* for women are far more frequent than Greek, Semitic, or mixed names, and this is true for the inscriptions from the town itself no less than for those from the territory.[52] The significance of all this comes out most clearly in contrast with, for instance, the material from Emesa, the city immediately to the north of Heliopolis. The only Latin inscriptions to be found there or in its territory are on milestones and official boundary stones.[53]

It is clear that the impact of the settlement of legionary veterans was quite remarkable for its long-lasting intensity. The existence of a distinguished school of Roman law at Berytus has always been seen as an indication of the Latin character of this town.[54] There is evidence of

---

ANRW ii 1 (1974), bibliography on 777 f. (nothing on the eastern provinces); L. A. Churchin, *REA* 87 (1985), 327–43 on those in Spain, with general discussion on 328 and 338. Churchin concludes that those in Spain have to be seen in their own context; this may be true for other provinces as well. For *pagi* at Ptolemais, below, p. 344 n.

[46] J.-P. Rey-Coquais, *Sociétés urbaines, sociétés rurales dans l'Asie Mineure et la Syrie hellénistiques et romaines: Actes du colloque organisé à Strasbourg (novembre 1985)*, ed. E. Frézouls (1987), 191–216, esp. 198–207, pls. ii–iv 1.

[47] *IGLS* vi 2935 and Rey-Coquais, pl. ii 2.

[48] *IGLS* 2946, cf. Rey-Coquais, 203.

[49] *IGLS* 2940, and cf. Rey-Coquais, loc. cit., who also sees mutual influence in the style of the stelae.

[50] Nos. 2781, 2786 f., 2793 f., 2795, 2796 f., 2798. No. 2795 mentions a member of a senatorial family which produced three consuls in the second century and is also mentioned at Berytus. Cf. G. W. Bowersock, *Atti del colloquio internazionale AIEQL su epigrafia e ordine senatorio, Roma 1981* (1982), ii 651–68, esp. 665 f., nos. 16–18.

[51] No. 2714: L. Antonius Silo. 2716: L. Julius Severus. 2781: L. Antonius Naso. Also the persons referred to in the previous note.

[52] Statistics do not prove anything, but the relationship is at least 3:1 for the period of the principate.

[53] See *IGLS* v, Émésène. Latin boundary stones: nos. 2549, 2552. Milestones: 2672, 2674–6; see also 2704, 2708.

[54] Sometimes this is even expressed in terms of racial prejudice, e.g. Vittinghoff, 134 f.: 'Den

at least two senators from Berytus, which shows that it produced members of the imperial upper class.[55] Equestrian officers are attested as originating from both Heliopolis (2) and Berytus (4 or 5).[56] Two or three of these are the only attested first-century equestrian officers from Syria, which is not surprising given the military background of the settlers. In numbers of attested officers these towns were surpassed only by Palmyra in the second century.[57] Epigraphic evidence proves that the effects of the settlement of veterans on the social and cultural life of both Berytus and Heliopolis, in the towns and the surrounding territory, lasted at least till the fourth century.

To sum up, Berytus and Heliopolis were very successful colonies, from a Roman point of view, but they did not pacify or garrison the Ituraean country. That was the work of the Roman army.

Southern Asia Minor

Barbara Levick has pointed out that the Roman colonies in Southern Asia Minor did not or could not suppress banditry in their own area.[58] A serious rising of the Isaurians in AD 68 had to be suppressed by the regular army under M. Plautius Silvanus.[59] There was also recurrent trouble in Cilicia.[60] The activities of Q. Veranius as governor of Lycia during the reign of Claudius are another indication of continued unrest.[61] Almost three centuries later the emperor Probus is reported to have said that 'it is easier to keep brigands away than to expel them'.[62] Whether he said it or not, it is a good aphorism. In 280, according to the same source, he settled veterans where the old veteran colonies had failed to keep the brigands under control. The veterans' sons were conscripted at the age of eighteen 'so that they would never learn to be brigands'.[63] The story is probably not authentic, but it may be taken as reflecting the realities of a later age.[64]

---

einzigen grossen Sieg einer römischen Kolonie gegen die hellenistisch-östliche Umwelt hat in Syrien die alte Hafenstadt und Veteranenkolonie Berytus . . ., eine "lateinische Insel im semitischen Ozean" (Cumont, *CAH* xi 626) errungen.'

[55] Bowersock, *epigrafia e ordine senatorio*, nos. 11 and 12: M. and S. Sentius Proculus, possibly brothers.

[56] H. Devijver, *DRBE*, 183.   [57] Devijver, loc. cit.

[58] B. Levick, *Roman Colonies in Southern Asia Minor* (1967), 173.

[59] Dio lv 28. iii; Velleius Paterculus ii 112. Cf. R. Syme, *Klio* 27 (1934), 139 ff. For the troubles in Isauria see further above, Chapter II.

[60] Tacitus, *Ann.* ii 42: AD 17; xii 55: 'saepe et alias commotae' (AD 52).

[61] A. E. Gordon, *Quintus Veranius, Consul AD 49* (Univ. of California, Publ. in Classical Archaeology, ii 5, 1952).

[62] SHA, *Probus* 16. 6. Cf. Levick, 173–5.   [63] SHA, *Probus* 16. 6.

[64] As argued by J. Rougé, *REA* 68 (1966), 284 ff.

Ptolemais (Acco)

The manner in which a colony could be useful even in wartime can be seen in the case of Ptolemais (Acco) in Syria-Phoenice.[65] It was founded following serious trouble between Jews and Samaritans in the reign of Claudius.[66] An investigation was carried out on the spot by the governor of Syria. The prefect of Judaea was dismissed in about 52. Veterans of the four Syrian legions were settled in a new colony at Ptolemais between 51/2 and 54, and a new road was constructed from Antioch in Syria to the colony.[67] The connection between the troubles in Judaea and these measures is not proved. Josephus does not mention the foundation of the colony, but the chronological sequence indicates a causal connection. Ptolemais lay just north and west of the boundary of Judaea and was situated in a sort of salient between the sea and the hills of lower Galilee which were occupied by Jews. It had the last good harbour north of Caesarea and was the last major town to be passed by anyone travelling from Syria to Judaea along the coast road. This was the road most frequently chosen by all those travelling over land from the north, north-west, and north-east, as may be illustrated by the following passage: 'Pappus and Lulianus set up tables from Acco to Antioch and provided for the immigrants from the diaspora.'[68] In Acts 21: 1 Paul is represented as sailing (in stages) from Ephesus to Tyre, 'for there the ship was to unload its cargo.' After spending a week in Tyre he travelled by boat to Ptolemais, and thence to Caesarea,

[65] L. Kadman, *The Coins of Akko-Ptolemais* (1961); N. Makhouly and C. N. Johns, *Guide to Acre* (1946); H. Seyrig, *RN* 4 (1962), 25–50; *Syria* 39 (1962), 192–207; Schürer, ii (revised ed. 1978), 121–5. Also *Encyclopedia of Archaeological Excavations* i 14–23; M. Avi-Yonah, *Gazetteer of Roman Palestine* (1976), s.v., 89; Isaac, *Talanta* 12–13 (1980–81), 37 f.

[66] Schürer, 458–60, 462. The element 'Germanica' in the names of the city, although first attested on pre-colonial coins of the reign of Claudius (Schürer, ii 125), almost certainly goes back to the eastern journey of Germanicus in the reign of Tiberius. The absence of information is irrelevant, for Acco did not issue coinage in the intervening period, and a parallel from Bithynia seems decisive: here the city of Caesarea Germanica issued coinage with a head of Germanicus on the obv. and a legend which mentions Germanicus as founder: B. V. Head, *Historia Numorum* ([2]1911), 511. I owe this reference to Mrs Alla Stein.

[67] The last pre-colonial coin-issue of Ptolemais dates from AD 51/2: Kadman, nos. 86–90; Seyrig, *RN* 4, 39. For further bibliography, A. Kindler and A. Stein, *A Bibliography of the City Coinage of Palestine* (1987), 5–18. The foundation by Claudius (died 54) is mentioned by Pliny, *NH* v 17. 75: 'Colonia Claudi Caesaris Ptolemais, quae quondam Acce . . .' Milestones of 56 record the construction of a road 'ab Antiochea ad novam coloniam Ptolemaida': R. G. Goodchild, *Berytus* 9 (1948–49), 91–123, esp. 120. For the legions see the founder's coins with *vexilla*, AD 66: Kadman, nos. 92 ff. There is no evidence for the statement by M. Avi-Yonah, *RE*, Sup. xiii, s.v. Palaestina, col. 382, that the colony was founded after Claudius' death in an effort by Nero's ministers to neutralize rumours of the late emperor's murder by honouring him.

[68] Genesis Rabbah 64, ed. Theodor-Albeck, 710; cf. G. Alon, *The Jews in their Land in the Talmudic Age* ii (1984), 436–8. The tables ('trapezin') presumably were banking centres where loans were offered to Jews from the diaspora on their way to Jerusalem.

presumably by land.[69] Ulpian describes Ptolemais as lying between Palaestina and Syria.[70] The town proved useful in 67, when it served as Vespasian's base of operations. This was precisely the sort of function that a veteran colony could perform.[71] The veterans at Ptolemais could not possibly fight the rebellious Jews, but they could provide the Roman army with a reliable base. The establishment of a veteran colony at Ptolemais must clearly be distinguished from the granting of privileges, also under Claudius, to several towns, such as Tiberias, which received the name 'Claudiopolis'.[72] The foundation of the colony involved drastic reorganization of the territory and land grants to veterans. The land, whether bought or confiscated was taken from its original possessors, and the infusion of veterans entailed the imposition of a new local leadership. Unlike the mere grant of a new name with accompanying privileges this was undoubtedly a project to the disadvantage of the existing population.

Aelia Capitolina

A colony which will also be discussed in the next chapter is Aelia Capitolina. It is true that veterans of the legion X Fretensis settled in this colony, but the town remained at the same time the headquarters of the legion. It would therefore be futile to claim that the veterans who settled there guarded the region, since a proper legion had its base in the colony. The nature of Hadrian's foundation is intriguing. After 70 Jerusalem became a legionary base. Hadrian refounded the city as a

[69] For Ptolemais as a port, also m. Nedarim 3. 6: '. . . such as those who sail from Acco to Jaffa . . .'

[70] Ulpian, *Dig.* L 15. 1. 3: 'Ptolemaeensium enim colonia, quae inter Phoenicen et Palaestinam sita est, nihil praeter nomen coloniae habet.' That is, the colony had no additional financial privileges, such as the *ius Italicum* or the exemptions from taxation enjoyed by Caesarea and Aelia Capitolina. Perhaps it received *ius Italicum* in the reign of Elagabalus, for city coins of his reign show Marsyas (Kadman, no. 163). However, that is an argument of dubious value. The statement by Ulpian is sometimes misinterpreted, e.g. Schürer, ii (1907), 148, followed by the revised version (1978), 125; Avi-Yonah, *Gazetteer*, 89.

[71] Only after the complete subjugation of Galilee did Vespasian move his headquarters to Caesarea: Josephus, *BJ* iii 2. 4 (29), 4. 2 (64 ff.), 9. 1 (409). Ptolemais was a military depot under the later Seleucids, Y. H. Landau, *IEJ* 11 (1961), 118–26 (*SEG* xix 904; cf. xx 413); cf. S. Applebaum, *Essays in Honour of C. E. Stevens*, ed. B. Levick (1975), 64 f., n. 48.

[72] 'Claudiopolis' appears on coins of the reign of Trajan and later: A. Kindler, *The Coins of Tiberias* (1961), 45 f.; and on an inscription in Rome, dated after 135: *IGR* i 132. Apamea received a similar privilege: J. and J. C. Balty, *ANRW* ii 8. 120 f. Also Gaba Hippeon: Schürer, ii (revised edn.), 165 n. 421; M. Rosenberger, *The Rosenberger Israel Collection*, ii (1975), 43, no. 1; see now A. Kindler, in B. Mazar (ed.), *Geva, Archaeological Discoveries at Tell Abu-Shusha, Mishmar Ha-'Emeq* (1988), 43 ff., with catalogue on p. 61 (in Hebrew). There are coins of Claudia Leucas bearing dates according to an 'era' that starts some time between 47/8 and 53/4 AD. Seyrig identifies the city with Balanea (*Syria* 27 (1950), 24). In *BMC, Galatia, Cappadocia and Syria*, those coins are listed as belonging to Leucas on the Chrysoroas.

Roman colony, and this led to an anomaly: the close proximity of an army base and a Roman colony. As John Mann has shown, veteran colonies were normally only founded at, or alongside, the site of a legionary base after the legion had moved on elsewhere, leaving the military site vacant.[73] What little evidence there is indicates that the citizens of Aelia Capitolina were veterans of Fretensis. This may be inferred from colonial coinage with *vexilla* and the emblems of the legion,[74] and from the few inscriptions of the period. Perhaps this anomalous situation was possible because the relationship between the army and urban settlements in the eastern provinces was different from that in the West (from where most of what we know derives): the fact that army units were frequently based in the cities in the eastern frontier provinces may have made it less anomalous. Moreover, Aelia was one of the last few veteran colonies founded in the Roman provinces.[75] It is conceivable that regular Roman practice was no longer held to be of essential importance.

Even if Hadrian did nothing to build up Aelia as a city the establishment of a veteran colony had advantages from a Roman point of view. It would induce discharged soldiers of the legion to settle there, especially since it enjoyed the same exemptions from taxation as Caesarea.[76] The veterans and their descendants would be a focus of loyalty in the middle of Judaea, and the latter might, like the citizens of Caesarea, provide the provincial army with recruits.[77]

There are not many inscriptions from Aelia Capitolina, but it is worth observing that all of the sixteen inscriptions datable to the period from the destruction in 70 until Constantine are in Latin. These include two military inscriptions set up before Hadrian,[78] a number of honorary inscriptions for emperors,[79] one inscription for a legionary legate,[80] but also a few tombstones of veterans,[81] and, most significant, tombstones of civilians inscribed not in Greek but in Latin with Roman names.[82] While the Byzantine inscriptions, far greater in number, are

[73] Mann, *Recruitment*, 60–3; id., *BJb* 162 (1962), 162–4.
[74] L. Kadman, *The Coins of Aelia Capitolina* (1956), nos. 1 (*vexillum*), 5 (eagle on shaft), 6 (boar). Further references: Kindler and Stein, *Bibliography*, 22–37. See also Isaac, *Talanta*, 31–54.
[75] Mann, *Recruitment*, 60 f., 65.
[76] Ulpian, *Digest* L 15. 1. 6; Paulus, *Digest* L 15. 8. 7.
[77] For recruits from veteran colonies, Mann, *Recruitment*, 65 f. Mann observes that in the East the practice of drawing on veteran colonies for recruitment is largely unknown. In the case of Aelia there is no evidence either, but on general grounds it may be considered likely that the descendants of the veterans at Aelia did join the army.
[78] *AE* 1978. 825; *CIL* iii 13587.
[79] e.g. *CIL* iii 1168 (6639).　　[80] *CIL* iii 6641 (12080a).
[81] *CIL* iii 14155. 3; *AE* 1939. 157; J. H. Iliffe, *QDAP* 2 (1932), 123, no. 4.
[82] J. E. Hanauer, *PEFQSt* 35 (1903), 271, whence P. Thomsen, *Die griechischen und lateinischen*

in Greek, the pattern formed by the pre-Constantinian inscriptions reminds one of that observed in the material from Heliopolis. Aelia Capitolina seems indeed to have had the characteristics of a veteran colony in the East. Its citizens spoke Latin and preferred to be identified with Rome rather than the Hellenized Orient. The legion was still in Jerusalem in the mid third century, as shown by a city-coin of Herennius Etruscus with emblems of the legion.[83] Eusebius mentions the legion as based at Aela on the Red Sea in his time (*c.*260–*c.*340).[84]

Local Militias

In 4 BC Berytus provided Varus, on his way to Judaea, with 1500 infantry.[87] It has been suggested that this was an expression of the military character of Berytus as a veteran colony.[88] If so, the troops would have been veterans back in active service; and indeed Josephus, in the *War* uses the word ὁπλῖται, which may denote legionaries. But in the *Antiquities* he refers to them as ἐπίκουροι (auxiliaries), a term he uses also to describe the soldiers collected in large numbers from Syrian cities by Cestius Gallus in 66, again for an expedition into Judaea.[89] 'These', he says, 'though lacking the experience of the regulars, made good their deficiency in technical training by their ardour and their detestation of the Jews.' This assessment is demonstrated by the description of the first stage of the campaign: Cestius Gallus sacked the city of Chabulon and its territory and returned to Ptolemais. 'But while the Syrians and in particular those of Berytus were still occupied in pillage, the Jews, understanding that Cestius had departed, recovered courage and, falling unexpectedly on the troops which he had left behind, killed about two thousand of them.' These troops, therefore, showed a lack of wartime experience and discipline characteristic of a local militia. Moreover, it is clear that Berytus was but one of the Syrian cities which had such troops.[90] In Judaea Gaba provided auxiliaries to the Roman forces early in the First Jewish Revolt.[91]

Inscriften der Stadt Jerusalem (1922), no. 179; *CIL* iii 14155. 4; E. L. Sukenik and L. A. Mayer, *The Third Wall of Jerusalem* (1930), 45 f., whence Thomsen, *ZDPV* 64 (1941), no. 182a.

[83] *BMC, Palestine*, 100, no. 104.   [84] Eusebius, *Onomasticon* 6. 17–20 (Klostermann).

[85] Tacitus, *Ann.* xiv 27. 4; Hyginus, *Grom.* pp. 160, 176.

[86] Mann, 8; Keppie, *Colonisation*, 110 ff.

[87] Josephus, *BJ* ii 5. 1 (67); *Ant.* xvii 10. 9 (287).   [88] Bowersock, *Augustus*, 71.

[89] *BJ* ii 18. 9 (502; 506). Titus, too, had such troops during the siege of Jerusalem: *BJ* v 1. 6 (42).

[90] For the long-lasting impact of veteran settlement at Berytus and Heliopolis, see above.

[91] See below, p. 329.

Mommsen has collected evidence of irregular auxiliaries in the provinces.[92] Relevant examples from the East are taken from Tacitus, who reports that in AD 51 Paelignus, the equestrian governor of Cappadocia, called out the provincial militia.[93] Arrian appears to mean the same type of forces when he lists as allied troops, in addition to the legionaries, infantry from Armenia and Trapezus, Colchians, and Rizian λογχοφόροι (i.e. spearmen from Rize, east of Trabzon).[94] Note the mention of troops from Trapezus, a town which had a regular garrison. A different kind of troops may be meant in *Annals* xv 3: Corbulo in AD 62 placed his legions on the bank of the Euphrates and armed a band of irregular provincial auxiliaries.[95] It is not quite clear what exactly is the difference between these irregulars and the '*iuventus*, armed and trained as a militia', mentioned elsewhere.[96] At least a part of these troops may have carried out local police duties since there was no regular police apparatus in the provinces during the principate. That seems to be clear from Ovid (in Tomi)[97] and from the fact that there was an officer for the suppression of banditry at Nyon (Julia Equestris).[98] There is now evidence of the existence, at Syrian Antioch, of a citizens' militia as well; they collaborated with legionary vexillations and auxiliary cohorts in the construction of a canal near the city.[99]

It is clear then that there were military or para-military organizations in the provinces, and there is no reason why these should not have existed in colonies as well as elsewhere. That is consistent with the view that Roman colonies performed only very limited military functions.[100] This is not to say that citizen militias are always ineffectual. A well-

---

[92] Mommsen, *Gesammelte Schriften*, vi, 'Die römischen Provinzialmilizen', 145 ff.

[93] *Ann.* xii 49. 2: 'auxiliis provincialium contractis.'

[94] *Ectaxis* 7, cf. 14.

[95] 'tumultuarium provincialium manum armat.' 'Tumultuarius' is common for troops levied in an emergency, e.g. *Ann.* i 56. 1: 'Igitur Germanicus quattuor legiones, quinque auxiliarium milia et tumultuarias catervas Germanorum . . . tradit.'

[96] *Hist.* i 68: 'hinc Caecina cum valido exercitu, inde Raeticae alae cohortesque et ipsorum Raetorum iuventus, sueta armis et more militiae exercita.' Cf. *Hist.* iii 5: 'igitur Sextilius Felix cum ala Auriana et octo cohortibus ac Noricorum iuventute ad occupandam ripam Aeni fluminis, quod Raetos Noricos que interfluit, missus.'

[97] Ovid refers again and again to troubles caused by Getae, e.g. *Ex Ponto* i 2. 808 ff. The townspeople themselves had to cope with this at times: i 8. 5–6; iv 14. 28. But the regular army also interfered: iv 7.

[98] See above, n. 23.

[99] See the milestone of 75 which may have marked a canal in the neighbourhood of Antioch, as read by D. van Berchem, *BJb* 185 (1985), 85 ff.

[100] The only Roman colony of which I know that it succeeded in beating off a dangerous attack was a citizen colony, Salona, which withstood an attack by the leader of the Illyrian revolt in AD 6: Dio lv 29. 4. For Salona, J. J. Wilkes, *Dalmatia* (1969), 220–38. At the same time a large force of veterans still serving under the colours in a remote region was exterminated: Velleius ii 110. 6.

trained citizen army can be very forceful in defence of its home ground, as observed in the case of the Mesopotamian cities in the Byzantine period. But this requires a high degree of motivation, intelligent leadership, and an awareness of a common danger. These qualities were absent among the Syrian townsmen who accompanied Cestius Gallus. They were pillaging other peoples' possessions and not defending their homes. Hence the disaster.

Herodian Settlements

Settlements of quite a different nature, function, and social composition were established by Herod in his kingdom. For the present we are concerned only with those which had a clearly military component in their population; Herod's contribution to the urbanization of the region will be discussed below. We should, however, note in passing that Josephus himself was of the opinion that several Herodian towns which were not settled with veterans also served to provide security. In the *Antiquities*, after explaining how Herod kept the city of Jerusalem under control,[101] he goes on to describe his measures for ensuring the security of the rest of the country.[102] These were, first, the establishment of settlers and the re-foundation of Samaria as Sebaste, and then the founding of the city of Caesarea (one of his major projects), Gaba in Galilee, and Esbon (Heshbon) in Peraea. 'These were the measures which he kept thinking up one after the other, while distributing garrisons everywhere among the people, so as to reduce as much as possible their habit of lunging into turmoil independently, as they did constantly, given the smallest provocation, and so that it would not escape him if they did make disturbances, thanks to the constant proximity of people who could discover and prevent it.'

In Josephus' view, therefore, an important function of these settlements, whether inhabited by former soldiers or not, was that they constituted loyal elements living near or among the Jews who tended to be rebellious. The settlers were not themselves expected to keep the Jews under control, but they would keep Herod informed of any dangerous activity among them. It may be observed that Roman veteran colonies could serve precisely the same purpose for the Roman authorities.

It is doubtful whether Heshbon was a military colony; Josephus does not say so:[103] Caesarea was purely civilian, although it supplied

---

[101] See above, ch. VI.   [102] *Ant.* xv 8. 5 (292–5).

[103] Schürer, ii (1978), 166 n. 429, is convinced that Josephus, *Ant.* xv 8. 5 (294), means to say

recruits for the army. Sebaste and Gaba, however, were military colonies. There was also the military settlement of Zamaris in Trachonitis, although that was entirely different in nature and organization. More needs to be said about these last three.

Sebaste—Samaria

'[Herod] endeavoured to settle [at Samaria] many of those who had fought for him in his wars and many of the neighbouring population. He did this out of ambition to found as a new town one which had not been significant before, and more still because he strove eagerly after security for himself. He changed its name, calling it Sebaste, and from the territory he assigned to the settlers the best lands in the neighbourhood.'[104] In a shorter reference in the *War* Josephus tells us that the settlers were six thousand in number and that Herod gave the town an 'excellent constitution'(?).[105] This foundation resembles a Roman veteran colony in many respects, consisting as it did of a mixed population of veterans and local people and being assigned the best land in the area. Josephus insists that security was an important consideration for Herod in initiating the project. Yet we do not hear of the Sebastenians being engaged in actual fighting. They did, however, provide several generations of recruits for the local army, and the city supported the Romans after Herod's death and, apparently, in the First Jewish Revolt.[106] That surely is all that could be expected of such a town.

Gaba

'And in the Great Plain he allotted land to selected men of his own cavalry, and he founded the place called Gaba near (*or* for the domination of) Galilee. . .'[107] The identity of the place used to be

---

it was a military colony. But Caesarea, mentioned in the same passage, certainly was not a military colony. The passage is obscure, cf. Schürer, 164, n. 417. For the city coinage, Kindler and Stein, *Bibliography*, 117–19.

[104] Josephus, *Ant.* xv 8. 5 (296): τότε δὲ τὴν Σαμάρειαν ὡρμημένος τειχίζειν, πολλοὺς μὲν τῶν συμμαχησάντων αὐτῷ κατὰ τοὺς πολέμους, πολλοὺς δὲ τῶν ὁμόρων συμπολίζειν ἐπετήδευεν, ὑπό τε φιλοτιμίας τοῦ νέαν ἐγείρειν καὶ δι' αὐτοῦ πρότερον οὐκ ἐν ταῖς ἐπισήμοις οὐσαν, καὶ μᾶλλον ὅτι πρὸς ἀσφάλειαν αὐτῷ τὸ φιλότιμον ἐπετηδεύετο, τήν τε προσηγορίαν ὑπήλλαττε, Σεβαστὴν καλῶν, καὶ τῆς χώρας ἀρίστην οὐσαν τὴν πλησίον κατεμέριζε τοῖς οἰκήτορσιν, ὡς εὐθὺς ἐν εὐδαιμονίᾳ συνιόντας οἰκεῖν. καὶ τείχει καρτερῷ τὴν πόλιν περιέβαλε. . . . For Herod's building works at Samaria see below, pp. 341 n.

[105] *BJ* i 21. 2 (403).

[106] References in Schürer, ii 163.

[107] Josephus, *Ant.* xv 8, 5 (294): ἔν τε τῷ μεγάλῳ πεδίῳ τῶν ἐπιλέκτων ἱππέων τῶν περὶ αὐτὸν ἀποκληρώσας χωρίον συνέκτισεν ἐπὶ τῇ Γαλιλαίᾳ Γάβα καλούμενον . . . Cf. *BJ* iii 3. 1 (36). For further references, Schürer, ii 164 f. Note in particular Pliny, *NH* v 19. 75; Eusebius, *Onomast.* 70.

uncertain. But thanks to the discovery of several inscriptions,[108] one of which contains the name 'Gaba', as well as many coins of Gaba,[109] at Tel Shush, about three kilometres north-west of Megiddo, there is no longer any doubt that this is the site. Like Sebaste it supported the Romans in the First Revolt. Early in the war it served as the head-quarters of the decurion who commanded the troops in the Valley of Jezreel and provided him with auxiliaries.[110] Here again we see how a veteran colony could be useful in wartime long after its foundation, when none of the original settlers was alive anymore. It served as a convenient headquarters and placed its militia at the disposal of the Roman army. The militia, however, was, like that of Berytus, of dubious efficacity.[111]

Babylonian Jews in Batanaea

A Herodian settlement of a wholly different kind was planted in Batanaea. As explained by Josephus, the aim was, first of all, to protect the Jewish region against banditry from Trachonitis.[112] Herod first settled three thousand Idumaeans in Trachonitis itself.[113] Nothing is known of this settlement, how long it survived or whether it had any success. Later, however, he 'decided to found between Trachonitis and the Jews a village virtually a town in size and to make his territory hard to invade while he could then attack the enemy from nearby and strike them by swift raids'.[114] He settled a group of Babylonian Jews, consisting of five hundred horsemen and a hundred relatives in Batanaea, which borders on Trachonitis, 'for he wished to acquire the settlement as a bulwark, and he promised that the land would be exempt from tax and that they themselves would be immune from all the customary levies. . .'[115] Zamaris, a Babylonian Jew, received the land and built forts and a village which he named Bathyra.[116] 'This

---

9 (Klostermann); Hierocles, *Synecdemus* 720. 11 (Parthy, 44). The last two show that the place continued to exist as a modest settlement in the Byzantine period.

[108] For the inscription that mentions the name of the town, A. Siegelmann, *PEQ* 116 (1984), 89–93. See also Mazar, *Geva*, 224 f., for two relevant inscriptions.

[109] For the coinage, Kindler and Stein, *Bibliography*, 120–4; Kindler, in Mazar, *Geva*, 43–67.

[110] Josephus, *Vita* 24, 115. It had earlier been attacked together with several other pro-Roman towns: *BJ* ii 18. 1 (459).

[111] *Vita* 24. 116: Aebutius relied on his cavalry in particular.

[112] For banditry in Trachonitis see above, ch. II.

[113] *Ant.* xvi 9. 2 (285).

[114] *Ant.* xvii 2. 1 (23 f.): Τότε δὲ βουλόμενος πρὸς Τραχωνίτας ἀσφαλὴς εἶναι, κώμην πόλεως μέγεθος οὐκ ἀποδέουσαν ἔγνω Ἰουδαίων κτίσαι ἐν μέσῳ, δυσέμβολόν τε ποιεῖν τὴν αὐτοῦ, καὶ τοῖς πολεμίοις ἐξ ἐγγίονος ὁρμώμενος, ἐκ τοῦ ὀξέος ἐμβαλὼν κακουργεῖν.

[115] Ibid. (25): βουλόμενος πρόβλημα τὴν κατοίκησιν αὐτοῦ κτᾶσθαι, ἀτελῆ τε τὴν χώραν ἐπηγγέλλετο, καὶ αὐτοὺς εἰσφορῶν ἀπηλλαγμένους ἁπασῶν . . .

[116] Schürer, ii 14 f.; i 338, 419 f., 479; G. Cohen, *TAPA* 103 (1972), 83–95.

man served as a bulwark against Trachonitis both for the indigenous population and for the Jews who came from Babylonia to sacrifice in Jerusalem, so that they did not suffer from banditry from Trachonitis.'[117] Josephus says that the settlement flourished even though, in the course of time, the settlers lost their privileges, for Philip imposed some taxes, Agrippa I and his son more. Subsequenty the Romans preserved their free status, but utterly oppressed them by the imposition of taxes. The son and grandson of Zamaris provided the kings with a troop of horsemen as bodyguards and trained the royal army. In the Jewish revolt they supported Agrippa II against the rebels.[118] Literary and epigraphic evidence proves the presence of Jews in Batanaea in later centuries.[119]

The important difference between this settlement and Roman veteran colonies was that Zamaris' men were not veterans but military men who received land in return for the performance of specific military duties, unlike the veterans settled after their retirement in newly founded towns.[120] The Babylonians were well equipped for this as they were skilled archers, just like the inhabitants of Trachonitis.[121] Their duties were, however, clearly restricted, for the number of soldiers, five hundred men, was limited.[122] Their settlement was not a *polis*, but a village—it did not issue coinage. The colonists had to protect their own lands and prevent infiltration by bandits. This was, in essence, local police duty. They would have had to man the forts which they built on various spots. It is significant that remains of a Jewish settlement have been found at Nawa, a site on the main road from Galilee through Hippos to Damascus, precisely the route which many Jewish pilgrims from Babylonia would follow.[123] Josephus mentions the protection of these travellers as one of the main duties of the settlers. Another Jewish settlement was at Tafas, on the road from Nawa to Der'a.[124] It may be noted that Josephus twice uses the term 'bulwark' πϱόβλημα to describe the function of the settlement, the immediate equivalent of *propugna-*

---

[117] *Ant.* xvii 2. 2 (26).

[118] Cf. Josephus, *Vita* 46–61, 177–80, 407–9; also *BJ* ii 17. 4 (421). See also *OGIS* 425; *IGR* iii 1144: à dedication to one of the officers who served under Agrippa II (AD 75 or 80). The find spot is significant: Sur in Trachonitis.

[119] References in Schürer, ii 14 f., n. 46.

[120] Cohen emphasizes the similarities both with Hellenistic feudal villages and in particular with a Ptolemaic military colony which existed in Ammonitis around 260 BC.

[121] As pointed out by Cohen, 84 f. See *BJ* ii 4. 2 (58), for archers from Trachonitis in Herod's army.

[122] On this see Cohen.

[123] T. Bauzou, *Hauran* i, ed. J.-M. Dentzer (1985), 137–65, for the road-system in Southern Syria.

[124] Frey, *CII* 861.

culum, used by Cicero and Tacitus to describe older citizen colonies, not settled with veterans.

The settlers were not expected to engage in major action in Trachonitis, but their settlement could serve as a base for Herod and his army if he wanted to undertake expeditions there. In this respect the project did resemble veteran colonies. Note in particular the parallel case of Berytus and Heliopolis, which, it has been argued, were never capable by themselves of suppressing Ituraean banditry in the Lebanon. Most important, the long-term effect was the same. The descendants of the Babylonians, like those of the Sebastenians, furnished loyal troops to the descendants of the founder of the settlements. At moments of crisis they turned against the rebels. And even after centuries they, like the citizens of Berytus and Heliopolis, preserved a distinct identity, clearly reflected in literary and epigraphic sources.

To some extent even non-military settlers planted in a new town could serve the monarch. Note the terms in which Josephus describes Sepphoris, re-founded by Herod Antipas after its destruction by Varus: 'a city built as a stronghold against (the people of the surrounding countryside) in a very powerful position and which would stand guard over the whole nation.'[125] The population was Jewish and yet firmly supported Rome in the First Revolt.

The settlements founded by Herod and his sons are instructive, even in a discussion of Roman veteran colonies, because the relatively full information on their function provided by Josephus enables us to see to what extent they could serve the monarchy, even if there were no military elements among the population, and what such settlements could never do, even if they were populated by soldiers on active duty.

Conclusions

Roman colonies were incapable of defending themselves in times of full-scale warfare. While they could not pacify a hostile region they might serve as bases of operations for an army. There is evidence of this in the case of Berytus and Ptolemais-Acco. At best they might send members of their local militia as participants in an imperial campaign. They do not seem to have done well on such occasions.

---

[125] *BJ* iii 2. 4 (34): μεγίστην μὲν οὖσαν τῆς Γαλιλαίας πόλιν, ἐρυμνοτάτῳ δ' ἐπιτετειχισμένην χωρίῳ καὶ φρουρὰν ἔθνους ἐσομένην. Note the use of ἐπιτειχίζειν 'to build a fort on the frontier of the enemy's country to serve as the basis of operations against him' (Liddell & Scott). For other references to Sepphoris as the strongest town in the region, *BJ* ii 18. 11 (511); *Vita* 45 (232), 65 (346). For the foundation see also below, p. 341.

There may have been expectations that they would guarantee local security at the level of internal police-duties. However, as has been seen in several instances, they did not provide a solution to the problems of banditry.[126] Colonies, unlike Herod's military settlement in Batanaea, could not replace army-units on active duty. That is not to deny that they were 'instruments of empire', in the sense that they formed a social, political, and economic complement to military power. The veterans and their descendants served for centuries as loyal representatives of the ruling class, firmly established on land taken from the subjugated natives. Local government was well organized. Like other cities in the provinces the colonies would take financial responsibility for the territories assigned to them. The colonists became the landowning class in the cities and could therefore be trusted to see that taxes were paid. Veterans will often have sent their sons to the army.[127]

The colonies were thus 'instruments of empire', but in a sense different from that intended by those who believe that they were outposts to hold barbarian tribes in check. As often in this book, it can be argued that this is an opinion which springs from an apologetic conception of the empire and its institutions. As long as it is maintained that the colonies defended the empire against barbarian attack their foundation can be morally justified in modern eyes. To suggest that they were instrumental in the consolidation of conquest and subjugation is less pleasing to modern scholars who admire the Romans. Yet it can be maintained that this concept better reflects the spirit of those who built an empire.

[126] As noted above, in Chapters II and IV, the Ottoman authorities occasionally attempted to reduce the problems of Nomadic raids by planting settlers on strategic spots, but for various reasons this had little effect.

[127] For the colonies as a reservoir for recruitment into the army, Mann, *Recruitment, passim*.

VIII

URBANIZATION

It is natural to suppose that the greatest number, as well as the most considerable of the Roman edifices, were raised by the emperors, who possessed so unbounded a command both of men and money.[1]

What was merely a natural assumption for Gibbon became a certainty for many others. Yet Gibbon does not really say anything in support of his hypothesis. Augustus rebuilt Rome in marble, but Rome is a special case. 'Scarcely had the proud structure of the Coliseum been dedicated at Rome, before edifices of a smaller scale indeed, but of the same design and materials, were erected for the use, and at the expense, of the cities of Capua and Verona. The inscription of the stupendous bridge of Alcantara attests that it was thrown over the Tagus by the contribution of a few Lusitanian communities.'[2] Gibbon then devotes two pages to the munificence of Herodes Atticus, the wealthy Athenian, before returning to public buildings erected by the emperors in the city of Rome. He is careful in noting who paid for the work in Rome and who did so in the provinces. 'The public monuments with which Hadrian adorned every province of the empire were executed not only by his orders, but under his immediate inspection.' Here, however, Gibbon does not say Hadrian paid for the work. The question therefore is: did the emperors pay for public buildings in the provinces? More important still, what was the role of the imperial authorities in the urbanization of the provinces?

The impact of Roman provincial administration on urban development in the provinces has been interpreted along widely divergent lines. While it is clear that the number of cities increased under Roman rule, the Roman role in furthering this process is a matter of dispute. A. H. M. Jones writes in his classic work *The Greek City*: 'At the same time the Roman government, now that it had become monarchical, adopted the traditional policy of the Hellenistic kings and regarded it as its mission by promoting the growth of cities to advance the civilization of

---

[1] E. Gibbon, *The Decline and Fall of the Roman Empire*, ch. II.
[2] Gibbon, loc. cit.; *ILS* 287, 287a.

the Empire.'[3] He goes on to quote with approval ancient authors such as Aelius Aristides, *To Rome*: 'the shores of the sea, and the inland regions are filled with cities, some founded, some enlarged under your sway and by your act.' Rostovtzeff, while allowing for the fact that the development of urbanization was a natural process which could not be imposed from above,[4] nevertheless throughout his work on the Roman Empire impresses his readers with the notion that the emperors consistently fostered urbanization and were responsible for the growth of urban life in the provinces. Again and again he asserts that emperors 'created' *municipia* and towns, often on no other grounds than that they bore an emperor's name. We read that 'it is safe to assert that after Augustus, Claudius, Vespasian and Trajan he (Hadrian) was the emperor who did most to urbanize the Empire . . . Despite the efforts of Claudius, the Flavians, and Trajan, urban life was still in its infancy in most of the Danube provinces . . .'[5]

For another view we may cite J. C. Mann: 'The Romans had no great interest in urbanization as such. Their policy was to create organizations of local government which would take responsibility, especially financial responsibility, for the territories assigned to them. To this end they placed power firmly in the hands of the moneyed class in the cities.'[6] It must be observed, first of all, that the belief in an active policy of support for urbanization takes for granted a remarkable change in the attitude of the Roman upper class toward subject peoples. To be subject to the Romans is considered the equivalent of slavery, as is emphasized again and again. Obviously a city of the empire inhabited by free Roman citizens had a different status, but is it reasonable to assume that the ruler considered it his duty to pay for buildings in the provinces? The extent of the Roman emperor's financial responsibility towards the cities of the empire was, naturally, quite different in nature from his obligations towards the capital or any other city where he resided. It is possible that every emperor saw it as his responsibility to adorn the capital, while accepting no obligation to do the same for provincial towns.

Roman activity in this domain could in principle include large-scale imperial plans for urbanization, imperial creation of wholly new urban centres, or such action by governors; the emperor's initiation of particular building projects; imperial financial contributions to build-

---

[3] *The Greek City from Alexander to Justinian* (1940), 60.
[4] *The Social and Economic History of the Roman Empire* (²1957), 560 n. 10.
[5] Ibid. 366.
[6] Review of G. Rupprecht, *Untersuchungen zum Dekurionenstand*, in *Germania* 54 (1976).

ing activity initiated locally; imperial permission for particular building projects; the granting of new status or giving of new names.
However, in this chapter discussion will be confined to the evidence of
imperial involvement in the physical development of cities.

It is true that there is no lack of sources, like Aelius Aristides,
containing the sort of flattering platitudes that suggest the emperor was
constantly busy founding cities. Dio Chrysostom—to mention just one
other—writes: 'He (sc. the ruler) attends to one of the matters which
require his attention, he acts swiftly where speed is needed, achieves
something which is difficult to do, examines an army, pacifies a
country, founds a city, builds bridges across rivers, or roads through a
country.'[7] The present chapter will investigate whether there is concrete evidence that the imperial government engaged in such activities
as a standing policy rather than just by way of exception.

Recourse will be had to concrete evidence only, such as inscriptions
that record donations or contributions made by an emperor, for the
mere appearance of an emperor's name does not prove anything.
Statements made by literary authorities must be checked in each
instance. We may assume for instance, that Josephus, through his
source, had reliable information on Herod's activities as a builder, and
the same may be assumed for Pausanias as regards the initiatives taken
by Hadrian. On the other hand, we have no reason to believe that
Malalas, writing in the sixth century, really knew whether Julius
Caesar made donations for buildings raised in Antioch six centuries
before. It is better to assume that the many statements found in
Malalas reflect no more than the presence of names of rulers seen on
buildings by the author.[8] In the present chapter Malalas will therefore
not be accepted as a trustworthy source on building activity by past
emperors.

The subject is included here for two reasons. First, it is of interest in
an analysis of Roman frontier policy in a specific area to see whether
this included active measures fostering urbanization. Second, it will be
seen that the evidence clearly brings out an elementary distinction
between the rule by client kings and Roman provincial government.

---

[7] Dio Chrysostom iii 127.

[8] G. Downey, *A History of Antioch in Syria* (1961), 651, observes that Malalas seems to have
thought it appropriate that important buildings should be planned and constructed under the
personal supervision of the ruler, and to have felt that such operations must have been undertaken
during personal journeys; these would therefore have been occasions of such great moment that
they could only have been made after successful campaigns. Yet, in discussing individual building
projects carried out at Antioch, Downey seems to assume throughout that Malalas is a reliable
authority on these matters. On Malalas as a source of information on Antioch see further Downey,
38–41.

The area under consideration is that conquered by Pompey in 63 BC, which forms a good starting point.

Gabinius

It is usually claimed that Pompey refounded many cities which were then physically reconstructed by Gabinius, proconsul of Syria in 57–55 BC.[9] This would have been a programme of tremendous scope: in a newly annexed region, it is supposed, a whole series of cities was first refounded and then physically reconstructed by the Roman authorities. The modern literature invariably takes for granted that this was the case. It mentions the programme as a whole without reservations and refers to individual towns as having been rebuilt by Gabinius on the sole evidence of Josephus' list.

There are two points to examine: first, we must consider what Josephus actually says, or means to say, about the urbanizing activities of Pompey and Gabinius. In other words, is Josephus interpreted correctly in the modern literature? Second, the information in Josephus' works must be checked for internal consistency and trustworthiness, for only thus can we determine whether we are justified in applying whatever Josephus says Gabinius did to individual towns. Third, it must be seen whether there is any independent evidence of large-scale urban development in Judaea in this period. As regards Pompey's intervention Josephus says in the *Antiquities* that he refounded (ἀνέκτισε) Gadara—

and gave back to their inhabitants the cities of Hippos, Scythopolis, Pella, Dium, Samaria, Marissa, Azotus, Jamnia, and Arethusa. Apart from those which had been destroyed he set free these cities and assigned them to the province (of Syria) and also the cities on the coast, Gaza, Joppa, Dora, and Straton's Tower . . .[10]

The sense of the passage is that Pompey ignored ruined cities and

---

[9] A. H. M. Jones, *The Cities of the Eastern Roman Provinces* ([2]1971), 257; Schürer, *The History of the Jewish People in the Age of Jesus Christ*, ii (revised edn., 1978), 91 f., following the original Schürer, *Geschichte des Jüdischen Volkes im Zeitalter Jesu Christi*, ii (1907), 102.

[10] xiv. 4. 4 (75 f.): καὶ Γάδαρα μὲν μικρὸν ἔμπροσθεν κατασκαφεῖσαν ἀνέκτισε, Δημητρίῳ χαριζόμενος τῷ Γαδαρεῖ ἀπελευθέρῳ ἑαυτοῦ, τὰς δὲ λοιπὰς . . . τοῖς οἰκήτορσιν ἀπέδωκεν. καὶ ταύτας μὲν ἐν τῇ μεσογείῳ χωρὶς τῶν κατεσκαμμένων . . . πάσας ὁ Πομπήιος ἀφῆκεν ἐλευθέρας καὶ προσένειμε τῇ ἐπαρχίᾳ. The Loeb translation by Ralph Marcus contains a serious error: 'And not only these cities in the interior, in addition to those that had been demolished . . .' χωρὶς with genitive is never 'in addition to' but always 'apart from'. Jones, loc. cit., seems to have made the same mistake: 'Many of these cities had been ruined and their citizens dispersed, and Pompey in most cases did no more than order their restoration. . .'

annexed existing towns to the province of Syria. Josephus says the same thing, slightly more verbosely, in the *Bellum Judaicum*:

He refounded Gadara which had been destroyed by the Jews, to please his Gadarene freedman Demetrius. He liberated from their rule those cities in the interior which had not been destroyed, Hippos, Scythopolis, Pella, Samaria, Jamnia, Marisa, Azotus, and Arethusa, as well as the cities on the coast, Gaza, Joppa, Dora and Straton's Tower . . . All these he gave back to their own citizens and assigned them to the province of Syria.[11]

In other words, none of the ruined cities were revived save Gadara, which was refounded, as an exception, to please Demetrius, Pompey's freedman. The intact cities were merely transferred from Jewish rule to Roman provincial authority.

As regards Gabinius, in the *Antiquities* Josephus says the following:

He made a journey through the rest of Judaea and ordered the refoundation of all destroyed cities. And so Samaria, Azotus, Scythopolis, Anthedon, Raphia, Adora, Marisa, Gaza, and many others were refounded. And the people did what Gabinius ordered, and as a result cities were safely inhabited that had long been desolate.[12]

In the *Bellum Judaicum* we read:

Gabinius made a journey, establishing order in cities that had not been destroyed and refounding those in ruins. Thus, upon his orders, were reoccupied the cities of Scythopolis, Samaria, Anthedon, Apollonia, Jamnia, Raphia, Marisa, Adoreus, Gamala, Azotus, and many others, while settlers gladly established themselves there.[13]

There is no reference anywhere in these passages to building or physical organization being initiated, let alone carried out, by the Roman authorities. The general sense of the information is that Pompey took an administrative measure in transferring a number of towns from Judaea to the province of Syria, re-founding Gadara only as a favour to an individual. Gabinius then refounded a number of cities in Judaea that had been abandoned. Josephus speaks of settling, not of building.

That might leave the possibility that the information in Josephus is

---

[11] i 7. 7 (155 f.): ἀνακτίζει δὲ καὶ Γάδαραν ὑπὸ Ἰουδαίων κατεστραμμένην, Γαδαρίτῃ τινὶ τῶν ἰδίων ἀπελευθέρων Δημητρίῳ χαριζόμενος. ἠλευθέρωσεν δ' ἀπ' αὐτῶν καὶ τὰς ἐν τῇ μεσογείῳ πόλεις, ὅσας μὴ φθάσαντες κατέσκαψαν . . . ἃς πάσας τοῖς γνησίοις ἀποδοὺς πολίταις κατέταξεν εἰς τὴν Συριακὴν ἐπαρχίαν.

[12] xiv 5. 3 (88).

[13] i 8. 4 (166): Γαβίνιος δὲ . . . αὐτὸς ἐπῄει τὰς μὲν ἀπορθήτους πόλεις κατιστάμενος, τὰς δὲ κατεστραμμένας ἀνακτίζων. συνεπολίσθησαν γοῦν τούτου κελεύσαντος . . . καὶ ἄλλαι πολλαί, τῶν οἰκητόρων ἀσμένως ἐφ' ἑκάστην συνθεόντων.

valuable if only it is interpreted correctly, but that is not the case, for there are too many discrepancies in his various lists. However, it is not so much these discrepancies that are particularly disturbing as the obvious contradiction between the measures attributed to Pompey and those allegedly carried out by Gabinius. When speaking of Pompey Josephus definitely states that the cities mentioned were not destroyed and that they were incorporated into Syria. A few years afterward we are led to believe that Gabinius resettled a ragbag of desolate cities, five or six of which (we were told earlier) had been still standing in 63. The table lists the cities recorded by Josephus as having been 'assigned to the province of Syria' by Pompey or 'refounded' by Gabinius. For further comparison, towns are added in column 5 which Josephus says were held by Alexander Jannaeus (103–76).[14]

Pompey		Gabinius		Held by Jews
Antiquities	*BJ*	*Antiquities*	*BJ*	
Gadara	—			
Hippos	Hippos	—	—	—
Scythopolis	Scythopolis	Scythopolis	Scythopolis	Scythopolis
Pella	Pella	—	—	Pella
Dium	—	—	—	—
Samaria	Samaria	Samaria	Samaria	Samaria
Marisa	Marisa	Marisa	Marisa	Marisa
Azotus	Azotus	Azotus	Azotus	Azotus
Jamnia	Jamnia	—	Jamnia	Jamnia
Arethusa	Arethusa	—	—	—
Gaza	Gaza	Gaza	—	Gaza
Joppa	Joppa	—	—	Joppa
Dora	Dora	Adora(?)	Adoreus(?)	Adora(?)
Straton's Tower	Straton's Tower	—	—	Straton's Tower
—	—	—	Apollonia	Apollonia
—	—	—	Gamala	Gamala

It will be clear that many towns 'refounded' (or, as some suppose, reconstructed) by Gabinius are said to have been held by the Jews

---

[14] *Ant.* xiii 15. 4 (395). Only those towns are listed here which correspond with those which occur in the other columns. The complete list is longer.

earlier in the same century. It would be idle to pretend that this is material from which we can legitimately derive concrete historical information for each of these cities, and yet that is generally assumed to be the case. Jones combines these lists without further ado and even adds the cities that use the Pompeian era on coins which are sometimes of much later (third-century) date[15]—thus further complicating already confused matters by introducing a different category of evidence, the significance of which is itself not clear. We may note that Josephus, or a source from which he copied, uses everywhere the standard terminology of imperial propaganda of all ages: cities are not conquered but liberated, suppression of resistance to occupation is termed the establishment of law and order, and so on. That may serve as a warning not to rely too much on this information. However, even those who insist on accepting the sources as they stand, contradictions and all, will have to agree that no mention is made anywhere of building or construction, but of 'refoundation' and 'resettlement'. Yet these pronouncements are invariably interpreted and even translated as if they mentioned rebuilding in a physical sense. However, 'foundation' can be a mere administrative measure. 'Building' entails organization, finance, supervision, responsibility. Gabinius, in the course of one journey, 'ordered' numerous cities 'to be refounded'. Even if Josephus had claimed that he built anything it is not clear how he could have done this in such a brief period.[16]

There is no evidence anywhere of building activity. Gabinius is not mentioned on a single extant building inscription. No excavations can confidently attribute building activities to these years. Only at Samaria-Sebaste have houses been uncovered which allegedly could be attributed to these years.[17] Something must therefore be said of the evidence regarding this town.

About 107 BC it was conquered by the sons of John Hyrcanus after a long and difficult siege, for it was a very strong city.[18] It was destroyed,

[15] For the Pompeian era used by cities in Syria, J.-P. Rey-Coquais, *JRS* 68 (1978), 45 f. For bibliography of the city coinage, A. Kindler and A. Stein, *A Bibliography of the City Coinage of Palestine* (1987).

[16] Coins of Commodus minted by the city of Kanatha show that the city bore the name 'Gabinia'. For references, Schürer, ii (1978), 141 and n. 292; for discussion, H. I. MacAdam, *Studies in the History of the Roman Province of Arabia: The Northern Sector* (1986), 75–9. Gabinius appears also on a coin of Scythopolis: M. Reshef, *Alon* 5 (1) (1973), 7 f. (in Hebrew); also: Y. Meshorer, *City-coins of Eretz-Israel and the Decapolis in the Roman Period* (1985), no. 103 on p. 40 and p. 113. This does not necessarily mean more than that Gabinius gave these cities a new status. Such names are often attested on coins of much later date.

[17] G. A. Reisner, C. S. Fisher, and D. Gordon Lyon, *Harvard Excavations at Samaria* (1924), 50–4.

[18] Josephus, *Ant.* xiii 10. 2 (275–83); *BJ* i 2. 7 (64 ff.).

and the inhabitants were reduced to slavery.[19] We should note that, in his description of the siege, Josephus says that Samaria was later refounded by Herod, ignoring his own statement elsewhere that Gabinius refounded it.[20] Those who excavated the site, moreover, attribute houses to Gabinius only tentatively. The second expedition, in the thirties of this century, stated in its report: 'When Gabinius was governor walls were built round a new city.'[21] However, this must refer only to the houses and a section of wall excavated by the first expedition early this century. Josephus, however, says explicitly that Herod built a new wall.[22] It was further assumed as a matter of course that the town had been abandoned from its alleged destruction by John Hyrcanus around 107 BC till its presumed reconstruction by Gabinius in the fifties. This assumption in the modern literature contradicts Josephus' explicit statement that it was one of the towns held by the Jews earlier in the first century. There is actually no evidence of a gap in occupation to be found in the excavation report, but the belief that there was one suited Kathleen Kenyon's *a priori* assumption that the pottery usually called 'eastern sigillata' cannot antedate the second half of the first century BC.[23] This pottery is found at Samaria in connection with the stage attributed to Gabinius.

It seems safest on all accounts to accept that Gabinius took various measures of an administrative nature, the impact of which may have been of considerable importance for the population of many cities. There is no evidence, however, that he himself was involved in actual reconstruction. If ever the inhabitants called themselves 'Gabinians' this may merely indicate their gratitude for administrative measures.[24]

Herod and his Dynasty

In contrast to Gabinius' activities, there is nothing shadowlike in those of Herod, who was, of course, no Roman governor but a dependent king. His building enterprises are described in detail by Josephus, and numerous buildings are mentioned by name. His projects were of two kinds: first, the foundation or refoundation of entire cities, including their physical organization, which he undertook only in his own

[19] *Ant.* xiii 10. 3 (281); *BJ* i 2. 7 (65).

[20] *Ant.* xiii 10. 2 (275). For Herod's activities see below.

[21] J. W. Crowfoot, G. M. Crowfoot, and K. Kenyon, *The Objects from Samaria* (1957), 5.

[22] See below, n. 26.

[23] See the conclusions by J. Gunneweg, I. Perlman and J. Yellin, *The Provenance, Typology and Chronology of Eastern Sigillata* (Qedem 178, 1983), 78. I owe this point to Dr M. Fischer.

[24] This is mentioned only by Cedrenus, ed. Bekker, i, p. 323 in an otherwise confused passage.

kingdom; and second, the erection of public buildings both in cities in his own kingdom and elsewhere. Both kinds of activities are well documented in the writings of Josephus and attested through inscriptions and archaeological remains.[25] There is no need to go into details here.[26] All over Judaea the projects ascribed to Herod by Josephus are clearly visible: the extended platform of the temple in Jerusalem, one of the towers of his palace in Jerusalem, the constructions at Herodion, Masada, and Caesarea with its harbour, and so on.[27] All these sites are very well-known. What needs to be emphasized here is that there is a crucial difference, not merely in quantity but in kind and quality, between the tangible proof of massive Herodian construction in many parts of the country and the vague references to 'foundations' by Gabinius.

Of Herod's successors his son, the tetrarch Herod Antipas, is also known as an active urbanizer. In his realm he founded or refounded three cities. The refoundations are Sepphoris and Livias.[28] Josephus says that he made of Sepphoris an 'ornament of all Galilee'.[29] Livias received a town wall.[30] So far no archaeological remains have been uncovered clearly belonging to this phase, but there is no reason to doubt Josephus' information. The new city was Tiberias, the most important and enduring of Antipas' foundations.[31] The population was of mixed origin, and the tetrarch, according to Josephus, provided the settlers with land and houses equipped at his own expense.

Philip established two towns. Caesarea Philippi (Banias), his capital, was an existing settlement transformed into a town.[32] Herod

---

[25] References in Schürer, i (1973), 304–8.

[26] But since his new settlement at Samaria-Sebaste was mentioned above it is of interest to note that, as well as a strong wall, briefly described by Josephus, he also built a temple there in an enclosed precinct: *Ant.* xv 8. 5 (296–8); *BJ* i 21. 2 (403). These have been identified by excavation: J. W. Crowfoot, K. M. Kenyon, and E. L. Sukenik, *The Buildings at Samaria* (1966), 31–3.

[27] For concise bibliography, Schürer, i 304–8; for the harbour of Caesarea, several essays in *Harbour Archeaology: Proceedings of the First International Workshop on Ancient Mediterranean Harbours 1983*, ed. A. Raban (1985). See also the relevant entries in M. Avi-Yonah and E. Stern, *Encyclopedia of Archaeological Excavations in the Holy Land* (1975–8).

[28] For Sepphoris, Schürer, ii 172–6; L. Waterman et al., *Preliminary Report of the University of Michigan Excavations at Sepphoris* (1937); Avi-Yonah and Stern, iv 1051–4. S. S. Miller, *Studies in the History and Traditions of Sepphoris* (1984). The town is now again under excavation. For numismatic literature, Kindler and Stein, 230–8. For Livias, Schürer, ii 176–8; also S. Waterhouse and R. Ibach, *Andrews University Seminar Studies* 13 (1975), 227 f. for the remains visible on the surface.

[29] *Ant.* xviii 2. 1 (27): πρόσχημα τοῦ Γαλιλαίου παντός.

[30] Ibid.

[31] *Ant.* xviii 2. 3 (36–8); *BJ* ii 9. 1 (168); cf. Schürer, ii 178–82; Avi-Yonah and Stern, iv 1171–7; A. Kindler, *The Coins of Tiberias* (1961); Kindler and Stein, 239–48.

[32] *Ant.* xviii 2. 1 (28); *BJ* ii 9. 1 (168). Cf. Schürer, ii 169–761; for the coinage, Y. Meshorer, *INJ* 8 (1984/5), 37–58; Kindler and Stein, 188–93.

had built a temple for Augustus there.[33] Agrippa II further enlarged it.[34] To the village of Bethsaida, north of the lake of Tiberias, he granted city status, naming it Julias; he added settlers and strengthened the fortifications.[35] Archaeological or epigraphic evidence of these activities is so far lacking, but the statements in literary sources are so specific that there is no reason to doubt them. We may conclude then that both Herod and his sons were active builders.

Berytus and Heliopolis

Herod contributed substantial sums for public buildings in cities outside his realm. Thus we are told that at Berytus and Tyre he built exedrae, porticoes, temples and forums.[36] Agrippa I built an extraordinarily expensive and beautiful theatre at Berytus, as well as a costly amphitheatre, baths, and porticoes. He donated spectacles and provided great numbers of gladiators for the amphitheatre.[37] Agrippa II built (another?) expensive theatre at Berytus and donated annual spectacles costing thousands of drachmas. He gave grain and distributed olive oil to the citizens and adorned the whole city with statues and replicas of ancient sculptures.[38] Epigraphic confirmation has been found in the form of an inscription recording the restoration by Berenice and Agrippa II of a building erected by Herod the Great.[39] The munificence of the three Herods at Berytus is of particular interest, for this was a Roman colony, and if we might expect imperial support for urban development anywhere it would be for a new settlement of legionary veterans established by imperial decree, the most privileged category of communities in the empire. Before considering the epigraphic evidence there are two remarks to be made. First, whatever Herod or his successors gave was clearly not built by the Roman authorities: this must mean, for instance, that Berytus, founded no later than 14 BC, did not have a theatre and amphitheatre until Agrippa I built them fifty or more years later. Second, no mention is made in these

---

[33] *Ant.* xv 10. 3 (363); *BJ* i 21. 3 (404).

[34] *Ant.* xx 9. 4 (211).

[35] *Ant.* xviii 2. 1 (28); *BJ* ii 9. 1 (168); cf. Schürer, ii 171 f.

[36] He also built *gymnasia* for Tripolis, Damascus, and Ptolemais, a wall for Byblus, theatres for Sidon and Damascus, an aqueduct for Laodicea on Sea, baths, fountains, and colonnades for Ascalon, not to mention the works he donated to Greek cities. *BJ* i 21. 11 (422).

[37] *Ant.* xix 78. 5 (335–7).

[38] *Ant.* xx 9. 4 (211). Agrippa also enlarged Caesarea Philippi, according to the same passage.

[39] R. Cagnat, *Musée Belge* 32 (1928), 157–67; cf. *MUSJ* 25 (1942–3), 31 n. 1. A photograph can also be found in J. Lauffray, *ANRW* ii 8. 135–63, pl. ii 5. See also id., *BMB* 7 (1944–5), 13–80, esp. 56; E. Gabba, *Iscrizioni greche e latine per lo studio della bibbia (1958)*, 102 f.

passages of Heliopolis, which clearly supports the opinion of those who do not believe that this was established as a separate colony by Augustus.

The epigraphic evidence from Berytus is less accessible than that of Heliopolis, but what has been published is of interest.[40] The material known to me seems on the whole to be relatively late. The earliest building inscription that mentions an emperor refers to Claudius.[41] Next there is the inscription just mentioned, of Berenice and Agrippa II. Vespasian occurs on one inscription.[42] The absence of early inscriptions in itself proves nothing, but it can at least be said that we have no positive indication of a systematic build-up in the early years of the colony. So there is no reason to doubt Josephus' claim that the Herods systematically funded the development of public buildings in that city.

The legal status of Heliopolis need not concern us here. It was probably part of the territory of Berytus till the reign of Severus when it is on record as a separate colony. In any event the region was taken over by veterans in the time of Augustus. It is therefore of interest to see what inscriptions tell us of the urban development of this town and its vicinity. The material has been published in Volume VI of *IGLS*. Here too evidence is lacking of an immediate or early development following the settlement of veterans. The earliest imperial texts from the area are two rock-cut inscriptions along the Heliopolis–Damascus road which mention Nero.[43] In the town Vespasian is mentioned on a dedication (not a building inscription).[44] An inscription set up by the public for Agrippa I or II as patron of the colony (Berytus or Heliopolis) confirms again the obligations of the community toward that king.[45] Dedications for Samsigeramus of Emesa and his son, the latter also a patron of the colony, attest a similar relationship.[46] No building inscriptions from Heliopolis record imperial initiative or financial support. The exception, as always, is a limited number of milestones. At least one of these shows that the city was responsible for the repair of the roads under Caracalla.[47]

---

[40] R. Cagnat, *Syria* 5 (1924), 108–12, esp. 109, 111 f.; Lauffray, *BMB* 7, 13–80; 8 (1946–8), 7–16; R. Mouterde and J. Lauffray, *Beyrouth ville romaine* (1952); R. Mouterde, *Regards sur Beyrouth* (1952, repr. 1966); Lauffray, *ANRW*, 135–63.

[41] *AE* 1958. 163. Cf. the development of Hadrian's Antinoopolis, where settlement was a continuing process: P. V. Pistorius, *Indices Antinoopolitani* (1939), 91–3; also the republican colonies discussed in ch. VII.

[42] An inscription which honours Liber Pater (= Marsyas?): Cagnat, *Syria* 5, 111, no. 7.

[43] *IGLS* vi 2968 f.   [44] Ibid. 2762.

[45] Ibid. 2759.   [46] Ibid. 2760. See also 2917.

[47] *IGLS* vi 2918: 'vias et milliari[a] per D. Pium Cassium praesidem prov. Syr. Phen. Colonia

The establishment of a Roman colony at Ptolemais (Acco) has been discussed above. Very little is known of this foundation. There are not many inscriptions, but the few that have been found fit the pattern established at Heliopolis.[48] As noted above, the imposition of the veteran colony was a measure which had a drastic impact on the existing community and cannot have been welcome, unlike the mere grant of a name of honour or privileges to the existing community (which Ptolemais and several other towns had received a few years before). There is too little information to say much more. There is one hint that families of distinction may have lived in the city. It produced at least one distinguished person: the consular Flavius Boethus, governor of Palestine, 162–6, known from the works of Galen as a scholar and philosopher with an interest in medicine.[49]

The Flavian Period

Syria and Arabia

In the reign of Vespasian roads were constructed in Syria, clearly as part of the military reorganization of the wider area.[50] It has been argued that there is evidence as well of an active policy fostering urbanization through building enterprises.[51] That is relevant for the present discussion and must be scrutinized.

Building activity at Bostra by the last Nabataean king, Rabbel II, has been connected with the presence of Marcus Ulpius Traianus, father of the emperor, as Vespasian's governor of Syria. But it seems unnecessary to think of Roman influence or pressure in considering building activity by client kings. As observed above, Herod alone was far more active in building and construction than all Roman governors together.[52] The development of Bostra as capital of the Roman prov-

---

Julia Aug. et Hel (r)en(o)v[a]vit.' This must be taken as it stands and cannot be construed as if it were a boundary stone marking the limit of the territory of the colony (as interpreted in the comments on the inscription and on p. 36). I have observed in many publications that milestones in Judaea and neighbouring provinces do not refer to territories. See also nos. 2900, 29–58, 29–63, and, for the Heliopolis–Emesa road, *IGLS* v 2675 f., 2672, 2674.

[48] M. Avi-Yonah, *QDAP* 12 (1946), 85 no. 2: 'Imp. Ner. Caesari Col. Ptol. Veter. Vici Nea Com. et Gedru.' There is no reason to connect this inscription with road building as the editor does. Ibid. 86 n. 3, 'Pago Vicinal(i)', shows that the territory, like that of Heliopolis, was organized in *pagi*. For literature on *vici* and *pagi*, ch. VII, n. 45. See also Y. Soreq, *JQR* 65 (1975), 221–4. A centurial *cippus* was found 1½ km. south of the first inscription: J. Meyer, *Scripta Classica Israelica* 7 (1983/4), 119–25, with an appendix by S. Applebaum, 125–8. Not far from this spot a fragment of another Latin inscription was found: ibid. 117 f.

[49] References in E. M. Smallwood, *The Jews under Roman Rule* (1981), 552.

[50] See ch. I.   [51] G. W. Bowersock, *JRS* 63 (1973), 133–40.

[52] For pre-Roman Bostra, M. Sartre, *Bostra, des origines à l'Islam* (1985), 56–62. See also J.-M. Dentzer, *Berytus* 32 (1984), 163–74, for soundings near the Nabataean arch.

ince of Arabia will be further discussed below. At Palmyra the early town-wall has been attributed to Vespasian.[53] However, it has been observed that 'the walls owed nothing to Roman influence, but were probably constructed by the Palmyrenes themselves' well before the Flavian period.[54]

At Gerasa a new city-plan was adopted in the first century. It has been suggested that the whole project might have been the initiative of M. Ulpius Traianus.[55] The excavators, however, believe that it was started in the sixties or even earlier.[56] There is, moreover, no indication that the work was initiated by imperial authorities. The building inscriptions give an impression of the speed of the development of Gerasa in the first and second centuries. The earliest of these record the construction of a temple for Zeus Olympios: the first is dated AD 22/3 and notes that a private citizen, a former priest of Tiberius Caesar, paid for the building.[57] The next building inscriptions belong to the reign of Nero.[58] Under the Flavians the building of the north-west gate, dated 75/6, was followed by much further activity.[59] Building activity reached a peak in the second half of the second century.[60] This included the erection between 161–6 of a new temple of Zeus in place of the old one built in the reign of Tiberius and of the Temple of Artemis, the central feature of the town plan and Gerasa's greatest monument. Of the numerous buildings constructed in the first and second centuries none is said to have been paid for by the imperial authorities. In the third century a stoa was built.[61] Two other inscriptions may be connected with buildings.[62] There are numerous building inscriptions of the fifth and sixth century.

Several other points are worth noting. First, six inscriptions for the procurator of Arabia and another set up by his *cornicularius*.[63] As there

[53] Bowersock, *JRS* 63, 137.   [54] J. F. Matthews, *JRS* 74 (1984), 161.

[55] Bowersock, *JRS* 63, 138, discussing inscription no. 50, dated 75/6 from Gerasa which records the building of the Northwest Gate. (The inscription numbers in this and the following notes are those of C. H. Kraeling, *Gerasa: City of the Decapolis* (1938)).

[56] Kraeling, 39 ff., esp. 41: 'The upper limit for the date of the adoption by Gerasa of its new plan is fixed at 75/6 by the Northwest Gate [inscription no. 50]. If we could be sure that inscriptions no. 45 and 46 of 66/7 AD referred to the city's wall rather than to some other enterprise, we might be able to lower the *terminus ad quem* by a few years. The *terminus a quo*, however, remains obscure. . .' He concludes that the new city plan was adopted between 22 and 76, perhaps about the middle of the first century.

[57] No. 2; cf. nos. 3–10.   [58] Nos. 45 f. of AD 66/7 (above, n. 56); no. 49 of 67/8.

[59] See nos. 51 f. and the inscriptions recording the construction of the theatre when Lappius Maximus was governor of Syria, AD 90/1: J. Pouilloux, *Liber Annuus* 27 (1977), 246–54; 29 (1979), 276–8. For Rostovtzeff's curious notions on Flavian activity in Transjordan see below, p. 347.

[60] No. 53, AD 119/20 and no. 58, of 130 are followed by nos. 60, 63–5, 69.

[61] No. 74 of AD 259.

[62] Nos. 105 f. of AD 293–305 and 286–305.   [63] Nos. 173, 175–9, 207 f.

are no such texts from Bostra, the provincial capital—where, however, there are numerous inscriptions honouring or mentioning the governor, who was also commander of the legion stationed in the city—it appears that the financial administration of the province was based at Gerasa, which was more important commercially and financially than Bostra. However, the governor (of Syria, after 106 of Arabia) is also present on many inscriptions.[64] It seems that an army unit was based in or near the city, a familiar phenomenon in the eastern provinces. Inscriptions set up for serving soldiers of the *ala I Augusta Thracum* strongly suggest that this unit spent some time there.[65] Other inscriptions refer to soldiers of the legion III Cyrenaica or to the legion itself.[66] Quite a few citizens of Gerasa served in the army. Several combined army and municipal careers, as was the case in Heliopolis.[67] Some combined procuratorial and municipal careers.[68] Local dignitaries maintained the imperial cult.[69] The emperors are duly honoured.[70] The Hellenistic pantheon is represented by numerous inscriptions and a series of temples, and their cult is reflected in many personal names. The inscriptions convey an image of a comfortable upper and middle class who did well for themselves in the empire and played the role expected by the authorities. The personal names are also interesting. Most of them are mixed Greco-Roman, some fully Roman; very few are Semitic.[71] The language of the inscriptions is almost exclusively Greek, Latin being restricted to inscriptions set up by or for imperial officials

[64] For the governor of Syria, above, n. 59 and no. 50; for the governor of Arabia, e.g. nos. 160–2, 165, 170. No. 1 honours a Nabataean king, the last Aretas or Rabbel. This need imply no more than the existence of friendly ties.

[65] Nos. 199–201.

[66] Nos. 23, 31, 211, 213. Note also no. 171, a Hadrianic inscription which mentions VI Ferrata: C. B. Welles, *ap.* Kraeling, 435, no. 171; cf. D. Kennedy, *HSCP* 84 (1980), 298 f.

[67] No. 52: veteran and *decurio*. 62: a centurion whose son was an *eques, bouleutes, strategos* (= duovir), and ex-priest of the city. 102 and 219: Aelius Germanus, *primipilarius*. 183: a centurion. 119: T. Flavius Flavii Cerealii f. Quirina Flaccus (AD 115/6), almost certainly a descendant of a man who served in Judaea in V Macedonica, under the command of Sex. Vettulenus Cerialis, and received citizenship as a result. Cerealis is named Cerealius by Josephus, e.g. in *BJ* iii 7. 32 (310). For Cerialis, Schürer, i 515; for similar cases of the adoption by soldiers of the name of their commander, B. Isaac, *Heer und Integrationspolitik*, eds. W. Eck and H. Wolff (1986), 259–62. 164 of AD 152: L. Ulpius Cerealis, perhaps a descendant of a man recruited by Vettulenus Cerialis and discharged as well as enfranchised under Trajan.

[68] Nos. 62, 189 f. Note also no. 53, set up in 119/20 by a man who served as priest in the imperial cult at Antioch for his son as *agoranomos*.

[69] Nos. 2 (above, n. 57), 10, 53.

[70] Trajan in 115: nos. 56/7, 119; Hadrian when he visited the town in 129/30: 143–5 and 58 (triumphal arch).

[71] e.g. no. 15: Malchos son of Demetrios son of Malchos; 16: Ameros the son of Rhagelos; 29: Leonidas son of Malchos.

and soldiers.[72] There is not much in the inscriptions from Gerasa to remind one of the background of the native population.

Comparison with the material from Heliopolis is of interest. At Heliopolis a social class is represented which did not exist at Gerasa, where no evidence has been found of local *equites* or senators, let alone of consuls.[73] Latin is not used at Gerasa by the local population, but in both cities the Semitic background is hardly noticeable. On the other hand, as we shall see below, the contrast with the material from Bostra is striking.

Judaea

'The Palestinian war of AD 70 led to the attempt of the Flavian emperors to surround the Judaean centre of fanaticism by chains of Hellenistic cities, and thus to enclose Judaism in an iron ring of Hellenism. . . . Vespasian and Domitian settled strong groups of Roman veterans in Transjordania, either of Greek origin or thoroughly Hellenized.'[74] Rostovtzeff clearly had no more sympathy for rebels against imperial authority than old Cato the Censor. This is a matter of choice and ideology. But the notion that the Flavian emperors surrounded Judaea with chains of cities and veteran settlements can be tested and thus confirmed or refuted. It entails assumptions about the Roman response to revolt and activism in the promotion of urban development as a means of controlling hostile groups in the empire.

We have seen above that there is in fact no evidence of Flavian activity in fostering urbanization in Syria and Transjordan. However, that still leaves the possibility that we might find evidence of a Flavian 'iron ring of Hellenism' elsewhere around Jewish territory.[75] In the province of Judaea we know to some extent what was done. Josephus has the following to say:

About the same time Caesar sent intructions to Bassus and Laberius Maximus, the procurator, to dispose of all Jewish land. For he founded there no city

---

[72] I counted five Latin inscriptions set up by civilians, five Greek inscriptions set up by soldiers, and three bilingual inscriptions set up by soldiers.

[73] See G. W. Bowersock, *Epigrafia e ordine senatorio*, 651–8: no senators from Judaea/Palaestina or from Arabia. For the *equites*, see below.

[74] M. Rostovtzeff, *Caravan Cities* (1932), 67.

[75] Flavian urbanization in Palestine after the revolt is also assumed by M. Avi-Yonah, *RE* Supp. xiii (1974), s.v. Palaestina, col. 398; *The Holy Land* (revised edn., 1977), 111 f. It is not entirely clear how Avi-Yonah views the process. The assumption appears to be that an administrative decision to turn a community into a municipality will foster the growth of a town on the spot.

of his own while keeping their territory, but only to eight hundred veterans did he assign a place for settlement called Emmaus . . .[76]

In this passage, often misunderstood, Josephus wants to emphasize that Vespasian gave instructions to sell all confiscated land in Judaea. No Jewish land was granted to foreign settlers, for he did not found a new Flavian city (i.e. a veteran colony) to replace Jerusalem. That, of course, would have been the first link in any 'chain of Hellenistic cities' such as envisaged by Rostovtzeff. Josephus explicitly mentions the modest settlement at Emmaus as an exception. The site can be identified without doubt with Moẓa.[77] It lies in one of the most fertile and pleasant valleys around Jerusalem, well-watered with ample farm land and situated on the main road from the coastal plain to the city. Even this veteran settlement—it was too small to receive the status of a colony—has left an imprint. The village still bore the name 'Qolonia' in the nineteenth century, and the tombstone of a young girl with a Roman name was found on the spot, inscribed in Latin.[78]

The available evidence regarding the military organization of Judaea after the Jewish War has been discussed in Chapter III. The garrison was reinforced, and Jerusalem became the site of the legionary headquarters. Josephus' information in this respect has been confirmed as well. There is, however, no evidence of large-scale construction by the troops from Vespasian to Hadrian. Two cities of Judaea received the name 'Flavia', Joppe (Jaffa) and Neapolis.[79] These were both communities that had been ravaged in the war.[80] There is no evidence that new settlers were planted in these towns or that the original communities of respectively Jews and Samaritans were disenfranchised. At Joppe a substantial Jewish cemetery has been found.[81] A Jewish *agoranomos* is attested in the reign of Trajan.[82] Under Domitian

[76] *BJ* vii 6. 6 (216) as translated and interpreted by B. Isaac, *JJS* 35 (1984), 44–50.

[77] Schürer, i (revised edn.), 512 n. 142; the results of a recent survey are forthcoming in M. Fischer, B. Isaac and I. Roll, *Roman Roads in Judaea*, ii. It must be emphasized that this was not a settlement with the status of a *polis*, let alone of a Roman colony. It does not appear in the lists of Roman colonies in the Digest, is not mentioned as a colony by Pliny, and did not issue coinage.

[78] Y. H. Landau, *Acta of the Fifth International Congress of Greek and Latin Epigraphy, Cambridge 1967* (1971), 389: 'Valeria L.f. Sedata vix(it) an(nos) iiii.'

[79] Joppe: on coins from Caracalla to Severus Alexander, A. Kindler, *Museum Haaretz Yearbook* 20/21 (1985/6), 21–36; cf. Kindler and Stein, 157–9. Neapolis: on coins of Domitian, not before 82/3, *BMC Palestine*, 45, no. 2. Cf. Pliny, *NH* v 13. 69: 'intus autem Samariae oppida Neapolis, quod antea Mamortha dicebatur . . .'; Josephus, *BJ* iv 8. 1 (449). Cf. Kindler and Stein, 162–76.

[80] For Joppe, Josephus, *BJ* ii 18. 10 (507–9); iii 9. 2–4 (414–31). For Neapolis, formerly Ma'abartha at the foot of Mount Gerizim, *BJ* iii 8. 32 (307–15).

[81] Frey, *CII* ii, nos. 892–960.

[82] *SEG* xxxi 1410: an inscribed mould for lead weights dated AD 107 and 110. The *agoranomos* is named Judas.

Neapolis issued coinage which avoided pagan types. Caesarea received colonial status from Vespasian, but it is clear that this was not accompanied by the settlement of veterans in the town.[83] It was a reward for support in the Jewish war and probably commemorated the fact that in Caesarea Vespasian was proclaimed emperor by his own troops—hence the name of the colony: *Colonia Prima Flavia Caesarea*.[84] The grant of colonial status will have had a profound impact. It meant that some of the citizens of the town received Roman citizenship; tax privileges were granted as well.[85]

What can we say of the Flavian activity in Judaea on the basis of all this? The garrison was strengthened. The only evidence regarding veteran settlement concerns the small community at Emmaus. Jerusalem was left in ruins. Three towns received various privileges. There is, however, no evidence at all of concrete steps to foster the reconstruction of towns after the war. At Caesarea there are monuments of Herod and an aqueduct built under Hadrian. It is possible that there was building activity under the Flavians, but there is no proof of this, and there is no basis for the assumption that the imperial or provincial authorities financed or even stimulated urban development. What is remarkable about Flavian policy in Judaea is the absence of large-scale reorganization and reconstruction. Rostovtzeff's pronouncements on Flavian measures represent at best what he himself thought the Romans should have done.

Trajan: Arabia

Trajan annexed the Nabataean kingdom. A Roman legion and auxilia formed the garrison, and a great new road was built from Bostra in the North to Aela on the Red Sea.[86] The legionary headquarters were established at Bostra, which also became the seat of the governor and was renamed 'Nova Traiana'.[87] One might expect this to have resulted

---

[83] See the arguments cited in *Talanta* 12–13 (1980–81), 39–43.

[84] 'Prima' indicates that the city was 'first in loyalty'. There are no chronological implications, for the same title was given to or adopted by the Flavian veteran colony at Paestum: 'Colonia Flavia Prima Paesti'. See L. Keppie, *PBSR* 52 (1984), 100–3, esp. 101.

[85] Paulus, *Dig.* L 15. 8. 7: 'Divus Vespasianus Caesarienses colonos fecit non adiecto, ut et iuris Italici essent, sed tributum his remisit capitis: sed divus Titus etiam solum immune factum interpretatus est. Similes his Capitulenses esse videntur.' Ulpian, *Dig.* L 15. 1: 'In Palaestina duae fuerunt coloniae, Caesarienses et Aelia Capitolina, sed neutra ius Italicum habet. Divus quoque Severus in Sebastenam coloniam deduxit.'

[86] For the city, A. Kindler, *The Coinage of Bostra* (1983); Sartre, *Bostra*. Also F. E. Peters, *JAOS* 97 (1977), 266–75, for Bostra in the period before the Roman annexation.

[87] Sartre, 76 f.; for the municipal institutions, 78–87. The new name is first attested in *IGLS* xiii 1 no. 91 and appears on coins of Antoninus Pius: Kindler, 105 f., nos. 2, 4.

in the rapid expansion of the city.[88] There are numerous building inscriptions from Bostra, yet all but two are dated between 259/60 and Justinian. There was, as would be expected, a temple for Rome and Augustus.[89] An altar dedicated by the town to Zeus Epicarpius is dated 181.[90] This may indicate that there was a temple as well. There is no further information on the physical development of the town in the period following the annexation of the Nabataean kingdom as a Roman province, let alone evidence of direct imperial stimulation or support. An exception is the fortification of the city in the third century. Here, as in Adraa, the work was initiated by the governor. The greatest number of building inscriptions belongs to the end of the fifth and the beginning of the sixth century.[91] Part of these again refer to the repair or construction of fortifications.

The epigraphic material from Bostra allows of various interesting observations. First, the local population and the military did not mix at any social level. Contrary to what was seen at Gerasa and Heliopolis no municipal magistrates or *bouleutai* seem to have served in the army,[92] nor do officers appear to have performed civic functions, as they did, for instance, at Palmyra.[93] It is significant that no senator is attested as originating from Bostra or any other city of Arabia.[94] Only six *equites* are known from this province, three of them uncertain.[95] The language of the inscriptions is to be noted as well. Of 229 grave-inscriptions in Greek, only five identify the dead as soldiers. Of 35 Latin grave-inscriptions only six record civilian burials. Military burials include stones set up by soldiers for their relatives or for soldiers by their relatives; among the mothers and wives there is not much evidence of local connections. Apart from grave-inscriptions there are well over 46 inscriptions set up by officials, army units, and individual soldiers; only six of these are in Greek, all the others are in Latin. Building inscriptions are all but one in Greek. The presence of the governor and the legionary headquarters is clearly expressed in the epigraphic material, but it is quite possible that the procurator of Arabia was based at Gerasa, because this town was more important as a financial centre.

---

[88] For the buildings of the city in the second and third centuries, Sartre, ch. IV.

[89] *IGLS* xiii 9143.

[90] *IGLS* xiii 9104.

[91] Sartre, 122–9.

[92] The only exception is Flavius Clemens, veteran and ex-*beneficiarius*: *IGLS* xiii 9422.

[93] H.-G. Pflaum, *Les Carrières procuratoriennes*, nos. 155 and 180; H. Seyrig, *Syria* 14 (1933), 152–68.

[94] See the list in Bowersock, *Epigrafia* ii 664–8. The emperor Philip the Arab was an *eques*.

[95] H. Devijver, *DRBE*, 191 f. He points out (198) that there are no equestrian officers at all from Cappadocia, Armenia, or Mesopotamia.

The onomastic material has recently been studied in detail.[96] It is not surprising that soldiers and imperial officials adhere to Roman nomenclature. The names are Greek and Roman. On the other hand, few civilians and local officials are clearly identified as Roman citizens by *nomen gentis* and *cognomen*. The only exceptions are *bouleutai*, mentioned on a few official inscriptions and two from graves.[97] Many civilians and very few soldiers bear Semitic names.[98]

To sum up. At Bostra the presence of the garrison commanded by the legate is clearly reflected in the inscriptions, but these do not provide evidence of the social and cultural integration of army and civilians characteristic of the material from Heliopolis and many western provinces.[99] It can perhaps be said that Bostra was a town of Hellenized rather than Romanized Arabs. To judge from the building inscriptions the city developed much more slowly than Gerasa. Bostra was the provincial capital, but there is in fact no indication that it was a flourishing 'caravan city' under the early empire. The material from Heliopolis, Gerasa, and Bostra shows for each of these cities the impact of Hellenistic culture and the Roman conquest. At Heliopolis, an important sanctuary and flourishing veteran colony, these characteristics can still be observed in the third century. Gerasa was a moderately prosperous town, inhabited by a thoroughly Hellenized population. It may have been the seat of the financial procurator of the province of Arabia. There is some evidence of the presence of army personnel there, but not comparable in scale with that at Bostra, which was a legionary headquarters and the seat of the governor of the province. At Bostra a clear division appears to be noticeable between the Hellenized Nabataeans and the army personnel and their relatives. It seems clear that the pattern observed at Heliopolis is typical of that of veteran colonies in the East, although there is far less evidence at Berytus, Ptolemais, and Aelia Capitolina.

One project for which there is concrete evidence of execution under Trajan is the construction of an aqueduct to Canatha in AD 106–14.[100]

---

[96] Sartre, ch. IV, with index and commentary.   [97] *IGLS* 9403, 9409.

[98] *IGLS* 9169; see also 9199. However, J. C. Mann, *Legionary Recruitment and Veteran Settlement during the Principate* (1983), 42, with Table 26, has shown that by the third century at least there were a number of recruits to III Cyrenaica, and it is very likely that at least some of these men came from Bostra or its territory.

[99] Coins of the mid-3rd cent. bear the reverse legend *Concordia Bostrenorum*, with Zeus-Ammon as the personification of the military garrison standing opposite the Tyche of the city of Bostra: Kindler, nos. 48 and 56. However, as pointed out by Kindler, 92 f., coins issued by the city as minting authority (as opposed to the provincial mint) do not have *vexilla* or the legend 'III Cyr.' like colonial coins of Aelia or Acco.

[100] *IGR* iii 1291; *OGIS* 618; cf. *SEG* vii 969.

It must be emphasized that the selection of cities studied in detail in this and the previous chapter is an opportunistic one. Palmyra has not been mentioned because it is unique, Antioch because, as an ancient metropolis, it is hard to determine what would be the impact of the Roman conquest. Yet the conclusions seem to be valid as far as they go.

Hadrian

Hadrian is credited with a wide range of activities. In the words of Schürer: 'Everywhere he went, he furthered works of civilization. Buildings were erected, ornamental and utilitarian, and games were celebrated: to all provinces he became a "restitutor".'[101] Hadrian indeed chose to be called 'restitutor', 'founder', and so on; and he certainly celebrated games. In the eastern provinces, however, there are not many buildings that can with certainty be attributed to his benefactions. Historians and archaeologists too easily believe that every building on which an emperor's name was inscribed had been paid for by him.[102] On the contrary there are inscriptions which dedicate a building to an emperor while mentioning specifically that the costs had been defrayed by a private person, for instance, at Lepcis Magna[103] and on the famous bridge at Alcantara.[104]

Various forms of bureaucratic activity can be traced. The imperial forests in Lebanon were carefully marked with inscriptions.[105] This is interesting material, for it shows the extent of the imperial domains in this area: the forests were in mountainous areas, and the cultivated plains were left as city territory.[106] Boundary stones were set up between the territories of Palmyra and Emesa.[107] A census was held in the Syrian cities.[108] The famous Tax Law of Palmyra was inscribed in Hadrian's reign.[109] Hadrianic road-building in Syria, Arabia, and

---

[101] Schürer, i 541 f.

[102] See e.g. the unjustified attack on L. Robert by Ch. Picard, *RA* (1963), 110 f. with fig. 3.

[103] *ILS* 5754: (Hadrian in abl.) 'Q. Servi[l]ius Candidus sua impensa aquam quaesit[a]m et elevatam in coloniam perduxit.'

[104] See above, p. 333.

[105] All are collected in *IGLS* viii 3, ed. Jean-François Breton (1980).

[106] It is not clear to me what the editor means when he writes: 'les inscriptions forestières attestent la pérennité d'un domaine impérial qui correspond approximativement au territoire de la colonie Béryte.'

[107] *IGLS* v 2550; cf. D. Schlumberger, *Syria* 20 (1939), 43–73. The boundary was first marked out by Creticus Silanus, governor from 11/12 till 16/17. See also J. Matthews, *JRS* 74 (1984), 175 n. 10.

[108] Rey-Coquais, *JRS*, 53 n. 114.

[109] Matthews, *JRS* 74, esp. 175 n. 10; H. Seyrig, *Syria* 22 (1941), 163–5.

particularly Judaea has been discussed above. That, however, is military organization.

What would be relevant for the present chapter is evidence of systematic urbanization, including support for the physical development of new and existing towns. We start with Judaea. Here we know of the existence of two buildings named 'Hadrianeion', at Caesarea and Tiberias.[110] Nothing is known of the nature of these buildings, and there is no evidence that Hadrian initiated their erection. A monumental building south of Scythopolis, perhaps a triumphal arch, apparently bore Hadrian's name.[111] It may have been connected with his visit to the province, but there is no indication who paid for its construction. Caesarea received an aqueduct built by legionary vexillations.[112] Aqueducts, however, were more often built by the army, all over the empire, than other structures, perhaps because they required a form of expertise which was not easily found among civilians.[113]

Hadrian's major project in the province was, of course, his new Jerusalem, Aelia Capitolina, founded, according to Cassius Dio, to replace the city that had been destroyed.[114] Dio adds that Hadrian 'built another temple for Zeus instead of the temple of the god'. We have here then an explicit reference to at least one temple built by orders of the emperor. In the modern literature, however, Hadrian is credited not merely with the initiative of founding a city, but with actually reconstructing the city which Vespasian had left in ruins. It is true that Byzantine sources list various public buildings in the town;[115] but we do not have to believe that a Byzantine author would know how much of Aelia Capitolina was actually built in Hadrian's time. The earliest eyewitness, the pilgrim from Bordeaux, visited the town in 333, after the activities of Constantine.[116] The only Roman structures mentioned are two imperial statues (*statuae duae Hadriani*) on the Temple Mount,[117] four porches at the pool of Siloam, the town wall

---

[110] References in Schürer, i 542; Smallwood, *Jews*, 432.   [111] See above, p. 307.

[112] For references, B. Isaac and I. Roll, *Latomus* 38 (1979), 59 f.

[113] See, however, W. Eck in *Die Wasserversorgung Antiker Städte*, ed. Frontinus-Gesellschaft (1987), on funding for aqueducts. Eck, 77, says the contribution by army units was not significant. On contributions made by the emperor, 76 f.

[114] Dio lxix 12. 1. For the revolt of Bar Kokhba which followed, B. Isaac and A. Oppenheimer, *JJS* 36 (1985), 33–60.

[115] *Chron. paschale*, ed. Dindorf, i, p. 474.

[116] *Itinerarium Burdigalense* 589–97, ed. P. Geyer, *Itinera Hierosolymitana*, CCSL clxxv 15–19.

[117] Cf. Jerome, *in Esaiam* i 2. 9 (*CCSL* lxxiiia 33): 'ubi quondam erat templum et religio Dei, ibi Hadriani statua et Iovis idolum collocatum est'; *Com. in Matt.* 24: 15 (*CCSL* lxxvii 226): 'potest autem simpliciter aut de Antichristo accipi aut de imagine Caesaris, quam Pilatus posuit in templo, aut de Hadriani equestri statua quae in ipso sancto sanctorum loco usque in praesentem diem stetit.'

and, of course, Constantine's Church of the Holy Sepulchre. There is, therefore, no clear evidence that Hadrian personally, or the authorities at a lower level, were responsible for any construction. It is significant that Dio, even in the version of Xiphilinus, does not mention any urban development at Jerusalem, although he mentions Hadrian's initiatives elsewhere. He is said to have constructed theatres in several cities.[118] In Egypt he restored Pompey's monument and built Antinoopolis.[119] He gave money for the Olympieion in Athens. Yet at Jerusalem we are told merely that he founded a city and built a temple.

All this would be irrelevant if there were archaeological finds, especially inscriptions, to show that Jerusalem was rebuilt under Hadrian. There is, however, not a single Hadrianic building inscription from Jerusalem. The earliest colonial inscription, on a statue base, mentions Antoninus Pius,[120] and the next two dated inscriptions are Severan.[121] Neither is a building inscription. Since there are not many inscriptions from the period from Hadrian to Constantine it could be argued that the lack of Hadrianic inscriptions is in itself not very significant. Combined with the archaeological evidence, however, it is important. In the years since 1967 extensive excavations have been carried out in the southern part of what was Aelia Capitolina.[122] No remains of any structures dating to the second and third centuries have been found.[123] The least that can be concluded is that Aelia Capitolina developed slowly. The fact that Jerusalem became in the Byzantine period a centre of Christian pilgrimage and imperial patronage is no basis for assuming that Aelia was a flourishing town from Hadrian to Constantine. The only structure which is attested without doubt as constructed by legionaries is an aqueduct.[124]

In Syria and Arabia there seems an equal lack of inscriptions attesting building activity initiated by Hadrian. A triumphal arch set up at Gerasa to celebrate the imperial visit is clearly a declaration of

---

[118] Dio lxix 10. 1.   [119] lxix 11. 1–2.

[120] *CIL* iii 116 (6639).

[121] M. Avi-Yonah, 'The Latin Inscription from the Excavations in Jerusalem', in B. Mazar, *The Excavations in the Old City of Jerusalem, Preliminary Report of the First Season, 1968* (1969), 22–4. *CIL* iii 6641 (12080a).

[122] For the results of excavations carried out in Jerusalem, H. Geva, *IEJ* 34 (1984), 239–54. See also below, p. 427, for the headquarters of X Fretensis in Jerusalem.

[123] Geva, 240–4, 2351. On the extensive excavations carried out in the southern part of Jerusalem only brief preliminary reports and popular accounts have been published: N. Avigad, *Discovering Jerusalem* (1983); M. Ben Dov, *In the Shadow of the Temple* (1985). In the latter book, 195–8, mention is made of one room which produced objects and coins of the second and third centuries; see also 199–205 for photographs of various finds of this period.

[124] See the centurial inscriptions collected by L. Vetrali, *Liber Annuus* 17 (1967), 149–61, figs. 1–5.

loyalty on the part of the citizens rather than a contribution to urban development by the emperor.[125] The same must be said of an inscription set up by the city of Palmyra to thank a citizen for his munificence on the occasion of Hadrian's visit in 130. He had provided oil, helped in every respect with the reception of the imperial expedition and, in particular, paid in person for the construction of the temple of Zeus (otherwise known as the temple of Baalshamim) 'with the front hall and the other colonnades'.[126] If the emperor himself made benefactions during his visit the evidence has disappeared.

Hadrian is generally known as the emperor who more than any other initiated and supported building projects in cities. Although this book is concerned only with the eastern frontier provinces it might be useful to test the general validity of the conclusions drawn in this chapter by considering what evidence we have of Hadrian's works elsewhere. This is by no means an attempt to give a full description of building projects in Hadrian's reign, but merely a sketch based on perusal of material easily available. This seems a legitimate procedure, as it is not the odd exception but the bulk of the material which indicates a pattern of activity. The material is drawn from Weber's work on Hadrian, supplemented with epigraphic material published later.[127] The *Historia Augusta* claims that Hadrian 'built something and gave games in almost all the cities'.[128] And it also states that, 'while he built an infinite number of buildings everywhere, he inscribed his name only on the Temple of his father Trajan'.[129] These are not pronouncements to be accepted without solid corroboration. How did the author know of all these Hadrianic buildings if the emperor's name did not appear on them?

Pausanias, writing in the middle of the second century, states: 'Some temples of the gods he built from the beginning and some he embellished with dedications and equipment; he gave gifts to Greek cities and also to barbarians who asked him: all these are registered in the Pantheon at Athens.'[130] Here, in a contemporary source, mention is made only of temples and gifts. Dio claims more for Hadrian: 'He aided virtually all (cities) giving to some an aqueduct, to some harbours, and

---

[125] Welles, *ap.* Kraeling, no. 58; for other inscriptions related to Hadrian's presence in town, nos. 30, 143–5.

[126] *IGR* iii 1054.

[127] W. Weber, *Untersuchungen zur Geschichte des Kaisers Hadrianus* (1907, repr. 1973).

[128] SHA, *Hadrian* 19. 2: 'in omnibus paene urbibus et aliquid aedificavit et ludos edidit.'

[129] Ibid. 19. 9: 'cum opera ubique infinita fecisset, numquam ipse nisi in Traiani patris templo nomen suum scripsit.'

[130] i 5. 5.

to others food, public works, money, and various honours.'[131] This indeed is a record of donations made by Hadrian for building projects in cities.[132] The authors, however, describe this as exceptional and we still do not know the scale of these works. Only the epigraphic evidence can give us an impression, and here it is important not to be misguided by the grandiose language of some inscriptions.

A remarkable case of misinterpretation is that of the well-known inscriptions on Hadrian's gate in Athens, which read on one side 'This is Athens, formerly the city of Theseus' and on the other 'This is the city of Hadrian and not of Theseus'.[133] The obvious way to read these two inscriptions will lead to the conclusion that they say the same thing: 'This is no longer the city of Theseus for it has been refounded by Hadrian'. It is a megalomaniac claim by the emperor to have superseded the mythical Theseus as founder of Athens.[134] Yet all modern commentators known to me follow an ancient scholiast who writes: 'When Hadrian visited Athens and extended the town wall he wrote where the old wall had been: "Theseus founded this and not Hadrian." Where he himself had made his foundation he wrote: "Hadrian built this and not Theseus."'[135] It is clear that the scholiast misread the inscriptions. Yet it is usually stated that these texts show that the arch marked the boundary between the old city of Athens and a new part built by Hadrian. There is no good evidence of the existence of such a quarter.[136] The most important building in Athens known to have been built with funds made available by Hadrian is the temple of Zeus, a building in which he will have had a personal interest.[137] Pausanias mentions also a temple of Hera and Zeus Panellenios, a pantheon, a

---

[131] lxix 5. 2: καὶ τὰς πόλεις τάς τε συμμαχίδας καὶ τὰς ὑπηκόους μεγαλοπρεπέστατα ὠφέλησε. πολλὰς μὲν γὰρ καὶ εἶδεν αὐτῶν, ὅσας οὐδεὶς ἄλλος αὐτοκράτωρ, πάσαις δὲ ὡς εἰπεῖν ἐπεκούρησε, ταῖς μὲν ὕδωρ ταῖς δὲ λιμένας σῖτόν τε καὶ ἔργα καὶ χρήματα καὶ τιμὰς ἄλλαις ἄλλας διδούς.

[132] See also *Orac. Sibyll.* 12. 163–75, which mentions temples.

[133] *IG* iii 401: Αἵδ᾽ εἴσ᾽ Ἀθῆναι Θησέως ἡ πρὶν πόλις. *IG* iii 402: Αἵδ᾽ εἴσ᾽ Ἀδριανοῦ καὶ οὐχὶ Θησέως πόλις. See in general P. Graindor, *Athènes sous Hadrien* (1934).

[134] Or, if not that, a sycophantic gesture on the part of the Athenians towards an emperor who expected it. Cf. the inscription honouring Hadrian as founder of Plataea (*AE* 1937. 8).

[135] Schol. Aristid. Panath. iii 201. 32 Dind.: μείζονα γὰρ τοῦ περιβόλου ποιήσασθαι ὕστερον. διὸ καὶ ὁ Ἀδριανὸς ἐλθὼν καὶ μείζονα ποιήσας τὸν περίβολον, ἔνθα μὲν ἦν πρὸ τείχους τὸ πεζόν, ἔγραψε τοῦτο ὁ Θησεὺς ἔκτισε, καὶ οὐκ Ἀδριανός, ἔνθα δὲ αὐτὸς ἔκτισεν, ἔγραψε τοῦτο Ἀδριανός, καὶ οὐ Θησεύς, ᾠκοδόμησεν.

[136] SHA, *Hadrian* 20. 4: 'Et cum titulos in operibus non amaret, multas civitates Hadrianopolis appellavit, ut ipsam Carthaginem et Athenarum partem.' This merely confirms that Hadrian *renamed* part of Athens, not that he built it. If it means anything—we do not know that any part of Athens was called Hadrianopolis—it could be taken as a confused reference to the *phyle* 'Hadrianis' mentioned by Pausanias i 5. 5.

[137] Pausanias i 18. 9 and a corrupt passage in Stephanus Byz. s.v. Olympieion. See also *AE* 1916. 24 f.

library and a gymnasium.[138] Dio, however, modifies this somewhat.[139] He says that Hadrian permitted the Greeks to build in his honour the sanctuary called 'Panhellenion'. Pausanias is a contemporary source, and his silence regarding Hadrian's 'New Athens' is decisive. Dio makes no mention of it either.[140] It is possible that Hadrian initiated numerous projects in Athens, but it cannot be said that there is reliable evidence.[141]

Antinoopolis in Egypt may have been an exception. Here we do know that Hadrian founded a new city, and it is possible that he actually saw to its physical development as well, although this is assumed rather than proved.[142] The construction of the Hadrianic road, discussed in Chapter III, was connected with this foundation, but not part of the urban development of the place.

Elsewhere the evidence is meagre. It is clear that Hadrian gave money for temples, as stated by Pausanias.[143] Philostratus reports that Hadrian paid for the costs of a grain-market, a gymnasium, and a temple at Smyrna.[144] At Ephesus funds were made available for the temple and the harbour.[145] Another port was built by Hadrian at Lupia.[146] His harbour at Trapezus has been mentioned above.[147] This confirms Dio's statement that Hadrian built harbours. Other buildings for which there is reliable evidence are a stoa at Hyampolis[148] and baths at Corinth.[149] Like other emperors, and as stated by Dio, Hadrian did build aqueducts. This was one service regularly provided by the authorities. The aqueduct of Caesarea-on-the-Sea has been mentioned.

[138] i 18. 6. For the Olympieion, Graindor, 218–25; for the library, ibid. 230–45.

[139] lxix 16. 1 f.

[140] lxix 16. 1 mentions only the Olympieion.

[141] See also *AE* 1912. 214.

[142] H. I. Bell, *JRS* 30 (1940), 133 ff., also P. V. Pistorius, *Indices Antinoopolitani* (1939); A. Bernard, *Les portes du désert* (1984), 23–107.

[143] x 35. 4: Apollo temple in Abai; i 42. 5: Apollo temple in Megara; viii 10. 2: restoration of Poseidon temple in Mantineia. This assumes that Pausanias distinguished between buildings which merely bore the emperor's name and those he actually paid for. If we may trust the Historia Augusta, Hadrian 12. 3, Hadrian paid for the restoration of the temple of Augustus at Tarraco. *AE* 1976. 114 from Nomentum is heavily restored and ambiguous.

[144] *Vit. Soph.* i 25. 531 K. The same author, *Vit. Soph.* ii 1. 548 K, tells a story regarding the building of the aqueduct of Alexandria Troas (Ilium) which contains a statement by the father of the famous Herodes Atticus to the effect that Hadrian had bestowed enormous sums on villages. The implication of the story is that Hadrian also made large sums available for the aqueduct, but the project was completed by Herodes Atticus and his father. Cf. F. Millar, *The Emperor in the Roman World* (1977), 199.

[145] *Syll.*² , 289.

[146] Pausanias vi 19. 9.

[147] See above, p. 48.

[148] Pausanias x 35. 6, who says that Hadrian built the stoa and that it bore his name.

[149] Pausanias ii 3. 5.

Other Hadrianic aqueducts are attested at Athens,[150] Sarmize-
gethusa,[151] Dyrrhachium, Corinth, and Nicaea.[152] At Alesia, Corsica,
some kind of water installation was constructed by (?) Hadrian.[153]
Otherwise there is only evidence of occasional support for cities struck
by disaster. This would have been considered the duty of every
emperor.[154] Finally, it is significant that of the numerous cities which
adopted the Hadrianic era, including Athens and Gaza, only two
obscure towns kept using it for some time after the emperor's death.[155]
This shows that the cities had no genuine cause for gratitude towards
Hadrian.

This survey is probably by no means complete, but it shows that the
evidence regarding Hadrianic initiative is far more modest than
ancient sources intimate and modern literature claims. Yet no emperor
is credited with greater munificence than Hadrian; if his activities were
modest what are we to expect of other rulers?

The restricted scale of his support for urbanization becomes all the
more evident in contrast with his activity in other spheres. There is no
need to insist on his elaborate military constructions in many provinces. His interest in administration and bureaucracy have been noted
in so far as they are attested in the eastern provinces: the delimitation of
imperial forests in Lebanon, the demarcation of various other
boundaries, the tax law of Palmyra. Numerous inscriptions prove
similar activities in other parts of the empire, notably the erection of
boundary stones.[156]

To sum up what we have seen of Hadrian's activities, there is indeed
evidence of various building projects supported or initiated by him but
it does not amount to very much. He had a particular interest in

---

[150] *CIL* iii 549; A. Kokkou, *Arch Delt.* 25 (1970), 150–72.

[151] *CIL* iii 1446: (Hadrian in abl.) 'aqua inducta colon. Dacic. Sarmiz. per Cn. Papirium
Aelianum legat. eius pr. pr.'

[152] Dyrrhachium: *CIL* iii 709. Corinth: Pausanias viii 22. 3; cf. W. Biers, *Hesperia* 47 (1978),
171–84. Nicaea: S. Şahin, *Die Inschriften von Iznik*, i (1979), no. 55. At Lepcis Magna an aqueduct
was built in Hadrian's reign, but it was paid for by a citizen (*ILS* 5754; *AE* 1977. 848).

[153] *AE* 1968. 283.

[154] Nicomedia was struck by an earthquake and received support: Weber, 127 f. with references
to literary sources; Robert, *BE* 1974. 571, p. 295. Inscriptions attest the restoration of temples,
baths and roads in and near Cyrene destroyed in the Jewish rebellion under Trajan (P. M. Fraser,
JRS 40 (1950), 77–90; S. Applebaum, *Jews and Greeks in Ancient Cyrene* (1979)).

[155] E. Schwertheim, *Epigraphica Anatolica* 6 (1985), 37–42, has shown that Hadrianoi and
Hadrianeia in Mysia used the Hadrianic era till the third century.

[156] *AE* 1981. 600 (Maritime Alps); *AE* 1936. 137 (Madura, Africa); *AE* 1981. 658 (cippus from
the Colonia Canopitana, Africa); *AE* 1939. 160 (Cirta, Algiers); *AE* 1938. 144 (cippus marking the
boundary between Dorylaeum and Nacolea in Asia Minor); *AE* 1937. 170 f., Robert, *BE* 1972.
270, p. 420 (repartition of lands for the benefit of Abdera in Thrace); *AE* 1924. 57 (Vilolishta,
Western Macedonia). See also *ILS* 5947a.

religion, and that resulted in a number of temples. There are several aqueducts and other waterworks, such as were often built by the Roman authorities for provincial communities. There were only two new foundations, Antinoopolis and Aelia Capitolina, and at the latter it has not been proved that there was any government-initiated construction. By contrast there is massive military construction in many provinces and a good deal of administrative activity.[157]

A final observation. It is definitely true that there is more evidence of support for building in the provinces under Hadrian than in many other periods. However, that in itself is not proof that this emperor took more initiative than others. As a travelling emperor Hadrian will have been exposed to far more pleas for support than others who stayed in the capital.[158] Generally speaking, when an emperor paid for a building project in a city this does not necessarily mean that he either initiated or actively supported it. It is merely proof of a successful request for aid.

Septimius Severus

Severus changed the status of many places in the area, often as a reward or punishment for attitudes during the civil war with Niger.[159] In Syria-Palaestina Beth Govrin and Lydda received city-status and became Eleutheropolis and Diospolis.[160] Because of the lack of archaeological and epigraphic material from these towns they cannot profitably be discussed, but there is no reason to assume that more than a change in legal status was involved. Sebaste received the status of a Roman colony.[161] This happened between 201 and 211, as appears from the colonial coinage, probably in 201/2.[162] Nearby Neapolis was temporarily deprived of city-status because of its support of Niger in 194.[163] It is possible that there was a connection between the temporary

[157] For Hadrian as bureaucrat see also the evidence in E. Mary Smallwood, *Documents Illustrating the Principates of Nerva, Trajan and Hadrian* (1966), ch. XV; note the boundary stones 455, 465–7.

[158] Cf. the anecdote told by Cassius Dio, lix 6. 3, about Hadrian, cited by Millar, *Emperor*, 3.

[159] See the lists in *Dig.* L 15. 1 and 8.

[160] City coinage of Eleutheropolis: A. Spijkerman, *Liber Annuus* 22 (1972), 369–84; Kindler and Stein, 112–16. Coinage of Diospolis: *BMC Palestine*, 141, nos. 1 ff.; M. Rosenberger, *City Coins of Palestine*, ii (1975), 28–31; iii (1977), 80: more than 10 types from Septimius Severus to Elagabalus; Kindler and Stein, 96–9.

[161] Paulus, *Dig.* L 15. 8. 7: 'In Palaestina duae fuerunt coloniae, Caesariensis et Aelia Capitolina, sed neutra ius Italicum habet. Divus quoque Severus in Sebastenam civitatem coloniam deduxit.'

[162] *BMC Palestine*, xxxix, 80, nos. 12 f.: COL L SEP SEBASTE. The latest pre-colonial coinage dates to 201/2; Kindler and Stein, 226–9.

[163] SHA, *Severus*, 9. 5: 'Neapolitanis etiam Palaestinensibus ius civitatis tulit, quod pro Nigro diu in armis fuerunt.'

punishment of one city and the enhancement of its neighbour.

At this time Sebaste was splendidly rebuilt. To this period belong the temple in its later form, the forum, colonnades, a basilica, a columned street, the theatre and stadium.[164] It has been assumed that there was a connection between the grant of colonial status and a subsequent building programme.[165] However, the excavators of Sebaste have concluded that several elements of the programme were perhaps already in existence, that is to say, that they preceded the change in status.[166] The buildings are not dated by any inscriptions.[167] It is quite possible that the prosperity of the citizens of Sebaste themselves gave them the means to carry out a substantial building programme. If this was the case, it is more likely that these circumstances contributed to the decision to grant colonial status than that the latter was accompanied by imperial munificence of which there is no record.

Severus organized the new province of Mesopotamia. Several cities received colonial status from him or from his successors: Rhesaena, Nisibis, and Carrhae.[168] Nothing is known beyond the mere fact of the grants themselves. Rhesaena was possibly the base of III Parthica, as the name of the legion appears on its coins.[169] This colony may therefore have been organized after the pattern of Aelia Capitolina, a town with colonial status where a legion was based. The other legionary base, Singara, where I Parthica was stationed, received colonial status at an uncertain date.[170]

---

[164] G. A. Reisner, C. S. Fisher, D. Gordon Lyon, *Harvard Excavations at Samaria* (1924), 50–4; J. W. Crowfoot, K. Kenyon and E. L. Sukenik, *Buildings*, 33–6.

[165] Such a connection is suggested by Smallwood, *Jews*, 490. For the conclusions of the excavators, Crowfoot et al., *Objects*, 6, 48; Crowfoot et al., *Buildings*, 35 f.

[166] *Objects*, 6: '. . . the colonnades in the stadium, the forum and the columned street were already perhaps in existence.'

[167] An inscribed architrave block from the basilica mentions *strategoi*, the common Greek term for the *duoviri* of a Roman colony, cf. Reisner et al., 250, no. 7 and pl. 59c. The rebuilding of the temple was assigned to the Severan period on the evidence of inscribed altars, ibid., 20, no. 30: 'Mil. Vexil. Coh. P. Sup. Cives Sisc.' (see Appendix I); 21, no. 31: no text published.

[168] A. H. M. Jones, *Cities of the Eastern Roman Provinces* (²1971), 220 f.; Kindler, *INJ* 6–7, 79–87. For Nisibis, A. Oppenheimer et al., *Babylonia Judaica in the Talmudic Period* (1983), 319–34.

[169] For the coinage, K. O. Castellin, *Numismatic Notes and Monographs* 108 (1946), 14 f., 45 f. It has been assumed that the reference to the legion on the coins of Rhesaena shows this to have been a veteran colony, but that is improbable. Mann, *Recruitment*, 43 f., has shown that *vexilla* and legionary inscriptions on city coins of this period no longer indicate real veteran settlement. It is also worth noting that the inscription 'Leg III P' is in Latin characters, although the coinage of the Mesopotamian colonies otherwise bears inscriptions in Greek, itself an unusual feature on coins of Roman colonies. Little is known of the town of Rhesaena; see also the references in *DE* iv, s.v. 'limes', 1333.

[170] Jones, *Cities*, 220. It is named AVR SEP COL SINGARA on coins of Gordian III: *BMC Arabia etc.*, cxii and 134–6, nos. 1–15. See also *DE* s.v. *limes*, 1330. It is now certain that I Parthica was based at Singara: M. Speidel and J. Reynolds, *Epigraphica Anatolica* 5 (1985), 31–5, and cf. *ILS*

Under Caracalla and Elagabalus the status of many cities in the eastern provinces was changed, but there is no evidence that this involved more than formal or administrative measures.[171] In Judaea, for instance, not only Emmaus but also Herod's foundation of Antipatris received city status from Elagabalus.[172] In Arabia Bostra and Petra were made colonies.[173] In Osrhoene Edessa was elevated to the rank of a Roman colony immediately after the deposition of the last king, Abgar IX.[174]

Philip the Arab and Philippopolis

Philip probably came from the village of Shahba to which he granted the status of a colony and the name of Philippopolis.[175] This was a city with all the usual amenities.[176] It is still listed as a bishopric of Arabia in the Byzantine sources and its representative took part in the council at Chalcedon.[177] It is natural to assume that Philip himself initiated the

9477. For references to the legion, to be added to those collected by Ritterling, *RE* xii, s.v. 'legio', Speidel and Reynolds, 34 n. 10.

[171] Survey in A. Kindler, *INJ* 6–7; Jones, *Cities*.

[172] For Emmaus, Jones, *Cities*, 279 and n. 72; Schürer, i 512–13 n; Kindler and Stein, 177–9. At present some seven coin types of Antipatris are known, all from the reign of Elagabal: *BMC Palestine*, xv f., 11; N. van der Vliet, *RB* 57 (1950), 116 f., nos. 11–12; Meshorer, *City-Coins*, nos. 149–52; Kindler and Stein, 41 f. The pilgrim from Bordeaux refers to it as a *mutatio* rather than a *civitas*: *It. Burd.* 600. 1. The decline is also apparent from Jerome's designation as a *semirutum oppidulum*: *Peregrinatio Paulae*, Ep. 108. 8. Later it is listed as a bishopric. It is represenated at Chalcedon (451): R. Le Quien, *Oriens christianus* iii, 579 f. It is also listed by Georgius Cyprius, 1001, ed. Gelzer, 51; Hierocles, *synecdemus* 718. 3, ed. Parthey, 43. Avi-Yonah, *Holy Land*, 145–7, is ignorant of the change in status in his fanciful description of the territory of Antipatris. See further *IGR* i 631, republished by L. Robert, *Les gladiateurs dans l'Orient grec* (1940), 103 f., no. 43, which mentions a *bouleutes* of both Antipatris and Neapolis; see also nos. 41 f. For further references, Schürer, ii 167 f.

[173] S. Ben Dor, *Berytus* 9 (1948–9), 41–3.

[174] A. R. Bellinger and C. B. Welles, *YCS* 5 (1935), 93–154; new edn. by J. A. Goldstein, *JNES* 25 (1966), 1–16.

[175] Aurelius Victor 28. 1: 'Igitur M. Julius Philippus Arabs Trachonites, sumpto in consortium Philippo filio, rebus ad Orientem compositis, conditoque apud Arabiam Philippopoli oppido Roman venit.' For the coinage of Philippopolis, *BMC Arabia*, 43–4, nos. 1–10; A. Spijkerman, *The Coins of the Decapolis and Provincia Arabia* (1978), 258–61; Kindler and Stein, 209–11. On Philip the Arab see G. W. Bowersock, *Roman Arabia* (1983), 122–7.

[176] For the antiquities of Philippopolis, Brünnow and Domaszewski, *Die Provincia Arabia*, iii (1909), 145–79; H. C. Butler et al., *Publications of the Princeton University Archaeological Expeditions* (1907–8), iia 359 ff.; H. C. Butler, *Architecture and Other Arts* (1903), 376–96; P. Coupel and E. Frézouls, *Le Theatre de Philippopolis en Arabie* (1956); A. Segal, *Journal of the Society of Architectural Historians* 40 (1981), 111, fig. 8; G. Amer and M. Gawlikowski, *Damaszener Mitteilungen* 2 (1985), 1–16. For the coinage, Spijkerman, *Coins*, 258–61. Philippopolis issued coins only in the reign of Philip.

[177] Georgius Cyprius, 1069, ed. Gelzer, 54, with comm. on p. 204; Hierocles, *synecdemus*, 722. 12, ed. Parthey, 46. For Hormisdas of Philippopolis who participated at Calchedon, references in Gelzer, loc. cit.

construction of the town wall and public buildings.[178] Indeed, there is a confused allusion to the enrichment of Bostra [and?] Philippopolis in the Sibylline Oracles (xiii 64–8). It has also been stated on stylistic grounds that the ruins now to be seen on the spot all belong to buildings raised in one short epoch.[179] However, that is an argument which cannot be verified. This was a community which might have flourished even without active imperial support. It lies in a densely populated part of the Jebel Druz and is accessible from the north-west and the south.

For concrete information it will be useful to consider the inscriptions from the city. A building inscription of 177/8 mentions the emperors, the governor of Syria P. Martius Verus, a centurion, and the local *strategos*.[180] This shows that at the time it was one of the many flourishing villages in southern Syria with their own administrators and a small garrison commanded by a centurion. Two *bouleutai* of the town are mentioned on inscriptions elsewhere.[181] Of particular interest is an inscription dated to 'Year One of the City'.[182] It is set up 'for the preservation of the emperor Philip and his son through the care of two *bouleutai*', but the emperors are not actually being thanked for any munificence toward the town. They are honoured in two other inscriptions, one set up by a neighbouring village,[183] the other by a procurator (*ducenarius*), almost certainly the financial procurator of Syria.[184] Neither thanks the emperors for donations or constructions. The same procurator honours the divine M. Julius Marinus, father of the emperor.[185] The latter is also honoured on two inscriptions affixed to the wall of a small temple and apparently signed by the legate of Syria

---

[178] Cf. Jerome ad a. 2264: 'Filippus urbem nominis sui in Thracia (*sic*) construxit.' This might support the assumption that Philip was responsible for the construction of the town, but Jerome did not know where it was and that makes the source suspect. Zonaras, *Ann.* xii 19, states that Philip built a city at Bostra, naming it after himself. Equally problematic is Cedrenus i, ed. Bonn, p. 451, 22, who says the same thing but places Bostra in Europe. The only good source is Aurelius Victor (above, n. 175), who merely says that Philip founded this city.

[179] Butler, *Architecture*, 376–96.

[180] Waddington, no. 2071, with comments. In the 2nd cent. this area belonged to the province of Syria.

[181] Waddington, nos. 2019 and 2506.

[182] Waddington, no. 2072: Ὑπὲρ σωτηρίας τῶν κυρίων Μ(άρκων) Ἰουλίων Φιλίππων Σεβαστῶν, ἐπ(ι)μελο[υ]μένων Ἰουλίου Σεντίου Μάλχου καὶ Ἀμωνί[ου] κὲ Ἀλεξάνδρου βουλ(ευτῶν), προεδρίᾳ Μαρρίνου, ἔτους πρώτου τῆς πόλεως.

[183] Waddington, no. 2073, set up by the *Eakkotai* (Eacca, Sacca, modern Shaqqa). For this place see also above, pp. 135 f.

[184] Waddington, nos. 2073 f. He is not listed in Pflaum, *Carrières*. The latter, 614, notes that *ducenarius* as a substantive is common in Greek. He also observes that, in the second half of the 3rd cent., the title came to be used for procurators of lower rank (950 f.). It is therefore conceivable that this was not the procurator of Syria.

[185] Waddington, no. 2075. Coins with the divine Marinus on the obverse: Spijkerman, 260 n. 1.

(*hypatikos*), which indicates that the temple was built by the provincial authorities for the worship of the emperor's father. In an inscription of the same years a *bouleutes* and *syndic* of the city honours the son of Julius Priscus, prefect of Mesopotamia,[186] who may well have been the brother of the emperor. A similar inscription was set up beside this by an *ex-beneficiarius* of the prefect.[187] Two further inscriptions are of later date.[188]

The number of inscriptions from Philippopolis is small, but it is of interest that seven out of nine are concerned with the emperor Philip and his relatives. The provincial authorities honoured them there, in their place of origin, and local dignitaries did the same. None of these inscriptions mentions financial donations or constructions carried out under the auspices of the emperor. We obviously cannot deduce from this that no such donations were made. It would be natural to assume that Philip made generous endowments, but the absence of any reference in a total of seven inscriptions is worth noting. It is possible that Philippopolis merely received the status of a colony and that the town was built up in the course of time with local funds.[189] It is also possible, although there is no evidence to confirm this, that the grant involved exemption from taxation.

In Arabia several cities received town walls in the second half of the third century. The evidence and the likely background have been discussed in Chapter III. In the same period the walls of Tiberias in Galilee were repaired. Here, however, the citizens themselves had to pay, according to a legal discussion in the Babylonian Talmud:[190]

R. Eleazar asked R. Johanan (Tiberias, *c.* 250–79): [When forcing members of a city to pay for the construction or repairs of its walls] does one collect according to the number of souls in (a family) or according to the (distribution of) wealth? He replied: One collects according to wealth, and, Eleazar, my son (i.e. pupil), fix this ruling with nails, (i.e. be sure to keep it). Others say: He asked him whether one collects according to wealth or proximity of houses . . .

The same text then goes on to relate:

R. Judah Nesiah (Sepphoris, *c.* 250–85) placed the expenses (of mending Sepphoris' city walls) upon the Rabbis [too]. Resh Lakish said to him: Rabbis do not need protection, (hence they should not participate in the expense). . .

---

[186] Waddington, no. 2077, with comments on the identity of Julius Priscus. The *bouleutes* is probably one of those mentioned in no. 2072.

[187] Waddington, no. 2078.

[188] Waddington, nos. 2079 f.

[189] Philip also granted colonial status to Damascus and Neapolis; K. W. Harl, *American Numismatic Society, Museum Notes* 29 (1984), 61–97, for Neapolis; ibid. 62 n. 3, for Damascus.

[190] b. Bava Batra viib–viiia. I cite the translation by D. Sperber, *JESHO* 14 (1971), 242.

The Fourth Century

The practice of awarding grants of higher status continued at least till the reign of Constantine. In Second Palestine, for instance, two communities received names and city status. One was Maximianoupolis, formerly 'Legio', the civilian settlement near the legionary base of the VI Ferrata just east of Megiddo.[191] The other, Helenopolis, is not even identified. It was presumably founded by Constantine, but nothing further is known.[192] These places have for us no history. Other projects of Constantine, however, are immediately relevant. In Jerusalem he ordered the construction of the basilica of the Holy Sepulchre.[193] His mother Helena supervised the construction of churches at Bethlehem and on the Mount of Olives.[194] A fourth church was built by order of the emperor at the shrine of Abraham at Mamre.[195] Apart from providing the means for the construction itself Constantine and his successors probably endowed these churches generously.[196] At Antioch in Syria Constantine is said to have initiated the construction of the octagonal Great Church. It is not unlikely that the emperor should endow the principal city of the eastern provinces with a fitting Christian monument. The evidence, however, is not reliable.[197]

On public buildings in Antioch we have information of great interest, particularly in the works of Libanius.[198] The emperor is rarely referred to as involved in construction. This is significant, since Antioch frequently functioned as imperial residence. Apart from the Constantinian church we have references to four projects in the area. Diocletian had a palace built at Antioch,[199] but that cannot be construed as

---

[191] References in Isaac and Roll, i 10 f.

[192] Georgius Cyprius, 1038, ed. Gelzer, 53; Hierocles, *synecdemus*, 720. 8, ed. Parthey, 44; cf. F.-M. Abel, *Géographie de la Palestine*, ii (1967), 205.

[193] Eusebius, *Vita Const.* iii 25 ff., 33 ff., iv 43 ff. Cf. E. D. Hunt, *Holy Land Pilgrimage in the Later Roman Empire, AD 312–460* (1982), 10–14; G. Stemberger, *Juden und Christen im Heiligen Land* (1987), 54–60.

[194] *V. Const.* 41, 43; cf. Hunt, 14 ff.; Stemberger, 61–4.   [195] *V. Const.* iii 51 ff; cf. Hunt, 15 f.

[196] Hunt, 141–5. There is not much evidence, and the endowment of churches in Rome has to serve as parallel. The validity of the comparison is dubious as, even in the Byzantine period, Rome cannot serve as a model for the treatment of provincial towns.

[197] See Downey, *Antioch*, 342/9, with full discussion. There are several brief references to the project and a little more information in Malalas, 317 f., which Downey, 650–3, has shown to be full of errors and distortions.

[198] Cf. P. Petit, *Libanius et la vie municipale à Antioche au IV* siècle après J.-C.* (1955), 314–30; W. Liebeschuetz, *Antioch* (1972), 132–6.

[199] The attribution to Diocletian rests on a statement by Malalas, 306, who says it was built by Diocletian on foundations laid by Gallienus. This was rejected by Downey, 259 n. 126, who assumed that Antioch was controlled by Palmyra throughout the sixties, so that Gallienus could

imperial initiative in urban development. Constantius completed a new harbour at Seleucia Pieria, probably the one which we hear of in the reign of Diocletian. This was a structure of military importance and hence the army was involved in its construction, at least under Diocletian.[200] To Antioch itself he gave porticoes and fountains.[201] Valens is reported to have built a forum at Antioch, but this is known only from Malalas.[202] Libanius asked Theodosius for the donation of a building in the city, but we do not know whether the request was granted.[203]

In provincial towns governors are mentioned in this period as normally taking the initiative in the construction of public buildings, for which compulsory labour and services were always used.[204] The council and its members apparently no longer had the authority to do so. That does not mean that the projects were financed by the fiscus. They were paid for from the civic revenue and with forced contributions from councillors. Men below the rank of councillors had to provide compulsory physical labour, such as the transport of building materials. As already noted in Chapter VI, peasants were burdened with the compulsory disposal of building rubble.

The Byzantine Period

After Constantine's donations the next church built in Palestine with funds provided by the emperor was the one dedicated in 407 at Gaza, for which the money was made available to the bishop Porphyrius by Eudoxia, wife of Arcadius.[205] For the origins of these funds it might be of interest to remember that Eudoxia had obtained quite considerable sums from the corrupt and rapacious general Arbazacius, whom she protected in exchange for part of his loot from Isauria.[206]

not then have begun to build a palace there. However, Fergus Millar, *JRS* 61 (1971), 8–10, has shown that there is no indication that Palmyra exercised any real influence in Antioch before *c.* 270. It is therefore not impossible that Gallienus laid foundations for a palace in Antioch, but naturally this does not prove that Malalas is right. For a description of the palace, Libanius, *Or.* xi 203–7; cf. Downey, 318–23.

[200] Libanius, *Or.* xi 263; Julian, *Or.* i 40 D; *The Expositio Totius Mundi*, 28, states that the port was constructed for the use of the city and the army; for further sources, Downey, 361, with n. 198.

[201] Julian mentions them in his panegyric in honour of Constantius (*Or.* i 40 D)—where the only other city singled out as having received donations is Constantinople.

[202] 338 f. Malalas is here particularly untrustworthy since he claims at the same time that Valentinian (Valens' colleague in the western empire) founded many buildings in Antioch.

[203] *Or.* xx 44. Libanius mentions a new palace at Daphne, constructed by Theodosius.

[204] *Cod. Theod.* xv 1.

[205] Marcus Diaconus, *Vita Porphyrii*, 53 f., 84; cf. Carol Glucker, *The City of Gaza in the Roman and Byzantine Periods* (1987), 47–9; Stemberger, 64–6.

[206] Zosimus v 1. 3–4; Eunapius, *Hist.* fr. 84. Cf. Zosimus, ed. Paschoud, iii 1, n. 52, p. 190.

Our knowledge of the benefaction at Gaza is, to a certain extent, a random piece of information. There may have been other churches paid for by emperors, but we know of nothing to match the extensive building programme at Jerusalem, initiated and organized by Eudocia, wife of Theodosius, during her visit in 437–8 and particularly when she lived there from 441/2 till her death in 460.[207] As had become usual in the Byzantine period, she built churches, monasteries, and hostels for pilgrims. In Jerusalem she is also credited with the extension of the city walls southward. Her most ambitious project there was the complex of the basilica of St Stephen.[208] Her church-building, however, was not confined to Jerusalem. At Constantinople she founded the church of St Polyeuktos.[209] This church was replaced by a bigger one in the sixth century (AD 524–7?) donated by Anicia Juliana, another noble lady connected with the imperial court.[210] At Jamnia Eudocia established a church with a home for the convalescent.[211] She endowed several monasteries in Palestine.[212] While on her way to Jerusalem she twice visited Antioch, combining demonstrations of literary talent with munificence. On the first occasion she is reported to have donated two hundred pounds of gold for the restoration of the Baths of Valens, which had been partly destroyed by fire.[213] Her second visit resulted in an extension of the city wall.

It is impossible to discuss Justinian and his works at length here. They are the subject of Procopius' *Buildings*, itself a problematic composition.[214] This work conveys the impression that one emperor single-handedly transformed a ruined empire into one full of flourishing fortified cities, provided with churches and everything else needed. This is not the place to decide how much or how little of this in general is true, but the question of Justinian's initiatives in urban restoration or development is a relevant topic.

First, it seems wise to distinguish in Procopius' work between lengthy and detailed descriptions, such as those of the fortification of

---

[207] See Hunt, ch. 10.

[208] An inscription from the altar of the church: *SEG* viii 192.

[209] C. Mango and I. Ševčenko, *DOP* 15 (1961), 243 ff. The church has been extensively excavated; R. M. Harrison, *Excavations at Saraçhane in Istanbul* i (1986); for the testimonia see 5–10. Apparently no remains of the earlier church have been identified.

[210] For Anicia Juliana and the background to her munificence, Harrison, 418–20. Note that this project was carried out in the imperial capital and is not typical of support for construction in the provinces.

[211] *Life of Peter the Iberian*, 114 f.

[212] References in Hunt, ch. 10. A remarkable recent discovery is a poem by the empress celebrating the baths of Gadara and inscribed on the spot: J. Green and Y. Tsafrir, *IEJ* 32 (1982), 77–91.

[213] Evagrius, *HE* i 20.   [214] Averil Cameron, *Procopius* (1985), 84–112.

Dara or the building of Hagia Sophia, and vague remarks which add, almost as an afterthought, that the emperor 'also built stoas, baths, and everything that a *polis* requires'. The former is to be taken seriously, the latter to be accepted only if there is corroboration. Such corroboration has occasionally been found. The remains of the huge *Nea* in Jerusalem, described at length by Procopius, have now been partly uncovered and a building inscription has been published.[215] The sixth-century remains of the monastery of St Catherine in Sinai can be identified and contemporary inscriptions are extant.[216] In Arabia one inscription records the restoration of Qasr el-Hallabat.[217] Two inscriptions mark building operations at Chalcis (Kinnesrin) in 550–1.[218] An unpublished inscription is said to record the gratitude of the people of Cyrrhus in Syria for the town wall donated by Justinian.[219] It can therefore be said that there is epigraphic confirmation of some of the military and ecclesiastical projects described by Procopius. In the absence of such confirmation of other projects we should not accept grandiose but imprecise claims regarding the reconstruction of entire cities. Without further information it is impossible to say what we should make of the statement that Justinian 'built the city of Justinianopolis which formerly was called Adrianoupolis'.[220] It is very likely that for 'built' we may substitute 'renamed'.

Second, in Procopius' *Buildings* there is in fact very little to be found about civilian urban projects. The main emphasis is on military construction, and it is very clear that the fortification of cities was, in this period, sometimes considered the responsibility of the emperor. That is an important fact in itself which goes back to the third-century fortifications in Arabia.[221] The construction of the fortifications of Dara by Anastasius was also undertaken with funds provided by the imperial treasury.[222] However, it would be incorrect to say that fortification, or

---

[215] N. Avigad, *IEJ* 27 (1977), 145–51. Several donations for ecclesiastical projects in Palestine were made at the request of Saba and are mentioned, not by Procopius, but by Cyril of Scythopolis, *Vita Sabae* 72–32, 75 (ed. Schwartz, 175 ff.).

[216] See above, ch. II, p. 94.

[217] D. Kennedy, *Archaeological Explorations on the Roman Frontier in North-East Jordan* (1982), 40, no. 4, pl. vi.

[218] W. K. Prentice, *Publ. of an American Archaeological Expedition to Syria, 1899–1900*, iii, *Greek and Latin Inscriptions* (1908), nos. 305 f.; C. Clermont-Ganneau, *Recueil d'archéologie orientale* vii (1906), 228–30; viii (1924), 81–8; Procopius, *de aed.* ii 11. 1, 8. The inscriptions themselves do not contain a description of the structures concerned. The first mentions the builder Isidoros, μηχανικός. The second refers to funding by the emperor ἐκ τῶν εὐσεβῶν φιλοτιμιῶν.

[219] D. Frézouls, in *Apamée de Syrie, Bilan de recherches archéologiques 1965–8*, Janine Balty (ed.) (1969), 90 n. 2.

[220] *De aed.* iv 1. 36.

[221] See above, p. 133.

[222] Cf. Zachariah of Mitylene, vii 8.

refortification, always depended on imperial initiative. The walls of Gaza were rebuilt under Justinian at the initiative of the local bishop Marcianus with the active support and cooperation of the governor, Stephanus, a native of the city, and of the leading citizens of the town.[223] There is no indication that Gaza lay under any real threat of attack at that time,[224] and the refortification may have been prompted rather by a desire of the leading citizens to enhance the beauty and the status of the city. The governor may have lent his support because he was a native of the city. Bishop Marcianus also achieved the construction of two splendid churches, the restoration of two others, the extension of the stoas lining the main streets, and the building of a new bath house in the city.[225] These projects are not mentioned by Procopius even though he was a native of the same province. Choricius, who discussed these projects in detail, does not mention imperial funding.

Procopius says explicitly that under Justinian churches anywhere in the empire were built or restored with imperial funds only.[226] The statement is definitely not true,[227] and this is of interest for our judgement of the author: he must have known it was untrue and that his readers were aware that it was untrue, like his passing remark that Justinian 'abolished' the *limitanei*.[228] He does, however, mention by name numerous churches which Justinian built or restored. He also devotes much attention to road-repair, canals, and aqueducts, the traditional responsibility of the Roman authorities.[229]

Civilian projects in cities, on the other hand, are mentioned only in the last place and usually described in the vaguest possible manner. In the eastern provinces, for example, we are told that at Helenopolis in Bithynia, the birthplace of Helena, mother of Constantine,[230] 'Justinian built an aqueduct, a bath, churches, a palace, stoas, lodgings

---

[223] Choricius Gazaeus, *Laud. Arat. et Steph.* 54 (63. 4–9); *Laud. Marc.* i 7 (4. 16–19); cf. the building inscription *SEG* viii 268. The project is not mentioed by Procopius. Discussion and further references in Glucker, 55–7, 140 f.

[224] Choricius, *Laud Marc.* ii 16 (32. 7–9).

[225] Glucker, 55.

[226] *De aed.* i 8. 5. We may assume that this supposedly includes the various connected installations such as hospices and monasteries which Procopius does not usually describe.

[227] Justinian, *Nov.* lxvii, states that churches and monasteries may be built only with permission of the bishop. Of course private individuals may build churches, and there is an abundance of inscriptions to show they did. The churches in Gaza already mentioned were clearly built by local initiative.

[228] See above, pp. 210–13.

[229] Averil Cameron observes that there are three themes in the *Buildings*: church building, fortifications, and the water-supply.

[230] *De aed.* v 2. 1–5. Constantine had given it city status but no buildings.

for magistrates and, in general, made it look like a prosperous city'. Similar claims are made for Nicaea, Nicomedia, Pythia in Bithynia, Mocesus in Cappadocia, Sergiopolis (Resapha) in Euphratesia, Antioch in Syria, and Edessa. When all is said it seems best not to assume that the reign of Justinian saw a radical departure as regards imperial priorities in building projects.

To sum up, the period from Constantine onward represented radical changes of imperial interest in Palestine because of its importance for Christianity. It cannot be said, however, that imperial involvement in the development of provincial towns in general was essentially different in this period. As in the early empire, there was no policy of active stimulation or support. Indeed the establishment of new cities became less frequent, presumably because a saturation point was reached. The frontier cities in Mesopotamia received special attention for political and military reasons, as explained in Chapter V; and Justinian is credited with the establishment of a few cities, none of them in the eastern provinces.[231] But financial or other initiative was the exception rather than the rule. The best-attested instances of support were the result of petitions, personal contacts at court,[232] or direct imperial patronage and involvement, such as that exercised by Helena and Eudocia. During the later empire, as before, financial support for building in the provinces was more often a result of successful requests for aid than of active imperial or official interference. The fact that constructing and repairing public buildings became one of the numerous compulsory and unpaid personal services established by law, like maintaining roads or transporting clothes for the army,[233] shows clearly that the imperial government did not expect to pay for it.

Conclusion

Military construction was, of course, the business of the state, civilian building was not. Emperors might take initiatives where they were interested in doing so for political or ideological reasons. Thus Hadrian built temples, and immense fortunes were spent on the Church by Constantine and some of his successors. The resources had to be made available by the provinces, for the emperor had to take from somewhere what he gave.[234] It is possible that the emperor's involvement in the

---

[231] Procopius, *de aed.* iv 1. 19–42.
[232] e.g. the results of the presence of Porphyrius and Saba at court.
[233] *Cod. Theod.* xi 16. 18 (5 July 390).
[234] Millar, ch. IV; for the funds made available to the church, 583 f. For the 4th and 5th centuries, Hunt, 142 f.

Church exceeded his former interest in the old pagan cults, although this is hard to determine. This would be only natural, for through the Church the imperial authorities had effective means to exercise power at even the lowest social level which no pagan cult had ever provided. From the fourth century onward Constantinople rather than Rome became the focus of architectural ambition, but the mechanisms appear to have remained the same. There was never any automatic support for urban development in the provinces. The grant of a new status did not necessarily result in large-scale construction initiated by the authorities. Imperial support for various projects in towns is occasionally found, but usually for specific categories of buildings, such as aqueducts. Emperors would provide support for cities struck by disaster, following requests made by the recipients. It is quite likely that in most other instances too imperial support for physical development was forthcoming only upon special request. There is hardly any substantial evidence to show that the authorities regularly took the initiative. This explains why a 'travelling emperor' like Hadrian gave more money for buildings in cities than one who stayed at home, like Antoninus Pius. The former was more accessible than the latter.

The development of towns was the result of local conditions and initiative, not the work of an imaginary 'State Ministry for Urban Development'. It was therefore a far more diverse process than would otherwise have been the case. It was far less dependent on the whims of individual emperors and far more on regional social and economic development. Only thus can the remarkable prosperity and activity of a number of settlements in the Negev be explained. In this chapter we have seen that many of the cities in the provinces discussed here appear to have developed at a far slower pace than has often been thought. Inscriptions reveal a remarkably varied pattern of social and cultural relations, exemplified by the differences between Heliopolis and Bostra.

The difference between the level of activity of the Roman authorities and that of the Herodian client kings is remarkable. All that has often been claimed for the Roman emperors was in fact carried out by these vassals. It is difficult to say whether their subjects had any cause for gratitude, but at least most, though not all, of their munificence was spent in their own territory and not on palaces in Rome or Constantinople. Josephus' observation that there was a serious danger of unemployment when the reconstruction of the temple in Jerusalem was finished is well-known.[235] Whatever the merits of these endeavours, it is

[235] *Ant.* xx 9. 7 (219–222).

essential to keep in mind the difference between vassal kingdoms and provinces in this respect.

If there is any single conclusion to be drawn from the material considered in this chapter, it is that the growth and decline of every city has to be studied in its own right and not with an exaggerated regard for the constructive power of the imperial will.[236]

---

[236] I am grateful to Dr Stephen Mitchell for showing me in advance of publication his article on imperial building and contributions to urbanization in Asia Minor, which has since been published in S. Macready and F. H. Thompson (eds.), *Roman Architecture in the Greek World* (1987). Dr M. Mango kindly showed me her 1984 D. Phil. thesis, 'Artistic Patronage in the Roman Diocese of Oriens, AD 313–641' (publication forthcoming). This work provides a comprehensive survey of the available evidence on buildings and patronage.

IX

FRONTIER POLICY—
GRAND STRATEGY?

> And war, most of all is confusion, on the field and in people's heads: half the time you can't even figure out who's won and who's lost. The generals decide that afterwards, and the people who write history books.
>
> (Primo Levi, *If not now, when?*, Chapter 1)

In the first chapter it was argued that the frontier policy of Rome in the East intermittently but persistently aimed at expansion. This is clear from actual Roman behaviour at least till the age of Diocletian. The positions taken up by the Roman army in Syria and Cappadocia from the Flavian period onward are better explained in terms of offence than defence. What little can be learned about the Roman perception of Persia before the Byzantine period does not confirm the popular notion that Persia was conceived as a major threat which required an active policy of defence. In Chapters II–IV it was argued that in Arabia and Judaea there was hardly a 'frontier question' to cope with. The army was engaged in internal police duties of various kinds. As could be seen in Chapter VI, policing the towns, particularly the main cities, required the presence of considerable forces from Egypt to Syria. In the Byzantine period some of the police duties of the army in the East were taken over by Saracen allies. The relationship with Persia changed. After Julian the Roman emperors no longer hoped to destroy the Persian empire or to follow in the footsteps of Alexander, but this did not result in an attitude of constructive cooperation, precisely when such a policy was needed for defence against nomad pressure from the north. In the wars between the two empires fighting was usually heaviest in Mesopotamia. Yet in Chapter V it could clearly be seen that there was no functioning system of defence even in this area and this period. There were forces whose function it was to prevent the penetration of nomad raids, but major expeditions easily crossed into enemy territory and then focused on the siege of heavily fortified cities whose defence first of all was the responsibility of the local population.

This is a description of Roman frontier policy in the East that differs in many respects from the views commonly held by modern scholars. The present chapter will attempt to consider Roman frontier policy in a wider perspective.

It is commonly assumed that Rome had a very clear idea of which boundaries would guarantee the safety and security of the empire. Foreign conquest, such as Trajan's campaigns, is often explained as motivated by the search for defensible boundaries. A recent book argues the same even for the period of the republic.[1]

First it must be observed that the evidence often consists of little more than an empty shell: an incomplete list of the disposition of units and camps in various periods and a body of literature that does not describe the working of the system. To begin with, we certainly have no accurate image of forces hostile to the expansion or even the maintenance of the empire. It is usually taken for granted that the existence of the empire was an achievement subject to constant pressure, and that disintegration threatened all the time. This may be incorrect. Again and again historians search for explanations why the Roman Empire declined and fell. It might be fruitful to begin with a consistent explanation of how it came into being and maintained itself. A series of hypotheses then might possibly be built on the reasoning that there was a period in which circumstances favoured rather than threatened the conglomeration of many peoples into one political unit. Such hypotheses would probably be impossible to prove, but they might well fit the known facts better than the old widely accepted assumptions that the Romans perceived a constant need to defend the frontiers and that this was what they were in fact doing.

The common approach presumes that under the principate the establishment of secure boundaries was the first concern of the Romans in their frontier policy. It takes for granted that the security of the inhabitants of the provinces was of primary importance to the authorities. In other words, it attributes sets of motives to the Romans that would have sprung from a clearly defined ideology: one which sees war as an evil which is sometimes necessary for those who want to protect the integrity of the state.

It is an approach which assumes that the decision by Rome to initiate a war was usually the result of rational considerations.[2] It further

---

[1] S. L. Dyson, *The Creation of the Roman Frontier* (1985); see the critical reviews by J. Rich, *Liverpool Classical Monthly* 11. 2 (1986), 29 f.; S. Mitchell, *JRS* 76 (1986), 288 f. The opposite view, namely that Roman warfare under the republic was expansionist and not defensive, is argued by W. V. Harris, *War and Imperialism in Republican Rome, 327–70 BC* (1979).

[2] This is argued carefully but with great conviction by J. B. Campbell, *The Emperor and the Roman Army 31 BC–AD 235* (1984), 133 ff., 382 ff.

assumes that most of the frontier lines established in the course of time were those consciously chosen by Rome. That depends on a further assumption that geographical factors decided the Roman attitude toward the shape of its empire; and this in turn implies that there were Roman planners who had a clear sense of geography to guide them in their policy. It also involves assumptions as regards the Roman attitude towards the defensive use of geographical features as national barriers, as well as the function of artificial barriers. It implies that Rome went to war in order to secure the peace in the provinces. Last, but by no means least, this reconstruction of Roman strategy invariably rests on an analysis of the physical remains discovered by archaeologists, including the artificial barriers constructed in several frontier zones. It is believed that one can deduce the strategic or tactical function of military units from these remains and the locations where they were found.

In the following pages it will be argued that one must be cautious about accepting these assumptions, some of which are inspired by notions of modern strategy and warfare. This is particularly true of the concept of 'defence in depth', which is now widely accepted as underlying Roman military organization in the fourth century. It must be remembered that this is the usual designation for the current Nato doctrine. Nato is organized for defence against an enemy that has an overt policy of attack and offence, supported by an army of superior size and fire power. Nato doctrine as it stands would make no sense without the possibility of rapid and massive reinforcement from overseas and the threat of nuclear retaliation. None of these factors applies to Roman policy or to the state of affairs in antiquity. Other notions regarding Roman policy are determined by personal preference, or stem from a belief that the Roman empire was an institution more capable of improving the lives of its citizens and subject peoples than other forms of social organization have proved to be.

This book attempts to show that a different point of view can legitimately be argued. This is not an attempt to give the empire good or bad marks as pacifists or aggressors. In passing moral judgement on the Roman empire we should have to compare it with other ancient empires, and it is not at all certain that any of them would receive high marks from a modern observer. It is useful, however, to gain an impression of which motives led to decisions to go to war and what were the aims of campaigns.

These questions are often discussed in terms of strategy, and it is assumed without further ado that the Romans were capable of realizing in practice what they could not define verbally.[3] The assumption is that we can distil theoretical concepts from a reality that can be grasped through the interpretation of literary sources and archaeological remains. There is, however, the danger of imposing on inadequate evidence an interpretation that seems attractive only because we know so little. To take a random example, modern historians may declare of a specific author that he 'was not interested in analysing any defensive strategy that may have determined the disposition of Roman forts'. But the omission of such an analysis need not result from a lack of interest; it was a matter of fundamental inability. No ancient author, whether he was a general or not, gives such an analysis. This is true for the Greek historians no less than the Romans. Thucydides gives various reasons why Brasidas chose to campaign in Thrace.[4] Yet it was Liddell Hart, not Thucydides, who described his motives in strategic terms, as 'a move directed against the roots, instead of the trunk, of the enemy power'.[5] Whether Liddell Hart was right or not in describing Brasidas' expedition as the first recorded instance of a 'strategy of indirect approach' is not the issue here. The point is that this is a form of abstraction and rationalization that is not found in ancient authors. To take an author closer to the subject of this study, Procopius, it is clear that he had no real insight into the function of various military installations. His elementary misunderstanding of the purpose of Justinian's fortification of the monastery at Mount Sinai has been noted.[6] Another random example is his description of Resapha (Sergiopolis) as a church surrounded by a wall.[7] The church accumulated treasures and came to be powerful and celebrated, and it was for this reason (according to him) that Justinian built a new wall and cisterns. He failed to recognize that it was an important station on a major strategic route and hence a place that needed to be fortified. Procopius was an assessor on the staff of Belisarius and, as an intelligent participant in his campaigns, had direct experience of military affairs. If he made mistakes at this level we clearly must be cautious about the degree of strategic insight we ascribe to Roman and Byzantine planners.

Luttwak observes:

Just as the Romans had apparently no need of a Clausewitz to subject their military energies to the discipline of political goals, it seems that they had no

---

[3] The most successful modern study is E. N. Luttwak, *The Grand Strategy of the Roman Empire* (1976).

[4] iv 80–1.   [5] B. H. Liddell Hart, *Strategy, The Indirect Approach* ([3]1954), 31 f.

[6] Above, p. 94.   [7] *De aed.* ii 9. 3.

need of modern analytical techniques either. Innocent of the new science of 'systems analysis', the Romans nevertheless designed and built large and complex security systems that successfully integrated troop deployments, fixed defenses, road networks, and signaling links in a coherent whole. In the more abstract spheres of strategy it is evident that, whether by intellect or traditional intuition, the Romans understood all the subtleties of deterrence, and also its limitations.[8]

This attitude towards the Romans and their army is not novel. The applicability of Roman tactics and strategy to modern warfare has been a highly popular notion ever since the rediscovery, in the fifteenth century, of Caesar's *Commentaries*, 'that masterpiece of official deception', in the words of Liddell Hart.[9] The traditional subject of study, however, has been ancient battles—Cannae, say, or Caesar's campaigns in Gaul. The kind of rationalization of the frontiers of the principate attempted by Luttwak is a more recent phenomenon. There is, however, an essential difference between these two fields of study.

Of the ancient battles there exist ancient descriptions. These may be one-sided or misleading. It has, in fact, been argued that Maurice of Nassau and Gustavus Adolphus, in their attempts to recreate the Roman legions, were chasing a chimera, having been led astray by Caesar's distorted descriptions.[10] But, whatever the shortcomings of various ancient accounts, they are there. They describe specific actions by forces in the field. The sixteenth-century generals who read the ancient authors when studying the ancient 'art of war' found concrete descriptions of technique and tactics.

No such descriptions support those who attempt to describe the aims of Roman frontier policy. Ancient authors do not always give a clear-cut explanation why the Roman campaigns of the principate were undertaken. When they do give explanations, these are often brief references to 'glory' or the desire to subdue a people. Roman literature offers little justification for the assumption that the Romans subjected their military energies to the discipline of political goals. The distribution of troops on the frontier and the rationale behind the location of forts are never the subject of discussion in ancient literature. This makes questionable Luttwak's assertion that, whether by intellect or traditional intuition, the Romans understood all the subtleties of strategy. If they understood by intellect they kept quiet about it.

---

[8] Luttwak, 3.

[9] B. H. Liddell Hart, *T. E. Lawrence: In Arabia and After* (1934), 277.

[10] John Keegan, *The Face of Battle: A Study of Agincourt, Waterloo, and the Somme* (1976), 62 f., 63–68, with a detailed comparison of a passage of Caesar with one of Thucydides, in favour of the latter.

Modern students, therefore, resort to the interpretation of the disposition of troops and to 'logical' assumptions about the meaning of actions for which no such explanation is given by ancient authors. But if all we are told about the process of decision-making at the imperial court is, for example, the statement of a contemporary senator that 'the emperor went to war in order to subdue the enemy and annex his kingdom', how can we then assume that, in reality, there was a sophisticated, but unexpressed doctrine regarding economy of force which motivated the emperor to go to war? In these circumstances it must be questioned whether the *a priori* assumption of the 'modernism' of the Roman imperial army is not just an anachronistic attitude resulting in a distorted view of Roman values and organizational capabilities. The present chapter argues that generally historians and archaeologists, in their study of the Roman frontier, have been chasing not merely a chimera, but Utopia.

Luttwak has described Roman strategy in a systematic manner. He assumes that there was a coherent system built up with an inner logic and that it is possible to describe the coherence and the dynamics of this system. We can admire his lucid analysis of the material, accept many of his insights, and appreciate his systematic approach, but we must still ask whether the system analysed did in fact exist. If we do ask this question, it is thanks to Luttwak's own admirable synthesis. However, his central assumption, that there existed a system whose object was to defend and enhance the security of the empire, is a hypothesis based on analogies with modern army organization. It is not based on an independent analysis of the ancient literary sources or the archaeological material, but derives from a lucid perusal of modern literature, and naturally the result is an approach already implicit in the writings of most specialists on Roman frontiers. The hypothesis suffers from a disadvantage familiar in the study of history: it cannot be proved or disproved by objective means. What we can do, however, is to test the basic assumptions which underly the hypothesis by referring to ancient sources and archaeological material. In this chapter it is argued that the results of such a test do not bear out the validity of the hypothesis as it stands.

Decision-Making and War Aims

It may be asked whether Roman decision-making at the highest level did indeed follow an unconscious inner logic and consistency. The words of an acute observer, speaking of the Second World War, are relevant:

In fact, it was rare for policy to be clearly thought out, though some romantics or worshippers of 'great men' liked to think so. Usually it built itself from a thousand small arrangements, ideas, compromises, bits of give and take. There was not much which was decisively changed by a human will. Just as a plan for a military campaign does not spring fully-grown from some master general; it arises from a sort of Brownian movement of colonels and majors and captains, and the most the general can do is rationalize it afterwards.[11]

Even today, it is clear, we cannot be certain how often politicians and generals are capable of realizing in practice a well-considered strategy which looks sound in theory. There are now nearly 300 Institutes of Strategic Studies in more than 50 countries, more than 95% of them having been founded within the past two decades. Future students will have to consider what influence these will have had on the course of history.[12] As already noted, the Romans did not even rationalize their actions afterwards.

Even where there is copious information it is hard to determine the aims of even one side, let alone both, in going to war. The stated cause of a war may be merely a convenient excuse. The aims any side professes may not be the real ones. When we are faced with ancient literary sources it is often difficult even to determine whether the aims on record were merely spread by rumour among the upper class, or officially declared. Aims may change in the course of a war, being adapted according to results. Initial modest aims may be replaced by ambitious ones as a result of a successful campaign. Aims may be reinvented in the light of the outcome of a war;[13] this is particularly relevant to our enquiry if it results from a failure of plans for expansion. It would be idle to pretend that we possess sufficient information on many Roman wars to dissect such complicated processes.

In dealing with the principate the following pattern occurs again and again: tribe T. is said to have carried out raids on Roman territory (did they really?). The emperor decides to go to war. He is said to have defeated tribe T. Tribe T. is then incorporated into the empire or not. For information on the initial aims and on the motives for later actions

---

[11] C. P. Snow, *The Light and the Dark*, ch. 34. Campbell, ch. IX and especially p. 393, argues that the emperor in matters of war and peace, foreign policy, the annexation of territory, and the organization and use of the army would in practice consult his advisers and confidants, who were drawn mainly from the upper classes. That may be conceded without admitting that it was a form of decision-making that led to a restrained use of the army.

[12] 'The Fog of War Studies', *The Economist* 16–22 April, 1988, 72.

[13] See B. Lewis, *History, Remembered, Recovered, Invented* (1975).

we depend on literary sources, often of doubtful quality. It is very hard to know whether the said raids were more or less serious than we are told, whether the emperor really intended to defend the province or was glad of an excuse to show his mettle, whether he hoped to expand the empire and did so or not, or whether annexation was an afterthought. All this may seem obvious, but these realities are often ignored in discussions of specific wars. It is particularly noticeable that modern historians find it easy to ignore literary sources when these state that a war of conquest was initiated by Rome out of sheer ambition on the part of the emperor. It is then often assumed that it cannot have been as simple as that. However, when the sources state that the emperor marched to the frontier because of the threat posed by tribe T. no such doubts are entertained.

Random factors often decided the objects of Roman wars. Every student of Roman history is familiar with the stories told by Roman historians of wars launched by ambitious generals during the principate, the campaigns of Germanicus in Germany, those of Corbulo in Lower Germany.[14] The location of the war was determined by the area of command of such leaders; and if the war was not pursued further this was because the emperor did not permit it. On the other hand, Pompey and Caesar and many republican generals before them did go on, because there was no one to stop them. The mere fact that there existed a *lex Iulia* which forbade a governor to start an unauthorized war shows that this was, in fact, common practice. The first encounter with the Teutones resulted from an unprovoked attack by the Romans—and it took place beyond the Alps, another example of Roman disregard for the alleged defensive value of natural obstacles.[15]

This is not a book about Roman imperialism in general, or in the East in particular, but the subject clearly must be touched upon in any discussion of frontier policy. Roman imperialism in Republican Rome is a controversial subject, and so is the imperialism of the principate. For the present discussion it will suffice to indicate a number of elementary differences between the earlier and the later period which affect the issue.

Decisions regarding war and peace were, under the principate, made by the emperor, whose power rested on the support of the standing army, precisely the body which was directly affected when a decision

---

[14] Tacitus, *Ann.* xi 18–20.

[15] For the *lex Iulia*, Cicero, *in Pisonem*, 21. 50; for the encounter with the Teutones, Appian, *Celt.* 13; both references taken from P. Brunt, *Historia* 10 (1961), 192.

was taken to fight.[16] The civilian population of the empire or of the capital would usually not gain much from such enterprises; but they did not vote for their emperor. Those who hold that wars were often fought to defend the frontier provinces will argue that the population in those areas benefited from enhanced security. Yet it is certain that, at any rate in the first instance, they suffered rather than profited from the passing of armies and the court through their territory. Pliny's correspondence with Trajan shows how much small towns suffered from the passing of travellers even in peacetime. Byzantium, which was a major station for crowds of soldiers on the march, received some support. Smaller frontier towns had to cope by themselves as best they could.[17] Elsewhere Pliny compares the passing of Trajan through the provinces (best case) with that of Domitian (worst):

'Vehicles were requisitioned without chaos, there was no fastidiousness regarding lodgings, food-supplies were the same for all. Your court was strictly organized and obedient . . . How different was the recent journey of another emperor! If it was a journey rather than a devastation, when billeting meant expulsion, and right and left everything was burnt and trampled as if another power or the very barbarians whom he fled had invaded.[18]

Dio's complaint regarding the cost of supplies to the army in the time of Caracalla shows that even senators considered such events a burden.[19]

On the other hand, it is clear that a successful war of expansion was profitable to all participating soldiers. The acquisition of booty in this period has not, as far as I know, been treated systematically, but there is no lack of sources to indicate that winning a war was lucrative.[20] It was a commonplace that 'in war it is the stronger man who loots'.[21] Following the capture of Jerusalem by Titus 'all troops were so loaded with plunder that in Syria the price of gold was depreciated to half its previous standard'.[22] Titus called up those who had been especially brave and 'placed crowns of gold upon their heads, presented them

---

[16] The subject of Campbell, *The Emperor and the Roman Army.*

[17] *Ep.* x 77 f. As Campbell, 250 f., points out, Trajan naturally assumes that most of the travellers who caused trouble were soldiers. For the position of Byzantium on the route of armies on the march see also Tacitus, *Ann.* xii 62. On the passing of armies through Asia Minor, S. Mitchell, *AFRBA*, 131–50.

[18] *Pan.* 20. 3–4.

[19] lxxvii 9. 3; 5–7 (382 f.). Cf. Rostovtzeff, *Roman Empire*, 358 ff., 424 ff.

[20] For brief remarks, V. A. Maxfield, *The Military Decorations of the Roman Army* (1981), 58 f.; for Caesar's Gallic war, L. Keppie, *The Making of the Roman Army* (1984), 100 f. G. R. Watson, *The Roman Soldier* (1969), 108–14, lists the donatives paid by emperors to the troops on their accession and on special occasions to gain their loyalty. He seems to imply that no payments were made after campaigns. Campbell does not discuss booty.

[21] Tacitus, *Agricola* 14.

[22] Josephus, *BJ* vi 6. 1 (317).

with golden neck-chains, little golden spears, and standards made of silver, and promoted each man to a higher rank; he further assigned to them out of the spoils silver and gold and raiments and other booty in abundance'.[23] It is no coincidence, of course, that these passages derive from the fullest account available of a military victory under the principate. The well-known career inscription of C. Velius Rufus, who was decorated in the Jewish war, is a clear illustration of the manner in which able men could obtain rapid promotion during and after a war.[24] There is more, however. Tacitus emphasizes the importance of booty in the speeches which he attributes to commanders before a battle. Corbulo 'exhorted his soldiers to secure both glory and spoil'.[25] And indeed, after the battle, the adult men were massacred, 'the civilian population was sold by auction, the rest of the booty fell to the conquerors'.[26] Suetonius, before the decisive battle against Boudicca, similarly spoke of glory and booty.[27] Effortless glory and slaughter (of men, women, and animals) without Roman losses were the happy outcome of the battle. In fact, after a victory licence to kill without inhibition seems to have been part of the prerogatives of Roman soldiers, as of other armies in the ancient and less ancient world.[28] The result is measured in the numbers killed rather than strategic gain.[29] Severus' army was allowed to plunder Ctesiphon and its surroundings at liberty.[30] Dio, critical of this campaign, says Severus did not accomplish anything else, as if plundering the place had been the only purpose of the expedition.[31] It can be argued, of course, that ravaging enemy territory and destroying his economic base is in itself an efficient strategy since he will then not easily be able to carry on the war, but Dio clearly did not think that this was Severus' aim, or if it was, that it was a sensible thing to do.[32] Herodian gives a similar description of Caracal-

---

[23] *BJ* vii 1. 3 (14 f.), trans. Thackeray, Loeb.

[24] *IGLS* vi 2796, cf. D. Kennedy, *Britannia* 14 (1983), 183–96.

[25] *Ann.* xiii 39: 'hortatur milites ut . . . gloriaeque pariter et praedae consulerent.'

[26] Ibid.: 'et imbelle vulgus sub corona venundatum, reliqua praeda victoribus cessit.'

[27] Tacitus, *Ann.* xiv 36. 4.   [28] Josephus, *passim*.

[29] *Ann.* xiv 37: 'clara et antiquis victoriis par ea die laus parta.' It was merely a decisive engagement in a costly and harmful rebellion.

[30] Dio lxxvi 9. 4 (347); Herodian iii 9. 10 f.; SHA, *Severus* xvi 5. 6. Here the permission to plunder and keep the booty is called 'an enormous donative'.

[31] See also SHA, *Sev.* 16. 5: '. . . donativum militibus largissimum dedit, concessa omni praeda oppidi Parthici, quod milites quaerebant.'

[32] On the practice of destroying enemy crops in Greek warfare, G. B. Grundy, *Thucydides and the History of his Age* ([2]1948), chs. ix and x. Grundy argues that, for social and economic, as well as military reasons, the Greek wars, fought by citizen armies consisting of hoplites, had to be short, sharp, and decisive encounters. The aim was to destroy the other party's crops and to return in time for the harvest. The aims of the Roman imperial army were, of course, dictated by different considerations and needs.

la's Persian campaign.[33] Both Dio and Herodian describe this as an expedition undertaken on a feeble pretext, without provocation.[34] The troops marched through Parthia till they were tired of looting and killing and then returned to the Roman province. Both Dio and Herodian consider it a useless war. Ammianus attributes to Julian the statement that the desire for booty often tempted the Roman soldier.[35] Libanius, Julian's friend, describes how he envisaged Julian's progress in his Persian campaign, assuming all went well: 'ravaging the countryside, pillaging villages, taking forts, crossing rivers, mining walls, occupying cities . . . the army had exulted in the slaughter of the Persians'.[36]

The suppression of internal unrest too could be profitable. Caracalla allowed his troops to plunder Alexandria in 215 and gave them a donative as well.[37] The army received a donative before as well as after Severus Alexander's Persian campaign.[38] Apart from the booty they took home, valorous soldiers were promoted after a war. This was common practice and is known from literary and epigraphic sources.[39]

A successful war was the best opportunity for soldiers and officers in the imperial army to improve their material and social status without cost to the empire. A letter allegedly written by Aurelian with suggestions how the soldiers are to be kept under control advises: 'let them earn a living from the booty taken from the enemy and not from the tears of the provincials'.[40] Aurelian is praised because he 'commanded the army, restored the frontier districts, gave booty to the soldiers, enriched Thrace with captured cattle, horses, and slaves'.[41] Whether this is the author's fancy or not, it clearly reflects his ideas of a sound ruler. In 360 Constantius gave up the siege of Bezabde very reluctantly because 'he was going back without results while, as it were, the door of a rich house was open before him'.[42] The language of Ammianus is clear enough, and so is his description of the preparations for the next campaign: 'recruits were enrolled throughout the provinces, every order and profession was troubled, furnishing clothes, arms, artillery,

---

[33] iv 11. 7 f.
[34] Dio lxxviii 1; Herodian iv 9. 10: Caracalla desired the title 'Parthicus' and an eastern victory.
[35] xxiii 5. 21.
[36] *Or.* i 132. For the same spirit cf. the fanciful description in SHA, *Claudius* 8. 6; 9. 6.
[37] Dio lxxvii 23 (401).
[38] Herodian vi 4. 1 (before the campaign); 6. 4 (after).
[39] Maxfield, 236–40, with numerous examples.
[40] SHA, *Aurelian* 7. 5: 'de praeda hostis, non de lacrimis provincialium victum habent.'
[41] Ibid. 10. 2: '. . . exercitum duceret, limites restitueret, praedam militibus daret, Thracias bubus, equis, mancipipis captivis locupletaret . . .'
[42] Ammianus xx 11. 31: 'quod velut patefacta ianua divitis domus, irritus propositi reverteretur.'

even gold and silver, great quantities of provision and various kinds of pack animals'.[43]

Dio levels an interesting accusation against Caracalla: in his desire to spend money on the soldiers he constantly demanded gold crowns from the civilian population on the pretext that he had defeated some enemies.[44] The importance of financial gain or losses was an enduring feature in Roman policy-making and did not diminish in the Byzantine period, as can be seen from the weight attached to the payments made for the garrison in the Darial pass in the fifth and sixth centuries.

The soldiers, on the other hand, did not profit so much from a state of peace: since their length of service was fixed, unlike that of soldiers under the republic, they did not obtain early discharge in peacetime.[45] The troops, it may be concluded, had many practical reasons to welcome a decision to fight. The existence of the standing army as a major factor in Roman politics may well have increased the political will to wage wars of conquest.[46] This tendency was reinforced by the circumstance that military glory would have enhanced the reputation of an emperor and strengthened his ties with the troops.[47]

This is not to suggest that these were simple processes. There was no powerful 'officer class' in Rome, and no centralized army command. If there was a stimulus to initiate wars on the part of the provincial army this would have reached the emperor only through the legionary commanders, provincial governors, and ex-governors. No emperor could rule if there was concerted action to depose him, but the army had no institutionalized means of exerting pressure on political decision-making as in modern military dictatorships. The absence of a class of higher career-officers with permanent commissions, the colonels who, in our times, not only organize military coups but exert constant influence on politics in their countries, made it impossible for the army to interfere in politics in this manner. The centurions, who held permanent appointments, did not have the social status required and those who did, senators and *equites*, did not have permanent appoint-

---

[43] xxi 6. 6.

[44] Dio lxxvii 9. 1. Note, by contrast, SHA, *Marcus Antoninus* 17, praising Marcus Aurelius because he financed the Marcomannic war by selling imperial property instead of taxation. After a profitable war he bought everything back.

[45] B. Dobson, 'The Roman Army: Wartime or Peacetime Army?', *Heer und Integrationspolitik: Die römischen Militärdiplome als Historische Quelle*, ed. W. Eck and H. Wolff (1986), 10–25.

[46] Campbell, ch. IX, rejects this possibility in his treatment of the role played by the army in politics. An example, chosen at random, is the mutiny against Severus Alexander in protest against his policy to trade peace with the Germans in exchange for gold, rather than marching out to fight them: Herodian vi 78. 9–10, and cf. SHA, *Alexander* 63. 5–6, *Maximini* 7. 5–7.

[47] On imperial honours, Campbell, 120–56.

ments. We know a good deal about the mechanism which provided Roman troops with the means to depose and impose emperors of their choice.[48] It cannot be said, however, that the army, as a body, put up emperors. Ambitious military leaders used the troops placed at their disposal to depose rivals and impose their friends or themselves on the empire. Rebellions were organized by commanders, not by the rank and file. There is hardly any evidence of influence being exerted by the army when there was no crisis.[49] It is clear, however, that any emperor was conscious of his dependence on the army. To strengthen his position among the soldiers was indeed imperative if only to avoid a crisis. A ruler enjoyed due respect among soldiers and significant parts of the upper classes only if he was known, among other things, as an experienced and effective warrior. At the same time the army was always a potential threat to the ruling class.

The annexation of new territory was profitable also if it could be achieved without war. It will suffice to refer to the results of the annexations of Cappadocia and of Commagene[50] or to Tacitus' description of the causes of the revolt of Boudicca.[51] While the governor was fighting in Wales the prosperous kingdom of the Iceni was being annexed following the death of its king. 'The kingdom was plundered by centurions, the royal house by (the procurator's) slaves as if they had been captured in war', an expression which merely indicates that this was the usual treatment of peoples conquered in war. The distinguished Iceni were stripped of their ancestral possesions. The Trinobantes, previously incorporated, joined the revolt out of resentment over the veteran colony Camulodunum, founded on expropriated lands. Tacitus, outspoken in these matters, says: 'plunder, slaughter and rapine, the Romans falsely call it empire; they make a desolation and call it peace'.[52]

Annexation remained profitable after the early stages. Aelius Gallus' Arabian expedition was, according to Strabo, undertaken for reasons of long-term profitability.[53] When Trajan reached the Red Sea in his Mesopotamian campaign customs duties were immediately imposed. That was intended to be an enduring source of income. Annexation further afforded a greater possibility of direct interference, as in the

---

[48] Campbell, ch. IX.
[49] The regular demands by the troops for salary rises and donatives did not in themselves constitute influence on politics in any other sphere than their own material position.
[50] After the annexation of Cappadocia taxes were reduced: Tacitus, *Ann.* ii 42. 6.
[51] *Ann.* xiv 31.
[52] *Agricola* 30. 6, attributed to a Caledonian chieftain.
[53] xvi 4. 22 (780).

giving of support to local Roman citizens. As Strabo heard from a friend who had visited Petra, there lived there 'many Romans and many other foreigners, and he saw that the foreigners were often involved in lawsuits with each other and with the natives, but the natives never prosecuted each other, but they kept absolute peace with each other'.[54] In Caesar's *Bellum Civile* we find as a sort of standard phrase a reference to 'all the people of Antioch and residing Roman merchants'.[55] Antioch had been part of a Roman province for only fifteen years by that time. It is obvious that the imposition of Roman law will have been advantageous to the Roman citizens. Cicero's *Pro Fonteio*, delivered some time after 70 BC, is an obvious case. The province of Gaul was so full of Roman traders that no business could be transacted without the interference of a Roman citizen, no money changed without it being recorded in Roman books.[56] Fonteius was accused of extortion by Gauls, and various groups of Roman citizens resident in the province served as witnesses for the defence. Cicero advised the jury not to accept the testimony of barbarians against that of loyal Roman citizens.

Information on the presence of Roman citizens in such areas is incidental, but the hatred their presence engendered comes out particularly well in the descriptions of the massacres that accompanied rebellions against Roman rule. Best-known are the thousands of Roman citizens who were killed in the province of Asia in 88 BC, evidence both of the numbers involved and the enmity bred by their presence.[57] When the Illyrians revolted in AD 6 'Roman citizens were overwhelmed, traders massacred, and a large number of veterans still serving with the colours in a region far from the commander were exterminated'.[58] The revolt of the Treveri in 21 began with a massacre of Roman business men.[59]

The two groups of Romans, then, that profited from a war of conquest and subsequent annexation were the military and the Romans resident among the subject population. However, that is not to suggest that wars of conquest were primarily undertaken in the interest of these classes or that they had a decisive influence on the process of decision-making at the imperial court in the principate or the later

[54] xvi 4. 21 (779).
[55] *BC* iii 102: '. . . omnium Antiochensium civiumque Romanorum, qui illic negotiarentur . . .'
[56] *Pro Fonteio* I. 1: 'referta Gallia negotiatorum est, plena civium Romanorum. Nemo Gallorum sine cive Romano quidquam negotii gerit; nummus in Gallia nullus sine civium Romanorum tabulis commovetur.'
[57] For Roman citizens in the provinces under the republic, Harris, 95–102.
[58] Velleius ii 110. 6.
[59] Tacitus, *Ann.* iii 42. 1; *Ann.* ii 62. 4 describes the presence of such *negotiatores* even among the Marcomanni.

empire. They happened to be the instruments of conquest and annexation and gained by it, but there is no indication at all that they played an active role in politics any more than the subjects in the frontier provinces. Unless we choose to ignore centuries of Roman historiography and literature, the decision to engage in a war of conquest was determined by the imperial will and not by pressures from definable groups with interests at stake.[60] Like generals of all times a Roman emperor could not wage war successfully if the fighting spirit of the troops was broken—as Dio describes that of Severus' army before Hatra.[61] However, the decision to fight was taken by the emperor alone, with the help of advice from those he chose to trust.[62]

These might belong to almost any class: his family, senators, *equites*, freedmen, or worse—in the eyes of noblemen—'jugglers and actors'. Those advising the emperor were not selected, and did not act, as representatives of specific interest groups.[63] The imperial advisers are sometimes referred to as a group: Dio usually speaks of a collective 'we', and sometimes they are singled out as powerful individuals. Their social class is considered important. A good emperor listens to well-educated senators, a bad one to boorish upstarts. It is not clear, however, that attitudes and ideologies favouring or opposing expansion can be linked to specific social groups. There were, in other words, no permanent 'lobbies' with the ability and the desire to further particular causes at court. Ancient sources frequently describe the emperor as consulting his friends on matters concerning war and peace.[64] Good emperors are described as having good friends.[65] Sometimes it is even stated as rather exceptional that an emperor would consult particular friends because of their expert knowledge regarding the issue involved.[66]

There is never any suggestion that friends were selected as representing a specific ideology. Character, class, and virtue, or the absence of those qualities, are the features described as decisive by ancient authors. Conflict between imperial advisers is invariably about matters of immediate personal interest: influence and wealth, not policy and the

---

[60] See F. Millar, *The Emperor in the Roman World* (1977), ch. III, 'Entourage, Assistants and Advisers'.

[61] lxxv 12.

[62] See in general J. Crook, *Consilium Principis* (1955); Millar, ch. III, 'Entourage, Assistants and Advisers'.

[63] Millar, 113.

[64] e.g. Tacitus, *Ann.* xi 19; xii 20.

[65] Suetonius, *Titus* vii 2; and, with the usual reservations: SHA, *Marcus Antoninus* 22. 3; *Severus Alexander* 66.

[66] Dio lvii 17. 9; SHA, *Severus Alexander* 16. 3.

affairs of state. The emperor normally did take advice from his friends on important issues, but he was free to ignore it, as Dio tells of Caracalla from personal experience.[67] Dio must have experienced the same under Septimius Severus, for he found the two major campaigns of this emperor useless and even harmful projects. Commodus was criticized for the opposite reason: he decided not to pursue the war in the north, against the counsel of his father's senatorial advisers.[68] Again, Caracalla spent far more money on the army than his mother and advisers found desirable, and Dio complains that his own class no less than wealthy individuals or communities suffered heavy losses. This was a policy which hurt the immediate, personal interests of the emperor's friends.

These are important points in determining the motives which persuaded an emperor to go to war. To return to a statement frequently cited in this book: Severus merely pretended, according to Dio, that he conquered Mesopotamia for the benefit of the province of Syria. His real motive was the personal desire to obtain military glory.[69] Similarly, Caracalla went to war with Parthia because of his preoccupation with Alexander, again according to Dio who knew him well.[70] Glory, honour, and particularly an identification with generals of the past were a real factor in determining the choice between war and peace. 'Corbulo considered it due to the grandeur of the Roman people to reconquer what once had been captured by Lucullus and Pompey.'[71] 'It is praiseworthy for a private house to retain its own, for a king to fight for another's property.'[72] In Rome there did not exist an established group with political influence and a vested interest in the preservation of peace, the protection of frontier zones, and the avoidance of military adventurism. The only objection to wars of expansion which an emperor was likely to encounter would have been raised by individuals who considered them a waste of money.

The Choice of Frontier Lines

It is unlikely that most Roman frontier lines were determined by choice and by a conscious decision to halt indefinitely all further advance. On

---

[67] lxxviii 11. 5; 18. 2–4.   [68] Dio lxxii 1–2.

[69] See also SHA, *Severus* 15: 'Erat sane in sermone vulgari Parthicum bellum adfectare Septimium Severum, gloriae cupiditate non aliqua necessitate deductum.'

[70] lxxvii 7–8.

[71] Tacitus, *Ann.* xiii 34. 4: 'et Corbulo dignum magnitudine populi Romani rebatur parta olim a Lucullo Pompeioque recipere.'

[72] *Ann.* xv 1. 5: '. . . et sua retinere privatae domus, de alienis certare regiam laudem esse.'

the contrary, in the second century at least, a governor who wanted to earn the respect of many of his fellow Romans would strive to gain 'the glory of expanding his province';[73] and therefore the view has been expressed that 'the frontiers congealed around the borders of the empire: they arose by default'.[74]

A few examples may illustrate this point. The campaigns across the Rhine in Germany represent a sustained effort, reluctantly given up, to re-establish Roman authority east of the Rhine early in the reign of Tiberius.[75] Domitian's war against the Chatti, 83–(?)85, was fought with five legions and a detachment from Britain, a substantial force, but it resulted in a very modest expansion east of the Rhine, in the Wetterau region. It has plausibly been suggested that the original plan had envisaged a far more ambitious advance; if so, the offensive must have petered out and been abandoned without obtaining the desired result.[76]

Strabo lucidly explains why there was no need to occupy Britain: 'Local chieftains have made the whole of the island virtually a Roman possession'. He continues to say that the Britons put up so readily with heavy import and export duties 'that there is no need for a garrison on the island.'It would require at least one legion and some cavalry to levy tribute from them, so that the expenditure on the army would equal the revenues, for customs duties would have to be reduced if tribute were imposed. Also there would be some danger if force is used.'[77] Strabo held that, on the whole, the Romans possessed all that was worth having. The unconquered part of the world was poor or inhabited by nomads.[78] Appian, writing in the second century, found the unoccupied parts of Britain not worth caring for, 'and even what they do have is not very profitable'.[79] These are sound reasons not to annex territory. They are echoed, more than two centuries later, by Dio's objections against the annexation of northern Mesopotamia.[80] All three authors find unprofitable expansion objectionable, but the implication of their words is that they would not resist profitable conquest. They do not disapprove of the subjection of foreign peoples for moral reasons, and they definitely do not say that warfare ought to be

---

[73] Tacitus, *Agricola* 14. 2: 'fama aucti officii.'

[74] J. C. Mann, 'The Frontiers of the Principate', *ANRW* ii 1 (1974), 513 f.

[75] It is clear that this was the goal of these campaigns. See e.g. the words ascribed to Germanicus by Tacitus, *Ann.* ii 14: 'propiorem iam Albim quam Rhenum neque bellum ultra, modo se, patris patruique vestigia prementem, isdem in terris victorem sisterent.' And cf. the text of the inscription cited at *Ann.* ii 22. 1.

[76] Schönberger, *JRS* 59 (1969), 158.   [77] iv. 5. 3 (200 f.).

[78] xvii 3. 24 (839); vi 4. 2 (288).

[79] *Praef.* 5.   [80] See above, pp. 26, 387.

defensive. More important still, the fact that Strabo clearly judged the conquest of Britain undesirable for economic and financial reasons shows that the eventual decision to conquer it was taken regardless of financial or economic considerations, although the army required was four times the size envisaged by Strabo. Claudius desired the honour of a legitimate triumph and chose Britain as the most suitable place to gain one.[81] Suetonius, as an imperial secretary, was an author who, like Cassius Dio and Strabo, clearly knew at what conceptual level important decisions were taken by emperors. Yet he had no difficulty in stating that these were the reasons for the conquest of Britain.

Later the frontier in Britain moved northward and southward on several occasions. Movements backward and forward appear to be a function of the ambition of the commander and what could be held in practice. Tacitus describes Agricola as wistfully repeating that he could have conquered Ireland with one legion and some auxiliaries, just the forces Strabo thought would keep Britain under control.[82] Severus undertook a campaign in Northern Britain for the education of his sons, because he saw that the legions were becoming enervated by idleness, and for the sake of personal glory. He desired to conquer the whole of Britain. It was, in other words, a war of choice initiated by the emperor, who used frontier trouble as an excuse. This is the information provided by a contemporary senator *amicus* of Severus and Caracalla, twice consul, *ordinarius* together with the emperor, a man, therefore, who knew exactly how decisions about war and peace were taken, whether he agreed with those decisions or not.[83] Severus advanced nearly to the farthest point of Scotland and died in York while preparing for a second campaign. Caracalla hastened back to Rome to consolidate his position. What was the original aim of the expedition? It has been argued that it served two major ends, the repulse of the Maeatae and the establishment of a new frontier system based on Hadrian's Wall.[84] This assumes that Dio is lying and that the modest results of the expedition had been its aim from the beginning. It is also

[81] Suetonius, *Claudius* 178. 1: 'Cum . . . vellet iusti triumphi decus, unde adquireret Britanniam potissimum elegit. . . .'

[82] *Agricola* 24. 3; cf. on this J. C. Mann, *Britannia* 16 (1985), 23 f.

[83] For the aims of Severus' British campaign, Dio lxxvi 11–12 (365–7); in particular 13. 1: Severus wanted to conquer all of Britain. Note also that the tribes were considered rebels when they continued their resistance beyond a certain stage: ibid. 15. 1; cf. Herodian iii 14. 2; 5. For Dio's career, F. Millar, *A Study of Cassius Dio* (1964), ch. I.

[84] Millar, *Cassius Dio*, 148, referring to K. A. Steer in I. A. Richmond (ed.), *Roman and Native in North Britain* (1958), 91–111; similarly S. Frere, *Britannia: A History of Roman Britain* (1974), 199–203. P. Salway, *Roman Britain* (1981), 227–31, does believe that the British campaign was defensive in nature and not a war of choice. M. Todd, *Roman Britain, 55 BC–AD 400* (1981), 175–80, allows for the possibility that the emperor altered his plans in the course of the expedition.

possible to argue that Dio (and Herodian) knew that Severus had intended to conquer all of Scotland, but that this plan was subsequently abandoned, either by Severus himself or by Caracalla after the death of his father.[85] There is evidence to suggest that the decision to withdraw was taken while Severus was alive.[86] In other words, one interpretation sees the war as defensive, contradicting contemporary sources; the other accepts contemporary descriptions of the expedition as a war of conquest which ended in failure. This explanation, of course, would make nonsense of the claim that we see here an example of Rome's intuitive understanding of the essence of deterrence. It is impossible to prove that either explanation is correct. But the statements made by contemporary sources place the burden of proof on those who claim that this was a defensive campaign.

Once it is accepted that there have been failed but costly attempts to expand the empire for the sake of expansion, glory, or greed it becomes possible to list several such endeavours. The *Historia Augusta* claims that Marcus Aurelius intended to create new provinces in the North.[87] One should mistrust ancient sources, and the SHA more than any other, when they speak of plans which were not carried out. Indeed, Dio does not speak of such intentions, but he asserts that Marcus Aurelius would have subdued that entire region if he had lived longer.[88] In fact, by the time of Marcus' death several of the elements of gradual incorporation could be observed. In 175 the Marcomanni, Quadi, and Iazyges were already allies on unfavourable terms, which implies that they were part of the empire.[89] The Iazyges, for instance, furnished cavalry to the Roman army.[90] In 178 there were Roman troops

---

[85] D. J. Breeze and B. Dobson, *Hadrian's Wall* (1978), 134–7.

[86] Coins with obv. 'Severus Pius Aug. Brit.', i.e. late 210 or 211, and 'Adventus Augusti' indicate that preparations were made for an early return of the emperor: *BMC* Emp. v 366, no. 50, pl. 54. 8. I owe this reference to Mrs Alla Stein.

[87] SHA, *M. Antoninus* 24. 5: 'Voluit Marcomanniam provinciam, voluit etiam Sarmatiam facere, et fecisset, nisi Avidius Cassius rebellasset sub eodem in oriente.' Ibid. 27. 10: 'triennio bellum postea cum Marcomannis Hermunduris Sarmatis Quadis etiam egit et, si anno uno superfuisset, provincias ex his fecisset.' These statements are accepted as true by C. Parain, *Marc-Aurèle* (1957), 164; A. R. Birley, *Roman Frontier Studies 1967* (1971), 10–12; see also id., *Marcus Aurelius* (1966), 222 f. and Appendix III. A. Mócsy, *Pannonia and Upper Moesia* (1974), 184, accepts the statement, but assumes that the plans were given up at an earlier stage. G. Alföldy, *Historia* 20 (1971), 84–109, argues that this was a defensive war from the start: Marcus Aurelius never intended to expand the empire or create new provinces, and Commodus acted in accordance with his father's plans when he withdrew following a negotiated settlement. See also further discussion by Alföldy in R. Klein (ed.), *Marc Aurel* (1979), 389 ff. and esp. 425–8; M. Stahl, *Chiron* 19 (1989), 289–317. [88] lxxi 21 (275).

[89] On the notion that clients and allies were considered part of the empire see Harris, 133 ff. (republic); C. M. Wells, *The German Policy of Augustus* (1972), 248 f. (Augustus).

[90] Dio lxxi 16 (263); cf. 18.

stationed among the Quadi and Marcomanni.[91] Dio says Commodus could easily have destroyed the Marcomanni, but was too lax to do so. He concluded a satisfactory settlement and withdrew the army.[92] The implication seems to be obvious: here again a war of conquest was interrupted because the successor failed to pursue the expansionist ambitions of his father. Marcus Aurelius fought in roughly the same areas as Trajan: the North and the East. We know that there was expansion in the East: following Avidius Cassius' Parthian campaign Dura-Europos (and other sites?) was permanently occupied. There is no good reason to deny that the wars in the North were fought with similar expectations.

It is legitimate to speculate that hostile sources contain unfair accusations against Commodus; he may have been sensible and used diplomacy to end a war which was costly and difficult, and the prospects for decisive actions may have been less good than Dio claims. But nothing is gained by explaining away the clear signs of plans for expansion in the North. As argued repeatedly in this book, it is a fallacy to believe that the results of a war were always those anticipated by Rome. The aims of a war are adjusted and modified by both sides in accordance with the course of the fighting.

As argued in Chapter I, in the East the existing boundary was never accepted as definitely satisfactory. Under Nero preparations were made for a Caucasian campaign, interrupted only by the revolt of Vindex. It can be said that there were occasional attempts to expand in Britain, in Germany, and in the North, even after Trajan, but the efforts to subdue the Persians in Mesopotamia were far more frequent and persisted after warfare in other areas had become mostly defensive. Even in those areas it would not have been impossible for the Roman authorities to decide that they might gain the initiative and expand the empire rather than stay where they were and repel barbarian raids. The clearest example of such an attitude is the reign of Justinian.

It is therefore impossible to maintain that there was a consistent

[91] Dio lxxi 20 (274 f.). The troops prevented the tribes from pursuing their normal economic life, and yet the Quadi were not allowed to emigrate. 'In acting thus', says Dio, '(Marcus) desired not to confiscate their lands, but to punish the people.' οὕτως οὐ τὴν χώραν αὐτῶν προσκτήσασθαι ἀλλὰ τοὺς ἀνθρώπους τιμωρήσασθαι ἐπεθύμει. I cannot agree with the interpretation of J. Dobias. *Corolla Memoriae Erich Swoboda Dedicata* (1966), 115–25, esp. 123: 'Er wollte also weniger das Land erobern, als vielmehr die Bewohner bestrafen.' See also Birley, *Roman Frontier Studies 1967*, 10 f.; id.. 'Die Aussen- und Grenzpolitik', in Klein, 488; Alföldy, in Klein (n. 87 above). Dio does not speak of conquest, of incorporation into the empire, or of annexation, but of confiscation of lands and the treatment of peoples newly subdued. They *were* part of the empire, although not yet part of a province. As observed below, it is not territory which is incorporated into a province but a people.

[92] Dio lxxii 1–3 (282–4).

quest for defensible borders in the early empire. Apart from the many wars of expansion that were fought successfully, there were other wars planned or actually fought which, for various reasons, were aborted or failed to achieve the intended result. It would not be difficult, either, to argue that some of the wars often described as defensive were, in fact, wars of conquest. Suetonius, for instance, says of Domitian's campaign against the Chatti that it was uncalled for and undertaken, against the advice of the friends of his father, merely in order to make himself equal to his brother in power and dignity.[93] As already observed, this war may actually have resulted in gains far less impressive than originally hoped for.

Herodian says of the Germanic campaign of Maximinus:

> . As soon as he had seized power he began to prepare for a military campaign. Since he believed that he had achieved his position because of his physical size, strength, and military experience, he wanted to confirm his reputation and the soldiers' opinion by deeds, and he attempted to prove that Alexander's delays and timidity regarding military undertakings had rightly been condemned. Accordingly he unceasingly trained and exercised the soldiers, wearing arms himself and urging on the army. Thus he completed the bridge, about to attack the Germans across the river.[94]

As so often in this book, it must be asked whether historians are justified in attributing to Roman decision-makers sets of motives and calculations that we do not find reflected in our sources, while ignoring statements actually made. There is no lack of pronouncements in ancient literature to show that the attainment of honour and glory was considered a legitimate reason to go to war. 'As it was good and honourable to acquire Gaul, Thrace, Cilicia, and Cappadocia, the richest and most powerful provinces, and also Armenia and Britain which were of no practical use but gained the honour of the empire great renown . . .'[95] Trajan went to war compelled by 'the dignity of empire', according to Pliny, who was not fond of military expeditions.[96] If we may trust his panegyric he approved of a state of peace which followed military victory rather than one based on negotiated conces-

---

[93] *Domitian* ii 1; vi 1; cf. Syme, *CAH* xi, 162–4.

[94] vii 1. 6 f. For Maximinus' ambitions in the North—and hypothetical chances of success: ibid. 2. 9 and SHA, *Maximinus* 13. 3.

[95] Florus, *epitome* i 47. 4 f.

[96] *Pan.* 178. 4: 'Meruisti proximas moderatione, ut quandoque te vel inferre vel propulsare bellum coegerit imperi dignitas, non ideo vicisse videaris ut triumphares, sed triumphare quia viceris.' See also 16. 1–5, where Pliny praises Trajan's moderation and restraint. Yet 'in the past our victory always followed contempt of our empire. Now, if any barbarian king should be so insolent and mad as to deserve your fury and indignation . . .' no obstacle in the world would protect him against Trajan's might.

sions. 'They ask and beg, we grant or deny however it suits the majesty of empire.'[97]

According to Ammianus, Julian went to war against Persia for three reasons: in order to punish the Persians for the previous war, because he was tired of idleness, and because 'he burned to add to the ornaments of his glorious victories the surname "Parthicus"'.[98] Ammianus cites him as saying in his speech before his troops: 'this most dangerous people must be annihilated . . . Our forefathers spent many ages in exterminating whatever vexed them.'[99] On the Persian war fought by Constantius after Constantine's death Julian himself is no more explicit in his panegyric in honour of Constantius. The enemy had broken the peace and was aggressive, so Constantius had to fight.[100] Constantine was successful, for he had been victorious on enemy territory and 'freed cities', that is to say, he had prevented the capture of Nisibis.[101] This, admittedly, is rhetoric regarding a moderately successful war, but even rhetoric could have given an indication of an awareness of what one was fighting for, of the aims of the war, if there had been such awareness.

Modern scholars often question the validity of each of these statements, and of many others not cited here, and substitute an image of Roman behaviour for which there is no explicit support in ancient literature. There is plenty of support, however, for a more sceptical approach. Scores of academic 'must have's' and 'certainly's' will not turn emperors into compassionate rather than ambitious and vain men. The ancient sources, unlike modern historians, do not attempt to persuade their readers to give Roman rulers the benefit of the doubt.

Another matter that needs to be considered, is the extent of responsibility for the safety of the provinces accepted by the Roman rulers. In modern times it is considered natural that the state should guarantee the physical safety of its citizens. But it is not evident that the Roman emperor considered it his duty to protect the inhabitants to the same degree as we now consider to be our right.[102] In Chapter V it has, in fact, been argued that self-defence was a permanent fact of life in Roman Mesopotamia. The subject peoples of the empire were essentially considered slaves. This comes out as an elementary truth in many sources. Tacitus speaks of rebels as 'not yet broken by servitude'.[103] In

---

[97] *Pan.* 12. 2.   [98] xxii 12. 2.   [99] xxiii 5. 19 f.

[100] Julian, *Or.* i 18 B.   [101] *Or.* 22 A–C.

[102] Luttwak, 130 ff. considers these matters in his discussion of the fourth-century army, but his conclusions appear to be based exclusively on the siting of forts and not on pronouncements in ancient texts.

[103] *Ann.* xiv 31. 4.

the speech attributed by Josephus to Agrippa it is emphasized again and again that subjection by Rome is the equivalent of servitude, hard to bear but unavoidable.[104] Florus succeeds in comparing subjection with 'the reins of servitude' and 'the yoke recently imposed' in one and the same sentence.[105] Obviously the citizens of a peaceful province incorporated long ago would be described in different terms. All the same it seems legitimate to question the assumption that protection against all forms of attack was taken to be a natural right. The empire may well have had other priorities, such as the integrity of the army and the sovereignty of the emperor, the safety of certain areas such as Italy, the levying of taxes. This is not to argue that protection against foreign aggression was considered unimportant, but merely that it may have been less important, in Roman opinion, than is sometimes thought.

Peoples and Territory

The next point to consider is the view commonly held that territorial motives determined Roman war-aims and that boundary lines were chosen in accordance with strategic considerations. For illustration two quotations will suffice: '(Vespasian) . . . immediately set about the establishment of a scientific frontier in the East. . .'[106] And '. . . as drawn on the map of the empire at the accession of Trajan, this frontier was scarcely tenable. . . . Opposite Antioch . . . the depth of the territory controlled by Rome was scarcely more than a hundred miles—not enough if the Parthian armies were to be contained . . .'[107] Dio, indeed, reports that Severus claimed exactly this, which shows that the notion existed, but he does not believe that it was Severus' real reason for going to war.[108] Dio, writing some time after the event, already knew that the expansion by no means served to protect Syria but, on the contrary, was itself a cause of further warfare. In fact, Severus' conquest of Mesopotamia did not prevent the capture of Antioch about 253 (and 260?). It may indirectly have caused it. Severus' claim that his conquest of northern Mesopotamia enhanced the security of the empire was as

---

[104] *BJ* ii 16. 4 (345–401).

[105] *Epitome* ii 21. 12: 'Nova quippe pax, necdum adsuetae frenis servitutis tumidae gentium inflataeque cervices ab inposito nuper iugo resiliebant.' See also 27. 17: '(Thraces) a Piso perdomiti in ipsa captivitate rabiem ostendere. Quippe cum catenas morsibus temptaverent, feritatem suam ipsi puniebant.'

[106] J. G. C. Anderson, *CAH* x 780. I have, without success, attempted to trace the origin of the curious term 'scientific frontier'. It brings to mind, however, the famous words of Marshal Saxe, who wrote in the eighteenth century: 'War is a science so obscure and imperfect (that) custom and prejudice confirmed by ignorance are its sole foundation and support'.

[107] Luttwak, 107 f.   [108] lxxv 3. 2.

disingenuous and incorrect as Agricola's insistence that the conquest of Ireland would provide the empire with a half-way station between Spain and Britain.[109]

More important, there can be no doubt that the focus of Roman imperialism tended to be ethnic rather than territorial or geographic. The Romans conquered peoples, not land. This is clear from the terminology used in numerous sources. Romans talked of the 'Imperium Populi Romani', the power of the Roman people, not of the 'Imperium Romanum' in any geographical sense.[110] Latin literature invariably speaks of war with a people or its king.[111] The Romans knew client-kings, *not* client-kingdoms. The arrangement was always with individual *kings*, not with individual *states*, as is amply illustrated by the confusion of the organization in Syria during the first centuries BC and AD. Note, for example, the manner in which Augustus in his *Res Gestae* formulates his expansion of the Empire: 'I expanded all provinces of the Roman people on which nations bordered which were not subject to our empire.[112]

The common description of what we refer to as 'the empire' is 'the peoples subject to Roman rule'.[113] The empire is not thought of as a territorial entity. Within the empire there were the provinces, and these could be geographically defined. Territorial limits of the empire, however, are rarely indicated in ancient sources. When they are mentioned this is done in a vague manner, by describing the farthest extent of a region or referring to some characteristic natural feature. Augustus goes on: 'I pacified the provinces of Gaul, Spain, and Germany, bounded by the ocean from Gades to the mouth of the Elbe.'[114] Another example is the text on his triumphal arch in the Alps: '. . . all Alpine peoples from the Adriatic Sea to the Mediterranean were

---

[109] Another point to be noted is that the Roman expansion beyond the Euphrates had already begun in the reign of Marcus and Lucius.

[110] e.g. the *Panegyricus* of AD 297 for Constantius, viii (v) 3. 3: 'Partho quippe ultra Tigrim redacto . . . aucta atque augenda res publica et qui Romanae potentiae terminos virtute protulerant, imperium filio pietate debebant.'

[111] Random examples: Aurelius Victor, *de Caesaribus* 13. 3 (on Trajan's conquests): '. . . cunctae gentes, quae inter Indum et Euphratem amnes inclitos sunt, concussae bello . . .' Festus xx: (Trajan) '. . . Armeniam recepit a Parthis . . . Albanis regem dedit, Hiberos, Bosphoranios, Colchos in fidem Romanae dicionis recepit, Osrhoenorum loca et Arabum occupavit . . . Seleuciam, Ctesiphontem, Babyloniam accepit ac tenuit . . . Provincias fecit Armeniam, Mesopotamiam, Assyriam . . .' Cities are mentioned as such, and so are provinces.

[112] *Res Gestae Divi Augusti* v 26: 'Omnium prov(inciarum populi Romani), quibus finitimae fuerunt gentes quae n(on parerent imperio nos)tro, fines auxi.'

[113] e. g. Josephus, *Ant.* xviii 8. 1 (258).

[114] 'Gallias et Hispanias provicia(s et Germaniam qua inclu)dit Oceanus a Gadibus ad ostium Albis flum(inis pacavi).' Cf. v 30: 'Pannoniorum gentes . . . imperio populi Romani s(ubie)ci protulique fines Illyrici ad r(ip)am Danui.'

subjected to the empire of the Roman People. Conquered Alpine Peoples . . .'[115]

Appian, writing in the reign of Antoninus Pius, clearly expresses the Roman attitude of his times:[116]

These emperors have added to their rule (ἡγεμονία) some peoples in addition to the original ones, and they have suppressed others which attempted to break away. On the whole, prudently possessing the best parts of land and sea, they choose to preserve their empire (ἀρχή) rather than extend it indefinitely over poor and profitless barbarian peoples. In Rome I have seen embassies of some of these offering themselves as subjects, but the emperor did not accept them as they would be useless to him. To other peoples, countless in number, they, the emperors, give kings while they do not wish to govern them. On some of the subject peoples they spend more than they receive, considering it shameful to give them up even though they are profitless.

We should note that the whole passage refers exclusively to peoples and kings. In this respect Appian's language reflects common Roman usage of all periods. Another element in this passage, however, is characteristic of only a few authors and typical of an ideology encountered in the middle of the second century, namely Appian's view that profitability, not the glory and honour of empire, is the sole factor determining the status of the subject peoples—although it is considered a disgrace to give up any part of the empire. The conception of political entities in terms of rulers and peoples is not confined to Roman thought, but distinctive of ancient political thought in general. To take merely one example, the Persian trilingual inscription commemorating Shapur's victories over Gordian and Aurelian has the same terminology.[117]

Appian speaks, not of 'the boundary of the empire', but of 'the boundary of the peoples subject to the Romans'.[118] D. Schlumberger has commented on the remarkable fact that there are no stones in existence marking the boundary of the empire. This suggests that the very concept of such a boundary had no relevance in antiquity.[119] An apparent exception is a boundary-stone delimiting the border between the province of Osrhoene and the Kingdom of Abgarus (AD 195).[120] But

---

[115] Pliny, *NH* iii 20. 136: 'gentes Alpinae omnes quae a mari supero ad inferum pertinebant sub imperium p.R. sunt redactae. Gentes Alpinae devictae . . .'

[116] Appian, *Praef.* 7/25–8; on other aspects of this passage, F. Millar, *Britannia* 13 (1982), 12. Note also Appian xii 17. 119–21 on the Mithradatic wars, which contains a number of references to the territorial extent of the empire in the first century BC.

[117] Text by A. Maricq, 'Res Gestae Divi Saporis', *Syria* 35 (1958), 295–360.

[118] *Praef.* 1: ἀναγκαῖον ἡγησάμην προτάξαι τοὺς ὅρους ὅσων ἐθνῶν ἄρχουσι Ῥωμαῖοι.

[119] *Syria* 20 (1939), 71.

[120] J. Wagner in *AFRBA*, 113 f.

it is only apparently an exception, since this was, in Roman eyes, a border between two parts of the empire, a province and a client kingdom,[121] and the boundary stone mentioned is that of a province, not that of an empire.[122] Even 'provincia', of course, was originally not a territorial concept, but expressed an office. Nevertheless, while there are no stones marking the border of the empire, stones marking the boundary of a province are rare, but they do exist.[123]

On the other hand, boundary-stones between administrative units within provinces—cities, villages, and other communities—are common all over the empire. The reason for this is obvious. Unlike the imperial and provincial borders such boundaries delimited taxable property. Provincial boundaries were recognized under the republic. They delimited certain forms of action of the governor, but they were not described as the frontier of the empire. Under the principate mention is sometimes made of 'the borders of the empire', but only in a vague and abstract manner: 'It was no longer the land and river boundaries of the empire, but the winter-quarters of the legions and the ownership of territories that were in danger.'[124] Or note the advice attributed by Tacitus to Augustus, quoted again and again by modern scholars: 'to confine the empire to its (present) limits'. 'Either from fear or out of jealousy', adds the author, but these words are usually omitted by those who praise the prudence of imperial frontier policy.[125] Even legal sources are remarkably vague when they refer to the borders of the empire: 'There is also the city of Palmyra in the Province of Phoenice situated near the barbarian peoples and nations.'[126]

When concrete, specific borders are mentioned, they are always

---

[121] Rome regarded all client kingdoms as part of the empire. Cf. P. Brunt in P. Garnsey and C. R. Whittaker (eds.), *Imperialism in the Ancient World* (1978), 168–70; Wells, 248 f.; Harris, 131 ff. See also the recent study by D. C. Braund, *Rome and the Friendly King* (1984).

[122] This is also the case on a milestone of AD 205, found 48 m. from Zeugma, which records the construction of a road in Osrhoene as follows: '. . . viam ab Euphrate usque ad fines regni Sept(imii) Ab(g)ari a novo munierunt, per L. Aelium Ianuarium, proc(uratorem) Aug(usti) prov(inciae) Osrhoenam (*sic*) . . .' (*AE* 1984. 920).

[123] In addition to the example above mention may be made also of *AE* 1973. 559 and 559 bis. These were inscriptions marking the coast road in Sinai, from Pelusium to the border of Syria-Palaestina. They showed the way to the border between the provinces of Egypt and Syria-Palaestina and were not intended to mark the border itself. They date to 233 and were probably connected with the Persian war, cf. B. Isaac, *PEQ* 110 (1978), 54 f. For the Latin concept of a 'province', A. Lintott, *Greece & Rome* 28 (1981), 53–67, esp. 54.

[124] Tacitus, *Agricola* 41. 2: 'nec iam de limite imperii et ripa, sed de hiberniis legionum et possessione dubitatum.'

[125] *Ann.* i 11: 'addideratque consilium coercendi intra terminos imperii, incertum metu an per invidiam.'

[126] *Digest* L 15. 1: 'Est et Palmyrena civitas in provincia Phoenice prope barbaras gentes et nationes collocata . . .'

defined in terms of a specific province: 'The emperor is about to cross the border of Raetia into barbarian [lands] in order to destroy the enemy.'[127] Milestones on the Trajanic road in Arabia read: '(Trajan) having organized Arabia as a province opened up and paved a new road from the boundary of Syria to the Red Sea.'[128] No imperial boundary is mentioned here, and the inevitable result for modern scholarship has been a good deal of confusion and discussion about the southern boundary of the province of Arabia.

The only ancient map we possess, the Tabula Peutingeriana, is highly instructive in this respect. The imperial boundary is nowhere indicated by signs or text. In the East two captions are worth noting. One, in Persia, says: 'Areae fines Romanorum'. This is merely a reference to the dividing line between two peoples; it says nothing about sovereignty. The other reads: 'Fines exercitus Syriaticae et conmertium Barbarorum'.[129] This refers to the farthest extent of military occupation by the troops of the province of Syria. Elsewhere important geographical features are occasionally marked, but boundaries are ignored.[130]

There are well-documented cases where the Roman army established a long-term presence beyond the borders of a province. In a forthcoming paper D. Graf shows this to be the case in the north-west of the Arabian peninsula. The Hejaz was definitely outside the area of Roman provincial organization, but the presence of the Roman army in the area is epigraphically attested.[131] It was also the case in southern Egypt. When the Ptolemaic kingdom was annexed as a province by Augustus the traditional southern border was maintained at Aswan and the First Cataract.[132] But Roman military occupation of the area south of the border is well-attested.[133] From 22 BC till the second

---

[127] *ILS* 451, Acta Arv. of 11 August 213: 'per limitem Raetiae ad hostes extirpandos barbarorum [*sc.* terram *vel sim.*] introiturus est . . .'

[128] See the catalogue of milestones by P. Thomsen, *ZDPV* 40 (1917), 1 ff.: 'redacta in formam provinciae Arabia viam novam a finibus Syriae usque ad mare rubrum aperuit et stravit . . .'

[129] Cf. *Expositio Totius Mundi* 19: '. . . Post hos sunt Persae, Romanis propinquantes . . .' 22: 'Post hos nostra terra est. Sequitur enim Mesopotamia et Osdroene.' Then follows a reference to the towns of Mesopotamia, notably Nisibis and Edessa where trade between the two empires is concentrated.

[130] Equally vague about the boundary between Persia and Rome is *Expositio Totius Mundi* 21.

[131] D. Graf, 'Qurā 'Arabiyya and Provincia Arabia', forthcoming in *Géographie historique au Proche-Orient, notes et monographies techniques*, 23.

[132] Strabo xvii 1. 12 (797); Pliny, *NH* v 10. 59; xii 8. 19; Aelius Aristides, *Or.* xxxvi 48 f. Cf. J. Desanges, *CE* 44 (1969), 139–47; L. P. Kirwan, *PBA* 63 (1977), 13–31; W. Y. Adams, *JARCE* 20 (1983), 93–104.

[133] Kirwan, *PBA*, 22 n. 2; *DE*, s.v *limes*, pp. 1376/11–15; Z. Zába, *The Rock Inscriptions of Lower Nubia* (1974), nos. (Latin) 236, 239, 240, 242, all from Kalabsha (Talmis), dated *c.*144–7 and referring to the cohors II Ituraeorum.

century a Roman military garrison was established at Primis (Qasr Ibrim), more than 150 kilometres south of the border.[134] Later, in the second century, the boundary seems to have been moved southward, followed by a withdrawal again in the time of Diocletian.[135] It has been observed that 'a beginning can perhaps be made by distinguishing between administrative, ethnic and military frontiers and recognizing that they do not always coincide'.[136]

In Germany during the reign of Augustus it has been concluded that the frontier was not identical with the forward line of military posts. 'Roman control extended as far as her arm could reach; and the army was very mobile.'[137] In a well-known passage Tacitus mentions 'lands kept unoccupied and reserved for the use of the soldiers' beyond the Rhine.[138] In the second century the Romans seem to have allowed the Germanic peoples to settle close to the line of Roman forts. It has been suggested that a sort of federate relationship existed.[139] An inscription found in Slovakia, north of the Danube, records the burial of a centurion who served among the Quadi as interpreter and officer in charge of trade relations.[140] In the same area a late-Roman building has been excavated in the middle of a Germanic settlement.[141] Such remains are evidence of the exercise of low-level interference, but they are relevant all the same.

Again, Nisibis in Mesopotamia was probably a military outpost before the annexation of the region as a province by Septimius Severus, for Dio tells us that in 195 the Osrhoeni and Adiabeni 'had rebelled and laid siege to Nisibis, and had been defeated by Severus . . .'[142] Dio also refers to other garrisons in the region which Severus refused to withdraw, and yet describes it as 'enemy territory'. The campaign of

---

[134] M. E. Weinstein and E. G. Turner, *JEA* 62 (1976), 125 ff.; Adams, 95–8.

[135] The Peutinger Table and the Antonine Itinerary are cited as evidence, but are not necessarily decisive; on the other hand the testimony of Philostratus, *Life of Apollonius* vi 2, is conclusive: 'For when he arrived at the border of Ethiopia and Egypt, and the name of the place is Sycaminus . . .'

[136] Adams, 98.   [137] Wells, 248.

[138] *Ann.* xiii 54. 2: 'agrosque vacuos et militum usui sepositos'; cf. 55. 3. North of the Rhine an inscription has been found which mentions 'prata Aureliana', and there was a military brick factory, the 'tegularia Transrhenana'; cf. H. von Petrikovits in J. E. Bogaers and C. B. Rüger, *Der niedergermanische Limes* (1974), 26–8. Marcus Aurelius compelled the Quadi and Marcomanni to leave unoccupied a strip 38 stades wide on the left bank of the Danube, and the Iazyges twice as much (Dio lxxi 16).

[139] Schönberger, 170. He cites a hypothesis regarding the origin of Germanic graves around Giesen, almost immediately north of the Wetterau line. These have been thought to belong to federate *exploratores* who lived in an otherwise sparsely settled region.

[140] T. Kolnik, *Act. Arch. Ac. Sc. Hung.* 30 (1978), 61–75 (*AE* 1978. 635): 'interprex leg(ionis) XV idem (centurio) negotiator.' Second half of the first century.

[141] T. Kolnik, *Akten des 11. Int. Limeskongresses* (1977), 181–97.

[142] lxxv 1. 2; cf. D. L. Kennedy, *ZPE* 36 (1979), 255; *Antichthon* (forthcoming).

198 was apparently undertaken for similar reasons. The Parthians, says Dio, had conquered Mesopotamia in a military campaign and had almost captured Nisibis.[143] The inference is that it was a region not yet subdued and organized as a province, but under partial occupation, presumably since the Roman campaign in the sixties of the second century.

The instances so far described are all based on a combination of literary and archaeological evidence. But there is a clear epigraphic expression of the manner in which Roman officials perceived the geographical extent of their responsibilities, obligations, and powers in the record of the governorship of Moesia by Tiberius Plautius Silvanus Aelianus in the sixties of the first century.[144] It lists six different forms of activity beyond the Danube. While the river is not explicitly referred to as a boundary, the phrase 'the river bank under his protection'[145] indicates a recognition of full responsibility for the security of the region south of the Danube, and it is clear from the inscription that it was only here that tribute was levied.[146] But the river was by no means the boundary of Roman authority or military activity. Apart from actions which could be explained as intended merely to defend the province,[147] 'kings previously unknown or hostile to the Roman people were brought to the river bank under his protection to pay homage to the Roman standards'. This can only have been the result of a campaign far into enemy territory. The author of the text does not pretend this was a defensive campaign; there was no need for a defence against 'kings previously unknown'. It is a straightforward claim that new kings had been made vassals of the empire. 'To the kings of the Bastarnae and Rhoxolani their sons were returned, and (to the king of?) the Dacians his brother(s) whom he had captured or carried off from their enemies. From some of these he accepted hostages, thus securing and expanding the peace of the province.' These are the classic forms of controlling vassals. There can be no doubt about the implications of the phrase 'to expand the peace of the province'.[148] The limit of Roman involvement

---

[143] lxxv 5.

[144] *ILS* 986. For a photograph and full references, A. E. Gordon, *Illustrated Introduction to Latin Epigraphy* (1983), no. 49, p. 127 and pl. 31. For comments, Millar, *Britannia*, 8; P. Conole and R. D. Milns, *Historia* 32 (1983), 183–200. The latter interpret the campaign as an entirely defensive operation.

[145] 'ripam quam tuebatur'.

[146] To Moesia were transferred more than a hundred thousand 'Transdanuviani' *ad praestanda tributa*.

[147] '. . . motum orientem Sarmatar(um) compressit . . .'

[148] Conole and Milns, 184 and n. 78, consider translating 'prolonged the peace'. Cf. Tacitus, *Agricola*, 30. 6: 'solitudinem faciunt et pacem appellant.' More recently: 'Take up the White Man's burden, the savage wars of peace . . .'

was the Crimea.[149] The attitudes and the actions described are traditional. The whole text, apart from the references to the emperor at the
beginning and the end, could in principle have been written under the
republic. It is true that the river here appears as the boundary of the
province, but there is nothing new in this. Under the republic the
provinces had boundaries, but they were not conceived of as imperial
boundaries, delimiting the influence and sphere of action of Rome.

In the fourth century, too, military frontier districts with subject
peoples in them could be organized beyond the provincial borders.
This can be seen, for instance, from the fact that Festus uses the
terminology of his own times, when there were frontier districts under
the command of a *dux*, in referring to the establishment by Trajan of an
eastern military frontier district (*limes*) beyond the Tigris,[150] and to its
re-establishment by Diocletian.[151] This district was seen as lying
beyond the province of Mesopotamia.

Geographical Concepts and Intelligence

As regards the importance of geography in determining the boundaries
of the empire, the best explanation of the irregular alignment of the
frontier in many areas is that it simply did not matter much to the
Romans where the boundary ran.[152] As pointed out by Fergus Millar,
what we know about ancient map-making indicates that the Romans
did not have a sufficiently clear or accurate notion of topographical

---

[149] 'Scytharum quoque rege{m} a Cherronensi, quae est ultra Borustenen, opsidione sum-
moto.' In 44 or 45 another governor of Moesia, Didius Gallus, interfered with troops to place his
own candidate on the throne of the Bosporan kingdom and was awarded triumphal insignia for his
achievements: Tacitus, *Ann.* xii 15–21; *ILS* 970. In the second century the Bosporan kingdom
apparently paid tribute through the governor of Bithynia and Pontus: Lucian, *Alexander* 57, refers
to envoys from King Eupator on their way to Bithynia, to deliver the annual tribute. For the
relationship between Rome and Bosporus from Caesar onwards, M. Rostovtzeff, *JRS* 7 (1917),
27–41, esp. 39 ff. The formal status varied, but the region was subordinated to Roman military
power throughout the first and second centuries. From the mid-third century dates the famous
Dura-Europos Shield with a simplified map of the Euxine coast from Odessos to Pantikapaion,
which was then ruled by a client prince but had a Roman garrison. For the shield, F. Cumont, *Syria*
6 (1925), 1–15 and pl. I; id. *Fouilles de Doura Europos, 1922–1923* (1926), 323–37, pls. CIX f.; O. A.
W. Dilke, *Greek and Roman Maps* (1985), 120–2; and an extensive treatment by R. Rebuffat, *Syria* 63
(1986), 85–105. Epigraphic evidence indicates that there was a *statio beneficiariorum* at or near
Chersonesos on the Crimea: E. I. Solomonik, *Akademiya nauk Ykrainskoi SSR, Institut Arkheologii*
(Kiev 1964), 121–32.

[150] *Breviarium* xiv, ed. Eadie, p. 57: 'et per Traianum Armenia, Mesopotamia, Assyria et Arabia
provinciae factae sunt ac limes Orientalis supra ripas Tigridis est institutus.'

[151] Ibid.: 'Mesopotamia est restituta et supra ripas Tigridis limes est reformatus, ita ut quinque
gentium trans Tigridem constituarum dicionem adsequeramur.' Cf. xxv: '(Persae)
Mesopotamiam cum Transtigritanis regionibus reddiderunt.'

[152] J. C. Mann, *ANRW* ii 1 (1974), 508–33.

realities to allow them to conceive of the overall military situation in global strategic terms.[153] Vegetius advises that all troop movements should be planned with the assistance of good *itineraria picta*, but that refers to road descriptions, of which we have a few examples, notably the *Tabula Peutingeriana*.[154] The best-preserved specimen of Byzantine cartography is the Madaba Map. Enough has been preserved to show that it must have been a pleasure to look at such a map, but here again it is immediately obvious that we are not faced with material that military planners of our age would find at all serviceable.[155] These maps could never help in forming a strategic conception. What we know about military campaigns and geography is mostly in the form of reports delivered after the completion of the war;[156] we have little information about preparation in advance. An apparent exception is Gaius Caesar's planned Arabian expedition, but all that the sources mention is the preparation of two treatises, and even so he is described 'ardentem fama Arabiae'.[157]

We have no indication that the Roman empire systematically collected and interpreted information beyond the territory under Roman control. As observed by Debevoise, Roman intelligence was notoriously bad in the East. There is no lack of evidence to show that the Romans would embark on major military campaigns without an elementary understanding of where they were going.

When Caesar decided to invade Britain 'nobody except traders travelled there without reason and even they knew only the sea-coast and the regions opposite Gaul. Consequently, although he summoned traders from everywhere, he could not find out the size of the island, the number or strength of the peoples who lived there, their methods of warfare, customs, or the harbours fit to receive numerous large

---

[153] *Britannia* 13 (1982), 15–20, esp. 15–18.

[154] Dilke, 102 f., briefly mentions a block of sandstone from France that shows signs of chiselling possibly representing the west coast of France. He suggests that this might be the work of a military surveyor. This is a speculation and, as Dilke observes, 'if military surveyors were map-minded in this way, it is surprising that no other doodles of this sort have emerged'. A genuine example of military cartography is the shield from Dura-Europos, above, n. 149.

[155] See now Y. Tsafrir, *DOP* 40 (1986), 129–45 on sixth-century maps of the Holy Land. The Madaba Map is still unique, although mosaics with architectural representations and depictions of towns of the same period are fairly common in Jordan: N. Duval, 'Architekturdarstellungen in Jordanischen Mosaiken', in *Byzantinische Mosaiken aus Jordanien* (1986), 175–80, with numerous examples in the catalogue by M. Piccirillo, 211 ff.; M. Piccirillo, *Liber Annuus* 37 (1987), 177–239.

[156] R. Sherk, 'Roman Geographical Exploration and Military Maps', *ANRW* ii 1. 534–62.

[157] Pliny, *NJH* xii 31. 56. One scholarly treatise was dedicated to Gaius by King Juba of Mauretania, according to Pliny, *NH* vi 31. 141; another was prepared for him by Dionysius of Charax, possibly a mistake for Isidore of Charax. See *NH* xii 31. 56; xxxii 4. 10; and cf. G. W. Bowersock, *JRS* 61 (1971), 227; F. E. Romer, *TAPA* 109 (1979), 205.

ships.'[158] Caesar therefore sent an officer ahead with a ship in order to explore as much as he could. 'Volusenus observed all the regions in so far as was possible for someone who did not dare to disembark and entrust himself to the barbarians. After four days he returned to Caesar and gave an account of his observations.'[159] Caesar, then, invaded Britain on the basis of intelligence gathered within a period of four days by a man on a ship.

Caesar was lucky, and his expedition did not result in disaster like that to South Arabia undertaken by Aelius Gallus, known to us from Strabo's contemporary description.[160] This was launched because Gallus had always been told 'that they were very rich and sold aromatics and the most precious stones for silver and gold, but never expended any part of their income to foreigners'. Aelius Gallus first built a fleet for which he had no use, and then got lost in the desert with an entire army, spending six months in reaching South Arabia, an area which the Romans never could have hoped to subdue if they had had any idea how it was situated. We are told that the Roman commander was purposely and treacherously misguided by the Nabataean ally Syllaeus.[161] That, however, is a common excuse for military disaster. It is found also in the descriptions of the disastrous expeditions of Crassus and Antonius against Parthia, both of which went hopelessly wrong because huge armies were taken through unfamiliar lands without adequate preparation and organization.[162] In fact, such dependence on local guides merely reinforces the impression that the Roman army itself did not possess adequate geographical information before it embarked upon major foreign campaigns.

In Central Europe, it has been argued, it was only after the loss of Varus' army that the Romans began to appreciate the size of the population they would have to keep under control if they wanted to hold Germany east of the Rhine.[163]

Strabo cites Posidonius as stating that the width of the isthmus between the Caspian Sea and the Euxine was 1500 stades (= *c.*280

[158] *BG* iv 20.   [159] *BG* iv 21.

[160] xvi 4. 22 (780) ff. Cf. S. Jameson, *JRS* 58 (1968), 71–84 (for the chronology); H. von Wissmann, *ANRW* ii 9. 1 (1976), 308–544; M. G. Raschke, ibid. 901–3; G. W. Bowersock, *Roman Arabia* (1983), 46–8; S. E. Sidebotham, *Latomus* 45 (1986), 590–602; id., *Roman Economic Policy in the Erythra Thalassa* (1986), 120–30. The tendency of some modern scholars to describe this expedition as a 'probe' rather than an ambitious failure derives from Pliny, *NH* vi 32. 160 f., who soft-pedals the affair.

[161] xvi 4. 23 (780).

[162] For the alleged tricking of Crassus by an Arab chieftain, Plutarch, *Crassus* 21 and 22; for Antony's expedition, Strabo xi 13. 4 (524); xvi 1. 28 (748); Plutarch, *Antony* 50. 2.

[163] Wells, 7 f.

km.). In reality it is about twice as much. Strabo, however, does not believe Posidonius, 'although he was a friend of Pompeius who made an expedition against the Iberians and Albanians, across the whole length from the Caspian to the Colchian Sea (Euxine)'.[164] This is a remarkable failure, as the question discussed is not complicated geography, but merely the distance between two points in a straight line which could be measured in days marched.

It is clear that there was no systematic evaluation of the geographic lessons to be learned from the military expeditions of the Roman army under the republic. That this remained true under the principate can be concluded from the confusion regarding the target of Nero's planned Caucasian expedition. Pliny has this to say:

> We must here correct an error made by many people, also by those who were recently on campaign with Corbulo in Armenia, for they have given the name of 'Caspian Gates' to the pass in Hiberia which, as we have said, is named 'Caucasian Gates', and sketches of the region despatched from there are inscribed with the former name. Also the threats of the emperor Nero were said to be directed at the Caspian Gates, although he intended to make for those which lead through Hiberia to the Sarmatians, while the Caspian Sea is hardly accessible through the mountain chain. There are, however, other Caspian Gates near the Caspian peoples, the distinction between which can only be understood from the (accounts of) those who took part in the expedition of Alexander the Great.[165]

Tacitus says that troops 'had been sent to the Caspian Gates for the war which he planned against the Albani'.[166] The Caspian Gates referred to here are the Darial pass—but this does not lead to the Albani.[167]

Here we have two authors incapable of explaining where Nero's

---

[164] xi 1. 5 f. (491).

[165] *NH* vi 15. 40: 'Corrigendus est in hoc loco error multorum, etiam qui in Armenia res proxime cum Corbulone gessere. namque hi Caspias appellavere portas Hiberiae quas Caucasias diximus vocari, situsque depicti et inde missi hoc nomen inscriptum habent. et Neronis principis comminatio ad Caspias portas tendere dicebatur, cum peteret illas quae per Hiberniam in Sarmatas tendunt, vix ullo propter oppositos montes aditu ad Caspium mare. sunt autem aliae Caspiis gentibus iunctae, quod dinosci non potest nisi comitatu rerum Alexandri Magni.'

[166] *Hist.* i 6. 2: 'quos . . . electos praemissosque ad claustra Caspiarum et bellum quod in Albanos parabat.'

[167] It appears from *Ann.* vi 33. 2 that Tacitus means the Darial pass. Hence the suggestion that we should read 'Alanos', but that is not a satisfactory solution. E. L. Wheeler, *Flavius Arrianus: A Political Biography* (Dissertation, Duke University, 1977), 117–23, assumes that Tacitus meant to say that the soldiers were sent toward the pass and not intended to cross the Caucasus; instead, they would move onward to the Caspian and fight the Albani. That is not what the Latin suggests. For the various passes, A. R. Anderson, *TAPA* 59 (1928), 130–7; for the Caspian Gates, J. F. Standish, *Greece & Rome* 17 (1970), 17–24. Ptolemy is the only ancient author who distinguishes between three passes: the Darial pass, the Derbent pass, and a set of defiles between Media and Parthia across Mount Caspius, a range which projects from the Elbruz Mountains. The latter are the Caspian Gates proper.

expedition was actually intended to go. Pliny tries to clarify matters, but with little success. It is significant that Pliny, who was confused but diligent, found the information regarding Alexander's campaigns of equal or greater value than the material sent home by troops in his own lifetime. The 'situs depicti' that he saw were clearly not staff maps in any modern sense, but sketches prepared by officers or soldiers. Neither Strabo, nor the less critical Pliny found information brought back from military campaigns trustworthy.

Tacitus tells us the advantages of conquering Ireland: it lies, he says, between Britain and Spain and also commands the Gallic Sea.[168] Yet this misinformation came to him from Agricola, a hard and competent general who reached Scotland in a successful campaign and was himself interested in an Irish expedition.

Septimius Severus sacked Ctesiphon, but did not occupy it, (according to Dio) 'just as if the sole purpose of his campaign had been to plunder this place. He was off again, owing partly to the lack of acquaintance with the country and partly to the dearth of provisions'.[169] It may be noted that Severus' expedition was the third in less than a century to operate in this area, a region which appears on the Peutinger Table. Dio may be wrong, and Severus may have had other reasons for leaving the area of Ctesiphon. But that does not affect the significance of the statement, for, whatever the actual reasons for Severus' actions, those alleged were clearly credible in principle to Dio and his audience. What was not credible to Dio—and yet is sometimes suggested in modern literature—is the assumption that the sole purpose of expeditions like that of Severus was to plunder Babylonia.

Severus' other major campaign, that in Britain, also took place on fairly familiar ground. Agricola had been there in the reign of Domitian, and Roman rule in Britain had more recently reached as far as the Antonine wall. Dio, who was in a position to obtain virtually all information accessible to those close to the emperor, gives a description of the enemy peoples, the Caledonii and Maeatae, that has been characterized as 'a strange compound of generalities and travellers' tales . . . practically worthless'.[170] The only concrete information he gives is the measurements of the island, and these are totally wrong. A contribution of Severus' expedition to geographical knowledge is said to have been the corroboration of Agrippa's conclusion that Britain is

[168] R. M. Ogilvie and Sir Ian Richmond, *Agricola* (1967), comments on 10. 2, pp. 166 f.

[169] lxxvi 9. 3–4, Boissevain, iii 347, trans. Cary, Loeb: οὐ μέντοι οὔτε τὸν Οὐολόγαισον ἐπεδίωξεν οὔτε τὴν Κτησιφῶντα κατέσχεν, ἀλλ᾽ ὥσπερ ἐπὶ τοῦτο μόνον ἐστρατευκὼς ἵν᾽ αὐτὴν διαρπάσῃ ᾤχετο τὸ μὲν ἀγνωσίᾳ τῶν χωρίων τὸ δ᾽ ἀπορίᾳ τῶν ἐπιτηδείων.

[170] Steer, in Richmond, *Roman and Native*, 93, cited by Millar, *Cassius Dio*, 149.

an island.[171] Dio is contemptuous of those who claimed it was a continent, but he himself explains that it lies parallel to Gaul and almost all of Iberia.[172]

On another campaign in Mesopotamia, that of Julian, John Matthews observes that Ammianus in his narrative 'does not define what the campaign was intended to achieve, and he seems very uncertain what was going on when the siege of Ctesiphon was abandoned before it even began and a retreat—or was it a further advance into Persia?—was ordered'.[173] Ammianus, who participated in Julian's Persian campaign, gives a rather extensive description of Persia the material for which was 'meticulously collected from the descriptions of the nations of whom very few tell any truth at all'.[174] This then is the result of more than four centuries living in proximity to the Persian kingdom.

It must be concluded that those who look at small-scale, or even large-scale maps, for conclusions regarding the strategy of the Romans use instruments and hence concepts that for the Romans did not exist. Moreover, there is ample evidence that the Romans on campaign did not behave in accordance with such concepts. On the subject of frontiers and geography it has been shown that the Romans thought in terms not of territory, but of populations, in their decision-making. Finally, to return to the subject of Chapters III and IV, there is no evidence to show that the Romans thought primarily in terms of defence when they established a boundary. This is obvious in the East, but equally true for other regions.

A related matter is the gathering of information among the subject peoples. There is no clear indication that the Roman empire had an institutionalized state-security police apparatus. Although there is evidence of various categories of military men serving in related capacities (*frumentarii*), little is known of the degree of organization behind these activities. In Chapter II we saw that there was a symptomatic failure to identify preparations for revolt among newly subjugated peoples in the sensitive stages of annexation and consolidation. Although mutiny in the army was a recurrent problem and eventually led to the period of crisis in the third century, we have no evidence that there was, either before or after the fourth century, a

---

[171] Dio xxxix 50 (ii 493 f.); cf. lxvi 20 (iii 155 f.).

[172] Todd, 177, assumes that Severus may have had the use of Agricola's despatches giving a detailed account of his occupation of eastern Scotland and perhaps of his campaigns. He believes imperial archives may have contained maps which could be used. There is no evidence to support any of these assumptions.

[173] J. F. Mathews, *DRBE*, 550.

[174] xxiii 6. 1.

branch of the army whose function was to exercise political control over the troops. The security of the emperor was protected, if at all, by personal guards and specific units which were not integrated into the regular army.

It is not until the Byzantine period that the gathering of intelligence for both Rome and Persia by paid agents or merchants is mentioned as a matter of routine. 'It is an old custom among the Romans and the Persians that spies are paid by the state to travel secretly among the enemy in order to examine the state of affairs accurately and report on it to their rulers upon their return.'[175] A law of AD 408/9 stipulates:

Not only merchants who owe allegiance to our government, but also those who are subject to the King of the Persians, must not hold markets beyond the places agreed upon at the time of the treaty concluded with the above-mentioned nation, in order to prevent the secrets of either kingdom from being disclosed (which is improper).[176]

Merchants may not travel beyond Nisibis, Callinicum, and Artaxata. The first two were border towns of the two empires, while Artaxata was the capital of Armenia.[177]

Yet these activities seem to have been remarkably restricted, if we may judge by the Byzantine handbook of military strategy, written about 600.[178] In general, it seems, the only purpose of intelligence is to gather information about enemy strength and movements in order to prevent surprise.[179] It is indeed stressed that 'the general should know the country well, whether it is healthy and safe or unhealthy for his troops and inhospitable, and whether the necessities such as water, wood, and forage are nearby. For if these are at a distance, then their procurement is difficult and dangerous, especially in the presence of the enemy.'[180] Yet it is not indicated how the general should acquire this information. Elsewhere the author notes that, before incursions into hostile territory, 'serious efforts should be made to capture inhabitants of the country alive in order to obtain information from them about the

[175] Procopius, *Bell.* i 21. 11–13. Procopius here tells a story of a spy who went over to the Romans and returned to Persia to convey misleading information. Cf. i 15. 6: bodyguards sent to spy out the enemy forces.

[176] *Cod. Iust.* iv 63. 4, trans. S. P. Scott, *Corpus Iuris Civilis, The Civil Law* (1932). See also A. D. Lee, *DRBE*, 455–61, where it is argued that the dispatch of embassies by the Roman and Persian empires with specific messages from their rulers presupposes prior information concerning the enemy's plans.

[177] According to *Expositio Totius Mundi* 22, trade between the two empires was concentrated at Nisibis and Edessa. The source mentions only that export of metal to the enemy is forbidden.

[178] *Das Strategikon des Maurikios*, ed. G. Dennis, trans. E. Gamillscheg, Corpus Fontium Historiae Byzantinae 17 (1981); *Maurice's Strategikon, Handbook of Byzantine Military Strategy*, trans. G. Dennis (1984).

[179] *Strategikon* vii 3.   [180] vii 2. 75, trans. Dennis, p. 89.

strength and the plans of the enemy'.[181] This method of gathering information is well-known and vividly and repeatedly illustrated on Trajan's column. However, it would be useful only in the course of an actual campaign and could never be an instrument in strategic planning. In the Byzantine handbook geography and topography are hardly mentioned; there is no suggestion that such information is needed before plans can be made or that such factors might influence war aims. The importance of information on enemy movements is indeed stressed, but that is not new. Such interest has always existed among nations at war.[182]

The Functions of Frontier Lines

The next subject to be discussed is how the Romans perceived the border of the empire, whether marked by artificial or natural barriers or not. The common term for a 'defended border' of the Roman empire in modern scholarly publications is *limes*. It was when the study of army organization in the frontier areas developed in the nineteenth century that the term *limes* came to be accepted as a concept expressing a system of defence in use along the border of the empire from the first century onward.[183] It has now become the standard practice of modern historians and archaeologists to apply the term to every frontier zone where the presence of Roman soldiers is attested. Once the term *limes* is applied it follows, or so it is thought, that we are faced with a system of defence. I have discussed the meaning of *limes* elsewhere, and the conclusions are repeated here.[184]

(*a*) There are a limited number of literary sources referring to Germanic campaigns in the first century which use the term in describing the construction of military roads.

(*b*) From the late first century till the third century it is used to indicate a demarcated land border of the empire. As such it does not refer to military structures or frontier organization, nor was it used to indicate a river boundary. The term is in fact rarely encountered before the fourth century.

---

[181] ix 3; trans. Dennis, p. 97.

[182] Frontinus, *Strategemata* i 2 is concerned with finding out the enemy's plans. The previous section stresses the importance of concealing one's own plans. The means included shrewd machinations for the provision of misinformation, e.g. i 1. 6; cf. Dio xlix 19. These are, of course, important elements of what is now called military intelligence, but as described by Frontinus they do not play a role in the process of decision-making at a strategic level.

[183] Gibbon, for instance, does not use the term.

[184] *JRS* 78 (1988), 125–147.

(*c*) From the fourth century onward it is the formal term used to designate a frontier district under the command of a *dux*. It denotes an administrative concept, again unconnected with the military structures which may have existed in the area. The *limes* is always mentioned as distinct from the frontier of the empire. In no single case is a *limes* described as something made or constructed, although the term is now used very frequently in that sense. The change in meaning coincides with the reforms of Diocletian and Constantine. In the course of time it came to be used as a geographic concept (instead of an administrative one), to indicate the eastern desert. The association with specifically Roman institutions was lost.

(*d*) More important, there is in Latin no term to indicate what modern frontier studies describe as a *limes*, a defended border, and there can be no justification for calling any chain of forts in a frontier area a *limes*.

It follows that the very concept of a frontier has to be revised. The preoccupation with border-lines and military frontiers is a modern one, and it cannot be shown that the concept was particularly important in Roman military thinking. In the words of Gibbon, 'From the reign of Augustus to the time of Alexander Severus, the enemies of Rome were in her bosom'.

If the word *limes* has indeed a different meaning, unconnected with military installations or border defence, we must allow for the possibility that the military installations served different purposes at different periods and in different areas. We must also allow for the possibility that we may not always be able to explain the original function or functions of army installations. The remains of military installations are of great interest, but it is a fallacy to assume that one can easily understand why a particular site was chosen for a fort. In the first place, it is usually assumed that the military authorities selected the best possible sites for their installations, whatever their aims. Anyone with experience of armies and other bureaucracies knows that numerous factors regularly prevent the best possible decision from being taken, and this includes the selection of sites for permanent bases.

To mention merely one possibility, in the course of a war a particular site is chosen by a small army unit just because this is a convenient spot to stay for a night or two. After the fighting ends the unit remains there for some time, and is replaced by a bigger unit which proceeds to make life bearable by erecting semi-permanent buildings etc. This then becomes an important army base. Only if the site is absolutely unsuitable will it be given up for another one. The soldiers on the spot may be unaware of the true explanation for their presence on this particular spot. No archaeologist would be likely to discover the truth. He would assume that the high command in its wisdom had chosen the perfect site for the strategy of the period. Even if sites were chosen in a purely rational manner it is not usually true that abandoned military installations provide an explanation why they were there in the first place—particularly if one does not know anything about enemy forces in the area or the native population to be kept under control.

The functions of any one military site may vary in the course of time. Let us consider the following scenario: A site serves as a temporary camp during the conquest of an area. It then becomes a supply-base for troops repelling a counter-attack. Next it serves as a base for a unit of engineers working on the military infrastructure in the area. Thereafter it houses troops that patrol the surrounding countryside. A long time afterward it is taken over by one of the units that attempt to halt the onslaught of the advancing enemy and, finally, is used as regional headquarters during the withdrawal. This is a perfectly feasible sequence for any camp of an army of occupation. Can the archaeologist who excavates the site after two millennia be expected to reconstruct all this?

There is in fact some concrete support for these suggestions, for there are many known instances where the Romans established permanent forts at places where they began by pitching temporary camps.[185] This can be shown in the case of sites that served as bases of operations and winter camps during Augustus' German campaigns and became permanent bases after Tiberius' recall of Germanicus (AD 16).[186]

Natural Barriers

In Chapter III it was observed that rivers, like highways, are not barriers but means of lateral communication and transport. It may be useful to consider what Roman literature has to say of the manner in which Romans perceived the strategic effect of natural barriers on the frontier. The first general to be confronted with the problems of having a major river as a frontier line was Caesar. Caesar showed the German tribes 'that an army of the Roman people could and would cross the

[185]   As observed by Wells, 162.

[186]   Bogaers and Rüger, 9, list Nijmegen-Kops Plateau, Vetera, Asciburgium, Novaesium, Mogontiacum. Carnuntum was the terminal point of the 'amber road', and in AD 6 the Roman forces under Tiberius were to attack the Marcomannic kingdom from there (Velleius ii 109. 5). In AD 14 it became the base of the legion XV Apollinaris; cf. E. Swoboda, *Carnuntum: seine Geschichte und seine Denkmäler* (⁴1964). A possible example in the East could be Satala, which may well have served as a logistic base for Corbulo's army and could for that reason have been chosen as the site of a legionary base in the reign of Vespasian.

Rhine'.[187] Caesar did not cross by boat, but built a bridge.[188] The German tribes, of course, crossed the river on boats and rafts. 'No marshes or forests check those born for war and guerrilla fighting.'[189] As Dio tells us, the Batavians were trained to swim the Danube with their arms.[190] In fact, the Batavi had always been known for swimming.[191] During Claudius' campaign Germans swimming in full armour across the Thames gained the Romans significant victories.[192] Tacitus attributes to Boudicca the statement that the Germans 'are (only) defended by a river, not by the Ocean (like the Britons)'.[193] The point emphasized is that the river is something of a barrier, although not an important one, but if any army was hampered by the river it was that of the Romans not the Germans. But Dio notes that rivers are bridged by the Romans without any difficulty, since the soldiers constantly practise bridging, like other military manoeuvres, on the Danube, the Rhine, and the Euphrates.[194]

There is no reason to believe that the role of the rivers changed in the course of the centuries. Particularly relevant is a passage in the anonymous *De rebus bellicis*:

First of all it must be recognized that frenzied native tribes, yelping everywhere around, hem the Roman empire in, and that treacherous barbarians, protected by natural defences, menace every stretch of our frontiers. For these peoples to whom I refer are for the most part either hidden by forests or lifted beyond our reach by mountains or kept from us by the snows; some, nomadic, are protected by deserts and the blazing sun. There are those who, defended by marshes and rivers, cannot even be located easily, and yet they tear peace and quiet to shreds by their unforeseen attacks. Tribes of this kind, therefore, who are protected either by natural defences such as these or by the walls of towns and towers, must be attacked with a variety of novel armed devices.[195]

Two points of great significance in this text, written perhaps about 368/9, must be noted.[196] First, these are genuine ancient comments on the value of natural obstacles as the frontier, made by a man with a

---

[187] *BG* iv 16. 1.   [188] *BG* iv 17 f.
[189] *BG* vi 35. 7.   [190] lxix 9. 6 (iii 230).
[191] Tacitus, *Ann.* ii 8; *Hist.* ii 17.
[192] Dio lx 20 (ii 681 f.). Regular troops also managed to cross the river (Medway?) somehow, without building a bridge. On the Thames troops got across by a bridge that was apparently already there.
[193] *Agricola* 15. 3: 'et flumine, non Oceano defendi.'
[194] lxxi 3. This is followed by a description of the technique.
[195] *De Rebus Bellicis* (BAR International Series 63, 1979), Part 2, the text ed. and trans. by Robert Ireland, vi, p. 28.
[196] As concluded by Alan Cameron, ibid., Part 1: Aspects of *De Rebus Bellicis*, 1–10.

professional intrest in military affairs. Far from being barriers that help
in repelling barbarian invaders they are seen as *obstacles* preventing
adequate action. This, from the Roman point of view, is the same
approach as that attributed to Boudicca by Tacitus. Second, for the
anonymous author the only strategy he can conceive of is preventive or
retaliatory attack across the frontier. This is clear also from the
equipment he designed, notably the transportable bridge.[197] An example of these methods in practice is the construction by Constantine of a
bridge across the Rhine at Cologne to facilitate the movement of troops
into enemy territory, while armed ships were present everywhere on the
river and soldiers were stationed ready for offensive action all along the
banks.[198] Permanent forts such as Köln-Deutz were established as
bridgeheads on sites across the river, and similar forts are found
elsewhere in the late Roman period.[199] Recently it has been argued that
in the Danube provinces composite detachments were established in
transdanuvian forts opposite the major forts to form a permanent
bridgehead for the better execution of an offensive military policy.[200]
Local defence in the frontier area should, according to the recom-
mendation of the *De rebus bellicis*, be the responsibility of local landowners, who were to construct a chain of forts and organize watches
and country patrols.[201]

The same attitude toward natural barriers can be found again and
again in the Latin Panegyrics. It is expressed clearly by Pliny: no
barbarian king will be defended against Trajan's anger 'by the sea in
between, by immense rivers or steep mountains'.[202] Florus, writing in

---

[197] Ibid., Preface, 14: 'Again, where difficult river-crossings are concerned, a design is proposed
for a new type of bridge which is not at all heavy to carry: a very few men, or about fifty pack-
animals, will be able to transport this bridge, which is essential for use across rivers or marshy
territory.' It is described in ch. xvi.

[198] In the words of the *Panegyricus* vi (vii) 13. 1: 'Insuper etiam Agrippinensi ponte faciundo
reliquiis adflictae gentis insultas, ne umquam metus ponat, semper horreat semper supplices
manus tendat, cum tamen hoc tu magis ad gloriam imperii tui et ornatum limitis facias quam ad
facultatem, quotiens velis, in hosticum transeundi, quippe cum totus armatis navibus Rhenus
instructus sit et ripis omnibus usque ad Oceanum dispositus miles immineat.'

[199] Schönberger, 183, with fig. 23: Köln-Deutz (for which see fig. 21), Engers, and Rheinbrohl
(perhaps), north of Remagen. South of Remagen, where troops had been withdrawn to the Rhine,
there are several forts on the right bank in this period: Wiesbaden, Mannheim-Neckarau, with a
landing place for ships, Breisach and Wyhlen across from Basle. Ammianus mentions forts further
inland in Germany: xvii 1. 11; xviii 2. 1 and 5.

[200] P. Brennan, *Chiron* 10 (1980), 553–67.

[201] *De rebus bellicis* xx: 'limitum . . . quorum tutelae assidua melius castella prospicient, ita ut
millenis interiecta passibus stabili muro et firmissimis turribus erigantur.' This has often been
seen as a reference to Hadrian's wall. However, as pointed out by J. S. Johnson, ibid., Part 1, p. 69,
'there is no mention of a wall as a continuous barrier to link these milecastles, rather the frontier is
to be understood as something almost separate from this system of *castella*.' The meaning of *limites*
here is 'frontier districts' in accordance with the normal usage of the period.

[202] Pliny, *Pan.* 16. 5; see also 12. 3: the frozen Danube fails to protect the enemy against Trajan's
resolute action.

the second century, says of the Dacians that they used to cross the Danube when it was frozen and ravage the neighbouring districts.[203] In other words, the river, at least in winter time, did not help in keeping them out. Yet they themselves were protected by the mountains 'which made them most difficult to approach'. On the occasion described by Florus the Roman army crossed the river and denied the Dacians access to it.[204] The same attitude recurs for instance in the following passage (written AD 310):

We are not now defended by the waters of the Rhine, but by the terror of your name. Nature does not close off any land with such an insurmountable wall that courage cannot cross it . . . Only that rampart cannot be stormed which is built with a reputation of valour.

The Franks no longer dare to live near the Rhine. 'The forts established at fixed intervals adorn rather than protect the *limes*.'[205]

In the sixth century Procopius observed that the Persians could cross every river without the slightest difficulty because on campaign they always carried bridging equipment with them which allowed them to cross any river quickly wherever they wanted.[206] So 'Belisarius was well aware that even a hundred thousand men would not be able to prevent Khusro from crossing (the Euphrates)'.[207]

This is not of course to deny that a river can play an important role in a military campaign, or that it will have been used as an obstacle by the Roman army.[208]

Artificial Barriers

Where the Romans built artificial obstacles, as in Britain, Upper Germany, and Raetia, it is important to keep in mind that we have no reliable information on the function of these obstacles. One can only speculate, and without adequate information such speculations are likely to be wrong. An example from another period may serve to illustrate this point. In 1661 the directors of the Dutch East India Company instructed Jan van Riebeeck—

that any idea of enlarging the colony beyond the limits of the Cape peninsula should be abandoned, and van Riebeeck had sought to accomplish this object by planting a great thorn hedge. The hedge had the advantage of being cheap;

---

[203] *Epitome* ii 28.
[204] Loc. cit.: 'Sic tum Dacia non victa, sed summota atque dilata est'; cf. *Res Gestae* 5. 30. Strabo, vii 3. 13 (305), considered them almost part of the empire.
[205] *Pan.* vi (vii) 11.
[206] *Hist.* ii 21. 21 f.
[207] ii 21. 18.
[208] See e.g. Ammianus xviii 7. 6; also Procopius, *Hist.* ii 30. 23–7 (on the lower Phasis, a deep and broad river with a very strong current).

it had the liability of being ineffectual. Neither thorn hedges nor other 'judicious measures' deterred the wanderings of the cattle Boer, and where he went governmental jurisdiction soon followed.[209]

It is conceivable that an archaeologist of the Roman empire, when discovering a similar structure, if one existed, would explain it as a line of defence for protection against barbarian attack.[210]

To return to Roman antiquity, a number of artificial barriers may be mentioned in areas that are not the subject of this book: first, Hadrian's Wall. There is an auxiliary fort at least every 7 kilometres. Small forts control gates every mile, with interval towers in between. Even so, it is not now thought that the wall ever served as a fighting platform. It has been suggested that it was built not to withstand large-scale attack but as a means of controlling traffic.[211] A similar hypothesis has been advanced for the Hadrianic *fossatum Africae* in Numidia.[212] It has been shown that there is no evidence of serious nomad pressure in Numidia before the second half of the third century. For a number of reasons the *fossatum* appears to have been of little military value.[213] This has led to the suggestion that, like the road system in Numidia, it was designed to control and direct the flow of traffic into and out of the occupied areas.

Next: the so-called 'Obergermanischer Limes' between the Main and Lorch in south-west Germany. It is a well-known structure, and reconstructions are often depicted.[214] Keeping in mind that Roman territory lies to the west and unoccupied land to the east, we see from west to east: a series of free-standing watchtowers surrounded by ditches; a road; a rampart; a deep continuous ditch; a palisade. As a consequence the view from the tower to the foreground eastward is blocked by the rampart and the palisade. That would be awkward if the soldiers on the tower were expected ever to be shot at from behind the

---

[209] John S. Galbraith, *Reluctant Empire, British Policy on the South African Frontier 1834–1854* (1963), 3.

[210] Similarly a future archaeologist faced with the Berlin Wall, but without historical sources, might be driven to regard it as something meant to defend West Berlin.

[211] D. J. Breeze and B. Dobson, *Hadrian's Wall* (1976). The purpose of the wall was first seen in this light by R. G. Collingwood, *The Vasculum* 8 (1921), 4–9. See now the survey of *limites* in John Wacher (ed.), *The Roman World* (1987). Here Breeze, i 208, suggests that the main purpose of the wall was to mark the southern limit of the military zone: 'it was the Roman equivalent of barbed wire.' On the other hand, Charles Daniels, in his survey of the military organization in Africa, i 226 f., argues that the Roman installations in the Eastern Desert constituted a *limes*.

[212] E. W. B. Fentress, *Numidia and the Roman Army* (1979), 66, 98 ff. See P. Trousset for comparable conclusions regarding southern Tunisia, in W. Hanson and L. Keppie (eds.), *Roman Frontier Studies, 1979* (1980), 931–42.

[213] As observed by van Berchem, *L'Armée de Dioclétien et la réforme Constantinienne* (1952), 42–9.

[214] See e.g. Schönberger, 144–97; D. Baatz, *Der römische Limes: archäologische Ausflüge zwischen Rhein und Donau* (1974), 39 f.; W. Beck and D. Planck, *Der Limes in Südwestdeutschland* (1980), 34.

palisade. The structures are often found on a slope falling away to the west—or to the south, in the case of those east of Lorch. That would have precluded the Romans from getting a proper view into 'enemy territory'. It is also worth noting that these towers have no means of defence whatever, not even the modest palisade depicted on Trajan's column. They are usually restored as having side windows; but those depicted on Trajan's column have no such windows and could be used for look-out purposes or signalling only by getting out on the balcony.[215] It may therefore be suggested that the whole structure was not intended to serve any purpose during hostilities of whatever scale.[216] It could only prevent infiltration in a situation where nobody dared to attack Roman troops, even if they consisted merely of four men on a tower.[217] Moreover, archaeological remains of settlement are rare beyond the barrier. The regions did not invite settlement.[218]

Significant differences between various kinds of artificial barriers have to be taken into account before any explanation of their purpose can be considered satisfactory. Just to mention one example: both walls in Britain are provided with a system of gateways which is an integral part of the structure. Although these are placed at rigidly fixed intervals that sometimes have no relevance to routes across the line Roman roads do in fact continue north of the walls, and military bases are found beyond them. In Germany occasional gateways have been found, presumably where they were actually needed, but the German barriers were not constructed so as to allow regular traffic across the line at many points. The main roads run along the rivers Rhine and Danube or parallel to the barrier and clearly afforded communication within the interior. There is no evidence that Roman roads leading to the forts on the line continued into Germany beyond the barrier.[219]

In chapters III and IV structures in the eastern provinces were discussed that were not even barriers, but roads with road-stations and forts.[220] It has been one of the aims of this book to show that we cannot

[215] As observed by Sir Ian Richmond, *Trajan's Army on Trajan's Column* (²1982), 38.

[216] For a different view, Baatz, 45, with a 'taktisches Schema zur Abwehr eines kleineren germanischen Überfalls am Limes'.

[217] Cf. Mann *ANRW*, 520: 'The fact that the palisade in upper Germany was re-inforced with a bank and ditch, while that in Raetia was replaced by a narrow stone wall . . . has of course no importance for the question of strategy. These changes seem to have little more than antiquarian interest.'

[218] Schönberger, 170.

[219] For bibliography, R. Chevallier, *Roman Roads* (1976), 247 f.

[220] It is usually agreed that there were no artificial barriers in the eastern provinces. See, however, I. Carnana, *Iraq* 48 (1986), 131 f., pl. xx, discussing an aerial photograph on which a line appears that looks like a wall. This has now been unmasked as a natural outcrop of rock: S. Gregory, *DRBE*, 325–8.

begin to understand Roman organization in the East unless the character of these lines as roads is clearly understood. Moreover, any theory regarding Roman strategy will have to take into account that the Romans did not often make innovations in their selection of routes in this area: many of the major roads existed long before they arrived and continue to exist today. There are of course exceptions where Roman technology and manpower allowed the construction of a road through densely wooded regions or swamps.[221] Another exception is the road through Trachonitis, which required large-scale security measures. Again, the preference for specific alignments may vary: in the early Islamic period roads through ravines came to be used which had been avoided by the Roman army whenever possible. The underlying fact, however, is that the Roman army was organized to secure and manage its own communications rather than to interdict movement to others.

Conclusions

It has been argued in this chapter that there was no Grand Strategy underlying Roman frontier policy. The paradox implicit in the notion of a Grand Strategy is that no Roman source formulates any clear-cut *aims* that this strategy was supposed to achieve. Even so it might be conceivable that there was a consistent strategy towards an aim that was tacitly accepted by the rulers of Rome. In this chapter, however, we have seen that the constituent elements of Roman frontier policy were not of a kind to produce a Grand—or even merely consistent— Strategy. The mechanism of decision-making was influenced primarily by the interests of the emperor in safeguarding his position and enhancing his glory. Preserving the peace and prosperity of the periphery contributed relatively little to either of these interests, in contrast to an even mildly successful war of expansion. And here it must be emphasized that any conflict which started as a genuine war of defence could be, and often was, turned into a war of conquest.

Modern students tend to overemphasize defence as a factor guiding Roman policy. Roman expansion may have been far less systematic than is often claimed. It was an aim in itself and therefore opportunistic. Rome expanded where it could, not where it should. The motive for a particular campaign was rarely the desire to reach a defensible boundary.[222] The choice of military frontier lines was hardly ever

---

[221] For a road through nearly impassable oak-forest and swamps, the Antipatris–Caesarea road, S. Dar and S. Applebaum, *PEQ* 105 (1973), 91–9, esp. 95, 97.

[222] *JRS* 78 (1988), 125–47. The inscription of Tiberius Plautius Silvanus cited above (p. 400)

dictated by the desire to establish rational systems of defence. If they were chosen rationally at all, they were meant to afford good communications and logistics. But often they were simply the frozen forward lines of advance that could be held following military campaigns.

The concept of an imperial frontier had little meaning for the Romans. Ancient imperialism saw control over peoples and towns as the essence of sovereignty, a point best illustrated by the continuing attachment to the *pomerium*, the boundary of the city, as the boundary of Rome, while the empire expanded. Territory was important only as a source of income. This was partly the result of an attitude of mind: in antiquity territory was not a factor constituting the essence of the state, as it is in our times. Another factor was a pragmatic attitude which allowed a great variety of systems of control to co-exist, involving more, or less, interference. Contrary to appearances, this phenomenon did not end in the first century, but lasted throughout the period under consideration in this book. Furthermore, Roman military policy was dictated by events in the field as a matter of necessity, for the Roman army did not have the geographical knowledge to permit a process of military decision-making at a higher level.

Considerable attention has been paid in this and other chapters to the difficulties of interpreting the physical remains of Roman army installations. Since it is clear that the Roman army did not possess good maps when organizing their military frontier and, for instance, laying out linear barriers, it follows that a proper understanding of such structures will not easily be gained from looking at the sort of modern maps that did not exist in antiquity. There are not many relevant statements in ancient literature. But it is noteworthy that natural barriers are repeatedly represented, not as a means of defence, but as an impediment to effective Roman action across the border. Artificial barriers are mentioned even less in the ancient literature and, where they exist, there is no reason to believe that they played a role in warfare. They will have controlled movements across the border in peacetime. If they are to be understood at all, this can only be achieved through insight into the relationship between the Roman authorities and the local population and into the Roman aims in the area.

On the many occasions when the Roman frontier came under serious pressure from outside there is no indication whatever that physical structures played a significant role in protecting the empire. An

deals with six different items of frontier policy without mentioning any *limes*. As already indicated, it refers to the *ripa* of the Danube as the boundary of full responsibility. But the river was by no means a military border.

apparent exception was the fortified cities in Mesopotamia, from the third century to the seventh (Chapter V); it is only an apparent exception, because cities as such were the focus of the struggle in this region. The history of these cities in the Byzantine period is also an excellent example of another basic fact, namely that the population in the frontier zone was not so much an object of care to the authorities as an instrument of empire.

A proper understanding of the organization of the Roman army will have to take into account the realities of an army in peacetime. These include numerous tasks, including suppression of local unrest, police-duties, periodical action beyond the provincial boundary in order to keep 'the barbarians' quiet, the maintenance of logistics and food-supplies, taxing the civilian population, and preparing for the next war. The latter, especially if it was fought in the East, was far more often offensive in nature than modern historians tend to admit.

EPILOGUE

A DIVERSITY of themes has been discussed in this book, concerning a large area and an extended period. It remains now to be seen whether, after all, common ground has been reached. Many of the conclusions, indeed, are negative and may leave nagging questions. But the elimination of misconceptions at any rate enhances clarity and may form a basis for future better understanding.

The book attempts to trace the limits of Roman physical involvement in the eastern frontier provinces, from their acquisition at the end of the republican age till the Islamic conquest. Four questions repeatedly asked throughout the book are: what were the aims of the Romans, what were their means to realize them, what problems did they face, and what were the results of their involvement? We have now reached the point where we must sum up to what extent answers could be given to these questions.

'Strategy' is the term applied nowadays when political and military planning as well as action at the highest level are discussed. But for a reliable reconstruction of past strategy it is necessary to be quite certain of the aims of policy. In the case of imperial Rome, it has been seen, anachronistic value judgements are often imposed. Those who think there was a Grand Strategy automatically assume that its aim would have been the protection of the provinces against foreign attack. In Chapter IX it has been argued that there was no Grand Strategy: Roman decision-making proceeded at a different conceptual level. This should be understood before any attempt can be made to describe it in a systematic manner. The moral qualities attributed by the Romans to good leaders were different from those demanded today. The interests and ambition of the emperors were very often served better by expensive conquests than by economic defence. The concepts of state, territory, and borders were different. The limitations of ancient geography and cartography resulted in views of the interrelationship between political power and military action unlike those held in our times. Modern logic cannot adequately explain the choice of ancient frontier lines.

Even if there had been a Grand Strategy, we have argued, it would have been a different one, for in antiquity defence was far less a preoccupation than conquest. As we saw in Chapter I, this can be observed most clearly in the East. The thought of expansion eastward, to follow in the footsteps of Alexander, was an obsession with one ruler after another, ever since Pompey had annexed large parts of the former Seleucid kingdom. But the military occupation of the desert and defence of the settled lands against nomad attack were of marginal interest. Policing the provinces was indeed one of the tasks of the army, but only in so far as necessary to maintain political and financial control.

The military means by which the latter was achieved were described in Chapter III. Army units were based in the interior, particularly in the cities. Since Roman interest in the desert was minimal, the military presence there developed at a correspondingly slow pace. The army served the Roman authorities as an instrument of control. It was not a police apparatus for the benefit of the population, and the cities themselves were therefore made responsible for policing roads and towns. The latter also levied taxes and transferred them to the provincial authorities.

Urbanization has rightly been considered a key element in maintaining Roman political and financial control in the provinces, and it has usually been supposed that this must have led to an active involvement in the physical development of urban life in the provinces. We have seen in Chapter VIII that this is not the case. While there was a standing policy of granting city status to communities that qualified, Roman initiative in the realm of construction and urban development was an exception rather than the rule. Urban development was the result of particular sets of circumstances that enabled communities to take initiatives at a local level, rather than an expression of the imperial will. But this did not in practice diminish the impact of Roman rule, since the empire created the circumstances in which cities could develop.

One particular type of city has often been credited with far-ranging achievements in the political and military control of the provinces, namely the Roman veteran colonies, discussed in Chapter VII. It should now be obvious that such settlements could never perform tasks properly undertaken by regular army units, nor did they ever attempt to perform them, for they were just as vulnerable as any other urban community. They did, however, play a long-lasting and remarkable role in regional, social, and economic control. Whether this had been intended by the founders or not is another matter. The descendants of veterans can be traced as representatives of the provincial upper class for centuries after the original foundation.

What problems did the Romans face in achieving their aims? The major challenge in the region was not Parthian/Persian expansionist imperialism. It was the fact that Rome never succeeded in subduing this rival empire. That was the ambition of many rulers, but Persia had resources which prevented its absorption by a power based beyond the Syrian desert. Distance and problems of logistics made imperial campaigns in such an environment expensive and hard to support. The Roman expeditions to southern Mesopotamia therefore tended to follow a fixed pattern. The region of Ctesiphon was reached, there was much slaughter, and a good deal of looting and pillaging, but the army would withdraw again to Roman territory, and essentially the status quo was maintained. It is hard to say why the Romans themselves thought this was a sensible form of campaigning. They perhaps reasoned along the same lines as those who in recent history advocated strategic bombing.

Another theme discussed (in Chapter II) is the activities of the army after the subjugation of an area. In newly conquered areas the process of consolidation required a far greater effort than is sometimes realized. After peoples were subdued Roman control was neither sure nor stable. Even where there is no reliable evidence it may be assumed that for years after the initial conquest the Roman army had to remain active in many ways. Yet it is remarkable how often the Romans failed to anticipate rebellions at this stage. While there is not much reliable information it is likely that the disposition of the Roman army in newly conquered territory reflected the need to maintain internal control.

ʻ This is particularly clear in the case of Judaea, which was exceptional in its long-term ideological rejection of Roman rule, described in a unique source, the work of Flavius Josephus. In the second century the Bar Kokhba war took place. It is known to have been fierce, although our information is entirely fragmentary. But we have been concerned in the present work not so much with the major wars as with the intermittent unrest when there was no open rebellion. On the period before the First Revolt we are well informed by Josephus. Thereafter Talmudic sources offer a remarkable impression of endemic political banditry. They also illustrate the fact that the sages never recognized Roman rule as legitimate. Later local sources again reveal that banditry was a fact of life, both in Palestine and in the various parts of Syria. However, there are no indications that the Roman army was very active in suppressing it, as long as it did not interfere unduly with the essentials of Roman control or the security of the upper classes. In Judaea it is clear that the resistance to Roman rule was countered by a widespread army presence all over the province. The primary function of the army there was to assert Roman control over the provincial population.

In some other regions a similar combination is encountered. One of the themes of this book is that it may be useful to consider the possibility that the Roman army elsewhere also was involved in the maintenance of internal security in cases where we have either information on internal troubles or evidence of widespread army presence in the interior of the province. This is not to deny that large sections of the empire accepted Roman rule with comparative ease.

The nomads of the desert hardly threatened the stability of life in the settled parts of the provinces. As noted in Chapter III, the Roman army did not take up fixed positions in the desert before the end of the second century (in north-eastern Jordan). In the Syrian desert Palmyra was dependable until its destruction in a blaze of glory, and this made it unnecessary for Rome to keep its own forces permanently on the Middle Euphrates. The Palmyrenes took care of the caravan trade and trade posts and did well for themselves. In the fourth and sixth centuries nomads attract attention in our sources, but primarily as allies of the two empires (Chapter V). Occasionally they were integrated in the regular armies or used as an internal police force in the provinces, but usually they were employed in the kind of warfare they were good at: swift raids resulting in economic damage and thus a weakened political position of the adversary. Throughout the Byzantine period some nomad groups enjoyed a formal status as subsidized allies under the command of a chief (*phylarch*). Their patterns of transhumance took them in and out of provincial territory, and they were responsible for keeping the edge of the settled lands reasonably quiet. Indications are that this was a successful policy. We know the names of a number of prominent leaders and gain an impression of the shifting power play which brought some tribal groups to prominence while others declined. The most notable feature of the Byzantine period, however, is the relative importance of these peoples as compared with the earlier period. Nomads, in short, had a role in the struggle between the two empires, but there is hardly any evidence that they were an important factor in their own right. When Rome and Persia were at peace the nomads did not feature significantly in Roman military policy.

In Chapter IV it was shown that the late third and early fourth centuries saw an unprecedented number of army units moved forward into the desert areas of Syria, Arabia, and Palestine. There is insufficient information on the reasons for this policy. We do not know what problems these forces were meant to solve. Various possibilities have been considered. It may have sprung from an acceptance of responsibility for the security of trade routes rather than the need to defend the provinces. Many of the units appear to have been withdrawn later in the fourth and fifth centuries, and there is no evidence that this resulted in widespread havoc. Like the Roman rulers, the Byzantine empire maintained financial, political, and military relations with the peoples living beyond the area of permanent military presence. Money and goods changed hands, titles were granted, and this system worked well, to judge from the prosperity of the northern Negev in the Byzantine period.

The scale of intervention brings us to the next point examined: the nature and function of the Roman installations in the frontier provinces. Since we are insufficiently clear about the problems the Romans faced there it is hard to define their aims and degree of success. Once it is accepted that the Roman army was never preoccupied with the defence of territory to the extent taken for granted by many modern historians, it is possible to think of other functions for the Roman remains in parts of the frontier provinces. It has been seen that it is a fallacy to interpret every square structure in the desert as part of a system of border defence, just as it is an error to think we can easily determine the original purpose of any military installation known exclusively by its plan. A number of edifices can be shown, and others can therefore be assumed, to have had different functions. These appear to have served as local administrative centres or road-stations. For other structures the same may be assumed. Many may tentatively be interpreted as centres of local authority, road-stations, or bases for patrols or campaigns. The organization in Mesopotamia from the fourth century onward appears to have been exceptional (Chapter V). The close proximity of the two rival empires in an area without natural barriers but with a relatively homogeneous population, together with the destructive employment of nomad raiders by both powers, induced the Byzantine authorities to organize a system of watch posts and frontier control. Paradoxically we know of this system mainly through literary sources. Archaeological exploration has not yet produced anything like an overall impression of the organization.

In Chapter V it was argued that the wars of the Byzantine period were as profitless as those of the early empire. In the region south of the Caucasus there was still an effort to change the balance of power—with little effect. Elsewhere they resulted in much looting and robbery, but little permanent change before the end of the sixth century. Yet there

was a difference in ideology in the politics and wars of this period. After
the fourth century the Byzantine rulers no longer dreamed of destroying the rival empire. The wars which were fought still aimed at
determining which was the stronger power, but the immediate causes
were different: religion played a role, but more important was the close
proximity of the two rival empires in Mesopotamia, where there was no
geographic or ethnic division to keep the two powers apart. This
resulted in local struggles for power and in a conflict about responsibilities for protecting the region against invasion from the North. The
matter of subsidies to Persia for guarding the Darial pass over the
Caucasus became a key issue. Yet controlling the pass, important as it
was, was an unproductive activity. It was merely a necessary means of
preventing disastrous invasions in a manner unknown in the early
empire.

In Mesopotamia the brunt of the wars was born by the citizens of the
fortified cities. In a sense this situation was the extreme outcome of the
earlier policy of making the cities responsible for security in their
districts. In Mesopotamia the wars were costly, but again unproductive in strategic terms. Neither power succeeded in achieving lasting
successes. The policy of the Byzantine rulers is perhaps best sum-
marized by stating that there was no longer any expectation of
significant territorial gains, while there was no willingness either to
withdraw or to expend what was required to maintain stability.

After considering the Romans' aims and methods and the problems
they faced we attempted to describe the results of imperial policy in the
eastern provinces. As the present book is not concerned with cultural,
social, or administrative history, many aspects of life in antiquity where
Roman rule is likely to have had its greatest impact are not considered.
Yet the general results of imperial policy in the eastern provinces
cannot be overlooked. In the first century BC Rome conquered a region
with many states, a variety of political systems, and as many different
loyalties. For seven centuries the area between the Cilician gates in the
west and the Euphrates in the east was an integral part of the Roman
empire. Apart from the Jews, the peoples of the region came to identify
themselves with the institutions of the Roman state. This was true to
such an extent that even the rulers of Palmyra in the desert, when they
made their attempt to set up a separate empire, chose to be honoured
with Latin milestone-inscriptions, proclaiming Vaballathus as
emperor with the usual Roman titles. Large parts of the eastern
provinces were transformed into territories of cities administered
according to a uniform pattern. Where there were no cities one often

encounters villages with city-type institutions. In the Byzantine period many areas were more densely settled than in any other pre-modern age. All this was the result of Roman rule.

However, the primary concern here is the direct, material impact of Roman rule, notably the military aspects. It may be concluded, first of all, that Roman rulers were incorrigible in their ambitions beyond the Euphrates. From Crassus to Julian pointless and expensive campaigns were undertaken out of sheer greed and ambition. Thereafter wars were fought without a clearly defined aim. Conquests were made that were too expensive to maintain and yet were not often given up. Apart from an interval of relative quiet in the fifth century, exhausting campaigns were undertaken without regard for the costs to the empire in money, food, and manpower. It is impossible to make any reliable calculations as to the expenditure on these campaigns, but our discussion of taxation and the Roman army has at least given an impression of the damage done. For the provincials the inevitable consequence of every imperial campaign was the ordeal of providing for the troops on the march. This had to be endured over and above the ordinary burdens caused by the presence of the permanent garrison in the provinces, particularly the troops quartered in cities. Another aspect of these expeditions was that they often provided an occasion for usurpation and civil unrest: emperors were murdered on campaign, generals were proclaimed emperor. The rise and fall of Odenathus and Zenobia of Palmyra had its inception in the former's successes against Persia.

Finally, then, how are we to characterize Roman frontier policy? As argued in Chapter IX, wars were undertaken for the glory of the commander and because various groups profited, even from relatively unsuccessful campaigns. Decisions were taken by ad-hoc groups: the emperor and his entourage. There was no professional officer class which could persuade or dissuade the emperor to go to war for 'professional' military or economic reasons. Again, it is clear that annexation of newly conquered areas was profitable. There was no Grand Strategy, conscious or unconscious, guiding the rulers in their decision to annex or not.

Far less thought was given to the defence of the frontier provinces against foreign attack. The natural response of the Roman army was always counter-attack, while the fate of civilians was at all times of marginal interest. Even if it had been of interest it is not at all clear whether much could ever have been done to protect the civilians in a war zone by means of a policy of defence. The course of the wars in Mesopotamia from the fourth to the seventh century appears to prove that the Byzantine empire was incapable of maintaining such a policy.

It was characteristic of the Roman frontier organization that the limits of military activity were not often marked by a fixed boundary. Even the river boundaries were to a large extent lines of communication rather than defence. In this respect the artificial barriers erected in some parts of the empire have had a misleading effect. Their importance has been exaggerated because of their visibility. Their layout was the result of convenience, not of sophisticated planning. The Roman army was a pre-modern army, and this had important consequences for the conceptual level at which it operated. Roman provinces had boundaries: these marked the extent of judicial and financial responsibility of the provincal authorities. The Roman army, however, acted where it thought fit, or found it could do so without undue losses. And this is true for the later empire as it is for the principate. The concept of a military border, whether defensible or not, was irrelevant to the Romans. (As noted above, an exception in this respect, the border in Mesopotamia during the later empire, is archaeologically little known). Few indications are found that territory played a role in military planning. Roman conceptions of power and military activity focused on peoples and towns rather than geography.

There is scope for revision of our views of the aim of Roman frontier policy, the means of carrying it out, and the influence thereof on the life of the population. Ever since Gibbon historians have been attempting to explain the decline and fall of the Roman empire. The present work does not pretend to shed any new light on that large topic. It may, however, be worth considering that we need to know more of the empire as it functioned before we can tell why it ceased to do so.

APPENDIX I
ROMAN ARMY SITES IN JUDAEA

Jerusalem

The garrison of Jerusalem before the First Revolt is discussed above, Chapter VI. In 70 the headquarters of the legion X Fretensis were established in Jerusalem to guard the former centre of the revolt. This is stated explicitly by Josephus on three occasions;[1] it follows from the text of a diploma of AD 93;[2] and it is also clear from inscriptions found in the town.[3] In a recent paper it has been stated that, in the areas excavated, no remains of a military base of the second century have been found.[4] This conclusion may have to be accepted. But it does not prove that there was not a base somewhere in the town, possibly at the Temple Mount or in the northern part of the city, where no excavations have been carried out. At Palmyra and Luxor the Roman army established military headquarters in a former sanctuary. The ancient literature of all periods insists on the fact that the Roman army never spent a single night without laying out a fortified camp.[5] As late as about 600 the Byzantine handbook of military strategy still observes that a fortified camp always must be set up, even while marching through friendly territory.[6] A remark by Tacitus is also relevant: Castra Vetera was never expected to come under attack,[7] and yet it did have walls, unlike the colony Camulodunum when attacked by Boudicca's rebels.[8] It is now clear that III Cyrenaica occupied a well-defined base of conventional shape in the northern part of Bostra, which may show that legions in cities were organized like those in the countryside elsewhere (see Chapter III, p. 123 f.). Similarly at Dura-Europos the military section of the town, including the *principia*, amphitheatre, baths, commander's house, and the palace of the *dux ripae*, was clearly defined by a wall separating the two parts of the town.[9] The same has been seen in Palmyra with its

---

[1] *BJ* vii 1. 1 (1); 2 (5); 1. 3 (17). See also *Vita* 76. 422.

[2] *ILS* 9059: 'qui militaverunt Hierosolymnis in legione X Fretense.'

[3] e.g. *AE* 1978. 825; *CIL* iii 12080 a; 13587 (vexillation of III Cyr., AD 116/17).

[4] H. Geva, *IEJ* 34 (1984), 239–54, with a survey of the results of excavations carried out in Jerusalem.

[5] Polybius vi 26. 10–32, 8; Josephus, *BJ* iii 5. 1 (76–84); Vegetius, *epitoma rei militaris* i 21–5; Ps.-Hyginus Gromaticus, *liber de munitionibus castrorum* (ed. Domaszewski).

[6] *Das Strategikon des Maurikios*, ed. G. Dennis (1981), viii 1 (26).

[7] *Hist.* iv 23.

[8] *Ann.* xiv 32. 4.

[9] *Excavations at Dura-Europos, 9th Season of Work*, 1 (1944), plan at end of vol. C. Hopkins, *The Discovery of Dura-Europos* (1979), 225: 'At Dura the city walls served as the camp defenses on two sides, and a strong mud-brick wall divided the camp from the city center. The palace of the commander (i.e. the *Dux Ripae*) lay outside this compound.'

tetrarchic fortress.[10] A lack of evidence from one partly excavated town should not, therefore, be used in support of theories that contradict the explicit statements of so many first-hand authorities.

Sites along the Jerusalem–Jaffa road

1. *Giv'at Ram (Sheikh Bader)*, 2.5 km. from Jerusalem. Brick-ovens and fort, excavated but unpublished.[11]

2. *Motza (Qolonia)*, 5–6 km. from Jerusalem, almost certainly to be identified with the veteran settlement established by Vespasian after the Jewish war (at a place named 'Ammaus' according to Josephus), possibly also with the village of Emmaus mentioned in Luke 24: 13.[12] The site is in a very fertile, well-watered valley. Its spring is mentioned in Byzantine sources and was guarded by a crusading fort. The Roman road passed over a bridge and through a narrow defile.[13] A Latin inscription was found on the spot:[14] 'Valeria L.f. Sedata vix(it) an(nos) IIII.' Although this is an isolated piece of evidence it is just the type of inscription that, in these parts, only a veteran settlement would produce. A brick stamp of X Fretensis was also found.[15]

3. *Abu Ghosh*, 13.5 km. from Jerusalem. Spring with remains of the Roman period. Inscription: 'Vexillatio Leg. X Fret.'[16] On top of a hill nearby (Kiriath Jearim, Deir el-Azhar) a second inscription: 'Vexillatio Leg. X Fret.' and a fragment: '. . . CO . . .'[17] The site of the spring always remained an important road-station. The hill nearby affords a commanding view of the vicinity.

4. *Emmaus-Nicopolis (Imwas)*, an important city at a major crossroads, 30 km. from Jerusalem. Josephus says that V Macedonica was stationed there in the Jewish War before the siege of Jerusalem.[18] Five inscriptions referring to V

---

[10] M. Gawlikowski, *Le temple Palmyrénien* (Warszawa, 1973), p. 11, fig. 1; J. Starcky and M. Gawlikowski, *Palmyre* (1985), figs. 3 and 8; R. Fellmann, *Mélanges d'histoire ancienne et d'archéologie offerts à Paul Collart* (1976), 173–91. See above, pp. 165–7.

[11] For a brief and unsatisfactory note, M. Avi-Yonah, *BIES* 15 (1950), 19–24, pl. 6 f. (in Hebrew). Cf. D. Barag, *BJb* 167 (1967), 244–67, for the stamped tiles produced here. This is only one of many interesting sites that have been excavated but remain unpublished.

[12] Joshua 18: 26: 'Hamotza'; m. Sukkah 4. 5: 'Motza'; y. Sukkah 54b, b. Sukkah 45a: 'Motza–Qaloniah'; Cyril of Scythopolis, *vita Sabae* 67 (Schwartz, p. 168): 'Kolonia'. For Vespasian's veteran settlement, Josephus, *BJ* vii 6. 6 (217). For later sources and problems of identification, Schürer, i (1973), 512 f., n. 142. Reservations there on the information in the Talmud are unjustified; L. H. Vincent and F. M. Abel, *Emmaüs, sa basilique et son histoire* (1932), 382–85; Fischer, Isaac, and Roll, *Roman Roads in Judaea*, ii (forthcoming). At this site too, excavations have been carried out, but the material is unpublished and inaccessible.

[13] The Roman bridge was in use till the nineteenth century, when it collapsed. It has now disappeared. The spring and the fort can still be seen.

[14] Y. H. Landau, *Acta of the Fifth International Congress of Greek and Latin Epigraphy, Cambridge 1967* (1971), 389.

[15] Barag, 267. It is frequently, but incorrectly, asserted that the settlement had the status of a Roman colony. While the Roman colonies of the region all issued coinage and are listed in the *Digest* neither is true of Emmaus.

[16] *AE* 1902. 230. For the site, R. de Vaux and A. M. Stève, *Fouilles à Qaryet el-'Enab Abu Gôsh* (1950). I have inspected the inscriptions of this site myself.

[17] *AE* 1926. 136; de Vaux and Stève, 54.   [18] *BJ* iv 8. 1 (445); see also v 1. 6 (42); 2. 3 (67).

Macedonica have been found there.[19] At least two of these are epitaphs of serving soldiers who died at Emmaus sometime in the later first century AD.[20] This shows that they stayed there long enough for a stone-mason's workshop to be set up. Another inscription mentions the *coh(ors) VI Ulpi(a) Petr(aeorum)*.[21] A fragmentary inscription mentions an unknown cohort.[22] It is therefore quite possible, although not certain, that army units were permanently based here. The military importance of the site is also discussed above.

5. In the village of *Kubab* now abandoned (near modern Mishmar 'Ayalon), *c*.5 km. from Emmaus, two inscriptions have been found, one of them certainly military.[23]

Another undated inscription may be mentioned: 'Leg X Fre / Coh IIX.' It is now in the Israel Museum, and the find-spot is unknown, but the inscription may indicate that the eighth cohort of the legion had a separate base somewhere.[24] A similar, Hadrianic inscription mentioning the first cohort was found in the north of the country (see below, p. 433).

Four other sites must be mentioned in this connection:

7. *Giv'at Shaul*, 4 km. from Jerusalem, 1.5 km. from site no. 1 (above). Excavation of a tower (10 × 9.25 m.), occupied in the first centuries BC and AD,[25] i.e. before the arrival of X Fretensis in Jerusalem after the Jewish War. A small fort, measuring 16 × 16 m., was built on the spot in the fourth century AD.

8. A similar small fort of the Byzantine period, excavated but unpublished, a little distance to the west.[26]

9. *Khirbet el-Qasr*, east of Emmaus, excavated by Dr M. Fischer.[27] The site was, like no. 7, occupied till the end of the first century AD, subsequently deserted, and occupied again in the Byzantine period.

10. On the parallel Beth Horon road a tower was recently excavated east of Upper Beth Horon. It was not occupied after the Jewish War.[28] Curiously, this tower stood along the section of the road where Cestius Gallus suffered severe losses in 66. That emphasizes the irrelevance of such structures in times of major warfare.

[19] *CIL* iii 6647; 14155. 11 and 12; J. H. Landau, *Atiqot* 2 1976), 98 f.

[20] As observed by L. J. F. Keppie, *DRBE*, 420. The formula 'H(ic) S(itus) E(st)' is not to be expected in the second century. Hence a date in the period of the Bar Kokhba Revolt may be excluded.

[21] *AE* 1924. 132; Vincent and Abel, 427, no. 4. The unit is listed on the diploma of AD 139 for Syria Palaestina (*CIL* xvi 87); possibly also on the fragment of 149–61 (Roxan, *RMD* 60); certainly not on that of 186 of this province (*RMD* 69).

[22] *CIL* iii 13588 and see n. 23.

[23] Ch. Clermont-Ganneau, *Archaeological Researches in Palestine*, ii (1896), 83 f.

[24] Y. Meshorer, *The Israel Museum Journal* 3 (1984), 43 f. (*AE* 1984. 915), provenance uncertain.

[25] V. Tzaferis, *IEJ* 24 (1974), 84–94, pls. 14–16.

[26] See the brief note by R. Amiran on 'Khirbet Ras el-Alawi', *Alon* 3 (1951), 43 f. (in Hebrew).

[27] For brief reports, M. Fischer, *RB* 86 (1979), 461 f.; 92 (1985), 426–8. Further discussion and reports forthcoming in Fischer, Isaac, and Roll, *Roman Roads in Judaea*, ii.

[28] Forthcoming report in Fischer et al.

The Road to Hebron

1. *Ramat Rahel*, 3.5 km. south of Jerusalem. Site on top of a hill controlling access to the city from the south. Roman bath-house, many tiles bearing the stamp of the legion. Peristyle villa. Various unidentified structures of non-durable material.[29] However, the military nature of the buildings has not been established beyond doubt.

2. Along the Jerusalem–Hebron road an aqueduct was constructed by the army. It served both the bath-house at Ramat Rahel and another in Jerusalem on the eastern slope of Mt Zion.[30] Here too stamped bricks have been found.

3. In or near the city of Hebron itself a *Cohors I Milliaria Thracum* was based.[31] Hebron is sited on a crossroads whence roads lead in all directions, one of them to Ein Gedi, where in 124 a centurion of the cohort is attested, occupying a *praisidion* flanked by soldiers' housing.

In the mountains of Judaea, south of Jerusalem, several ancient roads have been traced. Some of these were protected by a system of watchtowers, blockhouses, and small forts thought to be Roman. However, a series of such sites has been excavated and proved to be of Byzantine date.[32] In this area too the system by which entire roads were kept under constant observation does not belong to the Roman period; in that period of massive military presence in the province, it seems that larger units were kept together and occupied a limited number of essential towns and sites. There is evidence of engineering activity concerning the water-supply and bathing facilities.

The Road to the North: Neapolis and Samaria

1. *Neapolis, ancient Shekhem (Nablus)*, controls a crossroads whence roads lead to Jerusalem, to the coastal plain in the west, eastward to the Jordan Valley, and northward to Scythopolis (Beth Shean). This was the traditional centre of the Samaritans, dominated by Mt Gerizim, their holy site. The evidence of military presence is as follows: (*a*) A fragmentary inscription mentioning a *tribunus* and a *primus pilus* or *praepositus*.[33] (*b*) Countermarks of XII Fulminata on coins struck up to AD 86/7.[34] The coins were countermarked after AD 86/7 and probably before 156/7. This almost certainly shows that the legion (or

---

[29] Y. Aharoni, *Excavations at Ramat Rahel, Seasons 1959 and 1960* (1962), 24–7; ibid., *Seasons 1961 and 1962* (1964), 38–40, plan I.

[30] For the inscriptions on the aqueduct, L. Vetrali, *Studii Biblici Franciscani, Liber Annuus* 13 (1967), 149–61, figs. 1–5. For the bath on Mt Zion, cf. Barag, 266.

[31] Roxan, *RMD* i 69, said to come from Hebron. Cf. E. M. Smallwood, *The Jews under Roman Rule* (²1981), 422 n. 136; M. Speidel, *ZPE* 35 (1979), 170–2; cf. *AE* 1979. 633. For a centurion attested at Ein Gedi, cf. H. Polotsky, *IEJ* 12 (1962), 259, now published as N. Lewis (ed.), *The Documents from the Bar Kokhba period in the Cave of Letters: Greek Papyri* (1984), no. 11.

[32] For a brief report, Y. Hirschfeld, *Qadmoniot* 12 (1979), 78–84 (in Hebrew).

[33] Clermont-Ganneau, *Archaeological Researches*, ii 315 f.

[34] C. J. Howgego, *AFRBA*, 41–6.

part of it) was based at Neapolis in 115–17 or 132–5. (*c*) The tombstone of M. Ulpius Magnus, centurion of V Macedonica, presumably from the years of the revolt of Bar Kokhba.[35] (*d*) Tombstone of C. Valerius Longinus from Stobi, soldier of III Flavia, set up by his brother.[36] (*e*) Tombstone of Augindai eq(u)e(s) nomero(ru)m Maurorum.[37] (*f*) City coin: *obv.* Tribonianus Gallus (251–3); *rev.* COL NE[A]POLI and emblems of X Fretensis.[38] (*g*) City coin: *obv.* Volusianus Augustus (251–3); *rev.* COL NEAPOLIS and emblems of III Cyrenaica.[39]

2. *Samaria-Sebaste, ancient Shomron*, capital of the kingdom of Israel, military colony established by Herod. It controls the main north–south road. The evidence of military presence is as follows: (*a*) monumental inscription: 'Vexillatio Leg. VI Ferr';[40] (*b*) dedication to Jupiter by the 'mil(ites) v(e)xi(la-tionis) coh(ortium) Pa(nnoniae) Sup(erioris), cives Sisci(ani) (et) Varcian(i) et Latobici'.[41] These inscriptions have been discovered in excavations and their provenance is therefore certain.[42] (*c*) Certainly from Sebaste comes a fragmentary military tombstone: 'Arr[---] tesse[---] coh V[---] C R per C(aium) Sabin[---]'.[43] (*d*) Another fragmentary military inscription is said to have been found at Sebaste.[44]

The Jerusalem–Jericho Road

On a site on this road a military stamp has been found.[45] That is not, of course, conclusive. The fort at Maʿale Adumim, attested in Byzantine sources, is extant but unexcavated (see above, p. 91). It is not known whether it was occupied in the Roman period as well.

---

[35] F.-M. Abel, *RB* 35 (1926), 421–4, figs. 1 and 2. Abel suggests a connection with the events of AD 67 or with the Bar Kokhba war. The former is impossible in the case of an Ulpius.

[36] M. Avi-Yonah, *QDAP* 12 (1946), 92, no. 8.

[37] Ibid., 93, no. 9.

[38] Stella Ben Dor, *RB* 59 (1952), 251 f., pl. 9.1; Kenneth Harl, *American Numismatic Society, Museum Notes* 29 (1984), nos. 151 and 154, with comments on p. 68. In this paper it is assumed that legionary standards on city-coinage of this period indicate the possibility of veteran colonists. However, there is no evidence, after Hadrian, of the foundation of such colonies, cf. J. C. Mann, *Legionary Recruitment and Veteran Settlement During the Principate* (1983), 65–8. In this period military emblems are more likely to be an indication of the presence in town of a garrison. Of course that would not exclude the possibility that veterans of the garrison settled near their former base. The foundation of a veteran colony entailed settlement of retired soldiers *en bloc*, re-division of the city territory, and the reorganization of local administration. A grant of colonial status to an existing city would not in principle exclude settlement of individual veterans, but that is a measure different in scale and character from the foundation of a veteran colony.

[39] A. Kindler, *INJ* 4 (1980), 56–8.

[40] G. A. Reisner et al., *Harvard Excavations at Samaria* (1924), 251, pls. 59 f.

[41] *AE* 1938. 13.

[42] A dedication to Hadrian was originally said to come from Samaria, cf. *CIL* iii 13589, but this appeared to be incorrect, cf. below under Scythopolis.

[43] Avi-Yonah, *QDAP*, 94 f., no. 11.

[44] Ibid., 94, no. 11.

[45] *AE* 1902. 231 from Qa'adeh, not far from Jerusalem.

The Jerusalem–Gaza Road

Eleutheropolis (Beth Govrin). Monumental inscription, 'Vexillatio leg(ionis) VI Ferr(atae)', said to come from this town.[46] Near the town, at Erak Hala on the Roman road, the trunk of a life-size statue, apparently an emperor in military dress, was found.[47] Beth Govrin, which received municipal status under Septimius Severus, lies on an important crossroads with other Roman roads leading to Hebron, Ascalon, Lydda, and Emmaus.

The Scythopolis–Jericho Road

Tel Shalem, almost 11 km. from Scythopolis (near the seventh mile-station). An inscription mentions a vexillation of VI Ferrata.[48] On the site a bronze statue of Hadrian has been found,[49] and nearby fragments of a very large inscription which mentions Hadrian.[50] The site lies on the road in the area where the Valley of Beth Shean borders on the arid Jordan Valley.[51]

Caparcotna—Kefar ʿOtnay—Legio

The base of VI Ferrata was near the ancient site of Megiddo, a strategic spot where the Caesarea–Scythopolis road reaches the Valley of Jezreel. A branch makes for the hills of Lower Galilee and Sepphoris and thence to Ptolemais-Acco, while another leads to Ptolemais directly through the plain. Yet another road runs south-east to Samaria.[52] The legionary fortress lay on a site typical of many such installations. It reminds one somewhat of the old base at Vetera. The base was located near a strategic crossroads on a gentle slope that offered no tactical advantage, unlike nearby Megiddo, which lies on an easily defensible mount. An army base certainly existed there before the revolt of Bar Kokhba.[53] This was not an urbanized site. Kefar ʿOtnay was a village with a

---

[46] *AE* 1933. 158.

[47] Clermont-Ganneau, *Archaeological Researches*, ii 441 f.; 464; C. C. Vermeule III, *Berytus* 13 (1959), no. 288.

[48] N. Tzori, *IEJ* 21 (1971), 53 f. For the possible identification of the site, G. Fuks, *Scythopolis: A Greek City in Eretz-Israel* (1983, in Hebrew), 110.

[49] G. Foerster, *ʿAtiqot* 17 (1985), 139–60.

[50] The inscription has been mentioned in the daily press. It is now in the Rockefeller Museum where Dr G. Foerster kindly showed it to me. See also the brief note on the excavations carried out on the site: *Hadashot Arkheologiyot* 57/8 (1976), 17 f. The military character of the site was established and a small hoard of Hadrianic coins confirmed the date.

[51] There is no road leading to Neapolis from this spot, as stated erroneously in several publications.

[52] For the site of Caparcotna and the road-system, B. Isaac and I. Roll, *Roman Roads in Judaea*, i, *The Legio-Scythopolis Road* (1982), index.

[53] For the date see B. Isaac and I. Roll, *Latomus* 38 (1979), 54–66; *ZPE* 33 (1979), 149–56; 47 (1982), 131 f. W. Eck, *Bull. Am. Soc. Papyr.* 21 (1984), 55–67, has argued that Judaea had become a consular province under Trajan. That would entail the reinforcement of the garrison at the same time and thus, possibly, the contemporary establishment of a legion at Legio.

mixed Jewish and Samaritan population, according to Talmudic sources of the second century.[54] Kefar 'Otnay and Antipatris are mentioned as the two halting places on the usual route for Jews travelling from Galilee to Judaea and vice versa.[55] The legionary base was named after the village: 'Caparcotna', 'Caporcotani', or 'Kaparkotnei'.[56] It appears on the Peutinger Table as a road-station on the Caesarea–Scythopolis road. Later the name 'Legio' became common, and this name was retained after the departure of the legion at an unknown date in the third century.[57] The civilian settlement that developed near the base was important enough to receive city status as Maximianoupolis under the Tetrarchs.[58] This then was a rural site chosen for a legionary base because of its proximity to a strategic crossroads. The small town that developed there owed its existence to the base, like Raphanaea in Syria and Melitene in Cappadocia.

Scythopolis

Scythopolis was a substantial city which lay on an important crossroads. At the beginning of the First Jewish Revolt an *ala* was (temporarily?) based there.[59] A dedication to Hadrian by the first cohort of X Fretensis was said to come from Scythopolis, although this is not quite certain.[60] It certainly derives from that part of the country. Does such an inscription reflect temporary or long-term outposting of the entire first cohort of the legion? Or something else? An inscription certainly found in Scythopolis commemorates P. Aelius Capito, a Macedonian who served in XI Claudia. He died at the age of thirty-five after ten years service.[61] A vexillation of this legion participated in the suppression of the Bar Kokhba revolt.[62] It is possible that the unit spent some time in or

[54] m. Gittin i 5; vii 7; tos. Gittin i 4 and vii 9; tos. Demai v 3; tos. Bekhorot vii 3; cf. b Bekhorot 55a.

[55] tos. Gittin vii 9.

[56] Respectively on inscriptions from Asia Minor: *CIL* iii 6814–16, on the Tabula Peutingeriana, and by Ptolemy.

[57] The name is first attested on a milestone of Caracalla: Isaac and Roll, *Roman Roads in Judaea*, i 84 f., n. 27. It then appears, after the legion had left, in the *Onomasticon* of Eusebius, ed. Klostermann, *passim*. Note especially Jerome, ibid. 15. 20: *oppido Legionis*. This name could still be recognized in the name of the Arab village Lejjun. For Lejjun after the Islamic conquest, Isaac and Roll, *Roman Roads* i 24 f., n. 99.

[58] This name first occurs in the *Itinerarium Burdigalense* (AD 333): *Itineraria Romana*, i, ed. Cuntz, 95 f.; *CCSL* clxxv 13. It is uncertain whether it owed its name to Maximianus Herculius (286–304) or to Maximianus Galerius; Isaac and Roll, op. cit. 11. It is mentioned as a bishopric in 325, 347, 518, and 536 (for references, ibid., n. 61).

[59] Josephus, *vita* 24, 120 f.

[60] Clermont-Ganneau, *Études d'Archéologie Orientale* II (1897), 168–71. See in particular p. 171 for the origin of the inscription; cf. *CIL* iii 13589, which claims Samaria for its origin, and the correction under no. 14155. 14.

[61] M. Avi-Yonah, *QDAP* 8 (1839), 57–9 (*AE* 1939. 158): 'D(is) Manib(us) P. Aelius Capito natio(ne) Macedo mil(es) leg(ionis) XI Cl(audiae) vixit annix XXXV mil(i)tav[it] annis X Dol(enter) m[er](ito) fecit heres benef[i](ciatus) v(elut) t(estamento) i(ussus).'

[62] As appears from *CIL* iii 14155. 2 (Clermont-Ganneau, *CRAI* 1894, 13 f.)

near the town, but the evidence is ˙not decisive.[63] A recent discovery is a column bearing an inscription which mentions the *ala Antiana*,[64] i.e. the *Ala Gallorum et Thracum Antiana*, mentioned as based in Syria Palaestina on diplomas from 139 to 186.[65]

Tiberias

Aurelius Marcellinus, centurion of X Fretensis, was buried at Tiberias by his wife.[66] A Latin inscription mentions [P]ompeius [---]ullus, centurion of VI Ferrata from Europos.[67] That does not prove that their units were there, but either inscription may be the only surviving piece of evidence of a local garrison.

Galilee

Apart from the two inscriptions from Tiberias there is surprisingly little evidence of army units in Galilee. Yet it would be premature to draw conclusions from the absence of evidence. There are Talmudic sources regarding Sepphoris, one of the two main towns in the region,[68] but no archaeological or epigraphic material for confirmation. The Gospels contain a random piece of information that there was a centurion at Capernaum (Kefar Nahum),[69] which implies the presence of a unit of which we know nothing otherwise. A stamped tile of VI Ferrata was found at Horvat Hazon.[70] It is regrettable that so little is known of the excavations at Beth Yerah (Khirbet el-Kerak) on the south-western shore of the Sea of Galilee.[71] These produced the walls of a fort which looks like a fourth-century structure.[72] Nearby a Roman

---

[63] Compare the inscriptions relating to V Macedonica from Emmaus, above, p. 428 f. There is no reason to assume that the man fell in action.

[64] R. Last and A. Stein, *ZPE* 81 (1990), 224–8.

[65] *RMD* i, no. 3, 88 Nov. 7, Syria = R. Mellor, 'A New Roman Military Diploma', *The J. Paul Getty Museum Journal* 6–7 (1978–79), 173–84, esp. p. 182; *CIL* xvi 87, AD 139; *RMD* i, no. 60, AD 149/161; *RMD* i, no. 69, AD 186. The unit again appears in the *Not. Dig. Or.*, no. 33 in the list under the *Dux Palaestinae*, ed. Seeck, p. 73: *ala Antana dromedariorum*, based at Admatha.

[66] *IGR* iii 1204.

[67] M. Avi-Yonah, *QDAP*, 91, no. 7; note also no. 5 on p. 88, a Latin grave-inscription.

[68] See above, p. 117.

[69] Matt. 8: 5–9; Luke 7: 2.

[70] D. Bahat, *IEJ* 24 (1974), 160–9. Curiously it was found on the site of an underground hiding place, one of the first discovered in Galilee.

[71] B. Maisler et al., *IEJ* 2 (1952), 222 f. For brief summaries, P. Bar-Adon, *Eretz-Israel* 4 (1956), 50–5; R. Hestrin, *Encyclopedia of Archaeological Excavations in the Holy Land*, i 253–62, with plan on p. 254.

[72] In *IEJ* 2 the excavators state it dates to the second–third century. Elsewhere, however, they claim it belongs to the period of Vespasian; see Bar Adon, op. cit. No evidence has been published for this dating apart from a tentative identification with Ennabris (or Sennabris), mentioned by Josephus, *BJ* iii 9. 78 (4478); iv 8. 2 (455). They give the measurements as 60 × 60 m., but on the plan it measures *c*.60 × *c*.75 m. It has square projecting corner towers and a fortified gate.

bath was discovered.[73] The only building encountered in the fort was a synagogue, not contemporary, one may presume.

Eusebius, in his *Onomasticon* does not mention garrisons in Galilee, but that reflects fourth-century organization. In Chapter III it was observed that there is little evidence of the existence of Roman roads north of the Ptolemais–Tiberias road. That will be connected with the lack of urban development in the region.

[73] *IEJ* 2, 218–22, said to date to the fourth or fifth century.

APPENDIX II
ANTIOCH AS MILITARY HEADQUARTERS AND IMPERIAL RESIDENCE

Heavy Ares will not leave you, poor Antioch, as an Assyrian war will oppress you: for in your house will live the first of the warriors who will fight all the spear-throwing Persians, he who has become the royal ruler of the Romans. (Sibyll. xiii 59–63)

The city played a prominent part during Trajan's eastern wars.[1] If we may believe the *Historia Augusta* Lucius Verus remained in Antioch, Daphne, and Laodicea during the Parthian campaigns carried out in his name by Avidius Cassius, AD 162–6.[2] In 193 Pescennius Niger was proclaimed emperor by his own troops in Antioch and established his headquarters in the city.[3] It served as his principal mint, and Herodian claims that the city population supported him enthusiastically.[4] The punishment it suffered at the hands of Septimius Severus after his victory does not concern us here. The city may again have served as headquarters for Severus' Parthian war at the turn of the century.[5]

Caracalla stayed at Antioch during his Parthian campaign in 215,[6] and in 216.[7] In these years many cities in the region issued silver coinage, which was unusual, for city-coinage was normally bronze.[8] Apparently the coinage was struck for the payment of the troops. The mint at Antioch too was active. Here, however, it was not uncommon for silver to be issued, since that was normal for a provincial mint. While Caracalla was campaigning, his mother, Julia Domna, stayed at Antioch 'with orders to sort all the incoming mail to prevent the emperor from being bothered by a mass of letters while he was in the

---

[1] Dio lxviii 24 gives a good description: Trajan spent the winter there, and accordingly many soldiers and civilians had gathered there from all over the empire for their lawsuits, as ambassadors, for business, or as tourists. Cf. G. Downey, *A History of Antioch*, 212 f. For Antioch as military headquarters see also P. Petit, *Libanius et la vie municipale à Antioche au IVᵉ siècle après J.-C.* (1955), 179.

[2] Dio lxxi 2; SHA, *Verus* vii 6.

[3] Herodian ii 7. 9–8. 8. Cf. Downey, 236, 238 f.

[4] iii 1. 3; 4. 1.

[5] Cf. G. J. Murphy, *The Reign of the Emperor L. Septimius Severus from the Evidence of the Inscriptions* (1945), 21–4. The only literary reference is SHA, *Severus* 16. 8.

[6] Dio lxxvii 20 (399).

[7] Herodian iv 9. 8; *Cod. Iust.* ix 51. 1; J. Crook, *Consilium Principis* (1955), 82 f.

[8] For the coinage, A. R. Bellinger, *The Syrian Tetradrachms of Caracalla and Macrinus* (American Numismatic Society, Numismatic Studies, No. 3, 1940), 21–9.

country of the enemy'.[9] In other words, Julia Domna, who carried on most of
the administrative business for Caracalla even while the emperor was there,
continued to do so while he was campaigning, and Antioch was in effect the
centre of administration at this time.[10] Julia Domna was still there at the time
of Caracalla's murder, and Macrinus immediately went there to consolidate
his position.[11] He ordered Julia Domna to leave Antioch and go wherever she
desired, while Julia Maesa was instructed to return to her native Emesa.[12]
Macrinus stayed at Antioch for the duration of his reign, apart from a brief
Parthian campaign.[13] During the struggle for the throne in 218 Macrinus fled
from Apamea back to Antioch.[14] The battle between Macrinus and Elagabalus was fought near a village in the territory of Antioch.[15] Elagabalus
remained in Antioch till his position was consolidated.[16] Severus Alexander
again made Antioch his headquarters during his Persian War,[17] and the same
happened in the forties.[18] During the war in the fifties Valerian was certainly
in Antioch in 255 and 258.[19]

The role of Antioch at the time of Zenobia is mentioned in Chapter VI. The
next emperor who was at Antioch for extended periods was Diocletian.[20] He
certainly was in the town in 290 and spent at least two winters there, 297/8 and
298/9, at the time of the Persian campaign of Galerius. Diocletian and
Galerius celebrated a triumph there, and Diocletian entered on his seventh
consulship at Antioch on 1 January 299. Rescripts from 12 February, 26
March, and 25 June 300, and 4 July 301, were signed at Antioch. It is likely
that Antioch was his permanent residence from 299 to 303.

In Chapter VI it was noted that the presence of an expeditionary force at
Antioch caused famine on three occasions: in about 333, 354, and 360.
Constantius Caesar remained at Antioch from 333 for four years till the death
of Constantine. In 338 a division of the empire took place whereby Constantius
became Augustus of the East with Antioch as capital. He stayed there,
regularly conducting campaigns against Persia, till he became sole Augustus
in 350.[21] Gallus Caesar then was appointed Caesar of the East, and Antioch

---

[9] Dio lxxviii 4. 2–3 (405).

[10] Dio lxxvii 18. 1–3 (397): at winter-quarters in Nicomedia Caracalla prepared for the
Parthian war, while his mother took care of administration, held public receptions for distinguished persons, and still found time to study philosophy.

[11] Dio lxxviii 23 (428); Herodian v 1.

[12] Herodian v 3. 2; cf. Whittaker's note, Loeb ed., vol. ii 16.

[13] Herodian v 2. 3–5. For the career of Macrinus, *RE* xviii, s.v. Opellius (2), cols. 542 f. (von
Petrikovits); Pflaum, *Carrières*, no. 248; for Dio on Macrinus, F. Millar, *A Study of Cassius Dio*
(1964), 160–6. See further Downey, 247–50.

[14] Dio lxxviii 34. 5 (443).

[15] Dio lxxviii 37. 3–4 (446); 38. 2–4 (447).

[16] Dio lxxix 3 (455).

[17] As already noted in ch. V.

[18] Sibyll. xiii 59–63, cited above in translation.

[19] T. Pekáry, *Historia* 11 (1962), 123–8.

[20] For the evidence, *RE* vii A, cols. 2431; 2442 f.; 2445 f. (Ensslin).

[21] Downey, 352–62.

remained his residence till his downfall in 354. The turbulent sojourn of Julian at Antioch in 362–3 is well-known, thanks to his own writings and those of Libanius.[22] Jovian did not like the city any better. 'He stayed there for some time, suffering from the load of various tasks which had to be dealt with, and affected by an extraordinary desire to leave.'[23] Valens was Augustus of the East from 363 to 378 and chose Antioch as residence, from where he regularly campaigned against Persia.[24]

This brought to an end the period of virtually constant fighting with Persia and with it the intensive imperial involvement in the city. We hear of a visit by the empress Eudocia in 438.[25] As in Palestine, the combination of literary elegance and munificence made a deep impression. As noted in Chapter VI, in the last quarter of the fifth century Antioch served as headquarters for the various rebels against Zeno.

We may assume, although there is no concrete evidence, that Antioch played its usual role during the Persian war in the reign of Anastasius (AD 502–5). During the Persian wars in the reign of Justinian Antioch served as the military headquarters and communications centre of the Roman commander from 528 to 561.

The series of earthquakes, the raids and sack of the city in these years, as well as the plague that spread through the empire in 542 and recurred at times, had a lasting effect on its prosperity and brought about a substantial decrease in population.[26]

---

[22] Cf. Downey, ch. 13.
[23] Ammianus xxv 10. 4.
[24] Downey, 399 ff.
[25] Downey, 450–2.
[26] Downey, 546–57.

POSTSCRIPT

The following pages contain references to publications that reached me after the first edition of this book went to press in January 1989. Apart from the recent literature, I have included some additional older material that came to my notice after the book was published. References in bold type are to pages and footnotes in the text. These are followed by an additional bibliography, organized along the same principles as the main bibliography above.

Page 1 n. 1. C. R. Whittaker, *Les frontières de l'empire romain* (1989), 11–19, describes how modern, contemporary notions have shaped and even determined views of the Roman frontier.

Page 1 n. 3. R. Syme, *Classical Antiquity* 7 (1988), 227–51, esp. 247–51.

Page 16 f., 236, 266 f., 425. H. Delbrück, *Geschichte der Kriegskunst*, ii (1921³), 401–10, argues that it is typical of warfare in the Later Roman Empire that both Rome and her enemies did not have the resources to risk substantial losses in large-scale engagements. Shrewd tactics, ruses, and, above all, 'Ermattungsstrategie', a strategy of attrition, replaced the preference for decisive battles that was characteristic of earlier periods. Further arguments along these lines: W. E. Kaegi, *Some Thoughts on Byzantine Military Strategy*, The Hellenic Studies Lecture (Brookline, Mass., 1983).

Page 17 line 11. 'Bedouin allies'. As stated on p. 218 n. 1, I use the term 'Saracens' and avoid the term 'Bedouin' when referring to nomads in the pre-Islamic period. I am sorry to note that I have been inconsistent and refer occasionally to Bedouin when I should have written Saracens.

Page 20 n. 4. Whittaker, *Les frontières*, 15 f.: the alleged search for a natural border is in reality the expression of an aggressive attitude by an imperial power.

Page 24 n. 30. R. W. Davies, *Service in the Roman Army* (1989), 71–90.

Page 24 n. 35. For an examination of the military contribution of Syria to the Roman army, D. L. Kennedy, *EFRE*, 235–46.

Page 26 f. 'When another king of Rome will rule, then ruinous Ares with his bastard son will bring the disorderly races against the Romans, against the walls of Rome' (*Orac. Sib.* 13. 103–5); cf. *Orac. Sib.* 14. 165, 247. D. S. Potter, *Prophecy and History in the Crisis of the Roman Empire* (1990), 288 f., observes that, where no actual attack on the city of Rome is implied, the phrase should be taken figuratively. That is entirely convincing, but I cannot accept his subsequent assertion that such expressions refer explicitly to what he calls the *limes*. These passages, like similar utterances by Appian, *Praef.* 7/28; Aelius Aristides, *Roman Oration* 26. 29, 82–4; 35. 36; Herodian ii 11. 5, are vague analogies, describing the empire in terms of a Greek *polis*, surrounded by walls, an image far removed from the realities of Roman military policy in the frontier zone. None of these authors had ever seen Hadrian's wall, but all thought of the empire in terms of a city-state, which was the only relevant concept of a state in their eyes, and, to a large extent, in the view of Latin-speaking Romans as well. The sacred boundary of the city of Rome, the *pomerium*, retained throughout antiquity a significance which the border of the empire never had. Appian and Aelius Aristides are interpreted along these lines by Whittaker, *Les frontières*, 26–8, with further references. For the notion of an imperial boundary, see Chapter IX.

Page 28 n. 60. Note, however, the more balanced survey of M. Sartre, *L'Orient romain* (1991), chs. 1 and 2.

Page 31 n. 79. For the chronology of the 250's, Potter, *Prophecy and History*, 189–96, 290–7, 329–37. For the relevant sources in English translation: M. H. Dodgeon and S. N. C. Lieu, *The Roman Eastern Frontier and the Persian Wars (AD 226–363)* (1991), chs. 2 and 3.

Page 31 n. 80. English translation, ibid. chs. 2 and 3. Potter, *Prophecy and History*, 372–5, suggests that the wars between the first Sassanid kings and Rome were caused by the desire of Ardashir to establish control over the frontier client kingdoms like Hatra and Armenia which Rome considered part of her empire.

Page 32 n. 85. For Julian's Persian expedition, J. Matthews, *The Roman Empire of Ammianus* (1989), ch. VIII; for the events of 591, Theophylactus Simocatta v 6.7.

Page 32 n. 86. Potter, *Prophecy and History*, App. iii: Alexander Severus and Ardashir, 370–80.

Page 36 n. 105. Sartre, *L'Orient romain*, 71–5.

Page 42 n. 151. C. S. Lightfoot, *Epigraphica Anatolica* 17 (1991), 2, n. 7, points out that the stone was not discovered by D. Oates. More important is that I went too far in asserting that the discovery of a single inscription shows Roman units to have been based in the region.

Page 42 n. 153. D. Braund, *EFRE*, i, 31–43.

Page 44 n. 167. For photographs and discussion of the inscription, A. I. Boltounova, *Klio* 53 (1971), 213–22.

Page 50 n. 203. G. Lordkipanidse and D. Braund, *Roman Frontier Studies 1989* (1991), 335 f.

Page 63 n. 38. The second part of the name may derive from the Aramaic word for village, cf. Matthews, *Roman Empire*, 402 with n. 46.

Page 74 n. 89. See esp. xxii 5. 1–2 and, on Saracens as described by Ammianus, Matthews, *Roman Empire*, 342–53.

Page 73 n. 92. R. P. Lindner, *Past and Present*, 92 (1981), 3–19, observes a gradual process of sedentarization among the Huns in Central Europe, unlike those dwelling further east who retained their way of life.

Page 75 n. 94. On Isauria see now Matthews, *Roman Empire*, 355–67.

Page 99. Whittaker, *Les frontières*, 81 f., 90–2, observes that even the substantial migrations of foreigners such as the Goths into the Later Roman Empire represented a process of infiltration by small, unorganized groups rather than the massive movements of entire peoples as portrayed in the Roman rhetoric. Cf. Delbrück, *Geschichte der Kriegskunst*, 300–16.

Page 102 f., 410–13. Rivers do not function as barriers: Whittaker, *Les frontières*, 24 f. For logistics, supplies, rivers, and river-transport: Whittaker, ch. 2, esp. 54 f.

Page 107 n. 30. For a recently excavated Byzantine block-house in the Judaean desert on the road to En Gedi, Y. Hirschfeld and A. Kloner, *Bulletin of the Anglo-Israel Archaeological Society* 8 (1988–9), 5–20.

Page 125 n. 114. N. Lewis (ed.), *The Documents from the Bar-Kokhba Period in the Cave of Letters* (1989), no. 16.

Page 126 n. 114. For the site of Umm el-Qottein: D. L. Kennedy and D. N. Riley, *Rome's Desert Frontier from the Air* (1990).

Page 126 n. 115. Ibid., 74 f., 199–202.

Page 128 n. 123. For serious doubts regarding the notion of 'defence in depth' in antiquity, Whittaker, *Les frontières* (1989), 88 f.

Page 130 n. 137. For air photographs, a plan, and comments: Kennedy and Riley, *Rome's Desert Frontier*, 170–2, 197 f.

Page 136 n. 163. For the architecture of the alleged *praetorium*, Z. U. Ma'oz, *DOP* 44 (1990), 41–6.

Page 136 n. 167. Centurions are shown to have fulfilled police duties in the Middle Euphrates area in the third century, cf. the brief description of unpublished documents by D. Feissel and J. Gascou, *CRAI* (1990), 558.

Page 137 n. 171. A recently discovered tablet from Vindolanda, Inv. 946, shows centurions engaged in commercial activities on their own behalf: they trade in grain and hides, J. N. Adams, A. K. Bowman, and J. D. Thomas, *Britannia* 21 (1990).

Page 137 n. 175. In western provinces the *centurio regionarius* is well attested from the late first century onward: *RIB* 152. 583, 587, *CIL* XIII. 2958, *AE* (1944), 103 (and (1950), 105); cf. I. A. Richmond, *JRS* 35 (1945), 15–29, esp. 20; A. K. Bowman and J. D. Thomas, *Vindolanda, the Latin Writing Tablets* (1983), no. 22, 1.8 and comments on p. 110. According to Richmond such officers were charged with police duties and some administrative tasks in their districts. Richmond thinks these were imperial domain lands, but one could also think of less urbanized districts.

Page 150 n. 238. For the site of Ertaje (Biblada?), Kennedy and Riley, *Rome's Desert Frontier*, 224 f.

Page 140, n. 195. M. P. Speidel, *Epigraphica Anatolica* 10 (1987), 97–100, has discussed inscriptions which show that drafts of several army units were based near Apamea in Phrygia, in the very heart of Roman Asia Minor. There is no obvious reason for their presence there.

Page 152 n. 255. Kennedy and Riley, *Rome's Desert Frontier*, 105 f.

Page 152 n. 255. Ibid., 178 f.

Pages 164–55 n. 16. E. A. Knauf and C. H. Brooker, *ZDPV* 104 (1988), 179–81, discuss R. G. Khouri and D. Whitcomb, *Aqaba*

'*Port of Palestine on the China Sea*' (1988). They argue that the site excavated by Whitcomb represents the fourth-century legionary base. In reply D. Whitcomb, *ZDPV* 106 (1990) [1991], 156–61, states that the site was unoccupied in the pre-Islamic period. The legionary base may have been nearby. Note also H. I. MacAdam, *ZPE* 79 (1989), 163–71.

Page 165 n. 19. I am grateful to Prof. R. Fellmann for the information which he received in a letter from Henri Seyrig. There are no plans and no records. For the location of the camp: J. Starcky, *Palmyre* (1952), Pl. iii, no. 41 = J. Starcky and M. Gawlikowski, Pl. III, no. 32. Inscriptions of the *Ala Vocontiorum* are reported to have been seen there (Starcky, *Palmyre*, 42). There were no constructions of an earlier camp on the spot of the later 'Camp de Diocletien'.

Page 168 n. 22. For the site of Udruh, Kennedy and Riley, *Rome's Desert Frontier*, 131–3.

Page 168 n. 27. Interestingly Malatyah later served as a base for 4,000 Abassid soldiers, J. F. Haldon and H. Kennedy, *ZRVI* 19 (1980), 108. This clearly was a suitable site for a major garrison, no matter whether the army concerned faced eastwards or westwards.

Page 169 n. 32. Further discussion of the reading and interpretation by H. I. MacAdam, *EFRE*, 295–309. MacAdam reads *Dasianis* instead of Speidel's *Basianis* and, in 1.9: *A Basienisa M.P. XXX*.

Page 174 n. 63. For the use of *skenai* as soldiers' housing (not temporary tents) the editor refers to B. Kramer and D. Hagedorn, *Archiv für Papyrusforschung* 33 (1987), 13, note to l. 5, where the essential citations are Preisigke, *Wörterbuch*, s.v. 1; Photius and Hesychius, s.v., Polybius xii 8.4; xxxi 14.2. Prof. James Russell points out to me that it is possible nevertheless that in the present document actual tents are meant.

Page 176 n. 72. For the site of Azraq, Kennedy and Riley, *Rome's Desert Frontier*, 81–4, 108 f., 179–81.

Page 177 n. 78. *SEG* 36 (1986), no. 1277 for an inn, built AD 260, near Edessa on the road to Batnae.

Page 179 n. 97. G. T. Dennis (ed.), *Three Byzantine Military Treatises* (1985), ch. 9, p. 28.

Page 179 n. 98. For the site, Kennedy and Riley, *Rome's Desert Frontier*, 118–21.

Page 184 n. 124. Aerial photographs of one of the towers along the road to Jerusalem show that it has a wall all around, with a sort of *clavicula* in one corner. This is of some interest, for there are no pre-Flavian towers in NW Europe and Flavian towers are much simpler wooden structures: on the Gask ridge in Scotland for which see L. Keppie, *Scotland's Roman Remains* (Edinburgh, 1986), 37, fig. 20, and further references in D. J. Breeze, 'The Frontier in Britain, 1989', in V. A. Maxfield and M. J. Dobson (eds.) *Roman Frontier Studies 1989*, 35–43, esp. 38 and fig. 7.4. Note also those found in the Taunus or Odenwald. Stone towers are of later date: cf. comments by F. Lepper and S. Frere, *Trajan's Column* (Gloucester, 1988), 48, on the towers depicted on the column.

Page 185 n. 125. Kennedy and Riley, *Rome's Desert Frontier*, ch. 11: Towers.

Page 185 n. 126. See, however, the air photograph and discussion, ibid., 218–20.

Page 199 n. 174. R. E. Zitterkopf and S. E. Sidebotham, *JEA* 75 (1989), 155–89, for the Quseir–Nile road; Sidebotham, *et al.*, *JARCE* 26 (1989), 127–66, for excavations on the Red Sea coast.

Page 205 n. 194. For a complete bibliography: M. Staroiewski, 'Bibliographia Egeriana', *Augustinianum* 14 (1979), 297–317.

Page 207 n. 203. See also the air photograph in Kennedy and Riley, *Rome's Desert Frontier*, 196 f.

Page 216 n. 242. But see now P. Crone, *Meccan Trade and the Rise of Islam* (Princeton, 1987).

Page 216 n. 246. For Humayma also Kennedy and Riley, *Rome's Desert Frontier*, 146–8. For Umm el-Jemal: ibid., 183–5.

Page 220 1. 12. 'the Saracen (nomad) allies'. It must be noted that not all Saracen allies were nomads. Part of them were sedentarized Arabs, notably in the sixth century. On p. 240, and elsewhere in Chapter V, I occasionally use the term 'confederates of the Romans'. This is imprecise terminology, since there is no evidence to show that e.g. the Ghassanids were a confederation. 'Allies' is the correct designation, since they are described as *foederati* or *symmachoi* in the Latin and Greek sources.

Page 220 n. 2. Sources in translation: Dodgeon and Lieu, *The Roman Eastern Frontier* ch. 4, 68–110.

Page 221 n. 9. Potter, *Prophecy and History*, 392 f., thinks Odenathus was *corrector* rather than *restitutor*.

Page 225 n. 35. Ibid., App. iv, 381–94, for the career of Odenathus.

Page 226 n. 43. R. Delbrück, *Die Münzbildnisse von Maximinus bis Carinus* (1940), 160 f., observes on the coins of Vaballathus issued by the mint of Antioch: 'For his position between East and West it is characteristic that he wears both the royal diadem and the imperial laurel wreath. His hair is cut short according to Roman custom because he is a child. The coins issued at Alexandria show him wearing his hair long as King of Kings, following the Persian fashion. Later, as Augustus, he has short hair again and a laurel wreath.'

Page 239 n. 114. I. Shahîd, *Byzantium and the Arabs in the Fifth Century* (1989), 543, and photographs on pp. 484 f., reads the crucial designation of the Thamud in the Ruwwafa inscription as *šrbt* (tribe) instead of *šrkt* (confederation).

Page 240 nn. 125–7. Ibid., *passim*.

Page 240 n. 170. On Amorcesos and the Iotabe affair: ibid., ch. iv.

Page 224, n. 149. Ibid. 227–32 for discussion of *IGLS* 297.

Page 244 n. 150. The name of Mavia the Kindite stands for Mu'āwiya, with an *'ayin*, which is a man's name, cf. I. Shahîd, *BZ* 53 (1960), 59.

Page 247 n. 173. For Zokomos, Shahîd, op. cit., *passim*.

Page 248 n. 175. For Byzantium, Persia and Southern Arabia, Z. Rubin, *EFRE*, 383–420.

Page 250 n. 186. For similar conclusions regarding society in the north-western frontier zone, Whittaker, *Les frontières*, 34–42.

Page 252 n. 194. Dennis, *Military Treatises*, ch. 8, p. 26. Cf. P. Pattenden, *Byzantion* 53 (1983), 258–99.

Page 252 n. 196. H. Köchly and W. Rüstow, *Griechische Kriegsschriftsteller* (1853), ch. 9, p. 28.

Page 252 n. 197. Kennedy and Riley, *Rome's Desert Frontier*, 117–19.

Page 252 n. 218. For air photographs, ibid., 168–70, 213–15 (Ain Sinu), and 186–9, 215 (Tell Brak) with discussion.

Page 262 n. 239. Greek physicians are found also at the Achaemenid court: J. M. Cook, *The Persian Empire* (London, 1983), 21.

Page 262 n. 337. For Byzantium, Persia, and Southern Arabia in the reign of Anastasius, Rubin, *EFRE*, 383–420.

Page 278 n. 63. Cf. S. I. Oost, *Classical Philology* 56 (1961), 1–20. For army activity in Alexandria: O. W. Rheinmuth, *The Prefect of Egypt from Augustus to Diocletian* (1935).

Page 291 n. 148. Cf. Davies, 'The Supply of Animals to the Roman Army and the Remount System', *Service in the Roman Army* (1989), 153–73.

Page 294 n. 159. One of the parallel sources referring to the same period again mentions Jewish girls and nomad (Arab) horsemen on the road between Jerusalem and Lydda: Lamentations Rabbah i 48.

Page 301 n. 208. L. Neesen, *Untersuchungen zu den direkten Staatsabgaben der römischen Kaiserzeit* (1980), 142–5.

Page 303 n. 216. On recruitment in general, Davies, *Service in the Roman Army*, 3–30.

Page 318 n. 32. L. Okamura, *Historia* 37 (1988), 126–8; F. Millar in H. Solin and M. Kajava (eds.), *Roman Eastern Policy and Other Studies in Roman History* (1990), 7–23.

Page 321. A pay record from Masada (AD 72 or 75) mentions a legionary with an Italian name from Berytus: C. Messius, C. f(ilius) Fab(ia) Beru(tensis): H. M. Cotton and J. Geiger (eds.), *Masada, II* (1989), no. 722. 35 ff.; comments, 49 ff. In all likelihood this was a soldier of the *Legio X Fretensis*. For other recruits from Berytus, p. 50, n. 68.

Page 324 n. 77. Note, however, V. Kuzsinsky, *Aquincum* (1934), 176: 'D.M. Ael Silvano (centurioni) Leg II Adi domo Syria Pal Coloniae Capitolina(e).'

Page 326 n. 92. For additional evidence note the decree for volunteers from Thespiae who joined an expedition against the Costoboci in 170–1: A. Plassart, *Mélanges Glotz*, ii (1934), 731–8; *Nouveau choix d'inscriptions grecques*, l'Institut Fernand-Courby (Paris, 1971), no. 15. 85–94. The term *'neoi'* used there represents Latin *'iuvenes'*. This was an emergency and the participants were joining the army only for this campaign.

Page 334 n. 6. Similarly: Sartre *L'Orient romain*, 77 f.

Page 356 n. 136. For similar views and arguments, A. Adams in S. Walker and Averil Cameron (eds.), *The Greek Renaissance in the Roman Empire* (1989), 10–15, referring to an unpublished lecture by C. P. Jones.

Page 363 n. 189. A. Bianchi, *Aegyptus* 63 (1983), 185–98.

Page 380 n. 19. On campaign preparations in Late Roman–Persian warfare, A. D. Lee, *EFRE*, 257–65.

Page 384 n. 48. W. E. Kaegi, *Byzantine Military Unrest 471–843* (1981), observes that there was a measure of internal military stability in the east in the fourth and fifth centuries, followed by serious unrest in every reign and almost every decade between 471 and 842. Yet this does not mean that there was any form of army influence on politics in the modern sense.

Page 393 n. 98. Whittaker, *Les frontières*, 83–8, cites numerous examples to show that traditional attitudes towards foreign peoples and the Empire did not change in the later Roman Empire. At no time were the losses of the Empire in the third century and afterwards recognized and accepted officially. As argued by Whittaker, this was not bluff. The emperors believed in their propaganda.

Pages 394–401. Whittaker, *Les frontières*, 32 f., argues that the ancient frontiers were zones, not lines and cites Lucien Febvre who pointed out that 'fins, confins, limites' and 'frontières' were never considered to be identical before the nineteenth century: L. Febvre, *La terre et l'évolution humaine* (repr. Paris, 1970), 331; 'Frontière', *Rev. Synth. Hist.* 45 (1928), 31–44, esp. 32, which I have not seen.

Page 394 n. 106. The origin of the curious term 'scientific frontier' has been explained by C. R. Whittaker, 'Thorns in Rome's Side', *TLS* 22 Mar. 1991, 23. It 'was almost certainly coined by Lord Roberts during the Second Afghan War of 1890 to describe the untenable line he attempted to establish between Kabul and Kandahar'. See also Surendra Gopal, *TLS* 3 May 1991, with a correction of the date of the Second Afghan War, which lasted from 1878 till 1881. What Lord Roberts attempted to do in fact was apparently as impracticable as the military policies foisted on the Romans by modern scholars.

Pages 398 f. Whittaker, *Les frontières*, 49 f., cites additional examples of Roman military activity beyond the borders of the provinces.

Page 399 n. 140. *AE* (1974), 248 from Budapest records a *praepositus gentis Onsorum*. The Osii lived north of the Danube, cf. Whittaker, *Les frontières*, 36 f. Military supplies were regularly collected beyond the borders of the provinces: ibid. 65–8.

Page 402 n. 153. Syme, *Classical Antiquity* 7. 227–51, admits that the literary sources do not furnish direct evidence of a sound understanding of military geography, but argues that the wars in the reign of Augustus show a grasp of strategy in our sense of the term. As emphasized by R. J. A. Talbert, however, a comprehensive study of ancient cartography strengthens the impression that the majority of Greeks and Romans had only the most limited use for maps (*JRS* 78 (1987), 210–12; *Gouvernants et gouvernés dans l'Imperium Romanum* (1990), 215–23). Talbert, ibid. 217, observes that the ancient world seems to have relied on geographical descriptions rather than graphical representation. He notes another important phenomenon: the chronic underestimation of distances. This had obvious consequences for military planners.

Page 405 n. 154. See now the survey of ancient cartography by A. O. W. Dilke, 'The Culmination of Greek Cartography in Ptolemy', in J. B. Harley and D. Woodward (eds.), *The History of Cartography*, i (1987), 177–200; 'Maps in the Service of the State: Roman Cartography to the End of the Augustan Era', ibid. 201–11; 'Itineraries and Geographical Maps in the Early and Late Roman Empires', ibid. 234–57; and 'Cartography in the Byzantine Empire', ibid. 258–75. Dilke argues that the value of maps to the Roman state and its generals was widely accepted. However, he also concludes (p. 242) that the 'geographical manuscripts of Roman origin are of less cartographic interest than their Greek counterparts. Whatever the reason for this, no continuous tradition of writing in Latin about these subjects took root. It is often difficult to say if a Roman author composed with a map in front of him or indeed whether a map was drawn at all to illustrate a particular text.' Note also the definition proposed by Harley and Woodward, ibid. p. xvi: 'Maps are graphic representations that facilitate a spatial understanding of things, concepts, conditions, processes, or events in the human world.' If the graphic representations were lacking or deficient in the Roman world, how far went Roman spatial understanding? Finally, we may note the advice offered by the sixth century 'Anonymous Treatise on Strategy, 20', in Dennis, *Thee Byzantine Military Treatises*, 70 (trans. p. 71): When troops march into hostile territory or are getting close to the enemy, it is 'a good plan . . . to make sketches of the more dangerous places, and more so of locations suitable for an ambush, so that if we have occasion to pass that way again, we may be on our guard'. Cf. Vegetius' advice to use *itineraria picta*. It is perfectly clear from this statement that the Byzantine commander is not expected to have any proper maps at his disposal. The Treatise merely offers sound advice, which is proof that there was no standing order to keep a good record of any kind of an expedition into enemy territory.

Page 406 n. 173. See now Matthews, *Roman Empire*, ch. viii.

Page 406 n. 174. W. E. Kaegi, *Klio* 73 (1991), 586–94.

Page 408 n. 184. Here and in *JRS* 78 (1988), 125, reference ought to have been made to Delbrück, *Geschichte der Kriegskunst*, ii. 131–3, 164–6. Delbrück correctly interprets all the references to *limites* in passages on the Germanic campaigns of the first century as describing road construction into enemy territory rather than the erection of defence works.

Page 410–13. Similar arguments regarding natural barriers: Whittaker, *Les frontières*, 23–6.

Page 411 n. 194. The sixth century 'Anonymous Treatise on Strategy', 20, has a chapter on crossing rivers which contains a critical discussion of a raft designed by Apollodorus of Damascus (Dennis, *Three Byzantine Military Treatises*, 70.)

Page 430 n. 31. In a document of April 128 the *praisidion* and soldiers' housing are no longer there, so the unit was apparently withdrawn between 124 and 128: Lewis, *The Documents from the Bar-Kokhba Period*, no. 19, deed of gift (16 April 128), pp. 83–7; see also no. 20 of 130.

Page 432 n. 49. R. A. Gergel, *AJA* 95 (1991), 231–51.

BIBLIOGRAPHY

BOOKS AND MONOGRAPHS

ABBOTT, F. F., and JOHNSON, A. C., *Municipal Administration in the Roman Empire* (Princeton, 1926).

ABEL, F.-M., *Géographie de la Palestine*, 2 vols. (Paris, ³1967).

—— *Histoire de la Palestine depuis la conquête d'Alexandre le Grand jusqu'à l'invasion arabe*, 2 vols. (Paris, 1952).

ADAMS, R. McC., *Land Behind Baghdad: A History of Settlement on the Diyala Plains* (Chicago, 1965).

ADONTZ, N., *Armenia in the Period of Justinian* (trans. N. G. Garsoïan, Lisbon, 1970).

AHARONI, Y., *Excavations at Ramat Rahel: Seasons 1961 and 1962* (Rome, 1964).

—— *Excavations at Ramat Rahel: Seasons 1959 and 1960* (Rome, 1962).

ALFÖLDI, A., *Studien zur Geschichte der Weltkrise des 3. Jahrhunderts nach Christus* (Darmstadt, 1967).

ALFÖLDY, G., *Römische Heeresgeschichte: Beiträge 1962–1985* (Amsterdam, 1987).

—— *Noricum* (London, 1974).

ALLEN, W. E. D., *A History of the Georgian People from the Beginning Down to the Russian Conquest in the Nineteenth Century* (London, 1932).

—— and MURATOFF, P., *Caucasian Battlefields: A History of the Wars on the Turco-Caucasian Border* (Cambridge, 1953).

ALON, G., *The Jews in their Land in the Talmudic Age (70–640 CE)*, trans. and ed. G. Levi, 2 vols. (Jerusalem, 1980–84).

—— *Jews, Judaism and the Classical World: Studies in Jewish History in the Times of the Second Temple and Talmud* (Jerusalem, 1977).

ALT, A., *Die griechischen Inschriften der Palästina Tertia westlich der 'Araba* (Berlin and Leipzig, 1921).

ANDRAE, W., *Hatra, nach Aufnahmen von Mitgliedern der Assur-Expedition der Deutschen Orient-Gesellschaft* i, WVDOG 9 (Leipzig, 1908), ii WVDOG 21 (Leipzig, 1912).

APPLEBAUM, S., *Jews and Greeks in Ancient Cyrene* (Leiden, 1979).

—— *Prolegomena to the Study of the Second Jewish Revolt (AD 132–135)* (BAR Supplementary Series 7, Oxford, 1976).

—— (ed.), *Roman Frontier Studies, 1967* (Tel Aviv, 1971).

—— and GICHON, M., *Israel and Her Vicinity in the Roman and Byzantine Periods. The Seventh International Congress of Roman Frontier Studies, Notes Offered to Delegates* (Tel Aviv, 1967).

ASAD, T., *The Kababish Arabs: Power, Authority and Consent in a Nomadic Tribe* (London, 1970).

452 Bibliography

Ashkenazi, T., *Tribus semi-nomades de la Palestine du Nord* (Paris, 1938).

Avigad, N., *Discovering Jerusalem* (Jerusalem, 1983).

Avi-Yonah, M., *The Madaba Mosaic Map* (Jerusalem, 1954).

—— *Geschichte der Juden im Zeitalter des Talmud: In den Tagen von Rom und Byzanz* (Berlin, 1962).

—— *The Jews of Palestine* (Oxford, 1976, trans. of the previous title).

—— *Gazetteer of Roman Palestine* (Jerusalem, 1976).

—— *The Holy Land from the Persian to the Arab Conquest (536 BC–AD 640): A Historical Geography* (revised edn., Grand Rapids, Mi., 1977).

—— and Stern, E. (eds.), *Encyclopedia of Archaeological Excavations in the Holy Land*, 4 vols. (Jerusalem, 1975–8).

Baatz, D., *Der römische Limes: Archäologische Ausflüge zwischen Rhein und Donau* (Berlin, 1974).

Bagnall, R. S., *The Florida Ostraka: Documents from the Roman Army in Upper Egypt* (Durham, NC, 1976).

——, Sijpestijn, P. J., and Worp, K. A., *Ostraka in Amsterdam Collections* (Studia Amstelodamensia ix, Zutphen, 1976).

Baldus, H. R., *MON(eta) URB(is)–ANTIOXIA: Rom und Antiochia als Prägestatten syrischer Tetradrachmen* (Frankfurt, 1969).

—— *Uranius Antoninus: Münzprägung und Geschichte* (Bonn, 1971).

Balty, J. (ed.), *Apamée de Syrie: Bilan de recherches archéologiques, 1965–68* (Brussels, 1969).

—— and J. C. (eds.), *Apamée de Syrie: Bilan de recherches archéologiques, 1969–71* (Brussels, 1972).

Balty, J. C. and J. (eds.), *Actes du colloque Apamée de Syrie 1969–71* (1972).

Bandy, A. C., *Ioannes Lydus on Powers* (Philadelphia, 1983).

Barnes, T. D., *The New Empire of Diocletian and Constantine* (Cambridge, Mass., 1982).

—— *Constantine and Eusebius* (Cambridge, Mass., 1981).

Baur, P. V. C., and Rostovtzeff, M. I. (eds.), *the Excavations at Dura-Europos: Preliminary Report of Second Season of Work, October 1928–April 1929* (New Haven, Conn., 1931).

Bayer, E., *Grundzüge der griechischen Geschichte* (Darmstadt, 1964).

Beck, W., and Planck, D., *Der Limes in Südwestdeutschland* (Stuttgart, 1980).

Bell, H. I., Martin, V., Turner, E. G., and van Berchem, D., *The Abinnaeus Archive: Papers of a Roman Officer in the Reign of Constantius II* (Oxford, 1962).

Bellinger, A. R., *The Syrian Tetradrachms of Caracalla and Macrinus*, Numismatic Studies No. 3 of the American Numismatic Society (1940).

Ben Dov, M., *In the Shadow of the Temple* (Jerusalem, 1985).

Benvenisti, M., *The Crusaders in the Holy Land* (Jerusalem, 1970).

Berchem, D. van, *L'armée de Dioclétien et la réforme constantinienne* (Paris, 1952).

—— *Les routes et l'histoire*, ed. P. Ducrey and D. Paunier (Geneva, 1982).

Bernand, A., *De Koptos à Kosseir* (Leiden, 1972).

—— *Les portes du Désert: Recueil d'inscriptions grecques d'Antinoupolis, Tentyris, Koptos, Apollonopolis Parva et Apollonopolis Magna* (Paris, 1984).

BIRLEY, A., *Marcus Aurelius* (London, 1966).

BIRLEY, E., *Roman Britain and the Roman Army: Collected Papers* (Kendal, 1976).

—— (ed.), Congress of Roman Frontier Studies, 1949 (Durham, 1952).

BLOEMERS, J. H. F., *Rijswijk (Z.H.), 'De Bult': Eine Siedlung der Cananefaten*, 3 vols. (Amersfoort, 1978).

BOGAERS, J. E., and RÜGER, C. B., *Der niedergermanische Limes: Materialen zu seiner Geschichte* (Cologne, 1974).

BOWERSOCK, G. W., *Augustus and the Greek World* (Oxford, 1965).

—— *Roman Arabia* (Cambridge, Mass., 1983).

BRADSHER, H. S., *Afghanistan and the Soviet Union* (Durham, NC, 1983).

BRAUND, D., *Rome and the Friendly King: The Character of the Client Kingship* (London and New York, 1984).

BREEZE, D. J., and DOBSON, B., *Hadrian's Wall* (revised edn., Penguin, 1978).

BRÜNNOW, R. E., and DOMASZEWSKI, A. VON, *Die Provincia Arabia*, 3 vols. (Strasbourg, 1904–9).

BRYER, A., and WINFIELD, D., *The Byzantine Monuments and Topography of the Pontos*, i (Washington, DC, 1985).

BURCKHARDT, J. L., *Notes on the Bedouins and Wahabys*, 2 vols. (London, 1831, repr. 1967).

BURNEY, C., and LANG, D. M., *The Peoples of the Hills: Ancient Ararat and Caucasus* (London, 1971).

BURY, J. B., *History of the Later Roman Empire from the Death of Theodosius I to the Death of Justinian*, 2 vols. (repr. New York, 1958).

BUSCHHAUSEN, H. (ed.), *Byzantinische Mosaiken aus Jordanien: Katalog des Nö. Landesmuseums, Neue Folge, Nr. 178* (Vienna, 1986).

BUTLER, H. C., *Architecture and Other Arts* (New York, 1903).

—— et al., *The Publications of the Princeton University Archaeological Expeditions to Syria in 1904–5 and 1909*, 4 parts (Leiden, 1910–43).

CAGNAT, R., *L'armée romaine d'Afrique et l'occupation militaire d'Afrique sous les empereurs* (Paris, 1913).

Cambridge History of Iran: see Yarshater, E.

CAMERON, AVERIL, *Procopius* (London, 1985).

CAMERON, G. G., *History of Early Iran* (Chicago, 1936).

CAMPBELL, J. B., *The Emperor and the Roman Army* (Oxford, 1984).

CANTINEAU, J., STARCKY, J., and TEIXIDOR, J., *Inventaire des inscriptions de Palmyre*, 11 vols. (Beirut, 1930–65).

CASSON, L., and HETTICH, E. L., *Excavations at Nessana*, ii, *Literary Papyri* (Princeton, 1950).

CHAMPLIN, E., *Fronto and Antonine Rome* (Cambridge, Mass., 1980).

CHAPOT, V., *La Frontière de l'Euphrate de Pompée à la conquête arabe* (Paris, 1907, repr. Rome, 1967).

CHARLES, P. H., *Le Christianisme des Arabes nomades sur le limes et dans le désert Syro-Mésopotamien aux alentours de l'Hégire* (Paris, 1936).

CHARLESWORTH, M. P., *Trade Routes and the Commerce of the Roman Empire* (Cambridge, ²1926).

CHAUMONT, M.-L., *Recherches sur l'Histoire d'Arménie* (Paris, 1969).

CHEESMAN, G. L., *The Auxilia of the Roman Imperial Army* (Oxford, 1914, repr. Hildesheim).

CHEVALLIER, R., *Roman Roads* (London, 1976).

CHRISTENSEN, A., *L'Iran sous les Sassanides* (Copenhagen, ²1944).

CLERMONT-GANNEAU, C., *Archaeological Researches in Palestine*, 2 vols. (London, 1896–9).

——*Études d'archéologie orientale*, 2 vols. (1895–7).

——*Recueil d'archéologie orientale*, 8 vols. (Paris, 1888–1924).

COHEN, H., *Médailles impériales* (second edn., Leipzig, 1930).

COLLINGWOOD, R. S., and WRIGHT, R. P., *The Roman Inscriptions of Britain*, i, *Inscriptions on Stone* (Oxford, 1965).

COLT, H. D. (ed.), *Excavations at Nessana*, i (Princeton, 1962).

COMBEFIS, F., *Illustrium Christi Martyrum Lecti Triumphi* (Paris, 1660: sole existing edn. of the *Ammonii Monachi Relatio*).

COUPEL, P., and FRÉZOULS, E., *Le théâtre de Philippopolis en Arabie* (Paris, 1956).

CRAWFORD, M. H. (ed.), *Sources for Ancient History* (Cambridge, 1983).

CROOK, J., *Consilium Principis: Imperial Councils and Counsellors from Augustus to Diocletian* (Cambridge, 1955).

CROWFOOT, J. W., KENYON, K., and SUKENIK, E. L., *The Buildings at Samaria* (London, 1966).

——CROWFOOT, G. M., and KENYON, K., *The Objects from Samaria* (London, 1957).

CUMONT, F., *Fouilles de Doura Europos, 1922–1923* (Paris, 1926).

CUNTZ, O. (ed.), *Itineraria Romana* (Leipzig, 1929).

DAN, Y., *The City in Eretz-Israel During the Late Roman and Byzantine Periods* (Jerusalem, 1984, in Hebrew).

DAR, S., *Landscape and Pattern: An Archaeological Survey of Samaria, 800 BC–636 CE*, 2 vols. (BAR International Series 308, Oxford, 1986).

DASKHURANTSI, MOVSES., *The History of the Caucasian Albanians* (trans. C. J. F. Dowsett, Oxford, 1961).

DE LAET, S. J., *Portorium* (Brugge, 1949).

DE VAUX, R., and STÈVE, A. M., *Fouilles à Qaryet el-'Enab Abu Gôsh* (Paris, 1950).

De Rebus Bellicis, Part i, *Aspects of* De Rebus Bellicis*: Papers presented to Professor E. A. Thompson*, ed. M. W. C. Hassall; Part 2, *de rebus bellicis*: the text, ed. R. Ireland (BAR, International Series 63, Oxford, 1979).

DEBEVOISE, N. C., *A Political History of Parthia* (Chicago, 1938).

DEMOUGEOT, E., *De l'unité à la division de l'empire romain 395–410* (Paris, 1951).

DENNIS, G. (trans.), *Maurice's Strategikon* (Philadelphia, 1984).

——(ed.) and GAMILLSCHEG, E. (trans.), *Das Strategikon des Maurikios*, Corpus Fontium Historiae Byzantinae 17 (1981).

DENTZER, J.-M., *Hauran I: Recherches archéologiques sur la Syrie du sud à l'époque hellénistique et romaine*, 2 vols. (Paris 1985).

DILKE, O. A. W., *The Roman Land Surveyors: An Introduction to the Agrimensores* (Newton Abbot, 1971).

—— *Greek and Roman Maps* (London, 1985).

DILLEMANN, L., *Haute Mésopotamie orientale et pays adjacents: Contribution à la géographie historique de la région, du Ve siècle avant l'ère chrétienne au VIe siècle de cette ère* (Paris, 1962).

DOERNER, F. K., and NAUMANN, R., *Forschungen in Kommagene* (Berlin, 1939).

DONNER, F. McGRAW., *The Early Islamic Conquests* (Princeton, 1981).

DOUGHTY, C. M., *Travels in Arabia Deserta*, 2 vols. (third edn., London, 1936).

DOWNEY, G., *A History of Antioch in Syria from Seleucus to the Arab Conquest* (Princeton, NJ, 1961).

DUBOIS DE MONTPÉREUX, F., *Voyage autour de Caucase*, 4 vols. and atlas (Paris, 1839–40).

DUCREY, P., et al., *Mélanges d'histoire et d'archéologie offerts à Paul Collart* (Lausanne, 1976).

DUNAND, M., *Mission archéologique au Djebel Druse: Le musée de Soueida, Inscriptions et monuments figurés* (Paris, 1934).

DUNANT, C., *Le sanctuaire de Baalshamin à Palmyre*, iii, *Les inscriptions* (Institut Suisse de Rome, 1971).

DUSSAUD, R., *La pénétration des Arabes en Syrie avant l'Islam* (Paris, 1955).

—— *Topographie de la Syrie antique et médiévale* (Paris, 1927).

DYSON, S. L., *The Creation of the Roman Frontier* (Princeton, 1985).

EADIE, J., *The Breviarium of Festus* (London, 1967).

ECK, W., and WOLFF, H. (eds.), *Heer und Integrationspolitik: Die römischen Militärdiplome als historische Quelle* (Cologne, 1986).

EDDY, S. K., *The King is Dead: Studies in Near Eastern Resistance to Hellenism, 334–31 BC* (Lincoln, Nebraska, 1961).

ENSSLIN, W., *Zur Ostpolitik des Kaisers Diokletian* (Munich, 1942).

EUTING, J., *Sinaïtische Inschriften* (Berlin, 1891).

EVENARI, M., et al., *The Negev: Challenge of a Desert* (second edn., Cambridge, Mass., 1982).

FENTRESS, E., *Numidia and the Roman Army* (BAR International Series 53, Oxford, 1979).

FÉVRIER, J. G., *Essai sur l'histoire politique et économique de Palmyre* (Paris, 1931).

FIEY, J. M., *Nisibe, métropole syriaque orientale et ses suffragants des origines à nos jours* (CSCO vol. 54, Louvain, 1977).

FINLEY, M. I., *The Ancient Economy* (London, 1973).

FORSYTH, G. H., and WEITZMANN, K., *The Monastery of Saint Catherine at Mount Sinai: The Church and Fortress of Justinian* (Ann Arbor, 1973).

FRANK, T., *Roman Imperialism* (New York, 1929).

FRASER-TYTLER, W. K., *Afghanistan: A Study of Political Developments in Central and Southern Asia*, third edn., revised by M. C. Gillett (London, 1967).

FREEMAN, P., and KENNEDY, D., *The Defence of the Roman and Byzantine East: Proceedings of a Colloquium Held at the University of Sheffield in April 1986*, 2 vols. (BAR International Series 297, Oxford, 1986).

FRENCH, D. H., *Roman Roads and Milestones in Asia Minor*, Fasc. 1, *The Pilgrim's Road* (BAR International Series 105, Oxford, 1981).

FRERE, S., *Britannia: a History of Roman Britain* (London, ²1978).

FREY, J.-B., *Corpus Inscriptionum Iudaicarum: Recueil des inscriptions juives qui vont du IIIᵉ siècle avant Jésus-Christ au VIIᵉ siècle de notre ère*, 2 vols. (Rome, 1936–52).

FRYE, R. N., *The History of Ancient Iran* (Handbuch der Altertumswissenschaft: Abt. 3, Teil 7, Munich, 1984).

FUKS, G., *Scythopolis: A Greek City in Eretz-Israel* (Jerusalem, 1983, in Hebrew).

GABBA, E., *Iscrizioni greche e latine per lo studio della bibbia* (Milano, 1958).

GALBRAITH, J. S., *Reluctant Empire: British Policy on the South African Frontier 1834–1854* (Berkeley and Los Angeles, 1963).

GAUBE, H., *Ein Arabischer Palast in Südsyrien: Hirbet al Baida* (Beirut, 1974).

GAWLIKOWSKI, M., *Le temple palmyrénien: Étude d'épigraphie et de topographie historique* (Warsaw, 1973).

—— *Les principia de Dioclétien: Temple des Enseignes, Palmyre* viii (Warsaw, 1984).

GÉNIER, F., *Vie de Saint Euthyme le Grand (377–473): Les moines et l'église en Palestine au Vᵉ siècle* (Paris, 1909).

Geographical Handbook Series, *A Handbook of Mesopotamia*, 2 vols. (London, 1916–17).

—— *A Handbook of Syria (including Palestine)* (1920).

—— *A Handbook of Iraq and the Persian Gulf* (London, 1944).

—— *Western Arabia and the Red Sea* (²1946).

GERSTER, G., *Sinai, Land der Offenbarung* (1970).

GILLIAM, J. F., *Roman Army Papers* (Amsterdam, 1986).

GLUCKER, C. A. M., *The City of Gaza in the Roman and Byzantine Periods* (BAR International Series 325, Oxford, 1987).

GOODMAN, M., *The Ruling Class of Judaea: The Origins of the Jewish Revolt Against Rome AD 66–70* (Cambridge, 1987).

GORDON, A. E., *Quintus Veranius, Consul AD 49* (Univ. of California Publ. in Classical Archaeology ii, 5 Berkeley, 1952).

—— *Illustrated Introduction to Latin Epigraphy* (Berkeley and Los Angeles, 1983).

GORDON, CYRUS H., *The Bible World: Essays in Honor of . . .*, ed. G. Rendsburg et al. (New York, 1980).

GRAINDOR, P., *Athènes sous Hadrien* (Cairo, 1934).

GREGORY, S., and KENNEDY, D., *Sir Aurel Stein's Limes Report*, 2 vols. (BAR International Series 272, Oxford, 1985).

GRIFFIN, M., *Nero: The End of a Dynasty* (London, 1984).

GROUSSET, R., *Histoire de l'Arménie des origines à 1071* (Paris, 1947).

GRUNDY, G. B., *Thucydides and the History of his Age* (second edn., Oxford, 1948).

GRUNEBAUM, G. D. VON (ed.), *Studies in Islamic Cultural History*, Memoirs of the American Anthropological Association 76 (1954).

GUNNEWEG, J., PERLMAN, I., and YELLIN, J., *The Provenance, Typology and Chronology of Eastern Sigillata* (Jerusalem, 1983).

GUTSCHMID, A. VON, *Geschichte Irans und seiner Nachbarländer von Alexander dem Grossen bis zum Untergang der Arsaciden* (Tübingen, 1888).

GUTWEIN, K., *Third Palestine: A Regional Study in Byzantine Urbanization* (Washington, 1981).

HAALEBOS, J. K., *Zwammerdam—Nigrum Pullum* (Amsterdam, 1977).

HADIDI, A. (ed.), *Studies in the History and Archaeology of Jordan*, 3 vols. (Amman and London, 1982–7).

HALDON, J., *Recruitment and Conscription in the Byzantine Army c. 550–950: A Study of the Stratiotika Ktemata*, Oesterreichische Akademie der Wissenschaften, Phil.-Hist. Klasse, Sitzungsber., 357. Band (Vienna, 1979).

HANSON, W. S., and KEPPIE, L. J. F., (eds.), *Roman Frontier Studies 1979: Papers presented to the 12th International Congress of Roman Frontier Studies*, 3 vols. (BAR International Series 71, Oxford, 1980).

HARL, K. W., *Civic Coins and Civic Politics in the Roman East, AD 180–275* (Berkeley and Los Angeles, 1987).

HARMAND, L., *Libanius, Discours sur les patronages* (Paris, 1955).

HARRIS, G. L., *Jordan: Its People, Its Society, Its Culture* (New Haven, 1958).

HARRIS, W. V., *War and Imperialism in Republican Rome, 327–70 BC* (Oxford, 1979).

HARRISON, R. M., *Excavations at Saraçhane in Istanbul*, i (Princeton, 1986).

HASEBROEK, J., *Untersuchungen zur Geschichte des Kaisers Septimius Severus* (Heidelberg, 1921, repr. 1975).

HAUPT, D., and HORN, H. G. (eds.), *Studien zu den Militärgrenzen Roms*, ii, *Vorträge des 10. internationalen Limeskongresses in der Germania Inferior* (Cologne and Bonn, 1977).

HENDERSON, B. W., *The Life and Principate of the Emperor Nero* (London 1905, repr. Rome, 1968).

HENGEL, M., *Die Zeloten* (Leiden–Cologne, 1961).

HEYD, U., *Ottoman Documents on Palestine 1552–1615* (Oxford, 1960).

HILL, G. F., *Catalogue of the Greek Coins in the British Museum: Palestine* (1914, repr. Bologna, 1965).

—— *Catalogue of the Greek Coins in the British Museum: Phoenicia* (1910, repr. Bologna, 1965).

—— *Catalogue of the Greek Coins in the British Museum: Arabia, Mesopotamia, and Persia* (1922, repr. Bologna, 1965).

HOBSBAWM, E. J., *Primitive Rebels: Studies in Archaic Forms of Social Movement in the 19th and 20th Centuries* (Manchester, 1959).

—— *Bandits* (Penguin, [2]1985).

HOFFMANN, D., *Das spätrömische Bewegungsheer und die Notitia Dignitatum*, 2 vols. (Düsseldorf, 1969).

HONIGMANN, E., and MARICQ, A., *Recherches sur les Res Gestae Divi Saporis* (Brussels, 1952).

HOPKINS, C., *The Discovery of Dura-Europos* (New Haven, 1979).

HOWGEGO, C. J., *Greek Imperial Countermarks: Studies in the Provincial Coinage of the Roman East* (London, 1985).

HUNT, E. D., *Holy Land Pilgrimage in the Later Roman Empire AD 312–460* (Oxford, 1982).

HÜTTEROTH, W.-D., and ABDULFATH, K., *Historical Geography of Palestine, Transjordan and Southern Syria in the Late Sixteenth Century* (Erlangen, 1977).

ISAAC, B., and ROLL, I., *Roman Roads in Judaea*, i, *The Legio–Scythopolis Road* (BAR International Series 141, Oxford, 1982).

JARDÉ, A., *Études critiques sur la vie et le regne de Sévère Alexandre* (Paris, 1925).

JAUSSEN, A., *Coutumes des Arabes au Pays de Moab* (Paris, 1948).

JONES, A. H. M., *The Greek City from Alexander to Justinian* (Oxford, 1940).

—— *The Cities of the Eastern Roman Provinces* (Oxford, ²1971).

—— *The Later Roman Empire: A Social, Economic and Administrative Survey*, 2 vols. (Oxford, 1964, repr. 1973).

JONES, J. F., *Researches in the Vicinity of the Median Wall*, Selections Records Bombay Government, NS 43 (1857).

JULLIAN, C., *Histoire de la Gaule* (Paris, 1908–26).

KADMAN, L., *The Coins of Caesarea Maritima* (Corpus Nummorum Palestinensium, Jerusalem, 1957).

—— *The Coins of Aelia Capitolina* (Corpus Nummorum Palestinensium, 1956).

—— *The Coins of Acco-Ptolemais* (Corpus Nummorum Palestinensium, 1961).

KARNAPP, W., *Die Stadtmauer von Resafa in Syrien* (Berlin, 1976).

KEEGAN, J., *The Face of Battle: A Study of Agincourt, Waterloo, and the Somme* (London, 1976; Penguin, 1978).

KENNEDY, D. L., *Archaeological Explorations on the Roman Frontier in North-East Jordan: The Roman and Byzantine Military Installations and Road Network on the Ground and from the Air* (BAR International Series 134, Oxford, 1982).

—— and RILEY, D. N., *Rome's Desert Frontier From the Air* (London, 1990).

KEPPIE, L., *Colonisation and Veteran Settlement in Italy, 47–14 BC* (London, 1983).

—— *The Making of the Roman Army from Republic to Empire* (London, 1983).

KETTENHOFEN, E., *Die römisch–persischen Kriege des 3. Jahrhunderts n. Chr.* (Wiesbaden, 1982).

KIENAST, D., *Untersuchungen zu den Kriegsflotten der römischen Kaiserzeit* (Bonn, 1966).

KINDLER, A., *The Coins of Tiberias* (Tiberias, 1961).

—— *The Coinage of Bostra* (Warminster, Wilts., 1983).

KINDLER, A., and STEIN, A., *A Bibliography of the City Coinage of Palestine, From the 2nd Century BC to the 3rd Century AD* (BAR International Series 374, Oxford, 1987).

KLEBERG, T., *Hôtels, restaurants et cabarets dans l'antiquité romaine* (Uppsala, 1957).

KLEIN, R. (ed.), *Marc Aurel* (Darmstadt, 1979).

KLEIN, S., *Sefer Hayishuv*, i (Jerusalem, 1977).

KLONER, A., and TEPPER, Y., *The Hiding Complexes in the Judean Shephelah* (Tel-Aviv, 1987, in Hebrew).

KLOSTERMANN, E. (ed.), *Eusebius: Das Onomastikon der biblischen Ortsnamen* (Leipzig, 1904, repr. Hildesheim, 1966).

KNAUF, E. A., *Ismael: Untersuchungen zur Geschichte Palästinas und Nordarabiens im 1. Jahrtausend v. Chr.* (Wiesbaden, 1985).

KÖCHLY, H., and RÜSTOW, W., *Griechische Kriegsschriftsteller* (Leipzig, 1853).

KOKHAVI, M. (ed.), *Judaea, Samaria and the Golan: Archaeological Survey 1967–1968* (Jerusalem, 1972, in Hebrew).

KRAELING, C., *Gerasa: City of the Decapolis* (New Haven, 1938).

KRAEMER, C., *Excavations at Nessana, iii Non-Literary Papyri* (Princeton, 1958).

KRAFT, K., *Zur Rekrutierung der Alen und Cohorten an Rhein und Donau* (Berne, 1951).

KUHNEN, H.-P., *Nordwest-Palästina in hellenistisch-römischer Zeit: Bauten und Gräber im Karmelgebiet* (Weinheim, 1987).

KUHRT, A., and SHERWIN-WHITE, S. (eds.), *Hellenism in the East: The Interaction of Greek and non-Greek civilizations from Syria to Central Asia after Alexander* (London, 1987).

KURZWEIL, B. (ed.), *Yuval Shay: A Jubilee Volume, dedicated to S. Y. Agnon* (Ramat Gan, 1958, in Hebrew).

LABOURT, J., *Le Christianisme dans l'empire Perse sous la dynastie Sassanide* (Paris, 1904).

LANDER, J., *Roman Stone Fortifications: Variation and Change from the First Century AD to the Fourth* (BAR International Series 206, Oxford, 1984).

LANG, D. M., *The Georgians* (London–New York, 1966).

LAUFFRAY, J., *Halabiyya-Zenobia: Place forte du limes oriental et la Haute-Mésopotamie au vi^e siècle, i, Les Duchés frontaliers de Mésopotamie et les fortifications de Zenobia* (Paris, 1983).

LAUTERBACH, J. Z., *Mekilta de-Rabbi Ishmael* (Philadelphia, 1933–5).

LE BAS, P., and WADDINGTON, H., *Inscriptions grecques et latines recueillies en Grèce et en Asie Mineure, iii* (Paris, 1870).

LEPPER, F. A., *Trajan's Parthian War* (Oxford, 1948).

LEVI, A. and M., *Itineraria Picta: Contributo alla studio della Tabula Peutingeriana* (Rome, 1967).

LEVICK, B. M., *Roman Colonies in Southern Asia Minor* (Oxford, 1967).

LEWIS, A. SMITH, *The Forty Martyrs of The Sinai Desert and the Story of Eulogios: From a Palestinian Syriac and Arabic Palimpsest* (Cambridge, 1912).

LEWIS, B., *History, Remembered, Recovered, Invented* (Princeton, 1975).

LEWIS, N. N., *Nomads and Settlers in Syria and Jordan 1800–1980* (Cambridge, 1987).

LEWIS, N., *Inventory of Compulsory Services* (American studies in Papyrology 3, Toronto, 1968).

LIDDELL HART, B. H., *T. E. Lawrence: In Arabia and After* (London, 1934, repr. 1965).

——*Strategy, The Indirect Approach* (London, ^{3}1954).

LIEBESCHUETZ, J. H. G. W., *Antioch: City and Imperial Administration in the Later Roman Empire* (Oxford, 1972).

LINDER, A., *Roman Imperial Legislation on the Jews* (Jerusalem, 1983, in Hebrew).

LITTMANN, E., MAGIE, D., and STUART, D. R., *Publications of the Princeton University Archaeological Expeditions to Syria in 1904–5 and 1909*, iii, *Greek and Latin Inscriptions* (1921).

LUTTWAK, E. N., *The Grand Strategy of the Roman Empire, from the First Century* AD *to the Third* (Baltimore and London, 1976).

MA'OZ, M., *Ottoman Reform in Syria and Palestine, 1840–1861* (Oxford, 1968).

—— (ed.), *Studies on Palestine during the Ottoman Period* (Jerusalem, 1975).

MACADAM, H. I., *Studies in the History of the Roman Province of Arabia: the Northern Sector* (BAR International Series 295, Oxford, 1986).

MACDONALD, B., *Wadi El-Hasa Survey* (Wilfred Lauvier University, Waterloo, 1988).

McDOWELL, R. H., *Coins from Seleucia on the Tigris* (Ann Arbor, 1935).

MACKENSEN, M., *Resafa*, i, *eine befestigte spätantike Anlage vor den Stadtmauern von Resafa* (Mainz am Rhein, 1984).

MACMULLEN, R., *Soldier and Civilian in the Later Roman Empire* (Cambridge, Mass., 1963).

MAENCHEN-HELFEN, J. O., *The World of the Huns: Studies in their History and Culture*, ed. M. Knight (Berkeley and Los Angeles, 1973).

MAGIE, D., *Roman Rule in Asia Minor to the End of the Third Century after Christ*, 2 vols. (Princeton, 1950).

MAKHOULY, N., and JOHNS, C. N., *Guide to Acre* (Jerusalem, 1946).

MANN, J. C., *Legionary Recruitment and Veteran Settlement during the Principate*, ed. M. M. Roxan (London, 1983).

MARICQ, A., *Classica et Orientalia* (Paris, 1965).

MARX, E., *Bedouin of the Negev* (New York, 1967).

MATTINGLY, H., *Coins of the Roman Empire in the British Museum*, v (second edn., London, 1975).

MAXFIELD, V. A., *The Military Decorations of the Roman Army* (London, 1981).

MAZAR, B., *The Excavations in the Old City of Jerusalem: Preliminary Report of the First Season, 1968* (Jerusalem, 1969).

—— (ed.), *Geva: Archaeological Discoveries at Tell Abu-Shushah, Mishmar Ha'emeq* (Tel Aviv, 1988, in Hebrew).

MESHORER, Y., *City-Coins of Eretz-Israel and the Decapolis in the Roman Period* (Jerusalem, 1985).

—— *Jewish Coins of the Second Temple Period* (Jerusalem, 1967).

MICHAŁOWSKI, K., *Palmyre, Fouilles polonaises 1961* (contains: Première partie: camp de Dioclétien) (Warsaw, 1963).

MILLAR, F., *A Study of Cassius Dio* (Oxford, 1964).

—— *The Emperor in the Roman World* (London, 1977).

—— *The Roman Empire and its Neighbours* (London, ²1981).

MILLER, J. INNES, *The Spice Trade of the Roman Empire* (Oxford, 1969).

MILLER, S. S., *Studies in the History and Traditions of Sepphoris* (Leiden, 1984).

MITCHELL, S. (ed.), *Armies and Frontiers in Roman and Byzantine Anatolia* (BAR International Series 156, Oxford, 1983).

MITTMANN, S., *Beiträge zur Siedlungsgeschichte des nordlichen Ostjordanlandes* (Wiesbaden, 1970).

MÓCSY, A., *Gesellschaft und Romanisation in der römischen Provinz Moesia Superior* (Budapest, 1970).

—— *Pannonia and Upper Moesia: A History of the Middle Danube Provinces of the Empire* (London, 1974).

MONGAIT, A. L., *Archaeology in the U.S.S.R.*, trans. M. W. Thompson (Pelican, 1961).

MONTGOMERY, J. A., *The Samaritans* (Philadelphia, 1907).

MOUTERDE, R., *Regards sur Beyrouth, phénicienne, hellénistique et romaine* (Beirut, 1952, repr. 1966).

MOUTERDE, R., and LAUFFRAY, J., *Beyrouth ville romaine* (Beirut, 1952).

MURPHY, G. J., *The Reign of the Emperor L. Septimius Severus from the Evidence of the Inscriptions* (Philadelphia, 1945).

MUSIL, A., *Arabia Petraea*, 3 vols. (Vienna, 1907–8).

—— *Arabia Deserta* (New York, 1927).

—— *The Middle Euphrates* (New York, 1927).

—— *The Northern Heğaz: A Topographical Itinerary* (New York, 1926).

—— *The Manners and Customs of the Rwala Bedouin* (New York, 1928).

NAU, F., *Les Arabes chrétiens de Mésopotamie et de Syrie du VIe au VIIe siècle* (Paris, 1933).

NÖLDEKE, T. (trans. and comm.), *Geschichte der Perser und Araber zur Zeit der Sasaniden aus der arabischen Chronik des Tabari* (Leiden, 1879).

OATES, D., *Studies in the Ancient History of Northern Iraq* (London, 1968).

OERTEL, F., *Die Liturgie: Studien zur Ptolemäischen und Kaiserlichen Verwaltung Ägyptens* (Leipzig, 1917).

OGILVIE, R. M., and RICHMOND, I. A. (eds.), *Agricola* (Oxford, 1967).

OLINDER, G., *The Kings of Kinda* (Lund, 1927).

OPPENHEIM, M. VON, *Vom Mittelmeer zum Persischen Golf*, 2 vols. (Berlin, 1899–1900).

OPPENHEIMER, A. in collaboration with ISAAC, B. and LECKER, M., *Babylonia Judaica in the Talmudic Period*, Beihefte zum Tübinger Atlas des Vorderen Orients, B, 47 (Wiesbaden, 1983).

PARKER, H. M. D., *The Roman Legions* (repr. Cambridge, 1958).

PARKER, S. T., *Romans and Saracens, A History of the Arabian Frontier* (ASOR, Dissertation Series, 1986).

—— (ed.), *The Roman Frontier in Central Jordan: Interim Report on the Limes Arabicus Project, 1980–85*, 2 vols. (BAR International Series 340, Oxford, 1987).

PEKÁRY, T., *Untersuchungen zu den römischen Reichsstrassen* (Bonn, 1968).

PERKINS, A., *The Art of Dura Europos* (Oxford, 1973).

PETIT, P., *Libanius et la vie municipale à Antioche au IVe siècle après J.-C.* (Paris, 1955).

PFLAUM, H.-G., *Les Carrières procuratoriennes équestres sous l'Haut-Empire romain* (Paris, 1960–1).

PISTORIUS, P. V., *Indices Antinoopolitani* (diss. Leiden, 1939).

POIDEBARD, A., *La trace de Rome dans le désert de Syrie*, 2 vols. (Paris, 1934).

—— and MOUTERDE, P., *Le limes de Chalcis* (Paris, 1945).

PORTER, J., *Five Years in Damascus* (second edn., London, 1870).

PRENTICE, W. K., *Publications of an American Archaeological Expedition to Syria, 1899–1900*, iii, *Greek and Latin Inscriptions* (New York, 1908).

RABAN, A. (ed.), *Harbour Archaeology: Proceedings of the First International Workshop on ancient Mediterranean Harbours* (BAR International Series 257, Oxford, 1985).

RAJAK, T., *Josephus: The Historian and His Society* (London, 1983).

REISNER, G. A., FISCHER, C. S., and LYON, D. GORDON, *Harvard Excavations at Samaria (1908–1910)*, 2 vols. (Cambridge, Mass., 1924).

REY-COQUAIS, J.-P., *Arados et sa perée* (Paris, 1974).

—— *Arados et sa perée aux époques grecque, romaine et byzantine* (Paris, 1974).

REYNOLDS, J., *Aphrodisias and Rome* (JRS monographs 1, 1982).

RHOADS, D. M., *Israel in Revolution: 6–74 CE* (Philadelphia, 1976).

RICHMOND, I. A., *Roman and Native in North Britain* (London, 1958).

—— *Trajan's Army on Trajan's Column* (PBSR, 1935, ²1982).

RICKMAN, G., *Roman Granaries and Storage Buildings* (Cambridge, 1971).

ROBERT, L., *Études anatoliennes* (Paris, 1937).

—— *Les gladiateurs dans l'Orient grec* (1940, repr. Amsterdam, 1971).

ROSENBERGER, M., *City Coins of Palestine*, ii (Jerusalem, 1975); iii (1977).

ROSTOVTZEFF, M., *The Social and Economic History of the Hellenistic World*, 3 vols. (Oxford, 1941).

—— *Caravan Cities* (trans. by D. and T. Talbot Rice, Oxford, 1932).

—— *The Social and Economic History of the Roman Empire*, 2 vols. (second edn., revised by P. M. Fraser, Oxford, 1957).

—— et al., *The Excavations at Dura Europos: Preliminary Reports* (New Haven, 1929–56).

—— et al., *The Excavations at Dura Europos: Final Report* (New Haven, 1943–69; Los Angeles, 1977).

ROTHENBERG, B., *Tsephunot Negev* (In Hebrew: *Negev, Archaeology in the Negev and the Arabah*) (Jerusalem, 1967).

ROTHSTEIN, G., *Die Dynastie der Lahmiden in al-Hira* (Berlin, 1899).

ROUGÉ, J. (ed. and trans.), *Expositio Totius Mundi et Gentium: Introduction, texte critique, traduction, notes et commentaire* (Sources chrétiennes 124, Paris, 1966).

ROXAN, M. M., *Roman Military Diplomas 1954–1977* (London, 1978).

—— *Roman Military Diplomas 1978–1984* (London, 1985).

RUBIN, Z., *Civil-War Propaganda and Historiography* (Brussels, 1980).

STE CROIX, G. E. M. DE, *The Class Struggle in the Ancient Greek World from the Archaic Age to the Arab Conquests* (London, 1981).

ŞAHIN, S., *Die Inschriften von Iznik*, i (Bonn, 1979).

SALMON, E. T., *Roman Colonization under the Republic* (London, 1969).

SALWAY, P., *Roman Britain* (Oxford, 1981).

SALZMAN, P. C. (ed.), *When Nomads Settle* (New York, 1980).

SARRE, F., and HERZFELD, E., *Archäologische Reise im Euphrat-und Tigris-Gebiet,* 4 vols. (Berlin, 1911–20).

SARTRE, M., *Trois études sur l'Arabie romaine et byzantine* (Brussels, 1982).

—— *Bostra, des origines à l'Islam* (Paris, 1985).

SCHÄFER, P., *Der Bar Kokhba Aufstand* (Tübingen, 1981).

SCHIFF, Z., and YA'ARI, E., *Israel's Lebanon War* (second edn., London, 1986).

SCHLUMBERGER, D., *La Palmyrène du Nord-ouest* (Paris, 1951).

SCHUMACHER, G., *Across the Jordan, being an Exploration and Survey of Part of Hauran and Jaulan* (London, 1866).

SCHUR, W., *Die Orientpolitik des Kaisers Nero* (Klio, Beiheft 15/2 [1923]).

SCHÜRER, E., *Geschichte des jüdischen Vokes im Zeitalter Jesu Christi,* 3 vols. (Leipzig, 1901–9, repr. Hildesheim, 1970).

—— *The History of the Jewish People in the Age of Jesus Christ (175 BC–AD 135), A New English Version,* revised and edited by G. Vermes, F. Millar, M. Black, and M. Goodman, vols. i–iii. 2 (Edinburgh, 1973–87).

SCHWABE, M., and LIFSHITZ, B., *Beth She'arim, ii, The Greek Inscriptions* (Jerusalem, 1974).

SEDGLEY, J. P., *The Roman Milestones of Britain* (BAR 18, Oxford, 1975).

SEECK, O., *Geschichte des Untergangs der antiken Welt* (Berlin, 1920–21).

SEGAL, A., *The Byzantine City of Shivta (Esbeita), Negev Desert, Israel* (BAR International Series 179, Oxford, 1983).

SEGAL, J. B., *Edessa: 'The Blessed City'* (Oxford, 1970).

SESTON, W., *Dioclétien et la tétrarchie, i, Guerres et réformes (284–300)* (Paris, 1946).

SEYRIG, H., *Antiquités syriennes,* 4 vols. (Paris, 1934–65).

SHAHÎD, I., *Rome and the Arabs: A Prolegomenon to the Study of Byzantium and the Arabs* (Washington, 1984).

—— *Byzantium and the Arabs in the Fourth Century* (Washington, 1984).

SHERWIN-WHITE, A. N., *The Roman Citizenship* (second edn., Oxford, 1973).

SIDEBOTHAM, S. E., *Roman Economic Policy in the Erythra Thalassa 30 BC–AD 217* (Leiden, 1986).

SIMONS, J., *Jerusalem in the Old Testament* (Leiden, 1952).

SKEAT, T. C., *Papyri from Panopolis in the Chester Beatty Library, Dublin* (Dublin, 1964).

SMAIL, R. C., *Crusading Warfare* (Cambridge, 1956).

SMALLWOOD, E. M., *Documents Illustrating the Principates of Nerva, Trajan and Hadrian* (Cambridge, 1966).

—— *The Jews under Roman Rule from Pompey to Diocletian: A Study in Political Relations* (Leiden, 1981).

SPEIDEL, M., *Guards of the Roman Provinces: an Essay on the Singulares of the Provinces* (Bonn, 1978).

SPIJKERMAN, A., *The Coinage of the Decapolis and the Provincia Arabia* (Jerusalem, 1979).

STAEHELIN, F., *Die Schweiz in römischer Zeit* (third edn., Basle, 1948).

STARCKY, J., and GAWLIKOWSKI, M., *Palmyre* (Paris, 1985).

STARR, C. G., *The Roman Imperial Navy, 31 BC–AD 324* (second edn., Cambridge, 1960).

STEIN, E., *Histoire du Bas-Empire*, 2 vols. (Paris, 1949).

STEMBERGER, G., *Juden und Christen im Heiligen Land: Palästina unter Konstantin und Theodosius* (Munich, 1987).

STERN, M., *Greek and Latin Authors on Jews and Judaism*, 3 vols. (Jerusalem, 1974–84).

SUKENIK, E. L., and MAYER, L. A., *The Third Wall of Jerusalem: An Account of Excavations* (Jerusalem, 1930).

SWEET, L. E. (ed.), *Peoples and Cultures of the Middle East*, 2 vols. (New York, 1970).

SWOBODA, E., *Carnuntum: Seine Geschichte und seine Denkmäler* (Graz–Cologne, fourth edn., 1964).

SWOBODA, R. (ed.), *Corolla Memoriae Erich Swoboda Dedicata* (Graz–Cologne, 1966).

SYME, R., *Tacitus*, 2 vols. (Oxford, 1958).

—— *Ammianus and the Historia Augusta* (Oxford, 1968).

—— *Emperors and Biography: Studies in the Historia Augusta* (Oxford, 1971).

—— *Historia Augusta Papers* (Oxford, 1983).

TCHALENKO, G., *Villages antiques de la Syrie du nord*, 3 vols. (Paris, 1953).

TCHERIKOVER, V., FUKS, A., and STERN, M., *Corpus Papyrorum Judaicarum*, 3 vols. (Cambridge, Mass. and Jerusalem, 1957–64).

TEIXIDOR, J., *Un port romain du désert: Palmyre* (Paris, 1984 = *Semitica* xxxiv).

THOMSEN, P., *Die griechischen und lateinischen Inschriften der Stadt Jerusalem* (Leipzig, 1922).

TODD, M., *Roman Britain, 55 BC–AD 400* (Sussex, 1981).

TOUMANOFF, C., *Studies in Christian Caucasian History* (Washington, DC, 1963).

TRIMINGHAM, J. S., *Christianity Among the Arabs in Pre-Islamic Times* (London, 1979).

TSAFRIR, Y., *Eretz Israel from the Destruction of the Second Temple to the Muslim Conquest*, ii, *Archaeology and Art* (Jerusalem, 1984, in Hebrew).

TYLER, P., *The Persian Wars of the 3rd Century AD and Roman Imperial Monetary Policy, AD 253–68*, Historia Einzelschriften, Heft 23 (Wiesbaden, 1975).

ULBERT, T., *Resafa*, ii, *Die Basilika des heiligen Kreuzes in Resafa-Sergiupolis* (Mainz am Rhein, 1986).

UNZ, C. (ed.), *Studien zu den Militärgrenzen Roms III, 13. Internationaler Limeskongress, Aalen 1983, Vorträge* (Stuttgart, 1986).

VINCENT, L. H., and ABEL, F.-M., *Emmaüs, sa basilique et son histoire* (Paris, 1932).

—— and STÈVE, A.-M., *Jérusalem de l'Ancien Testament: recherches d'archéologie et d'histoire*, 3 vols. and pls. (Paris, 1954–6).

VITTINGHOFF, F., *Römische Kolonisation und Bürgerrechtspolitik unter Caesar und Augustus* (Wiesbaden, 1952).

VOGÜÉ, C. J. M. DE, *Syrie centrale: architecture civile et réligieuse du Ier siècle*, 2 vols. (Paris, 1865–77).

WACHER, J. (ed.), *The Roman World*, 2 vols. (London and New York, 1987).

Waddington: LE BAS, P., and WADDINGTON, W. H., *Inscriptions grecques et latines recueillies en Grèce et en Asie Mineure*, ii (Paris, 1870).

WAGNER, J., *Die Römer an Euphrat und Tigris, Antike Welt* (Sondernummer) 16 (1985).

——*Seleukia am Euphrat–Zeugma*, Beiträge zum Tübinger Atlas des Vorderen Orients (Wiesbaden, 1976).

WALSER, G., *Der Briefwechsel des L. Munatius Plancus mit Cicero* (Basle, 1957).

——and PEKÁRY, T., *Die Krise des Römischen Reiches: Bericht über die Forschungen zur Geschichte des 3. Jahrhunderts (193–284 N. Chr.) von 1939 bis 1959* (Berlin, 1962).

WARMINGTON, E. H., *The Commerce Between the Roman Empire and India* (Cambridge, 1928).

WATERMAN, L., et al., *Preliminary Report of the University of Michigan Excavations at Sepphoris* (Ann Arbor, 1937).

WATSON, G. R., *The Roman Soldier* (London, 1964).

WEBER, W., *Untersuchungen zur Geschichte des Kaisers Hadrianus* (Leipzig, 1909).

WEBSTER, G., *The Roman Imperial Army* (London, 1969; ³1985).

——*Boudicca: The British Revolt against Rome AD 60* (London, 1978).

WEISSLEDER, W. (ed.), *The Nomadic Alternative: Modes and Models of Interaction in the African-Asian Deserts and Steppes* (The Hague, 1978).

WELLES, C. B., FINK, R. O., and GILLIAM, J. F., *The Excavations at Dura-Europos*, Final Report V, Part I, *The Parchments and Papyri* (New Haven, 1959).

WELLS, C. M., *The German Policy of Augustus* (Oxford, 1972).

WETZSTEIN, J. G., *Reisebericht über Hauran und die Trachonen* (Berlin, 1860).

WHEELER, E. L., *Flavius Arrianus: a Political Biography* (Diss. Duke University, 1977).

WHEELER, R. E. M., *Rome Beyond the Imperial Frontiers* (London, 1954).

WHITCOMB, D., *Aqaba: 'Port of Palestine on the China Sea'* (Amman; booklet published in conjunction with an exhibition at the Oriental Institute, University of Chicago, 1988).

WIEGAND, T., et al., *Palmyra* (Berlin, 1932).

WILKES, J. J., *Dalmatia* (London, 1969).

WILKINSON, J. (trans.), *Egeria's Travels to the Holy Land* (Jerusalem, ²1981).

WINFIELD, D., *The Byzantine Monuments and the Topography of the Pontos*, 2 vols. (Washington, DC, 1985).

WINNETT, F. V., and HARDING, G. Lankaster, *Inscriptions from Fifty Safaitic Cairns* (Toronto, 1978).

WÖRRLE, M., *Stadt und Fest im kaiserzeitlichen Kleinasien* (Munich, 1988).

WOOLLEY, L., and LAWRENCE, T. E., *The Wilderness of Zin* (London, 1914–15).

WRIGHT, W., *The Chronicle of Joshua the Stylite Composed in Syriac AD 507, with a Translation into English and Notes* (Cambridge, 1882).

WROTH, W., *Catalogue of the Greek Coins in the British Museum: Galatia, Cappadocia, and Syria* (repr. Bologna, 1964).

WULZINGER, K., and WATZINGER, C., *Damaskus: die antike Stadt* (Berlin–Leipzig, 1921).

YARSHATER, E. (ed.), *The Cambridge History of Iran*, vol. 3 (i and ii), *The Seleucid, Parthian and Sasanian Periods* (Cambridge, 1983).

YAVETZ, Z., *Julius Caesar and His Public Image* (London, 1983, trans. from the German edn. 1979).

——*Augustus: The Victory of Moderation* (Tel Aviv, 1988, in Hebrew).

ZÀBA, Z., *The Rock Inscriptions of Lower Nubia* (Prague, 1974).

ZIEGLER, K.-H., *Die Beziehungen zwischen Rom und dem Partherreich: ein Beitrag zur Geschichte des Völkerrechts* (Wiesbaden, 1964).

ARTICLES

ABEL, F.-M., 'Chronique: (1) Nouvelle inscription de la Ve légion Macedonique', *RB* 35 (1926), 421–4.

——'L'île de Jotabè', *RB* 47 (1938), 510–38.

ADAMS, W. Y., 'Primis and the "Aethiopian" Frontier', *JARCE* 20 (1983), 93–104.

AGGOULA, B., 'Remarques sur les inscriptions Hatréennes, xii', *Syria* 63 (1986), 353–74.

AHARONI, Y., 'The Roman Road to Aila (Elath)', *IEJ* 4 (1954), 9–16.

——'Tamar and the Roads to Elath', *IEJ* 13 (1963), 30–42.

AL-KHALAF, M., and KOHLMEYER, K., 'Untersuchungen zur ar-Raqqa–Nikephorion/Callinicum', *Damaszener Mitteilungen* 2 (1985), 132–62.

ALFÖLDI, A., 'Die Hauptereignisse der Jahre 253–261 N. Chr. im Orient im Spiegel der Münzprägung', *Berytus* 4 (1937), 41–68 = *Studien zur Geschichte der Weltkrise des 3. Jahrhunderts nach Christus* (1967), 123–54.

——'Die römische Münzpragung und die historischen Ereignisse im Osten zwischen 260 und 270 n. Chr.', *Berytus* 5 (1938), 47 = *Studien zur Geschichte der Weltkrise des 3. Jahrhunderts nach Christus* (1967), 155.

——'Epigraphica, iv, Die Latrunculi der Bauinschriften der unter Commodus gebauten burgi et praesidia', *Archaeologiai Értesitö* 3/2 (1941), 40–48.

ALFÖLDY, G., 'Die Generalität des römischen Heeres', *BJb* 169 (1969), 233–46 = *Römische Heeresgeschichte*, 3–18.

AL-SALIHI, W. I., 'Mesene's Bronze Statue of "Weary Hercules"', *Sumer* 43 (1984), 219–29.

ALT, A., 'Aus der 'Araba, ii–iv', *ZDPV* 58 (1935), 1–78.

——'Jerusalems Aufstieg', *Kleine Schriften zur Geschichte des Volkes Israel* iii (1959), 243.

AMER, G., and GAWLIKOWSKI, M., 'Le sanctuaire impérial de Philippopolis', *Damaszener Mitteilungen* 2 (1985), 1–16.

AMIRAN, R., and EITAN, A., 'Excavations in the Courtyard of the Citadel, Jerusalem, 1968–1969 (Preliminary Report)', *IEJ* 20 (1970), 9–17.

—— —— 'Herod's Palace', *IEJ* 22 (1972), 50 f.

ANDERSON, A. R., 'Alexander at the Caspian Gates', *TAPA* 59 (1928), 130–7.

APPLEBAUM, S., 'Hellenistic Cities of Judaea and its Vicinity—some New Aspects', in *The Ancient Historian and his Materials: Essays in Honour of C. E. Stevens*, ed. B. Levick (1975), 59–63.

—— 'The Initial date of the Limes Palaestinae', *Zion* 27 (1962), 1–10 (in Hebrew, English summary).

—— 'The Zealots: The Case for Revaluation', *JRS* 61 (1971), 156–70.

—— 'Judaea as a Roman Province', *ANRW* ii. 8, 355–96.

—— DAR, S., and SAFRAI, Z., 'The Towers of Samaria', *PEQ* 110 (1978), 91–100.

ARIEL, D. T., 'A Survey of Coin Finds in Jerusalem', *Liber Annuus* 32 (1982), 273–326.

ASMUSSEN, J. P., 'Christians in Iran', *Cambridge History of Iran*, iii. 2 (1983), 924–48.

AVIGAD, N., 'A Building Inscription of the Emperor Justinian and the Nea in Jerusalem', *IEJ* 27 (1977), 145–51.

AVI-YONAH, M., 'Greek and Latin Inscriptions in the Museum', *QDAP* 2 (1933), 120–3.

—— 'Greek and Latin Inscriptions from Jerusalem and Beisan', *QDAP* 8 (1938–9), 54–61.

—— "Newly Discovered Greek and Latin Inscriptions", *QDAP* 12 (1946), 84–102.

—— 'The Samaritan Revolts against Byzantium', *Eretz-Israel* 5 (1956), 127–32 (in Hebrew).

—— 'The Latin Inscription from the Excavations in Jerusalem', in B. Mazar, *The Excavations in the Old City of Jerusalem: Preliminary Report of the First Season, 1968* (Jerusalem, 1969), 22–4.

BAATZ, D., 'The Hatra Ballista', *Sumer* 33 (1977), 141–52.

BAGNALL, R., 'Army and Police in Roman Upper Egypt', *JARCE* 14 (1977), 67–86.

—— 'Upper and Lower Guard Posts', *CE* 57 (1982), 125–8.

BAHAT, D., 'A Roof Tile of the Legio VI Ferrata and Pottery Vessels from Horvat Hazon', *IEJ* 24 (1974), 160–9.

BAILLIE REYNOLDS, P. K., 'The Troops Quartered in the Castra Peregrinorum', *JRS* 13 (1923), 168–89.

BALDUS, H. R., 'Syria', in A. M. Burnett and M. H. Crawford (eds.), *The Coinage of the Roman World in the Late Republic: Proceedings of a colloquium held at the British Museum in September 1985* (BAR International Series 326, Oxford, 1987).

BALTY, J. CH., 'Apamée (1986): Nouvelles données sur l'armée romaine d'Orient et les raids sassanides du milieu du IIIe siècle', *CRAI* (1987), 213–41.

BALTY, J. and J. CH., 'Apamée de Syrie, archéologie et histoire I. Des origines à la Tétrarchie', *ANRW* ii. 8, 103–34.

BANNING, E. B., 'Peasants, Pastoralists and *Pax Romana*: Mutualism in the Southern Highlands of Jordan', *BASOR* 261 (1986), 25–50.

—— 'De Bello Paceque', *BASOR* 265 (1987), 52–4.

—— and KÖHLER-ROLLEFSON, I., 'Ethnoarchaeological Survey in the Beidha Area, Southern Jordan', *ADAJ* 27 (1983), 375–83.

BAR-ADON, P., 'Sinnabra and Beth Yerah in the Light of the Sources and Archaeological Finds', *Eretz-Israel* 4 (1956), 50–5 (in Hebrew).

BARAG, D., 'The Countermarks of the *Legio Decima Fretensis* (Preliminary Report)', *International Numismatic Convention, Jerusalem, 27–31 December 1963* (Tel Aviv, 1967), 117–25.

—— 'Brick Stamp-Impressions of the Legio X Fretensis', *BJb* 167 (1967), 244–67.

BARNES, T. D., 'Imperial Campaign, AD 285–311', *Phoenix* 30 (1976), 74–93.

BARTHOLOMEW, P., 'Fourth-Century Saxons', *Britannia* 15 (1984), 169–85.

BAUZOU, T., 'Les voies de communication dans le Hauran à l'époque romaine', in J.-M. Dentzer (ed.), *Hauran i* (Paris, 1985), 137–65.

—— 'Deux milliaires inédits de Vaballath en Jordanie du Nord', *DRBE*, 1–8.

BEAUCAMP, J., 'Rawwafa et les Thamoudéens', *SDB* ix (1979), 1467–75.

BEIT-ARIEH, Y., 'Horvat 'Uzza—A Border Fortress in the Eastern Negev', *Qadmoniot* 19 (1986), 31–40 (in Hebrew).

BELL, H. I., 'Antinoopolis: A Hadrianic Foundation', *JRS* 30 (1940), 133.

BELLAMY, A., 'A New Reading of the Namarah Inscription', *JAOS* 105 (1985), 31–48.

BELLINGER, A. R., and WELLES, C. B., 'A Third Century Contract of Sale from Edessa in Osrhoene', *YCS* 5 (1935), 95–154.

BEN DOR, S., 'Petra Colonia', *Berytus* 9 (1948–9), 41–3.

—— 'Quelques rémarques à propos d'une monnaie de Néapolis', *RB* 59 (1952), 251 f.

BEN-DOV, M., 'The Crusader Fortress at Latrun', *Qadmoniot* 7 (1974), 117–20 (in Hebrew).

BERCHEM, D. VAN, 'L'annone militaire dans l'empire romain au IIIème siècle', *Mém. de la soc. nat. des antiquaires de France* 8/10 (1937), 117–202.

—— 'Recherches sur la chronologie des enceintes', *Syria* 31 (1954), 254–70.

—— 'Le premier rempart de Palmyre', *CRAI* 1970, 231–7.

—— 'Le plan de Palmyre', *Palmyre: Bilan et perspectives: Colloque Strasbourg 1973* (1976), 168–70.

—— 'Armée de frontière et armée de manoeuvre: alternative stratégique ou politique?' *SMR* ii (1977), 541–43.

—— 'Une inscription flavienne du Musée d'Antioche', *Museum Helveticum* 40 (1983), 185–96.

—— 'Le port de Séleucie de Piérie et l'infrastructure logistique des guerres parthiques', *BJb* 185 (1985), 47–87.

BERTINELLI, M. G. A., 'I Romani oltre l'Eufrate nel II Sec. d. C.', *ANRW* ii. 9, 3–69.

BIERS, W., 'Water from Stymphalos?', *Hesperia* 47 (1978), 171–84.

BINGEN, J., 'Un dédicace de marchands palmyréniens à Coptos', *CE* 59 (1984), 355–8.

BIRLEY, A., 'Roman Frontier Policy under Marcus Aurelius', *Roman Frontier Studies 1967* (1971), 7–13.

—— 'Die Aussen- und Grenzpolitik unter der Regierung Marc Aurels', in R. Klein (ed.), *Marc Aurel* (1979), 473–502.

BIRLEY, E., 'Hadrianic Frontier Policy', in E. Swoboda (ed.), *Carnuntina: Vorträge beim 2. internationalen Kongress der Altertumsforscher, Carnuntum 1955* (Graz–Cologne, 1956), 25–33.

BISHEH, G., in *Studies in the History and Archaeology of Jordan*, ii (1985), 263–5.

BIVAR, A. D. H., 'The Political History of Iran under the Arsacids', *Cambridge History of Iran* iii. 1 (1983), 21–99.

BLOCKLEY, R. C., 'The Division of Armenia between the Romans and the Persians at the End of the Fourth Century AD', *Historia* 36 (1987), 222–34.

BLOEMERS, J. H. F., 'Twenty-Five Years ROB Research in Roman Limburg', *Berichten van de Rijksdienst voor het Oudheidkundig Bodemonderzoek* 23 (1973), 238–42.

—— 'Periferie in Pre- en Protohistorie' (Inaugural Lecture, IPP Publication, no. 318, Amsterdam, 1983).

BOGAERS, J. E., 'Forum Hadriani', *BJb* 164 (1964), 45–52.

—— 'Civitates und Civitas-Hauptorte in der nördlichen Germania Inferior', *BJb* 172 (1972), 310–33.

BOSWORTH, A., 'Vespasian's Reorganization of the North-East Frontier', *Antichthon* 10 (1976), 63–78.

—— 'Arrian and the Alani', *HSCP* 81 (1977), 218–29.

BOSWORTH, C. E. 'Iran and the Arabs Before Islam', *Cambridge History of Iran*, iii. 1 (1983), 593–612.

BOWERSOCK, G. W., 'A Report on Arabia Provincia', *JRS* 61 (1971), 219–42.

—— 'Syria under Vespasian', *JRS* 63 (1973), 133–40.

—— 'The Greek-Nabataean Bilingual Inscription at Ruwwafa, Saudi Arabia', *Le monde grec: Hommages à Claire Préaux* (1975), 513–22.

—— 'A New Antonine Inscription from the Syrian Desert', *Chiron* 6 (1976), 349–55.

—— 'Limes Arabicus', *HSCP* 80 (1976), 219–29.

—— 'Mavia, Queen of the Saracens', *Studien zur antiken Sozialgeschichte: Festschrift F. Vittinghoff* (1980), 477–95.

—— 'Review of A. Spijkerman, *The Coins of the Decapolis and Provincia Arabia*, *JRS* 72 (1982), 197.

—— 'Roman Senators from the Near East: Syria, Judaea, Arabia, Mesopotamia', *Tituli* 5 (1982), 651–68.

—— 'Hadrian and Metropolis', *Bonner Historia-Augusta-Colloquium, 1982/3* (Bonn, 1985), 75–88.

—— 'Tylos and Tyre: Bahrain in the Graeco-Roman World', in S. H. A. Al Khalifa and M. Rice (eds.), *Bahrain through the Ages: the Archaeology* (1986), 399–406.

—— 'Arabs and Saracens in the *Historia Augusta*', *Bonner Historia-Augusta-Colloquium 1984/5* (Bonn, 1987), 71–80.

—— Review of S. E. Sidebotham, *Roman Economic Policy*, and of H. I. MacAdam, *Studies . . .*, *CR* 38 (1988), 101–4.

—— 'The Three Arabias in Ptolemy's Geography', *Géographie historique au Proche-Orient* (1988), 47–53.

BOWSHER, J., 'The Frontier Post of Medain Saleh', *DRBE*, 23–9.

BRAUND, D., 'The Caucasian Frontier: Myth, Exploration and the Dynamics of Imperialism', *DRBE*, 31–49.

BREEZE, D. J., 'Roman Forces and Native Populations', *Proc. Soc. Antiq. Scotland* 115 (1985), 223–8.

BRENNAN, P., 'Combined Legionary Bridgehead Dispositions', *Chiron* 10 (1980), 554–67.

BRIDEL, P., and STUCKY, R. A., 'Tel al Hajj, place forte du limes de l'Euphrate aux i^{er} et ive s. ap. J.-C.', in J. Cl. Margueron (ed.), *Le Moyen Euphrate, zone de contacts et d'échanges* (Leiden, 1980), 349–52.

BROCK, S., 'Syriac Sources for Seventh-Century History', *Byzantine and Modern Greek Studies* 2 (1976), 17–36.

BRULET, R., 'Estampilles de la IIIe légion Cyrénaïque à Bostra', *Berytus* 32 (1984), 175–9.

BRUNT, P. A., 'Charges of Provincial Maladministration under the Early Principate', *Historia* 10 (1961), 189–223.

—— Review of H. D. Meyer, *Die Aussenpolitik des Augustus und die augusteische Dichtung*, *JRS* 53 (1963), 170–6.

—— 'Conscription and Volunteering in the Roman Imperial Army', *SCI* 1 (1974), 90–115.

—— '"Did Imperial Rome Disarm her Subjects?', *Phoenix* 29 (1975), 260–70.

—— 'Josephus on Social Conflicts in Roman Judaea', *Klio* 59 (1977), 149–53.

—— 'Laus Imperii', in P. D. A. Garnsey and C. R. Whittaker (eds.), *Imperialism in the Ancient World* (1978), 159–91.

CAGNAT, R., 'Une inscription relative à la reine Bérénice', *Musée Belge* 33 (1928), 157–67.

CAMPBELL, B., 'Teach Yourself How to be a General', *JRS* 77 (1987), 13–29.

CAMPBELL, D. B., 'What Happened at Hatra? The Problems of Severan Siege Operations', *DRBE*, 51–8.

—— 'Auxiliary Artillery Revisited', *BJb* 186 (1986), 117–32.

CANTINEAU, J., 'Textes palmyréniens du Temple de Bêl', *Syria* 12 (1931), 116–41.

CAQUOT, A., 'Nouvelles inscriptions Araméennes de Hatra', *Syria* 30 (1953), 235.

CASKEL, W., 'The Bedouinization of Arabia', in G. E. von Grunebaum (ed.), *Studies in Islamic Cultural History* (1954), 36–46.

CHAUMONT, M.-L., 'L'Arménie entre Rome et l'Iran, i, de l'avènement d'Auguste à l'avènement de Dioclétien', *ANRW* ii. 9 (1976), 71–194.

—— 'A propos de la chute de Hatra et du couronnement de Shapur Ier', *Acta Antiqua Academiae Scientiarum Hungaricae* 27 (1979), 217–37.

—— 'Un document méconnu concernant l'envoi d'un ambassadeur Parthe vers Septime Sévère (P. Dura 60B)', *Historia* 36 (1987), 422–47.

CHEVALLIER, R., 'Cité et territoire: Solutions romaines aux problèmes de l'organisation de l'espace. Problématique 1948–73', *ANRW* ii (1974), 649–788.

CHURCHIN, L. A., '*Vici* and *Pagi* in Roman Spain', *REA* 98 (1985), 327–43.

CLERMONT-GANNEAU, C., 'Une dédicace de la légion Xe Fretensis à l'empereur Hadrien en Palestine', *Ét. d'Arch. Orientale* 2 (1897), 168–71.

—— 'Les inscriptions romaines de l'aqueduc de Jérusalem', *RAO* 4 (1901), 206–10.

—— 'Nouvelles inscriptions de Palestine', *RAO* 6 (1905), 182–203.

—— 'L'édit byzantin de Bersabée', *RB* ns 3 (1906), 412–32.

—— 'Inscriptions romaines d'Abila de Lysanias', *RAO* 2(1899), 35–43.

COHEN, G. M., 'The Hellenistic Military Colony—A Herodian Example', *TAPA* 103 (1972), 83–95.

COHEN, R., 'New Light on the Petra–Gaza Road', *Biblical Archaeologist* 45 (1982), 240–7.

—— 'Excavations at Moa 1981–85', *Qadmoniot* 20 (1987), 26–31 (in Hebrew).

COLES, R., 'The Barns Ostraka', *ZPE* 39 (1980), 126–31.

COLLART, P., 'Les milliaires de la Via Egnatia', *BCH* 100 (1976), 177–200.

COLLINGWOOD, R. G., 'The Purpose of the Roman Wall', *The Vasculum* 8 (1921), 4–9.

CONOLE, P., and MILNS, R. D., 'Neronian Frontier Policy in the Balkans', *Historia* 32 (1983), 82–200.

CONRAD, L. I., 'The *Qusūr* of Medieval Islam: Some Implications for the Social History of the Near East', *Al-Abhath: Journal of the Center for Arab and Middle East Studies, Faculty of Arts and Sciences, American University of Beirut* 29 (1981), 7–23.

—— '*Kai elabon tēn hēran*: Aspects of the Early Muslim Conquests in southern Palestine', Paper read at the Fourth Colloquium on: From Jahiliyya to Islam, July 1987, Jerusalem (forthcoming).

CRESWELL, K. A. C., 'Fortification in Islam before AD 1250', *PBA* 38 (1952), 89–91.

CROKE, B., and CROW, J. G., 'Procopius and Dara', *JRS* 73 (1983), 132–59.

CROW, J. G., 'Dara, a Late Roman Fortress in Mesopotamia', *Yayla* 4 (1981), 12–20.

—— 'A Review of the Physical Remains of the Frontier of Cappadocia', *DRBE*, 77–91.

—— 'The Function of Hadrian's Wall and the Comparative Evidence of Late Roman Long Walls', *SMR* iii (1986), 724–9.

—— and FRENCH, D. H., 'New Research on the Euphrates Frontier in Turkey', *Roman Frontier Studies 1979* (1980), 903–12.

CRUMMY, P., 'Colchester: the Roman Fortress and the Development of the Colony', *Britannia* 8 (1977), 65–105.

CUMONT, F., 'Le gouvernement de Cappadoce sous les Flaviens', *Académie royale de Belgique, Bulletin de la classe des lettres* (1905), 197–227.

—— 'Fragment de bouclier portant une liste d'étapes', *Syria* 6 (1925), 1–15.

DABROWA, E., 'Le limes anatolien et la frontière caucasienne au temps des Flaviens', *Klio* 62 (1980), 382–8.

—— 'Les rapports entre Rome et les Parthes sous Vespasien', *Syria* 58 (1981), 187–204.

—— 'The Frontier in Syria in the First Century AD', *DRBE*, 93–108.

DAGAN, Y., FISCHER, M., and TSAFRIR, Y., 'An Inscribed Lintel from Bet Guvrin', *IEJ* 35 (1985), 28–34.

DAN, Y., 'Palaestina Salutaris (Tertia) and its Capital', *IEJ* 32 (1982), 134–7.

DAR, S., 'Mount Hermon: An Ituraean Stronghold', *Cathedra* 33 (1984), 42–50 (in Hebrew).

—— and APPLEBAUM, S., 'The Roman Road from Antipatris to Caesarea', *PEQ* (1973), 91–9.

DAUPHIN, C., 'Dora-Dor: A Pilgrim Station on the Way to Jerusalem', *Cathedra* 29 (1983), 29–44 (in Hebrew).

DAVIES, R. W., 'Fronto, Hadrian and the Roman Army', *Latomus* 27 (1968), 75–95.

—— 'The Daily Life of the Roman Soldier under the Principate', *ANRW* i. 1 (1974), 299–338.

DE VRIES, B., 'Research at Umm el-Jimal, Jordan, 1972–77', *BASOR* 244 (1981), 53–72.

—— 'Umm El-Jimal in the First Three Centuries AD', *DRBE*, 227–41.

DENTZER, J.-M., 'Sondages près de l'arc Nabatéen à Bosrà', *Berytus* 32 (1984), 163–74.

DESANGES, J., 'Le statut et les limites de la Nubie romaine', *CE* 44 (1964), 139–47.

DEVIJVER, H., 'Equestrian Officers from the East', *EFRE*, 77–111.

DEVREESSE, R., 'Le Christianisme dans la péninsule sinaïtique, des origines à l'arrivée des Musulmans', *RB* 49 (1940), 216–20.

—— 'Arabes-Perses et Arabes-Romaines, Lakhmides et Ghassanides', *RB* 51 (1942), 263–307.

DOBSON, B., 'The Roman Army: Wartime or Peacetime Army?' in W. Eck and H. Wolff (eds.), *Heer und Integrationspolitik, Die römischen Militärdiplome als historische Quelle* (1986), 10–25.

DOMASZEWSKI, A. VON, 'Die politische Bedeutung der Religion von Emesa', *Archiv für Religionswissenschaft* 11 (1908), 223–42.

DOWNEY, G., 'Aurelian's Victory over Zenobia at Immae, AD 272', *TAPA* 81 (1950), 57–68.

DRIJVERS, H. J. W., 'Hatra, Palmyra und Edessa', *ANRW* ii. 8, 799–906.

DRURY, P. J., 'The Temple of Claudius at Colchester Reconsidered', *Britannia* 15 (1984), 7–50.

DUNAND, M., 'La strata Diocletiana', *RB* 40 (1931), 227–47.

—— 'La voie romaine du Ledjâ', *Mémoires présentés par divers savants à l'Académie des Inscriptions et Belles-Lettres* 13 (1933), 521–56.

DUNANT, C., 'Nouvelle inscription caravanières de Palmyre', *Museum Helveticum* 13 (1956), 216–25.

DUNCAN-JONES, R. P., 'Pay and Numbers in Diocletian's Army', *Chiron* 8 (1978), 541–60.

DYSON, L., 'Native Revolts in the Roman Empire', *Historia* 20 (1971), 239–74.

—— 'Native Revolt Patterns in the Roman Empire', *ANRW* ii. 3 (1975), 138–75.

EADIE, J. W., 'Humayma 1983: The Regional Survey', *ADAJ* 28 (1984), 211–24.

—— 'Artifacts of Annexation: Trajan's Grand Strategy and Arabia', in J. W. Eadie and J. Ober (eds.), *The Craft of the Ancient Historian: Essays in Honor of Chester G. Starr* (University Press of America, 1985), 407–23.

—— 'The Evolution of the Roman Frontier in Arabia', *DRBE*, 243–52.

—— and OLESON, J. P., 'The Water-Supply Systems of Nabataean and Roman Humayma', *BASOR* 262 (1986), 49–76.

ECK, W., 'Zum Konsularen Status von Iudaea im frühen 2. Jh.', *Bull. Am. Soc. Papyr.* 21 (1984), 55–67.

EGGER, R., 'Das Praetorium als Amtssitz und Quartier römischer Spitzenfunktionäre', *Österr. Ak. d. Wissensch., Phil.-Hist. Klasse* 250 (1966), 4. Abhandlung, 3–47.

EILERS, W., 'Iran and Mesopotamia', *Cambridge History of Iran*, iii. 1 (1983), 481–504.

EUZENNAT, M., 'L'olivier et le *limes*. Considérations sur la frontière romaine de Tripolitanie', *Bulletin archéologique du Comité des Travaux historiques et scientifiques* NS 79 (1983) [1985], fasc. B, 161–71.

FEISSEL, D., 'Deux listes de quartiers d'Antioche astreints aux creusement d'un canal (73–74 après J.-C.)', *Syria* 62 (1985), 77–103.

FELIKS, Y., 'Go and sow your Seed in the Sabbatical Year because of *Arnona*', *Sinai* 73 (1973), 235–49 (in Hebrew).

FELLMANN, R., 'Le "camp de Dioclétien" à Palmyre et l'architecture militaire du Bas-empire', in P. Ducrey et al. (eds.), *Mélanges d'histoire ancienne et d'archéologie offerts à Paul Collart* (1976), 173–91.

FIEY, J. M., 'A Roman Milestone from Sinjar', *Sumer* 8 (1959), 229.

—— 'Auteur et date de la chronique d'Arbèles', *L'Orient Syrien* 12 (1967), 265–302.

FIGUERAS, P., 'A Mosaic Pavement from Nabatiyeh in Southern Lebanon', *Liber Annuus* 35 (1985), 297–302.

FINKELSTEIN, I., 'Byzantine Monastic Remains in Southern Sinai', *DOP* 39 (1985), 39–75.

FISHWICK, D., 'Templum Divo Claudio Constitutum', *Britannia* 3 (1972), 164–81.

—— 'Note: Tacitean usage and the temple of *divus Claudius*', *Britannia* 4 (1973), 264 f.

FOERSTER, G., 'A Cuirassed Bronze Statue of Hadrian', *'Atiqot* 17 (1985), 139–60.

FORNI, G., et al., 'Limes', in *Dizionario Epigrafico* iv, fasc. 41–43/1–2, 4 (1982–5).

FORSYTH, G., 'The Monastery of St Catherine', *DOP* 22 (1968), 3–19.

FRANK, F. VON, 'Aus der 'Araba, i', *ZDPV* 57 (1934), 191–280.

FRASER, P. M., with a note by S. Applebaum, 'Hadrian and Cyrene', *JRS* 40 (1950), 77–90.

FRENCH, D. H., 'The Roman Road-System in Asia Minor', *ANRW* ii. 7, 698–729.

—— 'A Severan Milestone in the Antalya Museum', *Epigraphica Anatolica* 8 (1986), 84–90.

—— 'New Research on the Euphrates Frontier: Supplementary Notes 1 and 2', *AFRBA*, 79–101.

FREND, W. H. C., 'A Third-Century Inscription Relating to Angareia in Phrygia', *JRS* 46 (1956), 46–56.

—— 'Augustus' Egyptian Frontier Qasr Ibrim?', *Roman Frontier Studies 1979* (1980), 927–30.

FRYE, R. N., 'The Political History of Iran under the Sasanians', *Cambridge History of Iran*, iii. 1 (1983), 116–80.

FRÉZOULS, E., 'Inscription de Cyrrhus relative à Q. Marcius Turbo', *Syria* 30 (1953), 247 ff.

—— 'Recherches sur la ville de Cyrrhus', *Annales Archeologiques Arabes Syriennes* 4–5 (1954–5), 89–128.

—— 'Cyrrhus et la Cyrrhestique jusqu'à la fin du Haut-Empire', *ANRW* ii. 8, 164–97.

—— 'Les fonctions du Moyen-Euphrate à l'époque romaine', in J. C. Margueron (ed.), *Le Moyen Euphrate, zone de contacts et d'èchanges* (Leiden, 1980), 355–86.

GALSTERER-KRÖLL, B., 'Untersuchungen zu den Beinamen der Städte des Imperium Romanum', *Epigraphische Studien* 9 (1972), 44–141.

GARSOÏAN, N., 'Byzantium and the Sasanians', *Cambridge History of Iran*, iii. 1 (1983), 568–92.

GAUBE, H., 'An Examination of the Ruins of Qasr Burqu', *ADAJ* 19 (1974), 93–100.

GAWLIKOWSKI, M., 'Die polnischen Ausgrabungen in Palmyra', *AA* 83 (1968), 289–304.

—— 'Les défenses de Palmyre', *Syria* 51 (1974), 231–42.

—— 'Palmyre et l'Euphrate', *Syria* 60 (1983), 53–68.

—— 'Hadīta, Bēgān Island', *Archiv für Orientforschung* 29–30 (1983–4), 207.

—— 'Les princes de Palmyre', *Syria* 62 (1985), 251–61.

GEIGER, J., 'The Last Jewish Revolt Against Rome: A Reconsideration', *Scripta Classica Israelica* 5 (1979–80), 250–7.

GEVA, H., 'The Camp of the Tenth Legion in Jerusalem: an Archaeological Reconsideration', *IEJ* 34 (1984), 239–54.

GICHON, M., 'The Origin of the Limes Palaestinae and the Major Phases in its Developments', *SMR* i 175–93.

—— 'The Military Significance of Certain Aspects of the Limes Palaestinae', *Roman Frontier Studies 1967* (1971), 191–200.

—— 'Migdal Tsafit, a *burgus* in the Negev (Israel)', *Saalburg Jahrbuch* 31 (1974), 16–40.

—— 'Excavations at Mezad Tamar—"Tamara" 1973–75, Preliminary Report', *Saalburg Jahrbuch* 33 (1976), 80–94.

—— 'The Roman Bath at Emmaus. Excavations in 1977', *IEJ* 29 (1979), 101–10.

—— 'Research on the *Limes Palaestinae*: a Stocktaking', *Roman Frontier Studies 1979* (1980), 843–64.

—— 'The Military Aspect of the Bar Kokhba Revolt in the Light of the Exploration of Underground Hiding Places', *Cathedra* 26 (1982), 30–42 (in Hebrew).

GILLIAM, J. F., 'The *Dux Ripae* at Dura', *TAPA* 72 (1941), 157–75 = *Roman Army Papers* (1986), 23–41.

—— 'Romanization of the Greek East: The Role of the Army', *Bull. Am. Soc. of Papyrologists* 2 (1965), 65–73 = *Roman Army Papers*, 281–7.

GLUECK, N., 'Exlorations in Eastern Palestine', i, *AASOR* 14 (1934); ii, *AASOR* 15 (1935); iii, *AASOR* 18–19 (1939); iv, *AASOR* 25–28 (1951).

—— 'Wādī Sirḥān in North Arabia', *BASOR* 96 (1944), 7–17.

GOLDSTEIN, J. A., 'The Syriac Bill of Sale from Dura-Europos', *JNES* 25 (1966), 1–16.

GOLVIN, J. C., and REDDÉ, M., 'Archéologie militaire romaine en Égypte, la route de Coptos à Quseir', *CRAI* (1986), 177–91.

GOODCHILD, R. G., 'The Coast Road of Phoenicia and its Roman Milestones', *Berytus* 9 (1948), 91–127.

GRACEY, M., 'The Armies of the Judaean Client Kings', *DRBE*, 311–23.

GRAF, D. F., 'The Saracens and the Defense of the Arabian Frontier', *BASOR* 229 (1978), 1–26.

—— 'A Preliminary Report on a Survey of Nabataean-Roman Military Sites in Southern Jordan', *ADAJ* 23 (1979), 121–7.

—— 'The Nabataeans and the Hisma: In the Steps of Glueck and Beyond', in C. L. Meyers and M. O'Connor (eds.), *The Word of the Lord Shall Go Forth: Essays in Honor of David Noel Freedman* (1983), 647–64.

—— 'The Nabataeans and the Decapolis', *DRBE*, 785–96.

—— 'Qurā 'Arabiyya and Provincia Arabia', in *Table ronde, Géographie historique au Proche-Orient* (Notes et monographies techniques 23, CNRS, Paris, 1987), 171–211.

—— 'Rome and the Saracens: Reassessing the Nomadic Menace', *Colloque International sur L'Arabie préislamique et son environnement historique et culturel*, Strasbourg, June 1987 (Leiden 1989), 344–400.

—— and O'CONNOR, M., 'The Origin of the Term "Saracen" and the Raw-wāfa Inscriptions', *Byzantine Studies/Études Byzantines* 4 (1977), 52–66.

GREY, E. W., 'The Roman Eastern Limes from Constantine to Justinian—Perspectives and Problems', *Proc. African Class. Ass.* 12 (1973), 24–40.

GREEN, J., and TSAFRIR, Y., 'Greek Inscriptions from Hammat Gader: A Poem by the Empress Eudocia and Two Building Inscriptions', *IEJ* 32 (1982), 77–96.

GREGORY, S., 'Road, Wall or Rock: Interpreting an Aerial Photograph from the Jebel Sinjar', *DRBE*, 325–8.

HADAS-LEBEL, M., 'La fiscalité dans la littérature rabbinique jusq'à la fin du iiie siècle', *REJ* 143 (1984), 5–29.

HALFMANN, H., 'Die Alanen und die römische Ostpolitik unter Vespasian', *Epigraphica Anatolica* 8 (1986), 39–50.

HARDING, G. L., 'The Safaitic Tribes', *Al-Abhath* 22 (1969), 3–25.

HARL, K. W., 'The Coinage of Neapolis in Samaria, AD 244–52', *American Numismatic Society, Museum Notes* 29 (1984), 61–97.

HARPER, R. P., 'Excavations at Dibsi Faraj, northern Syria, 1972–74: a Preliminary Note on the Site and its Monuments', *DOP* 29 (1975), 319–37.

—— 'Two Excavations on the Euphrates Frontier 1968–1974: Pagnik Oreni (Easter Turkey) 1968–1971, and Dibsi Faraj (Northern Syria) 1972–1974', *SMR* ii (1977), 453–60.

—— 'Upper Zohar: A Preliminary Excavation Report, *DRBE*, 329–36.

HART, S., 'Some Preliminary Thoughts on Settlement in Southern Edom', *Levant* 18 (1986), 51–8.

—— 'Nabataeans and Romans in Southern Jordan', *DRBE*, 337–42.

HELLENKEMPER, H., 'Der Limes am Nordsyrischen Euphrat: Bericht zu einer archäologischen Landesaufnahme', *SMR* ii (1977), 461–71.

—— 'Legionem im Bandenkrieg—Isaurien im 4. Jahrhundert', iii (1986), 625–34.

HENRICHS, A., and KOENEN, L., 'Ein Griechischer Mani-Kodex', *ZPE* 5 (1970), 97–216.

HERZFELD, E., 'Hatra', *ZDMG* 68 (1914), 655–76.

HILL, G. F., 'The Mints of Roman Arabia and Mesopotamia', *JRS* 6 (1916), 135–69.

HILL, S., 'The "Praetorium" at Musmiye', *DOP* 29 (1975), 347–9.

HIRSCHFELD, Y., 'A Line of Byzantine Forts along the Eastern Highway of the Hebron Hills', *Qadmoniot* 12 (1979), 78–84 (in Hebrew).

HOPKINS, C., and ROWELL, H. T., 'The Praetorium', in *Excavations at Dura Europos, Preliminary Report of the Fifth Season of Work* (New Haven, 1934), 207–37.

HOPWOOD, K., ' "Towers, Territory and Terror", How the East was Held', *DRBE*, 343–56.

Horsley, R., 'Josephus and the Bandits', *Journal for the Study of Judaism* 10 (1979), 37–63.

—— 'Ancient Jewish Banditry and the Revolt against Rome', *Catholic Biblical Quarterly* 43 (1981), 409–32.

Howgego, C. J., 'The XII Fulminata: Countermarks, Emblems and Movements under Trajan or Hadrian', *AFRBA*, 41–6.

Iliffe, J. H., 'A Building Inscription from the Syrian Limes', *QDAP* 10 (1940–2), 62–4.

Ingholt, H., 'Deux inscriptions bilingues de Palmyre', *Syria* 13 (1932), 278–92.

Ingraham, M. L., et al., 'Saudi Arabian Comprehensive Survey Program: Preliminary Report on a Reconnaissance Survey of the Northwestern Province', *Atlal* 5 (1981), 59–80.

Invernizzi, A., 'Kifrin', *Archiv für Orientforschung* 29–30 (1983), 217–19.

—— 'Kifrin and the Euphrates Limes', *DRBE*, 357–81.

—— 'Traiano a Hatra?', *Mesopotamia* 21 (1986), 21–50.

—— 'Kifrin', *Mesopotamia* 21 (1986), 53–84.

Isaac, B., 'Milestones in Judaea, From Vespasian to Constantine', *PEQ* 110 (1978), 47–60.

—— 'Roman Colonies in Judaea: The Foundation of Aelia Capitolina', *Talanta* 12–13 (1980–81), 31–53.

—— 'The Decapolis in Syria, a Neglected Inscription', *ZPE* 44 (1981), 67–74.

—— 'A Donation for Herod's Temple in Jerusalem', *IEJ* 33 (1983), 86–92.

—— 'Judaea after AD 70', *JJS* 35 (1984), 44–50.

—— 'Bandits in Judaea and Arabia', *HSCP* 88 (1984), 171–203.

—— 'The Roman Army in Jerusalem and its Vicinity', *SMR* iii (Stuttgart, 1986), 635–40.

—— 'The Meaning of "Limes" and "Limitanei" in Ancient Sources', *JRS* 78 (1988), 125–47.

—— and Oppenheimer, A., 'The Revolt of Bar Kokhba, Scholarship and Ideology', *JJS* 36 (1985), 33–60.

—— and Roll, I., 'A Milestone of AD 69 from Judaea', *JRS* 66 (1976), 9–14.

—— —— 'Judaea in the Early Years of Hadrian's Reign', *Latomus* 38 (1979). 54–66.

—— —— 'Legio II Traiana in Judaea', *ZPE* 33 (1979), 149–56.

Jacobs, L., 'The Survey of the South Ridge of the Wadi 'Isal, 1981', *ADAJ* 27 (1983), 245–74.

James, S., 'Dura-Europos and the Chronology of Syria in the 250s AD', *Chiron* 15 (1985), 111–24.

Jameson, S., 'The Chronology of the Campaigns of Aelius Gallus and C. Petronius', *JRS* 58 (1968), 71–84.

Johns, C. N., 'Excavations at the Citadel, Jerusalem', *PEQ* 72 (1940), 36–58.

—— 'The Citadel, Jerusalem. A Summary of Work since 1934', *QDAP* 14 (1950), 121–90.

Jones, A. H. M., 'The Urbanisation of Palestine', *JRS* 21 (1931), 78–85.

—— 'The Urbanisation of the Ituraean Principality', *JRS* 21 (1931), 265–75.

Kasher, A., 'The relations between Ituraeans and Jews in the Hellenistic and Roman Periods', *Cathedra* 33 (1984), 18–41 (in Hebrew).

Kawar (Shahîd), I., 'Arethas, Son of Jabalah', *JAOS* 75 (1955), 205–16.

—— 'The Arabs in the Peace Treaty of AD 561', *Arabica* 3 (1956), 181–213.

—— 'Procopius and Arethas', *Byzantinische Zeitschrift* 50 (1957), 39–67; 363–82.

—— 'Ghassān and Byzantium: A New Terminus a quo', *Der Islam* 33 (1958), 232–55.

—— 'The Last Days of Salīḥ', *Arabica* 5 (1958), 145–58.

Kaygusuz, I., 'Neue Inschriften aus Ainos (Enez)', *Epigraphica Anatolica* 8 (1986), 65–70.

Keaveney, A., 'Roman Treaties with Parthia 95–circa 64 BC', *AJP* 102 (1981), 195–212.

—— 'The King and the Warlords', *AJP* 103 (1982), 412–28.

Kennedy, D. L., 'Ti. Claudius Subatianus Aquila, "First Prefect of Mesopotamia"', *ZPE* 36 (1979), 255–62.

—— '*Legio VI Ferrata*: The Annexation and Early Garrison of Arabia', *HSCP* 84 (1980), 283–309.

—— 'The Frontier Policy of Septimius Severus: New Evidence from Arabia', *Roman Frontier Studies 1979* (1980), 879–88.

—— 'C. Velius Rufus', *Britannia* 14 (1983), 183–96.

—— 'Cohors XX Palmyrenorum—An Alternative Explanation of the Numeral', *ZPE* 53 (1983), 214–16.

—— 'Milliary Cohorts: The Evidence of Josephus, BJ III. 4. 2 (67) and of Epigraphy', *ZPE* 50 (1983), 253–63.

—— 'The Composition of a Military Work Party in Roman Egypt (*ILS* 2483: Coptos)', *JEA* 71 (1985), 156–60.

—— 'Ana on the Euphrates in the Roman Period', *Iraq* 48 (1986), 103 f.

—— '"European" Soldiers and the Severan Siege of Hatra', *DRBE*, 397–409.

—— 'A Lost Latin Inscription from the Banks of the Tigris', *ZPE* 73 (1988), 325–8.

—— 'The Garrisoning of Mesopotamia in the Late Antonine and Early Severan Period', *Antichthon* 21 (1987), 57–66.

—— and Bennett, C. M., 'A New Roman Military Inscription from Petra', *Levant* 10 (1978), 163.

—— and MacAdam, H. I., 'Latin Inscriptions from the Azraq Oasis, Jordan', *ZPE* 60 (1985), 97–106.

—— —— 'Latin Inscriptions from Jordan', *ZPE* 65 (1986), 231–6.

Keppie, L. J. F., 'The Legionary Garrison of Judaea under Hadrian', *Latomus* 32 (1973), 859–64.

—— 'Colonisation and Veteran Settlement in Italy in the First Century AD', *PBSR* 52 (1984), 77–114.

—— 'Legions in the East from Augustus to Trajan', *DRBE*, 411–29.

KILLICK, A. C., 'Udruh—the Frontier of an Empire: 1980 and 1981 Seasons, a Preliminary Report', *Levant* 15 (1983), 110–31.

—— 'Udruh and the Southern Frontier', *DRBE*, 431–46.

KINDLER, A., 'Was there a Detachment of the Third Legion Cyrenaica at Neapolis in AD 251–253?', *INJ* 4 (1980), 56–8.

—— 'The Status of Cities in the Syro-Palestinian Area as Reflected by their Coins', *INJ* 6–7 (1982–3), 79–87.

—— 'Coinage of Joppe', *Museum Haaretz Yearbook* 20–21 (1985–6), 21–36 (in Hebrew).

—— 'Coins of the City Antipatris', *Eretz-Israel* 19 (1987), 125–31 (in Hebrew, English summary).

KIRK, G. E., 'Archaeological Exploration in the Southern Desert', *PEQ* 70 (1938), 211–35.

KIRWAN, L. P., 'Rome Beyond the Southern Egyptian Frontier', *PBA* 63 (1977), 13–31.

—— 'A Roman Shipmaster's Handbook', *GJ* 147 (1981), 80–5.

KLEIN, S., 'Zur Ortsnamenkunde Palästinas', *Monatschrift für Geschichte und Wissenschaft des Judentums* 82 / NS 64 (1938), 181–6.

KLONER, A., 'Underground Hiding Complexes from the Bar Kokhba War in the Judaean Shephelah', *Biblical Archaeologist* 46 (1983), 210–21.

KÖNIG, I., 'Zur Dedikation römischer Meilensteine', *Chiron* 3 (1973), 419–27.

KOERSTERMANN, E., 'Der pannonisch-dalmatische Krieg 6–9 n. Chr.', *Hermes* 81 (1953), 345–78.

KOLENDO, J., 'Le projet d'expédition de Néron dans le Caucase', in J.-M. Croisille and P.-M. Fauchère (eds.), *Neronia 1977, Actes du 2ᵉ colloque internationale d'études Néroniennes* (1982), 23–30.

KOLNIK, T., 'Cifer-Pac. Eine spätrömische Station im Quadenland', in J. Fitz (ed.), *Akten des 11. Int. Limeskongresses* (Budapest, 1977), 181–97.

—— 'Q. Atilius Primus, interprex centurio und negotiator', *Act. Arch. Sc. Hung.* 30 (1978), 61–75.

KRAFT, K., 'Die Rolle der Colonia Julia Equestris und die römische Auxiliar-Rekrutierung', *Jahrbuch RGZM* 4 (1957), 81–107.

LABROUSSE, M., 'Les *Burgarii* et le *Cursus Publicus*', *MEFR* 55 (1938), 151–67.

LANDAU, Y. H., 'A Greek Inscription from Acre', *IEJ* 11 (1961), 118–26.

—— 'Unpublished Inscriptions from Israel: A Survey', *Acta of the Fifth International Congress of Greek and Latin Epigraphy, Cambridge 1967*, 387–90.

—— 'Two Inscribed Tombstones', *'Atiqot* 11 (1976), 89–91.

LANDER, J., 'Did Hadrian Abandon Arabia?', *DRBE*, 447–53.

—— and PARKER, S. T., 'Legio IV *Martia* and the Legionary Camp at El-Lejjun', *Byzantinische Forschungen* 8 (1982), 185–210.

LANG, D. M., 'Iran, Armenia and Georgia', *Cambridge History of Iran*, iii. 1 (1983), 505–36.

LAUFFRAY, J., 'Forums et monuments de Béryte', *BMB* 7 (1944–5), 13–80; 8 (1946–8), 7–16.

—— 'Beyrouth Archéologie et Histoire, époques gréco-romaines I. Période hellénistique et Haut-Empire romain', *ANRW* ii 8, 135–63.

LEANING, J. B., 'The Date of the Repair of the Bridge over the River Chabina', *Latomus* 30 (1971), 386–9.

LEE, A. D., 'Embassies as Evidence for Movement of Military Intelligence Between the Roman and Sasanian Empires', *DRBE*, 455–61.

LEFKINADZE, V. A., 'Pontijski Limes', *Vestnik Drevnei Historij* (1969/2), 75–93.

LIEB, H., 'Zur zweiten Colonia Raurica', *Chiron* 4 (1974), 415–23.

LIEBERMAN, S., 'The Martyrs of Caesarea', *Annuaire de l'institut de philologie et d'histoire orientales et slaves* 7 (1939–44), 395–446.

—— 'Palestine in the Third and Fourth Centuries', *JQR* 36 (1946), 329–70.

LIEBESCHUETZ, J. H. W. G., 'The Defences of Syria in the Sixth Century', *SMR* ii (1977), 487–99.

LIEU, S., 'Urbanism in Hellenistic, Parthian and Roman Mesopotamia', *DRBE*, 507 f.

—— 'Captives, Refugees and Exiles: A Study of Cross-Frontier Civilian Movements and Contacts Between Rome and Persia from Valerian to Jovian', *DRBE*, 475–505.

LIFSHITZ, B., 'Sur la date du transfert de la legio VI Ferrata en Palestine', *Latomus* 19 (1960), 109–11.

—— 'Légions romaines en Palestine', in J. Bibauw (ed.), *Collection Latomus* 102, *Hommages à Marcel Renard*, ii (Bruxelles 1969), 458–69.

—— 'Un fragment d'un diplôme militaire de Hébron', *Latomus* 35 (1976), 117–22.

LINTOTT, A., 'What was the "Imperium Romanum"?', *Greece & Rome* 28 (1981), 53–67.

LOPUSZANSKI, G., 'La police romaine et les chrétiens', *L'antiquité classique* 20 (1951), 5–46.

—— *Cahiers de l'Institut d'études Polonaises en Belgique* 9 (1951).

LORIOT, X., 'Les premières années del la grande crise du IIIe siècle: De l'avènement de Maximin le Thrace (235) à la mort de Gordien III (244)', *ANRW* ii. 2, 659–787.

MacADAM, H. I., 'Epigraphy and Village Life in Southern Syria during the Roman and Early Byzantine Periods', *Berytus* 31 (1983), 103–15.

—— 'Some Notes on the Umayyad Occupation of North-East Jordan', *DRBE*, 531–47.

MacDONALD, B., 'The Wadi el-Hasa Survey 1979 and Previous Archaeological Work in Southern Jordan', *BASOR* 245 (1982), 35–52.

—— 'A Nabataean and/or Roman Military Monitoring Zone Along the South Bank of the Wadi el-Hesa in Southern Jordan', *Échos du Monde Classique/Classical Views* 28 (1984), 219–34.

MacMULLEN, R., 'Two Notes on Imperial Properties', *Athenaeum* 54 (1976), 19–36.

Maisler (Mazar), B., Stekelis, M., and Avi-Yonah, M., 'The Excavations at Beth Yerah (Khirbet el-Kerakh), 1944–1946', *IEJ* 2 (1952), 165–73; 218–29.

Malavolta, M., 'Interiores limites', *Ottava miscellanea greca et romana* (1982), 587–610.

Mallowan, M. E. L., 'Excavations in the Balih Valley, 1938', *Iraq* 8 (1946), 111–59.

—— 'Excavations at Braq and Chegar Bazar', *Iraq* 9 (1947), 1–87.

Mango, C., 'Who wrote the Chronicle of Theophanes?', *Zbovnik Radova Vizantoloskog Instituta* 18 (1978), 9–17.

—— and Ševčenko, I., 'Remains of the Church of St Polyeuktos at Constantinople', *DOP* 15 (1961), 243–7.

Mann, J. C., 'Colonia Ulpia Traiana and the Occupation of Vetera II', *BJb* 162 (1962), 162–4.

—— Review of G. Rupprecht, *Untersuchungen zum Dekurionenstand in den nordwestlichen Provinzen des römischen Reiches* (1975), *Germania* 54 (1976), 512–13.

—— 'Duces and Comites in the Fourth Century', in D. E. Johnson (ed.), *CBA Research Report* 18: *The Saxon Shore* (London, 1977), 11–15.

—— 'The Frontiers of the Principate', *ANRW* ii. 1, 508–33.

—— 'Power, Force and the Frontiers of the Empire', review of E. N. Luttwak, *The Grand Strategy of the Roman Empire*, *JRS* 69 (1979), 175–83.

—— 'Two "Topoi" in the Agricola"', *Britannia* 16 (1985), 21–4.

—— 'Appendix II: 'The "Palmyrene" Diplomas', in M. Roxan, *Roman Military Diplomas, 1978–84*, 217–19.

—— 'A Note on the so-called "Town-zone"', *Britannia* 18 (1987), 285 f.

Maricq, A., 'Hatra de Sanatrouq', *Syria* 32 (1955), 273–88.

—— 'La chronologie des derrières années de Caracalla', *Syria* 34 (1957), 297–305.

—— 'Les dernières années de Hatra: l'alliance romaine', *Syria* 34 (1957), 288–96.

—— 'Res Gestae Divi Saporis', *Syria* 35 (1958), 295–360.

—— 'La province d'"Assyrie" créée par Trajan. A propos de la guerre parthique de Trajan', *Syria* 36 (1959), 254–63.

Maróth, M., 'Le siege de Nisibe en 350 Ap. J.-Ch. d'apres des sources syriennes', *Acta Antiqua Academiae Scientiarum Hungaricae* 278 (1979), 239–43.

Matthews, J. F., 'The Tax Law of Palmyra: Evidence for Economic History in a City of the Roman East', *JRS* 74 (1984), 157–80.

—— "Ammianus and the Eastern Frontier in the Fourth Century: A Participant's View', *DRBE*, 549–64.

Mayerson, P., 'The Desert of Southern Palestine according to Byzantine Sources', *Proc. Phil. Soc.* 107 (1963), 160–72.

—— 'The First Muslim Attacks on Southern Palestine', *TAPA* 95 (1964), 155–99.

—— 'Observations on the "Nilus Narrations"', *Journal American Research Center in Egypt* 12 (1975), 51–74.

—— 'Procopius or Eutychius', *BASOR* 230 (1978), 33–8.

—— 'Mavia, Queen of the Saracens—A Cautionary Note', *IEJ* 30 (1980), 123–31.

—— 'The Ammonius Narrative: Bedouin and Blemmye Attacks in Sinai', in G. Rendsburg et al. (eds.), *The Bible World: Essays in Honor of Cyrus Gordon* (New York, 1980), 133–48.

—— 'The City of Elusa in the Literary Sources of the Fourth–Sixth Centuries', *IEJ* 33 (1983), 247–53.

—— 'The Beersheba Edict', *ZPE* 64 (1986), 141–8.

—— 'The Saracens and the *Limes*', *BASOR* 262 (1986), 35–47.

—— 'Libanius and the Administration of Palestine', *ZPE* 69 (1987), 251–60.

—— 'Palaestina Tertia—Pilgrims and Urbanization', *Cathedra* 45 (1987), 19–40 (in Hebrew).

MELLOR, R., 'A New Roman Military Diploma', *The J. Paul Getty Museum Journal* 6–7 (1978–9), 173–84.

MEREDITH, D., 'The Roman Remains in the Eastern Desert of Egypt', *JEA* 38 (1952), 94–111.

—— 'Eastern Desert of Egypt: Notes on Inscriptions', *CE* 28 (1953), 103–23.

—— 'The Roman Remains in the Eastern Desert of Egypt', *CE* 29 (1954), 281–7.

—— 'Inscriptions from the Berenice Road', *CE* 29 (1954), 281–7.

—— and TREGENZA, L. A., 'Notes on Roman Roads and Stations in the Eastern Desert, I', *Bull. Faculty of Arts, Fouad I University* 11 (1949), 1–30.

MESHEL, Z., and ROLL, I., 'A Fort and Inscription from the Time of Diocletian at Yotvetah', *Eretz-Israel* 19 (1987), 248–65 (in Hebrew, English summary).

—— and TSAFRIR, Y., 'The Nabataean Road from 'Avdat to Sha'ar Ramon', *PEQ* 106 (1974), 105–18; 107 (1975), 3–21.

MESHORER, Y., 'Two Finds from the Tenth Roman Legion', *Israel Museum Journal* 3 (1984), 41–5.

MEYER, J., 'A Centurial Stone from Shavei Tziyyon', *Scripta Classica Israelica* 7 (1983–84), 119–28, with appendix by S. Applebaum.

—— 'A Latin Inscription from A-Sumeiriya', *Scripta Classica Israelica* 7 (1983–84), 117 f.

MIHAILOV, G., 'La fortification de la Thrace par Antonin le Pieux et Marc Aurèle', *Studi Urbinati* 35 (1961), 42–55.

MILLAR, F., 'Paul of Samosata, Zenobia and Aurelian: The Church, Local Culture and Political Allegiance in Third-Century Syria', *JRS* 61 (1971), 1–17.

—— 'Emperors, Frontiers and Foreign Relations, 31 BC to AD 378', *Britannia* 13 (1982), 1–23.

—— 'Empire, Community and Culture in the Roman Near East: Greeks, Syrians, Jews and Arabs', *JJS* 38 (1987), 143–64.

—— 'The Problem of Hellenistic Syria', in A. Kuhrt and S. Sherwin-White (eds.), *Hellenism in the East* (1987), 110–33.

MILLER, J. M., 'Archaeological Survey of Central Moab', *BASOR* 234 (1979), 43–52.

MITCHELL, S., 'A New Inscription from Pisidia: Requisitioned Transport in the Roman Empire', *JRS* 66 (1976), 106–31.

—— 'R.E.C.A.M., Notes and Studies No. 3: A Latin Inscription from Galatia', *Anatolian Studies* 28 (1978), 93–6.

—— 'The Balkans, Anatolia, and Roman Armies across Asia Minor', *AFRBA*, 131–50.

—— 'Imperial Building in the Eastern Roman Provinces', in S. Macready and F. H. Thompson (eds.), *Roman Architecture in the Greek World* (Society of Antiquaries, 1987).

MITFORD, T. B., 'Some Inscriptions from the Cappadocian *Limes*, *JRS* 64 (1974), 160–75.

—— 'The Euphrates Frontier in Cappadocia', *SMR* ii (1977), 501–10.

—— 'The *Limes* in the Kurdish Taurus', *Roman Frontier Studies 1979* (1980), 913–26.

—— 'Cappadocia and Armenia Minor: Historical Setting of the Limes', *ANRW* ii. 7 (1980), 1169–228.

MITTMANN, S., 'Die römische Strasse von Gerasa nach Adraa', *ZDPV* 80 (1964), 113–36.

MONCHAMBERT, J.-Y., 'Le Moyen Khabour: Prospection préliminaire à la construction d'un barrage', *Annales Archéologiques Arabes Syriennes* 33/1 (1983), 233–7.

MOR, M., 'The Roman Army in Eretz-Israel in the Years AD 70–132', *DRBE*, 575–602.

MOREL, J.-M. A. W., 'The Early-Roman Defended Harbours at Velsen, North Holland', *SMR* iii (1986), 200–12.

MOUGHDAD, S., 'Bosra. Aperçu sur l'urbanisation de la ville à l'époque romaine', *Felix Ravenna* 111–112 (1976), 65–81.

MOUTERDE, R., and POIDEBARD, A., 'La voie antique des caravanes entre Palmyre et Hit, au IIᵉ siècle ap. J.-C.', *Syria* 12 (1931), 99–115.

MURRAY, G. W., 'The Roman Roads and Stations in the Eastern Desert of Egypt', *JEA* 11 (1925), 138–50.

NEGEV, A., 'Oboda, Mampsis and Provincia Arabia', *IEJ* 17 (1967), 46–55.

—— 'The Nabataeans and the Provincia Arabia', *ANRW* ii. 8 (1977), 520–686.

NÖLDEKE, T., 'Die Ghassanischen Fürsten aus dem Hause Gafnas', *Abhandlungen der königlichen preussischen Akademie der Wissenschaften zu Berlin* (1887).

OATES, D., 'A Note on Three Latin Inscriptions from Hatra', *Sumer* 11 (1955), 39–43.

—— and J., 'Ain Sinu: A Roman Frontier Post in Northern Iraq', *Iraq* 21 (1959), 207–42.

PARKER, S. T., 'A Tetrarchic Milestone from Roman Arabia', *ZPE* 62 (1986), 256–8.

—— 'Peasants, Pastoralists, and *Pax Romana*: A Different View', *BASOR* 265 (1987), 35–51.

—— and McDERMOTT, P. M., 'A Military Building Inscription from Roman Arabia', *ZPE* 29 (1978), 61–6.

PEETERS, P., 'Les ex-voto de Khosrau Aparwez à Sergiopolis', *Analecta Bollandiana* 65 (1947), 5–56.

PEKÁRY, T., 'Bemerkungen zur Chronologie des Jahrzehnts 250–260 n. Chr.' *Historia* 11 (1962), 123 ff.

PENNACCHIETTI, F. A., 'Il posto di Cipri', *Mesopotamia* 21 (1986), 85–95.

PETERS, F. E., 'The Nabataeans in the Hawran', *JAOS* 97 (1977), 263–77.

—— 'Byzantium and the Arabs of Syria', *AAAS* 27–8 (1977–8), 97–113.

PFLAUM, H.-G., 'Essai sur le cursus publicus sous le Haut-Empire romain', *Mémoires présentés par divers savants à l'Académie des Inscriptions et Belles-Lettres* 14 (1940), 189–391.

—— 'La fortification de la ville d'Adraha d'Arabie (259–260 à 274–275) d'après des inscriptions récemment découverts', *Syria* 29 (1952), 307–30.

—— 'Un nouveau diplôme militaire', *Syria* 44 (1967), 339–62.

PICCIRILLO, M., 'Rural Settlements in Byzantine Jordan', *Studies in the History and Archaeology of Jordan*, ii (1985), 257–61.

PIGANIOL, A., 'Observations sur le tarif de Palmyre', *Revue Historique* 195 (1945), 10–23.

POIDEBARD, A., 'Reconnaissance aérienne au Ledja et au Safa', *Syria* 9 (1928), 114–23.

—— and MOUTERDE, R., 'A propos de Saint Serge: aviation et épigraphie', *Analecta Bollandiana* (1949), 109–16.

POLOTSKY, H., 'The Greek Papyri from the Cave of Letters', *IEJ* 12 (1962), 258–62.

POUILLOUX, J., 'Deux inscriptions au théatre sud de Gérasa', *Liber Annuus* 27 (1977), 246–54.

—— 'Une troisième dédicace au théatre sud de Gérasa', *Liber Annuus* 29 (1979), 276–8.

RANKOV, N. B., 'M. Oclatinius Adventus in Britain', *Britannia* 18 (1987), 243–9.

RASCHKE, M., 'New Studies in Roman Commerce with the East', *ANRW* ii. 9 (1976), 604–1361.

REBUFFAT, R., 'Le bouclier de Doura', *Syria* 63 (1986), 85–105.

REEVES, C. N., 'A New Diploma for Syria-Palaestina', *ZPE* 33 (1979), 117–23.

REY-COQUAIS, J.-P., 'Syrie romaine, de Pompée à Dioclétien', *JRS* 68 (1978), 44–73.

—— 'Des montagnes au désert: Baetocécé, le *pagus Augustus* de Niha, La Ghouta à l'est de Damas', in E. Frézouls (ed.), *Sociétés urbaines, sociétés rurales dans l'Asie Mineure et la Syrie hellénistiques et romaines, Actes du colloque organisé à Strasbourg (novembre 1985)* (1987), 191–216.

RICHMOND, I. A., 'The Roman Siege-Works of Masàda, Israel', *JRS* 52 (1962), 142–55.

—— 'Palmyra under the Aegis of Rome', *JRS* 53 (1963), 43–54.

RILEY, D. N., 'Archaeological Air Photography and the Eastern Limes', *DRBE*, 661–76.

RODINSON, M., 'De l'archéologie à la sociologie historique. Notes méthodologiques sur le dernier ouvrage de G. Tchalenko', *Syria* 38 (1961), 170–200.

ROLL, I., 'The Roman Road System in Judaea', *The Jerusalem Cathedra* 3 (1983), 136–61.

—— and AYALON, E., 'Roman Roads in Western Samaria', *PEQ* 118 (1986), 114–34.

ROMER, F. E., 'Gaius Caesar's Military Diplomacy in the East', *TAPA* 109 (1979), 199–214.

ROMIOPOULOU, C., 'Un nouveau milliaire de la via Egnatia', *BCH* 98 (1974), 813–16.

ROQUES, D., 'Synésios de Cyrène et les migrations Berbères vers l'Orient (398–413)', *CRAI* (1983), 660–67.

ROSENTHAL, A. S., 'Leshonot Sopherim', in B. Kurtzweil (ed.), *Yuval Shay* (1958), 293–324.

ROSTOVTZEFF, M., 'Angariae', *Klio* 6 (1906), 249–58.

—— 'Synteleia tironon', *JRS* 8 (1918), 26–33.

—— 'Les Inscriptions caravanières de Palmyre', *Mélanges Gustave Glotz*, ii (Paris, 1932), 793–811.

—— 'Une nouvelle inscription caravanière de Palmyre', *Berytus* 2 (1935), 143–8.

ROTHENBERG, B., 'The 'Arabah in Roman and Byzantine Times in the Light of New Research', *Roman Frontier Studies 1967* (1971), 211–13.

ROUGÉ, J., 'L'histoire Auguste et l'Isaurie au IVᵉ siècle', *REA* 68 (1966), 282–315.

RUBIN, Z., 'Dio, Herodian, and Severus' Second Parthian War', *Chiron* 5 (1975), 419–41.

—— 'The Mediterranean and the Dilemma of the Roman Empire in Late Antiquity', *Mediterranean Historical Review* 1 (1986), 13–62.

—— 'Diplomacy and War in the Relations Between Byzantium and the Sassanids in the Fifth Century AD', *DRBE*, 677–95.

—— 'The Conversion of Mavia, The Saracen Queen', *Cathedra* 47 (1988), 25–49 (in Hebrew).

—— 'Sinai in the Itinerarium Egeriae' (forthcoming).

SAFRAI, S., 'The Commands regarding Shevi'it in Practice after the Destruction of the Temple', *Tarbiz* 35 (1966), 310–20 (in Hebrew).

—— 'A Note on *Burgarii* in Israel and its Vicinity', *Roman Frontier Studies 1967* (1971), 229 f.

—— 'The Relations between the Roman Army and the Jews of Eretz Yisrael after the Destruction of the Second Temple', *Roman Frontier Studies 1967* (1971), 224–29.

—— 'The *Nesiut* in the Second and Third Centuries and its Chronological Problems', *Proceedings of the Sixth World Congress of Jewish Studies, August, 1973*, ii (Jerusalem, 1975), 51–7 (in Hebrew), 412 f. (English summary).

SARTRE, M., 'Rome et les Nabatéens à la fin de la république', *REA* 81 (1979), 37–53.

—— 'La frontière méridionale de l'Arabie romaine', *La géographie administrative et politique d'Alexandre à Mahomet, Actes du Colloque de Strasbourg, 14–15 Juin 1979* (Leiden, 1981), 79–92.

—— 'Tribus et clans dans le Hawran antique', *Syria* 59 (1982), 77–91.

—— 'Le *dies-imperii* de Gordien III: une inscription inédite de Syrie', *Syria* 61 (1984), 49–61.

ŠAŠEL, J., 'Über Umfang und Dauer der Militärzone Praetentura Italiae et Alpium zur Zeit Mark Aurels', *Museum Helveticum* 31 (1974), 225–30.

SAUVAGET, J., 'Les Sassanides et Sergiopolis', *Byzantion* 14 (1939), 115–30.

SCHLEIERMACHER, W., 'Flavische Okkupationslimen in Raetien', *Jahrbuch RGZM* 2 (1955), 245–52.

SCHLUMBERGER, D., 'Bornes frontières de la Palmyrène', *Syria* 20 (1939), 43–73.

—— 'Les gentilices romains des Palmyréniens', *BEO* 9 (1942–43), 54–82.

—— 'L'inscription d'Hérodien: remarques sur l'histoire des princes de Palmyre', *BEO* 9 (1942–43), 35–50.

—— 'Le prétendu Camp du Dioclétien à Palmyre', *Mél. de l'Université St Joseph* 38 (1962), 79–97.

SCHÖNBERGER, H., 'The Roman Frontier in Germany: An Archaeological Survey', *JRS* 59 (1969), 144–97.

SCHWABE, M., 'The Burgos Inscription from Caesarea in Eretz Israel', *J. N. Epstein Jubilee Volume* (Jerusalem, 1950) = *Tarbiz* 20 (1950), 273–83 (in Hebrew).

—— 'A Greco-Christian Inscription from Aila', *HTR* 64 (1953), 49–55.

SCHWERTHEIM, E., 'Zu Hadrian's Reisen und Stadtgründungen in Kleinasien: Eine neue Gründungsära', *Epigraphica Anatolica* 6 (1985), 37–42.

SEGAL, A., 'Roman Cities in the Province of Arabia', *Journal of the Society of Architectural Historians* 40 (1981), 108–21.

SEGAL, J. B., 'Mesopotamian Communities from Julian to the Rise of Islam', *PBA* 41 (1955), 109–41.

SESTON, W., 'Du *Comitatus* de Dioclétien aux *comitatenses* de Constantin', *Historia* 4 (1955), 284–96.

ŠEVČENKO, I., 'The Early Period of the Sinai Monastery in the Light of Its Inscriptions', *DOP* 20 (1966), 255–63.

SEYRIG, H., 'L'incorporation de Palmyre à l'empire romain', *Syria* 13 (1932), 266–77 = *Antiquités Syriennes*, iii. 255–77.

—— 'Antiquités syriennes, 12: Textes relatifs à la garnison romaine de Palmyre', *Syria* 14 (1933), 152–68.

—— 'Antiquités syriennes, 37: Postes romains sur la route de Médine', *Syria* 22 (1941), 218–23.

—— 'Le Statut de Palmyre', *Syria* 22 (1941), 155–74 = *Antiquités Syriennes*, iii. 36 (1946), 142–61.

—— 'Sur les ères de quelques villes de Syrie, *Syria* 27 (1950), 5–56.

—— 'Le monnayage de Ptolemais en Phénicie', *Revue numismatique* 6/4 (1962), 25–50.

—— 'Divinités de Ptolemais', *Syria* 39 (1962), 193–207.

SHATZMAN, I., 'The Beginning of the Roman Defensive System in Judaea', *American Journal of Ancient History* 8 (1983), 130–60.

—— 'The Army and Security Problems in the Kingdom of Herod', *Milet* (Everyman's University, Studies in Jewish History and Culture, in Hebrew), 1 (1983), 75–98.

SHAW, B. D., 'Bandits in the Roman Empire', *Past and Present* 105 (1984), 3–52.

SHERK, R., 'Roman Geographical Exploration and Military Maps', *ANRW* ii. 1, 534–62.

SIDEBOTHAM, S. E., 'Aelius Gallus and Arabia', *Latomus* 45 (1986), 590–602.

SIEGELMANN, A., 'The Identification of Gaba Hippeon', *PEQ* 116 (1984), 89–93.

SIVAN, H. S., 'An unedited Letter of the Emperor Honorius to the Spanish Soldiers', *ZPE* 61 (1985), 273–87.

SOLOMONIK, E. I., 'New Epigraphical Documents from Chersonesos', *Akademiya nauk Ykrainskoi SSR, Institut Arkheologii* (Kiev, 1964), 122 ff. (in Russian).

SOREQ, Y., 'Rabbinical Evidences About the Pagi Vicinales in Israel', *JQR* 65 (1975), 221–4.

SPEIDEL, M. P., 'The Eastern Desert Garrisons under Augustus and Tiberius', *SMR* ii (1977), 511–15.

—— 'The Roman Army in Arabia', *ANRW* ii. 8 (1977), 688–730.

—— 'A Tile Stamp of the Cohors I Thracum Milliaria from Hebron/ Palestine', *ZPE* 35 (1979), 170–2.

—— 'The Caucasus Frontier. Second Century Garrisons at Apsarus, Petra and Phasis', *Roman Frontier Studies 1979* (1980), 657–60.

—— 'The Roman Army in Judaea under the Procurators. The Italian and the Augustan Cohort in the Acts of the Apostles', *Ancient Society* 13–14 (1982–3), 233–40.

—— 'The Roman Army in Asia Minor: Recent Epigraphical Discoveries and Research', *AFRBA*, 7–23.

—— 'The Roman Road to Dumata (Jawf in Saudi Arabia) and the Frontier Strategy of *Praetensione Colligare*', *Historia* 36 (1987), 213–21.

—— and REYNOLDS, J., 'A Veteran of Legio I Parthica from Carian Aphrodisias', *Epigraphica Anatolica* 5 (1985), 31–5.

SPERBER, D., 'The Centurion as Tax-Collector', *Latomus* 28 (1969), 186–9.

—— 'On Pubs and Policemen in Roman Palestine', *ZDMG* 120 (1970), 257–63.

—— 'Patronage in Amoraic Palestine', *JESHO* 14 (1971), 227–52.

SPIJKERMAN, A., 'The Coins of Eleutheropolis Iudaeae', *Liber Annuus* 22 (1972), 369–84.

STANDISH, J. F., 'The Caspian Gates', *Greece & Rome* 178 (1970), 17–24.

STEIN, SIR AUREL, 'The Ancient Trade Route past Hatra and the Roman Posts', *JRAS* 9 (1941), 299–316.

STROBEL, A., 'Observations about the Roman Installations at Mukawer', *ADAJ* 19 (1974), 101–27.

SULLIVAN, R. D., 'The Dynasty of Emesa', *ANRW* ii. 8, 198–219.

—— 'The Dynasty of Commagene', *ANRW* ii. 8, 732–98.

SYME, R., 'Galatia and Pamphylia under Augustus: the Governorships of Piso, Quirinius and Silvanus', *Klio* 27 (1934), 122–48.

—— 'Antonius Saturninus', *JRS* 68 (1978), 12–21.

—— 'Hadrian and the Vassal Princes', *Athenaeum* 59 (1981), 273–83.

—— 'Tigranocerta. A Problem Misconceived', *AFRBA*, 61–70.

—— 'Isaura and Isauria. Some Problems', in E. Frézouls (ed.), *Sociétés urbaines, sociétés rurales dans l'Asie Mineure et la Syrie hellénistiques et romaines, Actes du colloque organisé à Strasbourg (novembre 1985)* (1987), 131–47.

SIJPESTIJN, P., 'A New Document Concerning Hadrian's Visit to Egypt', *Historia* 18 (1969), 109–18.

THOMSEN, P., 'Die römischen Meilensteine der Provinzen Syria, Arabia, und Palaestina', *ZDPV* 40 (1917), 1–103.

—— 'Die lateinischen und griechischen Inschriften der Stadt Jerusalem und ihrer nächsten Umgebung. 1. Nachtrag', *ZDPV* 64 (1941), 201–56.

TIBILETTI, G., 'Ricerche di storia agraria romana', *Athenaeum* 28 (1950), 182–266; esp. 'colonie latine e colonie romane', 219–32.

TINH, T. T., 'Deux inscriptions sur l'invasion arabe', *Soloi, dix campagnes de foulles (1964–74)* (1985), 115–25.

TOYNBEE, J. M. C., 'Two Male Portrait-Heads from Hatra', *Sumer* 26 (1970), 231–5.

—— 'Some Problems of Romano-Parthian Sculpture at Hatra', *JRS* 62 (1972), 106–10.

TROUSSET, P., 'Signification d'une frontière: nomades et sedentaires dans la zone du limes d'Afrique', *Roman Frontier studies 1979* (1980), 931–42.

TSAFRIR, Y., 'St Catherine's Monastery', *IEJ* 28 (1978), 218–29.

—— 'The Maps used by Theodosius: On the Pilgrim Maps of the Holy Land and Jerusalem in the Sixth Century', *DOP* 40 (1986), 129–45.

TZAFERIS, V., 'A Tower and Fortress near Jerusalem', *IEJ* 24 (1974), 84–94.

TZORI, N., 'An Inscription of the Legio VI Ferrata from the Northern Jordan Valley', *IEJ* 21 (1971), 53 f.

VAILHÉ, S., 'La prise de Jérusalem par les Perses', *Revue de l'Orient Chrétien* 6 (1901), 643–9.

VAN RENGEN, W., 'L'épigraphie grecque et latine de Syrie', *ANRW* ii. 8, 31–53.

VASILIEV, A. A., 'Notes on Some Episodes Concerning the Relations Between the Arabs and the Byzantine Empire from the Fourth to the Sixth Century', *DOP* 9–10 (1956), 306–16.

VETRALI, L., 'Le iscrizioni dell'acquedotto romano presso Betlemme', *Liber Annuus* 17 (1967), 149–61.

VILLENEUVE, F., 'Ad-Diyateh: Village et castellum romains et byzantins à l'est du Jebel Druze (Syrie)', *DRBE*, 697–715.

VINCENT, H., 'Chronique—notes de voyage', *RB* 7 (1898), 424–51.

VOLKMAR, F., 'The Roman Fortress', in Y. Aharoni (ed.), *Beersheba i* (1973), 83–9.

WAGNER, J., 'Legio III Scythica in Zeugma am Euphrat', *SMR* ii (1977), 517–39.

—— 'Provincia Osrhoenae: New Archaeological Finds illustrating the military organisation under the Severan Dynasty', *AFRBA*, 103–30.

WARD-PERKINS, J. B., 'The Roman West and the Parthian East', *PBA* 51 (1965), 175–99.

WATERHOUSE, S. D., and IBACH, R., 'Heshbon 1973—The Topographical Survey', *Andrews University Seminar Studies* 13 (1975), 217–33.

WEINSTEIN, M. E., and TURNER, E. G., 'Greek and Latin Papyri from Qasr Ibrîm', *JEA* 62 (1976), 115–30.

WHITBY, M., 'Procopius and the Development of Roman Defences in Upper Mesopotamia', *DRBE*, 717–35.

—— 'Procopius' Description of Dara', ibid., 737–83.

WIDENGREN, G., 'Iran, der grosse Gegner Roms: Königsgewalt, Feudalismus, Militärwesen', *ANRW* ii. 9, 220–306.

WIESEHOFER, J., 'Iranische Ansprüche an Rom auf ehemals Achaimenidische Territorien', *Archaeologische Mitteilungen aus Iran* 19 (1986), 177–85.

WILL, E., 'Marchands et chefs de caravanes à Palmyre', *Syria* 34 (1957), 262–77.

—— 'Pline l'ancien et Palmyre: un problème d'histoire ou d'histoire littéraire', *Syria* 62 (1985), 263–9.

WINTER, E., 'Handel und Wirtschaft in Sasanidisch-(ost-)Romischen Verträgen und Abkommen', *Münstersche Beiträge zur antiken Handelsgeschichte* 6 (1987), 46–72.

WISSMANN, H. VON, 'Die Geschichte des Sabäerreichs und der Feldzug des Aelius Gallus', *ANRW* ii 9. 308–544.

YORKE, V. W., 'Inscriptions from Eastern Asia Minor', *JHS* 18 (1898), 306–27.

ZAWADZKI, T., 'La résidence de Dioclétien à Spalatum, sa dénomination dans l'Antiquité', *Mus. Helv.* 44 (1987), 223–30.

ZIEGLER, R., 'Antiochia, Laodicea und Sidon in der Politik der Severer', *Chiron* 8 (1978), 493–513.

MAPS

For most of the region discussed in this work detailed maps are not available to the general public. Here follows a list of those which have been accessible to me:

The Tactical Pilotage Charts produced under the direction of the Department of Military Survey, Ministry of Defence, UK, on a scale of 1:500,000 and of 1:1,000,000. These are available for the entire area and are excellent for topography.

The World Series produced under the same auspices and on the same scale. These are the best maps available for modern Turkey and Syria.

The only proper set of maps for any part of the region is that produced by 'the Survey of Israel', at a scale of 1:100,000 and 1:50,000. The latter has been my main source of reference for the relevant area. The 'Archaeological Survey of Israel', Jerusalem, has published a number of archaeological maps at a scale of 1:20,000.

For archaeological research the maps of the Survey of Western Palestine, published in 1880 are still invaluable.

The Archaeological Map of the Hashemite Kingdom of Jordan in three sheets (1:250,000). These are the best maps available to me for modern Jordan, but they contain very little archaeological information.

For the Roman archaeology of Jordan recourse must still be had to the maps produced by Brünnow and Domaszewski, *Die Provincia Arabia*, vol. i.

For Syria there are the maps in A. Poidebard, *La trace de Rome dans le désert de Syrie* (1934) and in Poidebard and P. Mouterde, *Le limes de Chalcis* (1945). The information from these maps and from that contained in the work of Sir Aurel Stein is conveniently reproduced in the main map in S. Gregory and D. Kennedy, *Sir Aurel Stein's Limes Report* (1985).

For the Roman road-system in Anatolia there are now various publications by D. French.

ADDITIONAL BIBLIOGRAPHY

BOOKS

ADAMS, A. in S. Walker and Averil Cameron (eds.), *The Greek Renaissance in the Roman Empire* (1989).

BOWMAN, A. K. and THOMAS, J. D., *Vindolanda: the Latin Writing Tablets* (1983).

COOK, J. M., *The Persian Empire* (London, 1983).

COTTON, H. M. and GEIGER, J. (eds.), *Masada ii, The Yigael Yadin Excavations 1963–1965: Final Reports, The Latin and Greek Documents* (Jerusalem, 1989).

CRONE, P., *Meccan Trade and the Rise of Islam* (Princeton, 1987).

DAVIES, R., *Service in the Roman Army*, ed. D. Breeze and V. Maxfield (Edinburgh, 1989).

DELBRÜCK, H., *Geschichte der Kriegskunst im Rahmen der Politische Geschichte*, 2 vols. (Berlin, 1921³, repr. 1966).

DELBRÜCK, R., *Die Münzbildnisse von Maximinus bis Carinus* (Berlin, 1940).

DENNIS, G. T. (ed.), *Three Byzantine Military Treatises: Text, Translation, and Notes* (Washington, DC, 1985).

DODGEON, M. H. and LIEU, S. N. C., *The Roman Eastern Frontier and the Persian Wars (AD 226–363)* (London, 1991).

FEBVRE, L., *La terre et l'évolution humaine* (repr. Paris, 1970).

FRENCH D. H. and LIGHTFOOT, C. S., *The Eastern Frontier of the Roman Empire: Proceedings of a Colloquium held at Ankara in September 1988* (Oxford, BAR International Series, No. 553, 1989).

GATIER, P.-L., HELLY, N., and REY-COQUAIS, J.-P., *Géographie historique au Proche-Orient (Syrie, Phénicie, Arabie grecques, romaines, byzantines)*, Actes de la Table Ronde de Valbonne, 16–18 Septembre 1985, Centre National de la Recherche Scientifique, Notes et Monographies Techniques No. 23 (Paris, 1988).

HALDON, J. F., *Constantine Porphyrogenitus: Three Treatises on Imperial Military Expeditions* (Vienna, 1990).

HARLEY, J. B. and WOODWARD, D., *The History of Cartography*, i, *Cartography in Prehistoric, Ancient, and Medieval Europe and the Mediterranean* (Chicago and London, 1987).

HORSLEY, R. A. and HANSON, J. S., *Bandits, Prophets and Messiahs: Popular Movements in the Time of Jesus* (Minneapolis, Minn., 1985).

KAEGI, W. E., *Byzantine Military Unrest 471–843: an Interpretation* (Amsterdam, 1981).

—— *Some Thoughts on Byzantine Military Strategy*, The Hellenic Studies Lecture (Brookline, Mass., 1983).

KEPPIE, L., *Scotland's Roman Remains* (Edinburgh, 1986).

LEPPER, F. and FRERE, S., *Trajan's Column: a New Edition of the Cichorius Plates* (Gloucester, 1988).

LEWIS, N. (ed.), *The Documents from the Bar Kokhba Period in the Cave of Letters: Greek Papyri*, with Y. Yadin and Jonas C. Greenfield (eds.), *Aramaic and Nabatean Signatures and Subscriptions* (Jerusalem, 1989).

LINDER, A., *The Jews in Roman Imperial Legislation* (Detroit, and Jerusalem, 1987).

MATTHEWS, J., *The Roman Empire of Ammianus* (London, 1989).

NEESEN, L., *Untersuchungen zu den direkten Staatsabgaben der römischen Kaiserzeit (27 v. Chr.–284 n. Chr.)* (Bonn, 1980).

NORTHEDGE, A., *et al.*, *Excavations at 'Ana* (Warminster, Wilts. 1988).

PLASSART, A., *Mélanges Glotz*, ii (1934).

—— *Nouveau choix d'inscriptions grecques*, l'Institut Fernand-Courby (Paris, 1971).

POTTER, D. S., *Prophecy and History in the Crisis of the Roman Empire: a Historical Commentary on the Thirteenth Sibylline Oracle* (Oxford, 1990).

SARTRE, M., *L'Orient Romain: Provinces et sociétés provinciales en Mediterranée orientale d'Auguste aux Sévères* (Paris, 1991).

SHAHÎD, I., *Byzantium and the Arabs in the Fifth Century* (Washington, DC, 1989).

STARCKY, J., *Palmyre* (1952).

WHITTAKER, C. R., *Les frontières de l'empire romain* (Besançon, 1989).

ARTICLES

ADAMS, J. N., BOWMAN A. K., and THOMAS, J. D., 'Two Letters from Vindolanda', *Brittania* 21 (1990).

BAUZOU, T., 'Les voies romaines entre Damas et Amman', *Table Ronde Valbonne*, 293 ff.

BIANCHI, A., 'Aspetti della politica economico-fiscale di Filippo l'Arabo', *Aegyptus* 63 (1983), 185–98.

BOLTOUNOVA, A. I., 'Quelques notes sur l'inscription de Vespasien, trouvée à Mtskhetha', *Klio* 53 (1971), 213–22.

BRAUND, D., 'Coping with the Caucasus: Roman responses to local conditions in Colchis', *EFRE*, 31–43.

DABROWA, E., 'Roman Policy in Transcaucasia from Pompey to Domitian', *EFRE*, 67–76.

DEVIJVER, H., 'Equestrian Officers from the East', *EFRE*, 77–111.

DILKE, O. A. W., 'The Culmination of Greek Cartography in Ptolemy', in J. B. Harley and D. Woodward (eds.), *The History of Cartography*, i (1987), 177–200.

—— 'Maps in the Service of the State: Roman Cartography to the End of the Augustan Era', ibid. 201–11.

—— 'Itineraries and Geographical Maps in the Early and Late Roman Empires', ibid. 234–57.

—— 'Cartography in the Byzantine Empire', ibid. 258–75.

DOBSON, B., 'The Function of Hadrian's Wall', *Archaeologia Aeliana* 5/14 (1986), 1–30.

EADIE, J. W., 'Strategies of Economic Development in the Roman East: The Red Sea Trade Revisited', *EFRE*, 113–20.

FEBVRE, L., 'Frontière', *Rev. Synth. Hist.* 45 (1928), 31–44.

FEISSEL, D. and GASCOU, J., 'Documents d'archives romains inédits du Moyen Euphrate (IIIe siècle après J.-C.)', *CRAI* 1990, 535–61.

GAWLIKOWSKI, M., 'La route de l'Euphrate d'Isidore à Julien, *Table Ronde Valbonne*, 77–98.

GERGEL, R. A., 'The Tel Shalem Hadrian Reconsidered', *AJA* 95 (1991), 231–51.

GOPAL, SURENDRA, *TLS*, 3 May 1991.

GRENET, F., 'Les Sassanides à Doura-Europos (253 ap. J.-C.), réexamen du matériel épigraphique iranien du site', *Table Ronde Valbonne*, 133–58.

HALDON, J. F. and KENNEDY, H., 'The Arab-Byzantine Frontier in the Eighth and Ninth Centuries', *Zbornik Radova Visantološkog Instituta* 19 (1980), 79–116.

HIRSCHFELD, Y. and KLONER, A., 'Khorbet el-Qasr: A Byzantine Fort in the Judaean Desert', *Bulletin of the Anglo-Israel Archaeological Society* 8 (1988–9), 5–20.

James, S., 'Dura-Europos and the Chronology of Syria in the 250s AD', *Chiron* 15 (1985), 111–24.

KAEGI, W. E., 'Challenges to Late Roman and Byzantine Military Operations in Iraq (4th–9th Centuries)', *Klio* 73 (1991), 586–94.

KENNEDY, D., 'The Military Contribution of Syria to the Roman Imperial Army', *EFRE*, 235–46.

—— and NORTHEDGE, A., 'The History of 'Ana, Classical Sources', in A. Northedge, *Excavations at 'Ana* (1988), 6–8.

KINDLER, A., 'The Numismatic Finds from the Roman Fort at Yotvata', *IEJ* 39 (1989), 261–6.

KNAUF, E. A. and BROOKER, C. H., review of R. G. Khouri and D. Whitcomb, *Aqaba 'Port of Palestine on the China Sea'* (Amman, 1988), *ZDPV* 104 (1988), 179–81.

KRAMER, B. and HAGEDORN, D., 'Zwei Ptolemäische Texte aus der Hamburger Papyrussammlung', *Archiv für Papyrusforschung* 33 (1987), 9–21.

LAST, R. and STEIN, A., 'Ala Antiana in Scythopolis: A New Inscription from Beth-Shean', *ZPE* 81 (1990), 224–8.

LEE, A. D., 'Campaign Preparations in Late Roman–Persian Warfare', *EFRE*, 257–65.

LIGHTFOOT, C. S. and HEALEY, J. F., 'A Roman Veteran on the Tigris', *Epigraphica Anatolica* 17 (1991), 1–7.

LINDNER, R. P., 'Nomadism, Horses and Huns', *Past and Present* 92 (1981), 3–19.

MACADAM, H. I., 'Fragments of a Latin Building Inscription from Aqaba, Jordan', *ZPE* 79 (1989), 163–71.

—— 'Ptolemy's Geography and the Wadi Sirhan', *Table Ronde Valbonne*, 55–76.

—— 'Epigraphy and the *Notitia Dignitatum (Oriens 37)*', *EFRE*, 295–309.

MACDONALD, D., 'Dating the Fall of Dura-Europos', *Historia* 35 (1986), 45–68.

MAYERSON, P., 'Saracens and Romans: Micro–Macro Relationships', *BASOR* 274 (1989), 71–9.

MESHEL, Z., 'A Fort at Yotvata from the Time of Diocletian', *IEJ* 39 (1989), 228–38.

MILLAR, F., 'The Roman *Coloniae* of the Near East: a Study of Cultural Relations' in H. Solin and Mika Kajava (eds.), *Roman Eastern Policy and Other Studies in Roman History: Proceedings of a Colloquium at Tvärminne, 2–3 October 1987* (Helsinki, 1990), 7–58.

MITFORD, T., 'High and Low Level Routes across the Taurus and Antitaurus', *EFRE,* 329–33.

OKAMURA, L., 'Western Legions in Baalbek, Lebanon: Colonial Coins (AD 244–247) of the Philippi', *Historia* 37 (1988), 126–8.

OOST, S. I., 'The Alexandrian Seditions under Philip and Gallienus', *Classical Philology* 56 (1961), 1–20.

PATTENDEN, P., 'The Byzantine Early Warning System', *Byzantion* 53 (1983), 258–99.

ROLL, I., 'A Latin Imperial Inscription from the Time of Diocletian Found at Yotvata', *IEJ* 39 (1989), 239–60.

RUBIN, Z., 'Sinai in the Itinerarium Egeriae', in *Atti del convegno internazionale sulla Peregrinatio Egeriae, 23–25 Ottobre 1987* (Arezzo, n.d.), 177–91.

—— 'Byzantium and Southern Arabia: the Policy of Anastasius', *EFRE*, 383–420.

SHAHÎD, I., 'Byzantium and Kinda', *Byzantinische Zeitung* 53 (1960), 57–73.

SIDEBOTHAM, S. E., *et al.*, 'Fieldwork on the Red Sea Coast: the 1987 Season', *JARCE* 26 (1989), 127–66.

SPEIDEL, M. P., 'Roman Troops at Aulutrene. Observations on Two Inscriptions,' *Epigraphica Anatolica* 10 (1987), 97–100.

STAROIEWSKI, M., 'Bibliographia Egeriana', *Augustinianum* 14 (1979).

SYME, R., 'Military Geography at Rome', *Classical Antiquity* 7 (1988), 227–51.

TALBERT, R. J. A., Review of O. A. W. Dilke, *Greek and Roman Maps, JRS* 87 (1987), 210–12.

—— 'Rome's Empire and Beyond: the Spatial Aspect', in *Gouvernants et gouvernés dans l'Imperium Romanum, Cahiers des Etudes Anciennes* 26 (1990), 215–23.

WHITCOMB, D., ' "Diocletian's" misr at 'Aqaba', *ZDPV* 106 (1990) [1991], 156–61.

WHITTAKER, C. R., 'Thorns in Rome's Side', *TLS*, 22 Mar. 1991.

ZITTERKOPF, R. E. and SIDEBOTHAM, S. E., 'Stations and Towers on the Quseir–Nile Road', *JEA* 75 (1989), 155–89.

INDEX

Abbahu, R. 87 f.
Abila 136
Abilene 294
Abokharabos (Abukarib) 248
Absarus 44, 45
abstention from alcohol 73
Abu Ghosh 428
Abyad, H. el 163, 176 f.
Acampsis 10
Acco see Ptolemais
Acre see Ptolemais
Acts of the Pagan Martyrs 278
ad Dianam (Yotvetah, Ghadyan) 164, 188–
    91, 212
adaeratio (tironia, aurum tironicium) 302–4
Adiabeni 339
adoption 266
Adraa
    walls of 133 f., 350
Adrianople (Hadrianopolis)
    battle of 25, 303
Aela 11
    base of X Fretensis at 11, 164, 168 f., 325
Aelia Capitolina 323–5, 353 f.
    see also Jerusalem
Aelius Capito, P. 433
Aelius Gallus 384, 403
Aerita (Ahire) 135
aggadah 7 f.
agraria statio 175 f., 235 n., 257
Agrippa II 28, 277, 330
Aha, R. 293
Ahire see Aerita
Ain Sinu 256
Aine 36, 294
akhsaniah (hospitium, compulsory
    billeting) 297–301, 380
Akiba, R. 84
Al-Mundhir 77
alae
    Constantiana 188 f.
    Gallorum et Thracum Antiana 434
    Herculana 143 n.
    Ituraeorum 60
    I Augusta Thracum 124 n., 346
    I Ulpia Singularium 143 n.
    II Felix Valentiniana 175 n.
Alani 48, 49, 261

Albani 9, 43, 229
Aleppo see Beroea
Alexander the Great 404
    emulation of 26, 121 n., 265
Alexandria in Egypt 12, 274 f., 277–9
    and massacre under Caracalla 278, 382
Amanus Mt. 11
Amida 252, 254
Ammaus see Emmaus (Motza, Qolonia)
Ammianus
    description of Arabia 171
    description of Persia 406
amoraim 7
Amorcesos (Imru'l-qais) 247
Ana (Anatha) 147, 150, 151, 152
Anastasius I 438
    and Darial pass 230 f.
    military constructions of 212
    and Persia 262
    and Samaritan revolt 90
    and troubles in the East 76
Anatha see Ana
angareia see *angaria*
angaria 291–7
    carts 293, 380, 382
    donkeys 292
    labourers 292
    oxes 293
    post-horses 291, 296
    and repair of roads and road-
        installations 294 f.
    and requisition of animals 293, 296, 382
    and supervision of stations 295, 296
Anicetus, rebellion of 40
annexation
    profitability of 384 f., 396
    see also Arabia, Cappadocia, Commagene,
        Judaea, Mesopotamia
annona militaris 282, 285–91, 293
    arms 291, 382
    barley 289
    bread 290, 296
    and campaigns 380, 382 f.
    chaff 289
    charcoal 296
    clothing 286, 287, 296, 382
    cow hides 289
    dough 286

annona militaris cont.
  foodstuffs 286, 382 f.
  and imperial visits 290 f.
  lime 296
  and *limitanei* 287 f., 295
  and payment for 287
  and payment in money instead of
    kind 287, 288 f.
  and requisition of animals 286, 296, 382
  meat 289
  timber 296
  use of pastures 289
  wine 286, 287
  wine skins 292
  see also supplies
annual fair(s) 256
anti-Oriental attitude(s) 20 f.
Anti-Lebanon 11
Antigonus 29
Antinoopolis 354, 357
Antioch in Syria 11, 35, 274 f.
  army unit(s) in 269–76
  as headquarters and rearbase 274 f., 276,
    Appendix II
  brigands in 97
  capture by Sassanians 15, 394
  corruption in 273
  donations made by Eudocia 366, 438
  Great Church in 364
  militia of 271, 326
  public buildings in 364 f.
  punished by Septimius Severus 436
  standing of 274 f.
  strife between Jews and gentiles 271, 272
  support for Avidius Cassius of 271
  support for Persia in 260, 271
  support for Pescennius Niger of 271, 436
  support for Zenobia 223, 227, 271, 275
Antipatris (Apheq) 361
Antitaurus 11
Antonia fortress 279, 280
Antoninus Pius 25, 27, 49
Antoninus (deserter), 31
Antony 29, 141, 403
Apamea 39, 281 n.
Appian
  against unrestricted expansion 27, 388
  on Roman empire 396
'Aqaba *see* Aela
aquae 174
aqueduct(s) 353, 357 f., 430
Arabia
  annexation of 119
  borders of 398
  disposition of army in 122–31
  equestrian officers from 350

permanent garrison of 118
  Trajanic activity in 349–51
Arabian expedition of Aelius Gallus 384,
  403
Ararat 10
'Aravah 11, 188 f.
  military presence in 128–31
Araxes 10, 11
Arcadius 266
archaeological evidence
  interpretation of 6–7, 133, 156 f., 162
archers 144, 225, 330
Ardashir 21
Arethas the Kindite 210, 243
Arethas the Ghassanid 242, 244, 249, 263,
  264
Aristides 27, 272
Armenia
  division of 234
  geography of 10 f.
  routes into 10 f.
  status of 16, 229
  uprising in 572 in 274
  war in under Nero 40 f.
armouries 280
  see also imperial armouries
army on campaign
  supplies for 380, 382 f.
army
  and politics 383 f.
army presence beyond border 398–400
Arnon (Wadi Mujib) 92 n., 170 f.
Arrian 46, 48
Artabanus III 21, 22, 23
Artaxata 10, 52, 231, 407
artificial barrier(s) 413–16
Ascalon 136
Ashqelon *see* Ascalon
Aspebetos 246 f.
Athens
  and Hadrian 356 f.
Athis *see* Dibsi Faraj
Augustus on the empire 395 f., 397
Aurelian 32, 223
Aurelius Marcellinus 136 n.
aurum tironicum (tironia, adaeratio) 302–4
aurum coronarium 301 f.
Avdat *see* Oboda
Avidius Cassius 15, 30, 270
  results of campaign of 51 f., 391
Azraq 126, 176, 178 n.

Babatha archive 125
Babylon 144
Babylonian Jews in Batanaea 329–31
Baku 44

Balikh 13
banditry Chapter II *passim*, 182, 183, 282, 318, 321
Bar Kokhba war 84, 85, 87, 248, 353, 431, 433
Barabbas 79 f.
Batanaea (Bashan)
    Babylonian Jews settled in 329–31
Batavi 411
Batavian revolt 58, 59
bath house(s) 174, 430
Bathyra
    Jewish settlers at 64
Bedouin 70 f., 214
Beer Sheva edict 287
Belisarius 210 f., 241
beneficiarii 127 n., 135, 401 n.
Beqa' valley 11, 12, 60, 318
Berbers 76
Beroea (Aleppo) 39
Berytus (Beirut) 12, 60 f., 318–21
    Herodian donations for 342 f.
    militia from 325
Beshir (castra Praetorii Mobeni) 164, 172 f., 174, 201 f., 203
Beth Horon 429
Beth Govrin *see* Eleutheropolis
Beth Yerah 434
Betthoro *see* Lejjun
Bewegungsheer 170
Bezabde 42 n., 168, 252, 382
Bijan 147, 150 n.
bishop(s) 178, 206, 250 n.
    authority of 246, 253, 298
blockhouse(s) 107, 430
    see also burgi
booty 380–2
Bosporan Kingdom 401
Bostra 13, 90, 124, 349–51
    Flavian emperors and urban development of 344 f.
    legionary fortress at 123 f., 165, 427
    received colonial status 361
    Trajan and urban development of 349 f.
    walls of 133, 350
Boudicca
    revolt of 58, 59, 384
bouleutes
    social status of 137
boundary stones 352, 358, 396 f.
Brasidas 375
brick-ovens 328
bridge(s) 41, 392, 411, 412, 413
bridgehead(s) 41, 412
bridging 411–13
Britain
    motive(s) for wars in 388–90

Bulla (bandit) 88 f.
burganin 182, 183, 184, 294
burgarii 132, 179, 180, 181, 183
burgasin 294
burgi 176, 178–86
Burqu Qasr 185
Byzantine military policy 265–8
Byzantium 380

Caecilius Bassus, Q 29
Caesarea in Cappadocia 275
Caesarea Philippi 341 f.
Caesarea Maritima 87 f., 90, 118, 181, 353
    granted colonial status 349
    Hadrianic aqueduct at 353
    Herod's harbour at 341
Caesennius Paetus 40, 41
camel raiding 72
camel rider(s) 225
    see also Dromedarii
Camulodunum (Colchester) 317 f.
Canatha 65, 136, 351
Caparcotna *see* Legio
Capernaum (Kefar Nahum) 137, 434
Cappadocia
    annexation of 384
    permanent garrison of 36–8
captives, information from 407 f.
caput viae 112
Caracalla
    at Antioch 436
    eastern campaign of 23, 30, 382
    grants of city status of 361
    in Britain 389 f.
    and massacre in Alexandria 278, 382
caravan(s) 144–7, 152 f., 168, 182
caravanserai 200, 201
Carrhae 221, 360
Carus 32
Caspian Gates 404 f.
Cassius 237
Cassius Dio
    against expansion 26, 388
    on Caracalla 23, 30, 382, 383, 387
    on Commodus 387, 390 f.
    on Hadrian 24, 355 f.
    on Septimius Severus 26, 88 f., 381, 387, 389 f., 394
    on Trajan 24 n., 26, 51
castra 173
castrum 176 f.
Cato the Elder 25
Caucasian Gates 404 f.
Caucasus 9, 42–50
    passes 47 f. 229 f.
cave(s) 63 f., 64, 85

centurion(s)
in charge of road-repair 294
and collection of taxes 287
as commanders of garrisons 125, 135–8,
174, 362
as interpreter and *negotiator* 399
social status of 137 f.
Cepha 168
Cestius Gallus 110, 325
Chabinas (Çendere) bridge 35
chains of wells 189
Chalcis (Kinnesrin) 367
Chatti 41, 392
choice of frontier line(s) 387–94
Christianization of empire 16
Christians in Persia 261, 264
churches built with imperial funding 364–9
churches in forts 206 f.
Cicero, Tullius M. 58 f.
on veteran colonies 313 f.
Cilician Gates 11
Circesium 165, 168
city coinage and legionary standards 431
civilian population and warfare 380 f.
see also militias
Claudius (bandit) 88 f., 98
client kingdom(s) 119, 396 f.
see also Albani, Arabia, Cappadocia,
Commagene, Emesa, Iberia, Judaea,
Nabataeans, Osrhoene
Clysma (Suez) 92 n., 205
Cohorts
Augusta 105
Dromedariorum 127
Gaetulorum 127
Italica 105
I Augusta Thracum 125
I Flavia Chalcidenorum Equitata 144 n.,
165 n.
I Flavia Urbana 317 n.
I Milliaria Thracum 38 n., 174, 430
I Salutaria 91
II Italica C. R. 105 n.
II Ituraeorum 398 n.
II Pia Fidelis 38 n.
II Thracum Syriaca 138
II Ulpia Equitata 151 n.
III Augusta Thracum 126 n., 151 n.
IV Phrygum 175 n.
VI Ulpia Petraeorum 429
IX Maurorum Gordiana 154
XII Palaestinorum 106, 151 n.
XIII Urbana 317 n.
XX Palmyrenorum 37, 144, 151 n.
Colchis (Lazica) 9, 43, 232, 233, 260, 264
comes Orientis 276

Commagene
annexation of 22, 39 f.
Commodus 387, 390 f.
communications
lines of 12, 14
security of 102 f.
compulsory labour 293–7, 365
and repair of *burgi* 294
compulsory billeting *see akhsaniah*
confiscation of land(s) 58, 317, 323, 348
conscription 58, 59, 302–4
Constantina 11, 168
Constantine 162 f., 393
and church building 364
Constantinople 366
Constantius 25, 32, 206, 254, 393, 438
consularis Syriae 276
Coptus 200
Corbulo 15, 27, 29, 40, 41, 56, 102, 379
and military discipline 24 f., 269
Crassus 29, 403
Cremona 313 f.
Crimea 401
crusader castles 198 f.
Ctesiphon 32, 221, 405
Cumanus 81
cursus publicus 173 f., 261, 291, 295
custom post(s) 125, 247, 255, 261
customs 127 n., 384
Cyrrhus 38, 139, 176, 274, 367
Cyrus (river) *see* Kura

Damascus 12, 138 f., 275, 281 n.
received colonial status 363 n.
Danaba 165, 166, 168 n.
Danube, as border 408
Dara 11, 231, 252, 254, 255, 260 n., 261, 264
Darb el-Haj 128
Darial pass (Krestovy, Juari, Georgian
military road) 43 f., 74, 230, 231, 261,
263, 383, 404 f.
Dead Sea 11
decision-making and war aims, Chapter IX,
passim
Decius 168
Dedan (al-'Ulah) 127
defence in depth 122, 127 f., 170, 374
defensible boundaries 373
Deir el Kahf 164
demai 209
deportation of captives 266
Der el-'Atrash 199, 202
Derbent pass 44, 404 n.
desert
military presence in 122 f., 125–33, 155,
157

problems of service in 132
withdrawal from 212
deserters 261
Dhiban 133 n.
Dibsi Faraj (Athis?) 257, 258 f.
Diocletian
  at Antioch 437
  military constructions of 164, 212
  military reforms of 162–71, 254
  and rebellion in Alexandria 278
  and Saracens 73
  visits to Egypt of 290 f.
Dionysias (Soada) 133, 178
Dioscurias (Sukhumi) 9, 44, 47 n., 48 n.
Diospolis *see* Lydda
Domitian 24, 41, 388, 392
donative(s) 380, 381, 382
Dromedarii 151, 225
  units of 59 f., 127
  see also camel riders
drunkenness 290, 293
Drusus 102
Dura Shield (map) 401 n., 402 n.
Dura Europos 13, 147–52, 427
dux limitis 208, 278
  Arabiae 210, 243, 244
  and collection of taxes 289
  et praeses Isauriae 75
  Mesopotamiae 243
  Palestinae 89, 92, 178, 208, 210, 243, 248, 288
  Phoenicis 176 f., 210, 243
  ripae 151 f.
dykes against nomad attack 241

earthquake(s) 276, 438
eastern desert (Egypt) 199–201
eastern frontier of Roman empire
  after Septimius Severus 15, 394 f.
eastern sigillata 340
Echmiadzin *see* Kainepolis
Edessa 11, 275, 361
Egeria 94, 205
Egypt
  borders of 398 f.
Ein Gedi 137, 174, 430
Ein Tamar 193
Ein Boqeq 190 f.
El Leja *see* Trachonitis
Elagabalus 361, 437
Eleazar ben Dinai 81
Eleutheropolis (Beth Govrin) 178, 359, 432
Emesa 40, 227 f.
Emmaus (Nicopolis) 81, 104, 118, 183, 361, 428 f.
Emmaus (Motza, Qolonia) 293, 348, 428

emperor and decisions on war Chapter IX
  passim
empire
  Roman concept of 14, 395–401
equites Mauri Illyriciani 280
equites promoti
  Illyriciani 257
  indigenae 204
Ertaje (Biblada?) 150
Esbus *see* Heshbon
ethnic slurs 73, 88
ethnic prejudice 20, 320 n.
Eudocia 366, 438
Eudoxia 206, 365
Euphrates 10 f., 13, 14
  as border 29 f.
  forts on 150 f.
Euphratesia 241
Europos 434
Eutherius 96
exactor 289
exemption(s) from taxation 295 f., 299 f.
expansion
  profitability of 380–5, 388 f.
expulsion of population 123
extortion 90, 276, 283, 284, 285, 289, 385
Ezekias (bandit leader) 78

famine 274, 437
Fertile Crescent 11, 13
First Jewish revolt 80, 81, 82, 83, 325, 380 f., 428 f.
fiscus Iudaicus 301
Fityan 198 n.
Flavian building activity
  in Syria and Arabia 344 f.
  in Judaea 347–9
Flavians
  and military organization in the East 34–42
  and policy in North-East 44 f.
Flavius Boethus 344
fleet 48, 127
fortified cities 252–9
  defended by militias 252–4
  functions of 254–6
fossatum Africae 414
fourth-century forts
  siting and function of 186–208
Frisii 56, 289
frontier lines
  ancient concept of 394–401
  and artificial barriers 413–16
  choice of 387–94
  functions of 408–16
  and natural barriers 410–13
  and peoples 394–401

Fronto 23 f., 269 f.
frumentarii, 2, 406
funding
  of town walls 134 f., 367 f.

Gaba Hippeon 325
  Herodian settlement at 328 f.
Gabinius and urban development of
    Judaea 336–340
Gadara 336 f.
Gadimathos 239
Gaius Caesar 402
Galerius 32
Galilee
  Herod as governor of 78
  no Roman roads in north of 112
  Roman troops in 434 f.
Gallienus 221, 224, 278
Gallus Caesar 274, 290, 438
Gamla (Gmeyla) 150
Garni *see* Gorneae
garrison(s) in cities 124 f., 139, 157, 269–82,
    427 f.
Gaza 11, 93, 206, 365, 368
geographical concepts and intelligence 401–8
Georgia 9
  see also Iberia
Gerasa 12, 345–7, 354 f.
  citizens of in the army 346
  military presence at 124 f., 346
  probable seat of *procurator* 345 f.
  urban development of 345
Germanicus 142
Germany
  campaigns in 388
  frontier zone in 414 f.
Ghadhyan *see* Ad Dianam
Ghassanids 240
Giv 'at Ram 428
Giv 'at Shaul 429
glory as motive for wars of expansion 381,
    383, 387, 388, 389, 392
gold crown(s) 383
  see also aurum coronarium
Gordian III 32
Gorneae (Garni) 52
Goths 49, 303
Gour 177
grand strategy 170, 419, Chapter IX *passim*
guerrilla warfare 60 f., 81, 85
guest-house(s) 184
  see also hostels, inns
Gulf of Elath / Aqaba
  difficulty of sailing in 168

Hadrian 307, 432

and Athens 356 f.
and bureaucracy 352
and building enterprises in the East 352–
    9
  construction of Antinoe-Myos Hormos
    road 201
  eastern policy of 23, 24, 25
  and foundation of Aelia Capitolina 323 f.,
    353 f.
  founded Antinoopolis in Egypt 354, 357
  and imperial forests 319, 352
  and military discipline 24 f.
  visit to Egypt of 290 n.
Hadrian's Wall 414
Hadrianic boundary stones 352, 358
Hadrianic milestones 111, 306, 307 f.
Hadrianic era 358
Hadrianopolis *see* Adrianople
halakhah 7 f.
Hallabat 126, 178 n., 194 n., 212, 367
Hanania ben Teradion, R. 83 f.
harbour(s) 45, 48, 67, 125, 168, 341, 365
Harmozica 44, 231
Hasa (Wadi) 186, 216 f.
Hatra 42, 152–4, 386
  Roman garrison at 154
Hatzevah 130, 193 n.
Hebron 430
Hejaz 398
Hejaz railway 120 f.
Helena 364
Helenopolis 364
Heliopolis (Baalbek) 60 f., 318–21, 342 f.
  soldiers on active duty in 61, 319
Helvetians 316
Herod
  building enterprises of 340 f.
  campaign in Arbela 79
  donations for Berytus 342 f.
  governor of Galilee 78
  military settlement(s) of 327–31
  ruler of Trachonitis, Batanaea, and
    Auranitis 62, 63, 64, 329 f.
  settled Idumaeans in Trachonitis 64, 329
Herod Antipas 341
Herod's palace in Jerusalem 280
Herodian
  on expansion 25, 27, 382
Heshbon (Esbus) 327
highway men 63, 87, 91, 96, 99, 282
Hirta 151 n.
Hit 150
Holy Sepulchre 364
Honorius 300
Horvat Hazon 434
hospitium see akhsaniah

hostel(s) 176 f., 183
  see also guest-houses, inns
Humayma 216
hunger 273, 274
Huns 16, 49, 74 f., 230, 232, 233, 261, 262
hydreumata 200, 201, 202
  see also watering stations
Hyrcanus 29

Iberians 9, 43, 48, 49, 229, 231
ideology
  and annexation 383
  and resistance to Roman rule 80, 82, 86,
    87
  and war 386 f., 388 f., 393 f.
Illyria
  revolt in 57
imperial adviser(s) 386 f.
  armouries 275
  boundary 396–401
  cult 142
  forests 319, 352
  post 180, 276
  see also *cursus publicus*
  visits
  and supplies 209 f.
imperialism Chapter I, IX *passim*
Imru' l-qais 74, 239 f., 249
Imru' l-qais (Amorcesos) *see* Amorcesos
Inat 181
inn(s) 136, 177 f., 182 f., 297, 298
  see also guest-houses, hostels
inscriptions
  interpretation of 158–60
Instuleius Tenax, A. 136 n.
interpretation
  of archaeological evidence 6–7, 133, 157,
    162
  of inscriptions 158–60
  of Talmudic sources 7–9, 85
interpreter 399
Iotabe 127 n., 247 f.
Ioustasa 89
Ireland 389, 395, 405
Isauria 68, 75 f., 140
Isaurians 75 f., 321
Islamic conquest 71
  causes of 80
itineraria picta 402
Ituraean army unit(s) 60
Ituraeans 60, 318
iuventus 326

Jaffa (Joppe) 348
Jaghjagh, river 255
Jamnia 366

Jawf 13, 126, 169
Jebel Druz 13
Jerusalem (Colonia Aelia Capitolina) 104 f.,
    118
  Antonia fortress in 279
  donations made by Eudocia in 366
  foundation of Aelia Capitolina 323 f.,
    353 f.
  garrison of before First Revolt 105 f.,
    279 f.
  Herod's palace in 280
  Herod's buildings in 341
  legionary fortress in 427 f.
  Nea church in 367
  topography of 104 f.
Jews
  accused of brigandage 66 f.
  in Alexandria 277, 278
  in Antioch 271
  conflict with Samaritans 110, 322
  martyrdom 79
  refusal to recognize legitimacy of Roman
    rule of 80, 82, 86, 87
  resistance to Rome 77
  resistance before AD 66 78–83
  resistance after AD 70 83–5
  resistance after Bar Kokhba war 85–9
  revolt(s) of 55, 80, 81, 82, 83, 84, 85, 87
  sympathy for Persia of 265 n.
Jezreel valley 12, 329
John Moschus 92, 93
Jordan valley 11, 12
Joseph ben Simai 117
Josephus
  and brigands 82
  description of Roman provinces of 277
  on Gabinius 336–40
  on independence 28
  on Herod's military settlements 327
  on zealots 79
Joshua ben Levi, R. 86, 116
Jovian 438
Judaea
  annexation of 119
  banditry in 77–89
  Herodian building enterprises in 340 f.
  permanent garrison of 105, Appendix II
  road-system of 107–13
  social conflict in 80–9
  urban development under Pompey and
    Gabinius 336–40
  urban development under Flavians 347–9
  see also *Jews, Palaestina*
Judah Hanassi, R. 286, 301
Julia Domna 436 f.
Julia Maesa 437

Julia Equestris (Nyon) 315 f., 326
Julian 25, 32, 245, 265, 382, 406, 438
    motives for Persian campaign of 393
Julias (Bethsaida) 342
Julius Aurelius Zenobios (Zabdilas) 225 f.
Julius Caesar 29
    bridged the Rhine 411
    British expedition 402, 411 n.
Julius Marinus, M. 362 f.
Justin I 266
Justin II 235, 252, 264
Justinian 92, 93, 207, 212, 249, 252, 263,
    438
    building enterprises 366–9

Kainepolis (Echmiadzin) 52
Kara 10
Kavad 262
Khabur 13, 257
Khabur, river 255 f.
Khan Kosseir 138
Khirbet el-Qasr 429
Khusro I 253
Khusro II 16, 32, 244, 245, 256
Kifrin 147
Kinda 240
King's Highway 12
Koke (Be Ardeshir) 32
Kubab 429
Kura river (Cyrus) 9, 11, 47
Kurdish Taurus 11
Kurnub *see* Mampsis

Labienus 29
lacci 200, 201
Lakhmids 240, 242
Latin
    used in eastern veteran colonies 319 f.,
        324 f.
latrunculi 179
Lawrence, T. E. 169
Lazica 232
    see also Colchis
Lebanon, Mount 11, 60–2, 318 f.
Legio (Caparcotna, Kephar 'Otnay,
    Maximianoupolis) 281, 432 f.
    received city status 364
Legio (Lejjun, Betthoro?) *see* Lejjun
legionary detachment(s) 36, 38, 125, 139,
    157, 169, 280, 295, 428, 431, 433
legionary standards and city coinage 431
legions
    I Illyricorum 165, 169
    I Italica 43 n., 169
    I Parthica 42 n., 360
    I Pontica 168
    II Parthica 36 n., 281 n.
    III Cyrenaica 123, 125, 126, 169, 222,
        280, 346
    III Gallica 36, 39 n., 135, 139
    III Parthica 42 n., 360
    IV Scythica 36, 135
    V Macedonica 118, 428 f., 431
    VI Ferrata 36, 39 n., 125, 139, 431, 432,
        434
    X Fretensis 38, 280, 323–5, 427, 428, 429,
        433
    XI Claudia 169, 433
    XII Fulminata 36, 45 n., 430
    XVI Flavia 36, 135, 136, 294 f.
Leja *see* Trachonitis
Lejjun (Betthoro?) 164, 168 n., 197 f., 281
Leuke Kome 125
Libanius 97–9, 273, 296, 382
licence to kill, after victory 381 f.
limes 33, 75, 128, 150, 161, 175, 205, 208,
    255, 288, 408 f., 414 n.
limitanei 208–13
    and *annona militaris* 287 f., 295
    and landed property 209
    as a police force 210
    not a peasant militia 208 f., 288
    on campaign 210 f., 288
lions 108
Litani 11
Livias 341
local guide(s) 403
local recruitment 138
Lod *see* Lydda
logistics 40 f., 168
loot *see* booty
Lucius Verus 436
    campaign of in the East 51 f.
    results of eastern campaign of 399 f.
Lucullus 28
Luxor
    fortress at 427
Lydda (Lod, Diospolis) 83, 92 n., 116 f., 359
Lyons 309, 316 f.

Ma'ale Adumim 91, 431
Ma'an 177
Macrinus 30, 73, 437
Mada 'in Salih 127
Madaba 125 n., 137 n.
Madaba Map 402
magister militum per Orientem 272, 276
maladministration 58, 82
Malalas 162
    on urban development 335
Malchus 96
Mamluk empire 69

Mampsis (Kurnub, Mamshit) 125
Mamre 364
Mamshit *see* Mampsis
mansiones 176 f., 200, 201, 205, 206, 295
Maratocupreni 63
marauder(s) 87 f., 200 f.
　see also raids, raiding
Marcus Aurelius 88
　Mesopotamia during reign of 399 f.
　and plans for expansion 390, 391
　northern wars of 390 f.
Mardin 11
Mareades 271
market(s) 407
　see also annual fair(s)
martyrdom 79
Martyropolis 10
massacre(s) of Roman citizens 385
Mavgai 181
Mavia 74, 244, 246
Maximianopolis (Shaqqa) 135 f.
Maximianoupolis *see* Legio
Maximinus Thrax 392
Mecca 215 f.
Melitene 11, 38, 42, 139, 168
　development of city 281 f.
merchants 407
　see also trader(s)
Mesene (Meshan) 71, 144
Meshan *see* Mesene
Mesopotamia (province) 42, 250–64
　annexed by Septimius Severus 360, 394 f.
　banditry in 95 f.
　frontier of 255–7
　Roman presence in, before Severus 399 f.
　Trajan and customs in 127 n., 384
Mezad Thamar (Qasr al-Juheiniya,
　　Thamara?) 193–5, 202 f.
midrash 7
migration(s) 246, 263
milestone(s) 108–12, 120 f., 158
　and development of road-system 108 f.
　and propaganda 304–9
　do not refer to territories 343 n.
　language of 305 f.
　of Vaballathus 223, 227
　scarce in the desert 111 f., 121, 304 f.
　set up by the local communities 295, 308
military diploma(s) 105 f.
military architecture 207 f.
military bases in cities 427 f.
military discipline 24 f., 269 f.
military intelligence 401–8
　and information from captives 407
military map(s) 402–8
militia(s) 37, 134, 208, 210, 247, 252–4,
　325–7, 329
　see also para-military organizations
milliaria 108 f.
Mismiyeh *see* Phaena
mistreatment of animals 293
Moa (Mo'ah, Moyet 'Awad) 129 f., 193
moderator of Arabia 90, 244
monasteries
　attacked by bandits 91–5
　military protection for 92, 94 f., 208
monophysite(s) 265 n., 272
Mount Gerizim 90, 139, 430
mountain warfare 25, 231
Moyet 'Awad *see* Moa
Mundhir, al 76 f., 210, 242, 243, 244, 245,
　262 n., 263, 264
Murat 10
mutiny 22, 273, 274, 406 f.
myrtle 295

Nabataean(s) 12
　army of 133
Nablus *see* Neapolis
Namara 74, 239
Narbo Martius 314 f.
natural barriers as boundary 410–13
navigability of rivers 48
Nawa 65, 330
nazirite 85
Neapolis (Nablus, Shekhem) 90, 139, 349
　military inscriptions from 430 f.
　punished by Septimius Severus 359 f.
　received colonial status 363 n.
Negev 11 f.
　military presence in 128–31
　urbanization of 215 f.
Nehardea 96 f.
Nela 135
Nero
　abortive eastern campaign of 43 f., 391,
　　404 f.
　Armenian war of 41
Nessana 206 f., 211 f.
　papyri from 209
Nicephorium-Callinicum (ar-Raqqa) 256 f.,
　407
Nicomedia 275
Nicopolis *see* Emmaus (Nicopolis)
Niha 319
Nilus 93
Nisibis 11, 23, 33, 42 n., 221, 252, 255, 261,
　393, 399, 407
　colonial status of 360
Nitzanah *see* Nessana
nomad allies 235–49
　and the treaty of AD 562 261

nomad allies *cont.*
  conversion to Christianity of 246, 247
  functions of 243–8
  inscriptions set up by 238 f.
  migrations of 246, 261, 263
  sedentarization of 246 f.
  tactics of 235–7, 241 f.
nomad raids 72, 74–6, 211, 235–7, 241–3,
    247, 255, 257, 265
  see also marauders, camel raiding, raiding
nomadic pastoralism 69–72, 96 f., 214–18
  see also transhumance
Notitia Dignitatum 161 f.
numeri Maurorum 431
Numerus Theodosiacus 207, 209 f., 211 f.
numerus 303

Oboda (Avdat) 130, 206 f.
Odenathus 32, 220–2, 224, 226
Oresa 165, 166
Orontes 11, 12
Osrhoene 142, 211, 361
Osrhoeni 399
Ostia 309
Ottoman Palestine
  road security in 113 f.
Ottoman empire 69
  fortresses in 183
  and nomads 214
  protection of trade in 145 f.
  and road-security 113–15
overpopulation 70

Pacorus 29
pagi 319 f., 344 n.
Palaestina
  banditry in Byzantine period 97
  unrest in Byzantine period 89–91
  see also dux, Jews, Judaea, *limitanei*
palatium 295
Palestine
  in Ottoman period 113–15, 214
Palmyra 13, 141–7, 166
  colonial status 144, 225
  Diocletianic fortress at 164, 165–7, 427 f.
  and eastern trade 141, 144–6
  equestrian officers from 146, 225
  extension of influence of 150
  extent of supremacy 223
  garrison at 144
  and Hadrian's visit AD 130 355
  inclusion in the empire 141–4
  independence in third century 220–8
  Pliny on 142 f.
  renamed Hadrianopolis 143
  senators from 146, 225

strategoi of 225, 226
  tax law 142, 352
  territory of 142 f.
  town wall of 345
Palmyrene archers 144, 225
Pappus and Lulianus 322
para-military organization(s) 325 f.
  see also militia(s)
Parthians
  attitude(s) towards Rome 22
  considered part of the Roman empire 21
  invasion in 40 BC 31
  tactics of 22
patron saints of soldiers 177
Pausanias
  against superfluous conquest(s) 27
  on Hadrian's building enterprises 355
payment(s)
  by Rome to Huns 245
  by Rome to Nomads 245, 248
  by Rome to Persia 231, 260, 261 f., 264
peace of Nisibis 229
Persian war(s) 28–32, chapter V *passim*
Pescennius Niger 271, 436
Petra 12, 361, 385
  military presence at 125
Petra in Georgia 233
Phaena (Mismiyeh) 135, 136, 298
Pharan 95, 205, 247
Pharasmanes 48
Pharisees 79
Phasis (river) *see* Rioni
Phasis (town) 9, 46 f.
Philadelphia 12
Philip the Arab 65, 361 f.
Philippopolis (Shahba) 361–3
phroura/phrouri 179, 180
phrouria 201, 252, 256 n.
phylarch(s) 210, 238, 241, 248
  functions of 243–8
  appointed bishop 246
physician(s) 262 n.
pilgrim(s) 94 f.
  military protection for 95
piracy
  on Black Sea 45
Pityus (Pitsunda) 49, 233
Pizos 180
Placentia 313 f.
Plautius Silvanus Aelianus 400 f.
Pliny
  on expansion 392
  on Nero's Caucasian campaign 404 f.
  on Palmyra 142 f.
  on war 392 f.
plunder *see* booty

Podosaces 74, 240
police duties 112 f., 115–18, 138, 210, 248, 326, 330
political murder 83
Pompey 28, 43, 60, 336, 338 f.
Pontus
  revolt in AD 69 in 45
population density 215, 217 f.
Posidonius 403 f.
Pozzuoli 309
praesidia 174 f., 177 n., 180, 201, 430
Praesidio (al-Khaldi) 175, 189, 197
Praesidium (Ghor el-Feife?) 175, 193
praetenturae 235 n., 257
praetorium 172 f., 202, 256, 295
praisidion see *praesidia*
preparations for campaign 380
primipilaris 136 n.
  as collector of taxes 289
Primis (Qasr Ibrim) 399
primus pilus
  social status of 138
principia of Palmyra 165
proconsul
  duties of 81
  of Palestine 90
Procopius
  misinterprets military installations 204, 375
  on expansion 27
  on Justinian's building activity 260, 366–9
  on *limitanei* 208–10
  on the desert 132
  on Melitene 281
  on Resapha 204, 260 n., 375
  on St Catherine's monastery 94 f.
promotion in wartime 380, 381, 382
propaganda 304–9
propugnaculum 313 f., 330 f.
prosecutio annonae 293, 295 f.
protection of trade 63
  in Ottoman empire 145 f.
protection money 93, 98, 247, 276
province, concept of 397
Ptolemais (Acco) 110, 322 f., 344
Pumbedita 97
Pyrgos 179
Qantara, el 164
Qasr Ibrim see Primis
Qasr al-Juheiniya see Mezad Thamar
Qolonia see Emmaus (Motza, Qolonia)
Quinctilius Varus 81, 109, 325
  as general 56 f.

Rabbatmoba 125, 137
raiding 60–4, 66, 141, 179, 180, 204

see also camel raiding, marauders, nomad raids
Ramat Rahel 430
ransom, payments of 86
Raphanaea (Raphniyeh) 39, 134, 139, 165, 166, 281
  inn at 177
Raphniyeh see Raphanaea
ravaging 381 f.
refugees 261
requisition see *angaria*, *annona*
Res Gestae Divi Saporis 23, 31, 152, 229
Resapha (Sergiopolis) 204, 211, 253, 256, 260 n., 375
Resh Laqish 283
Rhabdium 260 n.
Rhesaena 42, 360
Rhine 102 f., 410
Rhizus (Rize) 233
Rioni (Phasis) 9, 46, 233, 413 n.
riot control 272, 277, 278, 279
rivers
  and military bases 102 f.
  and warfare 410–13
road-station(s) 188, 204, 228, 295, 296
road-construction
  pre-Roman 34
  and forced labour 294 f.
road-repair 294 f.
roads
  Aelia–Oboda–Aela 189
  Antinoe–Myos Hormos 201
  Antioch–Ptolemais 110, 181, 182, 322
  Antipatris–Caesarea 416 n.
  Apamea–Palmyra 35
  Apamea–Raphanaea 35
  Berytus–Damascus 62, 318
  Bostra–Azraq 175
  Bostra–Dumata 169
  Chalcis–Emesa 35
  Coptus–Berenice 200
  Coptus–Leukos Limen 200
  Damascus–Emesa 138
  Damascus–Heliopolis 136, 294
  Damascus–Palmyra 34, 138, 143, 163, 176
  Damascus–Scythopolis 65, 136
  Damascus–Tiberias 136
  desert highway (Jordan) 122 f., 127 f.
  Emmaus–Jerusalem 81, 104
  Gaza–Aela 112
  Gerasa-Bostra 121
  in Syria 34–6
  Jaffa–Jerusalem 107, 429 f.
  Jaffa–(Beth Horon)–Jerusalem 429
  Jerusalem–Gaza 432
  Jerusalem–Jericho 90, 431

roads *cont.*
  Jerusalem–Hebron 430
  Jerusalem–Neapolis 430 f.
  Mampsis–Phaeno 130
  near Kainepolis in Georgia 52
  Nisibis–Hatra 154
  Palmyra–Sura 34, 138, 143, 167
  Palmyra–Hit 204
  Petra–Gaza 129 f.
  Scythopolis–Jericho 112, 305, 432
  Scythopolis–Legio 110
  Scythopolis–Pella–Gerasa 110, 122
  Sephoris–Tiberias 182
  south of Jerusalem 107
  strata Diocletiana 163, 171, 211
  through Trachonitis 65, 134 f.
  Trapezus–Commagene 37 f.
  via Nova Traiana 12, 120 f., 122, 305
Roman attitudes
  towards the army 24
  towards Persia 20–8, 393
Roman citizens
  resident in neighbouring territories 385
Ruwwafa 73, 126, 238

Saba 92, 93
Sabbatical year (Shevi'it) 284–6, 298 f.
Safaitic graffiti 72
Salih 240
Salt 125 n.
Samaria 12, 186
  alleged building activity under Gabinius
    at 339 f.
  Herodian settlement at 328, 340
  military inscription(s) from 431
  received colonial status from Septimius
    Severus 359 f.
Samaritans 81
  conflict with Jews 110, 322
  revolt(s) of 89 f., 210, 248
  and sympathy for Persia 265 n.
Samosata 11, 22, 39, 40, 139
Sampsigeramus (Uranius Antoninus) 227
sanctuaries and road-stations 188
Saracens 175, 179, 236, 241 f., 257
Sardis 275
Sassanians 15 f.
  and raids into Syria 31
  attitude towards Rome 23, 265 f.
  and Byzantium 260–8
Satala 11, 38, 42, 139, 168, 281, 410 n.
Scythopolis (Beth Shean) 433 f.
Sebastopolis 233
secret service men 116
sedentarization of nomads 246 f.
Seleucia Pieria 35, 273, 365

Sepphoris 81, 303, 331, 341, 434
Septimius Herodianus (Hairan) 221, 222
Septimius Severus 32
  and conquest of Mesopotamia 15, 22, 30,
    394
  and bandit(s) 88 f.
  and urbanization 359 f.
  and war in Britain 389, 405 f.
  attack on Hatra of 153, 386
  organized new province of
    Mesopotamia 360
  sacked Ctesiphon 405
Septimius Vorodes 226
Sergiopolis *see* Resapha
Severus Alexander 32, 143
Sextus Pompeius 29
Shapur (Sapor) I 23, 30, 31, 220, 227, 229
Shapur (Sapor) II 21, 23
Shaqqa *see* Maximianopolis
Sharon plain 67
Shimeon Hatemani 116, 298
Shimeon bar Yohai 284
Shimon ben Cahana 83
Sidon 139
siege(s) 250, 252–5
Silvinus 177
Sinai 94, 247, 248; *see also* St Catherine's
  Monastery
Singara 42, 252, 260 n., 360
singulares 270
Sirhan (wadi) 13, 126, 169
skenai 174
skopelarioi 113, 132, 200
slaughter 381
small military installation(s) 430
  burgi 178–86
  function of 172–86
  in Arabia 172–6
  in Syria 177 f.
Soada *see* Dionysias
social integration 136
Southern Asia Minor 321
speculatores 180 f.
spies 407
St Catherine's monastery 94 f., 204, 367
stathmoi 201
stationarii 113
stationes agrariae see *agraria statio*
Strabo
  and Roman imperialism 26, 388
  on nomads 132
strata Diocletiana 163, 171, 211
Strata dispute 211, 244, 263
strategic reserve 313
strategoi (duoviri) 225 f.
strategy 169 n., 187, 380, Chapter IX *passim*

Strymon 21
stubble 96 f.
subsidies *see* payment(s)
subterranean hiding place(s) 84 f.
suicide 79
Sukhumi *see* Dioscurias
Sulla 28
supplies 168, 290 f., 380, 382 f.
Sura 165, 166
swimming 411
synteleia tironon (compulsory
    conscription) 302–4
    see also tironia
Syria
    banditry in 97–9
    permanent garrison of 36–9, 134–9
    senators from 225

Tabula Peutingeriana 398, 402
Tacitus
    on Nero's Caucasian campaign 404 f.
    on veteran colonies 313 f.
tactics
    Parthian 22
    of nomads 235–7
talmudic sources
    as historical material 7–9, 85
    on Roman troops 115–18
    on taxation 282–304
tannaim 7
Tanukh 239
Tarphon, R. 84
Taurus 40
taxation 292–304
taxes 138, 282–304
    collection by army 282, 287, 289
Tbilisi 44, 49
Tel Shalem 12, 305, 307, 353, 432
Telbis (Talbus) 147 n.
telescope 21
Tell el Hajj 37 n.
Tell Brak 256
Tell Bali 256
temple in Jerusalem 279 f.
temporary camps made permanent 410
tetrarchic legions 169
    see also legions
Teutones 379
Thamara *see* Mezad Thamar
Thamudians 73, 126
Thannouris 179, 257
Theodosian Code
    on *annona militaris* 287
Thracians
    revolt of 58, 59
Tiberias 137 n., 301, 323, 341, 353, 434

walls of 133, 363
Tiberius 43
Tigranocerta 10, 40
Tigris 10 f., 14, 241
tironia (aurum tironicium, adaeratio) 302–4
Toloha 189
Tomi 326
town wall(s) 133
Trabzon *see* Trapezus
Trachonitis (Leja) 13, 62–6, 135, 136, 137,
    248, 329
trade route(s) 141, 144 f., 150, 152 f., 201,
    256
trade 144 f., 216
    disturbed by banditry 63
    protection of 63
trader(s) 62f.
    see also merchants
Trajan
    and Parthia 3
    and annexation of Arabia 119, 349–51
    attack on Hatra of 153, 154
    conquests of 15, 26, 30
    eastern war of 51
    invasion of Armenia 42
    provinces created by 58 n., 401
transhumance 69–72, 96 f., 176, 214–18
    see also nomadic pastoralism
transport
    requisition of *see angaria*
transportation of provisions *see angaria*
Trapezus (Trabzon) 11, 38, 40, 48, 50, 168,
    233, 326
treasuries 280
treaties between Rome and Parthia 28
treaties between Rome and Persia
    of AD 441–2 263 f.
    of AD 532 231
    of AD 562 231, 243, 260–4
tributum capitis 286
Tsafit tower 194, 196, 197
Tuwweiba (Wadi) 125
Tyre 139
Tzani 61

Udruh 122, 164 f., 167 f., 281
'Ulla son of Qoshev (Qosher) 116
Ulpius Magnus, M. 431
Ulpius Traianus, M. 35, 110, 345
Ummayad palaces 178
Umm el-Halahil 177
Umm el-Jemal 181, 216 n., 239
unoccupied land beyond border 399
Upper Zohar 191–3
Uranius Antoninus (Sampsigeramus)
    227

urban development
around legionary bases 281 f., 432 f.
of Judaea under Gabinius 336–40
urbanization
modern opinions on funding for 332 f.
Ursicinus 290
Uweinid 126, 174
'Uzza 130 f.

Vaballathus 222 f., 226 f.
Valash 262
Valens 303, 438
Valerius Longinus, M. 431
vehiculatio 296
see also imperial post, *cursus publicus*
Velius Rufus, C. 381
Vespasian
as general 57
Vetera (Xanten) 186, 427
veteran colonies 60 f.
and army bases 324
confiscation of land(s) for 317, 323
Latin used in 319 f., 324 f.
modern opinions about functions of 311–
13
personal names in 320
recruits from 324
social and cultural impact of 319–21
used as base of operations 319, 323
veterans
recalled into service 315
vexillation(s) *see* legionary detachments
via Nova Traiana 12, 120 f.
Vincentius 175 f.
Vologaeses I 22
Vologesias 142, 144

Wadi Barada 294

war(s)
decision(s) on 379–87
expansion and profit in 380–5
glory as motive for 381, 383, 387, 388,
389, 392
started by generals 379
war aim(s) 377–94
and frontier(s) 394–401
watchtower(s) 107, 136, 252, 430
in eastern desert 200 f.
see also burgi
water supply
protection of 176, 189 f., 191, 195, 197 f.,
200
watering station(s) 200
see also hydreumata
Way of Edom 130, 192 n.
withdrawal from desert 212

xenodochia 206

Yannai, R. 87, 285
Yohanan ben Zakkai, Rabban 183, 293 f.
Yotvetah *see* Ad Dianam

Zabdilas (Julius Aurelius Zenobios) 225 f.
Zamaris 329–31
Ze'ira, R. 295
Zealots 78, 82
Zeno
and Samaritan revolt 90
and Persia 262
Zenobia 222–24, 226, 227, 239
Zenobia (Halabiya) 252
Zenodorus 62, 63
Zeugma 11, 13, 35, 38, 139
Zigana pass 11
Zoroastrian religion 16
Zosimus 162 f., 273

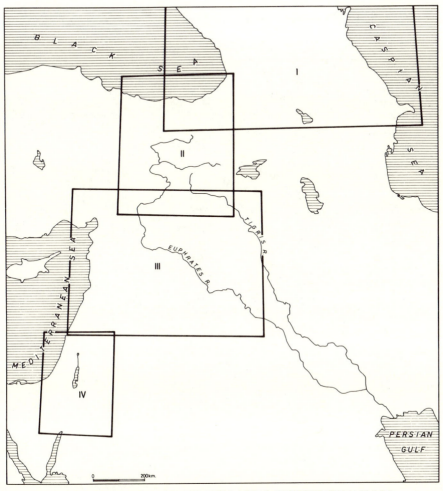

MAP A. THE NEAR EAST, SHOWING AREAS COVERED BY MAPS I-IV

In Maps I-IV ancient place-names are printed as e.g. PETRA and modern place-names as e.g. (Batumi)

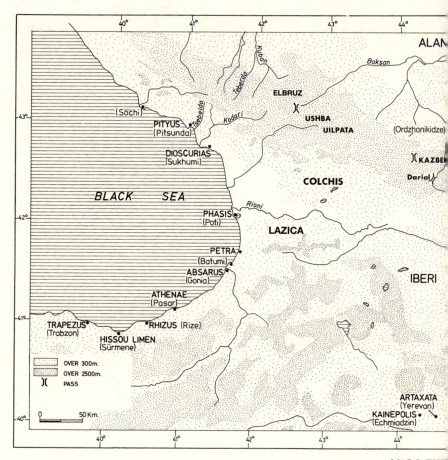

MAP I. THE

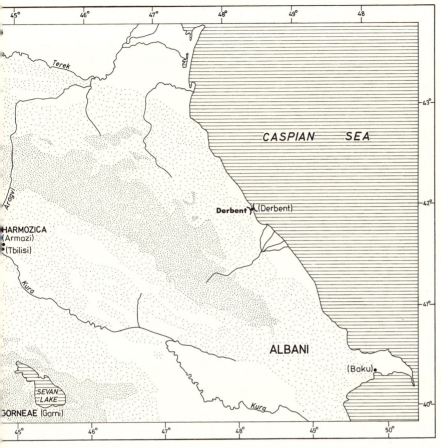

ORTH-EAST

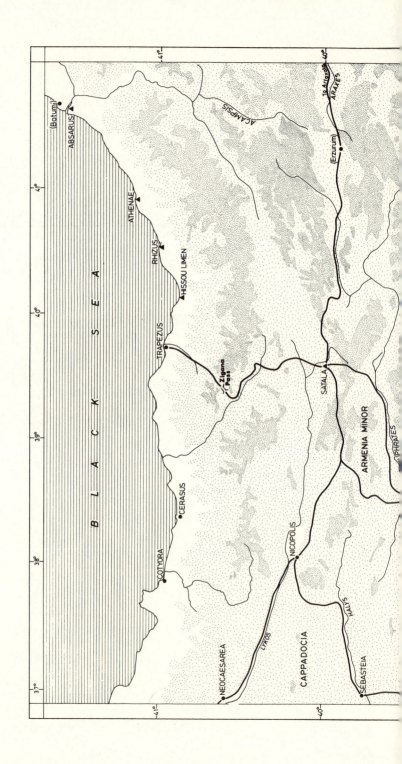

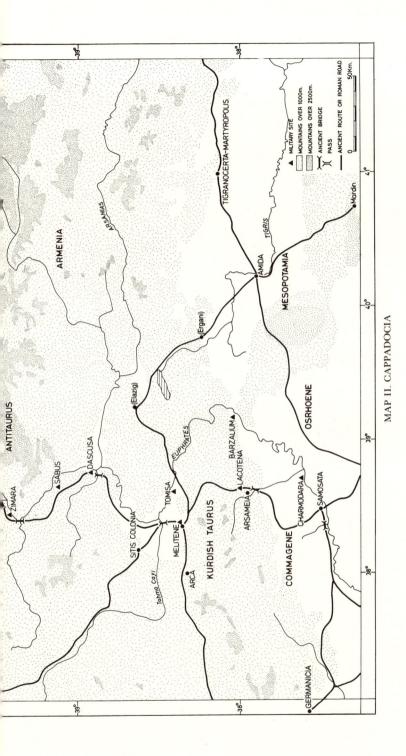

MAP II. CAPPADOCIA

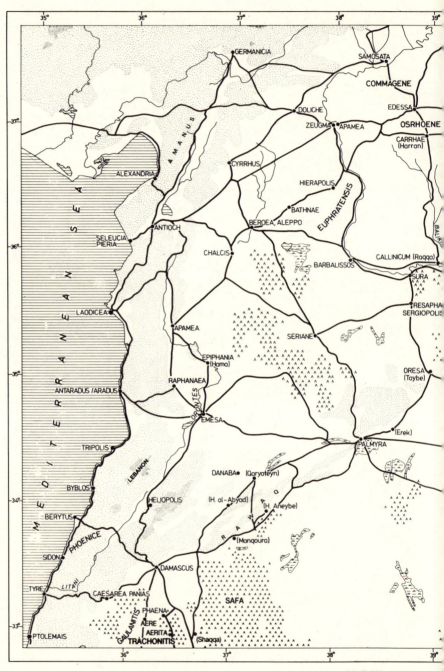

MAP III. SYRIA AND

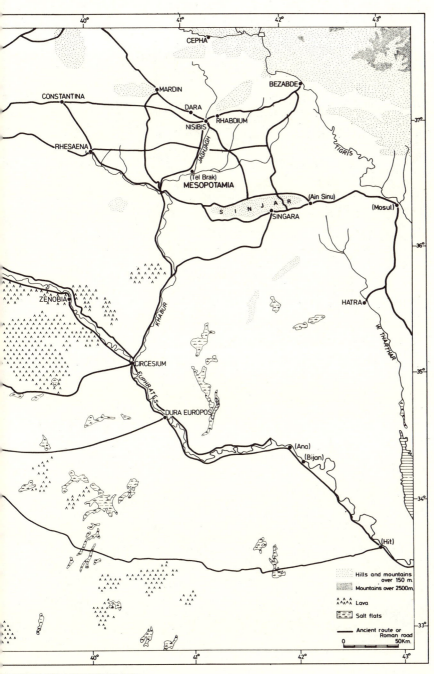

NORTHERN MESOPOTAMIA

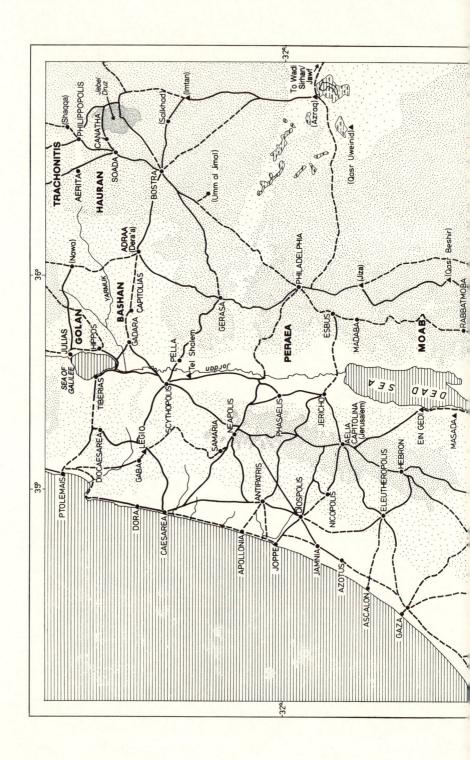

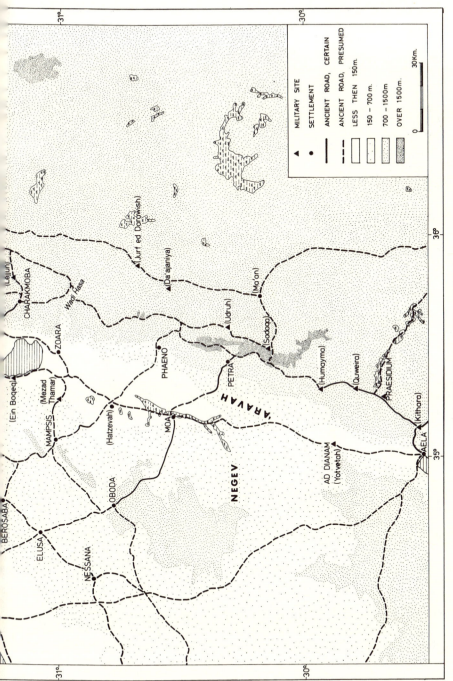

MAP IV JUDAEA AND ARABIA

MILITARY SITE

SETTLEMENT

ANCIENT ROAD, CERTAIN

ANCIENT ROAD, PRESUMED

LESS THEN 150m.

150 – 700 m.

700 – 1500m

OVER 1500m.

0   30Km.

(Lejjun)

CHARAKMOBA

ZOARA

Wadi Hasa

(Jurf ed Darawish)

(Da'ajaniya)

(Ma'an)

PHAENO

(Udruh)

(Sadaqa)

(Ein Boqeq)

(Mezad Thamar)

MAMPSIS

(Hatzevah)

PETRA

MOA

(Humayma)

BEROSABA

OBODA

NEGEV

(Quweira)

PRAESIDIUM

ELUSA

NESSANA

AD DIANAM
(Yotvetah)

AELA

(Kithara)

ARAVAH

31°

30°

36°

35°